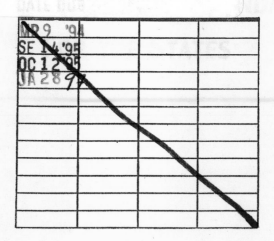

MAKING GOVERNMENT WORK: A CONSERVATIVE AGENDA FOR THE STATES

Foreword by
Ronald Reagan

Tex Lezar, Editor
President, Texas Public Policy Foundation

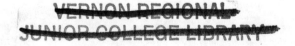

Manufactured in the United States of America
D. Armstrong Co., Inc.
Houston, Texas

This book is dedicated to Presidents Richard M. Nixon, Ronald W. Reagan, George H.W. Bush, and Gerald R. Ford. Together, they led America to maintain its national might during challenging times. They outdistanced the "Evil Empire" and won a new chance for free people and free markets both in America and throughout the world.

To the People of Texas & all Americans in the world—
   Fellow citizens & compatriots—

I am besieged, by a thousand or more of the Mexicans under Santa Anna— I have sustained a continual Bombardment & cannonade for 24 hours & have not lost a man— The enemy has demanded a surrender at discretion; otherwise, the garrison are to be put to the sword, if the fort is taken— I have answered the demands with a cannon shot, & our flag still waves proudly from the wall— I shall never surrender or retreat. Then, I call on you in the name of Liberty, or patriotism & of everything dear to the American character, to come to our aid, with all dispatch— The enemy is receiving reinforcements daily & will no doubt increase to three or four thousand in four or five days. If this call is neglected, I am determined to sustain myself as long as possible & die like a soldier who never forgets what is due to his own honor and that of his country— Victory or Death.

   William Barret Travis
   Lt. Col. Comdt.
   Last communication from The Alamo, 24 Feb. 1836

CONTENTS

FOREWORD

During my time as Governor of California I realized that the biggest problems we had regarding big government had to be solved in Washington, which was gradually but inexorably taking power from the states. We have now at least begun the process of returning to the states some of the powers they need to meet the needs of our citizens. That effort must be continued—and met by new proposals for action by the states and localities. That is the purpose of this book, to provide A Conservative Agenda for the States.

I'm reminded of something that James Madison said in 1788: "Since the general civilization of mankind, I believe there are more instances of the abridgement of the freedom of the people by gradual and silent encroachment of those in power than by violent and sudden usurpations." His friend and neighbor, Thomas Jefferson, thought much the same way. "What has destroyed liberty and the rights of men in every government that has ever existed under the sun?" he asked. And he then answered: "The generalizing and concentrating of all cares and powers into one body."

As Governor of California, I experienced how the federal bureaucracy had its hand in everything and was "concentrating all cares and power into one body." Washington would establish a new program that the states were supposed to administer, then set so many rules and regulations that the state wasn't really administering it—you were just following orders from Washington. Most of these programs could not only be operated more effectively but also more economically with greater state and local discretion.

The federal government didn't create the states; the states created the federal government. Washington, ignoring principles of the Constitution, has, however, too frequently tried to turn the states into nothing more than administrative districts of the federal government. And the primrose path to federal control has, to a large extent, followed the lure of federal financial aid. From our schools to our farms, Washington bureaucrats have tried to dictate to Americans what they could or could not do. They have portrayed bureaucratic control as the price Americans must pay for federal aid from Washington. The money comes with strings that reach all the way back to the Potomac.

Usually with the best of intentions, Congress passes a new program, appropriates the money for it, then assigns bureaucrats in Washington to disperse the money. Almost always, the bureaucrats respond by telling states, cities, counties, and schools how to spend this money.

To use Madison's words, Washington usurped power from the states by the "gradual and silent encroachment of those in power." Federal handouts frequently went to the states for programs the states would not have chosen themselves. But they took the money because it was there; it seemed to be "free."

Over time, states and localities became so dependent on the money from Washington that, like junkies, they found it all but impossible to break the habit. Only after becoming addicted did they realize how pervasive the federal regulations were that came with the money.

As all this was going on, the federal government was taking an ever-increasing share of the Nation's total tax revenues—making it more difficult for states and local governments to raise money on their own. As a result, states and localities became even more the captives of federal money, federal dictates, and federal governments surrendered control of their own destiny to a faceless national government that claimed to know better how to solve the problems of a city or town than the people who lived there. And if local officials or their congressmen ever tried to end a program they didn't like or they thought was unproductive and wasteful, they discovered that the beneficiaries of the program and the bureaucrats who administered it had formed too tight an alliance to defeat. Once started, a federal program benefiting any group or special interest is virtually impossible to end and the costs go on forever.

We have strayed a great distance from our founding fathers' vision of America. They regarded the central government's responsibility as that of providing national security, protecting our democratic freedoms, and limiting the government's intrusion into our lives—in sum, the protection of life, liberty, and the pursuit of happiness. They never envisioned vast agencies in Washington telling our farmers what to plant, our teachers what to teach, our industries what to build. The Constitution they wrote established sovereign states, not administrative districts of the federal government. They believed in keeping government as close as possible to the people. If parents didn't like the way their schools were being run, they could throw out the Board of Education at the next election. But what could they do directly about the elite bureaucrats in the U.S. Department of Education who sent ultimatums into their children's classrooms regarding curriculum and textbooks?

As President I tried to do as much as I could to return responsibility to the states and localities. Today, the hottest area of public policy making is now back in the states, or as the former House Democratic whip Representative William H. Gray III has recently said, "I don't think the federal government will be the engine of major change in the 1990s." Somehow I believe that our Administration's emphasis on turning back to the states areas of responsibility that had been wrongfully preempted by the federal government has encouraged the states as problem solvers.

For the states to provide real solutions to the problems and challenges of the 90s and the 21st Century beyond, state policymakers will need the benefit of research that is both practical and also reflects basic American principles—an emphasis on the individual, respect for private property, reliance upon government closest to the people, shared western values, and the dynamism of the free market.

The Texas Public Policy Foundation recognized that a guide to public policy on the state level reflecting those principles was needed. So they went about producing one. Under the leadership of Tex Lezar—who served as my Assistant U.S. Attorney General for Legal Policy—the Texas Public Policy Foundation has brought together specific proposals by some of the Nation's best authorities on the most important issues facing our states today. Working with Professor Mel Bradford and David Williams, Tex has assembled a remarkably sweeping conservative agenda backed by a who's who of conservative policymakers. They could also help to make state government much more effective in meeting the most difficult problems faced by Americans today.

For policymakers and interested citizens, this book should be the first stop on the road to turning the Tenth Amendment of the U.S. Constitution from a flabby invalid into a healthy and muscular individual. I know that in the days ahead I will frequently refer to *Making Government Work: A Conservative Agenda for the States* as my guide for state public policy. I urge all Americans to do likewise.

Ronald Reagan

Ronald W. Reagan

ACKNOWLEDGMENTS

Warren G. Harding once observed: "I wish we might have less condemnation of error and more commendation of right." In Harding's case, that wish was not fulfilled. I trust that, in the case of this book, it has been. This book is an effort to describe and propose what is right. A great many people have contributed to that effort. As a result, there are many who deserve commendation for what is right about the book—although the editor reserves to himself any condemnation for error.

The Texas Public Policy Foundation deserves special commendation. It recognized the need for a book that would compile many of the new conservative proposals to make state government an effective leader in our federalist system. I am certain that this is just one of what will be a multitude of positive contributions by the Texas Public Policy Foundation to the great State of Texas and her sister states.

I am especially indebted to the Board of Directors and Advisors who trusted me to edit this work and elected me to serve as President of the Texas Public Policy Foundation. Our Board of Directors and Advisors are special people. They care deeply about our state and our nation, contributing their time and efforts ceaselessly to better both. No one could ask for better counsel or greater support than has been provided by the co-founders of the Texas Public Policy Foundation, James R. Leininger, M.D., Chairman and Fritz S. Steiger, Executive Vice President. Without their vision and devotion, there would be no book and no Foundation. Without men like them, there would have been no Texas either.

Assisting in the editing of this book have been Professor Mel Bradford and David Williams. Neither needs an introduction to conservatives throughout America. Professor Bradford, one of this country's most passionate and learned advocates of conservative virtues for many, many years, has written the concluding chapter. Similarly, David Williams has worked long and hard on behalf of conservatism—even subjecting himself to a policymaking role in Washington, D.C. Both have contributed greatly to the design and crafting of this book.

Invaluable is the only way to describe the efforts of Brian Roberts (Research Director, Texas Public Policy Foundation) and Ed Valentine and Marci Tackett of Spaeth Communications. All three have worked through the nights as well as night and day to compile this book. They have each done whatever was asked of them in the effort to get the book done. The book certainly could not have been done so quickly or so well without their dedication and very hard work.

The staff of the Texas Public Policy Foundation have played a significant role in the development of the book through their administrative support and creative talent. Robin Leyendecker, Mike Watson and Claudia Harper have been tremendous in their assistance and support.

My wife, Merrie Spaeth, deserves separate mention for encouraging me to do this book, to serve as President of the Foundation, and to take time from my litigation practice for these nonpaying pursuits. As then-President Reagan's Director of the White House Office of Media Relations, Merrie herself is a well known conservative whose commitment and talents were surely tested—and found exemplary—in the writing and editing of this book. No one can appreciate her talents or commitment more than I.

Financial support is always an essential ingredient of any private effort to improve public policy. Various individuals, corporations, and foundations provided financial support that made this book possible. Our special thanks for that assistance go to:

> The J.M. Foundation
> The Roe Foundation
> The Armstrong Foundation
> The Adolph Coors Foundation
> The Patrick Henry Foundation
> The Strake Foundation

The Texas Public Policy Foundation is one of a growing number of independent, conservative public policy think tanks around the country. The members of these new organizations believe that real change must first occur in the states before it can take place in Washington, D.C. Several of these organizations have joined with the Texas Public Policy Foundation in a coalition effort to produce this national edition of *Making Government Work: A Conservative Agenda for the States*. Those think tanks also co-sponsoring this project (as of press time) include:

> The Georgia Public Policy Foundation
> The James Madison Institute for Public Policy Studies (Florida)
> The Indiana Policy Review Foundation
> The South Carolina Policy Council
> The Arizona Institute for Public Policy Research
> The Alabama Family Alliance
> The Southwest Policy Institute (Oklahoma)
> Center of the American Experiment (Minnesota)
> The Evergreen Freedom Foundation (Washington)
> The Tennessee Institute for Public Policy

There surely are others who deserve commendation, but the final commendation must go to those who read the chapters of this book with open minds. There is a great deal that must be done to make this country a better place in which to live. Many of the kinds of things that need to be considered are discussed in this book. In your hands rests the final decision, however. What will you do to make this a better country? Each of you who answers the call deserves commendation too.

CONTRIBUTORS

PATRICK R. ANDERSON is Professor of Criminology and Chairman of the Department of Sociology and Criminology at Florida Southern College. He is a recognized expert on gambling issues, especially state-operated lotteries, and has served as a consultant with the U.S. Department of Justice as well as a number of city and state agencies. He has published numerous articles in various academic journals and law reviews and is the author of a leading textbook, *Introduction to Criminal Justice, 5th Edition*. A graduate of Furman University, Dr. Anderson received his Ph.D. in Criminology from Florida State University.

JOHN A. BADEN is the Chairman of the Foundation for Research on Economics and the Environment. A former head of the Maguire Oil and Gas Institute in the Cox School of Business at Southern Methodist University, he also founded the Political Economy Research Center. An expert on environmental and economic issues, his list of publications includes *A Yellowstone Primer: Policy Reform via the New Resource Economics* and *The New Environmentalists: Money, Politics, and Nature*. A graduate of Wittenberg University, Dr. Baden received his Ph.D. in Government from Indiana University.

GARY L. BAUER currently serves as President of the Family Research Council, Inc., and Senior Vice President of Focus on the Family. He served as Assistant to President Reagan for Policy Development and Director of the White House Office of Policy Development. Prior to that, Mr. Bauer served as Under Secretary of the U.S. Department of Education. While at the Department, Mr. Bauer served as Chairman of President Reagan's Special Working Group on the Family. Along with Dr. James Dobson, Bauer is the author of *Children at Risk: The Battle for the Hearts and Minds of our Kids*. A graduate of Kentucky's Georgetown College, Mr. Bauer received his J.D. from Georgetown Law School in Washington, D.C.

M.E. BRADFORD is Professor of English at the University of Dallas, where he has taught for the past 23 years. He is one of America's foremost scholars in American political thought, the literature of the South, the English origins of American political thought, and the constitutional relationship of the states to the federal government. He is author of more than 250 articles and reviews and six books including: *A Better Guide Than Reason: Studies in the American Revolution, The Generations of the Faithful Heart: On the Literature of the South*, and *A Worthy Company: Brief Lives of the Framers of the United States Constitution*. A graduate of the University of Oklahoma, Professor Bradford received his Ph.D. in English from Vanderbilt University.

JOHN E. CHUBB has been a Senior Fellow in Governmental Studies at the Brookings Institution since 1984. Prior to that, he was a member of the faculty at Stanford University. He has also been a Visiting Professor at Johns Hopkins University and the Woodrow Wilson School of Public and International Affairs at Princeton University. An expert in education policy, Dr. Chubb has been awarded more than ten fellowships and grants and is author with Professor Terry M. Moe of *Politics, Markets and America's Schools*. A graduate of Washington

University, Dr. Chubb received his Ph.D. in Political Science from the University of Minnesota.

TERRY CONSIDINE has served as a Colorado State Senator since 1987. A leader of the term limitation movement, he is also Founder and Chairman of Coloradans Back In Charge, the Republican Leadership Program, and The Cairn Companies, a diversified company operating in fifteen states. Senator Considine received both his B.A. and J.D. from Harvard.

GREGORY S. DAVIDSON is currently the committee clerk for the Texas House of Representatives Committee on Public Safety and a graduate student at the University of Texas at Austin. He has also served as a legislative aide to Governor William P. Clements, Jr. and Texas State Representatives Ted Roberts, Fred Hill, and Bill G. Carter.

JOHN J. DiIULIO, JR. is Professor of Politics and Public Affairs, and Director of the Center of Domestic and Comparative Policy Studies at Princeton University. An expert on American national government, administrative theory, public management, criminal justice, military affairs, and political philosophy, he is also the recipient of numerous research grants, foundation fellowships, public service awards and teaching awards. He has been an advisor to the Bush Administration on drug policy. He is the author of numerous works on criminal justice including *Courts, Corrections, and the Constitution* and *No Escape: The Future of American Corrections.* Professor DiIulio is a graduate of the University of Pennsylvania and received his Ph.D. from Harvard.

DINESH D'SOUZA is a John M. Olin Research Fellow in Social Policy at the American Enterprise Institute. He has served as Managing Editor of *Policy Review* and as a Senior Domestic Policy Analyst at the White House in the Reagan Administration. He has published numerous articles on various aspects of politics and culture and is author of the best selling book *Illiberal Education-The Politics of Race and Sex on Campus.* Mr. D'Souza is a graduate of Dartmouth College.

THOMAS R. DYE is McKenzie Professor of Government and Policy Sciences at Florida State University. He has also served as President of the Southern Political Science Association, President of the Policy Studies Organization, and Secretary of the American Political Science Association. He has served as a visiting scholar at Bar-Ilan University in Israel and has taught at the University of Pennsylvania, University of Wisconsin, and University of Georgia. He is the author of numerous books and articles in American government and public policy, including his most recent work, *American Federalism: Competition Among Governments.* A graduate of Pennsylvania State University, Dr. Dye received his Ph.D. from the University of Pennsylvania.

JOHN C. GOODMAN is President of the National Center for Policy Analysis. An author of six books and numerous articles published in professional journals, he won the prestigious Duncan Black award in 1988 for the best scholarly article on Public Choice Economics. Dr. Goodman has taught and done research at Columbia University, Stanford University, Sarah Lawrence College, Dartmouth College, and Southern Methodist University. Dr. Goodman received his Ph.D. in Economics from Columbia University.

EDMUND F. HAISLMAIER is the Health Care Policy Analyst for The Heritage Foundation. His most recent papers examined proposals to mandate health insurance, the effects of the 1988 Medicare catastrophic legislation, and proposed changes in Medicare's physician reimbursement system. Mr. Haislmaier is also the principal author of Heritage's monograph on health care financing reform entitled, *A National Health System for America.* Prior to joining Heritage, Mr. Haislmaier was Vice President for Marketing and Public Relations at the Free Congress Foundation. He holds a degree in History from St. Mary's College of Maryland and studied Political Philosophy at Oxford University.

JOSEPH M. HORN is Associate Dean, College of Liberal Arts, University of Texas at Austin. He is Editorial Consultant for *Science* and *Behavior Genetics* and Research Proposal Reviewer for the National Science Foundation and National Institute of Mental Health. He is also a member of the editorial board for Acta Geneticae Medicae Gemillologiae. Dr. Horn received his B.S. in Chemical Engineering from Oklahoma State University and M.A. and Ph.D. in Psychology from the University of Minnesota.

CARL F. HOROWITZ is Policy Analyst for Housing and Urban Affairs at The Heritage Foundation. He received both his Ph.D. and M.C.R.F. in Urban Planning and Policy Development from Rutgers University and his B.A. in Economics is from the University of Kansas. He has taught Urban and Regional Planning at Virginia Polytechnic Institute. He has been an urban planner both in New Jersey and Virginia, and a Field Associate at the Brookings Institution.

PETER W. HUBER is a Senior Fellow of the Manhattan Institute for Policy Research, and Of Counsel to the Chicago, Illinois law firm of Mayer, Brown & Platt. He earned a doctorate in Mechanical Engineering from M.I.T., and served as an Assistant and later Associate Professor at M.I.T. for six years. He also holds a J.D. from Harvard and clerked for Judge Ruth Bader Ginsburg of the U.S. Court of Appeals for the D.C. Circuit and Justice Sandra Day O'Connor of the U.S. Supreme Court. Mr. Huber's professional expertise is in liability law and safety regulations. He is the author of four books, *Liability, The Geodesic Network, The Liability Maze* and *Galileo's Revenge.*

TEX LEZAR is President of both the Texas Public Policy Foundation and Associated Texans Against Crime. A founding partner in the Dallas and Houston law firm of Daniel & Lezar, he handles commercial and constitutional litigation and appeals. He has served as President Reagan's Assistant U.S. Attorney General in charge of Legal Policy, Counselor to U.S. Attorney General William French Smith, Staff Assistant and Speechwriter to President Nixon, and Vice

Chairman of the U.S. Attorney General's Commission on Pornography. He is a Board Member of numerous national conservative and professional organizations. He served as Assistant to William F. Buckley, Jr., immediately after graduating from Yale. Mr. Lezar received his J.D. from the University of Texas School of Law, where he was Editor in Chief of the *Texas Law Review*.

CHARLES H. LOGAN is a Professor of Sociology at the University of Connecticut, where he has taught since 1970. He has published widely on many issues in criminal justice and is the leading authority on privatization in corrections. Professor Logan served as a professional staff member on the President's Commission on Privatization and has been a Visiting Fellow in the U.S. Department of Justice at the National Institute of Justice and the Bureau of Prisons. His most recent publication is *Private Prisons: Cons & Pros*, published in 1990.

PATRICK B. McGUIGAN is chief editorial writer at the *Daily Oklahoman* in Oklahoma City. While at the Free Congress Foundation (1980-90), he edited the nation's only regular source of information on the politics of direct democracy; the initiative, referendum and recall. A member of the American Political Science Association, Mr. McGuigan has participated frequently in sessions of the Direct Democracy Research Group. He is the author of *The Politics of Direct Democracy: Case Studies in Popular Decision Making* and (with Dawn M. Weyrich) *Ninth Justice: The Fight for Bork*. He is also editor of six books on legal policy issues, including *Crime and Punishment in Modern America*.

MICHAEL McLAUGHLIN is currently a Congressional staff member. He formerly served as a Research Assistant in Domestic Policy Studies at The Heritage Foundation. He also served as Assistant Editor of the *Business/Education Insider*, a monthly guide for business leaders on education reform. He is the author of numerous papers, including *High School Dropouts: How Much of a Crisis?*, co-author of *A Businessman's Guide to the Education Reform Debate*, and *How Poor are America's Poor*. Mr. McLaughlin is a graduate of the University of Washington.

TERRY M. MOE is a Professor in the Department of Political Science, Stanford University. He is the author of numerous scholarly articles and two books, *The Organization of Interests* and, with John E. Chubb, *Politics, Markets, and America's Schools*. A graduate of the University of California at San Diego, Professor Moe received his Ph.D. from the University of Minnesota.

STEPHEN MOORE is Director of Fiscal Policy at the Cato Institute. He was formerly the Grover M. Hermann Fellow in budgetary affairs at The Heritage Foundation, where he headed a task force on federal budget process reform. He is the Founder and Executive Director of the American Immigration Institute, an organization devoted to promoting and studying the benefits of immigration. He is the editor of two books, *Slashing the Deficit: A Blueprint for a Balanced*

Budget by 1993 and *Privatization: A Strategy for Taming the Federal Budget.* Moore is a graduate of the University of Illinois.

WALTER K. OLSON is a Senior Fellow of the Manhattan Institute for Policy Research. He also launched and continues to direct the Institute's Judicial Studies Program, which explores the impact of litigation on American life. He is the author of *The Litigation Explosion: What Happened When America Unleashed the Lawsuit.* Olson graduated from Yale.

DUANE A. PARDE is Legislative Director for tax and fiscal policy at the American Legislative Exchange Council (ALEC). Mr. Parde is responsible for policy development, issue research and publication, and legislative analysis on state tax and fiscal policy. In addition, he serves as the staff director for ALEC's Task Force on Tax & Fiscal Policy. He has authored and edited several tax studies, including *State Tax & Expenditure Limits: A State-by-State Review* and *Less Taxation* and *More Democracy.* Prior to joining ALEC, he served as a Research Assistant for Legislative Affairs with the Kansas Attorney General's Office. Mr. Parde is a graduate of the University of Kansas.

ALLAN E. PARKER is a Professor of Law at St. Mary's University School of Law in San Antonio, Texas. He received his B.A. in Economics, *magna cum laude* from the University of Oklahoma, and J.D. at the University of Texas School of Law, where he was an Associate Editor of the *Texas Law Review.* He has been a Visiting Professor at the University of Texas School of Law, and has had significant civil trial practice with the firm of Gary, Thomasson, Hall & Marks in Corpus Christi, Texas.

ROBERT W. POOLE, JR. is President of the Reason Foundation and Publisher of *REASON* magazine. He was the first person in this country to promote the concept of "privatization" of government services. Poole founded the Local Government Center in 1976 as a think tank to research and publicize privatization. He served as a White House consultant on privatization in 1981, 1985, and 1986; and advised the President's Commission on Privatization in 1987-88. He is now on the Caltrans Privatization Advisory Steering Committee. Mr. Poole holds two engineering degrees from M.I.T.

ROBERT RECTOR is Policy Analyst for Social Welfare and Family issues at The Heritage Foundation. He is co-editor of *Steering the Elephant: How Washington Works,* a book on the internal management of the Presidency. At the Heritage Foundation, Mr. Rector has conducted a series of training seminars in policy development. He has written about income inequality, welfare, poverty, and family issues. He frequently testifies before Congress on these topics and played a key role in the development of President Bush's child care policy. Mr. Rector is a graduate of William and Mary College and holds an M.A. in Government from Johns Hopkins University.

LYNN SCARLETT is Vice President of Research at the Reason Foundation. President Bush's White House Office of Policy Development has utilized Dr. Scarlett's policy work on recycling and privatization. She has done work for the National Chamber Foundation, and The Heritage Foundation and confers frequently with the Office of Management and Budget on privatization issues. Currently, Dr. Scarlett is focusing on her own research on solid waste management issues. She received a B.A. and M.A. in Political Science and her Ph.D. in Economics and Political Science from the University of California at Santa Barbara.

LEWIS K. UHLER is the founder of the National Tax Limitation Committee—with the assistance of Milton Friedman, William A. Niskanen, Wm. Craig Stubblebine, Robert B. Carlson and others. The NTLC is now the largest grassroots taxpayer lobby in the United States. He served as a member of the California Law Revision Commission pursuant to appointment by then-Governor Ronald Reagan. He is now Of Counsel with the Newport Beach firm of Davis & Punelli. A graduate of Yale, Mr. Uhler received his J.D. from Boalt Hall School of Law, University of California at Berkeley.

DAVID A. WILLIAMS assisted in the editing of this book. He is a former Policy Analyst at The Heritage Foundation and served in the Health Care Financing Administration (HCFA) as well as the Department of Labor and Legal Services Corporation during the Reagan Administration. Mr. Williams also served as Senior Writer and Washington Correspondent for the physician's magazine, *Private Practice*. An alumnus of The King's College, he has been a member of the adjunct faculty of the University of Dallas and a television commentator in Virginia and Texas.

INTRODUCTION

A Conservative Agenda for the States
Problems, Principles, and Proposals

This book seeks to move people to improve their state governments. At the state and local level—like the federal level—liberal programs have not succeeded. As New York's Governor, Mario Cuomo, once admitted:

> If you're saying the test of whether you performed well is, did you solve the problems [of housing, health, education, welfare, and drugs], then I fail. I have a secret for you: Everybody is going to fail. The most you can do, it seems to me, is hope to make some difference.[1]

The failure of government to address the critical problems we face is neither necessary nor acceptable. Government can succeed, however, only by adopting different strategies and proposals—and by giving priority attention to those areas that are most important. Most importantly, government must recognize that it is the servant of people rather than their ruler. As the servant, government can succeed only if it elicits a new and greater degree of popular support for its actions.

This book concerns the failures of government today—and offers specific conservative prescriptions for improving government tomorrow. It calls for fundamental changes in the way government operates. As a result, it is not addressed primarily to those already in government. Through long service, too many in government have come to believe that the only way for government to be more effective is for it to tax and spend more. It is a central premise of this work that government must tax less—and pursue new and better approaches if it is actually to help to solve the most urgent problems the public expects government to address.

Instinctively, most Americans know that government has failed to do well those things that we all depend upon it to do. Most do not know, however, how to make government work better in meeting critical needs—such as the protection of our families from violent crime, the education of our children, and the fostering of greater economic opportunity for everyone. This book attempts to outline the basic principles that must guide government to become more effective—and it makes specific proposals based upon those principles.

The kinds of sweeping change in government necessary today can occur only if demanded by an informed and insistent electorate. As Abraham Lincoln observed at another critical moment in American history:

> In this and like communities, public sentiment is everything. With public sentiment, nothing can fail; without it nothing can succeed. Consequently he who moulds [sic] public sentiment, goes deeper than he who enacts statutes or pronounces decisions. He makes statutes and decisions possible or impossible to be executed.[2]

This book attempts to inform public sentiment. By doing that, it hopes to make better government possible.

Three other points must be mentioned in introducing this work. First, the principles and proposals are conservative. They seek to maximize freedom, to minimize government spending and intrusion, and to release the potential of people in their daily pursuits. They seek to empower individuals and provide them greater choice. They seek therefore to decentralize government and to use market forces to promote progress.

Second, we propose what government should do, rather than merely rejecting what government has done and denying the need for government to act at all. There are many things that government should not do. There are nevertheless a great many things in the modern world that government must do. It is our purpose to define what government should do, not just what it should not do. Like Abraham Lincoln, we believe:

> The legitimate object of government, is to do for a community of people, whatever they need to have done, but can not do, at all, or can not, so well do, for themselves—in their separate, and individual capacities. In all that the people can individually do as well for themselves, government ought not to interfere.[3]

Third, this book focuses upon state and local government—not the federal government. For too long, conservatism has been by necessity primarily an attack upon liberal adventurism by the national government. Always part of that critique was the admonition that much of what the government attempts to do at the federal level should be attempted in diverse ways at the state and local level. Nevertheless, the specifics of state and local governmental action have been too infrequently addressed by conservatives. This work attempts to redress that failing and provoke experimentation with new policies at the state and local level throughout America. It was a liberal, Justice Louis Brandeis, who put it so well more than 50 years ago:

> It is one of the happy incidents of the federal system that a single courageous State may, if its citizens choose, serve as a laboratory; and try novel social and economic experiments without risk to the rest of the country.[4]

Today, conservatives must enter that field—instead of playing solely upon the field of national government. It is upon the playing fields of state and local government that the battles of tomorrow in the Congress, the White House, and the federal courts will be won or lost. The failure to compete with vigor has left the field to liberals, who now dominate state and local government throughout America and gain practice for the national candidates of tomorrow. The liberal dominance of the states has, however, only been enhanced by the 1990 elections.

A true conservative revolution throughout this country will not occur until conservatives reemphasize the importance of state and local government—and demonstrate that conservative principles and proposals can be applied at the state and local level to improve the lives of our fellow citizens. The liberals have known this for decades—and have used the states as hothouses for new governmental growths. As has been often noted, the basic programs of the New Deal were not invented in Washington, D.C. Originally, they were experiments undertaken in New York State by Governors Al Smith and Franklin Delano Roosevelt, as well as in other states.[5]

Similarly, conservative policy experiments at the state and local level today could become the basis for improved federal policies tomorrow. Those experiments would take place without risk to the rest of the country, in Brandeis's words. But conservative successes in the states could save the country from a continuation of costly, but ineffective liberal policies at the national level.

The Problems

Crime

After several years of decline—following an explosive twenty years of growth—serious crime began to increase again in many areas of the country. Especially for minority and poor Americans, crime has become a new form of slavery. Inner city residents are most frequently the victims of crime—and the proliferation of drugs and gangs increasingly makes them the victimizers as well. According to the U.S. Department of Justice itself, five out of six twelve-year-olds will become the victims of an attempted or successful **violent** crime during their lifetimes if something better isn't done to combat crime.

Education

By most educational measures, American children do more poorly today than children in previous generations and other countries. Twenty-five percent of our children drop out of high school—in some large cities fifty percent—and only half go to college. Worse still, these figures have not improved in more than two decades. The failure of public education has made it even more difficult for minority students to break the bonds of poverty. The decline in public education has occurred despite a tripling of public spending per pupil during the last thirty years, which strongly suggests that more of the same is not the answer. But the poor—which also means most minority students—don't have any choice. They usually can afford to attend only local public schools. Of further concern, those who do attend college too often face a "dumbing down" of the curriculum by educational thought police more interested in political correctness than educational excellence. As a result, the value of higher education for Americans continues to decline in a more competitive world.

The General Public Welfare

Growing evidence suggests that long-standing government programs have been so ineffective that they have spawned the beginnings of a permanent underclass in American society. Throughout our history, Americans of the humblest origins have taken advantage of a continually expanding economy to move beyond poverty. In recent decades, even as government at all levels spent increasing amounts of effort and money in addressing the problem, the poorest of Americans—and especially African-Americans—have become mired in poverty. Many of these citizens have remained poorly educated and unhealthy. They have turned in large numbers to crime. They have experienced a widespread destruction of their families—and a remarkable increase in births to unmarried women without jobs.

Recent decades have witnessed what many believe to be a growing disrespect for individual human life itself. The phenomenon of dramatically increased abortions far beyond the numbers predicted by anyone and the effect of alcohol and drug abuse upon the unborn raise difficult questions for those on all sides of the abortion debate. Whether one favors or opposes abortion in specific circumstances—and most deem it permissible at least when a mother's life is threatened—nearly all Americans are concerned about the growing lack of emphasis upon individual responsibility and a basic respect for life itself. Very few who support a "right" to abortion nevertheless approve of its widespread use, especially as a birth control measure.

Indeed, the institution of the family itself has been severely weakened—among other things—by sexual liberalism, an exaggerated concern only for the self, and the use of abortion as a birth control technique. Concomitant with these stresses upon the traditional family, there is a growing pessimism about the opportunities and quality of life that will be available to our children. Throughout our history, Americans have sacrificed to ensure better educations and greater opportunities for their children. There is now a generalized questioning about the continuing viability of the American dream for our children. Through personal sacrifices alone can we do enough to ensure greater opportunities for our children?

More and more Americans worry that the future will see instead a growing competition for fewer resources and opportunities. America's historic faith in a future of greater opportunity produced by economic growth has been shaken. Adding to that breach of faith, government policies sometimes seem more intent on redistributing existing resources rather than encouraging the production of greater resources and promoting opportunity for all.

Most Americans, for example, now recognize the importance of conserving and preserving our physical environment and natural resources. Waste and thoughtless destruction impose high costs upon our future. Effective environmental policies will depend upon recognition of those future costs by the market. Only then can market forces be harnessed to develop approaches in the present to decrease or eliminate those threatening future costs.

Unfortunately, a powerful environmental lobby in America often seems more intent upon using government to discourage economic growth and energy development, rather than to improve the environment. Rather than seeking to foster innovative long-term solutions through the free market, this lobby seeks to promote government restrictions as a first response to scientifically uncertain environmental hazards.

In nearly every important area of policy, government has failed to emphasize or promote individual responsibility as a component of its initiatives. The results have been devastating for many Americans—and the country as a whole. We have spent more and more to help those in need—only to produce more need. We have had welfare, housing, and health policies that focused almost exclusively on providing something now. What we need are policies that provide something now, but that focus primarily upon making people self-sufficient in the future. Rather than creating a seemingly permanent and growing class of welfare recipients, policy should encourage personal conduct that promotes individual and familial responsibility and discourage conduct with the opposite effect.

There is, for example, a growing movement by the states—as well as the federal government—to respond to escalating public pressure to do something about the increasing costs of health care. How the states respond will influence policy approaches in other important areas in the immediate future. Thus far, a frightening rebirth of liberalism threatens to dominate health care policy.

Taxation and Spending

In 1991 state tax increases totaled about $18 billion—a record increase, which followed immediately upon $11 billion in state tax increases in 1990. Faced with a recession that decreased the earnings of so many Americans, states took more—not less—money from the people's pockets. And these increases occurred against a background of state revenues consuming more and more of the gross national product—some 8.4 percent today, a more than 60 percent increase since 1960 in the proportion of GNP consumed by the states.

Between 1980 and 1990 total spending by the states increased by more than 120 percent. During the first seven years of the 1980s, state and local expenditures from their own sources—as opposed to federal grants—grew at nearly twice the rate of federal per capita spending. Similarly, increases in the number of state and local government employees were more than three times the growth in federal civilian employment. And contrary to liberal mythology, federal aid to states and localities actually increased by 10 percent during the 1980s.

Historical evidence suggests that the drive to increase state taxes further—rather than significantly change the way states spend tax revenues—will result in further spending by the states. Nevertheless, government continues to adopt new means for separating citizens from their hard-earned cash—such as lotteries and other new forms of taxation (like a corporate income tax in Texas and a personal income tax in Connecticut).

A growing body of evidence also suggests that those states that increase their tax burdens relative to competing states—especially by so-called "progressive" income tax increases—threaten their overall economies. Increasingly, many states have followed an even more aggressive tax-and-spend strategy than the federal government. Absent a widespread tax revolt and new strategies for limiting state spending, the 1990s already promise more of the same.

Restoring Integrity to Government

Judged by voter registration figures and turnout at elections, American citizens have become alienated from our political process. A growing number of Americans no longer believe that their participation in that process would make a difference or that government would respond to their desires and beliefs. The growing number of scandals involving political perquisites and old-fashioned "pork" have further weakened public confidence in government itself—as has the creation of a protected class of professional political incumbents at all levels of government.

Adding to the sense of powerlessness in the heart of our democracy is the growth in activism by state courts, which increasingly interpret and overturn laws based upon nebulous legal reasoning. This new form of judicial activism has led state courts to interpret their own constitutions to provide greater rights than the federal Constitution in some 500 cases since 1975. And the trend is increasing. Instead of protecting the rights of our citizens, courts and the lawyers who practice in them seem more and more to be an impediment rather than an aid to settlement, security, or economic growth.

Federalism

Federal power, spending, and taxation in many ways inhibit more effective action by states and localities. Even as the power of states and localities to experiment with new and diverse policies must be encouraged, the federal government must give up some of its power, taxes, and spending. Just as centralization has occurred at the federal level, it has also arisen over the past century at the local level. The federal government frequently passes mandates requiring—or financial inducements encouraging particular actions by the states. Those requirements and inducements serve to deter state experimentation—as does the growing tendency of the Congress to pre-empt state activities in various areas of concern. Having caught the same sickness from the national government, states frequently now pass along costs and requirements to local governments, limiting the opportunity for experimentation at the level of government closest to the people. Florida, for example, had imposed some 445 such mandates upon its local governments through 1989—and New York State, some 2,700. In addition, both states and the national government have imposed costly requirements upon the next lower level of government without also ceding a part of their own revenue sources at the same time. As a result, the pressure to spend more and tax more has grown at all levels of government.

Principles & Proposals

The basic principles and proposals of liberalism still dominate state and local government in America. It is basic to liberal government to regulate what it condemns and to effect what it considers a fairer distribution of essential goods throughout society, especially to the disadvantaged and needy.

Similarly, conservatism is based upon basic principles as well. Like liberalism, conservatism seeks to promote the good society. But conservatism favors very different means from liberalism—and emphasizes a different hierarchy of values. It is the premise of this book that conservative principles allow the fashioning of specific proposals that would cause government to do a more efficient and effective job in promoting solutions to the domestic difficulties Americans now face. It is the first principle of conservatism that government works best by encouraging or discouraging specific actions of individuals and by promoting an ever-increasing abundance of resources—not by creating regulatory bureaucracies and redistributing existing resources. And conservatives believe that the free market can itself be utilized to improve the effectiveness and efficiency of governmental efforts, including those on behalf of the poor.

What then are the other basic principles of a conservative agenda for state government?

Public safety—the domestic defense—is the primary responsibility of government. It should be the first priority of government policymakers as well. Freedom from crime is a basic civil right. People choose to commit crime when the likelihood and severity of punishment are outweighed by anticipated gains. Common sense and social experience have demonstrated to the satisfaction of most Americans that crime is not the result of social problems. Crime is itself a social problem, which results from an individual choice. Only a society committed to punishing serious crime severely and swiftly—both by word and deed—can deter crime. Criminals must believe that they will be caught and will receive severe sanctions. Violent crimes and drug-dealing are the most severe crimes. Sentences determined as a matter of policy—not early release to conserve prison space—should be served in full by all who commit the most serious crimes or enter upon a career devoted to serious crime. Deterrence and incapacitation are the primary goals for the punishment of serious crime. Certainty of swift punishment—even a lesser punishment—and restitution should be the primary goals in dealing with less serious crime. Since the use of drugs clearly promotes crime, drug users should be treated while incarcerated and drug testing should be expanded as a requirement by employers and the providers of government services.

The best government programs are those that minimize bureaucracy and its costs by fostering self-help by recipients and private competition to provide services. Decentralizing government activities serves those goals—as does the development of market-driven programs. Regulation that sets narrow national or even statewide requirements can inhibit the innovation and experimentation necessary to solve social problems. Privatization should be made a priority for experimentation in all possible areas of government services.

Government spending should be reduced overall rather than increased. High rates of taxation or continuing tax increases retard economic growth, reduce individual personal income, and decrease the number of jobs that would otherwise be created. Further tax increases would produce greater costs to most Americans than any benefits that could flow from government expenditures.

Most parents want what is best for their children and will intelligently exercise choices available to them. And most children can learn so long as learning is expected and demanded from them. Parental involvement and schools that refrain from expecting too little as a tacit reward for relative obedience are critical to improving education. Discipline in the schools should be a key component of education—as should the teaching of moral values.

Government policy should encourage educational choice by parents rather than attempting to decree the choices that parents must make. Experimental choice plans for education should become the rule rather than the exception. By granting parents a choice, government will make the schools more accountable. Competition among schools will improve the quality of all schools and hence improve the education received by our children. To the maximum extent possible private education should be a component of choice in education—through vouchers.

Choice in education is so important that it must be tried. In the absence of governmental experimentation with choice plans, private business-es—whose future will surely depend upon the education received by employees—should fund private choice plans. Golden Rule Insurance Company has done so in Indianapolis, Indiana. And the Texas Public Policy Foundation's CEO (Children's Educational Opportunity) initiative is doing so in San Antonio, Texas. Together, they are allowing the families of more than two thousand low-income, inner-city children to choose a better education. If government educational bureaucracies continue to thwart publicly funded experiments with choice, businesses and individuals must ensure that they occur. In education and other areas, business should focus its eleemosynary efforts upon experimental programs that could serve as a model for improved governmental efforts in the future. Private pump-priming may force government to adopt promising new initiatives funded by the private sector.

Government should vigorously promote opportunity and attack all obstacles to opportunity based upon invidious discrimination, but it should never use quotas set by government to guarantee a particular distribution of results. Discrimination against individuals—especially because of their race—does exist. It must be vigorously and mercilessly attacked by government whenever it causes harm to identifiable individuals. Discrimination cannot, however, be successfully deterred by government's adopting reverse discrimination in favor of classes of people. Indeed, affirmative racial discrimination by government will not generally benefit the intended beneficiaries sufficiently to outweigh the harm it does to innocent individuals who have not themselves discrimi-nated against anyone.

The family has been critical to the development of civilized society. All government policies that weaken families should be forthrightly recognized as suspect and be re-evaluated. No matter how well-intended, some such policies have had a perversely opposite effect to what they intended. The forming and preserving of families should be encouraged, not discouraged.

The ability of the individual voter to influence governmental policy directly—and to recognize that influence—should be promoted. Initiative and referendum may well be the most important tool for constructing a more accountable government. Government must be generally reformed to ensure that it becomes more responsive to individuals and less the captive of special interest funding and professional incumbents. The adoption by states of term limits upon their elected representatives at the state and federal level could be an important step along the road of reform. In addition, the machinery of state government should be reformed to increase its effectiveness.

Government incentives to protect the environment are likely to be more successful than regulations or proscriptions—except in the case of clear hazards intentionally created. Promoting a healthier environment should be a key function of government, but government should not allow radical environmentalism or a desire for a seemingly instant policy panacea to retard economic growth or energy development.

Economic growth—coupled with a renewed emphasis on individual responsibility—is the most effective means to fight poverty. Government programs that sap economic growth generally cost more than they accomplish—and trap the intended beneficiaries in a web of dependence. Government actions to promote growth and to refrain from inhibiting growth—coupled with programs to enhance opportunities for all—are the key to reducing poverty. Rather than further restricting individual initiative in a necessarily ineffective effort to mandate progress, government programs should aim to empower individuals and local associations of individuals to develop diverse and innovative approaches to meeting their own needs.

Lawyers serve as instruments of the state in the services they perform. As a result, the activities of lawyers should receive special scrutiny to determine whether they benefit the public as much as they benefit themselves. In addition, it is time for a careful review and reform of laws and legal procedures that place American workers and businesses at a significant disadvantage in the world market.

Diversity and experimentation are critical to making government do a better job. Just as state governments are therefore better suited than the federal government to the development of improved policies in many areas, local governments are best suited to the development of many policies. Those mechanisms that encourage communities of interest to come together to meet shared problems are most important. Governmental policies that divide communities or give a little to every interest group are less likely to effect improvements.

These principles are the heart of the many proposals that follow. No one need agree with them all, but government would be significantly improved by experimenting with many of them. Emboldened by the international converts to our philosophy of free elections and free markets, it is time America renewed its own faith in the ability of ordinary people to do extraordinary things. The Texas Public Policy Foundation and the authors of the following chapters hope that this book encourages more Americans to make their state governments work more effectively on behalf of us all.

Endnotes

1. *New York Times*, 24 Oct. 1990, A16.

2. First Debate with Stephen A. Douglas at Ottawa, Ill., *The Collected Works of Abraham Lincoln*, Roy P. Basler, ed., vol. III (New Brunswick: Rutgers Univ. Press, 1953), 27.

3. Abraham Lincoln, written fragment, 1 Julyy 1854, *The Collected Works of Abraham Lincoln*, vol. II, p. 220.

4. *New State Ice Co. v. Liebmann*, 285 U.S. 262, 311 (1932) (Brandeis, J., dissenting).

5. *See, e.g.,* David Osborne, *Laboratories of Democracy* (Boston: Harvard Business School Press, 1988), 1 and accompanying notes 1 and 2.

GIVE CHOICE A CHANCE

Dr. John E. Chubb
Senior Fellow, The Brookings Institution

and

Prof. Terry M. Moe
Stanford University

A new wave of school reform is beginning to sweep the nation. From coast to coast, state legislatures and boards of education are looking at ways to use "choice," an innovative concept in educational organization, to boost school performance. This is encouraging because choice is a significant departure from traditional approaches to education reform. While past attempts at educational improvement have focused on schools, choice focuses on school systems. If the theory supporting choice is correct, traditional reforms have worked rather poorly because they have failed to get to the root of the problem. Choice promises much better results because it aims to correct the systemic problems that give rise to problems in the schools.

If choice is to fulfill its promise, however, policymakers must understand that choice is not just another approach to school reform. Choice is fundamentally different. Choice provides a blueprint for a new system of public education. Properly implemented, choice reallocates authority over schools, restructures the incentives facing schools, and reorders the priorities set by schools. Choice basically inverts the way schools are controlled. Today, schools are part of a vast education system, subject to multiple authorities at the federal, state, and local levels, and run from the top down through politics and bureaucracy. In a choice system, authority would be effectively decentralized to the local or school level. Schools would shape their own organizations and programs in response to concerns communicated from the bottom up—in response, primarily, to the demands of parents who would be empowered to choose their children's schools.

Properly understood, choice promises to improve schools by redistributing the power to govern them. If choice is implemented in ways that do not alter the balance of power over schools—if choice is implemented as are traditional reforms—choice will not make much of a difference. Despite all the support that the idea of choice is now attracting, including that of President Bush who has made choice a central part of his America 2000 Education Strategy, choice could easily go the ineffectual way of countless past reforms. If choice is to avoid this fate, policymakers must understand the inadequacy of traditional school reforms, the need to fundamentally restructure school systems, and the process by which choice will lead schools to work much better.

Policymakers must also understand that while choice promises to create a system of schools that is genuinely new, there is already a lot known about how such a system would operate and how schools within it would improve. Over the past decade we have been conducting research on school performance and its relationship to the way school systems are run. Most of that research has been based on a nationwide sample of some 500 high schools and over 20,000 students, teachers, and administrators, surveyed over a four year period. Last year the Brookings Institution published the final results of that work in our book, *Politics, Markets, and America's Schools*. The book provides extensive evidence on the effects of various factors—families, friends, schools, school systems—on student achievement, and recommends choice as a comprehensive strategy for boosting student achievement and improving schools more generally. The book concludes with a detailed proposal for a statewide system of choice. Our purpose in this paper is to distill the theory, evidence, and recommendations from the book into a form that is perhaps more useful to policymakers. Using a question and answer format, we will address the issues that policymakers most often raise about American education and school choice.[1]

1. Are America's schools really performing so poorly that we must consider wholesale changes in them?

Yes. Schools in the United States appear to be doing a worse job than schools in this country did in the past and than schools in other countries are doing now. We say appear because there are many factors that influence students besides schools, and these factors have never been adequately controlled in analyses of American students over time or in comparisons of American and foreign students. Nevertheless, a host of relevant indicators are disturbing.

The academic achievement of American students may be significantly lower today than it was twenty-five years ago. On the best known indicator of student ability, the Scholastic Aptitude Test or SAT, the average total score of college-bound seniors fell more than 90 points between 1963 and 1981, and remains more than 80 points below its high-water mark today.[2] Although some of this decline is explained by increases in the size of the test-taking population (a growing proportion of the population is attending college), similar declines were registered on many tests that do not present this problem of comparability.[3] Scores on the Iowa achievement test, administered to students in grades 6, 8, 10, and 12, dropped about as much as SAT scores during the late 1960s and 1970s. The same can be said of the tests administered to students at ages 9, 13, and 17 as part of the periodic National Assessment of Educational Progress (NAEP). True, not all test trends over the last twenty-five years have been bad. The gap between minority and non-minority test scores has closed significantly. And during the late 1970s and early 1980s, depending on the test, American students posted gains in performance. Unfortunately, those gains have now stabilized and/or ended. SAT scores, to cite a clear example of this, peaked in 1985, and since 1987 have suffered a 10-point fall.[4]

Another troubling trend is the persistently high rate of high school dropouts. Again, the facts depend to an extent on how the measurement is done. If dropouts include those young people of normal high school age who are not in school or out of school with a regular high school diploma—not equivalency credentials—the average dropout rate is currently around 20 percent nationally, and as much as 50 percent in some large cities.[5] If the dropout rate counts only those students who have failed by their late twenties to receive either a regular diploma or high school equivalency credentials, the rate is not as bad—12.6 percent in 1989.[6] But the disturbing fact about the dropout rate is that however it is measured, it has not declined much since the mid 1970s. After making great strides in increasing school attendance in the immediate postwar era—half of all adults did not have a high school education in 1950—American schools have virtually stalled out, far short of success, in reaching this modest educational objective.[7]

Trends aside, the knowledge and skills of American students today are simply not very impressive. The NAEP classifies only 10 percent of all 13 year olds as "adept" at reading, and less than 1 percent as "advanced."[8] Large percentages of the 17 year olds taking the NAEP tests answered questions requiring only basic skills or knowledge incorrectly. For example 47 percent could not "express 9/100 as a percent." Only 5 percent could calculate the cost per kilowatt on an electrical bill that charged $9.09 for 606 kilowatts of electricity. Twenty-six percent of the students did not know that Congress is part of the legislative branch of government. The same share could not define "democracy." On other NAEP tests, 43 percent of all high school juniors could not place World War I in the broad historical period of 1900-1950, and 75 percent could not place Abraham Lincoln's presidency in the era, 1840-1880.[9]

By international standards this sort of performance also fails to measure up. Eighth grade students in the United States placed next to last on a 1981-1982 mathematics test administered in 12 advanced industrial democracies.[10] The averages of Japanese students, the highest in the world, were about 15 percent higher than the averages of American students. In a 1982 comparison of the *best* math students in 11 nations, including many nations with which the United States competes economically, American students came in dead last in calculus and algebra, scoring at the same level as the median of *all* Japanese 17 year olds.[11] The most recent comparisons tell the same story. A new study conducted by the Educational Testing Service for the National Science Foundation and the Department of Education found American 13 year olds performing worse or no better in science and math than students in all of the countries in the study—the United Kingdom, Ireland, Spain, Canada, and South Korea.[12] In math, South Korean students, the highest performers, are achieving levels four times those of American students—an alarming statistic indeed, but far from an isolated one. By most measures American students are not doing very well, and their schools must bear some responsibility for this.

2. What have American schools been doing about the troubling trends in student performance?

For the last twenty years American schools have been trying in many and varied ways to improve student performance. School systems did not wait until the 1983 presidential report, *A Nation at Risk*, warned of a "rising tide of mediocrity" to begin seeking improvement. The national decline in test scores was apparent by the early 1970s, and efforts to turn that decline around—to boost student achievement—began in earnest at that time. For example, the 1970s ushered in the "back to the basics" movement. The 1970s also brought innovations in curriculum, instruction, and special programs almost as numerous as the state and local systems of education that implemented them. To be sure, the 1980s saw a stronger wave of reform sweep the nation. But the important point is that America's school systems first introduced reforms to boost academic achievement a generation ago, and have pursued such reforms even more vigorously since then.[13]

This experience should at least make reformers skeptical of new efforts to improve education through traditional means. While it would be premature to pass final judgment on the school reforms of the last five years, it is fair to say that the educational establishment can provide little evidence that its efforts to improve schools over the last two decades have paid off. There is also ample evidence that the dominant approaches to reform that the schools have been using, approaches that rely heavily on spending and regulation, have not been working out.

It may come as a surprise to some participants in the current educational debate, but public schools are increasingly well funded institutions. From 1970 to 1990 per pupil current expenditures increased 489 percent in nominal terms against an inflation rate of 213 percent. That's a real increase of 88 percent. Total expenditures per student in daily attendance reached $4,929 by 1990.[14] For the sake of comparison, that amount is more than twice the cost of educating a student in a Catholic school, where research indicates the education is superior.[15] Even during the 1970s, the period of steepest decline in student achievement, per pupil current expenditures in the public schools increased 41 percent in real terms.[16]

But what were these increased financial resources being used for? Some portion of the additional money was being used for two things that the educational establishment has long argued are vital to school improvement. Teacher salaries were increased and class sizes were decreased. From 1970 to 1990 the average teacher salary in the United States increased from $8,560 to $32,249, and the average ratio of pupils to teachers (a proxy for class size) fell from 22.3 to 17.2.[17] Moreover, the increases in teacher salaries purchased at least nominal gains in teacher quality. The percentage of teachers with master's degrees doubled by 1990, reaching 54 percent.[18]

These "improvements" account for less than half of the 88 percent real increase in per pupil education spending over the period. Although the increase in average teacher salaries amounted to only 20 percent in real terms, the increase had to be paid to 30 percent more teachers per student. The total cost of teacher salaries therefore rose 36 percent per student from 1970 to 1990. If the returns on this investment have been meager—and this apparently is so—there are several likely reasons. One is that reductions in pupil-teacher ratios or class sizes of the magnitude achieved during the seventies and eighties simply may not produce systematic improvements in student achievement. Another is that these reductions were not achieved through careful efforts to increase student-teacher contact but rather as a byproduct of efforts to minimize teacher layoffs during a period of declining student enrollments. A final reason is that the higher average salaries—actually 7 percent lower during the 1970s—were not being used to attract more talented teachers into the profession but to compensate those already in the aging teaching force for increasing experience and educational attainment.

If the increased investment in teacher salaries did not pay off as hoped, however, it had and still has a better prospect of improving education than most of the rest of the increase in public school spending that occurred from 1970 to the present. Schools are not spending more today than twenty years ago because of better books, materials, laboratories, equipment or other obvious improvements in instructional facilities—at least not much more. No, at least half of the 88 percent real increase in educational spending per pupil from 1970 to 1990 was consumed by such things as more expensive employee fringe benefits (which doubled their share of school system budgets); rising "fixed costs" such as rent, maintenance, and insurance; increasing use of "auxiliary teaching services" provided by aides and counselors; and last but not least, educational administration.[19] Indeed, after teacher salaries and fringe benefits, school bureaucracy may be the single largest beneficiary of the substantial increase in educational expenditures over the last two decades.

Because of problems of data availability and comparability it is impossible to estimate with confidence the size of the real increase in all administrative costs per pupil in America's public schools since 1970. But the data that are available describe very significant growth in public school bureaucracy. From 1977 to 1987, when the ratio of students to teachers nationwide fell 8.4 percent, the ratio of students to central office professional personnel dropped 21.0 percent.[20] In other words, administrative employment outside of schools was growing at two-and-a-half times the rate of instructional employment inside the schools. Between 1960 and 1980 local school spending on administration and other non-instructional functions grew by 107 percent in real terms, almost twice the rate of per pupil instructional expenditures.[21]

More instructional matters were also being taken out of the classroom: between 1960 and 1984 the number of non-classroom instructional personnel in America's school systems grew 400 percent, nearly seven times the rate of growth in the number of classroom teachers.[22] In 1987, full-time classroom teachers represented barely half (53 percent) of all local school employment; administrators represented 12 percent.[23] Whatever its precise magnitude, if the growth in bureaucracy did not help schools educate children more effectively, bureaucratization may explain some of the disparity between educational spending and student achievement over the last generation.

In due course, we will provide many reasons for concern about school bureaucracy. At this juncture, it is only important to recognize that school reform and bureaucratization have traditionally gone hand-in-hand. Two decades of school reform have substantially increased the regulation of public schools. The local public school is subject to far more federal and state mandates today than it was when the nation's educational slide began. Schools are more constrained in their use of personnel, their design of curriculum, their choice of instructional methods, their maintenance of discipline, and their provision of special programs. School reform is not solely responsible for this. Collective bargaining with increasingly powerful teacher unions has helped to constrain schools. And school systems, for their own reasons, have seen fit to take authority out of schools and to centralize it in district offices.[24] Still, from the countless special programs of the federal government—for example, compensatory education—to the curriculum specifications of state departments of education, to the implementation of these innovations by district offices, school reform has increased the regulation of local schools.

Since the early 1980s, moreover, this tendency has picked up pace. First, educational spending has increased more than anyone thought possible when *A Nation at Risk* called for a long list of expensive reforms. Between 1984 and 1990 aggregate spending on public elementary and secondary education increased in real terms by $49 billion.[25] Second, many new regulations have been written. Some of these regulations may be desirable (though research does not encourage optimism). For example, almost all states have imposed higher graduation requirements on high schools, and many states have required competency tests of new teachers. But much of the regulation—as we shall explain—has the prospect of backfiring. The increased regulation of student and teacher performance, now being widely implemented through evaluation and accountability systems composed of tests and a host of other "objective" criteria, could easily rob schools of vitality and undermine their performance. This is a fairly well-known danger, but it is a danger that educational systems, now so heavily dependent on central administration, seem willing to accept. It is also a danger that elected officials, ultimately responsible for these systems, can hardly avoid. With education organized as it is, political leaders anxious to improve school performance have little choice but to provide school systems with more money and then regulate how those systems use it. Within the existing system, reform options are limited.

3. What do other researchers have to say about the recent trends in learning and schooling?

The decline (and rise) in student test scores over the last twenty-five years is one of the most researched and least understood phenomena in education. As yet, researchers have produced no simple or adequate explanation for the changes in aggregate student performance. The trends appear to be the product of many factors, some educational but many non-educational. The most important factor, accounting for perhaps a fifth of the total decline, appears to be a change in the racial composition of the test-taking population.[26] American schools have been taking in different kinds of students, students who are more difficult to educate than students in the past. Influences in the home have also been changing.

The second most important cause of the test score trends appears to be changes in family size—larger families initially hampering achievement and then smaller families encouraging it.

It is also clear that the test score decline did not characterize all grades equally. The decline was comprised primarily of worsening scores among students born between 1946 and 1963, the "baby boom" generation.[27] As these students moved through the schools, test scores declined, pushing SAT scores down from 1964 to 1979. But as the baby boomers began to be replaced, around 1970, by a new cohort, the "baby bust" generation, test scores in the early grades began to climb. By 1980 the younger cohort, now in high school, was taking the SAT and posting the modest increases in SAT scores observed during the early eighties. Unfortunately, further gains have not been posted by subsequent cohorts, leaving achievement generally below the levels of twenty-five years ago.

The influence that so-called compositional and cohort effects have had on test score trends underscores the importance of factors beyond the control of schools in producing student achievement. Yet, even when the full range of non-educational factors is taken into account—alcohol and drug use, and exposure to environmental lead (both of which have had small effects on test score trends); single-parent households, maternal employment, and television viewing (none of which seems to have had a substantial effect on test score trends)—no more than a third of the variation in test scores over time can be explained.[28] That leaves a lot of room for educational factors to make a difference.

But researchers have made little progress in identifying significant educational factors. The most comprehensive study to date, by the Congressional Budget Office in 1987, found some evidence that schools might have undermined achievement by watering down the content of courses, assigning less homework, and using less challenging textbooks.[29] But the study found no impact, positive or negative, from other educational factors such as teachers' test scores, teachers' educational attainment, or state graduation requirements. The fact of the matter is, most of the relationship between schooling and learning over the last twenty-five years remains a mystery.

Some clues about the relationship can be found, however, in other kinds of research into student achievement, research that has not focused on test score trends but on differences in tests among schools at any given time. This research has reached some fairly strong, though negative, conclusions about the connection between schooling and learning. A recent survey of 147 statistical analyses of school performance, for example, found no consistently positive and significant relationship between student achievement and any of the major factors popularly assumed to influence achievement: teacher-pupil ratios, teacher education, teacher experience, teacher salaries, and per pupil expenditures.[30] In other words, much of what school systems have been doing to turn test scores around may have no systematic effect on school performance.

Nevertheless, we know that factors outside of schools do not adequately account for student achievement either. And we know, from casual observation, as well as careful case studies, that some schools are much, much better than others. The challenge remains to find out why. The research in which we have been engaged takes up that challenge.

4. Why does your research have anything new to say about the mysteries of student achievement and school performance?

The research that we have been doing on school performance differs from a lot of other such research in two important ways. The first has to do with the causes of school performance that we investigate, the second with the data that we employ to study those causes. Research into the causes of school performance and student achievement has been dominated by what are often called input-output studies.[31] Based on the economic concept of the production function, these studies have tried to explain educational "outputs," such as student test scores, with conventional economic "inputs," such as expenditures per student, teacher salaries, class sizes, and the quality of school facilities. The fundamental idea behind these studies is that schools, like any economic enterprise, ought to produce their products—educated students—with varying degrees of effectiveness and efficiency as the combination of capital and labor used in production varies. Years of study now suggest, however, that schools may not be like just any economic enterprise. Since the famous "Coleman Report" of 1966, input-output studies have been unable to establish any systematic relationship between school performance and a wide range of indicators of school resources.

The research that we have been doing takes a different approach than input-output studies. It focuses on the production process itself. It considers how schools are organized and operated—in other words, how inputs are actually converted into outputs. The production process may well be more important in public education than the economic theory of production functions would suggest. Schools are not part of a market where competitive forces can be assumed to encourage managers to organize firms to use capital and labor efficiently. Schools are part of political and administrative systems where the forces that managers— principals and superintendents—are exposed to cannot be expected to encourage efficient organization. It therefore becomes especially important in analyzing the performance of a public enterprise, such as a school, to study its organization. It is also important to examine those non-economic forces that lead schools to organize as they do. While our research also considers the conventional economic determinants of school performance, our emphasis is on the production process—how it works and what causes it to work in different ways. Because of this emphasis, our research may well have something new to say.

Our research also differs from traditional research in the data it employs. We are far from the first researchers to suggest that school organization is important, that it can help explain the weak link between school resources and school performance. Indeed, over the last ten years many researchers have completed studies that show that successful schools have distinctive organizations. Better schools appear to be characterized by such things as clear and ambitious goals, strong and instructionally oriented leadership by principals, an orderly environment, teacher participation in school decision making, and collegial relationships between and among school leaders and staff. The studies that have identified these characteristics—studies known collectively as "Effective Schools Research"—have not settled the issue of school performance, however.[32] There are serious doubts about the magnitude of the impact that school organization has on school performance and, indeed, about whether organization is a cause of performance at all: healthy school organizations may be a consequence of successful students, and not vice versa. It almost goes without saying that Effective Schools Research has provided few clues about the causes of school organization; the focus of that research has been on organizational consequences.

A primary reason for the doubts about Effective Schools Research is the methods that have been used in most of the studies. Research has been dominated by qualitative case studies of small numbers of schools, often reputed to be unusually successful. Those few studies that have used somewhat larger numbers of schools and employed quantitative analysis have still not examined representative samples. From one study to the next there has been considerable variation in the particular organizational characteristics said to be important. And the conclusion that organization is important, however frequently it has been drawn, is still based on impressionistic evidence, uncontrolled observation, and limited numbers of cases. In contrast, input-output research, however negative its conclusions, is based on rigorous statistical analyses of hard data in hundreds and thousands of schools nationwide. There is consequently more reason at this point to believe that the relationship between school resources and school performance is unsystematic than to believe that school organization provides a strong link between the two.

In our research we explore how strong that link may be by employing the methods that have been used in input-output analyses. Unlike most Effective Schools Research, we investigate the resources, organization, and performance of a large, random, national sample of schools in which all characteristics are measured with quantitative indicators, all relationships are estimated with statistical controls, and all inferences are careful to try to distinguish causes from effects.

Our data base is the result of merging two national surveys of American high schools—High School and Beyond (HSB), a 1980 and 1982 panel study of students and schools, and the Administrator and Teacher Survey (ATS), a 1984 survey (which we helped design) of the teachers and principals in half of the HSB schools. The merged data set includes over 500 public and private high schools—the privates providing a valuable look at school organization in a market setting—and approximately 9,000 students, 11,000 teachers, and the principals in every school in the sample. While no piece of research is ever definitive, and this is certainly true of research as new as ours, our work is a step in the right direction methodologically, and therefore a contribution that may well make a difference.

5. What did you find about the relationship between school organization and school performance?

If school performance is gauged by student achievement, school organization is a major determinant of effectiveness. All things being equal, high school students achieve significantly more—perhaps a year more—in schools that are "effectively" organized than in schools that are not. Indeed, after the aptitude or entering ability of the student, no factor—including the education and income of the family or the caliber of a student's peers—may have a larger impact on how much a student achieves in high school than how a school is organized to teach its students.

We reached these conclusions after analyzing the gains made by roughly 9,000 students on standardized tests—in reading, writing, vocabulary, math, and science—administered first during the sophomore year of high school and then again at the end of the senior year. It is important to recognize that by analyzing the gains on these tests, as opposed to analyzing only the final level of achievement on the tests, we have probably improved our chances of measuring the effect that schools actually have on achievement. Most studies of student achievement analyze test score levels, not gains. By high school, however, levels of achievement are heavily influenced by a host of factors preceding the high school experience. Our study looks at a variety of factors besides the school experience too, but our measures of student achievement are not contaminated by prior influences; the gain scores reflect only the learning that takes place during the high school years.

Besides school organization, the influences on student achievement that we examined included several that are generally beyond the control of schools: the education and income of the parents, the race of the student, the education and income of the families in the school (a proxy for peer group influences), and the aptitude of the student. We also examined some of the conventional influences over which the school has control: pupil-teacher ratios, expenditures per student, teacher salaries, graduation requirements, homework loads, disciplinary policies, and more. When these conventional school influences were examined simultaneously, and in various combinations, most did not make a significant difference for student achievement. Traditional measures of school resources and school policies were not systematically related to student performance. This is consistent with the results of numerous input-output studies that precede ours.

In the final analysis, only four factors consistently made a significant difference for achievement gains by high school students. In order of importance they were student aptitude, school organization, family background, and peer group influence. Over a four year high school experience the difference in achievement that would be expected to result from being in the top quartile rather than the bottom quartile on each of these factors, all other factors being equal, are as follows: aptitude, one-and-a-half years of achievement; school organization, a little more than one year of achievement; family background, one year of achievement; and peer group influence, less than a half year of achievement. In short, school organization may be as important to student achievement as the influence of families, a major influence indeed.

6. What are the organizational characteristics that seem to make schools effective?

Three general characteristics most distinguish effective school organizations from ineffective ones. The first is school goals. The objectives of effective schools are clearer and more consistently perceived than the goals of ineffective schools. The objectives of the more successful schools are also more academically ambitious. More than twice as many effective schools as ineffective ones make "academic excellence" their top priority. In contrast, the unsuccessful schools place more priority than do the successful ones on such objectives as basic literacy skills, good work habits, citizenship, and specific occupational skills. Overall, effective organizations seem more likely to possess a sense of "mission," something that many other observers of effective schools have noted.

The second distinctive characteristic of effective organizations is leadership. The better schools have principals who are stronger educational leaders. Specifically, effective organizations are led by principals who, according to their teachers, have a clear vision of where they want to take the school and the practical knowledge to get the school there. This is consistent with the sense of mission that characterizes school goals. But there is more to effective leadership. There is a strength of purpose in the better principals that comes through in their reasons for wanting to head a school. Principals in effective schools are much more likely than their counterparts in ineffective schools to report that they took the job of principal to gain control over the educational performance of the school—over personnel, curriculum, and other school policies—and much less likely to say that they simply preferred administration to teaching. In much the same vein, the successful school principals have more teaching experience and less ambition to leave the school for a higher administrative post. Overall, the principals in the successful schools seemed to be more oriented by teaching and less by administration. The successful principals seemed more like leaders, the less successful ones more like managers.

Finally, effective organizations were more professional in all of the best senses of that much abused term. Principals in the effective schools held their teachers in higher esteem and treated them more as equals. Teachers were more involved in decisions about various school policies and they were given more freedom within their classrooms. Teachers also treated each other more like colleagues. They cooperated with one another and coordinated their teaching more regularly, and held each other in relatively high regard. The teachers in effective schools behaved in another important way like professionals too; they came to school regularly and presented less of an absenteeism problem for principals. Finally, the teachers in effective schools exhibited stronger feelings of efficacy, beliefs that they could really make a difference in the lives of their students. And it is no wonder. In a school where everyone is pulling together, working as a team—the concept we think best captures the effective school—and in which teachers are trusted and respected to do their best, it stands to reason that teachers would tend to believe that they can actually succeed.

7. **How do you know that schools with effective organizations haven't simply benefitted from teaching bright kids or receiving the support of educated parents? In other words, how do you know that effective organizations promote student achievement rather than the other way around?**

There are several reasons why we are confident that effective school organization means a great deal for student achievement. The first is that in our analysis of student achievement, school organization competes directly with many characteristics of student and family background to explain the observed changes in test scores. In this competition school organization fares very well, coming in second. Now, it is true that school organization may be receiving undue credit for influences on test scores that are really the result of student body influences working through the school organization. But it is also true that student bodies may be receiving undue credit—credit that should go to school organization—for boosting test scores. After all, it is school reputations for organizational effectiveness that lead many parents to buy homes in the jurisdictions of better schools, and that, in turn, provide effective organizations with better students.

So, how should the alternative forms of "undue credit" be corrected? Should the influence of school organization be downgraded because organization may be influenced by student body characteristics? Or should the influence of organization be upgraded because student body characteristics are influenced by school organization? The correct answer is that both should be done simultaneously. Unfortunately, such a correction is statistically impossible with our data. We must, therefore, be content that our estimate of the effect of organization on achievement strikes a happy medium between over- and under-estimation.

But there is another reason for confidence in the influence of school organization. We analyzed a variety of possible causes of school organization and found that the characteristics of students and parents were not the most important sources of effective or ineffective organization. A school may be effectively organized whether it is teaching bright students or educationally disadvantaged students, and whether it is supported by educated parents or scarcely supported by parents at all. As a result, a properly organized school can have a positive, independent effect on students of any kind.

8.   What causes some schools to be more effectively organized than others?

This is an important question, and one that has too seldom been asked. If school performance is to be lastingly improved, it will not be enough to know what effective schools look like. Knowing that effective schools should have clear goals, strong leadership, and a professional structure will not necessarily help reformers make schools more effective. It may not be possible, for example, to train principals to be stronger educational leaders, or to encourage them to treat teachers like colleagues or true professionals. Yet reformers in every state are trying to do precisely these kinds of things today. Based on Effective Schools Research, many state departments of education have established effective schools programs to encourage or force their schools to develop more effective organizations.

Schools are being instructed to raise their expectations, to establish priorities, to make decisions more cooperatively, and so on. But this approach assumes that schools have become poorly organized because they did not know any better. Once schools know how to organize themselves more effectively, they will do so—or so it is assumed. This assumption, however, is likely to be wrong.

Unlike Effective Schools Research, which has shown little interest in those things that might cause schools to become ineffectively or effectively organized in the first place, our research is extremely interested in the determinants of school organization. We are struck by the fact that many schools in this country have become effective organizations without the benefit of any research showing schools the way. By the same token, we find it hard to believe that many of the worst school organizations in this country have reached their sad state because their superintendents, principals, or teachers did not know any better. More likely, schools have organized effectively or ineffectively in response to various political, administrative, economic, and educational forces that demand organizational responses. If this is correct, the key to school reform is understanding how those forces work, and then making adjustments to them.

We examined simultaneously the effects of a large number of such forces on school organization. Many mattered little or not at all. For example, when all else is taken into account, higher teacher salaries and more expenditures per pupil do not produce more effective school organizations. Even if expenditures are used to reduce student-teacher ratios, there is no significant impact. More effective organizations do not have more teachers per pupil, or by extension, smaller classes. Ultimately, more effective organizations are distinguished from less effective ones by but two kinds of forces. One kind emanates from the students in the school, the other kind is applied by politicians and administrators outside of the school.

High schools are much more likely to organize effectively—to set ambitious priorities, practice vigorous educational leadership, and operate professionally—if their students are well-behaved, have above average aptitude, and come from relatively well-educated and affluent families. If the students in a school exhibit any one of these traits, the organizational effectiveness of that school is likely to rank one or even two quartiles above that of a school whose students do not have these traits. This is not to say that the impact of school organization on student achievement is artificial, however. Students still register higher *gains* in schools that are effectively organized, all things being equal. But a school is more likely to get organized to provide this academic boost if its students are more academically inclined to begin with.

Not too much should be made of the organizational advantage of educating bright kids, however. The single largest determinant of whether a school is effectively organized is not associated with the caliber of the students in the school but with the strength of the pressures outside the school. Specifically, the more a school is subject to the influence of administrators, unions, and indirectly, school boards, the less likely the school is to be effectively organized. Schools that have relatively little control over curriculum, instruction, discipline, and especially hiring and firing are likely to fall more than two quartiles in overall organizational effectiveness below schools with relatively strong control over these matters. This is true, moreover, when the influences of students and parents are held constant. Schools with less academically able students can be organized quite effectively, and succeed, if they are given the freedom by politicians and bureaucrats to do so!

9. Why is autonomy from outside authority so important for effective school organization?

Autonomy is vital for many reasons, but two seem to be paramount. First, and clearly most important, if schools have control over their personnel, they are far more likely to develop many of the qualities of organizational effectiveness than if they do not. A principal who has the power to staff a school—to hire teachers, and if need be, fire them—is likely to fill the organization with teachers whose values, ability, methods, and behavior are compatible with his or her own. In other words, such a principal is likely to create a team whose members are deserving of trust. Team members are therefore more likely to be involved in school decisions, to be delegated more authority, and in general to be treated like colleagues. Because of all of these influences, teachers are also likely to treat each other more like colleagues. The end result, then, of vesting more control over personnel in principals is to increase the prospect that a school will pursue a coherent mission as an integrated, professional team.

The result of withholding control over personnel from principals is much the opposite. Stuck with staff that have been assigned to the school and cannot be easily removed, the principal will discover that teachers disagree with his or her educational objectives, and with the objectives and methods of each other. In this setting of conflict and disagreement, which the principal ultimately can do little about, the principal is going to be reluctant to involve teachers in school decision making or to delegate additional authority to them. Teachers are also less likely to feel great affinity for each other and therefore are less likely to work together closely. The school will tend, then, not to operate as a professional team but as a bureaucratic agency managed by explicit rules and careful supervision. Unfortunately, the personnel systems of many public schools leave principals so little discretion that the schools do tend to operate much like other, less professional government agencies.

The problem of personnel is not the only reason that autonomy is vital to school organization. Another reason, close in importance, is that successful teaching is more art than science. Teaching is a highly contingent process; its results depend on the interaction of teachers and students, who differ in their methods of instruction and their styles of learning. The outcomes of these interactions depend on the match between methods of instruction and learning styles and on the ability of teachers to adjust their methods to suit different student needs. Although methods of instruction can be specified with some precision and teachers can be trained to use them, much of the methodology of teaching—for example, motivating, challenging, and engaging students—must be learned by teachers on the job. As teachers experiment with different instructional techniques to discover what works for them, teachers develop different teaching styles. Because the effectiveness of teaching is so dependent on complex interactions between teachers, students, and alternative methodologies, school authorities cannot easily regulate the learning process. When authorities try to do so, they often make mistakes. The most common one is to limit teacher flexibility, which is detrimental to those teachers and students for whom the "one best method" is not effective. This problem is far from hypothetical: many researchers have identified the overregulation of curriculum and instruction as a serious problem in today's schools.[33] Our research is not alone in finding that schools with too little autonomy from external control often perform badly.

10. **Since school-level autonomy seems to be so important for effective school organization and performance, how is it that some schools have autonomy, but most do not?**

To aid us in figuring out how America's schools might be given more autonomy, we investigated why some schools already enjoy it. Much as we concluded when thinking about improving school organization, we decided that school autonomy was probably not a virtue that would come to schools just because researchers or reformers thought it was a good idea. Rather, it seemed that autonomy stood a better chance of being increased if the forces that reduced it were understood and then attacked. Thus, we examined a number of factors that we suspected would influence the degree of autonomy that a school would experience. The results support two generalizations, one about public schools, the other about private.

Public schools are given relatively high levels of autonomy only under very special conditions. All things being equal, public schools will fall at least two quartiles below private schools in autonomy from external control. To enjoy the kind of autonomy that the private school receives on average, the public school must exist in the most favorable of circumstances. To be permitted to control its own destiny, the public school must be located outside of a large city in a suburban school system. Its students must be making significant gains in achievement, and its parents must be in close contact with the school. In other words, when the public school is performing well, is being monitored by parents, and is not part of a large administrative system, it will be given relatively great control over its policies, programs, and personnel.

Unfortunately—and predictably—the public schools that now enjoy autonomy are not the ones that are most in need of improvement. The inner city public schools that most desperately require improvement are the ones that have so little of the autonomy they arguably need. It may even be that urban public schools are caught in a vicious cycle of deteriorating performance, increasing control, and eroding organizational effectiveness. Under political pressure to do something about city schools that are failing, school boards, superintendents, and administrators tend to take the only actions that they can. They offer schools more money, if it is available, but then crackdown on underachievement with tougher rules and regulations governing how teachers must teach and what students must "learn." The problem with crackdowns, however, is that they are seldom carried out with much sensitivity for those subject to them. Unfortunately, any intervention that deals clumsily with the complex needs of teachers and students may undermine school organization rather than build it up.

Private schools, even in urban systems with high percentages of poor students, generally do not face these troubling pressures. Private schools, almost regardless of their circumstances, tend to be free from excessive central controls by administrators, boards, and unions. The main reason for their liberty appears to be market competition. In a process much the reverse of the one in public schools, where political pressure leads to an increase in central control, competitive pressures lead to an increase in autonomy in private schools. To stay in business, private schools must satisfy parents—more than free public schools or alternative private schools. Private schools are therefore forced to organize themselves in ways that above all else respond to the demands of parents. One thing this clearly means is that private schools must vest a lot of control over vital school decisions—about personnel and curriculum, for example—at the school level where the wishes of parents can be more clearly perceived and accommodated. Strong external control is incompatible with the imperative that private schools face: satisfy parents or lose them to other schools. In contrast, strong central control fits public schools very nicely. Public schools need not satisfy parents first; indeed they must ensure that parents are not satisfied at the expense of other legitimate groups such as unions, administrators, and various special interests. External authorities are consequently encouraged to take decision making out of the schools—to limit autonomy—and set policy in political and bureaucratic arenas, far from schools, where parents will not have a political edge.

Because public schools are ruled by politics, and private schools by markets, public schools may be at a decided disadvantage in developing effective organizations and promoting student achievement. Private schools, without the benefit of any reform at all, are encouraged by competitive forces to operate autonomously and to organize effectively. And indeed, the private schools in our study have more of the attributes of organizational effectiveness than public schools, regardless of the quality of their students. Public schools, however, are usually not granted the autonomy that they need to organize effectively—political forces discourage this—and must therefore be periodically reformed from the outside.

11. What does your research suggest will be the consequences of the many school reforms of the 1980s?

Our research indicates that the school reforms that were pursued so aggressively during the 1980s will have disappointing results. We offer this assessment with some caution because our research does not examine the consequences of specific reform efforts. Nevertheless, it is fair to assume that the consequences of reform will depend on how reform affects those attributes of schools that are most strongly related to student achievement. Most recent reforms either fail to change those school characteristics that seem to matter most for student achievement or they change those characteristics in counterproductive ways.

Public school reform in the 1980s had essentially two thrusts, one to spend more money and the other to impose more standards. Thus, teacher salaries and per pupil expenditures were increased by sizeable amounts (as we explained in question 2), and graduation requirements, teacher certification and performance standards, and student achievement objectives were raised substantially too.

Spending reforms obviously do not have a very good track record. For example, per pupil expenditures increased over 40 percent in real terms during the 1970s (see question 2) while high school achievement slid downward. If our research is correct, the record of the 1970s will be repeated. The amount that a school spends on each pupil or on each teacher is unrelated to the amount that students in a school achieve, all things being equal. Many schools succeed in this country with relatively low levels of funding and many others fail with relatively high levels of funding. Because so many forces more powerful than money influence how a school performs, spending more money on schools probably will not transform the bad ones into good ones. In the long run, higher teacher salaries ought to attract more talented people into teaching and provide some improvement. But there is no evidence that in the short run higher teacher salaries, paid to poor and excellent teachers alike, will spur improvement. There is also little evidence that the small reductions in class size that might be purchased with greater school revenue will boost achievement either. Schools can succeed with relatively high pupil-teacher ratios and fail when those ratios are low. In sum, if schools are given more funds to employ in essentially the same ways funds have been employed in the past, there is little reason to believe additional spending will bring about improvements.

Of course, many school reformers are wary of throwing good money after bad. They recognize that past investments in public schools have not produced expected returns. Many reformers understand that giving poor schools and incompetent teachers more money will not turn either around. Reformers during the 1980s therefore got tough with schools, holding them to higher standards and telling them more explicitly what to do. Some of this may be helpful. It is hard to argue with competency tests that prevent the truly unprepared from becoming teachers.

But most of the well-intentioned crackdown that reformers launched on mediocrity during the 1980s may not help at all. Our research shows that student achievement is not promoted by higher graduation requirements or more demanding homework policies—two favorite targets of school reforms. And more fundamentally, our research shows that the regulation of teachers and teaching can be detrimental to school performance. Current reforms employ more extensive teacher evaluation systems, use more frequent standardized testing to keep track of student performance, and impose more detailed curricula and instructional methods. Yet, these are precisely the kinds of reforms that can rob schools of the autonomy that they need to organize and perform effectively.

School reformers are not ignorant of the dangers of excessively regulating schools. And some reformers are taking small steps to provide schools with autonomy. School systems are experimenting with school-based management and other forms of decentralization. For example, the entire Chicago school system is converting to a system of community control over schools. But these efforts must overcome major problems. First, the so-called autonomy that schools are being given is being circumscribed by regulations governing precisely how decentralized policies must be made—specifying, for example, decision processes and participation rules. Second, the use of autonomy is being monitored with elaborate performance accountability systems—for example, employing standardized tests—that threaten to distort how autonomy is used. Finally, autonomy is always vulnerable to political pressures that it be reduced. If schools utilize their increased authority in ways that are unwise or displeasing—and some inevitably will—school authorities such as superintendents and school boards will be pressured to intervene in school decision making and to return to the pre-autonomy ways of doing things. Increased school autonomy is simply not consistent with public education as it is now organized. Unfortunately, autonomy, not spending and regulation, seems to hold the key to school improvement.

12. Does your research suggest any promising approaches to school improvement?

Our research suggests that the key to better schools is more effective school organization; that the key to more effective school organization is greater school autonomy; and finally, that the key to greater school autonomy is school competition and parental choice. We therefore believe that the most promising approaches to school reform are those that promote competition between schools and that provide parents choice among schools—for example, magnet school programs, open enrollment systems, and voucher or scholarship plans. Not just any reform that increases competition and choice will do, however. To succeed, an arrangement employing competition and choice must ensure that the systemic forces now discouraging autonomous and effective school organization are fundamentally weakened. In effect, this means radically restructuring today's system of public education.

The greatest virtue of a system of competition and choice, and the virtue that sets such a system apart from the current system of public education, is that competition and choice make it possible to provide schools autonomy without relinquishing accountability. In a school system organized according to principles of competition and choice, the responsible government authority can permit schools to make virtually all decisions for themselves yet be confident that schools will not generally abuse the vast discretion delegated to them. If the principles of competition and choice are followed closely, schools are not guaranteed students or funds; enrollments and financial support come only when students and their parents choose to use particular schools. Schools that use their control over personnel, curriculum, discipline, and instruction to organize in ways that are displeasing to parents and students—and to teachers—will quickly find themselves struggling to stay open. Schools that use their authority to organize effectively, to provide the kinds of educational gains demanded by parents, will be well-supported. In a system of competition and choice, autonomous schools, schools that are substantially free from top-down regulatory control, are nonetheless held accountable for their performance.

As it is currently organized, public education does not permit autonomy and accountability to coexist comfortably. Indeed, the two forces work at cross-purposes. Efforts to enhance autonomy come at the expense of accountability, and vice versa. If public education were reorganized so that schools were forced to compete for the support of parents who had the freedom to choose, autonomy and accountability would work in harmony. Competitive pressures would encourage educational authorities to delegate power to the school level where it could be used most effectively to meet the demands of students and parents. The ability of parents to leave schools that were not meeting their demands would work as a powerful force on schools, holding them accountable for their performance.

To be sure, the accountability that would be provided by market forces in a reorganized system is different than the accountability provided by administrative and political forces in the current system. In a system of competition and choice, schools would be more accountable to students, parents, and teachers, and less accountable to bureaucrats, politicians, and the interest groups that influence them. While that may not be the kind of accountability that school reformers want, it is the only kind of accountability that is fully consistent with school autonomy, and by extension, with more effective school organization and performance.

13. In practical terms, how would a system of competition and choice work?

In an ideal world, one where a new system of public education could be created from scratch and previous systems would be of no consequence, a system of competition and choice would utilize educational vouchers or scholarships. The government would fully fund education with tax revenues, but the money would be distributed to students and their parents, in the form of vouchers or scholarships, and not distributed to the schools. The schools would receive their funds when they cashed in the vouchers from the students they were able to attract to their program. Beyond acting as a public education bank of sorts, the government's direct role in the system would be limited. The government would establish the criteria that a school would have to meet in order to qualify for vouchers—obviously, racial non-discrimination in admissions, and probably basic accreditation standards having to do with course offerings and graduation requirements. But most of the rest of the decisions—about curricula, personnel, discipline, instructional methods, priorities, etc.—would be made by the schools themselves—by teachers and principals—responding to their clients. While the government might want to be more involved in decision making for schools, and might well get more involved, the government would be under strong pressure from most schools and parents, for whom competition and choice would be working effectively, not to intervene.

Unfortunately, we do not live in an ideal world where we can organize public education anew. This means that we may need to employ less sweeping reforms than vouchers to implement competition and choice. The leading alternatives include district- or state-wide open enrollment systems and magnet schools. These practical alternatives to vouchers can work. Mechanisms other than vouchers can bring about many of the changes in school organization and performance generally promoted by competition and choice. But if the practical alternatives to vouchers are to make a significant difference in school performance they too must make basic changes in the way our systems of education are currently organized. They must make substantial changes on the demand side and the supply side of public education.

On the demand side the changes are straightforward. Parents and students must be given the right to choose the school that the student will attend. Students must not be assigned to schools on the basis of geographic proximity or for other strictly administrative reasons. All students should attend schools that they have chosen. This is not to say that all students will attend the school that is their first choice. Schools for which there is excess demand will have to turn some students away. But those students who are unable to have their first choice should not automatically be consigned to the school closest to their home, or to any other school they have not chosen. Students who lose out on their first choice should have the chance to attend the school that is their second choice—or third or fourth choice, if necessary. If students are denied the right to make more than one choice, the system will not work for those students who are not accepted at the school they most prefer. Magnet school programs generally have this defect. Students who win acceptance to the magnet schools are made better off; students who are not accepted are left behind, sometimes worse off, in their neighborhood schools.

The shortcoming of magnet school programs points up a deeper problem in grafting a system of competition and choice onto an established educational system. That is, while it is relatively easy for a school system to restructure its demand side—to provide parents and students with some choice—it is very hard for a school system to restructure its supply side. Unfortunately, if the supply side of public education is not restructured, changes on the demand side will not generate many benefits.

For a market to work properly, there must be enough suppliers, and enough potential for the entry of new suppliers into the market, so that suppliers cannot dictate to consumers. If there are too few established suppliers, and no prospect of new suppliers, consumers will have no choice but to take what existing suppliers provide (assuming the good or service has no substitutes—is a necessity—which is true of education). In a system effectively controlled by suppliers—a monopoly or oligopoly—the consumer is not sovereign; the demands of consumers do not drive the production of the good or service. The very point of creating a system of educational competition and choice, however, is to change the system of control—to increase the influence of the consumers of education and to decrease the influence of the monopoly suppliers. This cannot occur if parents and students are given the right to choose schools, but the schools from which they must choose are tightly controlled by a single authority.

So, how must the supply of schools be changed? To begin with, no school should be entitled to students. Schools that are not chosen by students—say as a first, second, or third choice—should be closed. No student should be forced to attend a school that is so bad that no parent would voluntarily have his child attend it. Closed schools could then be reopened under new management, with new objectives, new programs, and perhaps even a new teaching staff. Of course, this raises the question of what should be done with the principals and teachers in schools that students reject and that therefore are not entitled to financial support. In a private market, the employees of a failed business must seek employment elsewhere. In a public school system, where tenure and other rules negotiated by unions protect the jobs of teachers according to seniority, many of the staff of closed schools are likely to be reassigned to successful schools, however unwelcome those teachers may be. If a school system maintains all of the rules of job protection established prior to the installation of competition and choice, the supply of schools will ultimately fall short of satisfying parent and student demand, and of raising system performance. This has been a problem in magnet school programs where the most talented teachers win assignments to the magnet schools and the less talented teachers are permitted to continue toiling in the traditional schools.

An obvious way around this kind of rigidity in the supply system, the kind that may force students to attend undesirable schools, is to allow teachers, principals, or any qualified entrepreneurs, including parents, to start schools on their own. If the only schools that are created are the ones that central educational authorities permit to be created, the sovereignty of parents and students will be undermined. If, on the other hand, schools are free to be created by any educational entrepreneurs who can win parental support (and meet government standards of eligibility as a school of choice), the demand for the kinds of schools that are wanted is more likely to be satisfied.

So-called entrepreneurial schools might exist within established educational systems and therefore be subject to the same personnel rules as other schools. But if this were so, the kinds of rules—for example, tenure and seniority—that can impede the efforts of principals and teachers to organize effectively would come under strong pressure for change. If entrepreneurial schools operated outside of established systems, the staff in those schools would have the right to vote to bargain collectively for the same job protections. But chances are the staff of autonomous entrepreneurial schools would not want or need the kinds of personnel rules found in public school systems. In any case, once students are not forced to attend schools they have not chosen, and educators are permitted to create schools that they believe students will choose, the key changes in the supply of public education will have been made.

There is one other supply-side change that is crucial. Decision making about school personnel and policy should be delegated to the school itself. Where truly basic changes have been made, decentralization will tend to occur naturally. Competition induces decentralization. In public systems of educational choice where basic changes in the structure of supply and demand have not been made, decentralization will not be as strongly encouraged, but it will be vigorously pursued nonetheless. In a system where schools know that their resources are dependent on their ability to attract students, schools will insist that they have the authority to organize and operate according to their best judgments of what students want and need. Central authorities will be hard pressed to retain control over many of the matters that they now dictate.

The sooner central authorities recognize that only decentralized decision making—school autonomy—is consistent with the new kind of accountability provided by competition and choice, the better the chances a new system will have to work. In a competitive system of relatively autonomous schools, central authorities will still be able to contribute. They will be able to learn from the market who the weak principals and the less competent teachers are, and which schools are ineffective. Authorities can then use this information to work constructively with—or ultimately to discharge—problem personnel, and to preserve the autonomy of successful teachers and principals. Systems of open enrollment could readily operate with central authorities performing in this new capacity.

14. How successful have actual systems of competition and choice been?

Genuine systems of competition and choice do not yet have much of a track record. Magnet schools and limited forms of open enrollment have been tried in hundreds of school systems around the country. These experiments have generally proven popular with parents and students, and have been credited with improving the education of the students fortunate enough to attend schools of choice.[34] Magnet systems have also had some success in promoting desegregation, a goal that first brought many of the magnet programs into existence. But whatever the virtues of these innovations, they only hint at the prospective consequences of competition and choice. Virtually none of the existing innovations has made the kinds of changes in the demand and supply sides of public educational systems that are necessary for the results of competition and choice to be adequately observed. The results of experiments with competition and choice are encouraging, to be sure. But they are not definitive.

Nevertheless, there have been a few experiments with competition and choice that have made more radical changes in previous systems. These experiments support the concepts of competition and choice rather strongly. In East Harlem, New York, one of the poorest areas in the country, student achievement has been raised from the lowest in New York City to the median using a system of competition and choice that has multiplied the number, variety, and effectiveness of schools, while reducing the size and central control of them. In the state of Minnesota, students have been free to choose to attend any public school in any district in the state since the fall of 1987. The most comprehensive system of competition and choice in the United States, the Minnesota plan has not been operating long enough to gauge its effects on school performance. But the plan has proven to be administratively workable, and it has already resulted in abundant efforts by schools to reach out to students and parents. It has also encouraged school improvement without the actual transfer of many students—less than 10,000 so far. The mere threat of student departures seems to influence schools significantly. Finally, the Cambridge, Massachusetts educational system, faced with a segregation problem and the increasing flight of affluent parents to private schools, created a system of elementary school choice in the early 1980s that has won back parents and satisfied the first or second choices of the overwhelming majority of students.

15. What kinds of results should we expect from a genuine system of educational competition and choice?

In a system in which schools compete for their funding from parents and students who are free to choose among a range of existing and new schools, a number of desirable consequences are likely to result. Our research suggests, first, that the management of schools would be substantially decentralized. Schools would be given the autonomy to chart courses more consistent with the wishes of their clients. Second, this autonomy would be used by schools to shape their organizations in whatever ways proved most effective in meeting demands. All indications are that schools would tend to become more focused and mission-oriented, recruit stronger educational leaders, and develop more professional teaching staffs. Finally, schools and students would become more closely matched. A constellation of schools, different schools serving different kinds of students differently, would probably emerge. Each school would still accomplish the minimum goals set by the government—for example, promoting achievement in reading, writing, mathematics, and science—but each school would meet public goals in different ways and pursue its own objectives as well. Some schools, for example, might stress the fine arts, others the liberal arts, others math or science, still others business and assorted occupations. But whatever the orientation of the school, it would tend to match the interests of its students.

These kinds of developments will lead schools to perform those educational functions desired by parents more effectively than they are now performed by public schools. For example, high schools whose very reason for being is to teach computer science will prepare students better in that subject than comprehensive high schools do today. But there is also reason to believe that schools of choice will better promote student achievement more generally. To begin with, our research shows that autonomous, effectively organized schools are more successful in bringing about student achievement, regardless of the caliber or family background of the student. Second, the experiences of magnet schools suggest that students achieve more when schools motivate students according to their diverse interests. Finally, parents should become more interested in and supportive of schools when they have gone to the trouble of selecting the schools their children attend. This too has occurred in magnet school experiments. The sum total of these forces—organizational, motivational, and parental—stands to be higher student achievement.

16. In a system driven by the demands of parents and students, many of whom do not really know what is best for them, won't schools that are unsound but superficially attractive flourish?

While a choice system, driven partly by the demands of some frivolous parents, might encourage the development of academically unworthy schools offering easy courses, no homework, and diplomas for all who stay four years, competition would tend to drive unworthy schools out of business over time. Parents and students would quickly learn that the schools conducting flashy, superficial programs were awarding diplomas that employers and colleges did not respect, and providing "education" that left students unable to function effectively as adults. Parents and students would quickly discover that schools offering more effective and no less interesting programs were more deserving of support. Ultimately there is little reason to believe that parents would not choose those schools with a proven record of educating students over schools with records of failure.

17. Even if a lot of frivolous schools do not flourish in a choice system, won't the children of uninformed or disinterested parents end up in mediocre schools?

A properly designed system of competition and choice would not relegate the children of apathetic or uneducated parents to mediocre schools. To begin with, many of the benefits of a market can be enjoyed by consumers regardless of their sophistication or level of information. In a competitive system, schools would recognize that because many parents and students are making informed choices, a school that did not strive to meet demands for quality would risk losing financial support. Hence all schools would be encouraged to improve, and parents who knew little about school quality, and enrolled their children in schools based only on geographic proximity, would nonetheless know that their schools had survived the competitive test. The uninformed parent would be served in much the same way as the hasty shopper in a supermarket: even the shopper who pays little attention to unit prices or to other indicators of value is well-served by the market—by the informed choices of millions of shoppers and the competitive pressures on producers to serve those shoppers best. This is not to say that some uninformed parents would not be taken advantage of by some schools in the short run. But in the long run, competitive pressures would tend to force out of the market schools which did not serve parent needs relatively well.

Uninformed parents would not be served as well as informed ones, however. Those parents who care most about education would strive harder to match their children with the most appropriate schools. Of course this happens in today's educational system too. Parents who value education choose their homes based on the quality of local schools or, if they can afford to do so, send their children to superior private schools. But the inequities in the current system are no excuse for inequities in a new system.

To reduce inequities in a system of competition and choice, the government should take two measures. First, it should give schools a financial incentive to attract the children of uneducated, uninformed, and unconcerned parents. Schools that enroll students from such educationally disadvantaged families should receive additional support, perhaps $1,000 more per student. The government would need to decide what set of circumstances puts a student at an educational disadvantage, but it could use as a reasonable approximation the poverty standard it uses now for programs of compensatory education. The government could also use the money now spent at the federal and state levels for compensatory education to offer bonuses of $1,000 per student to schools enrolling the truly economically disadvantaged. These bonuses would not only encourage schools to reach out to those parents who would not make an informed choice; bonuses would also encourage schools to take on the greater challenge of serving students who do not come to school already well-prepared to learn.

The government could take one other step to reduce inequities in schools of choice. The government could take responsibility for informing parents about the choices available to them. The government could provide all parents with detailed information about school programs, orientations, faculties, and students. The government might also provide statistics on school performance such as graduation rates or test scores. Such statistics would have to be assembled with great care, however. The government could easily distort school programs by imposing narrow achievement measures that encourage schools to "teach to the tests."

As an alternative, and one that we believe might be superior, the government could allow schools to provide whatever information they thought most useful for attracting parents, and then regulate the accuracy of the information provided. Recognizing that schools of choice would have strong incentives to communicate their virtues to prospective students and parents—and this might well include the publication of test scores and graduation rates—the government could opt to ensure "truth in advertising" rather than to provide information itself. In either case, by ensuring that parents are informed, and providing schools financial rewards for enrolling the educationally disadvantaged, the government could go a long way toward reducing inequities in a system of choice.

18. Should schools participating in a public system of school choice be permitted to select their students?

Generally, schools and students should be given the maximum opportunity to match up voluntarily. Just as students should have wide latitude in finding schools that suit their interests and learning styles, schools should have ample opportunity to select a student body that fits the school's mission. For example, schools that wish to create relatively unstructured but very stimulating learning environments—say, Montessori schools—need to ensure that incoming students do not instead require highly structured instructional programs, as some students do. A school that wishes to provide sophisticated training in computer science may need to require incoming students to satisfy certain course prerequisites in mathematics. Schools work best for students when the match between school and student is right. Although students and parents know a great deal about whether a school is a good match, they do not know everything. Schools are also in a good position to judge whether they are likely to be helpful to a child. Schools should therefore have considerable say over which children they enroll.

Of course, schools also make judgments about which children are likely to be helpful to the school—helpful in maintaining order, posting good test scores, sending lots of graduates to college. Consequently, schools may prefer to admit well-behaved, academically able children over children who have problems in these areas. Some critics of choice fear that children with problems will consequently be relegated to inferior schools. Critics therefore insist that if choice is implemented, schools not be permitted to control admissions.

Our view is that in a full-fledged choice system schools could be given virtually complete control over admissions, subject to certain key limitations, without stratifying the supply of schools by ability. We would permit schools to admit students based on whatever criteria they believe relevant, so long as they publicly announce their requirements, standards, and enrollment capacity; accept students regardless of race (we would allow single-sex and religious schools); and accept students from a "safety net" process that would place children unable to find a school through the voluntary admissions process. With these protections as well as supplementary scholarships for students with special needs, a choice system should provide better educational opportunities for all children and not just the easiest to educate.

There are several basic reasons to believe this. The first is that schools must compete for the available clientele. All high schools cannot decide, for example, that they will specialize in preparing students for Ivy League colleges. There are very few students in such a market, and only a small number of schools can survive trying to serve that market. If a school is to survive, it must identify a market niche that it feels especially well-qualified to serve. And, since there are limits to the distances most parents are willing to have school children travel, a school must identify a niche that includes students who are nearby. The public and private schools in inner cities, for example, would need to find distinctive and successful ways to serve inner city children if they wanted to survive and prosper in a system where children and parents are free to choose. Just as there will be competition to serve those few children bound for Ivy League schools, there will be competition to serve children whose academic development is average or below.

It is also reassuring to observe that in systems where schools are selective, schools have not become sharply stratified by student ability. In East Harlem, the schools did not become differentiated in terms of "good" and "bad" or "best" and "worst." They became differentiated by curricular focus—for example, performing arts, math and science, and bilingualism—and by instructional style—for example, traditional, progressive, and even parochial. Although some schools in East Harlem are still better than others as measured by test scores, the academic performance of most schools is much better than it once was, and quality is not the main factor distinguishing one East Harlem school from another. It is also noteworthy that private schools, which have complete control over their student bodies have not generally discriminated in admissions on the basis of race. While some private schools, especially during the 1960s and 1970s in the South, have discriminated, private schools today are actually more integrated racially than public schools are.

Which brings us to a final reason for confidence in a system that permits both students and schools to choose. The question of school stratification in a choice system should not be answered in a vacuum. It should be answered in the context of the existing education system, which is the alternative if choice is not adopted. Public education today is in fact an extremely stratified system in which poor people often attend bad schools and middle and upper income people often attend better or good schools. Some of this stratification in quality has to do with money, which is often unequally allocated between the districts in which rich and poor people live. But most of the stratification is a result of a host of other factors, ultimately rooted in politics and bureaucracy, that money cannot change. Under a choice system, even one in which schools choose students, the poor would have alternatives—in public schools in other districts and perhaps in private schools—to the schools that their school systems now provide them. The districts that now have the poor as their captive customers will also be pressured to decentralize, reorganize, and improve. It is hard to imagine that in providing the poor with alternatives and influence that choice would produce greater and not lesser educational stratification.

19. Because of the costs of transporting students away from neighborhood schools, won't systems of educational choice be more expensive than current systems?

A system of educational choice need not cost more than current educational systems, and might cost less. Transportation only raises costs significantly if the supply of schools is restricted to public schools as they are now constituted. If the supply of schools is allowed to respond to demand, the supply is likely to expand, with relatively small numbers of large comprehensive schools being replaced by larger numbers of small, specialized schools. This expansion could easily occur without the construction or acquisition of new facilities if several schools shared a building. "Schools within a school," as this concept is usually known, were used to more than double the number of schools in East Harlem's choice system. But however the supply expanded, students would find a significant number of choices within a distance that is now served by the transportation arrangements of most public school systems.

Of course, if the supply of schools were not expanded, transportation would cost more, and either taxpayers or parents would have to pay for it. But these costs might not prove to be onerous, for they could be offset by administrative savings in operating a decentralized system. There is every reason to believe that the administrative structure of a public choice system would be less bureaucratized than today's public school systems, and look more like private educational systems, where competition compels decentralization and administrative savings. While the efficiency of a choice system might not reduce the total cost of education substantially—depending on how it is measured, administration only represents 5-20 percent of the cost of public education—the savings ought to be enough to offset any increased transportation costs.

20. Should private schools be permitted to participate in a choice system?

Private schools would not have to be included in a system of educational choice for such a system to work, but including private schools would raise the probability of success. The greatest obstacle to a successful system of educational choice is a restricted supply of schools. If students who are unable to attend the schools that they choose are compelled to attend schools that they would never choose, choice is not being permitted to operate effectively. Choice would be benefitting primarily those students fortunate enough to attend their chosen schools. Those students forced to attend the schools that students and educators are trying to flee would probably be made worse off. The solution to this problem, as we explained in our answer to question 14, is to decontrol the supply of schools—to allow unwanted schools to close and to encourage new, more responsive schools to open. Decontrol will be exceedingly difficult to accomplish within established systems of public education, however. Decontrol would be much easier to implement if private schools were made part of the educational supply.

If a system of educational choice is implemented without private school participation, a provision would need to be made to permit new schools to organize in response to parental demand. If schools can be organized only by central educational authorities, the chances are great that the supply of new schools will not be adequate to meet parent and student demand. Central authorities will be pressured by teacher unions and constrained by the rules of personnel systems not to close old schools or create new schools by transferring, dismissing, or even "counseling out" unwanted teachers. While competitive pressures will make it more difficult for central authorities to protect and maintain ineffective schools, central authorities will certainly not permit the supply of schools to respond to demand in the way a market of autonomous schools would respond. Unfortunately, to the extent that a system of competition and choices fails to shift school organization and control from top-down regulation to bottom-up self-determination, the new system will fail to improve school performance. Thus it is essential for even a fully public system of educational choice to permit principals, teachers, or entrepreneurs, free from central administrative control, to organize schools when they see the demand for particular kinds of schools going unfilled.

If any group of parents or any educational entrepreneur is free to organize a school to be funded by the public system of choice, however, it is but a small step further to include private schools. To illustrate, what would be the difference between a public school of choice organized autonomously by a group of educators and parents, and a private school? The autonomous public school would need to satisfy eligibility criteria—for example, requiring particular courses, and meeting safety standards—but private schools must already satisfy many state regulations, too. Indeed, a public choice system might well adopt the minimal kinds of regulations now imposed on private schools to specify what autonomous public schools of choice would have to do. But however autonomous public schools of choice came to be regulated, they would actually look a lot like private schools—provided the new public schools were genuinely autonomous. In an effective system of public school choice, then, there would be little difference, besides funding, between public and private schools, and less reason for prohibiting private school participation.

There is, moreover, a very good reason for including private schools in a choice system. Private schools would immediately expand the educational supply, the range of educational options. Private schools would ensure that the educational supply would not be dependent entirely on the entrepreneurship of educators willing to bear the risks of starting new schools or on the responsiveness of central educational authorities. Private schools would immediately inject competition into the educational system, for in most states private schools are in abundance. Nationwide, one out of every five schools is private.[35] If tapped, the ready supply of educational options in the private sector would ensure that more parents provided with school choice would actually have their demands fulfilled. Without private school participation, a choice system could easily prove less responsive.

21. Wouldn't private school participation in a choice system destroy public education?

In contemplating the effects of private schools on a system of educational choice, it is important to distinguish between public schools and public education. Private school participation in a system of educational choice might indeed cause some public schools to go out of business; some public schools could be destroyed. But this is not the same as saying public education would be destroyed. Far from it. The objective of a system of educational choice is to strengthen public education, to improve the quality of education that is provided with government funds under general government supervision. If a choice system were to raise the average level of achievement of American students by encouraging competition among and between public and private schools, that reform would revitalize public education, not destroy it. Educational reform should ultimately be evaluated in terms of its effects on students, not on schools.

It should be pointed out, moreover, that private schools might be changed as much as public schools by a choice system. Private schools that elected to participate in a choice system would become wholly, or almost wholly, supported by public funds, and fully subject to the (hopefully minimal) regulations imposed on public schools of choice. Participating private schools would therefore be hard to distinguish from public schools. And the distinction would literally disappear if participating private schools were not permitted to charge tuition on top of the payment received from public education authorities. Because most private schools now operate with far less revenue per pupil than public schools, many private schools would probably not object to operating without supplementary tuition. Any system that awarded private schools a sum approaching the current per pupil expenditure in public schools would leave most private schools better off.

Still, some schools, public and private, might want to charge tuition in excess of their per pupil allotment. Whether this should be permitted is not a question we can answer, for it depends heavily on value judgments that can only be made by the political process. Permitting participating private schools to charge tuition beyond the public expenditure would permit those parents wanting "more" education for their children, and able to pay more, to purchase a more expensive education without having to foot the whole bill themselves. The virtue in this is that more children would be able to avail themselves of a potentially (though not necessarily) superior education than are able to currently, either because they cannot now afford tuition at elite private schools or mortgage payments in the neighborhoods of elite public schools. But there is a possible price to pay for satisfying parents with high educational demand. Permitted to charge additional tuition, schools would have an increased incentive to try to attract affluent students, and the means to create new inequities in the student composition and financial resources of schools. These inequities may not be as large as those that plague public education today, but it remains the responsibility of the political process to decide whether those inequities are too great to justify the benefits that tuition add-ons might provide for many students.

It is also the job of the political process to settle one other issue of private school participation. The majority of private schools in this country are religiously oriented institutions. While there is plenty of reason to believe that these schools provide very good academic educations, better on average than public schools,[36] there is at least some reason to exclude religious schools from participation in a public system of educational choice. Americans may still believe, as they once did, that religion can interfere with the social integration that schools are trying to accomplish, and that religious schools should not therefore be aided by the government. The Constitution provides additional support for this view. But there are enough constitutional precedents for public support of students who choose to be educated in religiously oriented institutions—for example, government grants for private higher education, and special government programs for poor or handicapped children attending religious schools—to indicate that the courts would permit religious school participation in a choice system. Ultimately, the question of religious school participation hinges more on the views of the public and less on the views of the courts, since the courts have no clear cut precedents to guide them. Be this as it may, before religious school participation can be urged, value judgments must be made. We cannot say whether the potential benefits of opening up many good (and currently under-enrolled) religious schools to public school students are worth the potential costs of providing some public encouragement to the dissemination of religious values. Personally, we favor including religious schools. But the public's values, not ours, must decide this issue.

22. Isn't there a danger that participating private schools might become as regulated as public schools and thereby cease to provide the alternative to public education that they now offer?

There is always a chance that a government program, which choice would be, will be subject to continually expanding regulation. But there are, in the case of choice, at least two factors working against regulation. The first is that private schools are free to leave any choice system and operate as they do now, on their own funds and according to minimal regulation. Private schools are also free not to join a choice system in the first place. If policymakers value private school participation—and, of course, some policymakers will not—they will need to be careful not to impose regulations that would discourage private schools from taking part.

The other factor working against regulation is politics. Once a system of choice is up and running, the politics of choice are likely to change. Groups that now oppose choice or are apathetic will become strong supporters. Teachers, for example, will discover the benefits of genuine autonomy and fight to maintain it. Parents will discover the value of educational alternatives and the opportunity for greater school involvement, and work hard to preserve the system that provides them these new benefits. Once a system of choice is firmly in place, these new pressures will provide considerable resistance to traditional pressures to regulate. In a choice system, private schools would not be alone in resisting regulation; public schools would be campaigning for autonomy too.

23. Is there some way school systems can experiment with private school choice before deciding whether to employ or reject it?

Given the controversial nature of private school choice and the lack of practical experience with the concept, even those policymakers concerned with ensuring meaningful competition and choice might reasonably decide to begin including private schools only on a limited basis. Such a decision would give public schools additional time to prepare for competition with private schools and give policymakers an opportunity to observe how private schools actually behave in a publicly supported choice system. An incremental approach to private school choice would also stand a better chance of being accepted by legislators, governors, board members, and the general public.

Several school systems have already adopted the incremental approach to private school choice. The state of Minnesota has long encouraged school systems to provide at-risk children, dropouts, and other struggling students access to specialized schools and programs outside as well as inside their school system. Minnesota consequently offers many examples of school systems contracting with private schools to provide alternatives for students with special needs. Recently Minnesota expanded the list of schools eligible to provide an alternative educational experience to include religious schools. The state of Wisconsin last year began an experiment that permits up to 1000 low income families in Milwaukee to send their children to non-sectarian private schools. Other states are debating similar experiments.

It is important to recognize that these experiments have a common focus on at-risk children. Choice in general and private school choice in particular are often criticized for helping children who least need help—the able choosers and the students most likely to be chosen—and for relegating the children who most need help to schools that are too poor to help them. If only disadvantaged children are permitted the opportunity to choose private schools, however, choice cannot be so criticized. Children who least need help are not permitted to choose better schools, and private schools that want to become schools of choice will have to accept disadvantaged students—since only disadvantaged children are involved.

24. What, in conclusion, are the most important points for school reformers to bear in mind?

If our research into the causes of school performance is basically on target, it holds several simple but important lessons for school reformers. The first is that school performance can easily be undermined by school reformers. If reformers believe, as many certainly do, that greater effectiveness can be obtained from schools through enlightened regulation and training, reformers are likely to be proven wrong. The qualities that effective schools most need to possess—ambitious academic goals, strong educational leadership, professional teamlike organization—cannot easily be imposed or taught by education reformers or government authorities. Indeed, external efforts to force school change, however well-intentioned, can make schools worse. The reason is that the organizational requisites for effectiveness tend to develop not when schools are told how to operate, but rather, when they are given the autonomy to develop their organizations themselves.

The second lesson of our research, then, is that school reformers should provide more discretion and authority to the schools. More decisions about personnel, curriculum, instruction, and discipline should be made by principals and teachers, and fewer decisions should be made by state legislatures, school boards, and superintendents. Educational policymaking should be substantially decentralized.

The third lesson, however, is that decentralization must involve more than the restructuring of public school administration. If schools are to be provided with meaningful autonomy—the kind that gives schools adequate flexibility to tailor their staffs and their programs to the needs of their students, and thereby improve their performance—decentralization cannot be accompanied by elaborate administrative accountability systems. To the extent that schools are required to make decisions and produce outputs according to the specifications of central education authorities, the value of autonomy for school improvement will be reduced. The only way to preserve autonomy and accountability too is to move to an alternative system for ensuring accountability. If our research is correct, the most promising alternative to a system of political and administrative control is a system that controls schools through the market. Public educational systems governed by the forces of school competition and parental choice are far more likely than current educational systems to encourage the development of autonomous schools that perform effectively.

There is a fourth and final lesson, however. If a system of educational choice is to make a significant difference in school performance, it must be freed from a key source of control now exercised by public school authorities. It will not be enough for reformers to grant parents the right to choose their children's schools. If the schools from which parents must choose remain under the firm control of central education authorities, parents will not have a real choice, and the system will not be subjected to the market forces that promise to change school organization and performance. Choice is relatively meaningless if the choices are not permitted to change education. Hence, reformers should recognize that the most crucial reform for them to make, if parental choice is to promote real school improvement, is to end the monopoly that public school systems have long exercised over the supply of schools.

Limited forms of parental choice are steps in the right direction, to be sure. But partial measures are precisely the kinds of measures that public education systems are most likely to undo. If educational choice is to make a real difference, it must be given a real chance.

This article was originally adapted for the Wisconsin Policy Research Institute.

Endnotes

1. Because this paper was written primarily to inform education reformers about the practical implications of our research, this paper does not provide extensive primary or secondary documentation of our arguments or findings. Readers interested in detailed supporting material can find it in our other publications, especially John E. Chubb and Terry M. Moe, *Politics, Markets, and America's Schools* (Washington: The Brookings Institution, 1990); and John E. Chubb and Terry M. Moe, "Politics, Markets, and the Organization of Schools," *American Political Science Review*, vol. 82, no. 4 (Dec. 1988): 1065-1087. In this paper we will document only those arguments or conclusions not documented in our other published work. A version of this paper was published in David Boaz, ed., *Liberating Schools* (Washington, D.C.: Cato Institute).

2. U.S. Congressional Budget Office, *Trends in Educational Achievement* (Washington, Apr. 1986), ch. 3; Office of Educational Research and Improvement, U.S. Department of Education, *Youth Indicators 1988: Trends in the Well-Being of American Youth* (Washington, Aug. 1988), 68-69.

3. U.S. Congressional Budget Office, *Trends in Educational Achievement* (Washington, Apr. 1986), ch. 3.

4. The College Board, "News from The College Board" (27 Aug. 1991), table entitled, "SAT Averages for All College-Bound Seniors, 1969-1991."

5. National Center for Education Statistics, U.S. Department of Education, *Dropout Rates in the United States, 1990* (Washington, 1991), 36.

6. Office of Educational Research and Improvement, U.S. Department of Education, *Youth Indicators 1991: Trends in the Well-Being of American Youth* (Washington, Apr. 1991), 60.

7. *Ibid.*, 61-62.

8. This and the following examples are discussed in U.S. Congressional Budget Office, *Trends in Educational Achievement* (Washington, Apr. 1986), 43, 46. The results of the most recent NAEP are virtually identical. National Center for Education Statistics, *Trends in Academic Progress* (Washington, 1991), 15.

9. William J. Bennett, U.S. Secretary of Education, *American Education: Making It Work* (Washington, Apr. 1988), 13.

10. Office of Educational Research and Improvement, U.S. Department of Education, *Youth Indicators 1988: Trends in the Well-Being of American Youth* (Washington, Aug. 1988), 64-65.

11. William J. Bennett, U.S. Secretary of Education, *American Education: Making It Work* (Washington: Apr. 1988), 12.

12. Barbara Wobejda, "Survey of Math, Science Skills Puts U.S. Students at Bottom," *Washington Post*, 1 Feb. 1989, p. A1, 14.

13. On school reform in the 1960s and 1970s *see also* Diane Ravitch, *The Troubled Crusade: American Education 1945-1980* (New York: Basic Books, 1983). On more recent reforms, *see* Chester E. Finn, Jr., *We Must Take Charge: Our Schools and Our Future* (New York: Free Press, 1991).

14. Calculated from the following tables: U.S. Department of Education, National Center for Education Statistics, "Total and Current Expenditure Per Pupil, by Enrollment in Public Elementary and Secondary Schools: Selected School Years Ending 1950-1990." *The Condition of Education 1991* vol. 1 (Washington 1991), Table 1:25-4, p. 228; and U.S. Bureau of the Census, "Estimated Public School Expenditures, 1970, and Personal Income, 1968, by States," *Statistical Abstract of the United States*, 1970 (Washington, 1970), Table 181; Implicit Price Deflator from: *Economic Report of the President*, 1991 (Washington, 1991), Table B-3, p. 290.

15. Per pupil current expenditures in Catholic high schools averaged $2,690 in 1987-88. Conversation with Fred Brigham of the National Catholic Education Association, Washington, 8 Feb. 1989.

16. Calculated from the following tables: U.S. Bureau of the Census, "Public School Finances, 1975 to 1981, and by State, 1981," *Statistical Abstract of the United States*, 1982-83 (Washington, 1982), Table 271; and U.S. Bureau of the Census, "Estimated Public School Expenditures, 1970, and Personal Income, 1968, by States," *Statistical Abstract of the United States*, 1970 (Washington, 1970), Table 181.

17. Salary figures were obtained from: NCES, *Condition of Education, 1991*, vol. 1. "Estimated Annual Salary (in 1990 constant dollars) of Teachers in Public Elementary and Secondary Schools, and Percent Increase Since 1960: School Years Ending 1960 to 1990" Table 1:27-1, p. 234; and U.S. Bureau of the Census, "Public Elementary and Secondary Schools—Estimated Number and Average Salary of Classroom Teachers, States: 1970," *Statistical Abstract of the United States*, 1970 (Washington, 1970), Table 185. Pupil-teacher ratios were obtained from: U.S. Department of Education, *Digest of Education Statistics, 1989*, "Public and Private Elementary and Secondary Teachers and Pupil-Teacher Ratios, by Level: Fall 1955 to Fall 1990" (Washington, 1989), Table 56.

18. Eric A. Hanushek, "The Economics of Schooling: Production and Efficiency in Public Schools," *Journal of Economic Literature*, 24 (Sept. 1986), 1149; and C. Emily Feistritzer, *Profile of Teachers in the U.S.-1990* (National Center for Education Information, Washington, 1990), 18.

19. Glen E. Robinson and Nancy J. Protheroe, Cost of Education: *An Investment in America's Future* (Arlington, Va: Educational Research Service, 1987).

20. *Ibid.*, 18.

21. William J. Bennett, U.S. Secretary of Education, *American Education: Making It Work* (Washington, Apr. 1988), 46.

22. *Ibid.*

23. National Center for Education Statistics, U.S. Department of Education, "Staff Employed in Public School Systems, by Type of Assignment and by State: Fall 1987," *Digest of Education Statistics*, 1989 (Washington, Dec. 1989), Table 72.

24. On centralization and consolidation in American public education, *see especially* David B. Tyack, *The One Best System: A History of American Urban Education* (Cambridge: Harvard University Press, 1974); and Ronald I. Campbell, et al., *The Organization and Control of American Schools*, 5th ed. (Columbus, Ohio: Charles E. Merrill, 1985).

25. NCES, *The Condition of Education, 1991*, vol. 1, "National Index of Public School Revenues" (Washington, 1991), 88.

26. U.S. Congressional Budget Office, *Educational Achievement: Explanations and Implications of Recent Trends* (Washington, Aug. 1987), 30-31.

27. U.S. Congressional Budget Office, *Trends in Educational Achievement* (Washington, Apr. 1986), 31-39.

28. U.S. Congressional Budget Office, *Educational Achievement: Explanations and Implications of Recent Trends* (Washington, Aug. 1987), 32-35.

29. *Ibid.*

30. Eric A. Hanushek, "The Economics of Schooling: Production and Efficiency in Public Schools," *Journal of Economic Literature*, 24 (Washington, Sept. 1986), 1141-1177.

31. For the most recent comprehensive review of this literature *see Ibid.*

32. For a friendly, comprehensive critique of the Effective Schools Literature *see also* Stewart C. Purkey and Marshall S. Smith, "Effective Schools: A Review," *Elementary School Journal*, vol. 83, no. 4 (1983): 427-452.

33. For example, *see* Linda Darling-Hammond, "The Over-Regulated Curriculum and the Press for Teacher Professionalism," *NASSP Bulletin* (Apr. 1987).

34. For a survey of educational choice experiments *see especially* Mary Anne Raywid, "The Mounting Case for Schools of Choice," *Public Schools By Choice*, ed. Joe Nathan (St. Paul: The Institute for Learning and Teaching, 1989).

35. National Center for Education Statistics, U.S. Department of Education, "Number of Schools, by Level and Control and by State: 1982-83," *Digest of Education Statistics*, 1985-86 (Washington, Sept. 1986), Table 8.

36. *See especially* James S. Coleman and Thomas Hoffer, *Public and Private High Schools: The Impact of Communities* (New York: Basic Books, 1987).

EDUCATIONAL CHOICE:
IS IT PUBLIC EDUCATION UNDER
STATE CONSTITUTIONS?

Prof. Allan E. Parker
St. Mary's University School of Law

Introduction

Americans are so accustomed to thinking of public education as only that provided in government operated schools with government approved teachers following government approved standardized curricula in government owned facilities controlled by political bodies, that the idea of anything else is almost considered heresy. But today heresy is not only being advocated in academia and the highest levels of national government, but it is even reaching the implementation phase in the real world. Wisconsin has adopted the Milwaukee Parental Choice program which introduces parental freedom into this government dominated system by providing state funding for low income parents who send their child to either the child's regular public school or, heretically, to any private nonsectarian school of the parents' choice. The program, intended as a pilot project, is limited to families with income below 175 percent of the poverty level, with a maximum one percent of Milwaukee public school students allowed to enroll. The Milwaukee plan further protects the public school funding base by limiting private tuition reimbursement to $2,500, rather than the full amount of per pupil spending allocated to the public schools.

This chapter will analyze the constitutional policy issues implicit in educational choice, using models such as the Milwaukee plan and the choice plan advocated by Chubb and Moe[1] for analysis under various state constitutional provisions. The state constitutions reflect the social and political battles over control of education in the past and constitute the battleground of the future. While each state's constitution is unique in some sense, and certainly subject to varying judicial interpretations, certain patterns tend to recur just as in the finance equity area. Based on historical development and textual similarity these can be grouped into various categories with different results for the constitutionality of public/private choice. For example, it may be difficult for a choice plan to satisfy the requirements of a "uniform system" since one thrust of the free market choice approach is to allow more diversity among schools.

Public Education—The Competing Models

First, Second and Third Generation Education Systems.

Americans tend to think of education as a dichotomy between public and private institutions. This dichotomy is strengthened by the rigid limitation on government power with a consequent expansion of individual rights embodied in the Bill of Rights. This dichotomy is further reinforced by the metaphorical "wall of separation" between church and state since much of private education is sponsored or provided by religious groups. But this dichotomous view is not the only possible approach and the idea of public/private educational choice may introduce Americans to a third generation hybrid which combines the strengths of both models.

In order to understand the third generation hybrid concept, one must review the history of education in this country. In a somewhat generalized view, the first generation educational system was purely private education; privately financed, privately controlled, though with some government land grants and local funding and state support for colleges. In the early period of American history and in some states until the late nineteenth century, this was the dominant method for educating our youth. The system was adequate for imparting the necessary education of the time to those who could afford to participate in it. Its emphasis on classical learning produced a very literate population among those who participated. Its tremendous disadvantage was limited financing—the cost was borne primarily by the individual and the benefit was limited generally to those who could afford it.

The movement toward a second generation of public schools provoked a major political and social battle over public education. Who would pay for education? The individual or the state? Opponents of public education viewed as tyranny a tax on one man's wealth to pay for the education of another's child. Spending public money on educating individual children was seen as spending public money for a private purpose rather than the general welfare. These arguments, so passionately held, gave way eventually to the second generation educational system still dominant today which combined the public school supported by taxation, provided in government operated schools (approximately 87 percent of students) and privately financed, privately controlled schools (approximately 13 percent of students). As the early opponents of public education predicted, if one good is free while the other is costly, more consumers will choose the free good and thus public schools came to dominate the market. The second generation is thus a public/private mix with the public school predominant since it alone receives state funding.

Advocates of public/private choice argue it will provide a third generation hybrid with the best of both worlds—strong public financial support through taxation for the education of all students, rich or poor; with the democratization, individualized attention and efficiency that free market competition would provide. Another reason for calling public/private choice a third generation system is that it may even introduce three types of schools into the system instead of the current two, at least initially, or under some plans. The first two would be the current publicly operated school and the privately operated school that accepts no state funds, and the new third type would be a "quasi-public" or chartered private institution that accepts some state funds and some state regulation and thus becomes part of the overall system of public education.

Educational Choice Models

How would a public/private choice system operate? In general, all public funds raised for education would be allocated on a per pupil basis rather than a district (or other governmental entity) basis. Each pupil could take his proportionate share, called the scholarship or voucher, to any school of choice, public or private. Formulas reflecting differing costs for educating different types of students could be used. The private schools and public schools would thus compete for funding and schools which satisfied parental demands would flourish, while schools which drove their students away would languish, and perhaps expire, to be replaced by teachers and schools eager to satisfy the market demand.

The first model to be discussed will be the full liberty model.[2] Reprinted with permission. Conceptually it is purposely designed to include the broadest possible range of choice, including public and private schools, religious and non-religious schools, and even home schools. Under the full liberty choice plan, any group can start a school, any child can attend any school, public or private. Funding for all schools, public and private will be based on how many students voluntarily attend that school, though still compelled to attend somewhere. Funding will follow the child, not district boundaries. Traditional public schools will compete with two other types of schools to attract students. The first would be new "free schools," i.e., private schools which accept students with state scholarship funding. They are free in the sense of being tuition free and free of state regulation. The second would be totally private schools for those who wish to refuse state funding and charge a higher tuition fee. In order to provide a real choice, private school autonomy is protected from any regulation by the state other than standardized testing and publication of the results.

This full liberty model incorporates complete liberty between public and private choice with equal funding for public and private schools, with only two equitable and egalitarian limitations on full competition. First, in order to prevent involuntary segregation, no school may refuse to accept applicants on the basis of race, religion, ethnic or national origin.[3] Second, so that educational access is not dependent on income, a school that accepts state funds may not charge extra tuition. Thus education is tuition free for each child, as it is currently.

Pure economic analysis would lead to the adoption of the full liberty model as described above. The gravest problem with the current system is the limited supply of good schools. Thus increasing the supply of available schools is critical to the effectiveness of real choice. Allowing choice when only one school is allowed to exist, or when all schools must comply with such rigid regulations that they are all the same is not choice—calling it such would be a cruel hoax. If the public schools are to be subjected to the refining influence of competition, the playing field in theory should be level with equal funding for the public and private sector.

However, current educational choice models have been proposed with less than full liberty and full competition. For example, a proposal placed on the Oregon ballot by initiative in November 1990 was a wide open supply side model but with a funding bias toward public education over private education. Under the Oregon initiative a child could attend any school, public or private, religious or non-religious, or home school. However, if a child attended private school, the parent or custodian would receive a tax credit of only $2,500 rather than a full share of the per pupil expenditure for that child in public education.

A bias towards public education as embodied in the Oregon proposal probably has a political advantage over the full liberty equal funding model. It avoids the emotional argument that choice will drain funds from public education. When a child leaves public school, the remaining children are not worse off, but better off since the child has left part of his share of public funding with them so that per pupil expenditures will actually rise rather than remain equal with his departure.[4] Further, if enough students leave and receive less funding, real cost savings can accrue to the system as a whole.

The final, most restrictive model which still includes any element of choice is public school choice. Under these plans children can attend any public school within their district, or perhaps even statewide as under the Minnesota open enrollment plan. Private schools are not included. These plans, even though the most restrictive form of competition, have proven successful at measurably increasing student achievement.[5] However, since only public schools are involved, these proposals cause few state constitutional problems (except in districting) and will not be discussed further.

State Constitutional Approaches To Public/Private Educational Choice

The interpretation of a state constitution by a state's highest court is a matter of great judicial sensitivity. Though varying somewhat by state, most courts in determining whether a specific educational plan such as public/private choice is constitutional will generally look to at least the following factors: 1) the constitutional text itself; 2) intent of the original drafters and ratifiers; 3) the evil to be remedied; 4) constitutional convention debates; 5) its own prior interpretations of its constitution; 6) how other states have interpreted the same or similar constitutional provisions; 7) economic and sociological background data.[6] Judges differ in the extent to which they are originalists, i.e., guided solely or primarily by the original intent of their state's constitution's ratifiers and framers, or activists, i.e., they view the constitution as an evolving document which must be shaped by courts to fit the tenor of the times. While judges seldom acknowledge it publicly (although more frequently accusing other judges of it), response to political pressures does play a role in some instances. Political pressure is more likely to be the case with education, a volatile, highly charged issue affecting almost every citizen of the state, especially in states with elected judges.

In some states the courts may even refuse to address the problem of structural reform of education on political question grounds. The political question doctrine states that if the state constitution directs the legislature to set up a system of public education, not the courts, the question of what is a suitable education and how it should be delivered is a question solely for the legislature.

One danger of which state courts need to be aware is that constitutionalizing the educational choice debate may reduce the power of states to experiment with new ideas. The Milwaukee Parental Choice Program was upheld in a 4-3 ruling by the Wisconsin Supreme Court in March 1992. The decision rebutted the teacher's union argument that choice by its very nature is unconstitutional. One of the strengths of a federal system is that each state is free to experiment, if the courts will allow it, and other states can copy successful programs. Of course, state constitutions can also be changed by the people, though with varying degrees of difficulty. It is invariably harder to change a constitution than to pass a law. The Oregon plan was proposed as a direct constitutional amendment to avoid both education clause and religion clause problems.

Granted that state courts can adopt different interpretations of even identical constitutional provisions, five broad state constitutional interpretive problems will be discussed: 1) express provisions; 2) efficiency clauses; 3) uniformity clauses; 4) public purpose clauses; and 5) liberty clauses.

Express References to Educational Choice

Sometimes the easiest constitutional interpretation involves provisions which expressly answer the question the court is attempting to answer, but not always. In the area of language, meaning may vary with the speaker or interpreter. An argument that may seem silly and quite outside constitutional boundaries to one judge might cause another to exclaim "Glory," meaning "There's a nice knock-down argument for you."[7] Confronted by the rude apologist for fixed meanings for constitutional language, few judges of this type have the forthrightness of Humpty Dumpty who said "when I use a word, it means just what I choose it to mean—neither more nor less," though they express the same scornful air. Humpty Dumptyism is not unknown among judges, though usually dressed up in terms of a living or organic constitutional interpretation. The stronger and more clearly an express provision is written, the more difficult it is for courts to give it an entirely different meaning.

In the area of educational choice, a state constitution may completely prohibit it. Usually this is done by completely prohibiting state funding to support schools which are not controlled by state school authorities. For example, California's Constitution expressly states:

> The Public School System shall include all kindergarten schools, elementary schools, secondary schools, technical schools, and State colleges, established in accordance with law and, in addition, the school districts and the other agencies authorized to maintain them. No school or college or any other part of the Public School System shall be, directly or indirectly, transferred from the Public School System or placed under the jurisdiction of any authority other than one included within the Public School System.[8]

This type of language on its surface seems clearly designed to prohibit completely any publicly funded public/private choice system. The California constitution goes on to forbid any appropriation for any school "not under the exclusive control of the officers of the public schools."[9] Proponents of choice in states with this type of language will probably need to enact choice through constitutional amendment or face probable invalidation by the courts.

The term "public school system" has been interpreted by the California courts to import a "unity of purpose," "an entirety of operation," and one system "applicable to all the common schools of the state."[10] On the other hand, despite this strong language, California courts upheld a school district lease of its facilities to a private organization to operate a completely independent, private summer school.[11] Allowing private schools to use government facilities, or categorizing all private schools as public schools chartered "in accordance with law" might also circumvent the prohibition clause and allow educational choice.

Clearly, this type of clause attempts to define a public school system as one exclusively under public control. It is in fundamental conflict with choice proposals which define public education as any publicly funded education, whether privately controlled or publicly controlled. For example, Chubb and Moe argue that their choice proposal is not privatization, but "a truly public system and a democratic one."[12] However, even Chubb and Moe recognize that their plan, as do all publicly funded public/private choice plans, would be a fundamental restructuring of public education.[13] The purpose of public/private educational choice is directly to allow private control, so competition will be increased. Educational choice sounds radical, and though it has been used successfully in other countries,[14] it may alter the educational structure outside the bounds of state constitutions like California's.

This type of constitution seems to forbid all public money for private schools, whether directly or indirectly granted, which we will see is very important. In California, the courts struck down a provision giving money directly to Stanford, a private school, to increase medical school enrollment. However, the Court in dictum stated that a voucher plan with aid given directly to students might well be constitutional even in California.[15] The Court stated a student voucher system is a direct benefit to the student and only indirectly benefits the school, thus not violating the California constitution.[16]

This indirect benefit theory has been used broadly by a variety of courts, including the U.S. Supreme Court, to support aid to private education, despite apparent constitutional prohibitions against such aid. Under this theory, the state's public purpose is to see that all children are educated. If it chooses to do this by paying all students a certain amount of money for their education, the money has been appropriated to a legitimate government purpose. Then, if students voluntarily exercise their free choice to attend private institutions, the state has not benefitted these institutions, only private individuals have done so. The chain of causation from appropriating money directly to these private schools, which would clearly be unconstitutional, is broken by the new, independent and superseding causation of thousands of individual choices.

While the indirect benefit analysis may seem weak to some, a significant difference does exist between direct grants and direct appropriations to private schools and direct grants to citizens which are then spent at private schools. In the case of direct grants, the direct benefit belongs entirely to the institution which may use the money as it sees fit; under the voucher system, if the student is not satisfied and leaves the school, the benefits, both direct and indirect, go with the student and flow to a new school. The indirect benefit theory is consistent with the historical fact that most state governments made direct land grants to private schools prior to the 1850s. These direct grants were the evil to be remedied by such clauses.[17]

Recognizing that strong language would be necessary to prohibit any indirect aid to nonpublic schools, Michigan adopted an even stronger prohibition:

> No public monies or property shall be appropriated or paid or any public credit utilized, by the legislature or any other political subdivision or agency of the state directly or indirectly to aid or maintain any private denominational or other nonpublic, pre-elementary, elementary, or secondary school. No payment, credit, tax benefit, exemption or deductions, tuition voucher, subsidy, grant or loan of public monies or property shall be provided, directly or indirectly, to support the attendance of any student or the employment of any person at any such nonpublic school or at any location or institution where instruction is offered in whole or in part to such nonpublic school students. The legislature may provide for the transportation of students to and from any school.[18]

This express prohibition would probably prohibit all educational choice plans. Other states with at least some degree of prohibition against educational choice include: Alaska, Delaware, Florida, Hawaii, Kentucky, Mississippi, Nebraska, New Mexico, North Dakota, South Carolina, and Wyoming.[19]

At the opposite extreme from express prohibitions of educational choice, some state constitutions may expressly allow public funding for private schools. For example, Virginia's constitution states:

> ... the General Assembly may ... appropriate funds for educational purposes which may be expended in furtherance of elementary, secondary, collegiate or graduate education of Virginia students in public and nonsectarian private schools and institutions of learning, in addition to those owned or exclusively controlled by the State ... [20]

Under a provision such as this, a plan like the Milwaukee Parental Choice Program would obviously pass state constitutional muster. Ironically, it was an African-American legislator, Polly Williams, who pushed for the Milwaukee Plan, but it was white flight that prompted the Virginia provision, as discussed more fully under race problems *infra*.

Seven other states whose constitutions expressly allow choice are Alabama, Georgia, Illinois, Kansas, New Hampshire, Ohio and Vermont.[21]

Efficiency Clauses

After an express allowance, the next strongest provision for educational choice is an efficiency clause. For example, the Pennsylvania Constitution provides:

> The General Assembly shall provide for the maintenance and support of a thorough and efficient system of public education to serve the needs of the commonwealth.[22]

Twelve states with similar provisions include Arkansas, Delaware, Illinois, Kentucky, Maryland, Minnesota, New Jersey, Ohio, South Dakota, Texas, West Virginia and Wyoming.[23]

The importance of these clauses to educational choice is threefold. First, it places a mandatory duty upon the legislature to provide an efficient system. Second, it provides a constitutional basis for an attack on the current state controlled, political bureaucracy as inefficient. Third, it allows educational choice to be implemented by the legislature or mandated by the courts by constitutionally enshrining the value educational choice most implements, the efficiency of free markets.

That an efficiency clause can be a powerful attack in restructuring education is seen in the Texas Supreme Court decision which struck down unequal local property tax funding on the grounds that such was "inefficient."[24] Even more sweepingly, the Kentucky Supreme Court struck down the entire system of common schools on efficiency grounds, including the system and all its regulations, creation of districts, boards, etc.[25] Pennsylvania courts have construed "efficient" to refer to the qualifications of teachers and other basic matters associated with a school system.[26] New Jersey is a champion for the rights of children to a "thorough and efficient" education.[27]

As one would expect with a bureaucratic model, it will not be difficult for educational reform litigants to present evidence to document system-wide economic inefficiency in the current system.[28] A large body of research in estimating the educational production function exists, material which can be focused upon any state's school system.[29] Such studies already document widespread inefficiency in public schools, or at least suggest avenues for further interdisciplinary research.[30]

Educational choice advocates would identify constitutional efficiency as the traditionally narrow definition of productive efficiency rather than modern welfare economics notions of efficiency such as Pareto optimality or Hicks-Kaldor wealth maximization. Efficiency is the relationship between inputs and outputs, and a school is efficient when it produces a certain level of achievement with the minimum possible cost, or with little waste of resources as the Texas Supreme Court argues.[31]

While litigation may be a battle of experts, it is difficult to imagine the state finding a reputable economist who would argue that a government bureaucracy is more efficient than free markets. The plaintiffs in the case could probably obtain Nobel prize winning economic experts for their side.[32]

Experts for the proponents of educational choice such as the plaintiffs in the Illinois and Kansas City voucher cases will have fertile ground for presenting evidence that the current system has sadly failed to efficiently produce a general diffusion of knowledge, a constitutional criteria for an acceptable school system in Texas, Indiana, California, Maine, Missouri, New Hampshire, and Rhode Island.[33] The pockets of good schools should not blind one to the evidence that almost half of the students in public schools are not receiving even a minimum level education. National studies such as *A Nation at Risk* show the abysmal rate of failure, to which this article can do little to add. In some states a general diffusion of ignorance, not knowledge, seems to exist.

Sadly, the diffusion of knowledge among minorities is even less general. Further, the current bureaucratic system seems especially unsuited to meeting the special needs of low income students. Thus, the poor, who were to be the prime beneficiaries of public education when it was established are the most inefficiently served. One litmus test of the problems with the public schools may be the fact that a large proportion of public school teachers send their own children to private schools.[34]

By contrast, one of educational choice's greatest examples of achievement is in inner city, low income East Harlem I.S.D. In 1973, East Harlem's scores in reading and math ranked 32nd out of 32 city districts, with only 15 percent of students at grade level in reading. But public school choice was implemented in the early 1980s and by 1989 East Harlem had moved up to 16th out of 32 in test scores, and 64 percent read at or above grade level.[35]

Educational choice is a far more fundamental change, a fundamental restructuring, and thus more likely to produce efficiency than many single-shot reform proposals. For example, while it is politically difficult in any jurisdiction to change the boundaries of any school district, educational choice eliminates the relevance of all boundaries for attendance purposes. Children can attend school in or out of their district. Many states have a wasteful, inefficient duplication of administrations. Chubb and Moe's research documents that choice and local school autonomy will eliminate unnecessary administrative duplication.[36]

School district consolidation is a prime example of how the market would achieve efficiency far more painlessly than under the political system. Much educational research shows that school districts under 2,000 pupils are inefficient.[37] Allowing students to choose would keep the districts alive at first, but as better school districts attracted more students voluntarily, and then achieved economies of scale to increase their competitiveness further, the less efficient systems would eventually either improve or expire, without any political vote.

Even courts which have reformed unequal school funding recognize "that an efficient funding system will not, by itself, solve all of the many challenges facing public education."[38] But educational choice maximizes the efficiency and equality of the whole system, both funding and delivery, and will free the creative potential of teachers and parents to address those many challenges in many different ways. With thousands of immediate individual choices being made, rather than statewide, untimely bureaucratic changes, in theory the successful responses of innovators will flourish, and failing responses will languish and fade away rather than being imposed on all the children of the state uniformly. Eastern Europe and the Commonwealth of Independent States (the former Soviet Union) have learned that only markets can draw forth creativity on a regular basis, and creativity is certainly needed to address the abysmal state of public education today.

Who should most appreciate the freedom and efficiency of the market over their current system? The answer is good teachers. Under a bureaucracy, good teachers are underpaid and bad teachers are overpaid. Under choice proposals, teachers would be free to start their own schools and attract students with adequate funding.

The overwrought charge often levelled at a voucher system is that it will destroy the public school system.[39] While this is an exaggerated claim and competition may invigorate public education rather than destroy it, let's assume for a moment that the charge is true. If true, is it not really an admission that a state needs a voucher system? After all, the assumption behind the charge is that vast numbers of parents would leave the system if they had a true choice. The assumption is that more attractive schools would become or are readily available so people would choose these schools if they had the economic power to do so. If the current system is so bad it can only be sustained through compulsion, why bother to save it? Advocates of the status quo say "Give us more money." Unfortunately, an impressive body of scientific research demonstrates that more money is not the best corrective to low student achievement.[40]

Public Purpose Clauses and the Danger of Regulation

The public purpose doctrine is a broad prohibition against the expenditure of any state funds for a private purpose. There may be a specific constitutional clause to this effect,[41] or it may be a court imposed doctrine.[42] This doctrine may prohibit any spending on vouchers or tuition tax credits for private education. Even if educational vouchers were not prohibited, the doctrine may require that when a government "provides funds to a private entity to further a public purpose, the private entity must be under proper governmental control and supervision," as the teachers' unions argue in their attack on the Milwaukee Parental Choice Program.[43] This attack raises the danger of overregulation of private schools if they are included in public education.

Herbert J. Grover, Wisconsin Superintendent of Public Instruction, articulating this public purpose doctrine, stated in opposition to the Milwaukee Parental Choice Program:

> For all practical purposes, the private schools that are targeted to receive funds authorized by this legislation are subject to no effective controls or standards related to pupils whose education is funded by the state. As private schools in Wisconsin, they are not subject to the educational standards that apply to public schools. There is nothing in the legislation that directly requires the schools to be certified or the teachers employed to have any training in the education process itself or in particular disciplines or subject areas. Thus, there is no way of assuring that state funds earmarked for the education of our children will be accomplishing the intended purpose.[44]

Conceding that the *state* cannot regulate the private schools for a choice plan to truly offer any real choice does not mean they are "subject to no effective controls." It is as if Superintendent Grover assumes that parents do not exist and that markets have no discipline. The reason that parents with the financial ability to choose are leaving the public schools, or choosing neighborhoods with good schools, is because they know bad education when they see it, and they want better for their children. The philosophy of educational choice trusts parents, even minority parents, to control the education of their children and gives them power through choice to implement their decisions. Assuming in an imperfect world that neither the government nor parents will always make the right decisions, who is more likely to care deeply and be willing to sacrifice, parents or government? If the public schools can do a better job, they will keep the children, who voluntarily attend. If they cannot, Polly Williams, a black legislative supporter of the Milwaukee plan, says they should release the hostages.

Choice is premised somewhat on faith in parental concern and proudly proclaims that the poor and minorities love their children as much as affluent whites love theirs, and if given an economically viable choice will choose good schools over bad schools. Educators who have seen the harsh reality of unconcerned parents do not have as much faith in choice as its advocates do. No one can deny the fact that some parents, and in some communities a large percentage of parents, do not care about their children's education. However, markets may solve even this problem better than government regulation. The invisible, impersonal mechanism of the market responds to the most concerned consumers, thereby benefitting the least informed consumers. Because a small percentage of consumers care, the nutritionally ignorant get "lite" products galore. In electronics, the smart consumers brought everyone cheap, readily available VCR's and stereos, much of which is beyond the competence or concern of electronically illiterate law professors. So in schools of choice, even if we assume a nightmare scenario where fully half the parents care nothing for their children or their education, if half the parents care at all, and ten percent start actually leaving, the bad school will react to its lifeblood leaving and respond with changes before some parents are even aware a problem existed. But the political control model requires parents to organize, rouse a significant section of the community, lobby, organize, etc., then rely on bureaucrats to correct the problem. As an example of school response to the informed consumer, Minnesota began a limited choice experiment in 1985 to allow high school seniors and juniors to go outside the district for college or high school courses available in their district. Local school districts, faced with competition, have expanded the number of foreign language and advanced placement courses because students could go elsewhere to get those courses.[45] All have benefitted, and more students take advantage of the programs.

Superintendent Grover's fear of competition between unregulated and regulated schools is irrational. If the regulations are designed to achieve better schools, (which no doubt they are) and they, in fact, achieve that purpose (which is more doubtful) the public schools will win the competition for students who choose to remain in good public schools. If no regulation does a better job of producing good schools, the state can happily follow the market lead and abolish its self-imposed regulations. The whole thrust of Chubb and Moe's research shows that the regulatory process itself stifles education.[46] But choice allows the free flow of consumers; and if Chubb and Moe are wrong and public schools are in fact better, parents will stay with public schools. If the research showing public schools are better is correct, they have nothing to fear from choice.

The essential attack by teachers' unions and others against the voucher plan on constitutional grounds is that it is taking public money for private purposes. In other words, the argument is that private education is not public education and therefore cannot be supported by public funds. Yet the 1800's saw the uniform loss of this argument that education of all children was not a public function. Can public education be provided only by the government? Isn't the government's only legitimate interest in seeing that everyone is educated, not in whether it does the educating? In *Pierce v. Society of Sisters* the Supreme Court acknowledged that while the state may have a compelling interest in seeing that all are educated, the Constitution guaranteed a role for private education in fulfilling that need. If the system is designed for the benefit of children, not the state employees, shouldn't the children and parents have the power to make decisions?

The teaching unions don't want the tax money collected for education to be used for education unless they do the educating. The Wisconsin trial court rejected this argument. It is ironic that the reformist Moscow City Council has abolished its government-run uniform school programs and has instead given vouchers to parents to use as they see fit, including church schools if desired. Valery Borschov, a member of the Council, has suggested that Americans might be interested in this free-market choice system.[47] The only requirements for education to be truly public are that it be publicly financed, available to all, and that schools not exclude students on grounds that would constitute invidious discrimination. The state's only legitimate interest is in a minimal core curriculum, minimum competency measured by testing, and that truthful results of this testing are published and available widely so that parents can intelligently regulate performance.

Uniformity Versus Liberty Clauses

After an express prohibition of variety, state constitutional language requiring a uniform system may be the greatest obstacle to educational choice. For example, the Wisconsin Constitution states:

> The Legislature shall provide by law for the establishment of district schools, which shall be as nearly uniform as practicable;[48]

The Wisconsin teachers' unions have also attacked the Milwaukee Parental Choice Program on the grounds it violates this uniformity clause.[49] The trial court rejected this argument, but the unions are correct at least in principle that the value expressed in a uniformity clause is inimical to the value of diversity inherent in choice. Fourteen other states also have explicit uniformity language: Arizona, Colorado, Florida, Idaho, Indiana, Minnesota, Nevada, New Mexico, North Carolina, North Dakota, Oregon, South Dakota, Washington and Wyoming.[50] Minnesota highlights the tension between uniformity and efficiency by combining them into one clause:

> The stability of a republican form of government depending mainly on the intelligence of the people, it is the duty of the legislature to establish a general and uniform system of public schools. The legislature shall make such provisions by taxation or otherwise as will secure a thorough and efficient system of public schools throughout the state.

Perhaps Minnesota recognized the inherent conflict between uniformity and efficiency, and resolved it by seeking the most efficient uniform system that was possible.

One of the probable side effects of any true educational choice plan will probably be a greater variety of schools than presently exist. A characteristic of markets is that when consumers are given a choice, wide variety exists. Today, if one group wants "back to the basics" and another group wants "higher order creative thinking skills," we have a political fight for control of the school bureaucracy. Those competing groups may be parents, or teachers competing against other teachers, but political control and institutionalization of programs occur. Under a choice plan any group of back to basic teachers or "higher order types" would be free to start such a school, but they would have to persuade parents to send their children rather than coerce them. Some parents would choose strict discipline and structure, others would choose a Montessori approach. Decisions would be quick, individualized and efficient rather than political.

The value of uniformity in education is that it in theory promotes a healthy socialization that many people feel is necessary for group survival. Yet, uniformity can be the enemy of free thought. Teachers want to teach students to think for themselves, but ironically only under the control of a state-imposed curriculum with state employees guiding the way. On the other hand, many state constitutions embody a love of liberty and freedom of thought that education for all is supposed to advance. Under a strong liberty clause a court could allow or mandate educational choice as maximizing the liberty that an education system is supposed to protect. For example, the Texas Constitution states:

> A general diffusion of knowledge being essential to the preservation of the liberties and rights of the people, it shall be the duty of the Legislature of the State to establish and make suitable provision for the support and maintenance of an efficient system of public free schools.[51]

Eleven other states have strong liberty language: Arkansas, California, Idaho, Indiana, Maine, Minnesota, Missouri, New Hampshire, North Carolina, Rhode Island, and South Dakota.[52]

The values conflict between uniformity and liberty may be resolved expressly in a state constitution. If uniformity is stressed, educational choice is probably out. If liberty is stressed, educational choice is in. If the issue is unclear, the court will have to struggle with the balance, but the American character would seem to favor liberty, not government-imposed uniformity. The courts will have to struggle with the balance between the creation of a government controlled political community and individual freedom. Is mandatory governmental social grouping essential to democracy? Will choice increase stratification as like seeks like, or decrease it as the lower socioeconomic class is economically empowered to join the middle class rather than being residentially segregated into poor schools?

If courts strike down free choice in education because it will promote non-uniformity, the government has been given full power over what to teach. Education is essential to democracy and liberty, yet liberty would be denied in the name of survival of the state. An interesting analysis to apply to the arguments on educational choice is to ask how it fits a master-servant relationship. Is the state to be the master served by the people, or are the people to be the master served by the state? The state as master model advocates uniformity because the state (or educational establishment) knows best what to teach. It uses such language as "education is one of the most critical of government functions, a compelling state interest." If it is the most critical government function then it must be controlled by the government, not by private choice. It was for this reason that the Illinois Supreme Court struck down the Illinois plan for restructuring the public schools to give local autonomy in *Fumarolo v. Chicago Bd. of Education.*[53] The court invalidated a plan to allow only parents to vote for parents and only teachers to vote for teachers on local public school councils, because education was a governmental function in which the whole public had an interest and a right to vote.

In contrast, if the government is viewed as "of the people, by the people, and for the people," i.e., a servant rather than a master, then the government's role is to assist the people to obtain an education they desire. This role can be performed through providing tax dollars for all citizens to obtain an education, while allowing citizens greater liberty to choose instructional settings. Of course, society as a whole, the state, has an interest in a core curriculum, but only in that curriculum which is essential to a free government. This would include the basic liberal arts curriculum, writing, math, English, social studies and history, but would provide a logical stopping place to prohibit mandated curricula in such areas as sex education, suicide prevention, AIDS awareness, and other important but peripheral fields. It would be the responsibility of informed schools and parents to include these matters rather than state mandate.

Teachers have been crying for years for greater autonomy. Teachers themselves rate schools as either failing or receiving a "D" grade in the area of teacher autonomy.[54] Their oft-stated desire is to be treated like professionals. If teachers want real autonomy, they should dismantle the educational bureaucracy.[55] Educational research strongly supports the teachers' position that schools which give teachers autonomy and discretion are better schools.[56] Chubb and Moe have also shown that centralized educational monopolies are the poorest possible mechanisms for providing teacher autonomy, but teachers' unions continue the hopeless struggle for autonomy in bureaucracy.

Conceptually, choice for parents must be coupled with choice for teachers or it is a cruel hoax. To allow parents to send their child to any public school, or even a private school, but then to regulate such institutions in such detail that all schools, public and private, are essentially identical is to effectively deny any real choice. To limit the available supply is to deny choice.

Regulations are much more necessary in a centralized monopoly like the current educational system than in a voucher system, and this fact may limit the thinking of those like Superintendent Grover who have spent a lifetime in such a system. In a monopoly, the monopolists (the teachers and administrators) have little incentive to respond to the demands of the consumer; therefore regulation is needed. But in a market, the consumer and supplier's self-interest will regulate the market, with parents and students leaving when needs are not met.

Is educational choice the answer to our current pluralistic dilemma, i.e. the shattering of consensus? Is it even possible today to have uniform values in education? What the opponents of parent-controlled education want is government socialization of children. At one point in our history we were able to move from private education to public education because a consensus existed as to what schools should teach. From 1840 to 1890 the great debate was over who should pay for education, not over the content of education or educational philosophy as it is today. The consensus explains why even prominent religious leaders were in the forefront of the public education movement. These leaders fully expected public education to be Christian education, even though it was nonsectarian. The Bible was to be taught, of course, though sectarian doctrines were to be avoided. Thus, in reality the public education system was really the same as the private system; it was just publicly funded. This was how it gained public acceptance, by upholding and teaching widely held private values. All important sectors of public opinion could agree on the socialization content. Public schools were simply better financed private schools, with the cost distributed throughout society rather than borne solely on the backs of parents.

Today, of course, our society is divided into highly vocal, highly politicized, separate value groups and communities of interest, who differ vastly on educational content and theory. Traditionalists compete with feminists[57] and political protesters.[58] Must they all be forced into the same political/educational mold? Choice allows each to form their own school, and compete equally in the marketplace of ideas.

Do opponents of parent-controlled education basically fear that parents will not make the right choices, that is, choices with which they agree. Some desperately fear that parents will choose religious education over secular education. Some fear that parents will not choose sex education, bilingual education, AIDS education, environmentalism, and suicide prevention programs, but will rather stick to the basics. Some fear that some parents would choose reading assignments that show women as homemakers rather than as doctors, lawyers, police persons, and fire persons. They fear parents might choose Mark Twain over *Catcher in the Rye*. Or they fear that parents will choose sports, strict discipline, back to the basics, convenience, cosmetology, Africa-centered curricula, or some other choice with which they disagree. They have concluded that only they or their experts know what is best for students and that parents are incapable of making intelligent choices. The most often heard cry of the social reformer is "Our schools must teach (fill in your pet social project)."

As the history of public school development shows, public schools eventually became dominant because they were significantly better funded. School taxation became quite high, thereby depriving parents of dollars for private education. Of course, public schools also convinced parents they could do a better job because they were competing with private schools. But the spur of competition has been lost, and reinstating it could challenge public schools to do a better job. Eventually, public schools would probably win again because most Americans want a public school experience, but only by producing better results. The *Fumarolo* court emphasized that reforming public schools would help parents of children in private schools who could then return to public schools. Almost all public/private choice plans remain heavily weighted toward public schools; for example, both Milwaukee and Oregon proposals only give $2,500 per student, whereas the public schools spend thousands more per student, perhaps a measure of the public schools' inefficiency. If private schools can do more with less, even through private subsidization of the real costs of education, why not let them?

The current monopoly takes a monolithic view of education, whereas educational research increasingly shows that all children do not learn in the same way. A market system will usually provide whatever services a sufficient number of customers desire. While true choice in education will probably result in a broader variety of schools, this does not mean that "public education" is destroyed unless by public education we mean a uniform "one size fits all" mentality that according to Sapon-Shevin has shackled public education for too long, and which modern educational research shows does not reflect the learning styles of all students.[59]

Choice alone will not educate anyone: It is not an educational technique; rather, it is a catalyst, a spur to goad an entrenched bureaucracy. The rule is harsh—respond to needs of the students and parents or die, but the result is to empower parents and students.

Even some public schools have begun to recognize that because of the diversity of their populations and the current lack of consensus, a good school system is one that gives students a choice among many options. Cambridge, Massachusetts, Deborah Meier in New York, Richmond ISD in California, Caddo P.M. Sr. High School in Shreveport, Los Angeles, and Brooklyn, have all implemented public school choice.[60] While there is a basic core curriculum composed of reading and language arts, mathematics, science, history and social studies, under choice each individual school could emphasize a different specialty. At the elementary level, specialty programs could include classical studies, future studies, gifted and talented programs, international studies, Montessori, university laboratory, and whole language studies, or any other new idea someone finds in the *Harvard Education Review*. At the secondary level, specialty programs could take the form of applied arts and sciences; classical studies; math, science and technology; university laboratory, visual/performing arts and humanities. Rather than forcing children to attend those local schools which may have adopted any one of these programs, parents could enroll their children in any of the specialty schools offering the program they have selected, depending on what best suits the family's needs and schedules. Thus another advantage of choice is that educational fads are not forced on anyone.

Special Problems—Religion and Race

Should Religious Schools Be Included in Choice?

As outlined above, a purely economic analysis argues for the broadest possible supply of schools. Thus it is that including private religious schools in choice plans makes economic sense. In addition, the United States and all state constitutions protect far more than economic efficiency. They include one of the most fundamental liberties, freedom of religion. While raising questions of church and state beyond the scope of this article, the Oregon Office of the Legislative Counsel[61] and

Professor Michael McConnell[62] both have argued that the Oregon initiative's inclusion of religious schools did not violate the United States Constitution's establishment clause. Many other commentators[63] have agreed based on the rationale of *Mueller* [64](tax credits for religious education upheld) and Witters[65] (blind student must be allowed to spend state voucher for aid to the blind at seminary), with such analysis further strengthened by the recent *Mergens*[66] decision (school prayer which is voluntary and student-led protected constitutionally).

While almost all state constitutions have a similar or even stricter sounding prohibition of state aid to sectarian schools, it was usually designed to prevent the direct grant of public lands and monies to sectarian institutions. Vast public lands had been given directly to religious institutions in the nineteenth century. Under these grants, the benefit went directly to the school itself. The voucher system is entirely different since the school gets no direct grant, no long-term control over assets, but merely benefits indirectly from the parents' decision. If the parents change their mind, the benefit leaves with the child.

A choice plan would also pass the *Lemon v. Kurtzman*[67] test. First, because its secular purpose is to advance all education, which is clearly a legitimate state interest. Second, because the effect would not be to aid directly religious education, it would be the result of private action, not state action if it occurred at all. The reverse might actually occur as reinvigorated public education draws back those who have fled to religious schools for academic rather than religious reasons. Finally, the state would not be excessively entangled with religion since the whole theory of choice is to leave the private sector unregulated so that true choices may exist. This secular purpose meshes nicely with the constitutional prohibition against excessive government regulation of religion.

Segregation, Integration, Income and Racial Equality

Educating the poor through public funding was historically the reason for public education in this country. Even opponents of taxation who felt one man should not pay for the child of another's education supported public charity for the poor. However, the current public school system deprives only the poor of educational choice. The well-to-do can choose a good school by choosing an expensive neighborhood or paying private school tuition. Yet the poor who were supposed to be prime beneficiaries of the public school system have been deprived through the years of their choice. Logically, only educational choice, not even equal public school funding, will give all children, rich or poor alike, the same choice and opportunity to choose between state controlled, bureaucratic education or privately controlled education.

When discussing poverty and education, race inevitably needs to be discussed. Some will call educational choice racist, and indeed there is reason to be cautious since educational choice was tried as an attempt to avoid integration in the South in the 1950s and 60s. The United States Supreme Court was forced to strike down on equal protection grounds Virginia's educational choice plan which specifically allowed state funding to segregated private academies.[68] However, choice plans today and current law prohibit racial discrimination.[69] To call choice racist today may be anachronistic, to use labels to discourage rational analysis. Which sounds more racist? An educational choice plan that gives the parents of a poor black child $2,000-$5,000 for tuition and guarantees equal access to any public or semi-private school in the state (schools with excess applicants must fill positions by lottery); or a plan which says we cannot change the current system which keeps that black child in an all black school in a black neighborhood which he is compelled by state law to attend. Educational choice eliminates the residential segregation roadblock to integration without government quotas, redrawing neighborhood lines, forced busing or any other form of coercion other than outlawing admission exclusions based on race.

Under our current system of choice for the affluent, the affluent have left the mediocrity and declining achievement of public schools in droves, leaving our inner city schools overwhelmingly black or brown. If whites have already left, is it not more racist to oppose a plan that would allow minorities to leave as well? If choice were implemented, it would not be white flight that would occur, but minority flight as in Milwaukee, or white return to invigorated schools. If attendance is not based on residential districting, and private schools are prohibited from discriminating on the basis of race, integration can increase. If one is really serious about desegregation, a plan which breaks the connection between funding, attendance and residential segregation, as choice does, must be seriously considered.

The greatest single impediment today to real integration is residential segregation, which choice effectively overcomes, especially if transportation is provided. Even if transportation is not provided, the cost of private education has been reduced to that of bus fare, which would be within the reach of far more low income students than under current law.

Minority students are the most tragic victims of the current educational monopoly.[70] One minority fear of vouchers is that if parents are allowed to supplement the state voucher with their own funds for education, unequal educational opportunity will result and there will be inflation in the cost of education so that the poor will still receive the worst education. One solution is simply to make the vouchers available on a sliding scale basis with the amount of the voucher varying inversely with one's income. Thus, the poor would receive larger vouchers than the well to do, with the goal being to provide rough equalization at some average cost of education. Variations in education would vary only by the parents' desire to devote family resources to education, rather than on the availability of resources. Another alternative is to require any school accepting state money to agree it will not charge its students more than the amount of the state aid.

Conclusion

The educational establishment has fought for years to gain exclusive control over public funding for education. It will not willingly relinquish control over these dollars to parents and students who want more of a choice in where they attend school and more control over school organization and curriculum. The wall has come down in Berlin. Let freedom and competition come to the American school.

Endnotes

1. John E. Chubb and Terry M. Moe, *Politics, Markets and America's Schools* (Washington, Brookings Institution, 1990).

2. This section previously appeared in Allan Parker and Michael Weiss, "Litigating *Edgewood*: Constitutional Standards and Application to Educational Choice," 10 *The Review of Litigation* 599-624 (1991). Reprinted with permission.

3. *Runyon v. McCrary,* 427 U.S. 160, 96 S. Ct. 2586, 49 L. Ed. 2d 415 (1976) upheld { 1981's prohibition of admission exclusion on the basis of race by private, commercially operated, non-religious schools.

4. For example, assume an elementary school with three hundred students with an annual budget of $1.5 million, which would be a per pupil expenditure of $5,000, about the national average. When a public/private choice plan is adopted, ten percent (30) of the students leave, but take only $3,000 per student with them (total $90,000). The school is left with a lower budget of $1,410,000, but per pupil expenditure rises to $5,222. Those who believe that more money means a better education will happily remain in public school. Those who prefer a private education will feel better off, and a win-win situation is created.

5. East Harlem ISD in New York and Richmond ISD in California are two of the most prominent examples.

6. *See also* P. Bobbit, *Constitutional Fate—Theory of the Constitution* (1982) (listing six types of constitutional argument: historical, textual, doctrinal, prudential, structural, and ethical).

7. Lewis Carroll, "Through the Looking Glass," *The Works of Lewis Carroll* 174 (London: Paul Hamlyn, 1965).

8. Cal. Const. Art. IX, { 6.

9. Cal. Const. Art. IX, { 8.

10. *Cal. Teachers Assn. v. Bd. of Trustees,* 82 Cal. 3d 249, 146 Cal. Rptr. 850 (1978).

11. *Cal. Teachers Assoc. v. Bd. of Educ.,* 109 Cal. 3d 738, 167 Cal. Rptr. 422 (1980).

12. John E. Chubb and Terry M. Moe, *Politics, Markets and America's Schools* (Washington, Brookings Institution, 1990), 225.

13. *Ibid.*

14. *See, e.g.,* Louis and Van Velzen, "A Look at Choice in the Netherlands," 48 *Educational Leadership* 66 (Dec. 1990/Jan. 1991).

15. Bd. of Trustees v. Cory, 79 Cal. 3d 661, 145 Cal. Rptr. 136 (1978).

16. *Ibid.*

17. *For example,* in Texas, from 1839, when the first such grant was made to Dekalb College, until 1857, a total of 172,319 acres were given away to private colleges and seminaries. A.S. Lang, *Financial History of the Public Lands in Texas* 99 (1932) citing Land Office Report, Nov. 2, 1857.

18. Mich. Const. Art. III, { 2.

19. Al. Const. Art. VII, {1; Del. Const. Art. X, { 4; Fla. Const. Art. IX, { 5; Hawaii Const. Art. X, { 1; Ky. Const. { 186; Miss. Const. Art. 8, { 208; Neb. Const. Art. VII, { 11; N.M. Const. Art., XII, { 3; N.D. Const. Art. VIII, { 5; S.C. Const. Art. XI, { 4; Wy. Const. Art. 7, { 8.

20. Va. Const. Art. III, { 10.

21. Ala. Const. { 256; Ga. Const. Art. 8, { 7; Ill. Const. Art. X, { 1; Kans. Const. Art. 6; N. H. Const. Art. 83; Ohio Const. Art. VI, { 1; Vt. Const. Ch. 2, { 68. Vermont has one of the most extensive public/private choice plans in operation today.

22. Penn. Const. Art. 3, { 14.

23. Ark. Const. Art. XIV, { 1; Del. Const. Art. X, { 1; Ill. Const. Art. X, { 1; Ky. Const. { 183; Minn. Const. Art. XIII, { 1; N.J. Const. Art. VII, { 4; Ohio Const. Art. VI, { 2; S.D. Const. Art. VIII, { 15; Tex. Const. Art. VII, { 1; W. Va. Const. Art. XII, { 1; Wyo. Const. Art. 7, { 9.

24. *Edgewood v. Kirby*, 777 S.W.2d 391 (1989).

25. *Rose v. Council for Better Education*, 60 Ed. Law Rep. 1289, 790 S.W.2d 186 (Ky. 1989).

26. *Ehret v. School District of Kulpmont*, 5 A.2d 188, 333 Pa. 518 (1939).

27. *See* Broden, "Litigating State Constitutional Rights to an Adequate Education and the Remedy of the State Operated School Districts," 42 *Rutgers L. Rev.* 779 (1990).

28. *See* Parker and Weiss, "Litigating *Edgewood*: Constitutional Standards and Application," 10 *The Review of Litigation* 599, 612-613 (1991).

29. *See* Hanushek, "Conceptual and Empirical Issues in the Estimation of Educational Production Functions," 14 *J. of Human Resources* 351-388 (1979, No.3) and Hanushek, "The Economics of Schooling," 24 *J. of Econ. Literature* 1141-77 (Sept. 1986) for an extensive review of the literature.

30. *See, e.g.*, Symposium Issue, "Public and Private Schools," 51 *Harv. Educ. Rev.* (Nov. 1981), 481-545; Averch et al., "How Effective is Schooling?" *A Critical Review of Research* (a Rand Educational Policy Study) (Englewood Cliffs, N.J. 1974); Denis P. Doyle, "Public Funding and Private Schooling: The State of Descriptive and Analytic Research," *Private Schools and the Public Good: Policy Alternatives for the Eighties*, ed. E. Gaffney (South Bend, Ind.: Notre Dame Press, 1981).

31. *Edgewood v. Kirby*, 777 S.W.2d 391, 395 (Tex. 1989).

32. *See* Milton Friedman, *Capitalism and Freedom* (1962), 85-107. Friedman, "The Role of Government in Education," in *Economics and the Public Interest*, ed. R. Solo (1955). *See also* J. Coons and S. Sugarman, *Education by Choice: The Case for Family Control* (1978); Coons, *Making Schools Public, Private Schools and the Public Good: Policy Alternatives for the Eighties* ed. E. Gaffney (South Bend, Ind. Notre Dame Press 1981), 91. Adam Smith and Thomas Paine might also be called upon to testify through their acknowledged expert texts. A. Smith, *The Wealth of Nations* 737 (1937 ed.); West, "Tom Paine's Voucher Scheme for Public Education," 33 *S. Econ. J.* 378, 381 (1967).

33. Tex. Const. Art. VII, { 1; Ind. Const. Art. 8, { 1; Cal. Const. Art. IX, { 1; Me. Const. Art. VIII, { 1; Mo. Const. Art. IX, { 1(a); N.H. Const. Art. 83; R.I. Const. Art. XII, { 1a.

34. Task Force on Education of the City Club of Chicago, Educational Choice: A Catalyst for School Reform, Aug. 1989, p. 22 cited in Chubb, et al., *Choice in Education: Opportunities for Texas*, 25 (1990).

35. Hood, "Miracle on 109th Street," *Reason* (May 1989).

36. Chubb & Moe, *Politics, Markets and America's Schools* (1990).

37. M. Davis and K. Hayes, *Efficiency and Inefficiency in the Texas Public Schools, vol. 12* (National Center for Policy Analysis, 1990).

38. *Edgewood v. Kirby*, 777 S.W.2d 391 (Tex. 1989).

39. *See, e.g.*, Rose-Ackerman, *Social Services and the Market*, 83 *Colum. L. Rev.* 1405 (1983).

40. A rather large body of empirical research demonstrates that little positive correlation exists between spending and student achievement. *See, e.g.*, Eric A. Hanushek "The Impact of Differential Expenditures on School Performance," 45 *Educational Researcher* (May 1989) (summary of hundreds of studies over the last two decades produced "startlingly consistent results; variations in school expenditures are not systematically related to variations in student performance."

41. *See, e.g.*, Ind. Const. Art. 8, { 7.

42. *See, e.g., State ex rel Warren v. Reutter*, 44 Wis. 2d 201, 170 N.W.2d 790 (1969).

43. Appellant's Brief, *Davis v. Grover*, 90-1807-LU, Wis. Ct. of App., District IV, p.30.

44. Herbert J. Grover, Statement on the Milwaukee Parental Choice Program, Madison, Wisconsin, June 1990.

45. Meyers and Schwartz, "School Reform: Minnesota's Educational Choice Program Earns High Marks," *Beaumont Enterprise*, 29 Oct. 1990; Comment, "Open Enrollment: Social Darwinism at Work," 23 *Creighton L. Rev.* 441 (1990).

46. Chubb & Moe, *Politics, Markets and America's Schools*.

47. Roland Davis and Robert Novak, Inside Report, *San Antonio Express News*, 6 Aug. 1990, p. 8-A.

48. Wis. Const. Art. 10, { 3.

49. Appellant's Brief, *Davis v. Grover*, 90-1807-LU, Wisconsin Ct. of App., District IV at 36.

50. Ariz. Const. Art. XI, { 1; Colo. Const. Art. IX, { 2; Fla. Const. Art. IX, { 1; Idaho Const. Art. IX, { 1; Ind. Const. Art. 8, { 1; Minn. Const. Art. XIII, { 1; Nev. Const. Art. 11, { 2; N.M. Const. Art. XII, { 1; N.C. Const. Art. IX, { 2; N.D. Const. Art. VIII, { 2; Or. Const. Art. VIII, { 3; S.D. Const. Art. VIII, { 1; Wash. Const. Art. 9, { 2; Wyo. Const. Art. 7, { 1.

51. Tex. Const. Art. VII, { 1.

52. Ark. Const. Art. XIV, { 1; Cal. Const. Art. IX, { 1; Idaho Const. Art. IX, { 1; Ind. Const. Art. 8, { 1; Me. Const. Art. VIII, { 1; Minn. Const. Art. XVII, { 1; Mo. Const. Art. IX, { 1(a); N.H. Const. Art. 83; R.I. Const. Art. XII, { 1; S.D. Const. Art. VIII, { 1.

53. 566 N.E.2d 1283 (Ill. 1990).

54. *San Antonio Light*, 16 Aug. 1990.

55. Raymond J. Domancio, New York *Newsday*, 23 Oct. 1989, p. 52, Col. 1 (former policy analyst and evaluator for the New York City Board of Education from 1979 to 1987).

56. Chubb & Moe, *Politics, Markets and America's Schools*.

57. *See* Magda Lewis, "Interrupting Patriarchy: Politics, Resistance, and Transformation in the Feminist Classroom," 60 *Harv. Educ. Rev.* 467 (Nov. 1990).

58. Andrew David Gittin, "Educative Research, Voice and School Change," 60 *Harv. Educ. Rev.* 443 (Nov. 1990).

59. Sapon-Shevin, "The National Education Reports and Special Education: Implications for Students," 53 *Exceptional Children* 300 (1987).

60. *See* December 1990/January 1991 issue of *Educational Leadership: Journal of the Association for Supervision and Curriculum Development*, "Schools of Choice?" and "A System for Choice," Richmond Unified School District, Richmond, California (pamphlet).

61. Letter to Lee Penny, Joint Committee on Education, 29 Jan. 1990.

62. University of Chicago School of Law, Letter to Oregonians for Choice, 2 Aug. 1990.

63. *See, e.g.,* Monaghan and Ariens, "A Fairer Approach to the Establishment Clause," 29 *St. Louis L. J.* 115, 116 (1984); Anthony, "Conservative Judicial Activism and Parochial: An Open Door Policy Towards Funding Religious Schools?", 57 *West Educ. L. Rptr.* 13 (Jan. 18, 1990); Note, *The Increasing Judicial Rationale for Educational Choice: Mueller, Witters and Vouchers,* 66 *Wash. U.L.Q.* 363 (1988); Note, *The Constitutionality of Louisiana Aid to Private Education,* 44 *La. L. Rev.* 865, 868 (1984) (others).

64. *Mueller v. Allen,* 463 U.S. 388 (1983).

65. *Witters v. Wash. Dept. of Services for the Blind,* 474 U.S. 481 (1986).

66. *Bd. of Educ v. Mergens,* 496 U.S. 226, 110 S. Ct. 2356, 110 L. Ed. 2d 191 (1990).

67. 403 U.S. 602 (1971).

68. *Griffin v. County Sch. Bd. of Prince Edward Co.,* 377 U.S. 218 (1964).

69. *Runyon v. McCrary,* 427 U.S. 160 (1976).

70. *See* Chambers, *Adequate Education for All: An Achievable Goal,* 22 *Harv. C.R.-C.L. L. Rev.* 55 (1987); McDermott & Klein, *The Cost Quality Debate in School Finance Litigation: Do Dollars Make the Difference?*; Yudof, *Effective Schools and Federal and State Constitutions: A Variety of Opinion,* 63 *Tex. L. Rev.* 865, 867-868 (1985).

EDUCATION TODAY
AND HOW IT MUST CHANGE

Prof. Joseph M. Horn
University of Texas

Part I: The Problem

Americans are justifiably proud of our educational systems that strive to educate all of our citizens. We are the only country in the world that tries to make everyone eligible for college. Our plan is to graduate as many people as we can from high school, thereby eliminating the major barrier that every other country places between its students and higher education. Only the Japanese, with approximately 56 percent of their children still in school the year before college admissions begin, come close to the total effort we make to graduate everyone from high school.[1] Almost 70 percent of American children reach their senior year in high school. An equivalent figure for most European countries would be between 20 and 35 percent.

What most Americans don't realize is that we have achieved world leadership in educational quantity through fraud. Our curriculum is so easy, our standards for passing courses so low, that our high figures for graduation are really deceptive. Most of our graduates don't know enough to have earned a valid diploma. That they do graduate is more a result of the political demands for high graduation rates rather than of achievement. Needless to say, many of our colleges are expected to provide places for even the worst of these students.

Even though most Americans are unaware of these unsettling facts, there is also some evidence that a few influential people are beginning to learn the truth about education in the United States. Even the leaders of the educational establishment are beginning to face reality. Albert Shanker, President of the American Federation of Teachers, recently acknowledged that a high school diploma from American public schools is, in international terms, almost worthless.[2] He said, "95 percent of the kids who go to college in the U.S. would not be admitted to college anywhere else in the world." I would put the figure closer to 85 percent,

but the point remains. In our effort to graduate everyone from high
school, we have so degraded the curriculum that the diploma is, in terms
of genuine achievement, meaningless. High schools and colleges have
colluded in this embrace of mediocrity. If our universities had admissions
standards even close to those of foreign institutions, the vast majority of
our high school graduates could not matriculate.

Is there objective evidence that the situation is as bad as Shanker says
it is? The answer is yes. According to the National Assessment of
Educational Progress,[3] *only 51 percent* of our 17-year-olds can solve
simple problems of the types given below:

Which of the following is true about 87% of 10?

    A. It is greater than 10.

    B. It is less than 10.

    C. It is equal to 10.

    D. Can't tell.

    E. I don't know.

Refer to the following graph. This graph shows how far a typical car
travels after the brakes are applied.

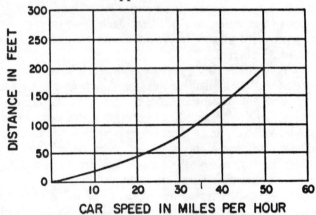

A car is traveling 55 miles per hour. About how far will it travel after
applying the brakes?

    O 25 feet   O 350 feet
    O 200 feet   O I don't know
    ● 240 feet

And *only six percent* of our 17-year-olds can solve slightly more difficult problems like these:

> Christine borrowed $850 for one year from the Friendly Finance Company. If she paid 12% simple interest on the loan, what was the total amount she repaid?
>
> Answer: $952
>
> The number of tomato plants (t) is twice the number of pepper plants (p). Which equation best describes the sentence above?
>
> A. t = 2p
>
> B. 2t - p
>
> C. t = 2 + p
>
> D. 2 + t = p
>
> Answer: A.

Clearly, half of our high school students who will graduate in a year (17-year-olds) cannot do high school level work. The question about 87 percent of 10 shows that many high school juniors do not even know the definition of percent. Equally clear is that 94 percent of these students cannot do the slightly more difficult problems we have every right to expect them to do in order to go on to college. But our system is geared to graduate them in spite of their deficiencies, and our colleges are expected to provide for them after that.[4]

The most reasonable interpretation of the foregoing is that America is unique among nations in preferring quantity to quality in education. We are committed to high graduation rates from high school because we believe that this diploma signifies that our graduates are knowledgeable and capable individuals. We forget that all the pressure we put on our schools to produce large numbers of graduates is much easier to deal with by lowering standards rather than raising achievement.

It is also important to recognize that our preference for quantity over quality is not a recent development, but was thoroughly fixed by 1960. From then on, every effort to improve the quality of public education has been defeated by a stubborn, seemingly congenital, resistance to *anything* that could cause the graduation rate to fall. In effect, by 1960 we had found a way to push large numbers of students through a mediocre curriculum and nothing that threatened this system could survive.

Examining a typical set of 1960s recommendations for educational improvements will show that even then, we knew what to do but remained incapable of doing it. In 1960 the Gallup Poll conducted a five-nation survey of educational systems. The results were published in *Look*

(31 Dec. 1960), under the title of "Is European Education Better than Ours?" The authors of this report concluded that we need to improve the quality of American public (government) education and their recommendations are given below:

How can we improve the quality of American Education?

Six points for a program of reform

To meet this problem of raising our standards, American educators—and their critics—have suggested a long list of possible reforms. Some are adaptations of European methods, some are not. Here are a few of the most promising ideas:

1. We can lengthen our school year and increase the amount of homework required.

2. We can re-examine our schools in the light of the German teachers' avoidance of personality training and stop insisting that our educators "be at once priest, physician, policeman, parent and more, as well as teacher."

3. We can think of our talented children as the European does—as an extremely valuable national resource—and give him as much attention as we do the retarded and handicapped.

4. We can set up national standards that would establish what a child should know when he leaves school, continuing the work begun by Dr. Paul R. Hanna, professor of education at Stanford University, two years ago, when he suggested a "national curriculum design."

5. We can set entrance standards for teachers' colleges so high that they no longer will be forced to make teachers out of inferior material.

6. We can review the pros and cons of Federal aid to education, realizing that it is already here, to a degree. In the school year 1959-60 the nation spent about $25,000,000,000 on education; of this about $2,400,000,000 came from Federal funds.

In the long run, whether the decisions are made by 45,000 school boards, by fifty state-wide commissions or by a centralized office of education, it is the American voter who is going to choose the path of American education. Ultimately he will decide whether he really does want better education for his nation's children. And he will decide how much he is willing to pay for it.

Taking these recommendations one by one, we can see that almost nothing has been done since 1960 to improve the quality of our schools.

1. Our school year remains the shortest among the industrialized nations,[5] and each of our 180 school days is about two hours of academic work shorter than each of the 230 days for the Germans and the Japanese. Adding the short-fall in days to the short-fall in hours, it is easy to see that our overall educational effort is about half that of our major economic competitors.

2. Rather than reduce the amount of time spent on extracurricular activities material, we have expanded it to include major segments on sex education, mental health, etc. Many of these topics merit inclusion, but over the years the time devoted to core topics has had to diminish to make way for this material. Rather than add an hour per day to the total instruction time, we have taken time away from essential and basic subjects.

3. We continue to focus our educational effort on the below-average student, even after we see how little improvement results.[6] One consequence of orienting the curriculum around the average or below-average student has been the decline in effort and achievement demanded of higher ability students. In 1972, college-bound students taking the Scholastic Aptitude Test reported that they spent only 4.55 hours per week on homework; by 1980 this figure had declined still further to a mere 4.05 hours per week.[7] Imagine, just one hour per day, four days a week, for students who will soon be in college. No wonder our achievement scores are low; no one need do any more than this to graduate and go on to college.

4. No progress at all here. Instead we hear an increasing volume of criticism of the very idea of standards. We are told now that all standards are exclusory racist barriers to the advancement of minorities.[8] Tests of any type are attacked by women's groups if the results don't yield an equal distribution of outcomes by gender.[9] National standards, if high enough, would put school districts on notice to improve actual achievement; but a shift to higher standards would only magnify the group differences in school achievement that already cause us to keep the curriculum mediocre.

5. Again, despite some stiffer college graduation requirements for education majors, not much real progress can be found here either. Teaching just isn't lucrative enough to attract the "best and the brightest."

6.   The sixth question raised in the report has been mooted by the
       studies showing that student achievement is not increased very
       much by raising per pupil expenditures and improving teacher
       qualifications.[10] Since we now know that these traditional
       remedies do not work, it is essential that we begin to focus on
       what good research shows does improve performance. This
       means that we have to dismantle the LOW PERFORMANCE
       CYCLE that is currently operating in our public schools, and
       replace it with a HIGH PERFORMANCE CYCLE. How to do
       this is the topic of the next section of this report.

Part II: An Outline of a Solution

Decades of research in industrial-organizational psychology have
produced a model of effective job performance that is strongly supported
by a wide variety of empirical studies.[11] The model is called the HIGH
PERFORMANCE CYCLE (HPC) and the key element is *difficult* goals.
Assigned goals are as effective as self-determined goals. But both types
of goals are effective only when they are difficult. Without high standards
for performance it is almost impossible to motivate workers (and
students) to perform up to their potential. Research confirms that people
respond well to challenges and will, if provided accurate feedback about
performance, enjoy the exercise and development of their talents that only
the adoption of difficult goals makes possible. Locke and Latham have
the following to say about the HPC and education:

> Another application of this model is to the field of education. It is
> widely recognized that, among the major industrial nations, American
> students are among the worst-educated, not only with respect to basic
> skills like mathematics but even with respect to knowing basic facts
> such as where the major countries of the world are on a map. Studies
> of in-school and out-of-school activities of U.S., Japanese, and
> Taiwanese students reveal that American students: spend less time in
> class doing actual work, spend less time taking core courses such as
> mathematics, have a shorter work day and a shorter work week, have
> a shorter academic year and have less homework (Stevenson, Lee, &
> Stigler, 1986). In other words, much less is demanded of the American
> students. In view of our model, it is not surprising that they learn a lot
> less than their Asian counterparts.
>
> The near illiteracy of many of our high school graduates and non-
> graduates, and sometimes even college graduates, makes them virtually

unemployable. Even those employed lack so many skills that it puts our organizations at a severe competitive disadvantage in the world marketplace. Perhaps more than any other institution in our society, our educational system needs to introduce the high performance cycle. The first step in introducing the cycle would be to demand more of our students, starting in elementary school. Teachers also need to persuade students that they are capable of accomplishing more than they are now accomplishing (Collins & Tamarkin, 1982) and to train students to use effective learning strategies. Constructive feedback needs to be provided showing progress in relation to goals and regarding the effectiveness of the learning strategies used. Increasing success in learning will enable students to feel more efficacious and to take greater pride in their performance. This, in turn will make them more committed to school and to learning. The ultimate extrinsic reward will be greater success in the job market and in life.

The important issue not addressed by these advocates of the high performance cycle in education is how to introduce more difficult goals into a school system dedicated to mediocrity. If higher standards should cause a higher percentage of students to fail, as happened in the famous case of the Boston Compact[12] and elsewhere, can we expect such standards to be maintained? I think the answer is clearly no, unless the public school system is drastically altered. With the current system, the major barrier to even the initial adoption of more difficult goals is the belief of the vast majority of teachers and administrators that a more difficult curriculum will increase the achievement differences between the top and the bottom of the class. They are probably correct. What then is to be done?

The first step is to recognize that the last four decades of educational reform in the United States have had the effect of lowering the educational challenges for our more capable students. Easier textbooks[13] and less homework are two obvious examples of innovative but harmful stratagems. The idea seems to have been that good students can take care of themselves and the major effort needs to be with the poorer students. This approach has been disastrous.[14] The current reality is that millions of American children with above average academic aptitudes are being intellectually underdeveloped by a curriculum that is literally "childsplay." Here I would remind the reader that our college-bound high school juniors are so unengaged that they report only four to five hours of study per week on the average. This means that hundreds of thousands are studying fewer than two hours per week. An educational system that permits such a neglect of talent doesn't deserve our support.

The second step is also one of recognition. We must realize that our better students will continue to be undereducated until political pressure to improve the curriculum is brought to bear on school boards. Such proposals will be castigated as elitist. We must not be intimidated. We should have at least as much elitism in education as we have in sports. We all know what would happen to individual and team athletic performance if coaches were required to spend most of their time with the poorer athletes. Aren't our talented intellects entitled to as much attention as our talented athletes?

The third step is to know that advocates for excellence have very few allies among professional educators. Rather than promote the intellectual growth of all children, educators have tended to emphasize the need for more attention and resources going to the various at-risk groups. These administrators and teachers are very uncomfortable with changes that could cause the achievements of the relatively gifted to spurt ahead. Although well-intentioned, this group of educators are more responsible for lowered standards and for the resulting educational crisis than the societal decay they tend to blame for their students' poor performance.

The absence of advocates for excellence among professional educators means that pressure for change must come almost exclusively from outside. This should not discourage us. The data supporting the need for change is overwhelming. The research reports referenced in this article have held up well under the toughest scrutiny.

Public knowledge of the waste and inefficiency in the public schools is increasing and this can be a powerful force for beneficial change. One recent, thorough report concludes "that increased expenditures by themselves offer *no overall promise* for improving education" (emphasis added).[15] Another study identifies what does work. James S. Coleman's study of public, private and Catholic high schools in Chicago shows that private and Catholic schools produce higher achievement levels than public schools *for students at all levels of aptitude.*[16] Concerning the reasons for the better performance:

> There are at least two important ways in which private schools produce higher achievement outcomes than public schools. First, given the same type of student (that is, with background standardized), private schools create higher rates of engagement in academic activities. School attendance is better, students do more homework, and students generally take more rigorous subjects (for instance, more advanced mathematics). The indication is that more extensive academic demands are made in the private schools, leading to more advanced courses and thus to greater achievement. This is a somewhat obvious conclusion, and the statistical evidence supports it. Second, student behavior in a school has strong and consistent effects on student achievement. Apart from mathematics coursework for seniors, the greatest differences in achievement between private and public schools are accounted for by school-level behavior variables (that is, the incidence of fights, students threatening teachers, and so forth). The disciplinary climate of a school,

such as the effectiveness and fairness of discipline and teacher interest, affect achievement at least in part through their effect on these school-level behavior variables.

Although these answers are only partial in that additional school factors may also explain the different outcomes in the sectors, they strongly suggest that school functioning makes a difference in achievement outcomes for the average student. And private schools of both sectors appear to function better in the areas that contribute to achievement.

Coleman's summary of the reasons private schools are better than public schools for students from any background is in good agreement with the data supporting the high performance cycle (HPC) in education. Coleman and HPC both show that everything depends on higher standards. Without difficult goals the motivation to do better is lacking and performance sags. And higher standards are better for everyone. Even the lower ability students do better when they are asked to strive for more difficult goals.

The key, then, is to demand more of our children in school. Recall from the beginning of this paper that only 51 percent of our 17-year-olds know that 87 percent of 10 is less than 10. It is certainly not asking too much for even 15-year-olds to know the answer to this and similar questions. But given the lenient inclinations of current school officials, we are going to have to insist on achievement tests as gatekeepers. Only with acceptable scores on nationally standardized achievement tests should a child be allowed to pass on to the ninth grade. As it is now, all students know that anyone who stays around will graduate. No need to really work at learning. This is the fact of life in our schools that destroys the incentive to learn. If people come to understand that they may not be able to go to high school, much less graduate, unless they perform well, their behavior is likely to change. One thing we do know for sure: without these enforced higher standards our current public school system is floundering, and the leniency in the system is hurting most those it was putatively designed to help.

The variety of current movements to increase parental choice in education are to be encouraged. Choice may be the only way to put people in charge who really care about high standards and improved performance. However, choice without higher standards will not work. The task at hand is to get our children to perform at levels that are not the lowest among the industrialized nations.[17] Choice will not, by itself, get us out of the achievement doldrums. Enforced higher standards will.

Endnotes

1. International comparisons of access to higher education use the statistic "percentage still in school the year before college" instead of "percent who graduate from high school" in order to measure how much "retentivity" is built into school systems. This is because most countries actually plan to limit college admissions to those students judged ready for high level work. The retentivity of students in the secondary school systems of these countries is quite low because the non-college-bound students leave school much before the age of 18, the year of high school graduation for most students in the U.S. In order to make international comparisons, allowances have to be made for the fact that only the U.S. tries to give higher education access to even its worst students in secondary school. *See* Torsten Husen, ed. *International Study of Achievement in Mathematics* (New York, N.Y.: John Wiley & Sons, 1967).

2. *Wall Street Journal*, 23 Aug. 1990, Review and Outlook section, p. A14.

3. *Crossroads in American Education*, Educational Testing Service, Feb. 1989.

4. Many readers might wonder about the effect of recently enacted requirements for prospective high school graduates to pass an exit achievement exam in order to graduate. Generally, these tests are so easy that the motivating potential of this approach is lost. That is, the typical exit test might catch the student who doesn't understand percentage, but would not cause the student to fail if he could not calculate simple interest.

5. Michael J. Barrett, "The Case for More School Days," *The Atlantic* (Nov. 1990), 78-106.

6. *Op. cit.*, 3.

7. *Excellence in High School Education: Cross-Sectional Study, 1972-1980*, Educational Testing Service, 1985.

8. Charles V. Willie, "Educating Students Who Are Good Enough: Is Excellence an Excuse to Exclude," *Change* (Mar. 1982).

9. "Court Ruling Rekindles Controversy Over SATs," *Science*, 17 Feb. 1989.

10. James S. Coleman, "Equality of Educational Opportunity," U.S. Department of Health, Education, and Welfare (Washington, 1966), and John E. Chubb and Terry M. Moe, *Politics, Markets, and America's Schools* (Washington, D.C.: The Brookings Institution, 1989).

11. Edwin A. Locke and Gary P. Latham, "Work Motivation and Satisfaction: Light at the End of the Tunnel," in *Psychological Science* 1 (July 1990).

12. William J. Spring, "A Public/Private Careers Service," in *School Success for Students at Risk* (Orlando: Harcourt, Brace, Jovanovich, 1988).

13. Harriet Tyson-Bernstein, *A Conspiracy of Good Intentions: America's Textbook Fiasco*.

14. *Op. cit.*, 3.

15. Eric A. Hanushek, "The Economics of Schooling: Production and Efficiency in Public Schools," *Journal of Economic Literature* 24 (Sept. 1986): 1141-1177.

16. James S. Coleman, *High School Achievement* (New York: Basic Books, 1982).

17. *Op. cit.* 1. *See also* Harold W. Stevenson, et al., "Mathematics Achievement of Chinese, Japanese, and American Children," *Science* 231, p. 693-699.

COMBATING POLITICAL CORRECTNESS
ON CAMPUS

Dinesh D'Souza
Research Fellow, The American Enterprise Institute

As the classes of 1992 walk down the aisle to accept their diplomas, and attention turns to next year's crop of students, it is an appropriate time for the discussion of the future of higher education to move to a more mature stage. Rather than exchange heated allegations of "racial insensitivity" and "political correctness," we need to begin a debate on concrete proposals to remedy the crisis facing our colleges and universities.

The testimony of many voices across the political spectrum indicates that liberal education is in danger of abandoning or even inverting three of its most cherished principles. At most universities, equal opportunity has given way to preferential treatment based on race. The goals of racial integration and the close interaction of diverse perspectives have been replaced by a new segregation on campus. Finally, standards, academic freedom and free speech are under attack at many colleges.

There are two reasons why such changes are worthy of close and careful examination. The first is that universities are facing questions that will soon confront the rest of the country. America is very rapidly becoming a multiracial, multicultural society. Immigration from Asia, Latin America, and the Caribbean has changed the landscape with an array of yellow, brown, and black faces.[1] Meanwhile, European immigration has shrunk from 50 percent of all arrivals between 1955 and 1964 to around 7 percent between 1975 and the present.[2] The recolorization of America is further enhanced by domestic minority birth rates, which exceed that of whites.

The result is a new diversity of pigments and lifestyles. When America loses her predominantly white stamp, what impact will that have on her Western cultural traditions? On what terms will the evanescent majority and the emerging minorities, both foreign and domestic, relate to each other? How should society cope with the agenda of increasingly powerful minority groups, which claim to speak for blacks, Hispanics, women, and homosexuals? These challenges are currently being faced by the leadership of institutions of higher education.

Universities are a microcosm of society. But they are more than a reflection or mirror; they are a leading indicator. In universities, an environment where students live, eat, and study together, racial and cultural differences come together in the closest possible way. Of all American institutions, perhaps only the military brings people of such different backgrounds into more intimate contact. With coeducation now a reality in colleges, and with the confident emergence of homosexual groups, the American campus is now sexually democratized as well.

Since the victim's revolution is transforming what is taught, both inside and outside the American university classroom, the second major reason to examine the changes is to discover what young people are learning these days, particularly on questions of race and gender, and the likely consequences for their future and that of their country.

This limited discussion will address three basic issues: **1) Who is Admitted?** How are preferential treatment policies justified which treat racial groups differently and admit some students based on academic merit, and others largely or exclusively based on their skin color? **2) What is Studied?** Why are universities expelling Homer, Aristotle, Shakespeare, and other "white males" from their required reading list? Is it true that a study of non-Western and minority cultures will liberate students from ethnocentrism, racism, sexism, and homophobia? **3) Life on Campus.** Should universities promote integration or separatism? Why do minority students attack exclusivity, yet seem to prefer segregated institutions for themselves? Is there a case for universal censorship of opinions that trespass on the feelings of blacks, feminists, and homosexuals?

Specific proposals are made as to how these issues could be handled more responsibly, so that the revolution of minority victims may more effectively achieve its legitimate aspirations, and all students may be better prepared for the challenges of career and citizenship in the society in which they will find themselves after graduation.

Admissions Policies: The Problem

Virtually all American universities have changed their admissions rules so that they now fill a sizable portion of their freshman class each year with students from certified minority groups—mainly blacks and Hispanics—who have considerably lower grade point averages and standardized test scores than white and Asian American applicants who are refused admission. Since it is often difficult for minorities admitted on the basis of preferential treatment to compete, most universities offer an array of programs and incentives, including cash grants, to encourage these students to pass their courses and stay in school.

At the University of California at Berkeley, black and Hispanic student applicants are up to twenty times (or 2,000 percent) more likely to be accepted for admission than Asian American applicants who have the same academic qualifications.[3] At Ivy League colleges, which are among the most competitive in the nation, incoming freshmen have average grade scores close to 4.0 and average SATs of 1,250 to 1,300. According to admissions officials, however, several of these schools admit black, Hispanic, and American Indian students with grade averages as low as 2.5 and SAT aggregates "in the 700 to 800 range."[4]

A similar pattern can also be found at state schools. Over the past five years, the University of Virginia has virtually doubled its black enrollment by accepting more than 50 percent of blacks who apply, and fewer than 25 percent of whites, even though white students generally have much better academic credentials.[5] At Pennsylvania State University, preferential treatment for black students extends beyond admissions; the university offers financial incentives to induce blacks to maintain minimum grades and graduate. All black students who maintain a grade average of C to C+ during the course of a year get checks from the school for $580; for anything better than that, they get $1,160. This official policy endures for all four years of college; it is not connected with financial aid; it applies regardless of economic need. White and other minority students are ineligible for the cash awards.[6]

Admissions Policies: The Solution

Universities should retain their policies of preferential treatment, but should alter their criteria from race to socioeconomic disadvantage. This means that admissions officers would take into account such factors as the applicant's family background, financial condition and primary and secondary school environment, giving preference to disadvantaged students so long as it is clear that they can be reasonably expected to meet the academic challenges of the university. Race or ethnicity, however, would cease to count either for or against any applicant.

Ordinarily the admissions policy of selective colleges should be based on academic and extracurricular merit. Preferential treatment is justified, however, when it is obvious that measurable indices of merit do not accurately reflect a student's learning and growth potential. Every admission officer knows that an SAT score of 1,200 out of 1,600 by a student from Harlem or Anacostia, who comes from a broken family and has struggled against negative peer pressure and a terrible school system, means something entirely different from the same score from a student from Scarsdale or Georgetown, whose privileges include private tutors and SAT prep courses.

Universities are entirely justified in giving a break to students who may not have registered the highest scores, but whose record suggests that this failure is not due to lack of ability or application, but rather to demonstrated disadvantage. Admissions officers are right to see the academic potential in these students.

Socioeconomically based affirmative action offers many advantages over the current race-based approach. No longer will the children of relatively affluent black and Hispanic families receive preference over the children of lower middle class and poor white and Asian families. Yet all minority groups would disproportionately benefit from such a program, because they are disproportionately represented in the ranks of the disadvantaged.

While it is true that extending affirmative action benefits to all groups would somewhat reduce the number of blacks and Hispanics at the most selective schools, this change could have the positive effect of placing many of these minority students into colleges where they would effectively compete with their peers, and graduate at comparable rates. Race-based preferences often have the effect of misplacing black and Hispanic students into academic environments where they are dramatically outmatched by their classmates, and this contributes to extremely high dropout rates among these groups.

Finally, socioeconomically-based affirmative action would not create the special stigma that is attached to racial preference. No longer would universities be forced to explain the anomaly of enforcing racial discrimination as a means to combat racial discrimination. The euphemism and mendacity currently employed to justify ethnic preferences can stop—the new program can be explicitly stated and defended. Students are to be judged as individuals, based on their ability, in the context of their circumstances.

Academic Curriculum and Self-Knowledge: The Problem

Most American universities have diluted or displaced their "core curriculum" in the great works of Western civilization to make room for new course requirements stressing non-Western cultures, Afro-American Studies, and Women's Studies. In 1988, the Stanford Faculty Senate voted 39-4 to change the Western culture course to a new three-course sequence called "Cultures, Ideas and Values."[7] The previous fifteen-book requirement was abandoned. Six common texts were chosen; professors could choose others they wanted to assign. Annually the six required texts would be reexamined, and changes made if necessary. The new requirement insisted that all courses study at least one non-European culture. Professors must give "substantial attention" to issues of race and gender. The reading list must include works by women and minorities.[8]

The change at Stanford reverberated across the country, reflecting powerful and well-organized movements for curricular reform and a new agenda for what should be taught—the basic raw material of a liberal education. "Core curricula" at such places as Columbia University and the University of Chicago are now under fierce attack in the aftermath of the Stanford transformation. At Mount Holyoke College, students are currently required to take a course in Third World culture although there is no Western culture requirement. At the University of Wisconsin, students must enroll in ethnic studies although they need not study Western civilization or even American history.

It is easy to sympathize with the feeling of inadequacy that many minority students experience when they encounter a curriculum that seems overwhelmingly dominated by whites. The claim by Stanford activists that other cultures count for something too is more in the nature of a psychological plea than a political demand. Even though the concerns of the students are legitimate, Stanford and other colleges have not had an easy time in coping with them. One important reason for this is the existence of some very inconvenient facts about the Third World.

The basic difficulty is that, by and large, non-Western cultures have no developed tradition of racial equality. Not only do they violate equality in practice, but the very principle is alien to them, regarded by many with suspicion and contempt.[9] Moreover, many of these cultures have deeply ingrained ideas of male superiority. Feminism is simply not indigenous to non-Western cultures. It is perhaps pointless even to bring up the issue of non-Western attitudes toward homosexuality or other "alternative lifestyles," which in various societies are enough to warrant segregation, imprisonment, even capital punishment.

Academic Curriculum and Self-Knowledge: The Solution

Universities should retain their core requirements emphasizing the classics of Western culture, but they should broaden the reading list to expose students to the greatest works of other civilizations as well. What Matthew Arnold termed the "best that has been thought and said" would remain the criterion for selection of books, only now the geographical range would not be limited to Europe but would cover the entire globe. In practice this means that Homer, the Bible, Shakespeare and Faulkner would be read in conjunction with the Bhagavad Gita, the Koran and the "Tale of Genji."

Young people must be familiarized with the fundamental texts of their own civilizations. Just as it would be embarrassing to encounter an educated Chinese who had never heard of Confucius, however well versed he might be in Mark Twain, so also it would be a failure of liberal education to teach Americans about Asia without immersing them in their own philosophical and literary tradition. American students of all races should know something about the Constitution and the Declaration of Independence, and about the Civil War and the civil rights movement.

In fact such self-knowledge can prepare Americans to better understand other cultures. And it is useful, as the world becomes a smaller place and as this country becomes more diverse, for students to move beyond their own cultural shores. For instance, young people should not graduate in the liberal arts without knowing something about the rise of Islamic fundamentalism, and for this purpose it is helpful to read the Koran. We hear about Max Weber's doctrine about the Protestant ethic and the rise of capitalism: is there a "Confucian ethic" that explains the enormous success of Asian entrepreneurs?

These sorts of questions constitute authentic multicultural education, which may be contrasted with the bogus multiculturalism currently practiced on many campuses, where texts are selected largely based on the race, gender or sexual habits of the author, and where non-Western study amounts to little more than ethnic cheerleading or Third World romanticism, combined with intemperate invective leveled against racism, sexism and homophobia in the West. If students learn to eschew such vulgar reductionism, then the greatest works of the human mind can help to liberate them from their provinciality and prejudice, so that they can develop stronger rational and moral bases for adopting the norms of others, or for reaffirming their own.

Life on Campus: The Problem

Most universities seek to promote "pluralism" and "diversity" on campus by setting up and funding separate institutions for minority groups; thus one finds black student unions, black dormitories and "theme houses," black fraternities and sororities, black cultural centers, black dining sections, even a black yearbook. Universities also seek to protect minority sensitivities by imposing administrative sanctions, ranging from forced apologies to expulsion, for remarks that criticize individuals or policies based on race, gender, and sexual orientation stereotypes. Since blacks, feminists, and homosexuals are regarded as oppressed victims, they are usually exempt from these restrictions and permitted considerable license in their conduct.

For example, graduate student Jerome Pinn checked into his dormitory at the University of Michigan to discover that his roommate had covered the walls with posters of nude men. When the young man told Pinn he was an active homosexual who expected to have partners over, Pinn approached the Michigan housing office and asked to be transferred to another room. "They were outraged by this," Pinn says. "They asked me what was wrong with me—what *my* problem was. I said that I had a religious and moral objection to homosexual conduct. They were surprised; they couldn't believe it. Finally they agreed to assign me to another room, but they warned me that if I told anyone of the reason, I would face university charges of discrimination on the basis of sexual orientation."

Although its handbook advocates racial integration, Cornell University supports a host of ethnic and minority institutions, most of which do not admit, and none of which encourage, white students as members: Cornell Black Women's Support Network; Gays, Bisexuals and Lesbians of Color; Society of Hispanic Professional Engineers.

At Michigan, Cornell and elsewhere, many minority students seek comfort and security among their peers who are in a similar situation. Thus many sign up for their campus Afro-American Society or Hispanic Students Association or ethnic theme house or fraternity, where they can share their hopes and frustrations in a relaxed and candid atmosphere, and get guidance from older students who have traveled these paths.

White students generally have no desire to set up their own racially exclusive unions, clubs, or residence halls, but they cannot help feeling that the university is practicing a double standard by supporting minority institutions to which whites may not belong. While it is possible to ignore minority self-segregation in principle, such indifference becomes harder when the groups serve as base camps for mounting ideological assaults against everyone else. "Pluralism" thus becomes a framework for racial browbeating and intimidation. Ultimately, this atmosphere produces one of the saddest effects remarked on by professor and students across the spectrum—that few true friendships are formed between white and black students.

When minority students demand that the college recognize and subsidize separatist institutions, the administration is placed in a dilemma.[10] The deans know that to accede to these demands is problematic, given their public commitment to integration of students from different backgrounds. At the same time, university leaders realize how dislocated many minority students feel, and how little the university itself can do to help them. Virtually every administration ends by putting aside its qualms and permitting minority institutions to flourish. There is a good deal of camaraderie and social activity in the distinctive minority organizations. Most of them, especially ethnic residence halls and fraternities, help to give newly arrived minority students a sense of belonging. They do not, however, offer any solution to the dilemma facing those students who are inadequately prepared for the challenges of the curriculum.

Life on Campus: The Solution

Universities should discourage the practice of minority self-segregation by refusing to recognize or fund any group that is racially separatist, or that excludes students based on skin color. Universities should, however, sanction groups based on shared intellectual or cultural interest, even if these groups appeal predominantly or exclusively to minority students.

What this means in practice is that universities would not permit a Black Students Association, but they would permit a W.E.B. Du Bois Society based on interest in the writings of the early 20th century author. Colleges would refuse to support a Latino Political Club but they would permit a Sandino Club based on interest in the thought of the Nicaraguan revolutionary hero. This principle could extend beyond race, so that universities would decline to fund a homosexual association but would fund a Sappho Society.

In all cases, university-funded groups should be built around intellectual and cultural interests, not skin color or sexual proclivity. Thought and expression are the currency in which universities trade and specialize. The consolidation of identity based on race or sexuality may be a project that some students ardently seek, but it is not always consistent with the mission of universities.

If this solution is adopted, no longer will universities have to justify the double standards that profess allegiances to cultural exchange, and then foster minority subcultures on campus; that encourage minority-pride groups and ethnic fraternities while prohibiting white-pride groups and segregated white fraternities.

There is no reason to think that a Malcolm X Society, for instance, would not attract any white or Hispanic or Asian students, but even if only blacks do happen to join, at least others would have been extended the opportunity. In some cases, perhaps, groups will be formed on the mere pretext of a shared idea, but inevitably this pretense will be challenged by some persistent outsider who insists on signing up and who cannot be refused membership.

Conclusion

As the situations described suggest, an academic and cultural revolution is under way at American universities. It is revising the rules by which students are admitted to college, and by which they pay for college. It is changing what students learn in the classroom, and how they are taught. It is altering the structure of life on the campus, including the habits and attitudes of the students in residence. It is aimed at what University of Wisconsin chancellor Donna Shalala calls "a basic transformation of American higher education in the name of multiculturalism and diversity." Leon Botstein, the president of Bard College, goes further in observing that the "fundamental premises of liberal education are under challenge. Nothing is going to be the same any more."

Parents, alumni, and civic leaders all invest substantial resources of time and money in American higher education. They are justifiably anxious about whether the new changes in universities will remedy these problems, or exacerbate them. Will the new policies in academia improve, or damage, the prospects for American political and economic competitiveness in the world? Will they enrich, or debase, the minds and souls of students? Will they enhance, or diminish, the prospects for harmony among different groups? In short, how well will the new project prepare the nation's young people for leadership in the multicultural society of the future?

This piece is an adaptation by the author of elements from his best-selling book, *Illiberal Education: The Politics of Race and Sex on Campus*, recently published by the Free Press/Macmillan and in paperback by Vintage Books.

Endnotes

1. According to the 1987 *Statistical Yearbook of the Immigration and Naturalization Service*, Asian immigration increased from 7.7 percent between 1955 and 1964 to over 40 percent between 1975 and 1987. Central and South American immigration rose from 7.6 percent between 1955 and 1964 to around 12 percent between 1975 and 1987. Caribbean immigration climbed from 7.1 percent between 1955 and 1964 to around 15 percent between 1975 and 1987. Washington, D.C., 1988, pp. i-ix.

2. *Ibid.*

3. These data have been confirmed with the office of Student Research, University of California at Berkeley.

4. This information was provided by officials who requested anonymity, and verified by alumni and members of judiciary committees with access to admissions data. While most admissions officers will privately admit its accuracy, they will not publicly release this sort of information "because we don't think it's anybody's business," in the words of a source at the Princeton admissions office.

5. Lawrence Feinberg, "Black Freshman Enrollment Rises 40 Percent at U-Va," *Washington Post*, 26 Dec. 1988, p. C-1.

6. "Black Incentive Grant," Office of Student Aid, Pennsylvania State University, 1989. *See also* Thomas DeLoughry, "At Penn State: Polarization of the Campus Persists amid Struggles to Ease Tensions," *Chronicle of Higher Education*, 26 Apr. 1989, p. A-30. This program is currently administered by Robert W. Evans, assistant vice president for student financial aid.

7. *See, e.g.,* Carolyn Mooney, "Sweeping Curricular Change Is Under Way at Stanford," *Chronicle of Higher Education*, 14 Dec. 1988, p. A-11; Bill Workman, "Stanford Puts an End to Western Civilization," *San Francisco Chronicle*, 1 Apr. 1988.

8. Mooney, "Sweeping Curricular Change."

9. *For example,* Iraqi writer Ibn al-Faqih writes, "The people of Iraq have sound minds, commendable passions, balanced natures, and high proficiency in every art, together with well-proportioned limbs, well-compounded humors, and a pale brown color, which is the most apt and proper color. They are the ones who are done to a turn in the womb. They do not come out with something in between blond, blanched and leprous coloring, such as the infants dropped from the wombs of the women of the Slavs and others of similar light complexion. Nor are they overdone in the womb until they are burned, so that the child comes out something in between black, murky, malodorous, stinking and crinkly-haired, with uneven limbs, deficient minds, and depraved passions, such as the Ethiopians and other blacks who resemble them." *See* Ibn Taymiyya, Al-Siyasa al-Shariyya, cited in Bernard Lewis, ed., *Islam: From the Prophet Muhammad to the Capture of Constantinople* (New York: Oxford University Press, 1987), 209.

Practical violations of equality are widespread in non-Western countries, including the caste system in India, tribal hierarchies in Africa, and a continuation of slavery in parts of China and the Arab world. *See, e.g.,* "Chinese Cracking Down on Thriving Slave Trade," *Washington Times*, 8 Feb. 1990, for reports on the traffic in women and children in Anhui province in Eastern China; Murray Gordon, *Slavery in the Arab World* (New York: New Amsterdam Books, 1989).

10. *For example,* Cornell president Frank Rhodes remarks, "We face an unresolved conflict between the natural impulse toward proud, separate racial and ethnic identity on the one hand and the genuine desire, on the other, for meaningful integration that transcends differences of background." *See* Frances Dinkelspiel, "In Rift at Cornell, Racial Issues of the 60s Remain," *New York Times*, 3 May 1989.

CRIME IN AMERICA: THE FACTS

Prof. Charles H. Logan
University of Connecticut

and

Prof. John J. DiIulio, Jr.
Princeton University

False ideas can have tragic consequences. For the last quarter-century, a network of anti-incarceration, pro-prisoner analysts, activists, lawyers, lobbyists, journalists, and judges has perpetuated a number of false ideas about crime and punishment in the U.S. For average law-abiding American citizens, if not for predatory street criminals and elite penal reformers, the consequences of these false ideas have been quite tragic indeed. As these ideas have been carved into federal, state, and local penal codes, they have succeeded in making it easier for the criminals to hit, rape, rob, burglarize, deal drugs, and murder with impunity. Worse, they have succeeded in concentrating such criminal mischief in economically distressed inner-city neighborhoods, inviting the criminal predators of these areas to repeatedly victimize their struggling underclass neighbors.

In this essay, we propose to identify and rebut ten deadly ideas about crime and punishment in the U.S. Before we do so, however, three cautions are in order.

First, we refer to these ideas as "myths." In *The American Heritage Dictionary*, myth is defined in four ways, including a "fiction or half-truth, especially one that forms part of the ideology of a society"; for example, "the myth of racial superiority." The false ideas about crime and punishment in the U.S. that we wish to challenge are myths in that sense. As we will show, in some cases, the ideas are flatly untrue; in other cases, they are more or less skillful, more or less well-publicized exaggerations of half-truths. But, in all cases, they are byproducts of an ideological vision in which punishing all save the most vicious chronic criminals is considered either morally illegitimate, or socially counterproductive, or both. For the purposes of the present essay we shall confine ourselves to the discussion of ten particular myths about crime and punishment in the U.S., driving our points through the gaping empirical and other holes in each of them, and suggesting what a truer, or at least a more balanced, vision of the realities in question might be.

Second, our list of ten is by no means exhaustive. There are other myths that could as easily come in for critical scrutiny, such as the myth that building new prisons encourages the courts to fill them up, while a moratorium on prison construction will prevent that outcome. Tempted though we are to try and clean up each and every myth, data availability, interpretive range, and space have limited us to rounding up the ten "worst offenders" below.

Third, we do not believe that most of those who have perpetrated these myths have done so with any sort of malicious intent. Instead, we believe that their intentions have been good, but that they have been blinded by ideology to the connection between the false ideas they have pushed, and the dire human and financial consequences that have resulted.

Myth One: *Crime in the U.S. is caused by poverty, chronic unemployment, and other socio-economic factors.*

Many academic criminologists, most of whom are sociologists, believe that capitalism produces pockets of poverty, inequality, and unemployment, which then foster crime. The solution, they believe, is government intervention to provide jobs, stimulate the economy, and reduce poverty and other social ills. There certainly is a correlation between the geography of crime and the geography of certain socio-economic factors, but to interpret the correlation as evidence that poverty causes crime is to get it just about backwards.

As James K. Stewart, former Director of the National Institute of Justice, has pointed out, inner-city areas where crime is rampant have tremendous potential for economic growth, given their infrastructure of railways, highways, electric power, water systems, and large supply of available labor.[1] There is every reason for these areas to be wealthy and, indeed, many of them have been rich in the past. But crime takes a terrible toll on physical, fiscal, and human capital, making it difficult to accumulate wealth and break out of the cycle of poverty. Criminals steal and destroy property, drive away customers and investors, reduce property values, and depreciate the quality of life in a neighborhood. Businesses close and working families move away, leaving behind a vacuum of opportunity. As Stewart says, crime "is the ultimate tax on enterprise.... The natural dynamic of the marketplace cannot assert itself when a local economy is regulated by crime."[2] What these areas need most from government is not economic intervention but physical protection and security. The struggling inner-city dwellers whom sociologist William Julius Wilson has dubbed "the truly disadvantaged" deserve greater protection from their truly deviant neighbors.

People who are poor, uneducated, unskilled, and unemployed may need and deserve help, but not because of their alleged propensity toward crime. In high crime urban areas, most poor people do not commit serious crimes. Fighting poverty and other problems only where, when, and because they are associated with crime would be an injustice to those who are neediest. It also would not succeed; that was the lesson of the 1960s and 70s, when the Great Society and its massive War on Poverty stemmed neither inner-city poverty nor crime.[3]

Economists, like sociologists, see a relation between economic conditions and crime, but the connection they make is much more straightforward. They see criminal behavior, like all behavior, as a rational response to incentives and opportunities. Statistical analyses have provided only mixed and limited evidence that levels of arrest and imprisonment may have deterrent effects, but as a matter of both theory and common sense, the belief that criminal behavior is responsive to reward and punishment has considerable strength.

Crime rates rose during the 60s and early 70s, then fell during the 80s. In contrast, imprisonment rates as a percentage of crimes fell during the 60s and early 70s, then rose during the 80s.[4] A deterrence-minded economist looking at these mirrored trends would say that crime rose and fell in response to its expected cost in terms of punishment.[5] An interpretation more favored by sociologists is that crime rose and fell as the "baby boom" cohort of young men in the population moved through their most crime-prone years. Economist Bruce Benson notes, however, that this "alternative" interpretation still requires some further explanation of why it is that young men are more prone to commit crimes. He provides an economist's answer: the opportunity costs of crime are lower for this group than for others. "Wages for young people are low, and their unemployment is always substantially higher than for the older population. In addition, punishment for young criminals tends to be less severe, particularly for those under eighteen who are prosecuted as juveniles. Even for those over 18, punishment may be less severe in a relative sense."[6]

Myth Two: *In the 1980s, the U.S. enacted all sorts of "get tough on crime" legislation and went on an incarceration binge.*

Prison populations have risen sharply over the last decade; that much is true. The myth is that this is due to an unprecedented and purely political wave of punitivity sweeping the nation, as epitomized by the War on Drugs and by legislative demands for longer and mandatory sentences. Several elements of this myth are shattered by a meticulous and authoritative article published recently in *Science* by Patrick A. Langan, a statistician at the Bureau of Justice Statistics.[7]

Langan examined the tremendous increase in state prison populations from 1973 to 1986. He determined that the growth was due to increases in prison admissions, rather than to (alleged but nonexistent) increases in sentence length or time served. He estimated that about 20 percent of the growth in admissions could be accounted for by demographic shifts in age and race. Increases in crime were offset by decreases in the probability of arrest, with the result that combined changes in crime and arrest rates accounted for only 9 percent of admissions growth. Increased drug arrests and imprisonments contributed only 8 percent.[8] By far the strongest determinant, explaining 51 percent of growth in prison admissions, was an increase in the post-arrest probabilities of conviction and incarceration.[9] Prosecutors convicted more felons, judges imposed more prison sentences, and more violators of probation or parole were sent or returned to prison. The data suggest that the system may have gotten more efficient but not harsher.

A column in the *Washington Post* captures well the form and spirit of the "imprisonment binge" myth.[10] In "The Great American Lockup," Franklin E. Zimring, a professor of law at Berkeley, claims that we are more punitive now than ever before in history, that the rising ride of imprisonment is a matter of overzealous policy rather than a response to need, and that we must come to our senses and reverse an essentially irrational imprisonment policy.

When Professor Zimring says that we are experiencing a "100-year peak in rates of imprisonment," he does not inform the reader that this is true only when you measure imprisonment on a crude per capita basis. If, however, you wish to describe the *punitivity* of our imprisonment rate, you need to measure the amount of imprisonment relative to the number of crimes for which people may be sent to prison. To get an even more complete measure of punitivity, you should multiply this probability of imprisonment by the length of time served. When just such an index is examined for all the years in which it is available, 1960 through 1986, it becomes clear that we have not been marching steadily forward to an all-time high in punitivity. Instead, this index of "expected days of imprison-ment" fell steadily from its high in 1959 (93 days) to about one seventh of that figure in 1975 (14 days). From 1975 through 1986 it returned to about one-fifth (19 days) of its 1960 level.[11] Even if we ignore the factor of time served and look only at prison commitments divided by crimes, we see much the same pattern. In 1960 there were 62 prison commitments per 1,000 Uniform Crime Index offenses; that number fell to 23 in 1970, remained relatively stable during the 1970s, then climbed from 25 back to 62 between 1980 and 1989.[12]

Thus, when we look at imprisonment per crime rather than per capita, and over 30 rather than 10 years, we see that our punishment level is not rocketing to a new high but recovering from a plunge. The myth of the imprisonment binge requires that we focus only on punishment and not on crime, and that we ignore all data prior to about 1980.

Myth Three: *Our prisons hold large numbers of petty offenders who should not be there.*

Tom Wicker, writing in the *New York Times*, asks: "Why does our nation spend such an exorbitant amount of money each year to warehouse petty criminals?"[13] He takes his question, and its underlying assumption, from a study by the National Council on Crime and Delinquency (NCCD), which he summarizes as finding "that 80 percent of those going to prison are not serious or violent criminals but are guilty of low-level offenses: minor parole violations, property, drug and public disorder crimes." Neither Wicker's account nor the NCCD's own summary, however, is supported by the data.[14]

The NCCD study involved interviews with 154 incoming prisoners in three states.[15] Based primarily on "facts" related by these new convicts, their crimes were classified as "petty," "medium serious," "serious," or "very serious." While the NCCD claims in its summary that the "vast majority of inmates are sentenced for petty crimes," we discover in the body of the report that "inmates" refers to just the entering cohort and not all inmates, that "vast majority" refers to 52.6 percent, and that "petty crimes" refers to acts that most Americans believe it is appropriate to punish by some period of incarceration.

Since more serious offenders receive longer sentences (and therefore accumulate in prison), the profile of incoming offenders differs significantly from that of the total population. The NCCD study is based on this distinction, but obscures it by referring always to "inmates," rather than "entering inmates."

A careful reader will find buried in the NCCD report sufficient information to calculate that 25.4 percent of the sample were men whose conviction offense was categorized by the researchers as "petty" but who revealed to the interviewers that they were high rate offenders who were committed to a criminal lifestyle. If that fact was revealed also to the judge, in the form of a prior criminal record, it would have been a valid factor in sentencing. In any case, shouldn't these 25.4 percent have been added to the 47.4 percent whose crimes were in some degree "serious" (i.e., more than "petty")? Then the study would show that nearly three-quarters of new admissions are either serious or high-rate offenders. And that does not even count 21 percent of the sample who, while not identified as high rate offenders, were described as having been on a "crime spree" at the time of their commitment offense.

The major fallacy in the NCCD study, however, was in concluding that certain property crimes are "petty"—and therefore undeserving of punishment by imprisonment—merely because they score low on a scale of "offense severity" developed in 1978. For example, burglary of a home resulting in a loss of $1,000 received a relatively low score on the severity sale, albeit higher than some descriptions of robbery, assault requiring medical treatment, bribery, auto theft for resale, embezzlement of $1,000, and many other offenses. A severity score, however, does not tell us what punishment is proper for any particular crime. In a recent survey, an overwhelming majority (81 percent) of Americans said that some time in jail or prison was a proper punishment for a residential burglary with a $1,000 loss. A clear majority (57 percent) thought jail or prison was appropriate even for a nonresidential burglary resulting in only a $10 loss.[16]

What the American public seems to understand, but NCCD does not, is that it is not just the amount of money or other material harm that makes a property crime like burglary or robbery serious rather than petty. It is the breach of an individual's security and the violation of those rights (to property and person) that form the foundation of a free society. Moreover, the NCCD dichotomy of crimes into "serious" and "petty" omits several factors that are very important both legally and morally. These include the number of counts and the offender's prior record, both of which the law recognizes as legitimate criteria in determining the culpability of offenders and the gravity of their acts.

Comprehensive national data from the Bureau of Justice Statistics show that U.S. prison populations consist overwhelmingly of violent or repeat offenders, with little change in demographic or offense characteristics from 1979 to 1986.[17] There may be individuals in prison who do not deserve to be there, and there may be some crimes now defined as felonies that ought to be redefined as misdemeanors or decriminalized altogether (some would argue this for drug crimes). But most people now in prison are not what most of the public would regard as "petty" offenders.

Myth Four: *Prisons are filthy, violence-ridden, and overcrowded human warehouses that function as schools of crime.*

There are two popular and competing images of American prisons. In one image, all or most prisons are hell holes. In the other image, all or most prisons are country clubs. Each image fits some prisons. But the vast majority of prisons in the U.S. today are neither hell holes nor country clubs. Instead, most American prisons do a pretty decent job of protecting inmates from each other, providing them with basic amenities (decent food, clean quarters, recreational equipment), offering them basic services (educational programs, work opportunities), and doing so in a way that ensures prisoners their basic constitutional and legal rights.

It is certainly true that most prison systems now hold more prisoners than they did a decade ago. The Federal Bureau of Prisons, for example, is operating at over 160 percent of its "design capacity;" that is, federal prisons house 60 percent more prisoners than they were designed to hold. When the federal prison agency's current multi-billion dollar expansion program is completed, it will still house about 40 percent more inmates than its buildings were designed to hold. That is by no means an ideal picture, and much the same picture can indeed be painted for dozens of jurisdictions around the country.

Contrary to the popular lore and propaganda, however, the consequences of prison crowding vary widely both within and between prison systems, and in every careful empirical study of the subject, the widely-believed negative effects of crowding—violence, program disruption, health problems, and so on—are nowhere to be found. More broadly, several recent analyses have exploded the facile belief that contemporary prison conditions are unhealthy and harmful to inmates.

For example, in a study of over 180,000 housing units at 694 state prisons, the Bureau of Justice Statistics reported that the most overcrowded maximum-security prisons had a rate of homicide lower than that of moderately crowded prisons and about the same as that of prisons that were not crowded.[18] By the same token, a recent review of the prison crowding literature rightly concluded that, "despite familiar claims that crowded prisons have produced dramatic increases in prison violence, illness, and hostility, modern research has failed to establish any conclusive link between current prison spatial and social densities and these problems."[19] Even more compelling was the conclusion reached in a recent and exhaustive survey of the empirical literatures bearing on the "pains of imprisonment." This conclusion is worth quoting at some length:

> To date, the incarceration literature has been very much influenced by a pains of imprisonment model. This model views imprisonment as psychologically harmful. However, the empirical data we reviewed question the validity of the view that imprisonment is universally painful. Solitary confinement, under limiting and humane conditions, long-term imprisonment, and short-term detention fail to show detrimental effects. From a physical health standpoint, inmates appear more healthy than their community counterparts.[20]

Normally, those who for ideological or other reasons are inclined to paint a bleaker portrait of U.S. prison conditions than is justified by the facts respond to such evidence with countervailing anecdotes about a given prison or prison system. Perhaps because good news is no news, most media pundits lap up these unrepresentative prison horror stories and report on "powder keg conditions" behind bars. And when a prison riot occurs, it is now de rigueur for "experts" to ascribe the incident to "overcrowding" and other "underlying factors." For selfish and short-sighted reasons, some prison officials are all too willing to go along with the farce. It is easier for them to join in a Greek chorus about the evils of prison crowding than it is for them to admit that their own poor leadership and management were wholly or partially responsible for the trouble (as they so often are).

Indeed, recent comparative analyses of how different prison administrators have handled crowding and other problems under like conditions suggests that the quality of life behind bars is mainly a function of how prisons are organized, led, and managed.[21]

Overwhelmingly, the evidence shows that crowded prisons can be safe and humane, while prisons with serious problems often suffered the same or worse problems before they were crowded. In short, the quality of prison life varies mainly according to the quality of prison management, and the quality of prison life in the U.S. today is generally quite good.

More specifically, contrary to the widely-influential "nothing works" school of prison-based criminal rehabilitation programs, correctional administrators in a number of jurisdictions have instituted a variety of programs that serve as effective management tools, and appear to increase the probability that prisoners who participate in them will go straight upon their release. Recent empirical studies indicate that prisoners who participate in certain types of drug abuse counseling and work-based programs may be less likely than otherwise comparable prisoners to return to prison once they return to the streets, as over 95 percent of all prisoners eventually do.[22]

Unfortunately, the recent spate of analyses that support this encouraging conclusion remain empirically thin, technically complex, and highly speculative. Moreover, each of the successful programs embodies a type of highly compassionate yet no-nonsense management approach that may be easier to describe in print than to emulate in practice or export widely. But, taken together with the more general facts and findings mentioned above, these studies—and the simple reality that most of those released from prison never return there—rebut the notion that most or all prisons in the U.S. are little better than crowded human warehouses that breed crime and other ills.

Myth Five: *The U.S. criminal justice system is shot through with racial discrimination.*

Most law-abiding Americans think that criminal sanctions are normally imposed on people who have been duly convicted of criminally violating the life, liberty, and property of their fellow citizens. Many critics, however, harbor a different, ostensibly more sophisticated view. They see prisons as instruments of "social control." To them, America is an oppressive, racist society, and prisons are a none-too-subtle way of subjugating the nation's poor and minority populations. Thus are roughly one of every nine adult African-American males in this country now under some form of correctional supervision—in prison, in jail, on probation, or on parole. And thus in the "conservative" 1980s was this "net of social control" cast over nearly a quarter of young African-American males in many jurisdictions.

There are at least three reasons why such race-based understandings of the U.S. criminal justice system are highly suspect at best. First, once one controls for socio-economic and related factors, there is simply no empirical evidence to support the view that African-Americans, or the members of other racial and ethnic minorities in the U.S., are far more likely than whites to be arrested, booked, indicted, fully prosecuted, convicted, be denied probation, incarcerated, disciplined while in custody (administrative segregation), or be denied furloughs or parole.

In one recent study, for example, the RAND Corporation found that "a defendant's racial or ethnic group bore little or no relationship to conviction rates, disposition times" and other adjudication outcomes in 14 large urban jurisdictions across the country.[23] Instead, the study found that such mundane factors as the amount of evidence against a defendant, and whether or not a credible eyewitness testified, were strongly related to outcomes. This study echoed the findings of several previous empirical analyses.[24]

Second, the 1980s were many things, but they were not a time when the fraction of African-Americans behind prison bars skyrocketed. In a recent report, the Bureau of Justice Statistics revealed that the number of African-Americans as a percentage of the state prison population "has changed little since 1974; 47% in 1974, 48% in 1979, and 47% in 1986."[25] It is certainly true that the imprisonment rate for African-Americans has been, and continues to be, far higher than for whites. For example, in 1986 the rate of admission to prison per 100,000 residential population was 342 for African-Americans and 63 for whites.[26] But it is also true that crime rates are much higher for the former group than for the latter.

Finally, it is well-known that most crime committed by poor minority citizens is committed against poor minority citizens. The typical victims of predatory ghetto criminals are innocent ghetto dwellers and their children, not middle- or upper-class whites.[27] For example, the best available data indicate that over 85 percent of single-offender crimes of violence committed by blacks are committed against blacks, while over 75 percent of such crimes committed by whites are committed against whites.[28] And if every credible opinion poll and victimization survey is to be believed, no group suffers more from violent street crime, "petty" thefts, and drug dealing, and no group is more eager to have courts, cops, and corrections officials crack down on inner-city criminals, than the predominantly minority citizens of these communities themselves.

The U.S. criminal justice system, therefore, may be biased, but not in the way that elite, anti-incarceration penal reformers generally suppose. Relative to whites and more affluent citizens generally, the system now permits poor and minority citizens to be victimized readily and repeatedly: The rich get richer, the poor get poorly protected against the criminals in their midst. The system is thus rigged in favor of those who advocate community-based alternatives to incarceration and other measures that return violent, repeat, and violent repeat offenders to poor, drug-ravaged, minority communities far from the elites' own well-protected homes, offices, and suites.

Myth Six: *Prisons in the U.S. are prohibitively expensive.*

Certainly, no sane citizen relishes spending public money on prisons and prisoners. A tax dollar spent to confine a criminal is a tax dollar not spent to house the homeless, educate the young, or assist the handicapped. There are many intrinsically rewarding civic ventures, but the imprisonment of wrongdoers is hardly at the top of anyone's list.

Nevertheless, it is morally myopic, and conceptually and empirically moronic, to argue that public money spent on prisons and prisoners is public money wasted. That, however, is precisely what legions of critics have argued.

To begin, nobody really knows how much the U.S. now spends each year to construct, renovate, administer, and finance prisons. Widely cited estimates range from $20 billion to over $40 billion. Corrections expenditures by government have been growing rapidly of late; in New Jersey, for example, the corrections budget has increased five-fold since 1978, and corrections threatens to become the largest single item in many state budgets. But viewed as a fraction of total government spending, in the 1980s the amount spent on corrections was trivial; for example, despite enormous growth in the Federal Bureau of Prisons, less than one penny of every federal dollar went to corrections. Just the same, estimating the costs of corrections in general, and of prisons in particular, is an exceedingly complex business to which competent analysts have given only scant attention.[29] Still, it is possible to get a conceptual and empirical handle on the financial costs and benefits of imprisonment in the U.S. today.

When critics assert that we are spending "too much" on imprisonment, we must ask "too much relative to what?" Is it the case, for example, that the marginal tax dollar invested in low-income housing, inner-city high schools, or programs for the disabled poor would yield a greater social benefit than the same dollar invested in constructing or administering new prison cells? The heart says yes, but the answer is far from obvious. Meaningful benefit-cost analyses of such competing public purposes are hard to conduct, and great difficulties attend any serious effort to quantify and compare the costs and benefits of this versus that use of public money. It is somewhat easier, but still problematic, to ask what benefits we would forgo if we did not use public money for a given purpose. For example, U.S. taxpayers now spend somewhere between $14,000 and $25,000 to keep a convicted criminal behind bars for a year. What would they lose if they chose instead to save their money, or apply it elsewhere, and allowed the criminals to remain on the streets rather than paying to keep them behind bars?

At least one thing they would lose is personal and property protection against the criminals. In simplest terms, if the typical street criminal commits X crimes per year, then the benefit to society of locking him up is to be projected against the X crimes he would have done if he were free. Thus, if the typical offender committed only one petty property crime per year, then paying thousands and thousands of dollars to keep him confined would be a bad social investment. But if he committed a dozen serious property or violent crimes each year, then the social benefits of keeping him imprisoned might well exceed the social costs of doing so.

Is imprisonment in the U.S. today worth the money spent on it? While critics assert that it is not, only a few serious efforts have been made to grapple with this question.[30] The first such effort was made in 1987 by National Institute of Justice economist Edwin W. Zedlewski.[31] Zedlewski surveyed cost data from several prison systems and estimated that the annual per prisoner cost of confinement was $25,000. Using national crime data and the findings of criminal victimization surveys, he estimated that the typical offender commits 187 crimes per year, and that the typical crime exacts $2,300 in property losses and/or in physical injuries and human suffering. Multiplying these two figures (187 times $2,300), he calculated that, when on the streets, the typical imprisoned felon was responsible for $430,000 in "social costs" each year. Dividing that figure by $25,000 (his estimate of the annual per prisoner cost of confinement), he concluded that incarceration in prison has a benefit-cost ratio of just over 17. The implications were unequivocal. According to

Zedlewski's analysis, putting 1,000 felons behind prison bars costs society $25 million per year. But not putting these same felons behind prison bars costs society about $430 million per year (187,000 crimes times $2,300 per crime).

There were, however, some flaws in Zedlewski's study. For example, he used dated data from a RAND prisoner self-report survey of prison and jail inmates in Texas, Michigan, and California. The inmates in the survey averaged between 187 and 287 crimes per year, exclusive of drug deals. He opted for the lower bound of 187. But the same RAND survey also found that half the inmate population committed fewer than 15 crimes per year, so that the median number of crimes committed was 15. There are plenty of good analytical reasons for using the median rather than the average in a benefit-cost study of this type. Making this one adjustment (using 15 rather than 187 for the number of crimes averted through incapacitation of an offender) reduces the benefit cost-ratio to 1.38—still positive, but more credibly and realistically so.

Last December one of us published a report on corrections in Wisconsin that featured an analysis of the benefits and costs of imprisonment.[32] The analysis was based on one of the largest and most recent scientific prisoner self-report surveys of inmates in a single system ever conducted. Among a host of other interesting results, the survey indicated that the prisoners committed an average of 141 crimes per year, exclusive of drug deals. The median figure was 12. Using the median to calculate, the study estimated the benefit-cost ratio to be 1.97.

In an attempt to satisfy the more reasonable critics, the Wisconsin data were reanalyzed and the results of the reanalysis were published in a recent edition of *The Brookings Review*, journal of The Brookings Institution.[33] But even after factoring in a host of assumptions that would be likely to deflate the benefits of imprisonment, the study reported a benefit-cost ratio of 1.84. This does not prove that "prison pays"; indeed, the Brookings study suggested that, for the lowest-level offenders, imprisonment probably is not a good social investment. But it does indicate that the net social benefits of imprisonment could well meet or exceed the costs.

At a minimum, the studies discussed above cast grave doubts over the notion that prisons clearly "cost too much," either in absolute terms or relative to alternate uses of the public monies that now go to build and administer penal facilities. What we simply do not know at this point is whether any given alternative to incarceration yields as much relative to costs as imprisonment apparently does. Recent studies have put question marks over several strictly supervised community-based correctional programs that might well represent a better investment than imprisonment for certain categories of low-level offenders.[34] Still, further research on the costs and benefits of imprisonment and other correctional sanctions is badly needed.

Myth Seven: *Interventions by activist judges have improved prison and jail conditions.*

In 1970, not a single prison or jail system in America was operating under judicial orders to change and improve. For most of our legal and constitutional history, prisoners were "slaves of the state," and judges followed the "hands-off" doctrine by normally deferring to the policies and practices of legislators and duly appointed corrections officials.

Today, however, over three dozen correctional agencies are operating under "conditions of confinement" court orders; many have class action suits in progress or population limits set by the courts; and several have court-mandated early release programs that put dangerous felons right back on the streets before they have served even one-tenth of their sentences in confinement. Despite the proliferation of Reagan- and Bush-appointed judges on the federal bench, activist federal judges continue to be the sovereigns of the nation's cellblocks, issuing directives on a wide range of issues, including health care services, staff training procedures, sanitation standards, food services, and the constitutionality of conditions "in their totality." Indeed, in some prison systems, the texts of court orders and consent decrees are now used as staff training manuals and inmate rulebooks, and everything from inmate disciplinary hearings to the exact temperature of the meat served to prisoners at supper is governed by judicial fiat.

There are at least three general points that can be safely made about the course and consequences of judicial intervention into prisons and jails. First, especially in the South, but in many jurisdictions outside the South as well, judicial involvement has substantially raised the costs of building and administering penal facilities.[35] Second, many of the most significant expansions in prisoners' rights, and most of the actual improvements in institutional conditions, made over the last two decades were conceived and implemented by professional correctional administrators, not coerced or engineered by activist judges.[36] Third, in the small but significant fraction of interventions that have succeeded at a reasonable human and financial cost, judges have proceeded incrementally rather than issuing all-encompassing decrees. In conjunction, they have vacated the serenity of their chambers for the cellblocks to get a first-hand understanding of things, working with and through the professionals who must ultimately translate their orders into action, rather than relying solely on self-interested special masters and neatly-typed depositions.[37]

Even taking into account the human and financial accidents caused by judges driving at breakneck activist speed through the intersection of corrections and the Constitution, the net of judicial involvement in this area is arguably positive. But there is at least as much evidence here for the thesis, articulated well by Nathan Glazer, Lon Fuller, and other scholars, that judges should limit themselves to doing what they are schooled to do; namely, to gather and weigh legal evidence, to analyze factual and legal issues, and to apply precedent standards in resolving disputes between parties.[38] At most, the idea that activist judges have helped to make prisons and jails more safe and humane is a half-truth.

Myth Eight: *The United States has the most punitive criminal justice system in the world.*

Over a decade ago, the National Council on Crime and Delinquency foisted on the media a statistic it produced in a 1979 report: in terms of severity of punishment, as measured by the number of prisoners per capita, only two countries in the world—the Soviet Union and South Africa—were more ruthlessly repressive than the United States. The media have been parroting this claim ever since, never asking the NCCD why they were so willing to accept Soviet figures at face value, nor why they did not include the four or five million prisoners held captive in the forced labor camps that have been indispensable to the Soviet economy.[39]

Well, maybe a sloppy attitude toward data didn't matter before; we merely would have been a more distant third. But now the NCCD, the Soviets, and the South Africans have all been trumped. According to The Sentencing Project, a Washington-based research group, the U.S. has moved into first place, with 426 prison and jail inmates per 100,000 population, compared to 333 in South Africa and 268 in the Soviet Union.[40] The media, including commentators as diverse as Tom Wicker and William Raspberry, have reached just as uncritically to the new figures as they did to the old ones.

While gullibility toward Soviet statistics is the most glaring, it is not the most fatal flaw in this comparison, which also shows American incarceration rates to be much higher than, say, those of European countries, for which we have more reliable figures. The fatal flaw is very simple and very obvious: to interpret incarceration as a measure of the punitivity of a society, you have to divide, not by the population size, but by the number of crimes.

More competent comparative studies have discovered that when you control for rates of serious crime, the difference between the United States and other countries largely, and for some crimes completely, disappears.[41] For example, after controlling for crime rate and adjusting for differences in charge reduction between arrest and imprisonment, the U.S. in the early 1980s had an imprisonment rate virtually identical to

Canada and England for theft, fell between those two countries in the case of burglary, and lagged well behind each of the others in imprisonments for robbery.[42]

In addition to the myth of the U.S. as the world's most punitive nation, the Sentencing Project perpetuates in its report several of the other myths we discuss in this essay. It notes that African-American males are locked up at a rate four times greater than their counterparts in South Africa. A fleeting reference to the very high crime rate among black males is immediately buried in an avalanche of references to root causes, poverty, diminished opportunities, the gap between rich and poor, and the failure of schools, health care, and other social institutions—all wrapped up as "the cumulative effect of American policies regarding black males." The report calls for increased spending on supposed "prevention policies and services" such as education, housing, health care, and programs to generate employment. In a truly wacky expression of faith in social engineering, the report urges the General Accounting Office "to determine the relative influence of a range of social and economic factors on crime."

Most of all, the Sentencing Project advocates the expanded use of alternatives to incarceration, but with a unique twist: they recommend racial quotas in the distribution of criminal justice. Independent of any preceding reduction in criminal behavior, the "Justice Department should encourage the development of programs and sanctions designed specifically to reduce the disproportionate incarceration rate of African-American males."[43] The Sentencing Project endorses the language of one such program designed to reduce the incarceration "of ethnic and minority groups where such proportion exceeds the proportion such groups represent in the general population." Methods recommended for such reduction include diversion from prosecution, intensive probation, alternative sentencing, and parole release planning, among others.

That crime rates are very high in this country, particularly among black males, is an unhappy fact. When that fact is taken into account, it exposes as a myth the argument that we are excessively punitive, relative to other countries, in our imposition of imprisonment. A related myth is that we have failed to consider sanctions other than incarceration.

Myth Nine: *We don't make enough use of alternatives to incarceration.*

According to this myth, we could reduce prison crowding, avoid new construction, and cut out annual operating costs if we would just take greater advantage of intensive probation, fines, electronic monitoring, community service, boot camps, wilderness programs, and placement in nonsecure settings like halfway houses.

It is important to distinguish the myth of a supposed need for "alternative" sanctions from the more valid assertion of a need for "intermediate" sanctions. Norval Morris and Michael Tonry, among others, argue that, for the sake of doing justice and achieving proportionality between crime and punishment, we need a greater variety of dispositions that are intermediate in punitivity between imprisonment and simple probation.[44] Most people will find that argument perfectly sensible, even if they disagree about what crimes deserve which intermediate punishments.

The myth that we need more sanctions to use as *alternatives* to imprisonment is based on the false premise that we do not already make the maximum feasible use of *existing* alternatives to imprisonment. Consider, however, the following figures for the most recent available years:[45]

2,356,486	(63%)	on probation
407,977	(11%)	on parole
771,243	(21%)	in state and federal prisons
195,661	(5%)	in jails, post-convicted
3,731,367	(100%)	Total

It is true that about two-thirds of convicted felons are sentenced to at least some period of incarceration.[46] (A felony, by definition, is punishable by a year or more in prison.) However, at any time after sentencing and prior to final discharge from the criminal justice system, the great majority of those under correctional supervision (74 percent in the figures above) will be in the community and not incarcerated. In other words, they will be experiencing an "alternative sanction" for at least some part of their sentence.

If one-third of convicted felons receive no incarceration at all, and three-quarters receive at least some time on probation or parole, how much room is left for expanding the use of alternatives to imprisonment? Some, perhaps, but probably not much, especially if you look at offenders' prior records when searching for additional convicts to divert or remove from prison. Two-thirds of inmates currently in state prisons were given probation as an alternative sanction one or more times on prior convictions, and over 80 percent have had prior convictions resulting in either probation or incarceration.[47] After how many failures for a given offender do we say that alternatives to imprisonment have been exhausted?

In sum, the idea that we have not given alternatives to imprisonment a fair chance is a myth. Any day of the week you will find three times as many convicts under alternative supervision as you will find under the watchful eye of a warden. And most of those in the warden's custody probably are there at least partly because they did not do well under some prior alternative.

Myth Ten: *Punishment is bad.*

Underlying all the myths we have discussed so far, and motivating people to believe them, is the biggest myth of all: that punishment itself is inherently wrong. It is largely because they are opposed to punishment generally and to imprisonment in particular that many people argue so strongly that we must address the root causes of crime, that our criminal justice system discriminates, that we are overly punitive and haven't considered alternatives, that prisons are too costly and overcrowded, and that we must look to the courts for reform.

The "Big Myth" is that punishment has no value in itself; that it is intrinsically evil, and can be justified as a necessary evil only if it can be shown to be instrumental in achieving some overriding value, such as social order. Even retributivists, who argue that the primary purpose of the criminal sanction is to do justice by imposing deserved punishment (rather than to control crime through such strategies as rehabilitation, deterrence, or incapacitation), can find themselves caught up in utilitarian terminology when they speak of the "purpose"—rather than the "value"—of punishment.

Andrew von Hirsch provides the major contemporary statement of the justice model in his book, *Doing Justice.*[48] Following Immanuel Kant, von Hirsch calls for penal sanctions on moral grounds, as the "just deserts" for criminally blameworthy conduct. Unlike Kant, however, von Hirsch sees deservedness only as necessary, but not sufficient, to justify punishment. There is supposedly a "countervailing moral consideration"—specifically, "the principle of not deliberately causing human suffering where it can possibly be avoided."[49] Accepting this principle, von Hirsch argues that for punishment to be justified, it must also be shown to have a deterrent effect. A utilitarian element has been added.

Von Hirsch's compromise is internally inconsistent, and is weaker than a purely retributivist justification. The principle that punishment for wrongdoing is deserved, and the principle against all avoidable suffering, are logically incompatible. To say that *some* suffering (i.e. punishment) is deserved is to say that we do *not* believe that *all* avoidable infliction of pain *should* be avoided. The justice model is stronger when the utilitarian requirement of deterrence is dropped.[50]

The best defense of punishment is not that it upholds the social order, but that it affirms important moral and cultural values.[51] Legal punishment is a legitimate and, if properly defined and administered, even a noble aspect of our culture. Imprisonment, in order to be respectable, does not need to be defined as "corrections," or as "treatment," or as "education," or as "protection of society," or as any other instrumental activity that an army of critics will forever claim to be a failure.

We must reject the false dichotomy between punishment and "humanitarianism." It is precisely within the context of punishment that humanistic concepts are most relevant. Principled and fair punishment for wrongdoing treats individuals as persons and as human beings, rather than as objects. Punishment is an affirmation of the autonomy, responsibility, and dignity of the individual.

Punishment in the abstract is morally neutral. When applied in specific instances and in particular forms—including imprisonment—its morality will depend on whether or not it is deserved, justly imposed, and proportionate to the wrongfulness of the crime. Where these conditions are met, punishment will not be a necessary evil, tolerable on utilitarian grounds only when held to the minimum "effective" level. Rather, under those conditions, it will have positive moral value.

This article originally appeared in the Winter/Spring 1992 edition of the *Wisconsin Interest*, a publication of the Wisconsin Policy Research Institute.

Endnotes

1. James K. Stewart, "Urban Crime Locks People in Poverty," *Hartford Courant*, 15 July 1986.

2. *Ibid.*

3. *See* Charles Murray, *Losing Ground: American Social Policy, 1950-1980* (New York: Basic Books, 1984); and James Q. Wilson, *Thinking About Crime* (New York: Basic Books, 1975).

4. *See* Myth Two, below.

5. Morgan Reynolds, *Crime in Texas*, NCPA Policy Report No. 102 (Dallas: National Center for Policy Analysis, Feb. 1991).

6. Bruce Benson, *The Enterprise of Law: Justice without the State* (San Francisco: Pacific Research Institute, 1990), 258.

7. Patrick A. Langan, "America's Soaring Prison Population," *Science*, 29 Mar. 1991, 1568-1573.

8. The war on drugs probably had a greater effect on state prisons after 1984 and undoubtedly has had a great effect on federal prisons, where over half of last year's admissions were for drug offenses.

9. *Ibid.*, 1572.

10. Franklin E. Zimring, "The Great American Lockup," *Washington Post*, 28 Feb. 1991.

11. Mark Kleiman et al., *Imprisonment-to-Offense Ratios* (Washington, D.C.: Bureau of Justice Statistics Report, Nov. 1988), 21; we are using his figures without adjustment for under-reporting by the UCR, since that adjustment is only possible from 1973 on.

12. Robyn L. Cohen, *Prisoners in 1990* (Washington, D.C.: Bureau of Justice Statistics, 1991), 7.

13. Tom Wicker, "The Punitive Society," *New York Times*, 12 Jan. 1991, sec. 1, p. 25.

14. James Austin and John Irwin, *Who Goes to Prison?* (San Francisco: National Council on Crime and Delinquency, 1990). The discussion here draws on Charles H. Logan, "Who Really Goes to Prison?" *Federal Prisons Journal* (Summer 1991): 57-59.

15. *See* Logan, *op. cit.*, for a critique of the study's methodology, including the sample.

16. Joseph E. Jacoby and Christopher S. Dunn, *National Survey on Punishment for Criminal Offenses* (Bowling Green, OH: Bowling Green State University, 1987).

17. Christopher A. Innes, *Profile of State Prison Inmates, 1986* (Washington, D.C.: Bureau of Justice Statistics Special Report, 1988).

18. Christopher A. Innes, *Population Density in State Prisons* (Washington, D.C.: Bureau of Justice Statistics, Dec. 1986).

19. Jeff Bleich, "The Politics of Prison Crowding," *California Law Review* 77 (1989): 1137.

20. James Bonta and Paul Gendreau, "Reexamining the Cruel and Unusual Punishment of Prison Life," *Law and Human Behavior* 14 (1990): 365.

21. *For example, see* Bert Useem and Peter Kimball, *States of Siege: U.S. Prison Riots, 1971-1986* (New York: Oxford University Press, 1989), and John J. DiIulio, Jr., *Governing Prisons: A Comparative Study of Correctional Management* (New York: Free Press, 1987).

22. For an overview, *see* DiIulio, *No Escape, ibid.*, ch. 3.

23. Stephen P. Klein, et al., *Predicting Criminal Justice Outcomes: What Matters?* (Santa Monica, CA: RAND Corp., 1991), ix.

24. *For example, see* Stephen Klein et al., "Race and Imprisonment Decisions in California," *Science*, Feb. 1990, 769-792.

25. Patrick A Langan, *Race of Prisoners Admitted to State and Federal Institutions 1926-86* (Washington, D.C.: Bureau of Justice Statistics, May 1991), 8.

26. *Ibid.*, 7.

27. *See* Stewart, *op. cit.*, and DiIulio, "Underclass," *op. cit.*

28. Joan Johnson et al., *Criminal Victimization in the United States, 1988* (Washington, D.C.: Bureau of Justice Statistics, Dec. 1990), 48.

29. For a good overview, *see* Douglas C. McDonald, *The Cost of Corrections: In Search of the Bottom Line* (Washington, D.C.: National Institute of Corrections Research in Corrections Report, Feb. 1989).

30. In addition to the efforts to be described in the remainder of this section, *see*: David P. Kavanaugh and Mark A.R. Kleiman, *Cost-Benefit Analysis of Prison Cell Construction and Alternative Sanctions* (Cambridge, Mass.: Biotec Analysis Corp., June 1990); Tara Gray et al., "Using Cost-Benefit Analysis to Evaluate Correctional Sentences," *Evaluation Review*, 15 (Aug. 1991): 471-481; and Peter W. Greenwood et. al., *The RAND Intermediate-Sanction Cost Estimation Model* (Santa Monica, CA.: RAND Corp., Sept. 1989).

31. Edwin W. Zedlewski, *Making Confinement Decisions* (Washington, D.C.: National Institute of Justice Research in Brief, 1987). The material in the remainder of this section is adapted from John J. DiIulio, Jr., *Crime and Punishment in Wisconsin: A Survey of Prisoners* (Milwaukee, WI.: Wisconsin Policy Research Institute, Dec. 1990), and John J. DiIulio, Jr. and Anne Morrison Piehl, "Does Prison Pay?", *The Brookings Review* (Fall 1991).

32. *See* DiIulio, *Crime and Punishment, op. cit.*

33. DiIulio and Piehl, *op. cit.*

34. *See* Joan Petersilia and Susan Turner, *Intensive Supervision for High-Risk Probationers: Findings from Three California Experiments* (Santa Monica, CA: RAND Corp., Dec. 1990).

35. Malcolm M. Feeley, "The Significance of Prison Corrections Cases: Budgets and Regions," *Law and Society Review* (1990).

36. Clair A. Cripe, "Courts, Corrections, and the Constitution: A Practitioner's View," in DiIulio, *Courts, op. cit.*, ch. 10.

37. John J. DiIulio, Jr., ed., *Courts, Corrections, and the Constitution: The Impact of Judicial Intervention on Prisons and Jails* (New York: Oxford University Press, 1990), especially ch. 11.

38. Nathan Glazer, "Towards an Imperial Judiciary," *The Public Interest*, (1978); Lon Fuller, "The Forms and Limits of Adjudication," *Harvard Law Review* (1978).

39. *See* Ludmilla Alexeyeva, *Cruel and Usual Punishment: Forced Labor in Today's U.S.S.R.* (Washington, D.C.: AFL-CIO Department of International Affairs, 1987); *see also* various editions throughout the 1980s of the State Department's annual *Country Reports* on human rights practices of governments around the world.

40. Marc Mauer, *Americans Behind Bars: A Comparison of International Rates of Incarceration* (Washington, D.C.: The Sentencing Project, Jan. 1991).

41. James Lynch, *Imprisonment in Four Countries* (Washington, D.C.: Bureau of Justice Statistics Special Report, February 1987); *see also* Alfred Blumstein, "Prison Populations: A System Out of Control?" in Michael Tonry and Norval Morris, *Crime and Justice: a Review of Research*, vol. 10 (Chicago: University of Chicago Press, 1988).

42. Lynch, *op. cit.*, 2.

43. Mauer, 12.

44. Norval Morris and Michael Tonry, *Between Prison and Probation: Intermediate Punishments in a Rational Sentencing System* (New York: Oxford University Press, 1990).

45. Figures are taken from the following Bureau of Justice Statistics Bulletins: *Probation and Parole 1988* (Nov. 1989); *Prisoners in 1990* (May 1991); *Jail Inmates, 1990* (June 1991).

46. Jacob Perez, "Tracking Offenders, 1988," *Bulletin* (Washington, D.C.: Bureau of Justice Statistics, June 1991); a study of offenders convicted of felonies in 14 states.

47. Christopher A. Innes, *Profile of State Prison Inmates, 1986* (Washington, D.C.: Bureau of Justice Statistics Special Report, Jan. 1988), combining information from Tables A and 8.

48. Andrew von Hirsch, *Doing Justice: The Choice of Punishments* (New York: Hill and Wang, 1976).

49. *Ibid.*, 553.

50. Charles H. Logan, *Private Prisons: Cons and Pros* (New York: Oxford University Press, 1990), 243, 298.

51. This discussion draws on Charles H. Logan and Gerald G. Gaes "The Rehabilitation of Punishment" (unpub..., 1991).

FIGHTING CRIME:
THE RECENT PAST AS A GUIDE
TO THE FUTURE

Tex Lezar

*President, Texas Public Policy Foundation and
Associated Texans Against Crime*

Providing for the domestic defense—securing our families against crime—should be the first priority of state and local government in our federalist system. For the fiscal year ending in 1988, however, all state and local governments in America spent a total of only $56.5 billion or $230 per capita on police protection and corrections.[1] State and local expenditures on police protection and corrections therefore only accounted for 6.8 percent of total state and local expenditures, which were $827 billion or $3,365 per capita.[2]

Partially explaining this relatively low level of spending, many politicians seem to prefer public expenditures that transfer dollars or some other tangible benefits directly into the view—if not the pockets—of voters. During much of the past three decades, that political predisposition was encouraged by an academic and bureaucratic mindset that viewed crime as the inevitable result of social deprivation. In other words, spending more on those—by various definitions—in need, sought both to win votes and to discourage crime. Recent years have revealed the bankruptcy of that liberal political mindset, which had an especially deleterious impact on criminal justice throughout America after infecting the federal judiciary.

At long last, more and more policymakers seem to be pursuing a more rational approach to fighting crime—although significant pockets of vestigial resistance remain. The safety of most Americans—particularly, minorities and the poor—depends upon the ability of state leaders to recognize that larger numbers of dangerous criminals must be imprisoned for longer periods in the years ahead.

The Threat of Crime

Pick up a magazine or newspaper. Listen to the radio or television. You'll soon learn that crime in America is bad and getting worse. But you'll also be told that, looking at the nation as a whole, the rate at which people are being victimized continues to decline. Both accounts are correct depending upon the measure used.[3]

In many places or for particular groups of Americans, however, crime is clearly increasing. In many of our cities, the amount and rate of violent crime—including murder—have begun to grow again.[4]

Between 1980 and 1989, the total number of serious crimes did grow by more than 6 percent, but the rate of serious crime fell. Nevertheless, even the rate of serious crime increased when you compare 1989 to 1984. In 1989, both the amount and the rate of violent crime were higher than in 1980. And although the amount of property crime fell by about 5 percent between 1980 and 1989, it grew from 1988 to 1989.[5]

In a very real sense, whether growing or not, crime has spread widely enough and strikes with such random violence that it threatens all of us. According to polling done for one new book, "fully 60 percent . . . of . . . adult Americans have been the victims of at least one crime."[6] And what could be more sobering than the U.S. Justice Department's own prediction only a few years ago that the trend was so bad that five out of six twelve-year-olds—our children—would become the victims of a successful or attempted violent crime during their lifetimes.[7]

By any measure there is enough crime in America today to justify worry by everyone. According to the most recent data—the Uniform Crime Reports for 1990—one violent crime occurred every 17 seconds, one property crime every 2 seconds, a murder every 22 minutes, a forcible rape every 5 minutes, a robbery every 49 seconds, an aggravated assault every 30 seconds and a burglary every 10 seconds.[8]

Why, if crime victimization is down, do people feel so much less safe? Is there greater awareness of crime because of television? Has the spread of drugs touched so many families? All of those, plus, as former U.S. Attorney General Edwin Meese III has written:

> On a deeper level. . .I believe that public concern about the danger of crime. . .grows out of a sense that some time back we took a wrong turn, that the basic institutions of our society fundamentally, and wrongly, changed their perspectives about how we should deal with the issues of crime and punishment. . . . [O]ur thinking about crime shifted from focusing on restraining and sanctioning criminals to finding "explanations" for criminal behavior.[9]

Some Americans face even greater risks from crime. The inner-city poor are most severely victimized by crime—and are most in need of protection against criminals.

In 1962 the Reverend Martin Luther King, Jr. counseled: "It may be true that the law cannot make a man love me. But it can keep him from lynching me, and I think that's pretty important."[10] Most Americans of every race have come to love or, at least, admire that man. But the law has not done enough to protect African-Americans from being murdered or otherwise victimized by crime.

In our long and continuing struggle to achieve equal rights for all, we have too frequently failed to recognize the most basic civil right: freedom from crime. Governments were first instituted among men to meet that most basic need, as former U.S. Attorney General William French Smith used to call it, the Domestic Defense.[11] In the words of the Preamble to our Constitution, "We the People" established our government to "insure domestic Tranquility." Fighting criminal wrongs should therefore be the first civil right.

In too many instances, however, government has failed to meet that most basic duty—especially in the case of minority Americans. Out of every thirty African-American men, one will be murdered—a risk six times greater than for Anglo-American men.[12] In fact, murder is the leading cause of death among urban African-American males nationwide.[13] For example, during the first eight months of 1991, nearly two out of three murder victims in my hometown of Dallas, Texas, were African-American and four out of five were African-American or Hispanic.[14]

The average African-American is twice as likely to be robbed—and 40 percent more likely to suffer a burglary.[15] An African-American woman is two and one-half times as likely to be raped. [16] Most distressing, over the course of three recent years, the number of African-American children murdered increased by 50 percent.[17] In a study of inner-city Baltimore, 24 percent of teenagers had actually witnessed a murder—and 72 percent knew someone who had been shot.[18] Almost one in eleven of the children in that study had been raped—and the life of one in five had been threatened.

African-Americans suffer the impact of crime in other ways as well. Too frequently, it is African-Americans who victimize other African-Americans. In a horrible tragedy, the most likely perpetrator of a violent crime against an African-American is another African-American. That is true for more than 80 percent of such crimes (a similarly high percentage of violent crimes against Anglos are committed by Anglos).[19] As a result, nearly one in nine adult African-American males is in prison, in jail, on probation, or on parole.[20]

The recent growth of youth gangs throughout this country has accentuated the tragedy for even more inner-city kids and their victims of all ages. According to the National Institute of Justice:

> A 1989 survey of law enforcement officials in 45 cities across the country produced the startling estimate of nearly 1,500 youth gangs

nationwide, with more than 120,500 members. African-Americans and Hispanics made up 87 percent of gang membership, far in excess of their representation in the general population. . . . The rate of violent offenses for gang members was three times as high as that for nongang delinquents.[21]

Overwhelming difficulties face the hard-working and law-abiding families who live in crime-ridden areas of our inner cities. According to studies done in Chicago, each one percent increase in the crime rate results in a 0.2 to 0.3 percent drop in home values.[22] Since nearly 40 percent of people in households living below the poverty line own their own homes, the impact of crime on families working so hard to develop modest capital is disastrous.[23] Poor households suffer the highest victimization rates for property and personal crimes—and they suffer a greater economic impact as well.[24]

Crime deters economic development in our inner cities. According to a National Institute of Justice study,[25] crime and the fear of crime can influence investment decisions more than high taxes or labor costs. The costs of operating a small business—in losses due to crime and in the costs of insurance and private security—doom many small businesses trying to serve the residents of high-crime areas. Prices are inevitably higher—even though the customers are less able to pay higher prices.

Like a new form of slavery, crime directly and indirectly shackles African-Americans who are working hard to improve their lives and the lives of their families. It preys especially upon the poor and most defenseless Americans. The failure of government to confront this dangerous reality and to do something about it is inexcusable neglect. Too many states and localities have hesitated too long—and made excuses instead of improving public safety. In the words of an extraordinary African-American named Reuben Greenberg—the Chief of Police in Charleston, South Carolina—it's past time to "Take Back Our Streets!"[26]   And taking back our streets and communities from crime should be the key civil rights goal of the 1990s.

Just as some groups have been victimized more than others, some states and cities have suffered more dramatically than others. Some areas of the country have failed more than others in confronting the facts of crime—and have been too slow in developing an effective counterattack. Texas provides a frightening, even if unexpected, example.

Throughout Texas, the crime problem is worse than in the whole country. Between 1977 and 1986, violent crime increased in Texas by 62 percent—more than twice the national increase. And property crimes in Texas increased at nearly six times the national rate.[27] In 1989, the rate of serious crime in Texas was nearly 40 percent higher than the country as a whole.[28] And Fort Worth, Dallas, San Antonio, Austin, Houston and El Paso are among the top 24 big American cities with the highest burglary rates.[29] And six Texas cities were among the 25 highest crime cities in America.

According to a recent report by the U.S. Senate Judiciary Committee, 1991 was likely a record year for murders in Texas, making Texas second in America.[30] Nearly 2,700 Texans may have been murdered in 1991— which would be some 300 more than 1990 and at least a 10 percent increase from the previous high in 1980.[31]

Some Texas cities fared even worse in homicides than Texas as a whole. By November 13, 1991, Dallas had already exceeded its record number of murders for all of 1990—passing the previous record set in 1990, which itself surpassed the previous record set just the year before.[32] By that same date, murders were up 62 percent in Ft. Worth, 39 percent in El Paso and more than 10 percent in Houston and Austin.[33] The year was especially bad for homicides in the entire Dallas-Fort Worth area. Not only did both Dallas and Fort Worth set homicide records, but seven of the ten larger area suburbs recorded homicide increases.[34]

Most Americans—New Yorkers included—have read articles or seen television reports about the horrors of violent crime in New York City—about the infamous jogger rapists, about the subway murders of tourists. Last year, however, a shocking *Dallas Morning News* headline[35] proclaimed:

New York beset by crime—but Dallas is still worse.

In spite of the much publicized rapes and murders in New York, the crime rate was 73 percent higher in Dallas during 1989. Our murder rate was one-third higher than New York's—and the rape rate in Dallas was 2.7 *times* as high as in New York City. In 1990, the murder rate in Dallas jumped by an astounding 24 percent—and violent crime increased nearly 19 percent.[36] In 1991, murder increased another 12 percent—and violent crime another 7.6 percent.[37]

Of course, Texas cities were not the only ones suffering from what seemed yet another jump upwards in crime.[38] Three (San Diego, Dallas, and Phoenix)—and possibly two more (Los Angeles and New York)—of the top ten American cities set homicide records. Washington, D.C., Oakland, Minneapolis, Columbus, Colorado Springs, New Orleans and Rochester also set homicide records.

Lessons of the Past and Prospects for the Future

The 1960s and early 1970s

There's an old story about two liberals who came upon a man lying in a ditch. Being liberals, they immediately climbed into the ditch to help. Between groans of pain, the injured man told how he was brutally beaten and robbed. The good Samaritans were visibly moved. And one said to the other: "How, horrible! We must find the man who did this. He really needs our help!"

During the 1960s and the 1970s, America suffered a long spell of liberalism in its criminal justice policy. Faced with mounting crime rates, we nevertheless spent billions of dollars on alternatives to incarceration. Many policymakers just wouldn't believe that so many criminals could be victimizing their fellow Americans without some grievous but remediable cause—such as poverty, lack of education, lack of family. The "desire to shift blame became so pronounced" that a Joint Economic Committee Report of the Congress proclaimed in 1976 that a "1.4 percent rise in unemployment during 1970 is directly responsible. . .for 1,740 additional homicides."[39]

During the 1960s, leniency and belief in rehabilitation caused rates of incarceration to drop by 17 percent—and the violent crime rate more than doubled.[40] Sociologist Charles Murray has written that during the 1960s, policy was developed based upon the belief that crime resulted from "poverty and privation."[41] As a result, there was an "explosive increase in crime" late in the 1960 and "slower but still troubling increases" during the 1970s. As Murray notes, there were 161 violent crimes per 100,000 people in 1960—but more than three times as many (581) at the peak in 1980. [42]

The increases in crime from the 1960s into the 1980s are clear—as are the correlative liberal criminal justice policies of the same era. They are so clear that they have been recognized across partisan boundaries. Indeed, it is worth quoting at some length the observations of Edward I. Koch while still the Democrat Mayor of New York City:

> The history of crime control policies in this country during the 20-year period prior to 1980 demonstrates that high crime rates are partly caused by policies that do not hold guilty defendants to account and impose upon them an appropriate punishment. . . .
>
> The crime control policies of the city, the state, and the nation in those years contributed to the huge increase of dangerous felons on our streets. In the early 1970s, as crime rates soared, the state was actually closing down prisons. . . . [A] policy of ever greater numbers of felons

being placed on probation, and no significant new prison construction took place. . . .

The federal government, through the Justice Department and its Law Enforcement Assistance Administration, committed during those years almost $7 billion to the major cities of America to, in large measure, underwrite diversion programs, unconventional theorizing, and non-institutional mechanisms for dealing with arrested criminals.[43]

And what were the results? Serious criminals spent less time in prison. In Koch's view:

By 1981, the grim consequences were all too clear. A New York police analysis of 235 career robbery specialists who had been operating over the previous decade, disclosed an average of 12 previous arrests, seven of them for felonies, with an average prior conviction rate of significantly less than one felony and four misdemeanors. The aggregate amount of time served for the 12 previous arrests was less than three months.[44]

In summary,[45] during the 1960s and early 1970s, imprisonment rates as a percentage of crime declined. And crime rates rose. As one member of the President's Commission on Organized Crime has observed, total prison population itself actually fell during the 1960s.[46] From a 1961 peak of 219,000, total prison population declined by 11 percent to 195,000 in 1968 and reached the 1961 level again only in 1972. During the decade of the 1960s, crime increased by some 135 percent.

The 1970s and 1980s

Dramatic changes began to occur in the 1970s—and escalated during the 1980s. Imprisonment rates themselves, and as a percentage of crime, rose—particularly during the 1980s. And crime rates fell during the 1980s.[47] In fact, prison population increased by more than 130 percent during the 1980s.[48]

As then U.S. Attorney General Thornburgh summarized things in 1991, imprisonment rates grew by almost 40 percent during the 1970s—and violent crime increased at about one-half its previous rate. According to national victimization surveys, violent crime grew by only six percent. During the 1980s, the imprisonment rate doubled. The official violent crime rate rose by only 11 percent during that period—and victimization surveys showed an actual decrease of 13 percent in violent crime.[49]

In fact, the number of inmates in state and federal prisons increased from 329,821 at the end of 1980 to 804,524 on June 30, 1991—an increase of nearly 144 percent in the last ten and one-half years.[50] And the rate of incarceration (inmates per 100,000 people) rose from 139 to 303—a 120 percent increase.

Did the increased incarceration rates of the 1980s cause a decrease in crime? No wholly conclusive answer exists. Differences between victimization surveys and uniform crime reports demonstrate the difficulty of knowing whether crime has increased or decreased. Nevertheless, the evidence is suggestive.

Besides the data above, consider the recent detailed analysis by U.S. Department of Justice statistician Patrick A. Langan in the magazine *Science*.[51] Langan analyzed the tripling of prison population in this country between 1973 and 1989. He determined that a relatively small amount of that growth in prison populations was caused by any of the following: the war on drugs, the baby boom, the increased use of mandatory sentencing laws, any increase in sentences received or served. Most of the increase was caused by an increase in the likelihood of someone receiving a state prison sentence once they were arrested. Langan also discovered that neither average prison sentences nor time served increased. Although Langan correctly concludes that it cannot be said "with certainty" that the increased incarceration rates of the period 1973 to 1989 reduced crime, "[t]hat possibility must be seriously weighed."[52] That is especially logical since, as Langan suggests, increased incarceration of criminals incapacitates repeat offenders from committing crime while in prisons. And the increasing likelihood of being sentenced after arrest, demonstrated by Langan's analysis, could have deterred more would-be offenders.

That an increased incarceration rate in the past two decades has decreased either the rate or amount of crime in America is supported by other evidence as well. Particularly intriguing is an analysis of "Imprisonment-to-Offense Ratios" done in 1988 by a group of U.S. Department of Justice statisticians.[53] The ratio of imprisonment rate per crime "represents the average effective burden (in days confined) placed by the justice system on each offense." In other words, it produces a measure of "punitivity" or "expected days of punishment," to use the words of Logan and DiIulio,[54] determined by multiplying the average sentence served by the probability of punishment. This measure fell from a high of just over 93 days of expected punishment in 1959 to a low of about 14.5 days in 1975. By 1986, it had risen to about 19.5 days—a nearly 35 percent increase.

Similarly, as also noted by Logan and DiIulio,[55] a Department of Justice analysis of the rate at which criminals are sent to prison compared to the amount of serious crime over three decades supports the same conclusion. In 1960, for every 1,000 serious crimes, 62 persons were actually sent to prison. By 1970, only 23 criminals were. The number remained in the mid-20s through 1980. In 1981 it reached 29 and continued to climb back to 62 by 1989.[56]

All of these studies show a correlation between rising and falling crime rates and rising and falling measures of imprisonment. A study done for the National Center for Policy Analysis by Professor Morgan Reynolds shows the same relationship.[57] Reynolds compares increases in the amount of serious crime with decreases in the probability of punishment over the period 1950 through 1988. To determine "probable punishment" or "expected days in prison," he multiplied the median prison sentences served for serious crimes by the probabilities of arrest, prosecution, conviction and imprisonment. According to Reynolds, "expected time in prison" for all serious crimes decreased sharply from 24 days in 1954 to 5.5 days in 1974—a 77 percent drop. Then, it began an increase to 8.5 days in 1988—nearly a 55 percent increase during the 1970s and 1980s. Thus, the Reynolds analysis supports the basic relationship and timing described by the Justice Department's earlier analysis of "Imprisonment-to-Offense Ratios."

Last, by looking at states that—like California—dramatically increased prison space during the 1980s, one can see the same pattern. As Attorney General Barr[58] and others[59] have emphasized, California more than quadrupled its inmate population during the 1980s. Prior to Governor Deukmejian's tenure commencing in 1982, California had not opened a new prison in at least 16 years. Deukmejian built eight new prisons and expanded seven others.[60] The murder, rape and burglary rates dropped between 24 and 37 percent from their peaks in 1982.[61]

A similar relationship between declining prison population and rising crime, as well as between an increasing prison population and a declining crime rate, was also observed in Michigan during the 1970s and 1980s.[62] For further comparison purposes, the experience of Texas is discussed at length below.[63]

Why Is Incarceration Important?

As suggested by Patrick Langan, "[t]heoretically, rising incarceration rates reduce crime in two ways. Through their deterrent effect, would-be offenders are deterred from committing crimes by the growing threat of a prison sentence. Through their incapacitative effect, increasing numbers of offenders are physically prevented from committing new crimes because they are behind bars."[64] Elaborating upon the argument for incapacitation, James Q. Wilson writes that incapacitation works if three conditions exist: "some offenders must be repeaters, offenders taken off the streets must not immediately and completely be replaced by new recruits, and prison must not increase the post-release criminal activity of those who have been incarcerated sufficiently to offset the crime prevented by their stay in prison."[65] As to point two, Wilson notes that for predatory street crime "there are no barriers to entry and no scarcity of criminal opportunities." As to point three—the often-repeated prison-as-a-school-for-crime thesis—"there is no evidence that the prison experience makes offenders as a whole more criminal." What of point one—are many offenders repeaters, recidivists? Surely, but how many? In fact, what are the characteristics of the prisoners in our state and federal prisons today? Are many petty offenders? Do we incarcerate—not too few—but too many?

As Logan and DiIulio note, "Comprehensive national data from the Bureau of Justice Statistics show that U.S. prison populations consist overwhelmingly of violent or repeat offenders, with little change in demographic or offense characteristics from 1979 to 1986."[66] Over 95 percent are violent offenders, repeat offenders (with two or more felony convictions), or violent repeat offenders.[67] Some 60 percent of those in state and federal prisons have been imprisoned two or more times; 45 percent, three or more times; and 20 percent, six or more times.[68] Two-thirds of state prisoners have previously received probation or some other alternative to prison for prior convictions, and over 80 percent have previously been incarcerated or given probation.[69] Although the number of prisoners committed for drug offenses has grown considerably in recent years, two-thirds of those offenders were convicted of trafficking or manufacturing illegal drugs.[70] Can anyone really believe that many of these offenders should not be imprisoned?

Although the rate of incarceration has risen significantly in recent years, that does not mean there are too many petty offenders in prison. Three-quarters of the convicted criminals who have actually been sentenced to some form of correctional supervision are on the streets, "many without supervision, most without meaningful supervision."[71] Alternatives to incarceration have grown even more swiftly than incarceration has. The rate of incarceration may have doubled during the 1980s, but the rate of community-based supervision tripled.[72] As noted above, two-thirds of current state prisoners have themselves previously received an alternative to prison for prior convictions. Two-thirds of convicted felons are not incarcerated—and three-fourths receive at least some time on probation or parole.[73]

In spite of these facts, an organization calling itself The Sentencing Project recently reported that America imprisons more people per capita than any other country—still, less than one-half of one percent of the population.[74] As Professors DiIulio and Logan show in the preceding chapter, that argument is fatally flawed: "you have to divide, not by the population size, but by the number of crimes." On that basis, the U.S. "lagged well behind" both England and Canada, for example, in imprisoning robbers.[75] In addition, Langan's "punitivity" measure clearly shows, "that our punishment level is not rocketing to a new high but recovering from a plunge."[76]

In fact, far from imprisoning too many criminals, America still imprisons too few. We must incapacitate violent and repeat criminals for longer periods because the same criminals commit so many serious crimes. As former U.S. Attorney General Edwin Meese III has suggested, parolees and probationers who "violate the terms of their suspended sentence by committing new crimes . . . should not only receive the penalty for the new offense but should be required to serve the sentence that had been conditionally withheld for the previous crime."[77]

Early release—and alternative sentencing—have become the norm in America. For every criminal in an American prison, there are five convicted criminals free on parole or probation.[78] Although the median time actually served by prisoners did not drop significantly between 1926 and 1983, the increased "hardening" of prisoners throughout America (including a 65 percent increase between 1933 and 1982 in the proportion of violent criminals in our prisons) suggests that inmates were serving much less time for more serious offenses.[79] Although the rate of incarceration has increased during the 1980s especially, it has not reached anywhere near its previous high levels.[80] If the increased rates of incarceration in the 1980s have helped—as I and many others believe— to reduce either the rate of crime or the rate of increase in crime, then we must incarcerate still more of the most dangerous criminals to have a greater impact on crime in the years ahead.

The figures on early release and alternative sentencing are cause for concern. A tremendous number of those who receive these dispensations go on to commit further crimes during the very time they would have been in prison for the earlier offense. An important study by the U.S. Department of Justice has found that 60 percent of prisoners released early are rearrested within just 3 years—and actually charged on the average with five new crimes each.[81] Rearrested prisoners were charged with having committed an average of about five new offenses within those three years. According to another Justice Department study, nearly one quarter of the new crimes for which persons were sent to state prison during 1979 could have been averted merely by not releasing those prisoners early.[82] In 1974, 16 percent of state prisoners were on parole or probation when last arrested; by 1986, however, 42 percent were.[83]

Nearly half of the felons who receive probation instead of a prison sentence either abscond or are imprisoned again within just three years.[84] And nearly one in five felony defendants released before trial was rearrested for another felony—and two-thirds of those rearrested on an additional felony were released yet again.[85]

Clearly, the American criminal justice system goes to great lengths to put dangerous repeat offenders back on the streets as quickly and as frequently as possible.

Studies clearly demonstrate that age is the key factor in predicting whether the serious criminals of today will repeat their offenses.[86] The younger a criminal when first arrested, the higher the rate of repeat offending. The older a prisoner when released, the lower the rate of repeat offending. Serious offenders who serve shorter sentences are released at an earlier age or, in the case of repeaters, more times at an early age. That guarantees more crimes will be committed.

Imprisoning the kinds of serious criminals being released early today throughout America would cost far less than releasing them. A 1987 study by the National Institute of Justice concluded that offenders on the loose cost society just over 17 times as much as it would cost to keep them behind bars.[87] Although the amount of savings continues to be debated, subsequent studies have confirmed the basic premise.[88] It costs less to keep today's serious criminals behind bars than it does to release them.

Imprisonment—and the need for new space in prisons—must remain the highest priority for state government in the immediate future. There are new studies that give some hope that rehabilitation may work for some low-level, less serious offenders.[89] Such efforts—like further research into drug and alcohol treatment as well as selective incapacitation[90]—should be supported. As Professor DiIulio has concluded, however, after a thorough review of the new literature of rehabilitation:

> There is little in the latest studies to give one hope that violent, repeat (two or more felony convictions), or repeat violent offenders can be rehabilitated. And . . . there is virtually nothing in these studies to enhance one's confidence in the rehabilitative efficacy of most prison- or jail-based programs.[91]

The security of all Americans depends upon government incarcerating more of the serious criminals now being returned into our communities after serving shorter and shorter sentences. Those that are released after serving longer sentences must receive greater supervision than they do at present.[92] Failing to do both will be felt most by those most in need of assistance: by minority citizens in the inner city and by other poor and working class citizens who live near those areas.[93] As Professor DiIulio has himself noted, "in 1980, 43 percent of New Jersey's prisoners came from ghetto areas in and around Newark. When released back to their communities, many of these deviant persons returned to prey on their disadvantaged neighbors."[94]

The Federal Courts and Our Prison Crisis

History

Early release has dramatically decreased the ability of our criminal justice system both to incapacitate and to deter. Why then has early release become so common throughout America? It has resulted in large part from the failure of many government leaders to build the prison space needed to incapacitate the growing number of dangerous and repeat criminals. It has also resulted from a misconceived effort by the federal courts to ensure revolutionary change in the conditions in state prisons and local jails. Even as liberals of the 1960s believed rehabilitation could be made to work, prisoners, their lawyers and organized liberal groups like the ACLU convinced federal judges to order states to make the environment in prisons more conducive to rehabilitation. Inevitably, the public proved unwilling to pay continually higher taxes to make prisoners more "comfortable"—whatever the rehabilitative purpose—especially at the direction of federal judges—placing ever greater pressure on state budgets generally and criminal justice budgets in particular.

All of the muscle being exerted by the federal courts to transform prisons is a quite recent phenomenon. Prior to the Warren Court activism of the 1960s, the federal courts had throughout our history maintained a hands off approach toward prisoners' attempts to challenge conditions in state prisons. In the early 1960s, the Warren Court opened the floodgates (*Cooper v. Pate*[95]) by allowing inmates to bring legal actions under section 1983 (of the Civil Rights Act of 1871) claiming that state officials had deprived them of their rights under the Constitution. Previously, courts had rejected prisoners' claims that their conditions of confinement amounted to cruel and unusual punishment forbidden by the eighth amendment to the U.S. Constitution. In rejecting those arguments prior to the 1960s, courts typically held that inmates had forfeited many of their rights by committing crimes and had become in effect "slaves of the state."[96] The latter language—"slaves of the state"—is not so surprising since the thirteenth amendment—which banned slavery—explicitly exempted incarcerated convicts from its ban on involuntary servitude and slavery.

What fueled overcrowding cases besides the desire of prisoners for easier conditions of imprisonment? "As late as 1970, not a single prison or jail system was operating under judicial orders to change and improve."[97] In 1972, the ACLU formed its National Prison Project to lead the fight against overcrowding nationwide—and through overcrowding suits to attack the premises of incarceration itself.[98] As one former head of that ACLU Project said:

> [The criminal justice system] must deemphasize its concern with
> traditional crime because the emphasis is misplaced. . . . The companies
> which knowingly manufacture unsafe products; the corporate executives
> who steal millions from the public by price-rigging and over-charging;
> the public officials who use their positions for personal gain; the
> industries that pollute our environment and the officials responsible for
> My Lais and Cambodias are the criminals we need to be concerned
> about.[99]

The ACLU launched its assault upon alleged overcrowding in our prisons
primarily as an attack upon the very concept of crime itself. And
Congress helped to fuel the attack in 1975 by explicitly authorizing the
payment of attorneys' fees and costs to the ACLU and other plaintiffs'
lawyers when they prevailed in court.[100]

The arbitrariness and subjectivity behind the overcrowding decisions
by the federal courts are as demonstrable as the increased crime they have
caused through the early release of repeat offenders. There are no clear
standards by which courts have been able to judge the constitutional
significance of alleged overcrowding.[101] As the result of the litigation
before Judge William Wayne Justice, for example, Texas' prison
population is capped at 95 percent of capacity.[102] The federal prison
system itself, however—long considered "one of the world's finest prison
systems"[103]—operates quite constitutionally at 165 percent of capacity.[104] Overall, state prisons were operating at an average of 115 percent
of capacity at the end of 1990.[105] Eighteen states were operating above
that average.[106] In addition to the federal prison system, the six states
of Massachusetts, Pennsylvania, Vermont, Ohio, Oklahoma and California
were all operating at 150 percent or more of capacity.[107] Overcrowding
has become a tool to attack the notion of incarceration itself—a device
to cause the release of large numbers of criminals from prisons.[108] And
sympathetic federal judges have too frequently succumbed to the growing
attacks.

Misinterpretations of the Constitution fueled by opponents of incarceration—like the ACLU—and adopted by the lower federal courts have
thrown open the prison doors. Judges have ordered some 40 states—like
Texas—to end overcrowding in their prisons.[109] All too frequently the
result has been the early release of dangerous criminals. In 1983 alone,
15 states ordered the early release of more than 21,000 inmates to ease
alleged crowding.[110]

Judicial intervention—although often justified on the basis of allegedly
unconstitutional overcrowding—has taken many forms. In the preceding
article, Professors Logan and DiIulio summarized the remarkable breadth
of judicial control:

> [A]ctivist federal judges continue to be the sovereigns of the nation's cellblocks, issuing directives on a wide range of issues, including health care services, staff training procedures, sanitation standards, food services, and the constitutionality of conditions "in their totality." Indeed, in some prison systems, the texts of court orders and consent decrees are now used as staff training manuals and inmate rulebooks, and everything from inmate disciplinary hearings to the exact temperature of the meat served to prisoners at supper is governed by judicial fiat.[111]

And, as Logan and DiIulio also emphasize, the excuse for intervention—allegedly "cruel and unusual" prison conditions—is not necessarily a sufficient excuse to justify sweeping judicial intervention. It is far from certain that so-called "overcrowding" in prisons has all the negative effects claimed by so many reformers and prisoners. Prisoners are even doing better physically than their peers at large.[112]

New Judges and New Law

During 1981, President Reagan's first Attorney General—William French Smith—reminded the Federal Legal Council:

> [B]asic changes in public sentiment can still portend changing judicial philosophy. Various doubts about past conclusions have already been expressed in Supreme Court opinions, concurrences, and dissents—which makes the next few years inviting ones to urge modifications upon that Court and other federal courts.[113]

Attorney General Smith had criminal justice issues very much in mind when he spoke those words—and his words were prophetic. It has, however, taken years—and the appointment of a majority of the U.S. Supreme Court and the federal bench by Presidents Reagan and Bush—for the federal courts to change direction.

Now, after two decades of increased crime fueled by early release, the U.S. Supreme Court has had enough. In a 5-4 vote, the Chief Justice and Justices appointed by Presidents Reagan and Bush have reinterpreted past precedent and erected a formidable obstacle to attacks on the conditions of incarceration.

In that case, *Wilson v. Seiter*[114], the Court held that the most difficult of prison conditions cannot be considered unconstitutionally cruel and unusual punishment unless they are the result of "intent" on the part of the state. Even assuming the prison conditions being challenged are sufficiently serious, they are unconstitutional only if they are the result of "deliberate indifference" on the part of state officials.

The broad scope of the Supreme Court's decision can be seen in the reaction of the four Justices who concurred only in the judgment. Writing for them,[115] Justice White warned that a challenge of "inhumane prison conditions" may henceforth be defeated "simply by showing that the conditions are caused by insufficient funding from the state legislature rather than by deliberate indifference on the part of the prison officials." Writing for the majority, Justice Scalia responded to that argument (interestingly, also made by the Justice Department): "Even if that were so, it is hard to understand how it could control" on the constitutional issue.[116]

On January 14 of this year, President Bush's new Attorney General— William Barr—moved quickly to take advantage of this change in approach by the high Court. General Barr announced a major new effort to restore reason to the states' criminal justice systems.[117] The U.S. Department of Justice would begin to help states to remove court-imposed caps on prison population. The new strategy reversed a decades-old federal policy that favored the comfort of convicted criminals over the safety of law-abiding citizens. The U.S. government planned henceforth to throw its weight in court behind localities that want to end early release and keep criminals behind bars.

For two decades our federal government—often acting through the Civil Rights Division of the Justice Department[118]—has sided in court with the ACLU and prisoners' rights attorneys. Liberal federal judges—like William Wayne Justice in Texas—were only too willing to order dramatic changes in prison conditions. Unable to ease overcrowding quickly enough, localities endured the early release of perhaps hundreds of thousands of dangerous criminals.

Can the Justice Department help convince the courts to allow Texas and other states to decrease early releases? Can it overcome consent decrees that federal judges often allowed prisoners' rights attorneys to coerce states and localities into signing?[119] Some quickly suggested that Supreme Court precedent might immunize such consent decrees from being modified even when their terms are not mandated by the U.S. Constitution.[120]

The day after Attorney General Barr announced the new Bush Administration policy, the U.S. Supreme Court decided that very issue in *Rufo v. Inmates of Suffolk County Jail*.[121] There, the high Court altered its own 60-year-old rule and made it easier to seek changes in existing judicial orders. Judges must be "flexible" and modify orders when there have been "significant changes in facts or law." The Supreme Court recognized that states may choose to settle lawsuits by accepting greater restrictions than the Constitution requires. That does not, however, mean that states cannot modify settlements they were bludgeoned into accepting by federal judges. In fact, the Supreme Court specifically recognized the propriety of a change when a party believed the Constitution required something it does not require. When facts and law change significantly or are different than the state believed—or when required by the public interest—a change is clearly proper.[122]

Texas—As A Case Study

Crime in Texas

Prior to the early 1980s, Texas had a deserved reputation for being tough on crime. During the 1970s, Texas imprisoned so many more of its robbers and burglars that a RAND corporation study found a much higher proportion of lower-level offenders in Texas prisons. In other words, burglars imprisoned in California admitted committing nearly four times as many burglaries as Texas's—and the ratio in Michigan was more than three times Texas's. For robbers, California inmates outdid Texas robbers by ten to one—and Michigan robbers admitted to six times as many robberies as Texans.[123]

The Texas prison system "had been hailed as one of the nation's best" from the 1960s into the 1980s.[124] In the seven years preceding 1980, fewer than 20 homicides occurred in Texas prisons—compared to seven times that number in California. Assaults within the Texas prison system were "well below the national average." Nevertheless, "costs per inmate were the lowest in the country" and Texas had the " only fully accredited prison educational system in the nation."[125]

By the 1980s, things had changed dramatically. Crime escalated wildly—and the prisons became an inadequate mess.

Texas began to pursue a policy of releasing dangerous criminals earlier and earlier. More convicted criminals are released early on parole in Texas than in *any* other state—including almost double the number in California and triple the number in New York.[126] One out of every five prisoners released on parole in the entire United States during 1989 was released from a Texas prison.[127] And every day Texas releases 150 more criminals early—including murderers, rapists, child molesters, and armed robbers.[128] One in every three of the prisoners Texas releases early is sent back to our own prisons within just two years.[129] The average time served by a Texas prisoner has declined from over one-half to less than one-twelfth.[130]

Although "expected punishment" for a serious crime rose in the nation as a whole, it dropped by 43 percent in Texas during the 1980s.[131] Since 1960, expected punishment for all serious crimes in Texas dropped by two-thirds—and the crime rate increased some 600 percent.[132] As Professor Morgan Reynolds determined:

> In 1980, when California had 24,569 state prisoners and Texas had 29,892, the Texas crime rate was 21.6 percent below California's. By 1989, California had more than twice as many state prisoners, its crime rate had dropped by almost 14 percent and the Texas crime rate was 17.2 percent higher than California's.[133]

Not only has crime spiraled out of control, but also the Texas prison system has. By 1984, the Texas prison system had also deteriorated badly. In 1984 and 1985, 52 prisoners were murdered—and 700 were stabbed.[134] In the words of Professor DiIulio: "More serious violence occurred during those two years than had occurred in the previous decade. As the disorder mounted, inmate participation in treatment and educational programs became erratic, the once immaculate inmate living quarters ceased to sparkle, and recreational privileges were curtailed."[135]

Besides management problems and the building-tender system "run amok," what other factor was at work according to DiIulio? Federal Judge William Wayne Justice, who has controlled the Texas prison system for two decades through the litigation surrounding *Ruiz v. Estelle*.[136]

As an expert on correctional institutions, Professor DiIulio's assessment of Judge Justice is well worth quoting at length. As conditions deteriorated in 1984:

> Judge Justice, who had not once set foot inside a TDC prison since the *Ruiz* case began, continued to pressure the agency. The court's actions came as repeated stabs against the officers' sense of mission and encouraged TDC workers at all levels to abdicate responsibility for the inmates, enervating any desire they might have had to go above and beyond the call of duty at a time when enormous demands were being made on them. Judge Justice and his staff made it clear they were out to revolutionize TDC, not to reform it, acting, as one of the court's aides later confided, on the assumption that TDC was "rotten from top to bottom, that everything had to change."[137]

What was the Judge's biggest error?

> Judge Justice's mistake in Texas was in attempting to punish corrections officials for their real or perceived slights against his authority. . . . [Of the federal judges who intervened into prisons and jails from 1970 to 1989] only Judge Justice reacted to the opposition in a way that even his most inveterate academic apologists admit created

an atmosphere of distrust, in addition to deepening efforts to resist court-approved reforms.[138]

In Texas, we have "revolving-door" prisons because of the decisions of Federal Judge William Wayne Justice—and the 95 percent cap on prison population enacted by the Texas Legislature to satisfy the Judge. As a result, in 1983 alone, Texas released over 7,000 inmates early—one-third of all the early releases in the nation.[139] And we have spent incredible amounts in an effort to meet the Judge's requirements.[140]

Texas did begin a substantial prison building program in the 1980s. By the mid-1990s, there were to be some 67,800 maximum-security beds. In November 1991, the voters approved a major bond program to add another 6,750 maximum-security beds, six 1,000-bed regional centers, one 500-bed psychiatric center, and 12,000 drug-treatment beds.[141] Unfortunately, having gotten behind the curve on increasing crime, that will not be enough to meet the state's needs. There are still at least another 10,000 state prison inmates in county jails—creating massive overcrowding in the jails.[142]

Between 1980 and 1991, Texas prisons expanded by some 77 percent.[143] For comparison purposes, during the same period, state prisons throughout the country expanded their populations by some 149 percent. That's why Texas does not have even one of the ten highest incarceration rates today—and, in fact, ranks 12th of 17 Southern states. In the first six months of 1991, for example, Texas prisons expanded by 1.1 percent—while other states expanded by four percent.[144] Indeed, in 1989 Texas ranked 39th in the country in admissions to prison per 1,000 serious crimes (with a rate more than 20 percent below the average for all states); in 1980, Texas had ranked 12th (with a rate more than 30 percent above the national average).[145]

Additional perspective on Texas's prison capacity and crime problem can be gleaned from its extensive use of alternative sentencing. As previously noted, Texas leads the nation in parolees and probationers. So extensive has the state's use of parole and probation been that in 1988, for example, only nine percent of Texas's convicted criminals under some form of correctional supervision were in prison. Although the country as a whole makes too great a use of parole and probation—especially in light of the inadequate resources provided in those areas—Texas uses them nearly twice as frequently.[146]

Not only has Texas not built enough prisons, the state's political leadership has not yet freed the prison system from Judge Justice's grip. Although the Legislature changed the law in June 1991 to make a 95 percent cap on prison population in Texas prisons unnecessary, the Attorney General of the state has yet to have a hearing before Judge Justice on the issue.[147] Instead, negotiations continue with prisoners' attorneys—and a hearing before Judge Justice is not even set before July 1992.[148]

Circumstances have changed since Judge William Wayne Justice forced the prison doors open. Innocent victims have paid for the Judge's constitutional conscience. The cap on prison population, which has caused so much harm to Texas, should be completely removed—and it can legally be removed. Still, the state seems to be dragging its feet. It is easy to believe that the old liberal mindset still grips some leaders. After all, it was only two years ago, that then-Treasurer and now-Governor Ann Richards told a Texas House subcommittee: "I can't look the taxpayers of Texas straight in the eye and tell them that building more prisons is a cost-effective corrections strategy."[149] In Texas—and throughout America—keeping more dangerous criminals behind bars through prison construction as well as better and more efficient prison management may be the only way to make our communities safe once again.

Conclusion

A decade ago, James Q. Wilson and George Kelling wrote their highly influential *Atlantic Monthly* article "Broken Windows."[150] They argued that violent crime arises from the breakdown of public order. A broken window—when left unfixed—shows that no one cares about the building. Inevitably, then, the other windows are broken as well. In a similar way, the spread of drunks, panhandlers, and prostitutes on the streets signals all criminals that no one cares. Unimpeded, the petty annoyance of today becomes the mugging or other violent crime of tomorrow. How much more true is that of a state or a nation? Faced with continued violence at an unbelievably threatening level, what signal is sent by the failure to imprison repeat and violent criminals for the time they once spent in prison in the not too distant past? Doesn't it say that we don't care enough? And doesn't the failure to take back our streets and communities indicate an unwillingness to do so? The single most important initiative for state governments is to build sufficient prison capacity to keep dangerous repeat criminals off our streets.

Endnotes

1. U.S. Department of Commerce, Bureau of the Census, *Statistical Abstract of the United States, 1991* (Washington, D.C.: GPO, 1991), 187.

2. *Ibid.*, 279.

3. For example, between 1984 and 1989, violent crime rose by 23 percent according to the FBI's Uniform Crime Reports. But the Bureau of Justice Statistics shows that victimization fell by about 15 percent from the early to the mid-1980s and then essentially leveled off. Whether these differences are the result of increased reporting to the police or differences between the types of individuals in the different databases remains uncertain. *See, e.g.,* Ben J. Wattenberg, *The First Universal Nation* (New York: The Free Press, 1991), 100-03, 394.

4. *See, e.g.,* "Homicide Records Set in 3 Big Cities," *New York Times*, 3 Jan. 1992, sec. A.

5. John W. Wright, ed., *1992 Universal Almanac* (Kansas City: Andrews and McMeel, 1991), 255.

6. James Patterson and Peter Kim, *The Day America Told the Truth* (New York: Prentice Hall Press, 1991), 173-76.

7. U.S. Attorney General Edwin Meese III, Press Release, U.S. Department of Justice, 9 June 1988, 1 [citing U.S. Department of Justice, Bureau of Justice Statistics, *Report to the Nation on Crime and Justice*, 2d ed. (Washington, D.C.: GPO, 1988)].

8. *The 1992 Information Please Almanac*, 45th ed. (New York: Houghton Mifflin Co., 1992), 824.

9. Edwin Meese III, "Crime and Punishment in Modern America," in Patrick McGuigan and Jon S. Pascale, eds., *Crime and Punishment in Modern America* (Washington, D.C.: Free Congress Research and Education Foundation, 1986), 10.

10. *Wall Street Journal*, 13 Nov. 1962.

11. *See, e.g.,* William French Smith, *Law & Justice in the Reagan Administration* (Stanford: Hoover Institution Press, 1991), 80.

12. Meese, Press Release, 9 June 1988, 3.

13. "Black-on-black crime is at crisis point, experts say," *Dallas Morning News*, 15 July 1990, sec. A.

14. "Dallas murders setting record pace," *Dallas Times Herald*, 14 Nov. 1991, sec. A.

15. James Q. Wilson and Richard J. Hernstein, *Crime & Human Nature* (New York: Simon & Schuster, Inc., 1985), 463.

16. Charles E. Silberman, *Criminal Violence, Criminal Justice* (New York: Vintage Books, 1980), 217.

17. Karl Zinsmeister, "Growing Up Scared," *Atlantic Monthly*, June 1990, 51.

18. *Ibid.*, 50.

19. *See, e.g.,* Charles H. Logan & John J. DiIulio, Jr, "Crime in America: The Facts," *supra* 97-98 and notes 27 and 28.

20. *Ibid.*, 17.

21. U.S. Department of Justice, *National Institute of Justice Reports*, No. 224, June 1991, 5.

22. *See* James K. Stewart, "The Urban Strangler," *Policy Review*, Summer 1986, 6.

23. Robert Rector, Kate Walsh O'Beirne, and Michael McLaughlin, "How 'Poor' Are America's Poor?" Heritage Foundation *Backgrounder* No. 791, 21 Dec. 1990, 9.

24. Stewart, "Urban Strangler," 6.

25. *Ibid.*, 7.

26. Reuben Greenberg, *Let's Take Back Our Streets* (Chicago: Contemporary Books, 1989).

27. Criminal Justice Center, Sam Houston State University, *Crime and Justice in Texas* (Oct. 1988), 7.

28. *1992 Universal Almanac*, 256.

29. "It's a crime," *Dallas Morning News*, 30 July 1991, sec. A, citing *Money*, Aug. 1991.

30. "U.S. killings are setting record pace," *Dallas Times Herald*, 5 Aug. 1991, sec. A.

31. *Ibid. See Crime and Justice in Texas*, 25.

32. "City breaks record for homicides," *Dallas Morning News*, 18 Nov. 1991, sec A.

33. "Dallas Murders setting record pace," *Dallas Times Herald*, 14 Nov. 1991, sec. A.

34. "Slayings increased in most suburbs during '91," *Dallas Morning News*, 6 Jan. 1992, sec. A.

35. *Dallas Morning News*, 16 Sept. 1990, sec. A.

36. *See* "City Breaks Record for Homicides," *Dallas Morning News*, 18 Nov. 1991, sec. A; "Overall Crime Down in '91," *Dallas Morning News*, 10 Jan. 1992, sec. A.

37. "Overall crime in Dallas down But violent offenses rose 7.6% from '90, Rathburn reports," *Dallas Morning News*, 10 Jan. 1992, sec. A.

38. "Homicide records set in 3 big cities," *New York Times*, 3 Jan. 1992.

39. Meese, "Crime and Punishment," 11.

40. U.S. Attorney General Dick Thornburgh, Speech, Bureau of Prisons' Conference on the History of Federal Corrections, Washington D.C., 28 Mar. 1991.

41. Charles Murray, "Crime in America," *National Review*, 10 June 1985, 37.

42. *Ibid.*

43. Edward I. Koch, "The Mugger and His Genes," *Policy Review*, No. 35, Winter 1986, 87-89, reviewing James Q. Wilson and Richard Hernstein, *Crime and Human Nature* (New York: Simon and Schuster, 1986).

44. *Ibid.*

45. *See* Logan and DiIulio *supra* 91-93 and notes accompanying.

46. Eugene H. Methvin, "Let's lock up more criminals—it works," *Houston Chronicle*, 10 Nov. 1991, sec. E.

47. *See* Logan and DiIulio *supra* 93-95 and notes accompanying.

48. *1992 Information Please Almanac*, 824

49. Thornburgh Speech, 28 Mar. 1991.

50. Robyn L. Cohen, *Prisoners in 1990* (U.S. Department of Justice, Bureau of Justice Statistics, May 1991), 1; U.S. Department of Justice, Press Release, "Four Percent More Prisoners in First Half of 1991," 13 Oct. 1991, 1.

51. Patrick A. Langan, "America's Soaring Prison Population," 251 *Science*, 29 Mar. 1991, 1568-73. *See* Logan and DiIulio *supra* 91-92.

52. Langan, "Prison Population," 1573.

53. Mark Kleiman, Kerry D. Smith, Richard A. Rogers and David P. Cavanagh, *Imprisonment-to-Offense Ratios* (U.S. Department of Justice, Bureau of Justice Statistics Discussion Paper, 15 Nov. 1988).

54. Logan and DiIulio *supra* 92.

55. *Ibid.*

56. *See* Cohen, *Prisoners in 1990*, 7.

57. Morgan O. Reynolds, *Crime Pays, So Does Imprisonment* (Dallas: NCPA Policy Report No. 149, Mar. 1990).

58. "Barr pushes for more prisons," *Dallas Morning News*, 12 Feb. 1992, sec. A.

59. *See, e.g.,* Charles R. Helms, Lisette McSoud and Dick Collins, *Crime and Punishment in Texas: A Comprehensive Analysis* (Dallas: ATAC Spring 1989), 26-30; Methvin, "Let's lock up more criminals."

60. "Running Hard, But Losing Ground," *Washington Post National Weekly Edition*, 6-12 May 1991, 31.

61. *See* sources cited *supra* notes 58 and 59.

62. Methvin, "Let's lock up more criminals."

63. *See* 16-20 *infra*.

64. Langan, "Prison Population," 1573.

65. James Q. Wilson, *Thinking About Crime* (New York: Vintage Books, 1985), 146-47.

66. Logan and DiIulio *supra* 94.

67. John J. DiIulio, Jr., *No Escape—The Future of American Corrections* (Basic Books, 1991), 4.

68. *1992 Universal Almanac*, 258.

69. DiIulio and Logan *supra* 104.

70. Cohen, "Prisoners in 1990," 8.

71. DiIulio, *No Escape*, 62.

72. *Ibid.*, 4.

73. Logan and DiIulio *supra* 104.

74. "U.S. leads in rate of incarceration," *Dallas Morning News*, 11 Feb. 1992, sec. A.

75. Logan and DiIulio *supra* 102-103.

76. *Ibid.*, 93.

77. Edwin Meese III, "Criminal Justice: A Public Policy Perspective," *Thinking About America*, eds. Annelise Anderson and Dennis L. Bark (Stanford: Hoover Institution Press, 1988), 435.

78. *Statistical Abstract* 1991, 194.

79. Speech by [Director, U.S. Department of Justice, Bureau of Justice Statistics] Steven R. Schlesinger, during 1987 to Conference of State Legislators.

80. *See* pages 91-93 *supra* and sources cited in accompanying notes 53, 54, and 57.

81. Allen J. Beck, *Recidivism of Prisoners Released in 1983* (Bureau of Justice Statistics Special Report, Apr. 1989), 1.

82. Lawrence A. Greenfeld, *Examining Recidivism* (Bureau of Justice Statistics Special Report, Feb. 1985), 1.

83. Langan, "Prison Population," 1572.

84. Patrick A. Langan and Mark A. Cuniff, *Recidivism of felons on probation, 1986-89* (Bureau of Justice Statistics Special Report, Feb. 1992), 1.

85. "Study says felony suspects often rearrested before trial," *Dallas Morning News*, 11 Feb. 1991.

86. *See, e.g.*, Beck, *Recidivism of Prisoners*, 5, 8, 11-12.

87. Edwin Zedlewski, *Making Confinement Decisions* (Washington, D.C.: National Institute of Justice Research in Brief, 1987).

88. *See* DiIulio and Logan *supra* 98-101 and accompanying notes.

89. *See* DiIulio, *No Escape*, ch. 2.

90. Research on selective incapacitation could prove exceptionally valuable. An overwhelmingly large amount of crime is committed by a remarkably small number of high-level offenders, the truly serious career criminal. If you could identify among those criminals already in prison the high-level recidivists, then you could ensure that they served the longest possible sentences. Similarly, you could release those who are not likely repeaters earlier. A great deal of promising research has already been done in this area. For example, two RAND researchers concluded in the late 1970s that requiring repeat offenders to serve five-year terms would cause an 18 percent decrease in the crime rate while increasing prison populations by some 190 percent. *See, e.g.*, Wilson, *Thinking About Crime*, 151-58.

91. *Ibid.*, 111.

92. In Los Angeles, a probation worker may have a caseload as high as 1,000; in New Jersey, a parole officer may have a caseload as high as 200. *Ibid.*, 63. Similarly, probation officers in New York City and elsewhere likely have several times the manageable caseload. *See* Editorial, *New York Times*, 20 June 1990.

93. *Ibid.*, 66.

94. *Ibid.*

95. 378 U.S. 546 (1964).

96. The language "slaves of the state" was perhaps first used in the subsequently often cited decision of the Virginia Court of Appeals in *Ruffin v. Commonwealth*, 62 Va. 790 (1871).

97. DiIulio, *No Escape*, 148.

98. *See, e.g.*, Daniel J. Popeo and George C. Smith, "Prisons, Priorities, and Judicial Fiat: The Need for Constitutional Perspective," in *Crime and Punishment*, eds. McGuigan and Pascale, 349-64.

99. *Ibid.*, 349.

100. *Ibid.*, 362.

101. *See, e.g.*, Jeff Bleich, "The Politics of Prison Crowding," 77 *California Law Review* 1125-80 (1989).

102. *See, e.g.*, *Crime and Justice in Texas*, 103.

103. DiIulio, *No Escape*, 54.

104. Remarks of U.S. Attorney General William Barr, *Dallas Morning News*, 15 Jan. 1992, sec. A.

105. Cohen, *Prisoners in 1990*, 6.

106. *Ibid.*

107. *Ibid.*

108. *See* Bleich, "Politics of Crowding."

109. *See* "Population of prisons," *Dallas Morning News*, 15 Jan. 1992.

110. *See* Bleich, "Politics of Crowding," 1173.

111. Logan and DiIulio *supra* 101.

112. *Ibid.*, 94-96.

113. Remarks by U.S. Attorney General William French Smith to the Federal Legal Council, in Reston, Virginia, Oct. 29, 1981.

114. 111 S.Ct. 2321 (1991).

115. *Ibid.*, 2330-31.

116. *Ibid.*, 2326.

117. *See, e.g.*, "Population of prisons may rise," *Dallas Morning News*, 15 Jan. 1992, sec. A; "U.S. Bid to lift prison sanctions praised in Texas," *Dallas Morning News*, 16 Jan. 1992; "Barr pans Texas prison ruling," *Dallas Morning News*, 5 Jan. 1992, sec. A.

118. *See, e.g.*, "Populations of Prison May Rise."

119. *Ibid.*

120. The argument concerns whether in consent decrees in prison-conditions cases can be modified only upon the "clear showing of grievous wrong," a standard which was set forth 60 years ago by the U.S. Supreme Court in *United States v. Swift & Co.*, 286 U.S. 106 (1932).

121. 112 S.Ct. 748 (1992).

122. *Ibid.*, 760-63.

123. James Q. Wilson, *Thinking About Crime* (Vintage: New York, 1985), 146.

124. *See, e.g.*, DiIulio, *No Escape*, 157; Ben M. Crouch and James W. Marquart, *An Appeal to Justice* (Austin: University of Texas Press, 1989), 46; Steve J. Martin and Sheldon Ekland-Olson, *Texas Prisons* (Austin: Texas Monthly Press, 1987), 24-25.

125. DiIulio, *No Escape*, 164.

126. *See, e.g.*, "In Texas, early release of convicts on the rise," *Austin American Statesman*, 9 Feb. 1991, sec. A.

127. *Ibid.*

128. *See, e.g., ibid.*; Peter Michel, "Proposition can shut revolving door," *Dallas Morning News*, 20 Oct. 1991, sec. A.

129. *See, e.g.*, Rider Scott (then general counsel to the Governor of Texas), "Tackling Crime," *Dallas Morning News*, 27 Mar. 1988, sec. A.

130. *See, e.g.*, Scott, "Tackling Crime"; Remarks of U.S. Attorney General Barr, "Barr pans Texas prison ruling"; Gregory Curtis, "Free to Kill," *Texas Monthly*, Sept. 1991, 5; "House panel OKs bill to boost prison capacity," *Dallas Morning News*, 2 May 1991, sec. A.

131. *See* NCPA, *Southwest Newswire*, March 5, 1991, 2; Editorial, *Dallas Morning News*, 19 May 1991, sec. A.

132. NCPA, *Southwest Newswire*, 3.

133. *Ibid.*

134. DiIulio, *No Escape*, 157.

135. *Ibid.*

136. *Ibid.*, 156-67.

137. *Ibid.*, 166-67.

138. *Ibid.*, 176.

139. *See, e.g.*, Anthony Champagne and Edward J. Harpham, eds., *Texas at the Crossroads—People, Politics, and Policy* (College Station: Texas A & M University Press, 1987), 249.

140. *See* Kenneth R. Mladenka and Kim Quaile Hill, *Texas Government—Politics and Economics* (Pacific Grove: Brooks/Cole Publishing Co., 1989), 312; Champagne and Harpham, eds., *Texas at the Crossroads*, 253.

141. *See, e.g.*, Editorial, *Dallas Morning News*, 3 Nov. 1991, sec. A.

142. *See, e.g.,* Editorial, *Houston Post,* 20 Jan. 1992.

143. *See 1991 Statistical Abstract,* 193; U.S. Department of Justice Press Release, 13 Oct. 1991; Cohen, *Prisoners in 1990; Crime and Justice in Texas,* 90.

144. U.S. Department of Justice Press Release, 13 Oct. 1991.

145. Cohen, *Prisoners in 1990,* 8.

146. *See 1991 Statistical Abstract,* 194.

147. *See* Rep. John Culberson, "Solution to prison problem waiting in the wings," *Austin American Statesman,* 5 Feb. 1992.

148. *See* "Prison negotiations result in an impasse," *Houston Chronicle,* 7 Feb. 1992; "Texas gets boost in effort to lift prison cap," *Houston Post,* 16 Jan. 1992.

149. Statement by then-Treasurer Ann Richards to Texas House Appropriations Subcommittee on Prison Alternatives, 25 Jan. 1989.

150. James Q. Wilson & George L. Kelling, Jr., "Broken Windows: The Police and Neighborhood Safety," *Atlantic Monthly* (Mar. 1982), 29-38.

A CONSERVATIVE'S GUIDE TO STATE-LEVEL WELFARE REFORM

Robert Rector
Policy Analyst, The Heritage Foundation

and

Michael McLaughlin
Staff Member, U.S. Congress

Introduction

Nearly three decades have passed since President Lyndon B. Johnson launched his "unconditional war on poverty in America." Despite the enormous financial and political resources which have been committed, Americans of nearly every ideological persuasion agree that the war was lost. A growing number of liberals and conservatives, in fact, agree that not only was the war lost, but in many important respects the condition of the poor today is worse than it was before the war began. When a majority of today's welfare programs were created, the problems facing the poor allegedly were lack of money and lack of opportunity. Given opportunity and enough resources, it was believed, a majority of the poor would move out of poverty and into self-sufficiency.

The problems facing the poor today, however, have less to do with low material living standards and more to do with the collapse of social norms and ethics which form the foundation of civilized life. Government programs have had no success in addressing problems like soaring illegitimate birth rates, inter-generational welfare dependency and reduced work effort. Growing evidence shows that most government welfare programs designed to alleviate material poverty have created a culture of self-destructive behavior among the poor. The problem today is not a lack of government spending on welfare programs; welfare spending is currently at an all-time high. The problem is that most, if not all, welfare programs contribute to a tangled social pathology of out-of-wedlock births, family disintegration, lack of work ethic, and long-term government dependence. Welfare has eroded the essential moral fabric within a large segment of U.S. society.

Washington's inability to enact meaningful welfare reform in the late 1980s has increased pressure on state lawmakers to handle the problem. Among middle and lower-middle income Americans there is a growing perception that a vast majority of the poor are not "pulling their own weight." Over 90 percent of the American people believe that able-bodied welfare recipients should be required to perform some work in exchange for assistance.[1] Moreover, as Uncle Sam's welfare state has stepped in as a surrogate father and breadwinner for millions of children, the traditional family has all but disappeared from some communities. In the eyes of the middle class, welfare has become a one-way handout, which harms rather than helps many of the poor. The combined effect of escalating state budgetary problems and a growing realization that government programs have created more problems than they have solved have improved the prospects for state-level welfare reform.

The Growing Welfare State

Throughout the 1980s, state lawmakers and the American public in general were inundated with media reports of draconian cuts in welfare spending. According to conventional wisdom, tax cuts for the "rich" and the Reagan Administration's defense buildup were being paid for, in part, by cutting spending for the poor.

Contrary to popular belief, however, welfare spending has risen steadily over the past decade and today is at an all-time high. The most comprehensive survey of welfare spending available is conducted by the Library of Congress' non-partisan Congressional Research Service (CRS). The CRS tracks federal, state and local spending on 75 "means-tested" programs, which are programs with benefits limited to persons with low or limited income. The CRS figures include programs targeted to low income persons such as Aid to Families with Dependent Children (AFDC), food stamps, and public housing. By contrast, the CRS does not include transfer programs available to the general population, such as Social Security. The 75 major means-tested welfare programs are listed in Appendix Table A.

According to Congressional Research Service figures, federal means-tested spending in constant, or inflation-adjusted, dollars rose from $114 billion in 1981 to $125.5 billion in 1988. State and local welfare spending also rose from $39 billion in 1981 to $48 billion in 1988. Total spending rose in constant dollars from $154 billion to $173 billion.[2] An additional $11.2 billion in Medicare spending on poor persons in 1988 was not included in the CRS total.[3] Thus in that year total welfare spending, including the CRS means-tested figures plus Medicare benefits for poor persons, was $184.2 billion. This is $5,531 for each poor person in the

U.S. Chart 1 shows the growth of welfare in constant dollars from 1975 to 1988.[4]

Chart 1
Expenditures on Major Welfare Programs

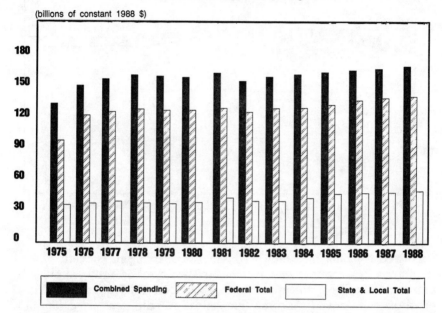

Sources: Vee Burke, *Cash and Non-Cash Benefits for Persons with Limited Income: Eligibility Rules, Recipient and Expenditures Data FY 86-88, p6; op. cit.,* U.S. House of Representatives, Committee on Ways and Means, *Background Material and Data on Programs Within the Jurisdiction of the Committee on Ways and Means: 1989 Edition* (Washington, D.C.: U.S. Government Printing Office, 1989). p. 152. Unpublished Congressional Budget Office data.

Moreover—despite claims of draconian cuts in welfare spending during the Reagan years—welfare spending as a share of the whole economy has changed little. Total welfare spending as a percentage of Gross National Product (GNP) is presented in Chart 2. Welfare spending as a share of GNP rose slightly during the recession of the early 1980s and then slowly declined as the recession ended. In 1988, total welfare spending remained at 3.5 percent of GNP, the same level as during the Carter presidency. Overall, welfare spending since the mid-1970s has kept pace with the growth of the economy.

Miscounting the Number of Poor Americans

Every year there is a ritual tearing of hair and gnashing of teeth among the press corps as the federal government announces that millions of Americans are still "living in poverty." The federal government has

Chart 2
Total Welfare Spending as a percentage of Gross Nation₌ⁱ Product

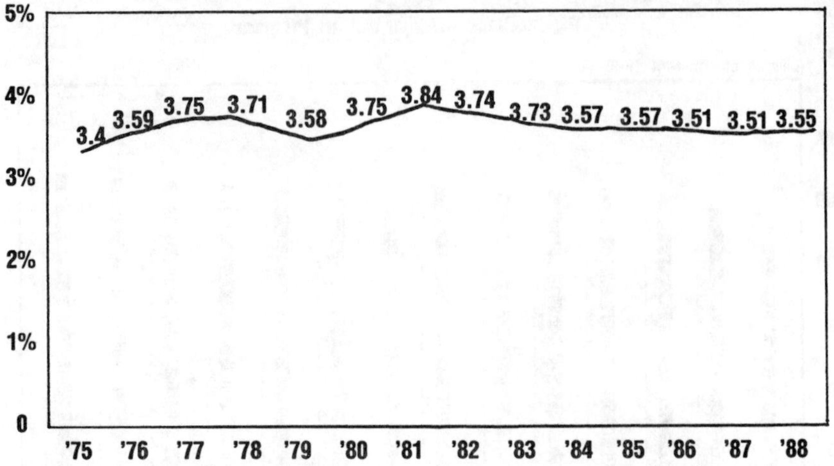

Source: See Chart 1.

attempted to count the number of Americans living in "poverty" every year since 1963. In that year, officials in the Social Security Administration at the U.S. Department of Health, Education and Welfare established quasi-official "poverty income thresholds" for different sized families. Families with apparent incomes below these thresholds were considered poor. Each year since 1963 the poverty thresholds have been adjusted for inflation. In 1989 the poverty income threshold for a family of four was $12,675.

Using these methods, the Census Bureau reported in 1989 that some 31.5 million Americans were living in poverty. It has become increasingly clear, however, that the Census Bureau's official poverty count dramatically underestimates the financial resources available to low-income Americans. While the Census Bureau counts as "poor" anyone with "cash income" less than the official poverty threshold, it completely disregards assets owned by the "poor," and does not even count much of what, in fact, is income. This is clear from the Census's own data: low income persons spend $1.94 for every $1.00 in "income" reported by the Census. If this is true, then the poor somehow are getting an additional $0.94 in income above every $1.00 counted by the Census. Indeed, the gap between spending and the Census' estimate of the poor's income has grown larger year after year.

A key reason that the Census undercounts the financial resources of the "poor" is that it ignores most welfare spending when calculating the "incomes" of persons in poverty. Thus, as far as the Census Bureau is concerned, billions of dollars of in-kind benefits to poor Americans have no effect on their standard of living. Of the $184 billion in welfare spending, the Census counts only $27 billion as income for poor persons. The bulk of the welfare system, including entire programs that provide non-cash aid to the poor, like food stamps, public housing, Medicaid, school lunch and breakfast programs, and the Special Supplemental Food Program for Women, Infants and Children (WIC) are completely ignored in the Census Bureau's calculations of the living standards of the "poor." The missing welfare spending that is excluded from the annual Census Bureau poverty reports comes to $158 billion, or over $11,120 for every "poor" household in the United States. The Census Bureau counts most persons receiving non-cash welfare as "poor" even if the total value of the welfare assistance received greatly exceeds the poverty income thresholds.

How "Poor" Are America's Poor?

Not surprisingly, the actual standard of living of persons defined as "poor" by the Census Bureau is far higher than most would imagine. In fact, government data on the possessions of officially poor households starkly contradict the American public's understanding of what it means to be "poor." For example, 62 percent of "poor" households own an automobile and 14 percent own two or more automobiles.[5] Fifty percent of the poor live in houses that are air conditioned.[6] Thirty-one percent have microwave ovens.[7]

The poor today are better housed, have better diets, and own more property than did the average U.S. citizen throughout much of the 20th century.[8] According to the Census Bureau's *American Housing Survey for the United States in 1987*, 38 percent of poor households own their own home, with a median value of $39,205 or roughly 60 percent of the median value of all homes in that year.[9] Nearly one-half million households defined as "poor" by the U.S. Census Bureau owned homes valued at over $100,000 in 1987.[10]

Whether owned or rented, the homes of "poor" households also are on average quite spacious by historic or international standards. By American standards, housing is considered "crowded" if more than 1.5 persons occupy each room. Using this definition, in 1987 less than 2 percent of "poor" households were "crowded" and only 7.5 percent of poor households had more than 1 person per room.[11] When measured by square feet per person, the homes of "poor" Americans have 4 times as much living space as the home of the average Russian and twice as much as the average Japanese. And the housing of poor Americans is generally in good condition.[12] The median age of such housing units is only seven years greater than the median age for the overall U.S. housing stock.[13]

According to the *American Housing Survey for the United States in 1987,* only 2.4 percent of housing units owned or rented by "poor" households had significant structural defects such as crumbling foundations or missing roof material.[14]

The diets of low income Americans are also significantly better than generally assumed. Surveys conducted by the U.S. Department of Agriculture show relatively little difference in overall food consumption between high and low income households. Though the food purchased by low income households normally is of lower quality and less expensive than that consumed by the upper middle class, there is little evidence of material shortages. For example, the average low income person eats 95 percent as much meat as the average person in the upper middle class. Measured in pounds of food consumed per week, low income persons actually consume 114 percent as much poultry, 109 percent as much fish and 92 percent as many fresh vegetables as consumed by the upper middle class.

The diets of the poor also provide a high level of nutrition. As Table 1 shows there is little difference in the average intake of essential

Table 1
Average Nutriments Consumed as a Percentage
of 1980 Recommended Dietary Standards

	Persons Eligible for Food Stamps	Poor Persons	Upper-Middle Income Persons
Protein	169	164	168
Vitamin B_{12}	142	171	171
Vitamin C	137	132	156
RiboFlavin	135	132	133
Phosphorous	131	125	139
Vitamin A	124	136	129
Thiamin	119	115	111
Niacin	118	119	125
Iron	99*	97*	101
Calcium	89*	81*	89*
Magnesium	87*	78*	86*
Vitamin B_6	75*	74*	77*

*Average Consumption falls below recommended dietary standards.

Source: U.S. Department of Agriculture, Human Nutrition Information Service, *Food Consumption and Dietary Levels of Low-Income Households November 1979–1980* (Washington, D.C.; U.S. Department of Agriculture, 1987), p. 126. U.S. Department of Agriculture, *Nutrition Monitoring in the United States—A Report from the Nutrition Evaluation Committee* (Washington, D.C.; Government Printing Office, July 1986), pp. 48–49, U.S. Department of Agriculture, Human Nutrition Information Service, *Food and Nutrient Intakes in 48 States, Year 1977–78* (Washington, D.C.; U.S. Department of Agriculture, 1984), passim.

nutrients between high income and poor Americans. Indeed, low-income Americans eat very rich diets compared to the rest of the world. For example, low-income Americans eat 75 percent more meat than the average Briton, 61 percent more meat than the average Italian and 150 percent more than the average Mexican.[15]

Hungry Children?

Children's "advocates" frequently express concern about malnutrition among the nation's poor children. In 1985 the Department of Agriculture conducted a thorough study of the food consumption and nutritional status of pre-school children. This study again found very little difference in the nutritional content of food consumed by low income as compared to affluent children. Children from families with incomes below 75 percent of the poverty line consumed 54.4 grams of protein per day compared to 53.6 grams for children in families with incomes above 300 percent of the poverty threshold (roughly $33,000 for a family of four in 1985).[16] Black pre-school children consumed 56.9 grams of protein per day compared to 52.4 grams for white children.[17] Surprisingly, protein and caloric consumption was slightly higher among children in the central cities than in the suburbs.[18]

Average consumption of nutrients was very high for pre-school children of all income classes. Protein consumption among children living in families with incomes below 75 percent of the poverty line equalled 211 percent of the recommended USDA standards.[19] Consumption of essential vitamins and minerals among both high income and poor children generally exceeded USDA standards, often by as much as 50 to 100 percent. Shortfalls were found in the average consumption of iron and zinc, but these were unrelated to income class or race.[20]

Material Poverty Versus Behavioral Poverty

Despite improvements in the general material condition of "poor" Americans, it would be a mistake to conclude that the War on Poverty was a success. To do so would ignore the emergence of widespread "behavioral" poverty, a breakdown in the values and conduct which lead to the formation of healthy families, stable personalities and self-sufficiency. The War on Poverty may have raised the material standard of living of some Americans, but at a cost of creating whole communities where work is rare or non-existent, and multiple generations have grown up dependent on government transfers.

Any attempt to reform the current structure of public welfare must begin with a realization that most programs designed to alleviate "material" poverty in general lead to an increase in "behavioral" poverty. While the poor were supposed to be the beneficiaries of War on Poverty's transfer programs, they instead have become its victims. If policy makers ignore or fail to recognize this relationship, the welfare state will continue to worsen, rather than improve, the lives of America's poor.

For the poor, one of the most devastating legacies of the past 25 years has been the dramatic reduction in work effort. For a growing number of poor Americans, the existence of generous welfare programs makes not working a reasonable alternative to long-term employment. During the late 1960s and early 1970s, social scientists at the Office of Economic Opportunity (OEO) conducted a series of controlled experiments to examine the effect of welfare benefits on work effort. The longest running and most comprehensive of these experiments was conducted between 1971 and 1978 in Seattle and Denver, and became know as the Seattle/Denver Income Maintenance Experiment, or "SIME/DIME."

Advocates of expanding welfare had hoped that SIME/DIME and similar experiments conducted in other cities would prove that generous welfare benefits did not adversely affect "work effort." Instead, the SIME/DIME experiment found that every $1.00 of extra welfare given to low income persons reduced labor and earnings by $0.80.[21] SIME/DIME's negative effect was even more pronounced among young, unmarried males: the number of hours worked per week declined 43 percent for those who remained unmarried during the experiment and 33 percent for those who married.[22] The results of the SIME/DIME study are directly applicable to existing welfare programs: nearly all have a strong anti-work effect like those demonstrated in the SIME/DIME experiment.

The effects of welfare in undermining the work ethic are readily apparent. In the mid-1950s nearly one-third of poor households were headed by an adult who worked full time throughout the year. Today, with greater welfare benefits available, only 16.4 percent of poor families are headed by a full time working adult. Thirty years ago the problem facing the working poor was low wages; today the problem is these adults don't work.

Perhaps the most distressing consequence of welfare is its devastating effect on family structure—and the black family in particular. At the outset of the Second World War, the black illegitimate birth rate was slightly less than 19 percent. Between 1955 and 1965 it rose slowly, from 22 percent in 1955 to 28 percent in 1965. Beginning in the late 1960s, however, the relatively slow growth in black illegitimate births skyrocketed—reaching 49 percent in 1975 and 65 percent in 1989. If current trends continue, the black illegitimate birth rate will reach 75 percent in ten years.[23]

Chart 3
Black Illegitimate Birth Rate

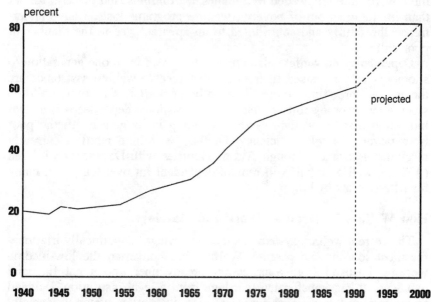

percent

Source: U.S. Department of Health and Human Services,
National Center for Health Statistics.

The onset of the "War on Poverty" directly coincided with the disintegration of the low-income family. Increasingly generous welfare benefits to single mothers directly contributed to the rise in illegitimate births. Recent research by Shelley Lundberg and Robert D. Plotnick of the University of Washington shows that an increase of roughly $200 per month in welfare benefits per family causes the teenage illegitimate birth rate in a state to increase by 150 percent.[24]

Similarly, high benefits discourage single mothers from remarrying. Research by Dr. Robert Hutchens of Cornell University shows that a 10 percent increase in AFDC benefits in a state will cause a decrease in the marriage rate of all single mothers in the state by eight percent. Welfare programs discourage young men and women from marrying and promote the disintegration of existing two-parent families. And because two parents are more likely to be able to sustain a family above the poverty level than a single parent, welfare, by increasing the number of single parent families, has led to an increase in the number of children officially counted as "living in poverty." According to the Census Bureau, a single parent family is six times more likely to be officially poor than a two-parent family.[25] In 1959, 28 percent of poor families were headed by females with no husband present. Today, 51.7 percent of families below the poverty line are headed by females with no husband present. Rather than lift families out of poverty, welfare programs instead have undermined the family and contributed to an apparent rise in the number of poor children.[26]

Dependency on welfare also appears to spread from one generation to another. Children raised in families that receive welfare assistance are themselves three times more likely to be on welfare than other children when they become adults.[27] This inter-generational dependency is a clear indication that the welfare system is failing in its goal to lift the poor from poverty to self-sufficiency. Of the 3.8 million families currently receiving assistance through Aid to Families with Dependent Children (AFDC), well over half will remain dependent for over ten years; many for fifteen years or longer.[28]

How Welfare Undermines Work and Marriage

The current welfare system has made marriage economically irrational for most low-income parents. Welfare has converted the low-income working husband from a necessary breadwinner into a net financial handicap. It has transformed marriage from a legal institution designed to protect and nurture children into an institution which financially penalizes nearly all low-income parents who practice it.

Across the nation, the current welfare system has all but destroyed family structure in the inner-city. Welfare establishes strong financial disincentives, effectively blocking the formation of intact, two-parent families. Example: Suppose a young man in the inner-city has fathered a child out of wedlock with his girlfriend. If this young father abandons his responsibilities to the mother and child, government will step in and support the mother and child with welfare. If the mother has a second child out of wedlock, as is common, average combined benefits will reach around $12,000 per year.

If, on the other hand, the young man does what society believes is morally correct (i.e., marries the mother and takes a job to support the family), government policy takes the opposite course. Welfare benefits would be almost completely eliminated. If the young father makes more than $4.50 per hour, the federal government actually begins taking away his income through taxes. The Federal Welfare Reform Act of 1988 will permit the young father to marry the mother and join the family to receive welfare, but only as long as he does not work.[29] Once he takes a full-time job to support his family, the welfare benefits are quickly eliminated and the father's earnings are subject to taxation.

It is important to note that under current welfare policy it is not even necessary for the father to live separately from the mother in order for the mother to receive AFDC benefits. As long as the parents do not actually marry, the father may hold a job and may co-habit with the mother on a near-permanent basis without jeopardizing the mother's welfare benefits.[30] However, the moment the mother and father marry, the welfare benefits are eliminated or sharply reduced.

Under the current system a welfare mother and her male partner may "pool" the financial resources available from the male's job and the mother's welfare as long as they remain unmarried. Welfare thus not only raises the rate of out of wedlock births, it also forms a permanent financial barrier to marriage for poor, single mothers. Example: A single mother on AFDC who has two children is receiving roughly $12,000 per year in welfare benefits from various programs. She has a stable relationship with a boyfriend who earns $12,000 per year. The AFDC mother and her boyfriend have a joint, after-tax income from welfare and earnings of roughly $22,000. If the mother marries the boyfriend, his earnings are included in the determination of the mother's welfare eligibility; most welfare benefits would be eliminated, and the couple's joint income would drop to between $12,000 and $13,000.

Current welfare may best be conceptualized as a system which offers each single mother a "paycheck" worth an average of between $8,500 and $15,000, depending on the state.[31] The mother has a contract with the government: She will continue to receive her "paycheck" as long as she fulfills two conditions:

1) she must not work; and

2) she must not marry an employed male.[32]

Low-income parents in the inner-city have responded to the destructive financial incentives of the welfare system. Single mothers on welfare drift through a series of "sequential common law marriages" with different males. Lacking the social, legal, and financial incentives which help to cement middle-class families, these sequential relationships do not flourish. Strong, permanent two-parent family units seldom emerge.

The behavior of males in the inner-city is also affected by welfare. As noted, the welfare system gives every incentive to fathers to abdicate their financial responsibility for their children; indeed, it severely penalizes those who accept such responsibility. Relieved of the financial necessity of supporting a family, the commitment of unmarried males to the labor force languishes. Even when jobs are [readily] available, low-income, unmarried men with fewer financial needs drift in and out of part-time jobs with frequent periods of non-employment.[33] While the continuous and full-time participation in the labor force among other workers leads to increased skills and earning levels, the half-hearted, intermittent labor history of unmarried males in the inner-city leads to stagnant skills and earnings.

Deprived of a role in financially supporting their children, these unmarried men also fail to assume their social and psychological roles as fathers. This, in turn, exacts a severe penalty on the children. Low-income children, growing up in inchoate family environments deprived of the vital, positive influence of a stable male parent, are themselves severely handicapped in their emotional, mental and moral development.

Groping for a Solution

America is a "fix it" society. By nature, Americans seem to believe that all problems have solutions. Therefore, American politicians and the public have difficulty believing that there are no easy solutions to the anti-marriage, anti-work incentives provided by the current welfare system. But there are *no* easy solutions. For example, a commonly proposed solution is to raise the earning capacity of low-income fathers. While this would be a step in the right direction, it would not eliminate the anti-marriage effects of conventional welfare. Even if the earning capacity of all low-income fathers were raised to the point where *every* working father could provide a standard of living for his family higher than the standard of living welfare provides to single mothers—low-income mothers and fathers would still be better off financially if they avoided marriage.

The economic logic of welfare is simple and cruel. If a mother and father do not marry their joint income equals: welfare for the mother plus the father's earnings.[34] If they do marry their joint income equals the father's earnings alone. Another way of expressing this dilemma is that the welfare system imposes an extraordinarily high marginal tax rate (i.e. income loss rate) on the act of marriage. If a man earning $10,000 per year marries a mother on welfare, their joint income (including the value of the welfare benefit) will fall by some 50 percent. If a man earning $20,000 marries a mother on welfare, the couple's joint income will fall some 30 percent.

There are only two ways to eliminate the anti-marriage incentives of the welfare system. The first would be to eliminate the $10,000 to $12,000 "welfare paycheck" given to single mothers. The second would be to provide exactly the same $10,000 to $12,000 in benefits to all two-parent families with a fully employed father. The first option is politically impossible; the second is financially impossible.

However, while it is impossible to eliminate the anti-work, anti-marriage incentives of welfare, it is possible to reduce these incentives, at least marginally. Thus a conservative approach to welfare reform would seek to reduce the harmful incentives of the current welfare system by increasing the economic benefits provided to two-parent working families with children relative to the benefits provided to non-employed single parents. This implies a two-fold strategy of:

1) reducing the aggregate welfare benefits given to non-employed single mothers[35]; and

2) providing new economic benefits to working, husband and wife families, especially those where the father is fully employed.

This amounts to turning the existing system on its head. This is not an approach which will be instantly understood by politicians and the press, nor is it politically pain-free. However, there is no alternative. If a reversal of the current incentive structure of the welfare system is not attempted—the result will be a continuing erosion of family structure and the work ethic within low-income communities.

Toward A Conservative Philosophy Of Welfare

The negative effects of the current welfare system should not come as a surprise; they are a direct result of liberal welfare philosophy. As practiced for the last twenty years, liberal welfare policy is based on a triad of dangerous premises. First, despite lip service to other goals, liberal policy is preoccupied almost exclusively with raising the material living standards of the less affluent through the provision of extensive cash transfers, food, housing and medical assistance. Second, nearly all assistance is unconditional: aid is given on the basis of perceived financial need. Liberal welfare programs are one dimensional and actuarial; they place no moral or social demands on recipients. The concept of reciprocal responsibility is avoided: the recipient is not expected to perform any service to society in exchange for the assistance given. The question of whether the recipient's behavior has caused his or her impoverished condition is ignored, and aid is not linked to a change in behavior. Third, liberal welfare policy rejects the idea that the poor will respond to the harmful incentives provided by the welfare system. Even if welfare heavily subsidizes non-work and single parenthood, this will not, it is believed, cause a serious increase in those behaviors.

The current welfare system is founded on a corruption of the concept of compassion derived from the Jewish and Christian religions.[36] In both the Jewish and Christian faiths, the idea of compassion is integrally linked to the moral responsibility of the beneficiary. In the Bible, both divine and earthly compassion are bestowed on those who repent and turn away from those behaviors which caused their misfortune.[37] Compassion in the traditional religious sense cannot be unconditional since its goal is to bring about a change of character and conduct.

The religious charity organizations which provided extensive aid to the poor throughout the U.S. in the late nineteenth century operated within this traditional view of compassion.[38] Based on a realistic understanding of human nature they knew that many would take advantage of aid that was given without the bond of reciprocal social and moral obligation. They realized that charity given unconditionally would have a corrupting effect on the poor more pernicious than poverty itself. While giving generously to meet the material needs of those who had fallen into poverty through no fault of their own, they never neglected the more permanent spiritual and psychic needs of those they aided. Religious charity was always intended to shape behavior in positive ways.

But the concept of "compassion" underwent a radical transformation beginning with the Social Gospel movement of the 1890s.[39] This change continued through the New Deal and found full fruition in the welfare explosion of the mid-1960s and 1970s. In this view the behavioral problems of the underclass poor are the result of vast social wrongs. Eliminating the undesirable behaviors of poor individuals requires not transforming the individual, but transforming society. Placing moral and social obligations on welfare beneficiaries was "blaming the victim," i.e., heaping added cruelties on those who had suffered enough. In its extreme form, social determinism (viewing all conduct as the by-product of the environment) has rendered liberals nearly incapable of punishing serious criminals, let alone capable of imposing middle-class norms of self-discipline, work, and family life on the "disadvantaged." Pending the radical transformation of society and economy allegedly needed to alleviate the "problems" of the poor, compassion has come to mean merely putting a larger welfare check in the mail, perhaps with a little voluntary job training on the side.

But the overwhelming share of material poverty today is the direct result of the specific behaviors of individuals which have undermined their capacity for a healthy, productive life: drug use, dropping out of school, having children out of wedlock, and failure to work consistently at available jobs (which erodes long-term productivity and wages). The *false compassion* of the current welfare system accepts and even rewards these very behaviors. False compassion in the long run can only harm the poor by trapping them deeper and deeper in a cycle of self-destructive behavior. *True compassion* begins by discerning those who are truly in need as opposed to those seeking a handout; it then places a moral obligation on beneficiaries and seeks to mold behavior in positive ways. True compassion expects the poor to live by the same standards and share the same aspirations sustained by mainstream society.

Principles of Conservative Welfare

Conservatives need to begin re-thinking the welfare system from the ground up based on the idea of true compassion. In shaping conservative welfare policy, six principles should be adhered to:

1) A conservative welfare policy must begin with a recognition that most government efforts to decrease material poverty through welfare have led to an increase in behavioral poverty: declining work effort; increased illegitimate birth rates and single parent-hood; and prolonged welfare dependency. There is an inherent contradiction between most efforts to decrease material poverty through welfare and efforts to reduce behavioral poverty, and there is no easy escape from this impasse. Conservative welfare policy should de-emphasize material poverty and place increasing concern on behavioral poverty.

2) Conservative welfare policy must also accept that there are some individuals who may have low incomes but are neither in need of nor deserve government aid. Single, non-elderly adults who are not supporting children are the most obvious category. Welfare to such individuals is not only a waste of funds, but is often counterproductive.

3) Conservative welfare policy must be based on a foundation of reciprocal responsibility between the recipient and society. Welfare should not be a one-way handout; a conservative welfare system must impose moral and social standards on those receiving benefits. Some, but not all, welfare recipients should be required to work in exchange for benefits given. A serious work test quickly weeds out those who do really need aid; it also restores dignity to the recipient and is essential in reducing long-term dependency.

4) A conservative approach to welfare would seek to provide strong incentives for healthy, constructive behavior and would seek to minimize rewards for self-destructive behavior. In particular, it would:
   A) seek to promote the formation of healthy, two-parent families as opposed to single parent families, and
   B) seek to reward work effort as opposed to idleness and dependence.

5) Conservative welfare policy should be based on an understanding that the U.S. already spends more than enough on welfare. The problem is not that we spend too little, but that most spending is

actually harmful. There should be an effort to shift funds from destructive programs into programs which provide positive incentives. Welfare spending should also be made as "transparent" as possible in order to make it clear to the public how much is being spent and how much aid a welfare recipient is receiving.[40]

6)   Legislators should recognize that many significant efforts to help the poor will occur outside the welfare system. Most low-income Americans can still significantly benefit from a growing economy, reduced crime, and dramatic reform of the education system. The poor will also absorb and benefit from—or be victimized by—changes in underlying American cultural values. Changes in general social norms concerning personal discipline, sexual behavior, religious belief, family commitment, and work ethic deeply affect the behavior and well-being of poor persons.

Advancing Welfare Reform

It has taken thirty years of bad policy to produce the current welfare mess. Reform may take equally as long. Conservatives must be patient. The first emphasis should be preventing the welfare system from doing even greater harm through increasing benefits in current counterproductive programs such as Aid to Families with Dependent Children.

Conservatives must launch an extensive public education campaign to inform the public about the disaster of the current welfare system. Conversely, the first line of defense for the liberal welfare system is disinformation. There is a virtual full-time industry in the U.S. devoted to advancing untruths about welfare and poverty: welfare benefits are low; welfare spending was slashed under Ronald Reagan; there is widespread malnutrition and severe poverty in the U.S.; welfare has few negative side-effects on the behavior of the poor; and the poor do not work because there are no jobs available for them. The press avidly repeats these falsehoods. Conservative reform must begin with a relentless public education campaign to set the facts straight about welfare.

The second line of defense for liberal welfare policies is the "Trojan Horse." Since the public is largely disgusted with the current welfare system, liberal efforts to expand conventional welfare must be camouflaged by conservative rhetoric and ideas. In 1987 Senator Patrick Moynihan proposed sweeping welfare reform legislation that he claimed would "require welfare mothers to work." In fact, the bill required no one to work and actually abolished some workfare programs. Moynihan's rhetoric about work was a successful smoke-screen for expansion of welfare benefits. Similarly in 1991 the National Commission on Children recommended placing limits on the amount of time a mother can spend on AFDC. In fact, the "time limits" were meaningless and were intended as a "bait and switch" ploy to promote vast increases in welfare benefits to single mothers. The National Commission also provided lots of rhetoric about promoting two-parent families while proposing a new government guaranteed income scheme for single mothers and illegitimate children.

Most welfare policy battles of the near future will be variants of the "Trojan Horse". Since the substance of public policy is always in the details, conservative legislators (most of whom lack expertise in welfare issues) are at a disadvantage. The best advice is to be patient and utterly suspicious. Pursuit of small, concrete changes will generally be better than grandiose reforms, i.e., it would be better to require a few AFDC mothers to work permanently in exchange for benefits (none now do) than to accept the nebulous "time limits" on AFDC in exchange for huge increases in benefit payment levels. Conservatives can afford to be patient; basic public attitudes support conservative policies and time is on our side.

Reforming Welfare: Specific Legislative Proposals

The following section provides sixteen legislative proposals which carry out the principles of conservative welfare policy.[41] These proposed reforms are grouped into five categories: Building a welfare data base; work requirements; general welfare reforms; financial incentives for two-parent families; and educational reforms.[42]

Building a Welfare Database

The average state legislator confronting welfare problems is like a man lost in the jungle without a guide, map or compass. The state legislator cannot even find out which welfare programs are operating in the state, how much money is spent, or the actual value of the benefits given to the average recipient. Data that are available will be incomplete and deliberately misleading. One thing is certain: The welfare bureaucracy will claim that nearly all programs are "successful." All that is needed is a little more money.

The lack of even rudimentary data on welfare spending and program effectiveness twenty-five years into the War on Poverty is no accident. Liberal advocates have long recognized that the best way to defend and expand the welfare state is to obscure the size of current welfare spending and the lack of effectiveness of current programs. The first step in designing conservative welfare policies must be to obtain accurate information about the existing welfare system.

1) Require Scientific Evaluation of Education and Training Programs Through Controlled Experiments.

Most job training programs are evaluated by "placement rates." For example, legislators may be told that 40 percent of the enrollees in a recent program have been placed in jobs. The implication is that none of these individuals would have obtained employment without the benefit of the training program. In reality, the use of placement rates to evaluate job training programs is highly misleading because many, if not all, of the trainees would obtain jobs without training. The use of "placement rates" to evaluate social services programs is a pseudo-scientific process that would not be accepted as evidence by any serious scholar. Unfortunately, many legislators are encouraged to treat this non-scientific data as a real measure of the effects of a program.

Instead, education, training and other social services programs should be evaluated by "controlled experiments." In a controlled experiment, a group of individuals eligible to participate in a program is randomly divided into two smaller groups: "controls," who do not participate in the program, and "experimentals," who do. After the training or education has been completed, the experimentals are compared to the controls. The difference between the two groups in employment, wage rates, and other factors gives a reasonable picture of the effectiveness of the program.[43] Often a scientific evaluation will show that a training program has no effect, or even negative effects. For example, an evaluation of a training program for AFDC-UP recipients in Maryland in the early 1980s showed that individuals who received training had lower employment rates than those who had not.[44]

Liberals often attempt to prohibit the use of controlled experiments on the grounds that it is unfair to deny services to the control group. There are two responses to this charge. First, few training or education programs provide services to all eligible persons; to deny services to a specific control group does not necessarily reduce the total volume of services provided. Second, it is grossly unfair to both the taxpayer and the program participant continually to offer "helpful" programs when there is no knowledge that the program actually works. For example, to offer a drug on the market, claiming it as a cure for a disease, without first evaluating the effects of the drug through controlled experiments would be a criminal offense. Unfortunately, politicians and government bureaucrats are not held to the same standards as drug companies.

2) Determine the Level of Aggregate Welfare Spending.

There are currently 75 major federal welfare programs operating in each state. In addition most states have extra welfare programs of their own design. At the present time *no* state government can provide even preliminary information on the total level of federal, state and local welfare spending in that state. Most press reports and political statements imply that spending is far lower than actual levels. This is no accident. The absence of data on current levels of welfare spending is a powerful tool for advocates of expanding welfare. By hiding the real level of current spending, they can always ask for extra spending to meet a new "crisis" or problem. Efforts to restrain the growth of welfare spending must begin with an accurate count of current spending levels. Without this information, conservatives opposing new welfare programs may appear merely indifferent to the "poor."

State legislators should require an annual tally of federal, state and local spending within the state on the 75 welfare programs listed in Appendix Table A, as well as any added state programs. In the average state, the total will be around $5,000 for each poor person or $20,000 for each family of four. Without accurate data on existing spending there can be no rational discussion of welfare policy. Once the data is available, the onus falls on the welfare state advocates to explain how so much can be spent with so little apparent effect.

3) Create a Study of Combined Welfare Benefit Levels.

Aid to Families with Dependent Children (AFDC) is the second largest welfare program in the United States. In an average month in 1989, 3.8 million families, comprising 10.9 million persons, received AFDC benefits. Among families currently receiving AFDC half will remain on welfare for over 10 years.[45]

The average AFDC benefit for a family of three in 1989 was $381. However, AFDC families are eligible to receive extra benefits from up to a dozen different programs. While few families actually receive benefits from all these programs, all receive benefits from more than one. In order to understand how much money is actually spent on the average welfare family, one must determine the value not of AFDC alone, but of the "combined welfare package" which the family receives from all programs. Neither the federal government nor any state government currently provides accurate information on the true cost of the combined welfare package received by the average AFDC family. All public figures understate the average benefit levels, and thereby implicitly provide ammunition to those who wish to increase welfare spending.

State legislators should require a survey of a sample of AFDC families within the state. This survey would include:

a) The percentage of AFDC families which also receive benefits from each of the following programs: food stamps, Medicaid, public housing or Section 8 housing, WIC, low-income energy assistance, school lunch programs, school breakfast programs, Head Start,

Emergency Assistance, Job Training Partnership Act, and any other welfare program.

b) The average cost of benefits received from each program listed above. (In the case of programs like Medicaid and public housing it is not necessary to calculate the value of services given to each specific family. Instead the average value of benefits for families of that size may be used.)

With these data, the value of combined welfare benefits for the average family on AFDC can readily be calculated. In the average state the value of combined welfare benefits will be more than twice the value of the AFDC grant itself.

Once the average value of the combined welfare benefits has been determined, it would be useful to compare it to the average cost of food and shelter for low-income persons in the state. The cost of food for low-income families of different sizes can be determined from the Thrifty Food Plan published by the U.S. Department of Agriculture. A separate survey should be undertaken to determine the average actual cost of non-subsidized rental housing in different localities for families living at or below the poverty level. In almost all cases, it will be shown that the average value of combined welfare benefits greatly exceeds the average cost of food and shelter for low-income families.

Required Work for Welfare Recipients

There are three types of initiatives generally included under the loose term "work program." They are:

Job Search. In a job search program the welfare recipient undertakes a supervised search for employment for a specified number of hours each week. A good job search program will provide: motivation, instruction on how to look for work and how to perform in a job interview, as well as close supervision. An example of a good job search program is a "job search phone bank," in which welfare recipients report to the welfare office each day and are placed in a phone bank room with other welfare recipients. Under close supervision, the welfare recipients phone a list of prospective employers looking for job openings; the welfare recipient remains continuously active in the phone bank throughout the day, leaving the welfare office only for actual job interviews.

Workfare or Work Experience. In a "work experience" program the welfare recipient works for a number of hours each week for a non-profit organization or government agency. A "work experience" program has three purposes: 1) it provides individuals unaccustomed to work with the basic skills of getting to work regularly and on time, of taking orders, decorum, and so on; 2) it establishes the moral principle that welfare should not be a one-way handout; that the welfare recipient should perform service to society in exchange for assistance; and 3) it makes welfare less attractive and real employment more attractive by attaching a cost to the welfare benefit. Thus it motivates individuals to leave the welfare rolls and obtain employment.[46]

Education and Training programs. Education and training programs are intended to raise the skill and wage levels of welfare recipients through either remedial education or specific job training.

Experiments with AFDC recipients have shown that job search, workfare, and education and training can all produce modest reductions in welfare dependency. Education and training programs, however, are much more expensive than job search or work experience and, therefore, are unlikely to reduce costs for the taxpayers. Moreover, education and training programs generally do not accomplish their goals of raising the skill and wage levels of welfare recipients.[47]

Over 90 percent of the public believe that able-bodied welfare recipients should be required to perform some work for the benefits received.[48] Liberals will pay lip service to this sentiment, but will adamantly oppose attaching serious work requirements to welfare beneficiaries. When liberals speak of "work requirements," they usually mean extra education and training programs for welfare recipients who wish to participate voluntarily. From a conservative perspective, workfare and job search are generally preferable to education and training. Some evidence indicates that a serious work requirement will dramatically reduce the number of welfare beneficiaries in some, but not necessarily all, welfare programs. However, serious workfare programs are rare, so the evidence is limited.

As a general rule of thumb, for both practical and ethical reasons, work requirements should be imposed first on those individuals who have the least justification to be unemployed, i.e., work requirements should be imposed first on single males and last (if at all) on unemployed single mothers with young children. Finally, in any serious workfare program, the number of hours of work required each week and the number of weeks the requirement will be continued will be key. Programs targeted toward volunteers should be avoided. Work and job search programs are successful to the extent that they motivate individuals to leave welfare, in part by making welfare less attractive. Volunteers are already motivated to leave welfare and will not benefit from most programs.

4) Collect Data on Work Requirements.

Many state legislators believe that large numbers of welfare recipients in their state are currently engaged in job search, workfare or training. This is almost never true. Statistics on this question are quite misleading. For example, a state welfare office may assert that 20 percent of adult AFDC recipients participated in work programs during a year, but many will have participated for only a few days or weeks. In most states only three percent to five percent of adult AFDC recipients will participate in job search, workfare or training during the average month.

State legislatures should require that their welfare departments reveal the percentage of adult welfare beneficiaries who actively participated in job search, workfare, education and training for each month throughout the year. The average hours of active participation per month should also be shown. These data should be provided for AFDC families, AFDC-UP families, General Assistance recipients and for single, non-elderly adults receiving food stamps.

5) Mandate Workfare for General Assistance Recipients.

AFDC provides aid to families with children. Supplemental Security Income (SSI) supports the elderly and disabled persons. General Assistance is a "catch-all" program run by the state governments for persons who are not eligible for either AFDC or SSI. Large numbers of General Assistance recipients are able-bodied, single adults who are unemployed. Since any single adult can support himself above the poverty level merely by working full time at a minimum wage job, there is little rationale for welfare assistance for this group. Even if a single adult cannot find any current employment, there can be no reasonable objection to requiring that such individuals perform public service in exchange for the welfare assistance received.

State governments should impose work requirements on all able-bodied single adult beneficiaries of General Assistance. Each General Assistance recipient should perform 40 hours of public service per week (or, alternatively, 25 hours of work and 15 hours of supervised job search). This work requirement should begin the first week assistance is given and should continue as long as General Assistance payments are received. Evidence suggests that such a work program may dramatically reduce General Assistance enrollments. Many General Assistance beneficiaries can readily obtain employment; many may, in fact, have part-time jobs which they have hidden from the welfare office.[49]

6) Mandate Workfare for Food Stamp Recipients.

Food stamps are provided to low-income working families, AFDC families, low-income elderly persons and the disabled. Food stamps are also provided to able-bodied adults who are unemployed. As in the case with the General Assistance program, there is little justification for this assistance; able-bodied, non-elderly adults without children receiving food stamps should be required to participate in a supervised job search program for 40 hours per week for the first eight weeks after initially receiving food stamp assistance. After this initial eight week period the individual should be placed in a workfare program for an additional 8 weeks. Federal law, however, limits required participation in a Food Stamp workfare program; the number of hours of required work per month may not exceed the value of the Food Stamps divided by the greater of the federal or state minimum wage. This means that, on average, single individuals receiving Food Stamps can be required to work two to three days each month. After 8 weeks participation in the workfare program, the individual should resume participation in a full-time, supervised job search program for an extra 8 weeks. If the individual is still receiving Food Stamps at the end of the second job search requirement, participation in the workfare program should recommence.[50] A serious work requirement and job search should cause a significant drop in the enrollment of such individuals in the food stamp program.

7) Establish Work Requirements for AFDC-UP Recipients.

The federal Welfare Reform Act of 1988 required all state governments to establish Aid to Families with Dependent Children—Unemployed Parent (AFDC-UP) programs. While normal AFDC is limited to single parents with children, AFDC-UP provides assistance to two-parent families with children. To be eligible both parents must be unemployed or have limited part-time employment. The average value of combined welfare benefits for an AFDC-UP family is between $12,000 and $14,000 per year. While there are practical difficulties with imposing work requirements on single parents with young children, work requirements seem much more reasonable for a family where both the father and mother are present and neither is employed. States should establish a 40 hour per week job search and workfare requirement on one parent in each AFDC-UP family. If a parent is employed part-time, the work requirement should be adjusted so that the job search, workfare and employment together equal 40 hours per week. The work requirement should continue as long as the family receives AFDC-UP benefits.[51] Most AFDC-UP fathers are readily employable. Attaching a serious, permanent work requirement to AFDC-UP will make welfare less attractive, thereby promoting quicker re-entry into the labor force and discouraging long-term dependency.

8)   Be Cautious About AFDC Workfare.

There were 3.07 million single mothers receiving AFDC benefits in an average month in 1989. Although there is a lot of rhetoric concerning work requirements for AFDC mothers, there are in fact very few AFDC mothers currently participating in job search, job training or work experience. Senator Daniel Patrick Moynihan made headlines in 1987 by declaring that he was going to require welfare mothers to work; in fact, Moynihan's original bill expanded welfare assistance but required no one to work or even to be trained to work. The final welfare reform legislation of 1988 requires roughly 6 percent of AFDC and AFDC-UP families to have one adult participating in job search, workfare or training in each month in 1992. This requirement is raised to roughly 10 percent in each month by 1995.

Most of the clamor about alleged work requirements for AFDC recipients is false. Many of those who talk the loudest on this issue are, in fact, the most opposed to serious workfare programs. Instead, they are interested in promoting added funds for education, training, daycare, transitional benefits and other welfare services under the rationale that AFDC mothers are now required to work. AFDC workfare is a classic "bait and switch" strategy. There will be lots of rhetoric about work, but when the smoke clears, spending for daycare, training and social services will go up while few, if any, welfare recipients will be required to even search for a job.

Conservative legislators who are seriously interested in work requirements for welfare recipients should focus their efforts on establishing serious, permanent work requirements for General Assistance, Food Stamps, and AFDC-UP recipients as outlined above. In most states, they will find that despite the glib rhetoric about work there is strong political opposition to real work requirements, even for these programs. Establishing work requirements for General Assistance, Food Stamps and AFDC-UP will be an uphill fight and will provide an opportunity to assess the limited prospects for establishing real work requirements for single mothers on AFDC.

However, if work requirements and training programs for AFDC mothers are to be established, the following principles should be followed:

a) Required participation in workfare, job search and training should be limited to mothers who do not have children under age five or who have been on AFDC for over 5 years.[52]

b) Job Search and workfare should be favored over training. Mothers who do not find employment through Job Search should participate in a 30 hour per week workfare program for at least 18 months.[53]

c) All Job Search, workfare and training programs should be evaluated by controlled experiments to determine their effectiveness and their cost or savings for the taxpayer.[54]

Job search and workfare are generally to be preferred to training.[55] Most AFDC mothers are employable; they lack the motivation and financial incentive to work, not the skills. Most training programs are expensive and are unlikely to significantly raise the earnings potential of the individuals enrolled in them.[56] AFDC work programs with a heavy emphasis on training are unlikely to save the taxpayer money.

It is particularly important to avoid imposing work requirements on AFDC mothers with children under age five. (The exception to this would be mothers in the Learnfare program. See proposal 16 below.) Nearly half of all AFDC mothers do not have any children under five. In most states AFDC job search, workfare, and training programs could be expanded five to ten fold without involving a single mother with a child under five. There is nothing in the federal law that requires or even encourages any work or training requirements for AFDC mothers with young children.

There are three reasons to avoid requiring AFDC mothers with pre-school children from participating in training, work and Job Search programs. First, if mothers with young children are forced to participate the state must pay the cost of providing daycare. While work programs for AFDC mothers without young children may save the taxpayer some money, programs involving mothers with pre-school children invariably will end up not saving money but costing the taxpayer more. Second, there is now a substantial body of evidence indicating that separating a young child from its mother for long periods of time has strong, negative effects on the child's development. This is particularly true for children under age two.[57] Third, we are currently witnessing a political and social struggle over the future of the American family. Some social theorists tell us that the traditional family where the parents care for their own children is a thing of the past; all children will soon be raised in daycare centers, they argue. They seek to create a system of government—funded daycare to support this "brave new world" of the future. Most find this vision of the future chilling.

Work requirements for AFDC mothers with pre-school children have a large, symbolic role in this debate over the future of the American family. In the odd logic of politics, promoting work requirements for AFDC mothers with pre-school children is transmuted into a ratification of claims that the traditional family is dead and that all mothers should be employed. Conservative politicians who argue firmly for putting AFDC mothers with young children to work will find themselves in a difficult position trying to stave off efforts to provide government daycare for children from middle-class families.

This has already occurred at the federal level where the Welfare Reform Act of 1988 with its extremely modest AFDC training requirements was immediately followed by the behemoth "Act for Better Childcare," an effort to establish the foundations of a federal daycare system for middle-class children. Advocates of this bill were quick to use the work requirements for AFDC mothers as a justification for building a government daycare system. Conservative members of Congress who had foolishly pushed for work requirements for AFDC mothers with three year-old children found it difficult to oppose government-subsidized daycare for working and middle-class families. Having argued that welfare children belong in daycare centers, they found it difficult to explain why it might be better to raise middle-class children in their own homes.[58]

Most individuals who call themselves conservative see the preservation of the traditional family and traditional parenting as essential to maintaining a free society. The prospect of converting America into a society like Sweden where most children are raised in government daycare centers is frightening. This overall question of the transformation of the family and the survival of traditional parenting is one of the most serious problems facing the United States; it is vastly more important than the issue of requiring AFDC mothers with young children to work. For this reason alone, conservatives should resist work requirements for AFDC mothers with young children.

Other Welfare Reforms

9)   Create an AFDC "Wed-fare" Program.

The current welfare system makes marriage unrewarding. The system instead rewards divorce and out-of-wedlock birth and discourages marriage by single mothers on welfare. While there is considerable discussion about increasing employment for single mothers on AFDC, there is little discussion of raising the marriage rate for single AFDC mothers. But more women leave AFDC through marriage than through employment. While promoting employment of single mothers may have some social benefits, the benefits of reducing single parenthood by promoting marriage are much greater.

State governments should consider a "wed-fare" program, providing a bonus of $4,000 to any woman who marries, leaves the AFDC rolls, and stays off for at least two years. The "marriage bonus" should be limited to women who have already been on AFDC for over two years and are likely to become long-term welfare dependents. The "marriage bonus" could be given to a mother only once. States should implement the "marriage bonus" on a small scale and evaluate the program's impact through a controlled experiment to determine if, in fact, it increases marriage rates and reduces AFDC dependence.

10) Reduce AFDC Benefits.

AFDC is the second largest welfare program in each state. Many of the social pathologies which beset low-income communities are, at least in part, the result of AFDC. AFDC undermines work ethic and parental responsibility; it corrodes family structure. The higher the monthly AFDC benefit level per family, the greater the negative effects. Raising the value of AFDC benefits per family in a state will cause: an increase in illegitimate births to teenage mothers; an increase in the number of single-parent families on AFDC; and a decrease in the number of single mothers leaving AFDC by marriage or re-marriage.

The monthly AFDC benefit level is the most important welfare policy variable within each state. State legislatures should never increase AFDC benefit levels faster than the rate of inflation. If politically possible, benefits should be reduced. Savings from this reduction could be used to fund other more beneficial welfare programs such as the Earned Income Tax Credit. The negative effects of increasing AFDC benefits are so significant that conservative policy makers should never consider raising AFDC benefits as a quid pro quo for other conservative reforms.

Families which receive both AFDC and public housing subsidies will generally have the highest welfare benefit packages within a state. An AFDC family which also receives housing subsidies will have, on average, a combined benefit package $2,000 to $5,000 a year higher than the benefits received by AFDC families without housing aid. Therefore reducing the benefits of AFDC beneficiaries who also get public housing aid may be more feasible than cutting benefits for all AFDC families. One practical way a state government could reduce AFDC benefits would be to reduce AFDC benefits by $40 for every $100 in housing subsidies received by a family.

11) Eliminate Extra AFDC Benefits for a Second Child Born While the Mother Is Already Receiving Welfare.

Governor Tommy Thompson of Wisconsin has proposed limiting the extra AFDC benefit given to mothers who have additional children while receiving welfare. He has pointed out that no taxpaying family has an automatic increase in income simply by having an additional child. Instead, parents must balance the important rewards of having children against the financial demands that a child brings. Working families must stretch limited financial resources to meet the pressure created by having more children. Governor Thompson has argued that, similarly, welfare mothers should not have an automatic and unlimited entitlement to extra income simply by having additional children. Under Governor Thompson's proposal, a mother on AFDC would not receive an increase in AFDC payments for additional children she had. If the mother decides to bear additional children while receiving welfare, she must accommodate the costs of raising the child within her existing budget. The scheme makes the welfare mother financially accountable for the decision to have additional children. Governor Thompson has proposed to use savings from the restriction of AFDC benefits to a variant of the "wedfare" proposal (see proposal 9 above). A similar proposal not to increase AFDC benefits for mothers who have additional children has been introduced by Representative Wayne Bryant, a black state legislator from New Jersey.

State legislators should follow these examples altering their AFDC systems so that AFDC benefits are not increased when a mother already enrolled and receiving AFDC benefits has an additional child. Funds saved from this limitation could be devoted to other programs such as a family wage supplement or wedfare.[59]

12) Establish Residence Requirements for Teenage Mothers on AFDC.

The Federal Welfare Reform Act of 1988 gives state governments the option to require any non-married teenage mother, who receives AFDC benefits for herself and her child, to reside with her parents. Permitting teenage mothers to receive welfare and set up separate households as if they were adults is neither in the interest of the mother nor the child. For many teenagers in the inner city, having a child out of wedlock and receiving welfare is a means of establishing financial and social independence. By leaving her home and using welfare to set up her own apartment, the teenage mother asserts her own identity and "adulthood." Requiring all teenage mothers to remain with their parents in order to be eligible to receive welfare will make welfare less socially desirable for many young women. This in turn may reduce the number of illegitimate births and the rate of welfare dependence.

Financial Incentives for Two-Parent Working Families

13) Create an Earned Income Tax Credit for Two-Parent Working Families.

Nearly all welfare programs reward counter-productive behavior: non-work and single-parenthood. The Earned Income Tax Credit (EITC) is an attempt to design a welfare system that rewards constructive rather than destructive behavior. In plain English, the EITC is a wage supplement for working families with children.

The U.S. government first established a federal EITC in 1975. The EITC, or wage supplement, differs from conventional welfare in four significant ways:

a) The EITC is targeted to those most likely to be in need: low income families with children.

b) The EITC is available to intact, two-parent families as well as single parent families. If properly designed it does not encourage family breakup and may even promote the formation of two-parent families.

c) Unlike other welfare programs, the EITC is linked to work.

d) Unlike other welfare programs, which pay lower benefits the more a parent works, the EITC provides positive work incentives by providing higher benefits as work effort increases.

Some welfare programs, such as Food Stamps and General Assistance, provide benefits to single, non-elderly able-bodied adults. Since any single adult can support himself above the poverty level merely by working at a minimum wage job and such jobs are plentiful, there is no justification for providing welfare to such persons. Indeed, the SIME/DIME experiment showed that low-income, single adults respond to welfare assistance by dramatically reducing the amount of work performed; welfare simply becomes a substitute for earned income.

By contrast, a parent with children may not always be able to provide adequately for his or her family even if the parent works full-time year round. A father with a low wage job paying less than $6.00 per hour cannot sustain a family of four above the poverty threshold even if he works full time throughout the year. In the case of such a parent struggling diligently to support a family, the provision of some welfare aid seems well justified. Indeed, in moral terms, offering a small amount of assistance to parents who are working hard but not quite making it, seems far more justified than giving aid to parents who do not work at all.

In contrast to many other welfare programs, the EITC is limited to parents with children. Both single-parent and two-parent families are eligible for the federal EITC. But the most striking difference from all other welfare programs is that the EITC is available only to parents who work; parents who do not work receive no benefits.

The final difference between the EITC and conventional welfare is in the benefit structure. In conventional welfare programs the more an individual works, the lower the benefits become. However, for low wage parents, the EITC actually increases the more the individual parent works. It thereby provides incentives for the parent to earn more to support his or her family in contrast to the disincentives provided in normal welfare programs. Charts 4 and 5 demonstrate the difference between conventional welfare programs and an EITC program.

In Chart 4, the maximum benefits are provided when the individual has zero income. With every dollar the individual earns the welfare benefits are reduced. Although the maximum benefit level and phase-out rate differ, most major welfare programs including AFDC, SSI, Food Stamps and Public Housing conform to this general pattern.

By contrast, in an EITC program benefits equal a percentage of earnings. EITC benefits increase as earnings rise up to a "threshold earnings level." Above the threshold earnings level, the EITC benefits are gradually reduced. Chart 5 shows a hypothetical EITC or wage supplement. The EITC benefit rate equals 10 percent of earned income for families with incomes below the threshold earnings level of $15,000. As the earned income in the family rises above $15,000, the EITC benefit is incrementally reduced. The EITC reaches zero when earnings reach the $25,000 level. Thus in this hypothetical model, a parent who did not work at all would get zero benefits. A family with $5,000 in earnings would get $500 in EITC benefits and a family which earns $15,000 gets $1,500 in EITC benefits. The EITC supplements the parents' wages. For all families with earned incomes below the "threshold earnings level" it provides a positive incentive for work and can encourage families to leave welfare.

Wage Supplement for Two-Parent Families

State legislatures should adopt a state-based wage supplement which would complement and add to the existing federal EITC. The state wage supplement should have the following features:

1) It would equal 10 percent of earned incomes for families with income below $15,000 and be reduced by $150 for each additional $1,000 in income above $15,000.[60]

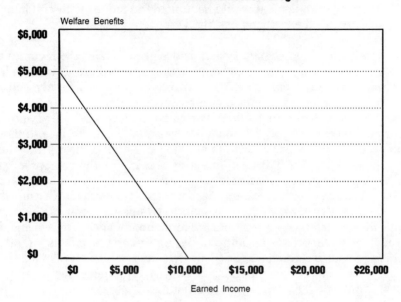

Chart 4
Benefits in Conventional Welfare Program

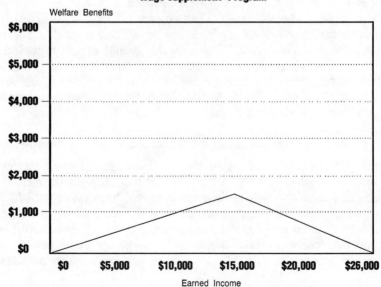

Chart 5
Benefits in a Model EITC or
"Wage Supplement" Program

2) The wage supplement would be provided on a quarterly basis. In any quarter in which the total work within the family was less than 350 hours the wage supplement would not be paid.

3) The wage supplement would be limited to families with children in which both the husband and the wife were present.[61]

This family wage supplement system is designed to raise the incomes of working, low wage parents relative to families on welfare. It is intended to reward low wage parents in their efforts to support a family and to promote the formation of intact, two-parent families.

Restricting benefits to families where there is at least 350 hours of labor per quarter (roughly 27 hours per week) targets assistance to those who need it most: a parent who is working full-time or nearly full-time at a low wage job. The 350-hour limitation avoids providing inappropriate and counterproductive assistance to families which have low incomes merely because neither parent has worked very much during the preceding quarter. By restricting benefits to two-parent families, the wage supplement is intended to promote the formation of such families and, in a small way, to offset the anti-family, anti-marriage effects of other welfare programs. The exclusion of single parent families is also justified by the fact that the federal EITC is already quite generous to single-parent families relative to two-parent families.

The proposed wage supplement is not perfect. For families in the $15,000 to $25,000 income range, it provides some work disincentives. The program also presents some administrative difficulties, though not necessarily more than other welfare programs. However, in comparison to other welfare programs, the positive aspects of the two-parent wage supplement would be enormous. The two-parent family wage supplement should be preferred to all other forms of welfare spending for non-disabled, non-elderly persons. But one should not expect miracles, the pro-work, pro-marriage incentives of the wage supplement are relatively modest in comparison to the huge anti-work, anti-marriage incentives of the AFDC, Medicaid, Food Stamps, and Public Housing programs. Nevertheless, the wage supplement is a step in the right direction.

14)   Reduce Income Taxes on Low-Income Working Families.

One of the simplest ways to reduce financial pressures on lower-income working families and to reward those families for their efforts to be self-sufficient is to reduce their tax burden. Those states with income taxes should raise the personal exemption in their income tax code for dependent children and dependent spouses. The rough goal should be to raise the exemption levels so that a husband and wife with two children with an income below $25,000 per year do not pay state income tax.

Assisting the Poor Through Real Reform in American Education

Despite nearly a decade of aggressive reform which followed the publication of the National Commission on Excellence in Education's *A Nation at Risk* in 1983, there is very little evidence to suggest that America's system of public education has improved. For low-income students trapped in decaying inner-city public schools, not only has student achievement stagnated or declined but the schools themselves have become virtual war zones. Every year nearly three million criminal acts are attempted or completed inside the schools and on school property; every month nearly 300,000 high school students are physically attacked. The Detroit school district was shut down for two days in 1987 after 102 school-age children under the age of sixteen were shot during a four- month period.[62]

In addition to rampant violence, low-income students in the inner-city must overcome the fact that their schools generally provide the lowest quality education. In the Milwaukee, Wisconsin public schools, for example, only two percent of black males have a grade point average above 3.0. In some inner-city school districts, the high school dropout rate routinely exceeds 40 percent. Even among those low-income, inner-city students who manage to survive the mayhem and stay in school long enough to receive a high school diploma, student achievement levels are chronically poor. For example, half of the Chicago public high schools rank in the bottom one percent of the nation in scholastic achievement.[63]

While the education reforms of the past decade have resulted in higher teacher salaries, higher per-pupil expenditures and smaller class sizes, the fundamental organization and delivery of education have changed very little. Because the poor cannot escape into private schooling, they bear the heaviest burden of the failure of the public schools. The large public school monopolies which exist in almost every major American city lack the incentive to improve the quality of education they provide because they know the poor have no alternative. In urban public school districts like Chicago, where the quality of education is notoriously low, those who can afford it usually send their children to private schools. In fact, 46 percent of public school teachers in Chicago—the very people who work in the system and know how bad it really is—send their children to private schools while only 22 percent of all people with school-age children do so.

Unlike nearly half of all Chicago public school teachers, the poor do not have the choice to "opt out" of dismal public schools. And unlike middle- and upper-class Americans, who can afford either to purchase homes in the suburbs or to choose private schools, the poor are "left behind" with an increasingly substandard education. The poor's inability to choose alternative providers of education leaves them little or no leverage in dealing with the public school bureaucracy. But poor children and their parents will gain leverage only when their status with the public school monopoly changes from "guaranteed clients" to "education consumers." The poor must be given the opportunity to take their business elsewhere.

15) Establish Education Voucher Programs.

The most promising education reform gaining momentum in the states is education vouchers. A voucher system would allow the poor to "opt out" of failing public schools and would force the public school monopoly to compete for students. The public school establishment (and the powerful teachers' unions in particular) vehemently opposes giving parents the right to choose non-government schools. Their opposition is usually shrouded in rhetoric about the "right of all Americans to a quality education" and the fear that vouchers would "leave the poor behind in the worst schools." Yet these arguments ignore the evidence which shows that a "quality education" is virtually non-existent in most inner-city public schools and that the existing public school monopoly has trapped the poor in substandard educational environments. Because the non-poor by and large already exercise choice in education, the poor would benefit most from a voucher system. Educational vouchers, which would allow parents to use their share of a state's per-pupil expenditure in any public or private school with the requisite funding "following them," would create a consumer-driven education system.

In the current public school monopoly, the needs of consumers (and especially poor consumers) are subordinate to special interests. The central office of the New York City public schools, for example, employs nearly 7,000 bureaucrats for its approximately 900,000 students—a ratio of one bureaucrat for every 155 students. The New York City Catholic schools, on the other hand, have fewer than 35 employees in the central office—a ratio of one for every 4,000 students.[64] Thus it is not surprising that in 1989 in New York City's public schools only 32 percent of the $6,107 allocated per pupil actually reached the classroom; the remaining 68 percent was "lost" in administrative costs and overhead.[65] It is also not surprising that the needs of poor parents are routinely ignored. The enormous size of public school bureaucracies and the politicized environment in which they function leave little room for innovation necessary to create the types of schools parents want. Without competition and the threat of losing students and the dollars that come with them, it is impossible for the public school monopoly to change.

The growing popularity of educational "choice" initiatives has forced traditional opponents of such ideas to reconsider their opposition. Albert Shanker, president of the American Federation of Teachers, for example, has publicly expressed his support for "choice." But the education establishment's support for choice is conditional: choice must be restricted to government schools. Any attempt to include even private, non-sectarian schools is vehemently opposed. Yet in cities like Washington, D.C. and Milwaukee, where nearly every public school is plagued by violence and learning is rare or non-existent, choice restricted to the public schools is essentially no choice at all. State legislators must recognize that the education establishment's rhetorical support for "choice" will do little to improve the quality of American education, and their opposition to allowing parents to choose private schools is an attempt to insulate a failing, bureaucratic monopoly from true competition.

Restricting choice to the public schools is unlikely to create effective schools or improve student achievement. According to the Brookings Institution Senior Fellow John E. Chubb and Stanford University professor of political science Terry M. Moe, reforms like "public school choice" and school-based management, which gained popularity in the mid- to late-1980s, failed because they relied on existing institutions to implement reform when those institutions themselves are the problem. Critiquing public school choice, Chubb and Moe assert:

> [C]hoice is usually restricted to a fixed set of existing schools, which reformers hope to improve through "competition" that choice will presumably stimulate. All these schools, however, have their existence and financial support guaranteed; actions are inevitably taken to ensure that no schools are "underenrolled" (a bureaucratic euphemism for what happens when schools are so bad no one wants to attend them); schools that do the worst are implicitly rewarded, because they tend to be the first in line for bigger budgets and more staff. . . . Under these conditions, giving parents and students choice among schools cannot in itself be expected to produce vigorous, healthy competition among schools.[66]

Chubb and Moe's exhaustive 10-year study of 500 schools and 20,000 principals, teachers and students concludes that the only way to improve the quality of American education is to dismantle the current bureaucratic organization of schools and replace it with one that is responsive to consumer demands and competition. They argue that competition will work to improve the quality of schools only when parents are given the opportunity to choose from a wide supply of school options including private schools.

It is also possible to design voucher programs to permit parents to send their children to religious schools. Many poor parents would strongly prefer to have their children educated in a religious environment. Research by Dr. Roger Freeman of Harvard University shows that black inner-city youth who have religious values are 47 percent less likely to drop out of school, 54 percent less likely to use drugs and 50 percent less likely to engage in criminal activities than those without religious values.[67] Despite liberal arguments to the contrary, the Supreme Court has indicated in *Mueller v. Allen* and *Witters v. Washington State Department of Services for the Blind* that vouchers or tax credits can be spent for religious education without creating constitutional problems. As long as the parent, not the government, decides where the voucher funds will be spent there is no violation of the religious establishment clause of the First Amendment.[68]

State legislators interested in implementing a voucher system should expect fierce opposition from both teachers' unions and organizations that represent the system's "administrators." It is essential that they be able to counter the establishment's egalitarian rhetoric concerning the poor and their arguments with regard to the separation of church and state. The successful passage of the Milwaukee voucher program for low-income children in 1990 offers proof that the opposition of the well-organized and heavily-funded education establishment can be defeated. The key lies in coalition building: much of the success occurred because the plan was promoted by a liberal, black Democrat and a conservative, white Republican together.

16)   Institute a "Learnfare" Program.

Even before the War on Poverty began, receiving an education was recognized as the best way to avoid poverty. Students who drop out of high school or who receive public assistance at an early age are much more likely to become welfare dependent than students who complete their education. In many inner cities, however, high school dropout rates in excess of 40 or 50 percent are commonplace.

To address this problem, states should enact a Learnfare program. Learnfare requires school-aged children receiving AFDC benefits to attend school regularly or face a reduction in AFDC benefits. It also requires teenage mothers on AFDC to continue school unless they have completed high school or have received an equivalency degree. Failure to meet attendance requirements (fewer than 10 full days of unexcused absences during the semester) results in the mother or child being removed from the AFDC until regular attendance is re-established.   The threat of reduced welfare benefits gives parents an incentive to make sure their children regularly attend school. The Learnfare program also ensures that young mothers on welfare will complete their education and thus reduces the likelihood of prolonged welfare dependency.[69]

Conclusion

American society spends nearly $200 billion per year on government welfare, a sum nearly 50 percent greater than the Gross National Product of Mexico. Even during the "draconian" Reagan Era, government welfare spending rose faster than the rate of inflation. It is politically inconceivable that government at all levels will not continue to spend enormous sums on welfare for the foreseeable future. Conservatives must be concerned not merely with how much is spent, but how it is spent and what the social consequences of spending are. Even if nearly all welfare functions were returned to private charity, all the ethical and policy questions raised in this essay concerning the structure of welfare assistance would remain—although the resolution of these issues would be far easier.

The invention of the "measurement of poverty" in the early 1960s has led government to throw money and benefits at low-income persons in an effort to raise their income above the poverty level. But since welfare spending reduces work effort and increases poverty-prone single parent families, raising welfare leads to an increased number of persons "needing" financial assistance. The welfare system is trapped in a vicious cycle, shoveling more and more dollars into a widening pit of splintered families and dependence. Meanwhile, the preoccupation with material poverty and "check-in-the-mail" welfare has distracted policymakers from the central questions of welfare's effects on behavior. Even if the royal family of Saudi Arabia were to offer to pay for all U.S. welfare costs, now and in the future, conservatives would still seek to eliminate the present welfare system—because it is a bad system. This is not to say that welfare is the only culprit in the current social pathology which afflicts low-income communities. Eroding norms of family life, sexual behavior, and personal responsibility occurring at all levels of society have also had their impact on the poor. But welfare has played a major role in the growing problems of low-income America: In the long run, welfare victimizes those it pretends to help.

Each of the recommended policies in this essay would be a positive, incremental step in reform. If all were enacted, they would substantially transform the welfare system within a given state (though still leaving a flawed and expensive system). But these changes would not miraculously erase the harm caused by the War on Poverty over the past quarter century. Even if the entire U.S. welfare system were dramatically overhauled tomorrow, the pathological effects of the present welfare system would leave deep scars on low-income Americans for generations to come. The struggle to reform welfare is not one for those seeking quick and easy victories; this haste only increases the credit to politicians who undertake the struggle.

Endnotes

1. Results from a Sindlinger and Company poll conducted for The Heritage Foundation in July 1985.

2. Vee Burke, *Cash and Non-cash Benefits for Persons with Limited Income: Eligibility Rules, Participant and Recipient Data, FY 1986-88* (Washington, D.C.: Congressional Research Service, The Library of Congress, 24 Oct. 1989).

3. Estimate of percent of total Medicare spending going to the "poor" is based on Congressional Budget Office figures showing that 12.8 percent of Medicare recipients are "poor."

4. The Census Bureau reported in 1988 that there were 33.3 million persons who were "poor" before receipt of welfare assistance. These individuals are generally termed the "pre-welfare poor."

5. U.S. Department of Commerce and U.S. Department of Housing and Urban Development, *American Housing Survey for the United States in 1987*, Current Housing Reports H-150-87 (Washington, D.C.: Government Printing Office, 1989), 46.

6. *Ibid.*, 40.

7. U.S. Department of Energy, Energy Information Administration, *Housing Characteristics: 1987* (Washington, D.C.: Government Printing Office, 1989), 87.

8. Robert Rector, Kate Walsh O'Beirne and Michael McLaughlin, "How 'Poor' Are America's Poor?" *Backgrounder 791* (Washington: The Heritage Foundation, 21 Sept. 1991), 2.

9. *American Housing Survey for the United States in 1987, op. cit.*, 34, 84, 114, and 304.

10. *Ibid.*, 114.

11. *Ibid.*, 38.

12. *Ibid.*, 34, 36, and 44.

13. *Ibid.*, 34.

14. *Ibid.*, 36.

15. *Ibid.*, 15. The comparison is between poor Americans and the general population in other countries.

16. Human Nutrition Information Service, U.S. Department of Agriculture, *Low Income Women 19-50 Years and Their Children 1-5 Years, 4 Days: 1985*, CSF II Report 85-5 (Washington, D.C.: U.S. Department of Agriculture, 1988), 50. Human Nutrition Information Service, U.S. Department of Agriculture, *Women 19-50 Years and Their Children 1-5 Years, 4 Days: 1985*, CSF II Report 85-4 (Washington, D.C.: U.S. Department of Agriculture, 1987), 42.

17. *Women 19-50 Years and Their Children 1-5 Years, 4 Days: 1985, op. cit.*, 42.

18. *Ibid.*

19. *Low Income Women 19-50 Years and Their Children 1-5 Years, 4 Days: 1985, op. cit.*, 72.

20. *Low Income Women 19-50 Years, op. cit.*, 73. *Women 19-50 Years, op. cit.*, 65.

21. Gregory B. Christiansen and Walter E. Williams, "Welfare Family Cohesiveness and Out of Wedlock Births," in *The American Family and the State*, eds. Joseph Peden and Fred Glahe (San Francisco: Pacific Institute for Public Policy Research, 1986), 398.

22. Charles Murray, *Losing Ground: American Social Policy From 1950 to 1980* (New York: Basic Books, 1984), 151.

23. U.S. Department of Health and Human Services, National Center for Health Statistics. Note: The black illegitimate birth rate is available only from 1969 on. The pre-1969 black illegitimate birth rates were calculated using the very similar "Non-White" rate.

24. Shelley Lundberg and Robert D. Plotnick, "Adolescent Premarital Childbearing: Do Opportunity Costs Matter?," June 1990, a revised version of a paper presented at the May 1990 Population Association of America Conference in Toronto, Canada.

25. Kate Walsh O'Beirne, "U.S. Income Data: Good Numbers Hiding Excellent News," *Backgrounder 667* (Washington,: The Heritage Foundation, 19 Aug. 1988), 4.

26. This, however, is at least partially due to the deficiencies of the Census Bureau measurement of poverty. According to the Census Bureau nearly all single parent families on AFDC are "poor." However, if the non-cash benefits received by such families were counted, many would have incomes above the poverty threshold.

27. M. Anne Hill and June O'Niell, *Underclass Behaviors in the United States: Measurement and Analysis of Determinants* (New York: City University of New York, Baruch College, Mar. 1990).

28. David Elwood, *Targeting "Would-be" Long-term Recipients of AFDC* (Washington, D.C.: U.S. Department of Health and Human Services, Jan. 1986), 5.

29. The 1988 federal welfare law required all states to establish an AFDC-UP program by Oct. 1, 1990. Prior to passage of the 1988 welfare law, 23 states did not have an AFDC-UP program and those states were allowed to limit AFDC-Up cash benefits to six months, but were required to continue to provide Medicaid as long as the family was otherwise eligible for AFDC. The 1988 law allowed states to require full-time participation by one parent in Job Opportunities and Basic Skills (JOBS) program, while mandating that the states require one parent to spend at least 16 hours per week in work activity. States must enroll at least 40 percent of their AFDC-UP caseload in work programs by fiscal 1994 and up to 75 percent by fiscal 1997 and 1998. Both the requirement for AFDC-Up coverage and the work requirement end Sept. 30, 1998.

30. Technically, the cohabiting male's income would be included in determining the AFDC mother's food stamp and public housing benefits, but it is unclear to what degree this principle is enforced.

31. This sum equals the value of welfare benefits from different programs for the average mother on AFDC.

32. Technically the mother may be married to a husband who works part-time at very low wages and still be eligible for some aid under the AFDC-UP program. However, if the husband works a significant number of hours per month even at a low hourly rate, his earnings will be sufficient to eliminate the family's eligibility to AFDC-UP and most other welfare.

33. Harry J. Holzer, "Black Youth Nonemployment: Duration and Job Search," in Richard B. Freeman and Harry J. Holzer, *The Black Youth Employment Crisis* (Chicago: University of Chicago Press, 1986), 64.

34. The general policy rule is that all means-tested welfare benefit programs have anti-marriage effects because the welfare benefits will be higher if a man and woman do not marry and they are treated by the government as separate "households" for purposes of calculating benefit levels. A partial exception to this rule is the earned income tax program which, because it is limited to employed parents, will encourage marriage between an employed man and a mother on AFDC who is not employed. However, the existing EITC would, in some cases, discourage marriage between an employed man and an employed single mother. Because of the small size of the EITC this effect is probably not great. The only programs which provide an unadulterated pro-marriage effect are

programs limited to two-parent families with children, for example, the two-parent wage supplement discussed in policy proposal 13 below.

35. Attaching a work requirement to AFDC or other welfare benefits is one means of effectively reducing the value of the welfare benefit package, since welfare benefits which are given in exchange for serious work clearly have less utility than benefits given to an individual at no cost. Thus serious work requirements attached to welfare benefits will reduce the anti-marriage incentives of the welfare system.

36. *See* Marvin Olasky, "Beyond the Stingy Welfare State: What We Can Learn from the Compassion of the Eighteenth Century," *Policy Review* 54 (Winter 1991): 2-14.

37. *Ibid.*, 8-9.

38. *Ibid.*

39. *Ibid.*, 10.

40. For example, if an individual receives a $5,000 voucher for housing assistance, the public is immediately aware that substantial assistance has been given to that individual. If, on the other hand, the same $5,000 is given indirectly through subsidies to builders or operating grants to public housing authorities, the true assistance level will remain largely hidden from policy makers and the public. Having an accurate estimate of the value of welfare benefits given to an individual is a necessary prerequisite to rational policy making. Thus, vouchers and cash assistance programs in which the value of the benefits given are immediately apparent to the public are to be preferred to indirect forms of aid in which the dollar value of the welfare benefits is hidden and difficult to obtain.

41. Specific draft legislative language to enact many of the following proposals is available in "Children, Family, Neighborhood, Community: An Empowerment Agenda," *The Source Book of American State Legislation: Volume VII* (Washington, D.C.: American Legislative Exchange Council, 1991). This publication is available from the American Legislative Exchange Council, located at 214 Massachusetts Avenue, N.E., Washington, D.C., 20002.

42. Some of these proposals require the state to request a waiver of federal law from the Secretary of Health and Human Services under Section 1115 of the Social Security Act. The Secretary has broad authority to waive federal law relating to the AFDC program at the request of state governments. The section 1115 waiver process will play an important role in welfare reform at the state level.

43. However, controlled experiments do not capture the effects of a training or workfare program in encouraging or discouraging individuals from enrolling in welfare. For example, a strong work requirement attached to AFDC or Food Stamps benefits is likely to dissuade many individuals from enrolling in welfare in the first place. Conversely, expensive education and training programs targeted to persons enrolled in AFDC or other welfare programs may actually encourage more people to enroll in welfare to benefit from the training. This apparently was the result from Governor Michael Dukakis' heralded Education and Training (ET) program, which actually increased welfare enrollments in Massachusetts. Since in a controlled experiment of the effects of workfare or training programs operated as part of larger welfare assistance programs, both the experimentals and controls will be individuals already receiving welfare benefits, the experiment will capture the effects of training or workfare in helping individuals to leave the welfare rolls but will not reveal the effects of the programs in encouraging or discouraging new enrollments in welfare. The effects on new enrollments may be imperfectly analyzed by examining changes in enrollment rates over time, or by comparing enrollment rates in counties or states which have a workfare program compared to those who do not. Despite these limitations, controlled experiments are a vast improvement over placement rates as a means of evaluation.

44. Daniel Friedlander, Gregory Hoerz, David Long, and Janet Quint, *Maryland: Final Report on the Employment Initiatives Evaluation* (New York: Manpower Demonstration Research Corporation, December 1985), 139-142.

45. David Elwood, *Targeting "Would-be" Long-term Recipients of AFDC, op. cit.,* 5.

46. Some state legislators feel that welfare recipients should be required to work in for-profit, private sector jobs. This is impractical because private sector firms do not want employees who have been literally forced to work. However, requiring welfare recipients to work in the public sector removes the option of receiving welfare without work. This makes welfare less attractive and will induce many recipients to leave welfare and take private sector employment.

47. *See* Robert Rector and Peter T. Butterfield, "Reforming Welfare: The Promises and Limits of Workfare," *Backgrounder 585* (Washington, D.C.: The Heritage Foundation, June 11, 1987).

48. Data from the Sindlinger and Company poll conducted for The Heritage Foundation, *op. cit.*

49. Blance Bernstein, *The Politics of Welfare: The New York City Experience* (Cambridge, Mass.: Abt Books, 1982), 48.

50. This complicated sequence of activities is a result of the restrictions of federal law and regulations. A Food Stamp recipient may be required to participate in a job search program for a period not longer than 8 weeks and for no more than a total of 16 weeks out of a single year. Participation in workfare may continue indefinitely but is subject to limits on the number of hours of required work per month.

51. This proposal would require submission of a waiver to the Secretary of Health and Human Services under section 1115 of the Social Security Act.

52. The exception would be young mothers in a Learnfare program. *See* page 31.

53. This policy would require a section 1115 waiver from the federal Secretary of Health and Human Services.

54. However, as with AFDC-UP Workfare, the controlled experiment will not capture the dissuasive effects of the workfare program on new AFDC enrollments.

55. Again, the exception is Learnfare.

56. *See* Robert Rector and Peter T. Butterfield, "Reforming Welfare: The Promise and Limits of Workfare," *op. cit.,* and Lawrence M. Mead, "Jobs for the Welfare Poor," *Policy Review* 43 (Winter 1988).

57. *See* Karl Zinsmeister, "Brave New World: How Daycare Harms Children," *Policy Review* 44 (Spring 1988): 40-48.

58. *See* Robert Rector, "Fourteen Myths About Families and Child Care," 26 *Harvard Journal on Legislation* 2 (Summer 1989).

59. This policy would require a section 1115 waiver from the federal Secretary of Health and Human Services.

60. This credit, if applied in conjunction with existing federal taxes, would create a relatively high marginal tax rate on families in the $15,000 to $25,000 income range. But the marginal tax rate would not necessarily be high in comparison to existing welfare programs. The credit would be most effective, however, if it were established in conjunction with an increase in the personal exemption for children in the federal income tax code or a similar reduction at the federal level. In that case, the phase-out rates on the wage supplement would not pose any particular difficulty.

61. Of course, it would be feasible to make single parents eligible for the wage supplement as well, although that modification would significantly reduce the positive pro-marriage effects of the program.

62. *Ibid.*, 50.

63. Bonita Brodt, "Inside Chicago's Schools," in *Liberating Schools*, ed. David Boaz (Washington, D.C.: The Cato Institute, 1991), 67.

64. Peter M. Flanigan, "A School System That Works," *Wall Street Journal*, 12 Feb. 1991.

65. Bruce S. Cooper and Robert Sarrel, *Managing for School Efficiency and Effectiveness: It Can Even Be Done in New York City*, 4-7. Paper prepared for the University of Chicago Department of Education, Aug. 1990.

66. John E. Chubb and Terry M. Moe, *Politics, Markets and America's Schools* (Washington, D.C.: The Brookings Institution, 1990), 207-208.

67. Michael Novak, *The New Consensus on Family and Welfare* (Washington, D.C.: American Enterprise Institute, 1987), 34.

68. *See* Clint Bolick, "Choice in Education: Part II - Legal Perils and Legal Opportunities," *Backgrounder* 809 (Washington, D.C.: The Heritage Foundation, 18 Feb. 1991), 8.

69. For mothers with children under age two, it is generally not desirable to separate the mother from the child for more than 20 hours per week. The Learnfare program for these mothers might be modified to require part-time school attendance.

Appendix Table A

The 75 Means-Tested Welfare Programs

MEDICAL AID

1) Medicaid
2) Medical Care for Veterans Without Service-Connected Disability
3) General Assistance (Medical Care Component)
4) Indian Health Services
5) Maternal and Child Health Services Block Grant, Title V of the Social Security Act
6) Community Health Centers
7) Medical Assistance to Refugees and Cuban/Haitian Entrants
8) Migrant Health Centers

CASH AID

9) Aid to Families with Dependent Children
10) Supplemental Sceurity Income
11) Earned Income Tax Credit
12) Pensions for Needy Veterans, their Dependents, and Survivors
13) General Assistance (Nonmedical Care Component)
14) Foster Care
15) Adoption Assistance
16) Emergency Assistance to Needy Families with Children
17) Assistance to Refugees and Cuban/Haitian Entrants (Cash Component)
18) Dependency and Indemnity Compensation and Death Compensation
19) General Assistance to Indians

FOOD AID

20) Food Stamps
21) School Lunch Program (Free and Reduced-Price Segments)
22) Special Supplemental Food Program for Women, Infants and Children
23) Temporary Emergency Food Assistance Program
24) Nutrition Program for the Elderly
25) School Breakfast Program (Free and Reduced-Price Segments)
26) Child Care Food Program
27) Summer Food Service Program for Children

28) Food Distribution Program on Indian Reservations
29) Commodity Supplemental Food Program
30) Special Milk Program (Free Segment)

HOUSING AID

31) Section 8 Lower Income Housing Assistance
32) Low-Rent Public Housing
33) Rural Housing Loans (Section 502)
34) Section 236 Interest Reduction Payments
35) Rural Rental Housing Loans (Section 515)
36) Rural Rental Assistance Payments (Section 521)
37) Section 235 Homeownership Assistance for Low-Income Families
38) Section 101 Rent Supplements
39) Farm Labor Housing Loans (Section 514) and Grants (Section 516)
40) Rural Housing Repair Loans and Grants (Section 504)
41) Indian Housing Improvement Grants
42) Rural Housing Preservation Grants (Section 533)
43) Rural Housing Self-Help Technical Assistance Grants (Section 523) and Rural Housing Site Loans (Sections 523 and 524)

EDUCATION AID

44) Pell Grants
45) Stafford Loans (Formerly Called Guaranteed Student Loans)
46) Headstart
47) College Work-Study Program
48) Supplemental Educational Opportunity Grants
49) Vocational Educational Opportunities, Disadvantaged Activities
50) Chapter 1 Migrant Education Program
51) Perkins Loans
52) Special Programs for Students From Disadvantaged Backgrounds (TRIO Programs)
53) State Student Incentive Program
54) Fellowships for Graduate and Professional Study
55) Migrant High School Equivalency Program
56) Follow Through
57) Health Professions Student Loans and Scholarships
58) Ellender Fellowships
59) Child Development Associate Scholarship Program
60) College Assistance Migrant Program

JOBS AND TRAINING AID

61) Training for Disadvantaged Adults and Youth
62) Summer Youth Employment Program
63) Job Corps
64) Senior Community Service Employment Program
65) Work Incentive Program
66) Foster Grandparents
67) Senior Companions

OTHER SERVICES

68) Social Services Block Grant (Title XX)
69) Community Services Block Grant
70) Legal Services
71) Emergency Food and Shelter Program
72) Social Services for Refugees and Cuban/Haitian Entrants

ENERGY AID

73) Low-Income Home Energy Assistance Program
74) Weatherization Assistance

VARIED AID

75) State Legalization Impact Assistance Group

HEALTH CARE

Edmund F. Haislmaier
Policy Analyst, The Heritage Foundation

Introduction

Few issues generate as much frustration among state policy makers as those related to America's ailing health care system. The frustration stems from the fact that the federal government exercises enormous influence over health care financing, and thus, over the health care delivery system as well. Confronted by a deteriorating system that continues to produce spiralling costs and declining access, state policy makers search for solutions, but often find their hands tied by federal programs, policies and regulations.

The federal government funds health care programs for the elderly, veterans and the poor. Additionally, federal tax policies and federal regulations of employers have a profound effect on health care financing and decision making in the private sector.

In contrast, the impact of state governments on the health care system is largely limited to the licensing and regulation of medical providers and health insurance companies, the ability to alter state laws concerning medical malpractice liability, and the funding and administration of health care programs for the poor and disadvantaged. Even in this last area, the ability of states to make changes is circumscribed by federal regulations governing those programs.

Accounting for over 12 percent of U.S. gross national product, health care is not only one of the biggest sectors of the American economy, it is also one of the sectors most heavily financed and regulated by government. True reforms in the system, and solutions to its problems, will come only when there is less, not more, government involvement.

While state lawmakers can take some steps to improve America's health care system, major reforms to address the underlying causes of soaring health care costs and a growing uninsured population must come at the federal level. With little ability to genuinely reform the present system, the danger is that many state lawmakers are looking to "solutions" that would actually make the present situation worse by imposing sweeping new government controls over the health care system in individual states.

Government Influence On Health Care

Approximately 30 percent of all U.S. health care spending is directly
funded by the federal government, and virtually all of the remainder is
influenced, to varying degrees, by federal policies or regulations. The
federally funded Medicare program pays for most of the health care of
the nation's elderly and is the largest government health program. Indeed,
it is the second largest government program of any kind, eclipsed only by
Social Security. At a cost of $110 billion dollars in 1990, Medicare alone
accounts for 17 percent of all U.S. health care spending. On the average,
30 percent of hospital revenues come from Medicare, and for many rural
hospitals the percentage is even higher. As a result, Medicare's reimbursement policies and regulations have a disproportionate impact on
health care providers and the services they provide to both Medicare and
non-Medicare patients.

The next largest program is the joint federal-state Medicaid program,
which funds health care for the poor and accounted for a total of $70
billion, or 12 percent, of U.S. health care spending in 1990. Medicaid is
not only the nation's second largest health care program, it is also its
largest welfare program. Roughly 55 percent of Medicaid funding is
provided by the federal government with the remainder paid for by the
states. Of all federal health care programs and policies, it is Medicaid that
frustrates governors and state legislators the most. Restricted by Medicaid
regulations and mandates imposed on them by the federal government,
state lawmakers in recent years have found Medicaid consuming an
ever-growing share of state budgets. On the average, Medicaid now
accounts for 15 percent of state budgets, and even higher shares in some
states.

Through the Veterans Department, the federal government also operates
a nationwide network of 172 hospitals, 229 outpatient clinics and 120
nursing homes, at a cost of $11 billion in 1990. It also funds a number
of targeted health care programs either directly, as in the case of the
Indian Health Service, or through block grants to the states, such as the
Maternal and Child Health Block Grant.

In spite of the size and cost of these programs, the federal government's greatest influence over the health care system comes in a much
less obvious area.

For the majority of working Americans and their families, most of their
health care is funded through a system of employer-sponsored health
insurance. It is the federal government's tax policies and regulations
relating to employer-sponsored health insurance which are primarily
responsible for determining the overall structure of America's health care
system.

While money spent on employer-sponsored health insurance is in reality part of employee wages, under federal tax law that money is not counted as income to workers. Thus, through this "tax exclusion" a worker avoids paying any federal or state income or payroll taxes on the portion of his income provided to him in the form of employer-sponsored health insurance.

Obviously, this tax exclusion is of great benefit to workers. Since its inception in the 1940s it has been the driving force in making widespread employer-sponsored insurance the dominant characteristic of the American health care system. Yet while this tax exclusion has served to expand access to health insurance and medical care, it has done so at the price of unintended, and increasingly unjustifiable, costs. Those costs are expressed in terms of an inequitable, inefficient, and increasingly expensive health care financing system.

The inequalities are fairly obvious. The tax exclusion provides greater tax relief to upper-income workers in higher tax brackets—the ones who least need help in paying for health care.

Furthermore, the tax exclusion provides no benefits to workers (and their dependents) whose employment is outside the traditional employment model. The self-employed are ineligible for the tax exclusion and are currently allowed to deduct only 25 percent of the cost of their health insurance.[1] At the same time, the cost or administrative complexity of employer-sponsored insurance often makes it uneconomical for firms to provide those benefits to part-time, temporary or seasonal employees. As a consequence, insurance companies do not offer coverage under group plans for such workers.

While Americans may deduct from their federal income tax money spent directly on health insurance and out-of-pocket medical care, they may only deduct those amounts which exceed 7.5 percent of their gross income, and only if they can itemize their deductions. Furthermore, both this deduction and the partial deduction for the self-employed apply only to income taxes and not to payroll taxes. In contrast, the tax exclusion applies to both.

Thus it is often the case that those who are in greatest need of assistance in buying health insurance and medical care—namely, low-wage workers and their dependents—receive little or no tax relief for those expenses.

Another effect of this combination of federal tax policies is to skew heavily health care purchasing decisions. In practical terms, health care tax relief is provided almost exclusively on the conditions that Americans purchase their medical care through insurance and purchase that insurance through their employers. This severely limits consumer choices and market competition, and generates scores of needless difficulties for workers and their families when they change jobs or suffer periods of unemployment.

It also produces a set of perverse incentives. The substantial tax relief for employer-sponsored insurance, combined with the complete absence of tax relief for purchasing medical care out-of-pocket, encourages over-insurance—that is, obtaining coverage for the more predictable or routine, low cost items which could more efficiently be paid for directly out-of-pocket. This adds disproportionate administrative costs to the system and spurs over-utilization of routine medical services.

On the other hand, to the extent employers limit over-insurance by increasing deductibles or restricting coverage, consumers are encouraged to forgo routine or preventive care not covered by their insurance, because they must pay out-of-pocket expenses with after-tax dollars, even though obtaining such care at an early stage could prevent much larger costs later if an untreated condition eventually became more serious.

Compounding these problems is the fact that employer-sponsored health insurance takes health care dollars out of the hands of consumers and places them in the hands of third parties (insurers), or actually fourth parties (employers who purchase the insurance on their behalf). This system doubly removes consumers from the money used to pay for their health care and dramatically distorts the normal market incentives of both consumers and providers. Consumers are not rewarded with more money in their pockets if they purchase health care wisely. Nor are providers rewarded with more patients, and thus higher incomes, if they offer good quality care at lower prices. Hence providers are encouraged to offer more services and to charge higher prices, while consumers are encouraged to consume more, regardless of cost, since their health benefits appear to be "free."

Even when consumers realize that their benefits aren't really "free," they still must "use them or lose them," since they often cannot choose to take the value of their health insurance in cash. Furthermore, because of federal tax policies, they would suffer a substantial net loss even if they took the cash value of their benefits and bought health insurance on their own.

Not surprisingly, escalating health care costs generated by federal tax policies, combined with inadequate, or non-existent, assistance for low-income families, have produced a growing population of uninsured Americans. These uninsured Americans, over three-quarters of whom are workers or the dependents of workers, have simply been priced out of the system.[2]

While the perverse incentives in health care spending created by federal tax policy are the primary causes of both escalating costs and declining access, it is virtually impossible for state lawmakers to correct them, and thus repair the system's fundamental flaws. Because of the substantial difference in the relative size of federal and state tax burdens, changing state tax policies would provide only marginal incentives and thus have only negligible effects on the behavior of consumers and providers.

In addition, the federal government has taken away from states even the ability to regulate directly employer-sponsored health insurance. A number of federal laws, most notably the Employee Retirement Income Security Act of 1974 (ERISA), give the federal government broad powers over employee benefit plans, and preempt state laws in this area.

For example, under ERISA, states are prohibited from requiring employers to provide health insurance to their workers as a condition of doing business in a state, or from directly imposing on employers any requirements or regulations governing the content or structure of their health benefit plans. While such policies would not be desirable in any event, states are denied even these options.[3]

In practice this means states can only indirectly regulate employer-sponsored health benefits by exercising the power they still retain to regulate health insurance companies and the policies which employers buy from them. But employers can avoid even these regulations by "self-insuring." A "self-insured" firm is one that designs its own benefit plan and pays its own health care bills, instead of purchasing a plan from an insurance company. In effect, self-insured firms act as their own insurance companies, but ERISA prevents states from taxing or regulating them as such.

This division of regulatory responsibility has become more significant for states in recent years as more companies dropped traditional insurance plans and began self-insuring as a way to reduce health care costs. Self-insured companies do not have to pay state insurance premium taxes and can structure their benefit plans as they see fit. In contrast, employers purchasing coverage from an insurance company can only choose from the plan designs which insurers are permitted to sell by state law. This can be a complex and expensive proposition for those firms, since the medical services commercial insurers are required to cover by state law vary significantly from state to state and can have a major impact on the cost of coverage.

As a consequence, the number of self-insured firms increased dramatically in the last fifteen years, until today about half of all workers are employed by firms with a self-insured plan. The remaining workers generally are employed by firms which are too small to assume the risks involved in self-insuring. Those businesses are forced either to pay the significantly higher costs of state-regulated commercial health insurance, or to decline from offering health insurance coverage to their workers.

In the end, federal policies and programs leave state lawmakers with little leverage to positively and effectively address major problems in the health care system. State lawmakers do have the ability to make important and much needed reforms in the regulation of health insurers, in medical malpractice and liability laws, and in providing better health care services to the disadvantaged. But in terms of making positive changes in the underlying policies and dynamics of the health care system, their hands are tied by the federal government.

The only remaining avenues available for lawmakers to change fundamentally the health care financing system at the state level are by pursuing policies which would, in the long run, make the system worse. Unfortunately, out of frustration, misguided zeal or a lack of understanding of the economic consequences, more state lawmakers are turning to embrace harmful "solutions." Chief among those "solutions" are proposals to provide universal health insurance at the state level by forcing employers either to "play-or-pay," or by creating a single, government-funded and -administered state health insurance plan.

Play-Or-Pay: The Wrong Approach

One approach to solving the problem of uninsurance favored by some lawmakers at both the federal and state levels is the idea of forcing employers to provide health insurance through a play-or-pay scheme.

The premise of the play-or-pay approach is that, since the majority (over 80 percent) of American workers and their dependents currently receive health insurance coverage through the workplace, those who now lack health insurance should also receive coverage in the same manner. It is assumed that the absence of universal employer-sponsored coverage is due to negligence on the part of some employers. The conclusion, based on this reasoning, is that those, presumably negligent, employers should be forced either to provide coverage by private means, (i.e., play), or fund the cost of government-administered coverage, (i.e., pay), for uninsured workers and their dependents.

On the surface, this approach appears attractive for several reasons. Federal and state lawmakers view it as an "off-budget" solution to the problem of uninsurance. Requiring employers to pay for health insurance is politically more appealing than raising taxes and creating new government programs to achieve the same end. Of course, a requirement imposed on businesses is really a tax, but it is a hidden tax, and thus less objectionable to most voters. At the same time, imposing an explicit tax on employers who fail to comply with the mandate, and then using the proceeds to buy insurance for the uninsured, can be construed more as a penalty for avoiding the law than as new taxing and spending by the government.

The added attraction for state lawmakers is that the play-or-pay approach allows them to circumvent the restrictions imposed by ERISA. States are prohibited by ERISA from requiring employers to provide insurance as a condition of doing business in a state. The play-or-pay approach effectively achieves the same result, but in an indirect manner.

Finally, some large businesses, with well-paid workers and generous benefit plans, view play-or-pay as a way to lower their own health care costs. Those businesses argue that their costs are unnecessarily high because providers increase charges to their insured workers to cover the cost of providing free or low-priced care to the uninsured. They believe a play-or-pay system would shift those costs back to the employers who do not provide insurance.

While the play-or-pay approach offers appealing simplicity, it would produce undesirable side effects, and its inherent structural flaws prevent it from ever effectively solving the problem of uninsurance.

The premise that the lack of universal employer-sponsored coverage is due to simple negligence or a desire by some employers to freeload off the system is largely wrong. Surveys show that workers consider the presence or absence of employer-provided health insurance to be a major consideration when choosing a job, and that employers feel competitive pressure to offer health insurance as a means of attracting or retaining workers.

The real reason most uninsured Americans lack coverage is simply that they and/or their employers have been priced out of the market. As the costs of health care and health insurance continue to escalate faster than general wages or prices, it is not surprising that more Americans are uninsured. Thus, the effect of a play-or-pay scheme would be to force employers or workers who cannot afford health insurance to buy it anyway, either privately or through the government, with money they cannot spare.

Furthermore, eliminating current health care cost shifting in which the cost of treating the uninsured is added to medical bills paid by the insured is not, contrary to the arguments of some large businesses, a valid reason for adopting a play-or-pay system.

If employers themselves paid for health insurance, there might be some justification to this argument. But they do not—employees pay for health insurance. Employee compensation equals cash wages, plus non-cash fringe benefits, plus payroll taxes paid by employers. Employees with tax-free employer-sponsored health benefits generally earn more than workers without such benefits. Thus, despite the inefficiencies of a system in which those with employer-provided health benefits cross-subsidize those without such benefits, in reality it is a far more progressive "solution" than imposing an added payroll tax on the uninsured, which would cut the cash wages of lower-paid workers.

The play-or-pay approach is also premised on the fallacious assumption that there is no difference between an incentive and a mandate. A targeted tax break, such as the current tax exclusion for employer-provided insurance, encourages people (to the extent they can afford) to obtain the goods or services in question. The size and structure of the tax break will determine how many people are induced to purchase and to what degree. In contrast, people seek to avoid, or limit the effects of, mandates.

Given that the existing incentive of tax relief for employer-provided insurance results in coverage for over 80 percent of the population,[4] the better way to provide coverage to the remaining population is by restructuring or expanding existing tax breaks. Simply mandating coverage will not give those who need it the funds to buy it.

A play-or-pay system will, however, create a perverse incentive for businesses currently providing health insurance to drop coverage for some or all of their workers. This is because the "pay" portion of this approach constitutes a payroll tax on uninsured workers.

Regardless of the size of the tax imposed, it will set in motion an unintended cycle of adverse selection. All businesses whose health benefits are comparable to the government plan, but whose costs exceed the payroll tax, will have an immediate incentive to pay the tax and dump their employees onto the government plan.

Raising or lowering the amount or percentage rate of the tax will only compound problems in one direction or another. The lower the tax, the greater the number of workers who will be dumped onto the public plan. The higher the tax, the fewer workers will be dumped, but those will be the workers who are most expensive to insure. It will never be in the interest of employers to pay the tax for workers who cost less to insure than the amount of the tax.

Thus, at every tax rate the cost of insuring those workers dumped on the government plan will exceed the revenues raised by the tax to fund their insurance, and the new government program will always operate at a deficit.

Regardless of whether employers comply with a play-or-pay system by buying insurance privately or by paying the payroll tax to cover their workers under the new public program, the effect will be the same. Mandating employer-provided benefits, raising the minimum wage or increasing payroll taxes all generate the same results. They artificially increase the cost of labor and thus depress cash wages or reduce employment. Furthermore, the cost of those actions is borne not by employers but by the workers themselves, and the hardest hit are the lowest wage workers—the same ones who are most likely to lack health insurance.

While economists debate the extent of such job losses, there is no question that they will occur under a play-or-pay system. Before enacting such a system, lawmakers should stop to consider the possibility that low-income families might consider a job to be more valuable than a government health plan.

Even worse, a play-or-pay system would give employers a strong, perverse incentive to dump costly workers and their families onto the government program or to avoid hiring workers whose families would be costly to insure. While in theory, anti-discrimination legislation could be enacted to prevent such behavior, in reality, such natural and logical discrimination would be very difficult to stop. Any anti-discrimination legislation would likely result in even more employers dumping their workers onto the public program to avoid potentially costly lawsuits.

Furthermore, if part-time workers are exempted from the play-or-pay mandate, employers will have an incentive to convert full-time positions into part-time positions. On the other hand, if part-time workers are included under the mandate, their jobs will be the first to be abolished.

Play-or-pay also increases costs. By legislating an arbitrary minimum benefit package employers must provide, and an equally arbitrary tax they must pay if they fail to provide those benefits, a state would force firms that have kept their health care costs under the tax level to make up the difference or drop their coverage. Thus the system would punish the firms that have done the best job in controlling costs.

Universal Health Insurance: Another Wrong Approach

Another proposed "solution" is for states to eliminate private health insurance entirely and instead replace it with a government-administered, tax-funded system of universal insurance modeled on one of the nationalized systems found in other countries. The effect would be to create a miniature "national health system" in any state that adopted such a plan.

The currently preferred model for this approach is the Canadian health care system. Under the Canadian system, physicians and hospitals are permitted to practice privately and patients are allowed to seek treatment from any provider. However, the government plan is the sole payer for medical care and covers all citizens. In contrast, under the British system, the government directly owns the hospitals, and most doctors function as salaried employees of the government.

The primary objection to adopting this approach at the state level is that the cost of the program, and the tax burden needed to sustain it, would be enormous. Depending on the state, funding such a system would require increasing the state's total budget by 50 to 100 percent. That would necessitate huge increases in income, payroll or sales taxes—any combination of which would cripple the state's economy, destroying jobs by the tens of thousands and sending businesses and citizens fleeing across the state's borders.

The state would also need to convince the federal government to relinquish control over the massive federal health care subsidies from which its citizens currently benefit. The federal government currently funds 55 percent of the average state Medicaid program. It also pays, through Medicare, for the vast majority of acute care medical treatments for the elderly, and through the federal tax system provides average tax relief of more than 30 percent for all current employer-sponsored insurance plans. In addition, the federal government funds health care for veterans and various public health programs in every state. To be simply no worse off, the new state plan would need to receive the combined value of those federal subsidies in a cash grant from the federal government.

Financing the cost, however, would not be the only problem. The majority of the state's population now covered by employer-sponsored insurance would not only lose their current tax breaks for that insurance, but would also face heavy new taxes to support the new program, presenting supporters with a major political obstacle.

Furthermore, offering health care (or anything) for "free" guarantees that demand will always outstrip supply. To prevent even greater escalation in health care spending, the state would need to impose budget caps on the new program similar to those in nationalized systems abroad. The state would then face the perennial and insoluble problem of reconciling unrestrained demand with restricted supply. The result would be shortages, most likely taking the form of waiting lists for numerous treatments. In the end, the program would be forced to deny the very thing it was designed to achieve—access to medical care.

Compounding these problems would be the misallocation of resources brought about by the inevitable politicization of government health care programs. While this phenomenon occurs in all nationalized systems, it would occur to a much greater extent in the U.S. were such a system adopted at either the federal or state level. Unlike countries with nationalized health care, the U.S. does not have a parliamentary system of government. Not only are the legislative and executive functions separated in the U.S. system, but even within the legislative arena congressmen and state legislators more closely represent the narrow interests of their constituents, have much more power to alter legislation, and are much less subject to party discipline than are their parliamentary colleagues in other countries.

Because of these significant political differences, any universal government health system in the U.S. likely would quickly degenerate into pork barrel politicking and legislative micro-management. In the end, the level of health care received by citizens would vary depending on how politically well connected they were, or according to the influence exercised by their particular state legislators.

A Conservative Philosophy Of Health Care

Ultimately, all debate over health care policy centers on the twin goals of efficiency and equity. Nearly everyone, regardless of ideology, wants a health system that achieves both of those goals. However, most of the present debate and disagreement results from either focusing on one objective at the expense of the other, or from confusing the two different objectives and the means of achieving them. In reality, efficiency and equity are two separate, though equally important goals. This realization should constitute the foundation of any conservative approach to health care reform.

An efficient health care system is one that provides optimum benefits—such as, quality, timeliness, and positive results—at minimum costs. In other words, a system that provides good value for money, both to individuals and to society as a whole.

An equitable health care system is one that provides the same benefits to the disadvantaged—the poor and afflicted—as to the more fortunate.

Conservatives recognize that the present system is neither efficient nor equitable, and so must be reformed. They also realize that, as in other sectors of the economy, freely functioning markets are the best way to generate efficiency in financing and delivering health care. However, free markets will not, in and of themselves produce equity. The poor and those afflicted with unusually chronic or severe illness are unlikely to be able to purchase the medical care they need at market prices with just their own resources.

The challenge for conservatives then, is to design a health care system that obtains the benefits of market driven efficiency while also meeting the needs of the disadvantaged.

Creating Efficiency

Arguments that health care spending can be controlled by government actions, up to and including nationalization of the entire system, are simply assertions that government monopolies are more efficient than free markets. In theory, through economies of scale, the elimination of profits, and reductions in administrative and marketing overhead, monopolies can achieve some initial cost savings. In practice, however, any such savings will be short lived. Over time, all monopolies, including those in health care, become increasingly inefficient due to the lack of competition, producing either rising costs or declining quality and benefit, or both.

True efficiency consists in providing value for money and that can only result from a free market in which consumers exercise the power of choice—something every monopoly prevents.

Only when consumers have strong incentives to seek good value, and when medical providers and health insurers have strong incentives to offer good value, will a more effective, efficient and less costly system result. Value is the relationship between cost and benefit. As such, value is largely subjective—it is in the eye of the beholder. In order for value to be accurately assessed, it is thus necessary that the beneficiary of the good or service in question also be the purchaser.

The current employer-sponsored insurance system divorces the two elements of the cost and benefit equation by, in general, establishing two distinct groups—those who benefit from medical care and insurance protection, and those who pay the costs. For the most part, workers and their dependents have substantial interest in benefit, but little interest in cost. On the other hand, employers have a strong interest in cost, but much less interest in benefit. In order for the market to become more efficient, with prices held in check and brought into line with perceived value, it is necessary to end this existing division.

The way to do this is by having the beneficiaries (i.e., consumers) pay for their own medical care and insurance directly, and not through their employers. Empowering consumers in this manner will in turn force providers to respond to consumer demand by offering good value for money in their products or services. This will hold true not only for those who directly provide medical services, such as doctors and hospitals, but also for those who help finance those services—namely, insurers.

Under the current system, insurers function largely as the agents of employers and not as the agents of beneficiaries. However, with consumers purchasing their health insurance directly, insurers would instead become the agents of beneficiaries and would be forced to respond to their needs and interests. This would bring about a significant change in the behavior of insurers.

For example, whether health insurance is purchased by employers or consumers, insurers have an incentive to restrain costs. But if consumers are paying the cost of their own insurance directly, it is in their interest to seek insurers who restrain costs by acting as the consumers' agents in locating providers who offer better results at lower prices. In contrast, if employers are paying, insurers can restrain costs by the simpler expedients of negotiating relative discounts with selected providers, regardless of the efficacy of their treatments, or by creating non-monetary obstacles to beneficiaries obtaining treatment or receiving payment for claims.

In addition, for managed care (or for that matter, preventive care) to be most effective, it requires the willing and active cooperation of patients. The strongest way to motivate beneficiaries to cooperate is by giving them a financial stake in the outcome of policy decisions. To the extent patients recognize it is in their financial interest—as direct buyers of medical care and insurance—to stay healthy or to minimize the extent and cost of illness, they will seek providers and insurers willing to act as their agents in achieving those goals.

Therefore, the first objective of conservative health care reform must be to create greater efficiency by reestablishing consumers as both the purchasers and beneficiaries of medical care and health insurance—thus giving them the means and incentives to seek the best value, which will, in turn, force providers and insurers to respond to consumer demand by offering good value.

But, for competition to be most effective it is necessary that competition occur not only within discrete segments of the market but also among those different segments. This means that government regulations and tax policies should not be biased in favor of particular methods of delivering or financing health care. For example, government should not provide a huge tax break for purchasing health insurance, but little or no tax relief for purchasing medical care directly out-of-pocket, as it now does. Any tax relief should apply equally to both. Similarly, government should not impose regulations which favor fee-for-service medicine over managed care, or vice versa. Nor should government regulations favor certain providers or treatments over others. There is no single "best" method for delivering or financing medical care in all situations. Different consumers will have different needs and desires, and will find different methods of delivering and financing medical care more or less to their liking.

True competition will also likely reveal that different methods of delivering and financing medical care each have their own strengths and weaknesses. Consumers will be best served by a system which encourages a variety of competing plans and practice patterns, together with normal market incentives for providers to experiment with new ones. A variety of plan designs and market prices will reveal to consumers the relative benefits of different health care financing options, allowing them to more effectively choose the option that best suits their individual needs and preferences. Furthermore, insurers will have the maximum flexibility to adjust their products and prices in response to changes in consumer demand, medical technology and practices, or new information.

Therefore, the second principle of conservative health care reform must be to create a level playing field on which all providers and insurers can compete, by eliminating distortions in the market caused by tax and regulatory policies.

Creating Equity

The greatest conflict and confusion in health policy centers around proposals designed to achieve social equity. Even some liberals may concede the superior efficiency of free markets. But free markets in and of themselves cannot meet demands for social equity. In a free market the poor would likely be unable to afford the medical care they need. Other individuals afflicted, through no fault of their own, unusually with frequent or severe illness, would suffer disproportionate hardship in financing the cost of their own care.

Liberals typically seek to correct for these disparities and achieve social equity, by heavily regulating, or eliminating entirely, the free market. In the process, they lose the efficiency that markets provide.

Conservatives must take a different approach to achieving social equity. The conservative approach should not be to tamper with the normal operation of free markets, but rather to provide the disadvantaged with the extra purchasing power they need to buy into the market on the same terms as the more fortunate majority.

An example of the contrast between these approaches can be seen in how different governments help the poor obtain food. In some socialist countries the government tries to make food affordable to the poor by setting artificially low prices. In the process, they destroy market efficiency and incentives. The results are poor quality goods, waste and shortages, which benefit no one. In contrast, in the U.S. the government leaves the market alone and instead taxes the more affluent to provide the poor with the extra funds they need to buy food at market prices, using a voucher program called Food Stamps.

In the case of health care, efforts to achieve social equity by tampering with the normal operations of markets primarily involve attempts to regulate health insurance prices. All such attempts result from misunderstanding the true nature and limits of health insurance, and from the fallacy of viewing health insurance not as a means of health care financing but rather as an end in itself. This error is common to all those who see the solution to America's health care problems in expanding access to health insurance, whether through employer mandates, the creation of a universal national health insurance system, or regulation of the health insurance industry.

In reality, health insurance is simply one means of financing medical care. In some circumstances it is an economically efficient, and thus superior means. In other circumstances it is an inefficient means, and thus inferior to purchasing medical care directly.

This is true of all forms of insurance. For any type of insurance to be cost efficient to provide or to purchase, two conditions must apply. First, the potential loss must be large enough to warrant the added administrative cost of insurance, as opposed to simply paying out-of-pocket to make good the loss should it occur. Second, the chance of incurring a specified loss must be sufficiently random and unpredictable, as opposed to losses which are certain or highly probable.

In the case of health care, there are wide variations in the risk of incurring many different illnesses and in the costs, of many different medical treatments.

For illnesses that are costly to treat but unpredictable or unlikely to occur, purchasing health insurance is a sensible solution. Through insurance premiums, each individual contributes a small amount to a collective pool against the likelihood that he may someday need the money in that pool to pay for an expensive medical treatment. Such a system is a much more efficient use of resources than each individual setting aside a large share of his resources just in case he needs expensive medical care someday.

But health insurance is not an efficient means of paying for low-cost, routine medical care. There is very little risk involved, since virtually everyone consumes at least some routine medical care on a fairly regular basis. As a result, the added administrative expense of buying routine medical care through insurance will make the eventual total cost greater than if the individual just purchased that care directly when needed. Even if an individual desires to "pre-pay" his routine medical care, there are less costly means of doing so than through traditional health insurance.

Nor is it possible to "insure" against the cost of an existing illness, anymore than it is possible to "insure" the cost of rebuilding a house that is already on fire. If the patient with an existing illness needs help paying his medical bills, or the person whose house is on fire needs help financing repairs, some method other than insurance must be found. Providing assistance in these or similar cases is beyond the natural limits of insurance, since there is no longer an element of risk involved.

Indeed, trying to push health insurance beyond its natural limits creates a whole set of new problems. They include: misallocation of health care resources, over-utilization and over-pricing of services, inefficient cross subsidies, risk avoidance by insurers and adverse selection by consumers.

All these are the result of government policies which regulate or distort the content, structure, or premiums of health insurance. Government regulations on insurers that arbitrarily limit premium increases (rate regulation), force insurers to charge everyone the same or similar premiums (community rating), limit the ability of insurers to charge premiums based on expected risks (underwriting restrictions), or force insurers to accept all applicants (guaranteed issue), all have the same basic effect. They artificially reduce the cost of insurance for some below true market prices, forcing insurers to compensate by raising the cost for others above true market prices. Naturally, those with subsidized benefits have a strong incentive to use them, while those who are being over-charged have a strong incentive to opt out of the system, or if that is not possible, to use their benefits on the theory that since they are forced to pay for them they might as well get their money's worth. Not surprisingly, the result is an escalation in costs across the board.

While such regulations are motivated by a desire to help disadvantaged individuals, they come at the price of destroying the natural efficiency of health insurance as a means of financing some types of medical care. In addition, more often than not they create new inequalities. As any patient on a waiting list for needed medical care in a national health system can attest, access to health insurance does not guarantee access to medical care.

Any private or government health insurance system that funds inexpensive or routine medical care, or charges premiums unrelated to true costs or true risks, will always generate these and other problems.

A natural health insurance market with minimum government regulation can provide an efficient system for financing unpredictable and expensive medical care. What health insurance will never do on its own, and can never be forced to do without loss of efficiency and the creation of new problems, is to achieve the social goal of helping disadvantaged individuals.

If it is to guarantee everyone access to medical care, and relieve the disproportionate burden of health care costs for the most afflicted, government must find other ways to subsidize the cost of medical care and insurance for the disadvantaged. This necessitates first understanding why some people are unable to afford health insurance and medical care. The next step is to then create new mechanisms for providing those low-income or high-risk individuals with the additional funds they need to purchase insurance and medical care in the marketplace as do more affluent or healthy individuals.

These goals can be realistically achieved through the use of mechanisms such as targeted tax credits, vouchers and public assistance programs, structured in any one of numerous variations, without sacrificing the efficiency of true markets in medical care and insurance.

Therefore, the third objective of conservative health care reform must be to achieve social equity, not by tampering with the normal market workings of health insurance, but rather by adopting policies which directly assist needy individuals—giving them sufficient purchasing power to obtain, whether directly or through insurance, the medical care they need at market prices.

What States Can Do

Achieving genuine health care reform that empowers consumers, invigorates market competition to control costs, and provides assistance directly to the needy, ultimately requires a major restructuring of federal tax policies and regulations. However, pending the requisite federal reforms, there are some steps state lawmakers can take to improve the health system. Among the most important are reforms in the regulation of health insurance—a responsibility that is still reserved to the states.

Mandated Health Insurance Benefit Laws

Under pressure from health care providers and advocates seeking coverage for various diseases, states have enacted mandated benefit laws requiring insurers to cover specified medical services or conditions. In 1973 there were only 93 state-mandated benefit laws in the entire country. Today they number close to 1,000.[5] The effect of these laws has been to guarantee markets for the favored health care providers with predictable results: an increase in the use of mandated services by policyholders and an increase in the fees charged by providers of those services.

Understandably, the growing number of mandated benefit laws encouraged employers to avoid these costly regulations by self-insuring. These laws also further discourage small companies from providing health insurance. Since they do not have large enough or predictable enough cash flows to consider self-insurance, they must choose between either increasingly regulated and expensive traditional insurance or no insurance at all.

One of the most important steps states could take to lower health care costs and bring market efficiency to health insurance would be to repeal these laws. However, for the foreseeable future this will likely be politically difficult to accomplish.

Providers who benefit from these mandates will lobby against their repeal. At the same time, many consumers view mandates as a way to force someone else (employers and insurers) to pay for their health care. Hence, they will be unsupportive or even hostile toward repeal efforts. Only when federal tax policies are changed to give consumers equal tax relief for out-of-pocket expenses and for health insurance purchased outside the workplace, will consumers see that it is they who ultimately bear the costs of mandates. When consumers are paying directly for their medical care and insurance, they will have an incentive to support repealing mandates as a way to lower the cost of their insurance.

In spite of these political obstacles, some states have recently taken positive, incremental steps to limit mandated benefit laws. One approach is to enact legislation requiring studies to assess the likely cost of any proposed mandate before it can be considered for adoption by the legislature. A similar and more aggressive approach is to enact legislation authorizing similar studies of the cost of some or all existing mandated benefits. If properly designed and conducted, such studies can provide valuable ammunition to use in defeating new mandates or in repealing existing ones.

Another approach is to legislate an exemption from some or all mandates for insurance provided to small employers (usually those with 25 or fewer workers). Legislation of this type has won passage in several states based on the argument that costly mandates contribute to making health insurance unaffordable for small businesses, thus exacerbating the problem of uninsurance.

Anti-Managed Care Laws

Similarly, states should also repeal so called "anti-managed care" laws. These are laws in some states which restrict the ability of managed care plans, such as Health Maintenance Organizations (HMOs), to contract with a limited number of providers to treat their enrollees, or limit what cost-sharing plans can impose on enrollees who seek treatment from unapproved providers.

Managed care plans use such practices to control health care costs or improve services for beneficiaries. Typically, a managed care plan designates selected doctors and hospitals as the preferred or exclusive providers of services to its enrollees. In return, the selected providers agree to accept the plan's reimbursement rates and any other agreed upon restrictions. The plan then encourages its enrollees to seek treatment from its approved providers by offering full payment for their services but lesser or no reimbursement for treatments obtained from an unapproved provider.

Laws which require plans to reimburse all licensed health professionals or to contract with any provider who accepts the plan's rates, effectively limit the ability of managed care plans to control costs, quality and service delivery through selective contracting. Similarly, laws which restrict the amount of cost-sharing managed care plans can impose on enrollees for obtaining treatment from unapproved providers, limits the ability of plans to steer enrollees toward more cost efficient providers—which is managed care's primary objective.

These laws effectively favor providers seeking to maintain a dominant position in the market. They are no more justified than laws restricting the ability of individuals or businesses to selectively contract for supplies or services provided by vendors in other lines of business, and should be repealed.

Reforming Insurance Practices

The current and common practice of employment-based, experience-rated, optionally-renewable, group health insurance is an anomaly. It is not the way insurers would normally write health insurance in a freely functioning market. Rather, it is the unintended consequence of government policies dating back to the 1930s and 1940s.

The practice of employer-sponsored insurance originated in the wage and price controls of World War II and the federal tax exclusion of non-cash benefits. With millions of men serving in the armed forces during the war, domestic employers faced a tight labor market. But wage controls prevented employers from increasing cash salaries to attract new workers. Employers turned instead to noncash benefits, particularly health benefits, as a backdoor way of offering employees additional compensation. Even though these benefits were really part of workers' wages, the IRS ruled that workers would not be required to pay income or payroll taxes on the money spent to purchase those benefits on their behalf. This, in effect, made employer-sponsored health insurance a huge tax break and very appealing to workers. As a result, the number of company-based plans continued to grow after World War II, even though the initial incentive of wage controls had by then been removed.

The practice of insurers experience-rating employer groups was first developed by commercial insurers to compensate for the market advantages enjoyed by Blue Cross and Blue Shield plans. The Blues derived their market advantage from the regulatory and tax exemptions granted them by state governments during the 1930s in exchange for requirements that they provide community-rated coverage. In the decades that followed, government policies further encouraged and entrenched both these practices.

But, absent these distorting government policies, optionally-renewable, experience-rated health insurance does not generally serve the interests of either insurance companies or their customers.

Not only is the need for medical care largely unpredictable, it is also rarely the clear and immediate result of an individual's behavior—unlike, say, auto accidents. In auto insurance, optionally-renewable, experience-rated coverage is the preferred method of writing policies because it offers powerful deterrents against risky behavior. But in a normal health insurance market, optionally-renewable, experience-rated policies would not provide customers with the protection they seek. Policyholders with major claims would face either cancellation of their insurance or steep, and often unaffordable, premium hikes when they tried to renew coverage. In practical terms, they could obtain affordable health insurance only so long as they remained reasonably healthy and filed little or nothing in claims.

In general, such policies would not benefit insurers either. Individuals who expect to need medical care would have strong incentives to obtain coverage, in the hope of getting an insurer to pick up their anticipated costs. This would force insurers either to suffer large losses or to invest considerable resources in screening applicants. At the same time, healthy individuals would have strong incentives to shop aggressively for the lowest rates and change policies frequently, which would increase the costs to insurers of marketing health insurance. Healthier individuals would also be inclined to go without insurance entirely, since in the end, such policies wouldn't really offer them long-term protection against costly illnesses. In either case, insurers would be unable to rely on premium income from healthy individuals needed to offset claims costs incurred by sick individuals.

The cumulative effect of writing insurance in this manner would be to create a highly uncertain and unstable market for both consumers and insurers. While managed care plans might dampen the effects somewhat, they would still be subject to the same basic dynamics, with much the same results. Not surprisingly, it is precisely this kind of unstable situation that is found today in the small group market. Both policyholders and insurers would be better served by coverage which instead spreads risks not only among a group but also over a longer period of time.

It would be much more in the consumer's interest to buy coverage which is "collectively-renewable." With collectively-renewable insurance, an individual policyholder's premium rate increases would be based on the collective claims experience of a large number of policyholders. The individual experience of a policyholder could never be used to drive rate increases. Furthermore, the insurer could not use an individual's claims experience to cancel his coverage.

As with other types of insurance, groups or individuals insured under the same or similar plans would be aggregated together. These groups, or risk pools, would actually be larger than those of almost any single employer. The consumer could expect to be assessed a risk-adjusted premium based on medical underwriting when he applied for insurance. But he could not be canceled or hit with an exorbitant rate increase if he incurred a major claim in future years. Policies which offered that kind of security would be a better value for consumers to purchase and retain than ones which are experience-rated and optionally-renewable. Furthermore, because such policies offer true insurance protection against expensive but unpredictable future events, healthy individuals would have a natural incentive to buy them.

With this kind of insurance it is likely that policyholders could obtain significant reductions in their premiums only by switching from an inefficient to an efficient carrier, by reducing their level of coverage (i.e., increasing the deductible), or by accepting more restrictions on their coverage, (i.e., converting to a managed care plan). Usually, the last two changes could be accomplished without switching carriers, and thus without the need for new underwriting. Of course, in the same manner, coverage could later be increased, if desired, for an additional premium.

Writing policies on this basis would also be in the interest of insurers. To the extent that they can use these more desirable policies to attract a variety of risks, they would have more stable groups over which to spread claims costs. Because more policyholders, including good risks, would likely renew their coverage for longer periods of time, insurers would avoid much of the underwriting and marketing cost they would otherwise incur in a more volatile market.

This is the kind of coverage which would naturally result in a true, free market for health insurance. It is also exactly the kind of coverage now sold in the current U.S. individual health insurance market, and even insurers who have stopped selling individual policies used to write those policies this way. Indeed, a number of years ago all insurers writing individual policies were forced by consumer demand and competitive pressures to discontinue the practice of writing optionally-renewable experience-rated individual insurance and switch to writing collectively-renewable policies. Furthermore, in the largely unregulated and undistorted British private health insurance market, the provision of collectively-renewable type policies is almost universal practice.

The only way optionally-renewable, experience-rated health insurance works even tolerably well, is by selling it on a group basis to relatively large and stable groups, each containing a reasonably random mix of different risks. This is why it has functioned in the large employer group market, though even there it has caused problems. However, as the size of the group becomes smaller, and/or the group becomes less stable, and/or the risk mix becomes more uniform, optionally-renewable, experience-rated insurance becomes more unpredictable. That is why there are so many problems today in the small employer group market.

It is also why there are problems even with Multiple Employer Trust (MET) plans. A MET combines a number of small businesses into one large group for the purpose of buying optionally-renewable, experience-rated group health insurance. While a MET may have a group that is as large as that of a major firm, a large firm has much greater stability than a MET. This is because business failures and employee turnover rates are always much higher for small businesses (such as those in a MET) than for large corporations.

In recent years various proposals have been advanced for states to make health insurance more affordable to small employer groups by imposing new regulations on health insurers. At their core, all of these reform proposals have some mechanism for limiting the effects of experience-rating. In general, they would do this by imposing floors and ceilings on the rates insurers can charge, often in conjunction with other complex restrictions on the marketing and underwriting practices of insurers.

Given that the intention of these proposed reforms is to limit the effects of experience rating, and given all of the problems generated by experience-rated, optionally-renewable insurance, particularly as group size diminishes, together with the difficulties and uncertainties it imposes on workers, the logical question is why retain such practices at all, even in a modified form?

Evidence shows that in a true free market insurers would be forced by consumer demand and competitive pressure to eliminate optionally-renewable, experience-rated policies, to the benefit of both themselves and their policyholders. While a true free market can be brought into existence only by changes in federal tax policies, states can undertake a vital reform in this area that would pave the way for future federal changes. What state lawmakers can do is simply enact laws eliminating the practice of experience-rating in the small group health insurance market and force insurers instead to write policies on a "collectively-renewable" basis—the same way policies are currently written in the individual health insurance market.

Under a collectively-renewable policy the consumer would have the right to renew without new medical underwriting, could not be hit with large future premium increases based on his own claims experience, and could only be canceled if the insurer takes the extreme, and unlikely, step of canceling all policyholders in the state and ceasing to do business there. The effect of such laws would be to force insurers to do what they would otherwise be forced to do by competitive pressure in a true free market where consumers paid directly for their own health insurance.

States could take an additional, positive step by enacting regulations which would limit the percentage increase in premiums that workers could be charged when they changed employers or shifted between group and individual coverage. The objective of such regulations would be to provide workers with more portable benefits, by limiting the degree of new underwriting when they switched plans.

Guaranteed Loss Ratios

Another reform of state insurance regulations would serve to increase the availability of individual health insurance. In recent years many insurers have left the individual market. In part, this is because current tax policies heavily favor employment-based group insurance, making it by far the bigger and more profitable segment of the market. Those tax subsidies also mean that it is in the financial interest of anyone with individual insurance to switch to employer group insurance whenever possible, even if the group insurance is more expensive. The results are inordinately high turnover, and much higher than normal marketing costs, in the individual insurance sector. But this exodus can also, in part, be blamed on increasingly arbitrary rate regulation of individual health insurance in some states. Several states have moved to remedy this problem by establishing "guaranteed loss ratios" as a mechanism for producing fair and predictable rate regulation for both consumers and insurers.

Under guaranteed loss ratio regulations, before an insurer offered a new type of policy on the market, he would negotiate with the state insurance regulatory authority an agreed upon minimum loss ratio for the policy. A minimum loss ratio stipulates the percentage of premium income that the insurer will pay out in claims on behalf of policyholders. For example, if the agreed upon minimum loss ratio for the policy is, say, 70 percent, the insurer agrees to pay out each year 70 cents in claims for every dollar of premium income, or refund the difference to policyholders. The remaining premium income (30 cents on the dollar, in this example), is retained by the insurer for administrative costs (such a billing, claims processing, agents' commissions and taxes) and profit. If the claims paid in a given year are more than the loss ratio, (say, 80 percent in this example), the insurer would have to absorb the loss for that year. But if the insurer anticipated higher claims costs for the next year as well, he would be able to get automatic approval for a premium rate increase for the coming year. Of course, if the insurer misjudged and its claims costs for the following year fell below the minimum loss ratio, he would have to refund the difference.

Thus, under this system, consumers would be protected because they would, collectively, be guaranteed receipt of a minimum amount of benefits from their policies, or a refund of the difference. At the same time, insurers would be guaranteed the ability, when necessary, to raise rates without costly delays or regulatory hearings. But insurers could not use rate increases in one year to recoup losses in previous years and therefore, would not be guaranteed a profit. Rather, insurers would have a strong incentive to control claims costs and administrative overhead, since any higher than expected claims or unnecessary administrative costs would reduce their profits.

The system could be further adjusted by insurers and regulators negotiating a pre-set series of loss ratios for each of the first several years of a new policy. For example, say, a ratio of 50 percent in the first year, increasing 5 percent each year until it reached 70 percent for the fifth year and thereafter. This would compensate for the fact that administrative and marketing costs for a new policy are initially high but then diminish over the first few years.

To save the state money, insurers could be required to, at their own expense, submit to the state regulatory authority annual audits conducted by an independent, certified outside accounting firm verifying the extent to which the claims paid by the insurer exceeded or fell short of the predetermined loss ratio.

In states with insurance regulation, the guaranteed loss ratio system would be an inexpensive, smoothly functioning system for providing fair treatment to both insurers and their customers.

Medicaid Reform

Besides insurance regulations, another area in which states could undertake positive reforms is in funding health care for the needy. This primarily involves Medicaid, a program for which the federal government still sets the rules. However, during the past ten years the federal government has permitted states some limited flexibility in administering their Medicaid programs.

The federal government requires states to administer their Medicaid programs in accordance with the existing set of numerous and detailed guidelines. To make even modest changes, states are required to petition the federal government for permission, in the form of a waiver, which is then either granted on a temporary or permanent basis, or denied. While designing and applying for waivers is a complicated and lengthy process, waivers do at least give states a limited avenue for reform. It is an avenue which states should aggressively pursue.

During the past decade, most states have used waivers to restructure Medicaid services and eligibility criteria or to introduce payment methods that change the incentives for health care providers.[6] States can now use competitive bidding arrangements to purchase services and medical devices. They also can suspend a physician's participation in Medicaid if his services do not meet recognized standards of care. And beneficiaries found to overuse expensive services may be required to use a specific provider selected for them.

States may also request waivers from federal requirements allowing them to manage their Medicaid programs in a cost effective manner. For instance, states may require beneficiaries to receive their medical care only from specific cost-effective providers and allow beneficiaries to share in savings resulting from their use of more cost-effective care. States also can enroll Medicaid beneficiaries in prepaid plans, such as Health Maintenance Organizations (HMOs), instead of relying solely on generally more expensive fee-for-service arrangements. Local jurisdictions may act as central brokers in helping beneficiaries choose from competing health care plans. Medicaid reimbursement for home- and community-based services is also authorized for beneficiaries who are otherwise eligible for admission to long-term care institutions.

Moving away from the virtually uncontrolled fee-for-service payment structure and toward managed systems of care has allowed states to shop around as purchasers to control costs and improve access to good quality, comprehensive medical services. In recent years, many states, with the cooperation of the U.S. Department of Health and Human Services' Health Care Financing Administration (which oversees Medicaid), have launched health care demonstration projects and alternatives to traditional Medicaid programs. As expected in any trial-and-error process, some projects have cut costs and improved care, while others have failed and been discontinued. All have taught valuable lessons to aid in the redesigning of health care policy for lower-income Americans, and the information that they yield is very useful to states in further refining their programs.

All of the demonstration projects encountered some problems. Besides the usual start-up difficulties, the most serious concern, faced by most of the demonstrations, was inadequate participation by providers. This sometimes resulted in very limited choices for patients, and thus little competitive incentive to keep costs down.

The lack of provider participation has several causes. The main reasons appears to be that states were too optimistic about the immediate savings that could be achieved. Because of this, states tended to set the capitation fees their programs paid to providers at too low a rate. As a result, providers were often reluctant to join a program because they perceived the financial risks as too great. Providers also expressed disinterest in participating in programs with small enrollments, because the potential market was insufficient to warrant the administrative costs. In addition, programs with voluntary participation were generally not successful because both patients and providers lacked strong incentives to participate. Also voluntary programs tended to suffer from adverse selection—that is, enrolling only those patients who anticipated needing substantial medical care. If the state pays providers or HMOs a fixed fee for all patients under a voluntary enrollment program, but only high-cost patients choose to enroll, the providers or HMOs face large financial losses.

Another problem is that these demonstrations are being undertaken in a volatile health services market. Many factors such as other public program reforms (especially changes in Medicare reimbursements), cost-saving initiatives in the private sector, and the growth of various types of alternative health care delivery systems have had an impact on the demonstrations, making accurate assessments very difficult. Program managers thus have been forced to be flexible and willing to modify their programs in order to adapt to constant changes in the market.

As the initial state demonstration programs matured, rate setting emerged as a major concern for program managers. Rate setting lies at the heart of government health care programs for the poor. The rate set for each enrolle determines the bottom line for the state and the health care provider. With rates set too low, providers are discouraged from joining the program, as they are very reluctant to enroll potentially high-cost individuals. With rates set too high, potential savings to the state disappear. Yet determining the ideal rate is very difficult. The pattern in the successful state demonstrations thus has been to start with a relatively simple formula and then modify as needed.

The longer that demonstration programs have been in place, the greater is the attention given to reviewing the use and quality of services. By the second year of their operation, most programs had put in place medical and financial audits and some type of system for monitoring the quality of care given to patients. In addition, improved patient education procedures significantly reduced costly out-of-plan services, such as beneficiaries seeking care for minor illnesses at expensive hospital emergency rooms instead of low-cost outpatient clinics.

In general, most of the programs still in operation, whether on the basis of a demonstration status or a permanent waiver, appear to be successful in offering economical alternatives to the traditional Medicaid program. They provide recipients with quality medical care, and in the cases where cost data is available, exhibit significant cost savings over traditional Medicaid programs.

Ultimately, there is no single, ideal system for financing the health care of the poor. Indeed, the poor do not constitute a uniform group in any state, and thus it is unlikely that they can ever all be adequately helped by a single, uniform health care delivery system. For some, mandatory assignment to a primary care physician or a managed care plan, paid on a capitated basis, may be the best answer. For others, vouchers allowing them to enroll in private plans of their own choice may be a better solution. In some cases, carefully constructed cost-sharing arrangements can help them buy the care they need while discouraging them from seeking unnecessary services.

While state policy makers are understandably frustrated that there is no set solution to the problem of financing health care for the poor, they at least have some ability to try innovative experiments—provided they are willing to invest the necessary time, effort and attention to detail. It is an opportunity they should pursue.

High-Risk Pools

Several states and localities have separate programs to provide medical assistance for low-income individuals who are ineligible for federal income assistance or Medicaid and for high-risk individuals unable to obtain affordable insurance. These programs generally cover basic health care expenses and catastrophic care.[7]

Many of these programs use insurance risk pools. These pools for high-risk individuals provide insurance to those unable to find affordable coverage in the private market because of their poor health status. Under such programs, the health status of the subscriber is eliminated as a barrier to health insurance, since subsidized low-cost insurance is available through the pool. States generally operate the pool by forming an association of all health insurance companies doing business in the state. One insurer normally is selected to administer the plan under specific guidelines for benefits, premiums, and deductibles.

Insurance for high-risk individuals obviously is more expensive than that for standard risks. But in a risk pool, premiums are set at a level affordable by those enrolled in the pool. This means that the enrollees pay less in premiums than the cost of the services that they use. The most common approach to cover the losses incurred by the pool is to require insurance companies to contribute in proportion to their share of the state health insurance market. Some states partly offset this assessment through some form of tax credit against premium taxes or other state taxes.[8] Thus the state taxpayers also make a contribution. Other states pay all the pool's losses directly out of their general funds,[9] while still others tax hospital patient revenues to raise the funds necessary to support operation of the program.[10]

Of all these options, the most desirable one is for a state to fund its risk pool program out of general revenues. Both insurance premium taxes and hospital taxes are insufficient and inequitable. Because ERISA exempts self-insured company plans from state insurance premium taxes, the cost of those taxes is borne exclusively by workers whose firms purchase insurance from traditional insurance companies. They are also the workers and firms who are most likely to have difficulty affording health insurance in the first place. Hospital taxes avoid this ERISA problem and are paid by both patients covered under self-insured plans and those with coverage from traditional insurers. However, hospital taxes are also inequitable since they are taxes on the sick, in particular those with illnesses severe enough to require hospital care. In contrast, funding high risk pools out of general revenues is the most equitable way to spread the cost among all state taxpayers.

As with Medicaid, there is no single, ideal way to structure state high risk pools. Most states now operate them as a single unit, either administering them directly or contracting out the administration to an insurer. However, states could instead fund vouchers for high-risk individuals. The eligibility criteria would be that an individual have annual medical and insurance costs in excess of a set percentage of his income. The state would then provide him with the extra funds he needs to purchase medical care and insurance. For such a system to work, however, it would necessitate that the state first enact the insurance reforms discussed above.

Reforming insurance practices to eliminate experience rating and guarantee renewability would encourage more young healthy individuals to purchase and retain coverage. They would not be dropped or dumped out of the private system when their health status declined. While more accurate risk assessment would initially create a larger group needing government assistance, over time their numbers would decline.

Also, enacting the conversion regulations discussed earlier would, over time, reduce even further the number of people needing government assistance. The effect of those regulations would be to ensure that once an individual entered the private insurance system, he would stay in the system. Because changes in policies or carriers governed by the conversion regulations would occur mainly for non-health reasons, such as changes in employment, no single insurer could be expected to suffer disproportionate rates of adverse selection.

States might also find it cost effective to keep individuals in the private insurance system by helping to pay their premiums if they are temporarily unemployed.

Certificate of Need Laws

State certificate of need (CON) programs regulate capital expenditures on facilities and equipment and expansions of services by hospitals and other health care providers. Only those proposed expansions or capital expenditures which the relevant state authority certifies as "needed" may be undertaken by providers. These programs are primarily the result of the 1974 federal National Health Planning and Resources Act, which required states to establish them as a condition of receiving federal health care funds.

Federal and state CON legislation was based on an unique rationale. Under normal market conditions, when supply exceeds demand, prices drop until equilibrium is restored. Conversely, when demand exceeds supply, the opposite occurs. However, this did not hold true in the health care market, where instead, as supply increased, demand and price increased as well. Thus, policymakers concluded that the health care market didn't function according to the normal laws of economics, and that the only way to restrain demand and prices was by controlling supply through government regulation.

What was missing from this logic was the reason why the health care market seemed to be unlike other markets. It was not due to any natural market failure, but rather to distorted health care reimbursement policies.

Because patients pay little directly for either their medical care or their health insurance, they have every incentive to demand more services and ignore the cost of those services. Unlike other areas, in health care a consumer who obtains fewer services or shops for lower prices doesn't pocket any savings.

Compounding this situation was the fact that those who do pay for health care (governments and private employers and insurers), from the 1940s through the 1970s reimbursed hospitals on a "cost-plus" basis. Under such a system, the more services provided and the higher their cost, the more money a hospital received. Thus, hospitals had a powerful incentive to compete, not by lowering prices, but by adding new facilities and expensive equipment, knowing that they would be fully reimbursed for them, regardless of their actual need or use.

However, beginning in the early 1980s both public and private sector health care payers shifted away from cost-plus reimbursement and toward payment systems based on price competition and utilization review. The present situation is still nowhere near as effective as a normal market system in which consumers pay for their own medical care and health insurance and thus are financially rewarded for pressuring providers to restrain prices, reduce overhead and eliminate unnecessary services. But the change in reimbursement policies by governments and private insurers and employers (acting as surrogate consumers) has been sufficient to eliminate any rationale for the continued existence of CON programs.

Recognizing this, the federal government in 1982 lifted the penalties on states without CON programs, and in 1986 eliminated all federal funding for such programs. The continuation of CON programs is now entirely at the discretion of individual states. One quarter of all states now have no CON programs at all, while in some others they are scheduled to terminate soon. Furthermore, virtually all states which still operate CON programs have, to varying degrees, made them less restrictive in recent years. Those remaining states should take the final step of abolishing their CON programs.

In addition to now being irrelevant, a growing number of studies have found that CON programs also not only don't reduce health care costs but actually increase them. This happens in three ways. First, the regulatory process itself is costly to both health care providers and state governments. Second, while the initial goal of CON programs was to prevent supply from exceeding true demand, in some states CON programs now restrict supply below true demand, resulting in higher costs. For example, a CON induced shortage of nursing home beds may lead to longer stays by some patients in more expensive acute care hospitals. Also in states where CON programs have restricted the number of hospital beds to the point where there is virtually no excess capacity, private and public payers (such as the state Medicaid program) have no leverage to negotiate discounted prices. Offering a hospital more patients in exchange for lower rates doesn't work if the hospital is always full anyway.

Finally, CON programs favor existing providers at the expense of new ones by erecting barriers to market entry. New, more innovative and cost efficient providers are kept out of the market, leaving existing providers in a monopoly position. As with any industry protected from competition, the result is increased prices and diminished sensitivity to consumer desires.

Rather than being a solution to the problem of rising health care costs, CON programs have become one more part of the problem. Repealing them would enhance competition in health care delivery and give payers (including state governments) more leverage to negotiate discounts with providers. States might even further stimulate competition by requiring medical providers to disclose prices or estimates in advance for non-emergency care.

Malpractice Reform

The one remaining area where states could, on their own, significantly improve the U.S. health care system and dampen its soaring costs, is by reforming their medical malpractice liability system. As a result of the explosion in liability litigation and damage awards, doctors today can be faced with annual malpractice insurance premiums in the six-figure range. Obviously, they must pass those costs on to their patients.

The current malpractice crisis imposes other costs as well. An increasing number of physicians, faced with the daunting task of having to raise such sums on top of their other, considerable, practice costs and own income, are simply quitting the practice of medicine entirely or refusing to practice in specialties where they are more likely to face lawsuits. This has created shortages of doctors in certain localities or specialties. In addition, many physicians have adopted "defensive medicine" practices. Defensive medicine is the practice of doctors prescribing additional tests or procedures, not because they are medically necessary, but because the doctor wishes the defense, in court, to be able to say that he did "everything possible" for the patient. These costs are, of course, also passed on to patients.

Ultimately, the issues involved in medical malpractice are beyond the scope of the health care system and involve the whole area of liability law. Consequently, they are the subject of another essay.

Endnotes

1. This provision is not a permanent feature of the tax code, and must be voted on periodically by the Congress.

2. Employee Benefit Research Institute, "A Profile of the Nonelderly Population Without Health Insurance," *Issue Brief* 66 (May 1987). Based on tabulation of the Census Bureau's March 1986 Current Population Survey.

3. Congressional Research Service, Library of Congress, *Health Insurance and the Uninsured: Background Data and Analysis*, 77-86.

4. EBRI, *op. cit.*, Table 2, 3.

5. *Health Benefits Letter*, vol. 1, no. 15, 29 Aug. 1991.

6. American Enterprise Institute Studies in Health Policy, "The Health Policy Agenda: Some Critical Questions" (Washington, D.C., 1985), 38.

7. Alaska, Maine, Minnesota, Rhode Island, Oklahoma and South Dakota have catastrophic health insurance programs that serve primarily near-poor or middle-income residents.

8. Florida, Indiana, Iowa, Maine, Minnesota, Montana, Nebraska, New Mexico, North Dakota, Tennessee and Washington.

9. Ohio.

10. Maine.

REGULATION OF HEALTH INSURANCE BY STATE GOVERNMENTS

Dr. John C. Goodman

President, National Center for Policy Analysis

Increasingly state governments are yielding to special interest pressures and passing laws that relentlessly increase the price of health insurance and the amount of health care spending. States are both mandating that specific benefits be provided and that employers provide health benefits. What is being requiered? And what have the effects been?

Health Insurance Benefits[1] Mandated by State Governments

Mandated health insurance benefits laws require that health insurance contracts cover specific diseases, disabilities and services. In some cases, laws require insurers to offer a benefit as an option for an additional premium. In 1970, there were only 48 mandated health insurance benefit laws in the United States. Yet as Figure 1 shows, in recent years there has been an explosion of such laws, and they now number close to 1,000.[2]

Mandated benefits cover diseases ranging from AIDS to alcoholism and drug abuse. They cover services ranging from acupuncture to *in vitro* fertilization. They cover everything from life-prolonging surgery to purely cosmetic devices, from heart transplants in Georgia to hairpieces in Minnesota. They cover liver transplants in Illinois, marriage counseling in California, pastoral counseling in Vermont and sperm-bank deposits in Massachusetts.

These laws reflect the politicization of health insurance. Special interest lobbies now represent almost every major disease and disability, group of health care providers and type of health care service. As a result, health insurance is being shaped and molded by political pressures, rather than by competition and consumer choice in a free market.

Mandated benefits legislation invariably makes health insurance more expensive. Yet under federal law, companies with self-insured health care plans are exempt from these state regulations, and virtually all large companies and many small and medium-sized ones are now self-insured. Federal employees and Medicare recipients also are exempt. State governments often exempt their own state employees and Medicaid recipients as well. As a result, mandated benefits regulations fall heavily on employees of small firms and on the purchasers of individual and family policies—people who typically lack economic and political power.

Figure 1

Number of Mandated Health Insurance Benefits Enacted by State Governments

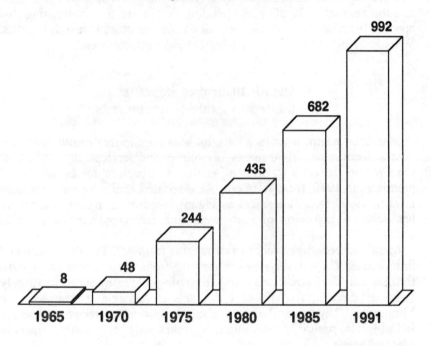

Source: Greg Scandlen, *Health Benefits Letter*

The Alternative to Mandated Benefits

Before looking at specific regulations, let's first consider some alternatives. In many, perhaps most cases, mandated benefit laws merely represent the legislative success of special interests. However, in other cases they address issues that many people care about: preventive care (including mammograms), well-child care, maternity expenses, medical expenses for adopted children, medical expenses for AIDS patients, etc. Legislators often mandate these benefits out of a desire to remove financial barriers to obtaining health care or relieve families of great financial burdens.

Even if the goal is humane and desirable, the method is not. In passing mandated benefit laws, state legislators are attempting to create benefits without paying for them. The cost is then imposed on other people through higher health insurance premiums. When legislators attempt to benefit one group, they raise the cost of insurance for another.

The result is a redistribution of costs and benefits which usually is highly regressive. Those most likely to gain are special groups of middle-income families. Those most likely to be harmed are lower income families who are priced out of the market for health insurance as premiums rise to cover the cost of the new mandates.

A more efficient and humane way to accomplish the same objectives is through direct subsidies, funded by taxes paid by all citizens. State governments, for example, could make direct payments to low-income families with particular health disabilities. The payments could be income-related so that financial help is targeted to those who need it most. Another technique is to subsidize purchases of particular medical services (such as prenatal care), again with the subsidies targeted to low-income families. A third strategy is to directly subsidize the health insurance premiums of people with particular disabilities (such as AIDS), based on their income.

Each of these alternatives allows the health insurance marketplace to continue to function—allowing people options among different types of coverage and allowing premiums to reflect the real cost of the options. Each alternative also requires legislators to pay for the benefits they confer and makes it more likely that the subsidies will go to people who most need them and that the costs will be borne by those who can best afford them.

Apart from more expensive medical services, there is a trend toward state mandates for relatively inexpensive preventive services such as pap smears, mammograms and well-child care. The vast majority of people can pay such expenses out-of-pocket and can include planning for such expenses in a family budget. Legislators are concerned, however, that when family budgets get tight, people will skimp on medical care. Yet, the evidence still suggests that using insurers to pay small medical bills is costly and inefficient. A better solution is to encourage people to establish and use Medisave accounts for small medical bills.

Misguided Attempts to Shift Costs from the Public to the Private Sector

An important principle of insurance is that the insured event must be a risky event—one which has not already occurred. In this sense, pure insurance is a gamble. Yet a number of states require insurers to insure people who are already known to have an illness that will generate future medical costs in excess of the premiums they pay. The result is that all other policyholders must pay higher premiums.

Another important principle of insurance is that individuals must not be able to collect as a result of their intentional behavior. Yet a number of states require that health insurance cover treatment for alcoholism and drug abuse for those who engage in substance abuse at the time the policy is issued.[3] The result is that social drinkers, teetotalers and non-drug users pay higher premiums to cover these costs.

Such regulations are partly the result of lobbying pressures from health care providers and high-risk groups. But they also reflect a desire on the part of state legislators to force the private sector to pay costs that would otherwise be paid for by government.

AIDS. The cost of treating AIDS patients currently runs between $75,000 and $150,000.[4] Since most AIDS patients are unable to pay these costs from their own resources, the cost often is paid by government. In an effort to shift these costs to the private sector, the District of Columbia enacted a law prohibiting insurers in the District from refusing to issue a policy or charging a higher premium to individuals *already* diagnosed as having AIDS.[5] A number of states are moving in this same direction. (See Table 1.) In California, insurers may not test insurance applicants for the presence of AIDS antibodies. Three states (Florida, New Jersey and Wisconsin) prohibit AIDS testing for group insurance and a similar regulation has been proposed in Rhode Island. In 12 states, insurers may not ask applicants if they have ever been tested for AIDS, and similar regulations are being proposed in five other states.[6]

Alcoholism and Drug Abuse. Substance abuse can be even more expensive to treat than AIDS. This is partly because the treatment is prolonged, typically takes place in an expensive facility and requires intensive use of trained personnel. In addition, the patient often must return for further treatment. As in the case of AIDS, the government might have to bear the cost of much of this treatment unless private health insurance pays for it.

TABLE 1

**RESTRICTIONS ON HEALTH INSURANCE
RELATING TO AIDS**
(As of June 1, 1988)

Regulation	States With the Regulation	States Where Regulation Is Proposed
1. HIV testing prohibited for all insurance.	1	0
2. HIV testing prohibited for group insurance.	3	1
3. Insurers may not discriminate on the basis of sexual orientation.	13	4
4. Insurers may not use sexual orientation, occupation, age, sex or marital status to predict whether an individual will develop AIDS.	10	3
5. Insurers may not ask questions about sexual orientation or lifestyle.	13	4
6. Insurers may not ask if the applicant has been tested for HIV or ask the results of such tests.	12	5
7. Insurers may not ask if the applicant has had a blood transfusion.	2	0
8. Insurers may not ask if the applicant has been rejected as a blood donor or been advised not to donate blood.	2	0

Source: Information compiled by Security Life of Denver

Forty states now have regulations governing health insurance for alcoholism. Of these, 29 states make such coverage mandatory and 11 states require that the insurer offer it as an option. Twenty-seven states have regulations governing health insurance for drug addiction. Of these, 19 states make benefits mandatory, and eight require coverage as an option. In some cases, the regulations are ludicrous from the point of view of genuine insurance. For example, in Louisiana, group insurers are required to offer optional coverage for treatment of alcoholism or drug abuse—an option few policyholders would choose unless they intended to file claims. In Connecticut, insurers are required to provide at least 30 days of inpatient care for the "accidental ingestion" of cocaine, marijuana, morphine, amphetamines, barbiturate, hallucinatory drugs and other controlled substances.

Adopted Children. Twenty-five states have regulations mandating coverage for adopted children, usually requiring that adopted children be covered like other dependents. In Minnesota, however, an insurer must cover preexisting conditions. This means that if an adopted child has an expensive-to-treat condition, the insurance company (and therefore other policyholders) must bear the costs. This regulation encourages families to adopt children who might otherwise remain in state institutions at taxpayer expense. Yet while saving money for some Minnesota taxpayers, it raises the cost of health insurance for others.

Special Interest Pressures from Health Care Providers

All health insurance contracts require some specification of who is authorized to diagnose and treat illness. Under traditional contracts, this authority was reserved to licensed MDs. Thus the treatment of mental illness would include psychiatrists, but not psychologists. Diagnosis and treatment of eye diseases would include ophthalmologists, but not optometrists. In general, podiatrists and chiropractors were excluded.

In recent years, however, we have witnessed a flood of regulations designed to open the market for health insurance reimbursement to scores of allied practitioners. Take chiropractors as an example. Currently, 45 states mandate coverage for the services of chiropractors. In general, chiropractors have the right to diagnose and treat diseases (including taking diagnostic x-rays) under standard insurance policies. In Nevada, insurers must reimburse chiropractors at the same rate as physicians performing similar services, even though the chiropractor's fee to uninsured patients may be one-half to one-third less.

These regulations can significantly raise the cost of conventional health insurance. In general, patients of chiropractors tend to be heavy users of services. Chiropractors often will diagnose illnesses that would be dismissed by MDs and prescribe courses of treatment that would not be prescribed by MDs.

As Table 2 shows, chiropractors are not an isolated example. In California, if an insurance policy covers the services of a psychiatrist, it must cover similar services by marriage counselors and child and family counselors. In Alaska and Connecticut, insurers must cover the services of naturopaths. In Nevada, New Mexico and Oregon, insurers must cover acupuncture, and in California acupuncture coverage must be offered as an option. The potential for further mandates covering allied practitioners is almost endless. Currently there are at least 142 health-related professions, with as many as 240 occupational job classifications.[7]

TABLE 2

MANDATED BENEFITS: SELECTED PROVIDERS
(As of July 1991)

Type of Provider	States with Mandates[1]
Optometrists	46
Chiropractors	45
Dentists	40
Podiatrists (Chiropodists)	37
Psychologists	36
Nurse Midwives	24
Other Types of Nurses[2]	23
Social Workers	22
Physical Therapists	16
Psychiatric Nurses	9
Speech/Hearing Therapists	8
Professional Counselors[3]	7
Occupational Therapists	5
Acupuncturists	4
Naturopaths	2

[1]Includes mandated coverage and mandated offerings.
[2]Includes nurses, nurse practitioners and nurse anesthetists.
[3]Includes marriage, family and child counselors.
Source: *Health Benefits Letter*, vol. 1, no. 1, 29 Aug. 1991.

Building Constituencies for Specific Diseases and Disabilities

As in the case of AIDS, legislators frequently face pressure from people who are afflicted with a particular disease or disability or at risk of affliction. In terms of the number of regulations, it would appear that

TABLE 3
MANDATED BENEFITS: SELECTED SERVICES
(As of July 1991)

Type of Service	States with Mandates[1]
Alcoholism Treatment	40
Mammography Screening	39
Mental Health Care	29
Drug Abuse Treatment	27
Maternity	25
Home Health Care	20
Well-Child Care	12
TMJ Disorders	12
Ambulatory Surgery	12
Breast Reconstruction	11
Pap Tests	8
In Vitro Fertilization	7
Cleft Palate	7
Hospice Care	7
Diabetic Education	5
Rehabilitation Services	5
Second Surgical Opinions	5
Long Term Care	3
Prescription Drugs	3

[1]Includes mandated coverage and mandated offerings.
Source: *Health Benefits Letter*, vol. 1, no. 15, 29 Aug. 1991.

the blind have the most effective special-interest lobby. Beyond blindness, constituencies extend from pregnant women exposed to cancer-causing substances to individuals concerned with virtually every form of mental illness. The following are some examples.

DES Mothers. In the 1950s and 1960s, a number of pregnant women took the drug diethylstilbestrol (DES) to control morning sickness. Subsequently it was discovered that DES exposure could cause cervical and uterine cancer in the daughters of these women. At least six states limit the ability of insurers to act on this knowledge. For example, in

California an insurer may not charge higher premiums or refuse to cover an individual either because the person has conditions attributable to DES or has been exposed to DES.

Sickle-Cell and Other Genetic Traits. Some individuals carry a genetic trait which does not affect the health of the carrier but may produce a disease or disability in the person's offspring. Examples are the sickle-cell trait (found almost exclusively in black men) and Tay-Sachs disease (almost exclusively affecting persons of Jewish descent). When an applicant is known to have such a genetic trait, many states restrict insurers from acting on this knowledge. For example, at least six states regulate the sale of insurance to individuals who have sickle-cell trait. In California, Florida and North Carolina, insurers may not deny coverage or charge a higher premium based on the likelihood that the trait may affect an individual's offspring. In North Carolina, the same restriction is extended to individuals with hemoglobin C trait. In California, the restriction applies to all genetic traits.

Physical and Mental Handicaps. Most states regulate the sale of health insurance to the handicapped or disabled. For example, at least 34 states have regulations covering all physical handicaps or all general handicaps and disabilities, at least 29 have regulations specifically covering mental disabilities, and at least 35 have regulations specifically covering blindness or partial blindness.

In general, these regulations inhibit insurance companies from selling policies for actuarially fair prices. As a result, the cost of insurance is higher for all other policyholders. In many states, insurers cannot refuse to cover the handicapped, but may charge higher rates based on actuarial experience. In North Carolina, insurers have flexibility with respect to handicapped adults but must cover handicapped minors at the same rates as other children.[8]

When insurers are allowed to charge higher premiums to handicapped persons, the insurance company usually bears the burden and expense of proving that the rate differentials are justified. For example, in Missouri, insurance regulators assume no differential risk among classes of people unless the insurers can produce statistical evidence. In Minnesota, insurers may not charge higher premiums unless they can prove significant differences in health care costs for people who have those disabilities.

On the surface, it might seem fair to ask that differential premiums be related to differential costs of insurance. Yet the burden of proof may be too costly or even impossible for insurers to bear. For example, in Louisiana, insurers must cover individuals with spinal cord injuries, amputations, autism, epilepsy, mental retardation and any other neurological impairment. A higher premium may be charged only if insurers can justify it on the basis of actuarial experience. In many cases, however, the disability is so rare that no actuarial tables exist.

As a result of these restrictions, the premiums charged are less fair than they would otherwise be. Handicapped policyholders often are undercharged, and all other policyholders are overcharged to make up the difference.

Misguided Attempts at Cost Control

A number of mandated benefits regulations are designed to encourage substitution of outpatient for inpatient surgery and of home care for hospital care, second and even third opinions prior to surgery, and certain types of preventive medical care. Although these regulations may have been encouraged by provider groups, some also appear to have been influenced by the desire to reduce health care costs. In all cases, the regulations are misguided attempts to substitute political judgment for personal choice.

Outpatient Care. Twelve states require insurers to cover outpatient care as an alternative to inpatient care, and six of these states require that the benefits be identical. Surgery performed in an independent outpatient clinic usually costs less. Yet hospitals are setting up their own outpatient services and the costs of these services may be higher than inpatient care.

Home Health Care. At least 20 states have regulations governing home health care. In 14 of these, coverage is mandatory and in six others, it must be offered as an option. New Jersey, for example, requires coverage in the home for anything that would have been covered in a hospital on the same reimbursement basis. Yet because it often consumes more services over a longer period, home care can cost more.

Second Opinions on Surgery. Five states require insurers to cover a second opinion prior to surgery, and Rhode Island requires coverage for a third opinion if the first two physicians disagree. Yet the experience of large corporations has been that blanket policies requiring second opinions save very little money. Second opinions are costly, and for many procedures the cost may be greater than the benefit.[9]

Preventive Medical Care. Eight states require coverage for Pap smears and 39 states mandate coverage for mammograms. Florida has mandated coverage for a specific number of physician visits for children at different ages, with a requirement that the insured not be charged any deductible in connection with the visit, and similar legislation is being considered by other states. The American Academy of Pediatrics is lobbying for 12 mandated well-child physician's visits for children from birth through age six, implying that this investment in preventive medicine will save Americans money.

The evidence says otherwise. On the basis of cost-benefit analysis, it is hard to justify *any* well-child physician's benefits.[10] This type of preventive medicine may have important benefits for parents (relief of anxiety, reassurance, etc.), but it is not necessarily a wise way to spend scarce health care dollars. Even where preventive care can be cost-justified, paying for it through third-party insurers is almost always wasteful.

Case Study: Maternity and Childbirth

No issue illustrates the pressures on state legislators better than pregnancy and childbirth—in terms both of the emotional impact and of the influence of medical providers and their potential patients. Every state has some regulation governing health insurance for newborns, and at least 45 states require that newborn care be included both in individual and group policies.[11] It's not hard to understand why. In 1986, the Sheraton Corporation spent $1.2 million (about 10 percent of its total health care costs) on three premature babies born to company employees. In 1984, Sunbeam Appliance Co. spent $500,000 (half of its entire employee health care costs) on four premature babies. That same year Ameritrust Corporation spent $1.4 million on one premature baby.[12]

Clearly, having a child is a risky and potentially costly event. Yet many state regulations force health insurers to ignore that fact. For example, Arizona requires that a policy covering an insured person's dependents must also cover newborns, including premature babies and those with congenital abnormalities, with no increase in premium. In Montana, coverage for a newborn is mandated even if other dependent children are not covered. In Minnesota and Ohio, a policy covering a dependent's daughter must also cover a newborn child of the (unwed) daughter. Since newborns are more expensive to insure than older children, the costs of these mandated benefits must be borne by other policyholders—including single men and childless women.

At least half the states also have regulations covering the costs of maternity and complications of pregnancy. At least 15 states prohibit discrimination on the basis of marital status—despite the fact that unwed mothers have a higher incidence of complications of pregnancy. For example, in Colorado and New Jersey, single and divorced women must receive the same coverage on the same terms as married women.

Nor is that all. Even if pregnancy is viewed as a risky and unplanned event, surely the same cannot be said for *in vitro* fertilization. Yet, five states—Arkansas, Hawaii, Maryland, Massachusetts and Rhode Island—mandate benefits for *in vitro* fertilization, and in Connecticut and Texas it must be offered as an option. Moreover, because the procedure can cause multiple conceptions, leading to multiple abortions or multiple births, and because unsuccessful couples may repeat the procedure an almost endless number of times, the resulting health care expenses can be quite high.[13]

Other Types of Mandated Benefits

In addition to the medical benefits described above, a number of states regulate the terms and conditions on which policies may be sold. For example, some mandate that a policy must be "guaranteed renewable" for a certain period of time. This means that an insurer cannot stop covering a group of people, regardless of actuarial experience. Some also mandate that Medicare supplemental policies must be "guaranteed issued." This means that the insurer cannot refuse to sell the policy, regardless of the applicant's health. In some cases, states refuse to allow coordination of insurance claims among companies covering the same individual. This means that an individual with coverage by more than one insurer can collect full benefits under each policy and "profit" from being sick.

As with other types of mandated benefits, little is known about how much any single type of regulation adds to the rising cost of health insurance. However, Golden Rule Insurance Company has estimated how some regulations have increased the average policy premium in some states. Because Texas mandated that major medical plans must be guaranteed renewable for the first five years, Golden Rule's premiums in the state were increased by 15 percent. Because Georgia does not allow claims to be coordinated among insurance carriers, Golden Rule policies in that state are 15 percent higher than they otherwise would be. Maryland's requirement that Medigap policies be guaranteed renewable adds 13 percent to premium prices. Michigan's requirement that Medigap policies be guaranteed renewable and guaranteed issued adds 30 percent. Because of unisex legislation prohibiting differential premiums for men and women in Montana, Golden Rule no longer markets insurance in the state.[14]

Guaranteed renewable is not a bad feature of health insurance policies—especially if people are willing to voluntarily pay a higher price to obtain it. When health insurance more closely resembled real insurance rather than prepayment for the consumption of medical care, guaranteed renewable was a common feature of policies sold in a competitive insurance market. Guaranteed issue is not a normal or natural consequence of a competitive insurance marketplace, however. Its adverse consequences will be discussed more fully below.

Price Regulation, Insurance Company Profits and High-Risk Individuals

As Lloyd's of London has shown us, almost any risky event is insurable for a price. Lloyd's not only insures communications satellites headed for upper earth orbit, it also has insured Bruce Springsteen's voice and the beards (against fire or theft) of 40 members of the Whiskers Club in Derbyshire, England. When Cutty Sark offered $2 million to anyone who could capture the Loch Ness monster alive, Lloyd's insured Cutty Sark against having to honor its promise. Prior to and during Operation Desert Storm, Lloyd's wrote coverage for vessels in or near the conflict. In fact, it opened its doors on Sunday for the first time in its 303-year history to accommodate new customers as hostilities broke out.

If Lloyd's of London can insure endangered ships, men's whiskers and promotional stakes, why can't many Americans buy health insurance? One answer is that in almost every state, health insurance premium prices are regulated.

Since health insurance costs are continually rising, such regulation usually consists of a restriction on how much premium prices may increase to cover those costs. In most states, insurance companies may not increase premium prices unless benefits paid are at least equal to a certain percentage of premium income. In all cases, regulation of premium prices translates into regulation of insurance company profits. Without sufficient annual profits, the companies cannot build reserves to cover costs that are unusual enough to occur once in every five, ten or 20 years. This type of regulation, in turn, can make it virtually impossible for individuals with a higher-than-average probability of illness to obtain health insurance.

Risk and Profit. A basic principle governing all financial markets is: The higher the risk, the higher the rate of return. For example, to induce investors to purchase riskier financial assets (stocks, bonds, etc.), the sellers must convince the buyers they can earn more than on less risky assets. If we made it illegal to earn more than, say, a 10 percent return in the bond market, investors would be unwilling to purchase bonds from any but the most financially sound corporations. If we made it illegal to earn more than 8 percent on bonds, investors might be willing to purchase only government securities.

A similar principle applies to the market for health insurance: When insurers sell policies to high-risk individuals, they take on more financial risk. Other things equal, the more high-risk policyholders an insurer has, the more risky the total portfolio. Insurers voluntarily accept additional risk only if they can earn a higher return. When state governments limit the rate of return, the inevitable result is that higher risk individuals are unable to obtain health insurance at any price. One way to think of many mandated benefits laws is to see them as an attempt by state governments to force insurers to sell policies to individuals who have been regulated out of the market by state insurance regulators.

Such attempts are destined for failure. When state governments force insurers to take on additional risk and forbid them to earn a higher rate of return, insurers simply quit selling policies in the state. For example, primarily because of the regulation of premium prices, in September 1988, Golden Rule Insurance Company ceased marketing its policies in seven states: Alabama, Georgia, Massachusetts, Mississippi, North Carolina, New Mexico and West Virginia.[15]

The Creation of Risk Pools. One way in which state governments have attempted to provide health insurance for high-risk individuals is through risk pools. These are mandated benefits in the sense that, usually, all insurers operating in the state are forced to participate in the pool.

Currently, 15 states have risk pools, and 22 others are considering similar legislation.[16] Under this arrangement, insurance is sold to individuals who cannot obtain policies outside the pool. Premium prices are regulated, and generally are set as a percentage of the prices of similar policies sold in the marketplace. For example, in most states, the premium for risk pool insurance is 50 percent higher than for comparable policies.[17] In Florida, however, risk pool premiums may be twice as high, and in Montana they may be four times as high. In Minnesota, the most generous state, risk pool insurance is only 25 percent more expensive.

Since all states cap the price of risk pool insurance, risk pools almost always lose money.[18] In most cases, losses are covered by assessing insurers—usually in proportion to their share of the market. However, in Maine, losses are covered by a tax on hospital revenues, and in Illinois, by general tax revenues. In most states that assess insurers for risk pool losses, companies are allowed to fully or partially offset their assessment against premium taxes paid to state governments.[19]

Problems with Risk Pools. The most serious problem with risk pools is that they raise the cost of health care and/or health insurance for everyone not in the pool. When risk pool losses are paid by a tax on hospital revenues, the burden is placed on sick people. When losses are covered by assessing insurers, the burden is placed on other policyholders. And when insurers are allowed to offset their assessments against state taxes, additional pressure to maintain (or even increase) taxes on insurance premiums is created and causes further distortion in the health insurance marketplace.

Some Consequences of Mandated Benefits by State Governments

The flood of mandated benefits legislation at the state level has had two major consequences: (1) all those who can opt out of regulated health insurance and purchase nonregulated insurance tend to do so and (2) among those who cannot obtain unregulated insurance, an increasing number have no insurance at all.

Ironically, those without insurance tend to represent both extremes on the spectrum of the potentially ill. Those who are very healthy and have a low probability of becoming ill choose to remain uninsured because the price of regulated insurance is too high. At the other extreme, those who have a high probability of becoming ill are uninsured because insurers go to considerable lengths to avoid them.

The Escape from Regulation by Large and Medium-Sized Firms. On January 1, 1988, the Circle K Corporation, the nation's second largest convenience store chain, sent an interesting letter to its 8,000 employees. The letter announced that the company would no longer provide health care coverage for certain "life style-related" illnesses, including alcohol and drug abuse, self-inflicted wounds and AIDS (unless acquired accidentally through a blood transfusion).[20] Since the Circle K Corporation operates in 27 states, it undoubtedly operates in states where health insurance benefits for the excluded diseases are required by state law. Yet because the company does not purchase insurance, federal law exempts it from state regulations mandating health insurance benefits.[21]

The Circle K Corporation is not alone. Just as there has been an explosion of mandated benefits legislation over the last decade, there has been an equally dramatic increase in the number of companies that self-insure and manage their own employee health care plans.[22] Today, roughly 50 percent of all employees work for an employer who is self-insured.

One reason for self-insurance is that companies are better able to manage their own health care plans and hold down rising costs. Another is that self-insured companies avoid state taxes on insurance premiums and other costly and inefficient regulations. Yet the most important reason may be that self-insured companies bypass the regulations and costs of mandated health insurance benefits.[23] In other words, employers who self-insure are free to tailor that insurance to the wants and needs of their employees. They are doing what any sensible consumer would do, were it not for government interference.

When companies self-insure, they usually institute cost management techniques that are at odds with the direction of state health insurance regulations. For example, while the trend in regulation has been to increase the number and types of services required under conventional health insurance, the tendency among self-insured companies has been to restrict and limit employee choices—to certain physicians, hospitals and types of care.[24]

With few exceptions, mandated health care benefits legislation raises the cost of conventional health insurance. Moreover, as more and more companies self-insure, the burden and costs of these regulations are being imposed on a smaller and smaller proportion of insured individuals. In some states, it is believed that as much as 75 percent of the workforce is covered by self-insured plans. This means that the full burden of mandated benefits regulation falls on the remaining 25 percent.[25]

In an effort to determine how state health insurance regulations affect the decision of firms to self-insure, health economists Jon Gabel and Gail Jensen looked at a sample of 280 firms that were not self-insured in 1981. By 1984, 24 percent chose self-insurance. Using a model that correctly predicted a firm's decision to self-insure 86 percent of the time, they found that increasing the state premium tax from 1 percent to 3 percent increased the probability of self-insuring from 20 percent to 24 percent. Imposing a risk pool and mandating continuation of coverage increased the probability by 55.8 percent and 165.6 percent, respectively.[26]

The Gabel and Jensen study found that mandates for psychologists raised the probability of self-insuring (by 93.2 percent,) as did mandates for alcohol treatment (5.9 percent) and drug dependency (58.8 percent) although the latter two mandates were not statistically significant. The impact of all state regulations taken together caused half the firms which self-insure to make that decision.[27]

Escape from Health Insurance by Small Firms. As noted earlier, all federal employees and all people covered under Medicare also are exempted from state mandated benefits by federal law, and states commonly exempt their own employees and all Medicaid patients. The upshot is that the burdens and costs of mandated health care benefits fall on the rest of the population: people who work for small firms, the self-employed and the unemployed.

As a result, an increasing number of small firms are discontinuing their health insurance plans for employees or choosing not to offer health insurance in the first place. Gabel and Jensen found that each new mandate lowered the probability that a small firm would offer health insurance by 1.5 percent. Raising premium taxes from 1 percent to 3 percent or imposing a risk pool lowered the likelihood of a small firm offering health insurance by at least 10 percent and continuation of coverage mandates lowered the likelihood by 13 percent. In the absence of all these regulations, 16 percent of small firms that do not now offer health insurance would do so.[28]

Higher Premiums for All Insured People. Mandated benefits legislation raises the cost of regulated health insurance in a variety of ways. As we have seen, some regulations force insurers to pay for the health care of people who are already sick (e.g., AIDS victims); other regulations force insurers to cover procedures related to people's choices (e.g., *in vitro* fertilization, and marriage and family counseling) rather than to well-defined, risky events; and many regulations expand the definition of illness and the cost of treatment by expanding the range of covered providers (e.g., to acupuncturists and naturopaths).

Consider coverage for the services of chiropractors. A study by Peat Marwick Main & Co. found that, under Hawaii's current practice of not mandating coverage for chiropractic services, there was no evidence that lack of chiropractic coverage resulted in inadequate care or financial hardship for people using those services. On the other hand, were Hawaii to mandate coverage, the total cost of the mandated benefit would be as high as $8.1 million.[29] (See Table 4).

In a separate study, Peat Marwick found no evidence that lack of coverage for well-baby care resulted in inadequate care or financial hardship. Yet mandating coverage for well-baby care in Hawaii would increase health insurance costs by as much as $1.7 million.[30] Researchers also found only anecdotal evidence that lack of coverage for alcoholism and drug dependence resulted in lack of treatment. Yet the cost of mandating coverage for alcoholism and drug abuse in Hawaii would be as much as $2.3 million.[31] The cost of mandating coverage for inpatient mental health care in Hawaii was estimated to be as high as $12.3 million, and for outpatient treatment of mental illness, as high as $6.8 million.[32]

Further evidence of the costs of specific mandates has recently been gathered by Gail Jensen at the Wayne State University and Michael Morrisey at the University of Alabama at Birmingham. The Jensen-Morrisey study attempted to estimate the effect on premiums of various insurance policy provisions, whether or not they are mandated.

The results of this study are presented in Table 5. As the table shows, second surgical opinions and home health care costs appear to have no individual statistically significant effect on premium prices of the primary insured, but second surgical opinions, in combination with other mandates, may cause premium prices for dependents to be higher than otherwise. Coverage for substance abuse is very costly—increasing premium prices by 6 to 8 percent. Coverage for outpatient mental health care is even more expensive—increasing premium prices by 10 to 13 percent. Psychiatric hospital care apparently has little effect on premium prices for employees. But if dependents are covered, premium prices can rise by as much as 21 percent.

TABLE 4

THE COST OF PROPOSED
MANDATED BENEFITS IN HAWAII

Benefit	Low Estimate	Middle Estimate	High Estimate
Chiropractic Services[1]	$2,734,000	$6,245,000	$8,089,000
Well-Baby Care[2]	1,267,750	1,521,280	1,774,810
Alcohol and Drug Abuse[3]	284,088	414,048	2,305,308
Inpatient Mental Health Care[4]	948,175	2,657,315	12,325,305
Outpatient Mental Health Care[5]	892,164	3,556,098	6,815,627
Total	$6,126,177	$14,393,741	$31,310,050

Note: These estimates would be considerably higher were it not for the fact that many Hawaiian insurance policies already have full or partial coverage for the benefits.

[1]Peat Marwick Main & Co. and the Office of the Legislative Auditor, *Study of Proposed Mandatory Health Insurance for Chiropractic Services: A Report to the Governor and the Legislature of the State of Hawaii*, Jan. 1988, Table 4.2, p. 46.

[2]Peat Marwick Main & Co. and the Office of the Legislative Auditor, *Study of Proposed Mandatory Health Insurance for Well-Baby Services: A Report to the Governor and the Legislature of the State of Hawaii*, Jan. 1988, Table 4.5, p. 45.

[3]3Peat Marwick Main & Co. and the Office of the Legislative Auditor, *Study of Proposed Mandatory Health Insurance for Alcohol and Drug Dependence and Mental Illness Services: A Report to the Governor and the Legislature of the State of Hawaii*, Jan. 1988, Appendix A, p. 108.

[4]*Study of Proposed Mandatory Health Insurance for Alcohol and Drug Dependence and Mental Illness Services*, Appendix B, p. 111.

[5]*Study of Proposed Mandatory Health Insurance for Alcohol and Drug Dependence and Mental Illness Services*, Appendix C, p. 114.

Another interesting finding of the Jensen-Morrisey study is that self-insurance raises insurance costs by as much as 19 percent, possibly because many companies are not skilled at operating their own health insurance programs. The additional cost may be worth it, however, if the firm saves a significant amount of money by avoiding state-mandated benefits.

Excessive Premiums for Low-Risk Individuals. A basic principle governing the health insurance marketplace is that, in any given year, a

TABLE 5

EFFECTS ON INSURANCE PREMIUMS
OF SPECIFIC HEALTH INSURANCE BENEFITS

Feature	Change in Individual Premium	Change in Dependents' Premium
Front-End Cost Sharing[1]	- 7.6 %	- 11.4 %
Second Surgical Opinion	+ 5.0 %*	+ 7.7 %
Home Health Care	+ 0.1 %*	- 5.0 %*
Extended Care	- 0.4 %*	- 5.1 %*
Substance Abuse Treatment	+ 7.9 %	+ 6.2 %
Psychiatric Hospital Care	- 1.7 %*	+ 20.8 %
Psychologists Visits	+ 10.4 %	+ 12.6 %
Routine Dental Care	+ 23.8 %	+ 11.8 %
Self-Insurance[2]	+ 19.0 %	+ 8.7 %
Commercial Insurance[2]	+ 8.6 %	+ 5.0 %*
1 or 2 HMOs[3]	+ 5.2 %	+ 6.0 %
3 HMOs[3]	+18.4 %	+5.6 %*

* = not statistically significant
[1]Presence of a deductible
[2]Relative to Blue Cross premiums
[3]Employee options
   Source: Gail A. Jensen (Wayne State University) and Michael A. Morrisey (University of Alabama at Birmingham), "The Premium Consequences of Group Health Insurance Provisions," Sept. 1988, mimeograph.

small percentage of people will generate a majority of the health care costs. For example, a survey of employers by Johnson and Higgins found that about one percent of all employees account for 22 percent of company health care costs, and about 5.6 percent account for 50 percent of the costs.[33]

The experience of employers undoubtedly reflects the experience of the health insurance market as a whole. Accordingly, a major objective of health insurers is to expand coverage for the vast majority who will generate few claims or small claims and avoid those likely to generate large claims. One purpose of mandated benefits legislation, as we have shown, is to try to force insurers to cover the high-risk population.

To the extent that the regulators are successful, insurers cover more and more high-risk individuals and attempt to pay for this coverage by overcharging the low-risk population. As average premiums rise, health insurance becomes less and less attractive to people who are at low risk and fewer of them buy insurance. As a result, a vicious cycle occurs: As fewer low-risk people buy insurance, the pool of the insured becomes increasingly risky—leading to higher premiums and even fewer low-risk people choosing to insure.

The Impossibility of Obtaining No-Frills Catastrophic Health Insurance Tailored to Individual and Family Needs. Another factor which encourages people (especially low-risk people) not to insure is that mandated benefits legislation prevents them from buying insurance tailored to their needs. In some states, couples who cannot have children cannot buy policies that do not provide coverage for newborn infants. Moderate drinkers and people who abstain from using drugs cannot buy policies that do not cover alcoholism and drug abuse. People who do not intend to see chiropractors, psychologists or marriage counselors cannot buy policies that exclude such coverage. As a result, people cannot buy insurance for a price which reasonably reflects their wants and needs.

The Lack of Availability of Health Insurance for High-Risk Individuals. An unintended consequence of mandated benefits legislation is that it probably makes it more difficult for higher risk individuals to obtain insurance. When insurers are prevented from charging a premium that reflects the risk they incur they will not insure. As low-risk individuals drop out of the market, insurers face even more pressure to avoid high-risk policyholders. At the extreme, as we have seen, insurers can refuse to sell any insurance within a state.

The Growing Number of Uninsured Individuals. From World War II until the mid-1970s, the percentage of the population covered by private health insurance grew steadily. For example, the percentage of the population covered by private health insurance for hospital care grew from 69 percent in 1960 to 83 percent in 1978, while the percentage covered for physician care grew from 46 percent in 1960 to 78 percent in 1974.[34] Since the mid-1970s, however, this trend has been reversed. Specifically, the percentage of people with private hospital insurance fell from a peak of 83 percent to 79 percent by 1984. The percentage of people with private physician insurance fell from a peak of 78 percent to 73 percent by 1984.[35]

As noted earlier this book, different studies arrive at different estimates of the number of people without any health insurance. One study, using the same methodology for different years, concluded that the number of people without health insurance rose from 24.5 million (11.1 percent of the population) in 1980 to 33.3 million (13.5 percent of the population) in 1990.[36]

Why is this growth occurring? One reason may be tax reform.[37] Another may be a shift in employment from manufacturing to services and the retail trades.[38] But it's hard to escape the conclusion that an increasing number of consumers are being regulated and priced out of the market for health insurance.

To What Extent Are Mandated Benefits Causing People to Be Uninsured?

An econometric model of the health insurance marketplace has been developed by John Goodman and Gerald Musgrave of the National Center for Policy Analysis.[39] This is believed to be the first model that produces statistical estimates of the factors causing people to be without health insurance. Although certain information about the market for health insurance is not available to researchers, the model nonetheless explains 94 percent of the variation in the percent of the population without health insurance across the 50 states.

Various versions of the model were tested, and in each test the number of mandated benefits was a strong and statistically significant cause of lack of health insurance. Specifically, as many as 25.2 percent of all uninsured people lack health insurance because of mandated benefits.

The number of mandated benefits varies considerably among the states—from a low of four in Delaware and Idaho to a high of 32 in Maryland. Moreover, the impact of the mandates is mitigated by other factors, such as the prevalence of employer-provided insurance and/or the ability to escape regulation through employer self-insurance. For these reasons, the impact of mandated benefits is substantially different in different states. As Table 6 shows, the number of who lack health insurance because of mandated benefits exceeds 60 percent of the uninsured population in Connecticut, Maryland and Minnesota, 41 percent in New York and exceeds 30 percent in California, Maine and New Jersey.

Massachusetts is of special interest. Legislation passed in Massachusetts at the urging of Michael Dukakis was a costly attempt to make health insurance available to all Massachusetts residents. Yet as Table 6 shows, up to 28 percent of the state's uninsured population already lack health insurance because of regulations imposed by the state government.

Positive Signs of Change

This essay has been pessimistic in its description of the explosion of state regulations during the 1980s and the negative impact of those regulations. There are, however, some signs that legislators are increasingly aware of the harmful effects of state mandated benefits.

Following the lead of Washington, Arizona and Oregon, more than a dozen states now require social and financial impact statements prior to

TABLE 6

EFFECTS OF MANDATED HEALTH
INSURANCE BENEFITS
(Selected States in 1986)

**Percent of People Who Lack Health Insurance
Because of State Mandates**

Arizona	20%
Arkansas	15%
California	32%
Connecticut	64%
Florida	18%
Kansas	27%
Maine	32%
Maryland	60%
Massachusetts	28%
Minnesota	60%
Missouri	30%
Montana	21%
Nebraska	26%
Nevada	30%
New Jersey	34%
New Mexico	16%
New York	41%
Ohio	28%
Texas	18%
Virginia	30%
Washington	30%

Source: Gerald Musgrave. Calculations reported in John Goodman and Gerald Musgrave, "Freedom of Choice in Health Insurance," National Center for Policy Analysis, NCPA Policy Report No. 134, Nov. 1988, Appendix A.

the passage of any additional mandates.[40] For example, because of concern about costs, in 1983 Washington state began putting the burden of proof on its proponents to show that the benefits of a mandate exceed the costs. As a result, no new mandates were adopted by the Washington legislature for several years.[41] These laws have clearly slowed the passage of mandated benefits, if only because the proponents of mandates need more time and money to overcome the new legislative hurdles.

A more positive sign is that fewer mandates are being passed and a number of states have actually rolled back mandates for small businesses. As Table 7 shows, in the three years prior to 1990 state governments passed an average of 71 mandates per year. In 1990 and 1991, however,

TABLE 7

NUMBER OF NEW STATE MANDATED
HEALTH INSURANCE BENEFITS

Year	New Mandates
1987	62
1988	51
1989	99
1990	29
1991	37[1]

Source: *Health Benefits Letter*, vol. 1, no. 15, 29 Aug. 1991.
[1]As of July 1991.

they passed only 29 and 37 mandates respectively. Moreover, at leaststates have now rolled back mandated benefits for small businesses and a dozen other states are considering similar legislation.[42]

Take Washington state, for example. Normally, health insurance policies there would be subject to 28 mandates—covering alcohol and drug abuse, mammographies, and the services of chiropractors, occupational therapists, physical therapists, speech therapists, podiatrists and optometrists. Under a law passed last year, however, firms with fewer than 50 employees can now buy cheaper insurance with no mandated benefits.

States also have taken other actions to encourage small businesses to purchase health insurance for their employees. Several exempt small-business policies from premium taxes, and at least six states extend tax credits to employers who are first-time buyers of health insurance. Iowa, for example, exempts "bare bones" policies from premium taxes and provides a tax credit to employers who pay at least 75 percent of the premium for low-income employees and half of the premium for the employees dependents.

Premium taxes also have been waived for small businesses in Nevada, New Mexico and West Virginia. Other states that give employers tax credits for the purchase of health insurance include Kansas, Kentucky, Montana, Oklahoma and Oregon. The credit is $15 per employee per month in Oklahoma and up to $25 in Oregon.

The Threat of a Counterrevolution

Now for the bad news. In a review of the fine print of the new legislation, Greg Scandlen (*Health Benefits Letter*) finds that many state reforms are less substantial than they seem. Some states have repealed some mandates but not others. Missouri, for example, has repealed only eight of its 18 mandates.

The definition of a "small business" is often quite restrictive. In 14 states an employer must have no more than 25 employees. In addition, many states allow a small business to qualify only if it has been without insurance for some period of time. In seven states, the qualifying period is at least one year; in Kansas, Maryland and Rhode Island, two years; and in Kentucky, three years. In these states, small employers who currently provide insurance coverage are penalized for doing so. All the benefits from the new legislation go to their uninsured competitors.

In another unfortunate trend, some states have subjected bare bones policies to new mandates while freeing them from the burdens of old ones. For example, numerous states require coverage for mammograms and well-child care, even though the same laws allow insurers to skimp on catastrophic coverage.

Perhaps the worst development is a new set of regulations governing insurance pricing. At least five states now require insurers to sell to any small business, regardless of the health of its employees (with limits on the premiums that can be charged). While the objective may seem humane, these laws encourage perverse behavior. If people know they can always get insurance after they are sick, they have an incentive to wait until they are sick to buy it. Yet if only sick people buy health insurance, the premiums will be extremely high.

Another perverse development is the trend toward "community rating." Virginia, for example, requires that all applicants be charged the same premium, regardless of the likelihood that they will get sick and incur medical costs. Other states have severely limited the ability of insurers to price risk accurately, causing healthier people to be overcharged and sicker people to be undercharged.

States that require insurers to take all comers and prevent insurers from charging premiums that reflect real risks usually set up "reinsurance pools"—industry gobbledygook forcing profitable companies to subsidize the losses of unprofitable ones. The net result is that all premium prices will be higher than they would have been.

Insurance industry experts estimate that the removal of all current state mandates would reduce the cost of health insurance by about 30 percent. But this gain could be totally wiped out by the cost-increasing effects of new regulations.

Furthermore, bare bones policies often sell at a lower price not because of reduced regulation but because of reduced coverage for basic medical risks. Annual insurance benefits may be capped at $100,000 per employee in Arkansas and $50,000 in New Mexico and Nevada. Such policies leave people exposed for truly catastrophic medical episodes and undermine the real purpose of insurance. Since the option to reduce coverage in this way was generally permissible even before insurance reform, it's not surprising that bare bones policies have not made much of an impact in the half-dozen states where they are now being marketed.

Mandating Employer-Provided Health Insurance

As has been noted, costly state regulations contribute to the increasing number of people who lack health insurance. Yet, as we shall see, the lack of health insurance does not necessarily keep people from getting medical care. But to the cost-plus mentality, those who lack health insurance are a problem that demands political solutions—solutions designed to put people back into the cost-plus system.

At the urging of Governor Michael Dukakis, Massachusetts passed legislation intended to provide all state residents with health insurance beginning in 1992. Other states are considering similar legislation. Several bills in Congress—including a bill introduced by Senate Democrats and one introduced by the Chairman of the House Ways and Means Committee, Dan Rostenkowski—would implement the Massachusetts plan at the national level. Other legislation to require employers to provide health insurance for all employees nationwide has been introduced in Congress by Senator Edward Kennedy. It appears that the principal problem addressed by these proposals is that of unpaid hospital bills. Yet the proposals carry a concealed price tag many times greater than any benefits the forced insurance coverage could provide.

What Difference Does Lack of Health Insurance Make?

It is believed widely in this country, and even more prevalently in Europe, that uninsured residents of the United States are routinely denied health care. This belief is quite wrong. What is true is that the existence or nonexistence of health insurance makes a big difference in determining how care is paid for. What follows is a brief summary of how and why health insurance makes a difference.

What It Means to Lack Health Insurance. Americans have been repeatedly told that 34 million people in this country lack health insurance. But what does that mean? Most discussions of the uninsured imply that they are a well-defined class of people. But Figure 2 shows that is not the case. Over a 28-month period, about 28 percent of the population will be uninsured, if only for a brief period of time. On any given day, about half that number will be uninsured, however. And, over the entire 28 months, only 4 percent will be continuously uninsured. The pool of uninsured, then, is one which many people enter and leave over a period of several years. Only a small number of people remain there permanently.

In this respect, being uninsured is comparable to being unemployed. Most people will probably be unemployed at some time during their worklife. At any point in time, however, only about 6 percent of the population will be unemployed, and only a very small percent of people will remain continuously unemployed for long periods. Like unemployment, being uninsured is generally viewed as an undesirable state of affairs. Most people will experience both without any long-term serious consequences.

Health Insurance and Access to Medical Care. A number of apparently contradictory studies have attempted to determine how the lack of health insurance affects access to health care. Some studies claim that the uninsured get less health care. Others claim that, once they see a doctor or enter a hospital, the uninsured receive as much as or more care than the insured. These studies are not necessarily inconsistent, but often they amount to comparing apples and oranges.

FIGURE 2
How Many People Are Uninsured?

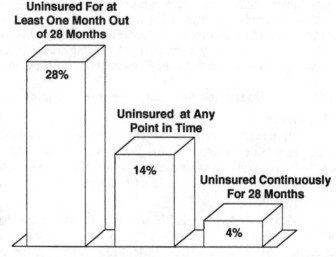

Source: C. Nelson and K. Short, *Health Insurance Coverge: 1986 to 1988*, U. S. Bureau of the Census Report, p. 70, No. 17, 1989. Reported in Louis P. Garrison, Jr., "Medicaid, the Uninsured, and National Health Spending: Federal Policy Implications," *Health Care Financing Review*, 1990 Annual Supplement, p. 169.

In comparing two groups of people, it is important to know much more than whether one group is insured and the other is not. For example, people with higher incomes and higher levels of education tend to place a greater value on health care and to spend more of their income on it. On the other hand, people who are sicker use more medical services than people who are healthy, and poor health tends to be correlated with low income and low levels of education.[43]

Age also matters, since younger people tend to be healthier. Interestingly, the uninsured have lower incomes, lower levels of education and at the same time are younger (two-thirds are under age 30, for example.)

Table 8 shows that if we ignore all other differences among the groups of people, there is very little difference between the insured and the uninsured in the number of physician's visits (among those who see a physician) or in the number of days in a hospital (among those who enter a hospital). This generalization also applies to people known to have low health status. In fact, among people with below-average health, those without health insurance make more trips to physicians and spend more days in the hospital than those with insurance.[44]

TABLE 8

USE OF MEDICAL SERVICES[1]

Medical Services	People With Insurance	People Without Insurance
Annual Physician's Visits[2]		
1-2 Visits	52.9%	51.4%
3-5 visits	24.9%	22.1%
6 or more visits	22.2%	26.6%
Annual Hospital Stays[3]		
1-5 days	56.9%	59.8%
6-10 days	22.3%	19.1%
11 or more days	20.8%	21.2%

[1]Refers to nonelderly people.

[2]Refers only to people who saw a physician.

[3]Refers to people who entered a hospital.

Source: National Health Interview Survey. Reported in Attiat F. Ott and Wayne B. Gray, *The Massachusetts Health Plan: The Right Prescription?* (Boston: Pioneer Institute for Public Policy Reserach, 1988), Table 2.15, p. 36.

More careful analysis shows that there are significant differences among the two groups, once all the relevant variables are accounted for. A study by Stephen Long and Jack Rodgers, for example, weighted the probability of using health care services by health status, age, sex, marital status, family size, income, education, employment status and residence. The results are depicted in Figure 3.

As the figure shows, the uninsured are about 25 percent less likely to see a physician and about half as likely to enter a hospital as people who have health insurance. Once in the health care system, the uninsured see physicians about 13 percent less often and spend one-third as much time in the hospital. Overall, the uninsured consume about half as much health care as the insured, when adjusted for all the variables listed above.

These results are consistent with a Rand Corporation study. Whereas the Rand study showed that a deductible in the range of $1,000 to $2,500 reduced health care spending by one-third,[45] the Long-Rodgers study showed that the absence of any health insurance reduces health care spending by one-half.

The Rand study also found that although the presence of a high deductible reduced health care spending considerably, the reduced spending had no apparent effect on people's health. Can the same be said of people who have no health insurance? That's not clear. But it seems likely that for the vast majority of people, the absence of health insurance for brief periods has no effect on health—especially considering that most health care is elective (and therefore can be delayed) and that most people have a great deal of choice over whether to be insured or not.

According to the National Health Interview Survey (1984), more than half of those without health insurance gave "cannot afford" as the primary reason. Less than one percent indicated "poor health" or "age" as a reason.[46] Note that the answer "cannot afford" should not be taken literally. Better phrasing would be: "The price is too high." In Massachusetts, which recently enacted a universal health care plan, 58.1 percent of the people who lack health insurance live in families with annual incomes of $20,000 or higher.[47]

Legal Rights to Health Care. Access to medical care by those who cannot pay for it is guaranteed by numerous state and federal laws. Currently, 47 states require state, county and/or city governments to provide care for the indigent and the uninsured, and numerous court decisions are upholding the right of hospitals to sue state and local governments for reimbursement for such care.[48] Moreover, federal law now requires all hospitals treating Medicare patients to accept all patients with emergency health problems and prohibits them from transferring

Figure 3

Use of Health Services by the Uninsured
(Relative To People Who Have Health Insurance)[1]

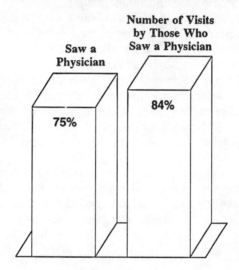

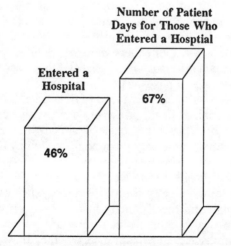

[1]Compares use of services over a 12-monthy period by those who were continuously unin-sured/insured over the 12-month period. Probabilities of use are weighted by age, sex, income, health status and other characteristics.

Source: Stephen H. long and Jack Rodgers (Congressional Budget Office), "The Effects of Being Uninsured on Health Services Use: Estimates From the Survey of Income and Program Participation," unpublished, Table 3, p. 11.

indigent patients unless the patient's condition is stabilized or is requested by the patient or medically indicated because of superior facilities at another hospital.[49]

Health Care Rationing in the Public Sector. Most discussions (and most studies) of the uninsured make little distinction between people insured in the private sector and those insured by public programs. Yet if there is a major difference in access to health care in the United States, increasingly the difference is in whether or not patients rely on public hospitals and clinics—whether or not they have health insurance.

One survey of public hospital emergency rooms in large cities discovered that patients could wait up to 17 hours to see a physician. In the face of such waits, many patients leave in frustration, without receiving care.[50] Waits can also be lengthy at outpatient clinics. A pregnant woman in Chicago, for example, had to wait 125 days to see a public clinic physician for free care to which she was presumably entitled.[51]

Casual (newspaper) descriptions of conditions in public hospital emergency rooms in the United States are very similar to the descriptions of emergency rooms in Canada, Britain and other countries with national health insurance. In these countries, everyone is theoretically insured. The problem of access is created by public sector health care rationing.

Health Insurance and the Protection of Financial Assets. If health insurance is not a prerequisite to health care, for most people, why does anyone purchase it? For the same reason people purchase life, automobile liability, and fire and casualty insurance—to protect assets. A major, catastrophic illness can wipe out a family's savings and investments. To protect these assets against unexpected medical bills, people purchase health insurance. It is hardly surprising that the more assets people have, the more likely they are to have health insurance.

If people with few assets choose not to purchase health insurance, their choice may be rational. It does, however, have social consequences. If society is committed to providing basic health care to all who need it, including the uninsured, some way must be found to pay the medical bills of the indigent uninsured. This is the reason usually given for the political support for universal health insurance.

Most proposals for mandatory health insurance, such as the Massachusetts health care plan and the Kennedy bill, are not primarily proposals to insure access to health care. Instead, they are proposals designed to force people to purchase health insurance whether they want to or not. The argument generally used in favor of mandatory health insurance is that it will reduce the burden of hospital bad debts and charity care.

For example, Susan Sherry, a spokesperson for Health Care for All (a coalition of consumer activist groups supporting the Massachusetts health care plan), explained to the *Washington Times* why individuals should not have the choice to buy or not buy health insurance. "That's not fair to the rest of us who have to pay when that person gets into an accident," she said.[52]

Why Are People Uninsured?

Why do so many people lack health insurance? Part of the reason is that, for many, health insurance has little value. Since lack of health insurance is not a major barrier to receiving health care, health insurance is of value primarily to those who wish to protect their assets against catastrophic health care expenses. For those with few or no assets, the price of health insurance may far exceed its value.

Contrary to widespread impressions, most of the uninsured are healthy. Two-thirds of them are under age 30,[53] in age groups that have the lowest health care costs. Because they tend to be young and healthy and have few assets, they are likely to be price-sensitive and to voluntarily forego health coverage if the price is too high. Yet at least three government policies cause the uninsured to face higher prices than most other people.

Because of the tax law, the self-employed, the unemployed and some employees of small business face after tax prices for health insurance that are as much as twice as high as the prices paid by people who have health insurance. Because of state regulations, the uninsured face premiums that are 20 to 30 percent percent higher than many people who have health insurance. And because of employee benefits law, people working in the small business sector find that health insurance is increasingly more expensive.

Ironically, our tax laws and employee benefits laws were originally designed to encourage greater health insurance coverage for more people. Today, the laws are having the opposite effect. Before imposing new costs on small businesses and creating yet another layer of bureaucracy, it would make sense to get rid of bad policies and give the market a chance to work. Instead, many are proposing more laws and more regulations.

Employer Mandated Health Insurance in Hawaii[54]

Hawaii is currently the only state that can require all employers—even self-insured employers—to provide health insurance to their workers. Under the federal Employee Retirement Income and Social Security Act (ERISA), companies that self-insure are exempt from state regulations. As a result, states such as Massachusetts that want to force all employers to provide health insurance have resorted to "pay or play" plans to get around the ERISA exemption. Under the "pay or play" approach, discussed below, state governments impose a per-employee tax on employers who do not offer health insurance. Hawaii passed its employer mandate in 1974, and after the Supreme Court invalidated the law in 1981 (declaring it in violation of ERISA), Hawaii got an ERISA exemption from Congress. Under Hawaii law, employers are required to provide a minimum package of health insurance benefits to employees, but not to their dependents. The contribution of employees is limited to 1.5 percent of wages.

It is not clear to what degree the state law forces employers and employees to do something they would not have done anyway. By one estimate, only 5,000 additional people acquired health insurance as a result of the law out of a population of 1.1 million. During the period from 1981 to 1983, when the law was invalidated by the Supreme Court, very few employers dropped health insurance coverage. And employer-provided benefits are commonly more liberal than the minimum benefits required by the state.

One reason why Hawaii has had fewer problems than other states could expect is that the state's population is apparently healthier and medical costs are much lower. The state has an extensive system of HMOs and per capita hospital expenses in Hawaii in 1988 were only $506, compared to $960 in Massachusetts.

Interestingly, mandated health insurance benefits imposed by the state have been more controversial than the required minimum health care package. Over the years, the state has mandated *in vitro* fertilization, mental health, alcohol and drug abuse treatments, psychological services and other benefits. These mandates force employees to take more of their compensation in the form of benefits they may not want or need instead of higher wages. The state has imposed additional mandates on employers who offer optional coverage for the dependents of workers, which has undoubtedly discouraged Hawaii employers from offering dependent coverage.

Hawaii's mandates are not free. One cost is in employment growth. In the period 1980-86, Hawaii's employment grew by only 9 percent compared with 13 percent for the nation and 20 percent for the U.S. Pacific coast states. Another cost is reduced money wages. In 1975, when the law first went into effect, Hawaii was 25th in average annual employee wages. By 1986 Hawaii had fallen to 36th.[55]

The Massachusetts Health Care Plan

On April 21, 1988, Governor Michael Dukakis signed legislation requiring employers to contribute toward health insurance premiums for their employees. Perhaps because of confusion created by 1988 election-year rhetoric, this plan has been widely misunderstood. The following is a brief attempt to clarify it.[56]

1. **Employees in Massachusetts are still not covered under the plan.** Despite 1988 election campaign statements that everyone in Massachusetts has health insurance, the law was not supposed to take full effect until 1992. Moreover, at the time of this writing, there is a reasonable chance the law will be repealed before it is fully implemented. Currently, the Massachusetts Legislature wants to delay the entry of private business into the program until 1995 and the governor wants to kill the program altogether.

2. **The Massachusetts law will require employers to spend money on health insurance for their employees but will not mandate a specific package of health insurance benefits.** Technically, employers will be assessed a state tax equal to 12 percent of salary up to $14,000 for each employee. However, employers may deduct from the tax any amount spent on health insurance for the employee. This means that employers must spend (either in taxes or on health insurance) $1,680 for employees earning $14,000 or more per year. Massachusetts would be in violation of federal law (ERISA) if it attempted to dictate specific benefits to self-insured plans.

3. **The Massachusetts plan is not "universal health insurance"; it will leave many uninsured people with the option of purchasing health insurance.** Technically, the only Massachusetts residents who will be "forced" to have health insurance are college students. All employees not covered by employer-provided health insurance and all nonworking people will have the option of buying health insurance from the state. But they may choose not to buy the state's health insurance, just as many now choose not to buy private health insurance.

4. **Under the plan, Massachusetts residents may not all have access to "affordable" health insurance.** The clear intention of Massachusetts is to offer health insurance at subsidized prices to low- and moderate-income families. Yet since the specifics of the benefit package are unknown, the cost of the policies and the subsidies also is unknown. Nor is it known how many people will rely on the state for health insurance. Moreover, given Massachusetts' well-publicized financial trouble, the state may not be able to offer its residents affordable health insurance.

5. **Although Massachusetts intends to force the private sector to provide health insurance to employees, the system may evolve**

into a state-run version of national health insurance. This is because the required contribution of employers is low relative to the cost of health insurance, and the benefits in the state insurance policy are likely to be quite liberal. Nationwide, the average employer contribution for an employee's health insurance in 1991 was about $1,739—$1,292 for single coverage and $2,887 for family coverage. Since health care costs are higher in Massachusetts, employer contributions to health insurance are likely to be $500 or $600 higher than the national average.[57] Moreover, the state insurance plan will include benefits such as mental health care and well-baby care not now included in many private plans. Thus many employers may decide to pay the state health insurance tax (12 percent of wages) and turn the obligation of providing health insurance over to the state. Indeed, given the difficulties employers now have in managing health care plans, it would be surprising if they did not.[58]

6. **After the plan is enacted, the number of uninsured Massachusetts residents may actually increase.** Because employers have the option of paying the state tax and not providing employee health insurance, many may choose that option, including employers who currently have health insurance for their workers. Because uninsured individuals do not have to purchase insurance from the state, many may decline to do so. As a result, the number of uninsured people in Massachusetts may actually increase. The more perverse the incentives created by the state plan, the higher the increase will be.

Economists Attiat Ott and Wayne Gray have estimated the minimum costs of the plan. Based on requirements already written into law, they concluded that the plan will force Massachusetts businesses to increase spending on employee health insurance by at least 32 percent. The additional cost will be at least $642 million in the first year of operation. Because of the increased costs of employing workers, as many as 9,000 jobs will be lost, with low-paid employees the likely losers.[59]

While it is difficult to generalize to the rest of the nation, Wayne Gray estimates that if the Massachusetts health care plan were adopted nationally, the additional cost to business would be $23 billion and as many as 358,000 jobs would be lost nationwide.

Despite the considerable cost of the plan, Ott and Gray found little evidence of a problem that needed to be solved. For example, Massachusetts already has a health care risk pool, designed to spread the cost of uncompensated hospital care among all hospitals and thus among all patients. Moreover, there is virtually no evidence that the uninsured in Massachusetts lack access to adequate health care, and most of the state's uninsured are far from poor. More than 58 percent have family incomes of $20,000 or higher, and 15 percent have family incomes in excess of $50,000.[60]

Actions by Other State Governments

Many other states are considering forcing people to purchase health insurance by making health insurance a condition of employment. Often, these states' legislators are trying to solve the problem they created by passing costly regulations. In almost every case, the natural legislative response is not to repeal bad laws but to pass more laws. Many of the legislatures which are considering forcing people to buy health insurance are the ones driving up health insurance costs by mandating more and more health insurance benefits.

At this writing, California, Illinois and Wisconsin are among the states where employer-mandated health insurance is being taken most seriously. Wisconsin is considering following the Massachusetts model by forcing employers to purchase health insurance on behalf of their workers and by imposing statewide taxes to pay for health insurance for the uninsured unemployed. As in Massachusetts, such a plan will be costly for the private sector.

A study conducted by Aldona Robbins and Gary Robbins estimated the effect of the Wisconsin plan on the state's economy. The study found that requiring private firms to provide health insurance for employees would cost businesses $417 million, reduce state output by $45 to $100 million a year and destroy 1,400 to 3,000 jobs annually. The study also found that creating a program of public health insurance for the uninsured with incomes below 155 percent of the poverty level would cost between $149 and $327 million and destroy as many jobs as the mandated insurance plan.[61]

The Need for Real Reform

The most basic problems with insurance reform are the refusal of state governments to allow a real market to develop and the refusal of the federal government to give the currently uninsured the same tax and regulatory breaks given to employees of large companies.

To summarize then, most people who lack health insurance are healthy. Two-thirds are less than 30 years of age, in the healthiest segment of our population. Most have below-average incomes and very few assets. As a result, they are especially sensitive to price.

Most of the uninsured have *voluntarily* decided not to purchase health insurance for a very good reason: The price is higher than that faced by other people for comparable benefit levels. Whereas 90 percent of insured people purchase health insurance with pretax dollars through an employer, uninsured individuals must pay with after-tax dollars. Whereas most employees of large corporations are exempt from silly state regulations, since their employers "self-insure," most of the uninsured are the victims of those regulations.

What most young, healthy people need is the opportunity to buy no-frills health insurance at a fair price. Aside from giving these people the same income tax break and the same options routinely given to others, politicians can help most by repealing bad laws and getting out of the way.

This article is adapted from John C. Goodman and Gerald Musgrave, *Patient Power: Solving America's Health Care Crisis*, to be published by the Cato Institute.

Endnotes

1. Many of the statistics in this chapter were obtained from various sources in the health insurance industry. The interpretations of the statistics are those of the authors and do not constitute legal opinions. In many states, lawsuits currently are underway to determine the exact meaning of various statutes and regulations.

2. Information obtained from *Health Benefits Letter*, vol. 1, no. 15, 29 Aug. 1991. For a discussion of the growth of mandated benefits, *see* Greg Scandlen, "The Changing Environment of Mandated Benefits," in Employee Benefit Research Institute, *Government Mandating of Employee Benefits* (Washington, D.C.: EBRI, 1987), 177-183.

3. Whether or not alcoholism and drug abuse are properly classified as "diseases," they are results of purposeful behavior. Thus, insurance against alcoholism or drug abuse often is not insurance against the possibility that someone "accidentally" will become a substance abuser but is instead a commitment to pay medical expenses for one who already is.

4. In certain "managed care" programs, the cost may be as low as $35,000. *See* Roger Rickles, "Firms Turn to 'Case Management' to Bring Down Health Care Costs," *Wall Street Journal*, 30 Dec. 1987, p. 13.

5. In 1989, Congress passed an appropriations bill that contained language forcing the District of Columbia to repeal this law. In effect, Congress told the District that no federal funds would be available unless the law was rescinded.

6. With the exception noted above, insurers may conduct their own tests, but such testing is expensive and adds to the overall cost of insurance.

7. John B. Welsh, Jr., "Legislative Review of Third-Party Mandated Benefits and Offerings in the State of Washington," in *Government Mandating of Employee Benefits*, 194.

8. In this instance, as in most other cases discussed in this section, the insurer is not required to pay the cost of treating a preexisting illness. However, the insurer is precluded from charging a higher premium even when a disability increases the likelihood of future claims.

9. *See* Glenn Ruffenbach, "Health Costs: Second Thoughts on Second Opinions," *Wall Street Journal*, 27 July 1988, p. 21.

10. *See* Judith Wagner, Roger Herdman and David Alpers, "Well-Child Care: How Much Is Enough?" *Health Affairs* (Fall 1989).

11. Linda L. Lanam, "Mandated Benefits—Who Is Protected?", in *Government Mandating of Employee Benefits*, 186.

12. Rickles, "Firms Turn to 'Case Management' to Bring Down Health Care Costs," 13; and Cathy Trust, "Corporate Prenatal-Care Plans Multiply, Benefiting Both Mothers and Employers," *Wall Street Journal*, 24 June 1988, p. 15.

13. It is estimated that one in six couples experiences infertility and the nation is currently spending $1· billion a year to address the problem. Success with *in vitro* fertilization usually comes after two cycles. However, unsuccessful couples may try an endless number of cycles. *See* "Business Bulletin," *Wall Street Journal*, 19 Oct. 1989.

14. Information obtained from Golden Rule Insurance Company.

15. Information obtained from Golden Rule Insurance Company.

16. For a state-by-state survey of risk pools, see Aaron K. Trippler, *Comprehensive Health Insurance for High-Risk Individuals*, 2nd edition (Minneapolis: Communicating for Agriculture, 1987).

17. *Ibid.*, 23-24.

18. Among operating pools, Florida is the only state that has not had losses. *Ibid.*, 47.

19. *Ibid.*, 35-37.

20. Kenneth B. Noble, "Health Insurance Tied to Life-Style," *New York Times*, 6 Aug. 1988, p. 1.

21. In the fall of 1988, Circle K rescinded the policy in response to pressure from special-interest groups. Failing to comply with state mandates, however, is common practice among self-insured employers.

22. For a description of the types of employer self-insurance and the benefits of self-insurance, *see* John Goodman and Gerald Musgrave, "The Changing Market for Health Insurance: Opting Out of the Cost-Plus System," National Center for Policy Analysis, NCPA Policy Report no. 118, Sept. 1985.

23. U. S. Congress, Office of Technology Assessment, *Medical Testing and Health Insurance*, OTA-H-384, (Washington, DC: U. S. Government Printing Office, Aug. 1988), 7.

24. Rhonda L. Rundle, "Insurers Step Up Efforts to Reduce Use of Free-Choice Health Plans," *Wall Street Journal*, May 1988.

25. Scandlen, "The Changing Environment of Mandated Benefits," 182.

26. Jon Gabel and Gail Jensen, "The Price of State-Mandated Benefits," *Inquiry*, vol. 26, no. 4 (Winter 1989), 419-431.

27. *Ibid.*

28. *Ibid.*

29. Peat Marwick Main & Co. and the Office of the Legislative Auditor, *Study of Proposed Mandated Health Insurance for Chiropractic Services: A Report to the Governor and the Legislature of the State of Hawaii*, Jan. 1988.

30. Peat Marwick Main & Co. and the Office of the Legislative Auditor, *Study of Proposed Mandatory Health Insurance for Well-Baby Services: A Report to the Governor and the Legislature of the State of Hawaii*, Jan. 1988.

31. Peat Marwick Main & Co. and the Office of the Legislative Auditor, *Study of Proposed Mandatory Health Insurance for Alcohol and Drug Dependence and Mental Illness: A Report to the Governor and the Legislature of the State of Hawaii*, Jan. 1988.

32. *Ibid.*

33. Reported in Rickles, "Firms Turn to 'Case Management' to Bring Down Health Care Costs."

34. U. S. Department of Commerce, Bureau of the Census, *Statistical Abstract of the United States, 1987*, Table 137, p. 89.

35. *Ibid.*

36. John Sheils (Lewin/ICF), testimony before the Senate Committee on Labor and Human Resources, 24 July 1991.

37. Under federal tax law, employer-paid premiums for health insurance are not counted in the taxable income of employees. This tax subsidy is not available to the self-employed or to people who purchase health insurance on their own, although the Tax Reform Act of 1986 does allow self-employed people to deduct 25 percent of their premium payments. The tax subsidy for employer-provided insurance becomes less important at lower marginal tax rates, however. Thus, the lowering of tax rates in the 1980s also reduced the attractiveness to employees of employer-provided health insurance. *See* Gary A. Robbins, "Economic Consequences of the Minimum Health Benefits for All

Workers Act of 1987 (S. 1625)," testimony presented to the U. S. Senate Committee on Labor and Human Resources, 4 Nov. 1987.

38. More than one-half of uninsured workers in 1985 were employed in retail trade and services. *See* EBRI, *Issue Brief no. 66*, p. 15.

39. *See* John Goodman and Gerald Musgrave, "Freedom of Choice in Health Insurance," National Center for Policy Analysis, NCPA Policy Report no. 134, Nov. 1988, Appendix A.

40. "Mandated Benefits: Mixed Signals From the States," *Health Benefits Letter,* 13 Mar. 1991.

41. Employee Benefit Research Institute, "Employee Benefit Notes," vol. 8, no. 9 (Sept. 1987) 7.

42. The discussion that follows is largely based on *Health Benefits Letter*, vol. 1, no. 8 and no. 13.

43. *See* Attiat F. Ott and Wayne B. Gray, *The Massachusetts Health Plan: The Right Prescription?* (Boston: Pioneer Institute for Public Policy Research, 1988), 26, 31.

44. *Ibid.*, Table 2.15, p. 36.

45. *See* Robert Brook et al., "The Effect of Coinsurance on the Health of Adults" (Santa Monica, Cal.: RAND, 1984).

46. *Ibid.*, Table 2.11, p. 30.

47. *Ibid.*, Table 2.2, p. 17.

48. Patricia Butler, "Legal Obligations of State and Local Governments for Indigent Care," in the Academy for State and Local Government, *Access to Care for the Medically Indigent*, 13-44.

49. Deborah J. Chollet, "Financing Indigent Care," in *The Changing Health Care Market*, ed. Frank B. McArdle (Washington, D.C.: Employee Benefit Research Institute, 1987), 188.

50. Philip J. Hilts, "Many Leave Emergency Rooms Needing Care," *New York Times,* 27 Aug. 1991.

51. *Chicago Tribune,* 25 Nov. 1990. Cited in Emily Friedman, "The Uninsured: From Dilemma to Crisis," *Journal of the American Medical Association*, vol. 265, no. 19, p. 2494.

52. Michael Hedges, "Study Finds Massachusetts Health Law Will Cut Jobs, Help Non-Poor," *Washington Times*, 6 Oct. 1988, p. A 4.

53. Jill D. Foley, *Uninsured in the United States: The Nonelderly Population Without Health Insurance* (Washington, D.C.: Employee Benefits Research Institute, Apr. 1991), 16.

54. This section is based largely on Emily Friedman, "Health Insurance in Hawaii: Paradise Lost or Found?", *Business and Health,* June 1990, pp. 52-59.

55. Rita Ricardo-Campbell, "Business Health Care Costs and Competition," Working Papers in Economics, No. E-91-6 (Hoover Institution, Stanford University, Feb. 1991), 34.

56. This section is based largely on Ott and Gray, *The Massachusetts Health Plan;* and Gail R. Wilensky, "The 'Pay or Play' Insurance Gamble: Massachusetts Plan for Universal Health Coverage" (Paper presented to the House Wednesday Group, Washington, D.C., 26 Sept. 1988).

57. Ott and Gray, *The Massachusetts Health Plan,* 51.

58. The plan does create tax-credit subsidies to encourage small businesses to provide employee health insurance during the first two years, however.

59. Ott and Gray, *The Massachusetts Health Plan.*

60. *Ibid.*, Table 2.2, p. 17.

61. Aldona Robbins, Gary Robbins and Richard Rue, *Mandated and Public Health Insurance* (Heartland Wisconsin Institute, Oct. 1989).

TOWARD MARKET-BASED
STATE HOUSING POLICY

Dr. Carl F. Horowitz
Policy Analyst, The Heritage Foundation

The past decade has seen enormous growth in the involvement of state government in creating opportunities for rental and homeownership affordability. Before 1980, for example, only 44 state housing programs were in existence. Between 1980 and 1987, however, the states created another 112.[1] Three states in particular—Maryland, Connecticut, and Massachusetts—accounted for this growth.[2] Below-market interest financing for housing construction, rehabilitation, and purchase; mandatory inclusionary zoning for local housing construction; state-private sector partnerships for neighborhood revitalization; environmental review of large-scale housing proposals; issuance of mortgage revenue bonds and housing tax credits; rehabilitation of vacant buildings into emergency shelters for the homeless; takeover of local rent control administration—state government has gotten involved in all of these activities, whether as initiators or as participants in federal or local programs.

The record has been mixed. To the extent that state government housing activity minimally disrupts market choice while benefitting those in need, it generally has been beneficial. To the extent that it supplants market choice—whether by federal mandate, or by its own design—it generally has been harmful. In recent years, as administrative, legislative, and judicial pressures for localities to build "affordable" housing have increased, state housing policy innovation increasingly has become coercive, and thus undesirable.

The kinds of organizations lobbying for an expanded federal presence in the housing market are working at the state level, too. Real estate trade organizations, homebuilding associations, construction trade unions, and low-income housing advocacy groups all promote the view that the U.S. is going through a worsening and potentially intractable shortage in affordable housing, which among other things, has contributed to an increase in homelessness. Governors, legislators, and state government associations are program advocates themselves, even prone to repeating the falsehood that a huge cut in the federal housing budget early during the Reagan years from $32 billion to $8 billion (yet to be restored) requires far greater intervention by the states.[3]   Since Washington presumably has abdicated its responsibilities, and since the market cannot provide affordable housing for the poor and near-poor, they argue, the states have no choice but to assure an adequate supply of affordable housing. Typical of this view is a comment by the Council of State Community Affairs Agencies (COSCAA): "Why is housing becoming a major policy issue for many states? During the past seven years, federal funding for housing, especially for constructing additional units of housing for low- and moderate-income households, has been substantially reduced, much more so than for most domestic programs."[4]

Challenging the notion of an ever-worsening housing crisis, far from being a frivolous exercise, is essential for defending any market-based housing policy. The most costly and inefficient state housing programs, regardless of region, usually came about because state officials were convinced of this crisis. The need for prudent state involvement in the housing market, therefore, can best be justified by combating the assertion that America is suffering a deep nationwide housing crisis.

By any reasonable measure, the existing stock of owner and renter-occupied housing is improving in both quantity and quality. Consider the following:[5]

- During 1980-89, the U.S. population grew by only 10 percent, while the housing inventory grew by 19 percent;

- During 1980-87, incomes rose by 46 percent, while housing prices rose by only 32 percent;

- In 1980, the rental vacancy rate was 5.2 percent, yet in 1989 it was 7.3 percent;

- In 1977, 7.0 percent of all renter-occupied units were characterized by the U.S. Department of Housing and Urban Development (HUD) as "severely inadequate," yet in 1987 only 2.6 percent of these units could be described as such.

On the other hand, there are real housing problems. The "national" housing market, after all, is the sum total of local and regional markets, which markedly differ from each other in economic, demographic, and geographic characteristics. Some markets in certain Northeastern and California metropolitan areas remain expensive in relation to everywhere else, despite their widespread declines in house prices and rents during this young decade. How large is this variation? In 1990, for example, median home purchase prices in the Boston, New York City, Orange County (California), and San Francisco areas were $166,200, $166,000, $240,300 and $247,400, respectively; in the Detroit, Minneapolis, Dallas/Fort Worth, and Denver areas, median figures were $94,100, $96,900, $90,600, and $91,400, respectively.[6] For too many families with children in the first group of areas, being able to afford safe, adequate housing and other necessities requires two full-time wage earners in the household.

Moreover, there still is a substantial stock of deteriorating and substandard housing, both occupied and vacant. This is increasingly true for the 1.4 million rental units in the public housing system, the taxpayers having been all but locked into permanently subsidizing them by recent federal housing legislation. America's housing problem can be summarized not by any "shortage" of housing itself, but by: 1) the *lack of market incentives* to operate housing in low-income areas and, if necessary, to sell, upgrade, or demolish the housing and to put it to a higher and better use; and 2) the decay of numerous neighborhoods due to *welfare dependency and crime* that characterize so much of lower-class culture.

Initiatives for the Nineties

The challenges facing the states in housing policy can be grouped under two general categories: 1) stimulation of housing construction, rehabilitation, and purchase in a cost-efficient manner that primarily reaches those most in need; and 2) reduction and streamlining of excessive housing regulation and high residential property taxation, the effects of which are to constrict the housing supply. Some of these initiatives already exist at the state level; others, based on the evidence from empirical studies or program experience, should.

The discussions center around initiatives that have or could come from states themselves. Where states are participants in federal programs, only those programs where states can exert real influence are discussed. On occasion, the analysis will make references to actions that the states should avoid (or as the case may be, discard).

The recent Report of the Advisory Commission on Regulatory Barriers to Affordable Housing, supervised by HUD Secretary Jack Kemp, recommends a strong role for the states to remove impediments to homeownership and rental affordability. This kind of federal support should make the states' load somewhat lighter.[7]

Section A. Strategies to stimulate housing construction, rehabilitation, and purchase in a cost-efficient manner.

1) Convert Mortgage Revenue Bonds to Mortgage Credit Certificates.

State governments, through their respective housing finance agencies (HFAs), have become major sources of funds for housing development, both in their own programs and in tandem with federal programs. The State of New York created the first HFA in 1961, and thereafter several other states did likewise. Currently, all fifty states, the District of Columbia, and several U.S. territories have HFAs.

At the time, the primary purpose of these agencies was to attract private investment funds for lenders to provide below-market interest rate mortgages for low- and moderate-income rental construction. This activity received a major boost from Washington in the federal Housing Act of 1968, which encouraged states to use such agencies as a means of leveraging federal rent subsidies, particularly the newly created Section 236 program. Beginning in the mid-70s, the emphasis shifted. States began to issue tax-exempt bonds—mortgage revenue bonds (MRBs)—to raise capital for lending to creditworthy mortgage applicants, especially first-time buyers, who likely otherwise would be turned down for assistance. Typically, the mortgage loans required a low down payment, and their interest rates were set at two percentage points below market rates. Their popularity grew quickly, and by 1978, over 60 percent of the capital raised by HFAs went for this purpose.[8] By the end of 1990, the states had issued about $70 billion in revenue bonds, close to $300 for every person in the U.S.[9]

Revenue bond programs have "worked" well in that they have helped numerous households, but in the process they have revealed their inherent dilemma. Though HFAs use them to help households in need, the bonds are secured only through repayment of mortgage principal and interest; they can be effectively marketed only if investors are convinced that homebuyers benefitting will not default. Thus, borrowers tend to be households who do not especially need the assistance.

The creation by the federal government of the Mortgage Revenue Bond Program under the Mortgage Subsidy Bond Tax Act of 1980 proved a major boost to these state revenue bond programs. Among the program's provisions were that only persons not having owned a home in the last three years were eligible for assistance; 20 percent of bond proceeds had to be used in "targeted" economically distressed areas; and the home, new or existing, could not cost more than 90 percent (110 percent in distressed areas) of the average purchase price in the preceding year in the area where the mortgage was placed.

With the help of this program, by late 1990, state HFAs had helped more than 1.25 million households to become homebuyers. Supporters of the federal revenue bond program point to this figure as proof that the program should be further expanded; that the program is a bulwark against falling rates of homeownership among young adults, especially in economically distressed regions and states. What they overlook is that the program has put the states at sizeable financial risk, without being particularly effective. In 1988, the U.S. General Accounting Office released a report entitled *Home Ownership: Mortgage Bonds Are Costly and Provide Little Assistance to Those in Need.*[10]

The GAO had gathered information on almost 178,000 buyers who received loans from the federal MRB program during 1983-87, and reported a federal treasury loss of $150 million for every $1 billion in bonds issued, with much of the money going to bond underwriters (who sell the bonds on behalf of the government) and bond holders. Even more troubling, the GAO found that the median reduction in monthly mortgage payments was only $40, and that incomes of recipient households and first-time homebuyers were, generally, similar. For these reasons, the GAO concluded that 56 percent of the assisted buyers could have purchased the same house without bond assistance, and at market interest rates. Another 12 percent could have bought the same home using a market-determined adjustable-rate mortgage. Moreover, the GAO noted that even those who "needed" the assistance (i.e., would not have qualified for either a conventional or an adjustable-rate loan) within several years would have qualified anyway. It is fair to say, then, that the overwhelming majority of assisted buyers did not truly need MRB assistance.

Given that during the 90s, mortgage interest rates have hovered within the relatively low 8 to 10 percent range, and given that Federal Housing Administration (FHA) and Veterans Administration (VA) mortgage insurance programs are still available, and on sounder financial footing than in the 80s, the federal MRB program appears even less justifiable today. Falling interest rates, in fact, can be problematic for state HFAs. In 1986, for example, the Texas Housing Agency had to call in about $90 million of its $110 million bond issue of a few months before because the bond-assisted rate was no longer attractive to homebuyers.[11] HFAs are apparently no more adept than lenders at predicting interest rate shifts.

States can improve this program by converting Mortgage Revenue Bonds to Mortgage Credit Certificates (MCCs). The MCC is a tax credit as opposed to a bond issue program. It allows a homebuyer to credit a portion of home mortgage interest toward taxable federal income. Provisions in the 1986 Tax Reform Act permit state (and local) housing finance agencies to receive $1 of MCC authority for each $4 of MRB authority they relinquish.

The states have shown great enthusiasm for the program; roughly half of the states have converted MRB authority to MCC authority, and have saved the taxpayer money in the process. According to a study by the California Association of Realtors, the loss to state and federal treasuries for each homebuyer using a certificate was only $17,700; for each buyer using bonds, the figure was roughly $40,000.[12]

Homeownership deservedly continues to be promoted as a cornerstone of national housing policy, and the states are justifiably part of the promotion. The evidence is persuasive, however, that all states should opt to relinquish MRB authority in favor of MCC authority. To be sure, the tightening several times since 1980 of borrower eligibility requirements, and the imposition of "recapture" provisions for borrowers with rising incomes to give back to the federal government a share of resale profits, are laudable, as they reduce MRB usage as a middle-class subsidy. Likewise laudable are efforts by state agencies, such as the Virginia Housing Development Authority (VHDA), to concentrate assistance upon those most in need. That said, the certificate program is more efficient, easier to administer, and works with the market, avoiding the tendency of revenue bonds to inadvertently raise market interest rates in the overall tax-exempt bond market.[13] For bond programs originating with a state, the administering agency should institute an equivalent program to convert bond authority to tax credit authority.

2) Encourage shallow one-time housing subsidies for construction and rehabilitation.

Whether in tandem with federal housing subsidies or as free-standing programs, the states have gotten heavily involved in stabilizing and upgrading conditions in neighborhoods. Very often, they work with nonprofit organizations to assess housing needs as well as improve housing.

A general rule, to be heeded by states as well as the federal government, is that housing programs succeed when government provides modest front-end assistance with a minimum of red tape. They fail, on the other hand, when they commit government to long-term obligations to house only the poor (and to annually recertify their incomes and assets), thus giving beneficiaries no incentive to move somewhere else, or even find work, lest they lose their subsidy.

Misguided housing "advocates" view with alarm the possibility that hundreds of thousands of privately-owned rental dwellings might lose their federal subsidy during the 90s, and thus require "preservation" laws that discourage owner mortgage prepayment, and mandate voucher payments to all displaced tenants. They successfully convinced Congress in 1987 to enact such features on an emergency basis, and in 1990 to make them permanent. States should not follow suit, and should avoid committing themselves to Section 8-style subsidy programs that lock rather than free the housing stock.

Worthy of support are housing programs that are low-key, gain support (or at least tolerance) from people not benefitting from subsidies, and involve a tax credit or a moderate one-time subsidy for people demonstrating a capacity to support all their housing expenses. Unworthy of support are long-term doles either for the nonworking poor incapable of paying for any of their housing, or the middle-class not needing assistance. Examples of better programs include:[14]

- Real Estate Tax Abatement Program (Pennsylvania). Established in 1983, the program grants authority to local governments to exempt property taxes for ten years on housing construction and rehabilitation undertaken in an economically distressed area.

- Community Contribution Tax Incentive Program (Florida). This program provides a 50 percent tax credit for corporations donating housing to approved community development projects conducted by nonprofit corporations. Housing must be in enterprise zones or some other area deemed distressed. Tax credits are available up to $200,000 per year.

- Equity partnerships with HFAs (various states). In Boulder, Colorado, for example, a developer and the Colorado Housing and Finance Authority are equal-equity partners in a 124-unit mixed-income project. When they sell the project after 10 years, they will split the profits.

- Subsidy/deregulation combinations (various states). The Maryland Community Development Administration, for example, has raised capital at slightly below market interest rates to assist the nonprofit Baltimore City Homes, Inc. in its purchase and moderate rehabilitation of over 200 row houses in imminent danger of abandonment. At a per-unit cost of $23,000 (including purchase price), a figure well below the $50,000-$75,000 per unit cost usually incurred by full-scale rehabilitation, the units are now inhabited by low- and moderate-income working families. As a result, the surrounding neighborhoods are in less danger of serious decline.

- Affordable Homeownership Development Program (New York). Begun in 1985, this program provides modest homeownership grants and loans to construct 1 to 4 unit structures. For-profit as well as nonprofit companies, along with municipalities, are eligible applicants. Many persons can be reached at minimal cost, and by leasing other units of their building to tenants, they can remain homeowners even with low incomes.

States should emulate such efforts, but should also attempt more frequently to include for-profit builders as eligible sponsors. There is no reason why a successful program cannot accommodate for-profit businesses as participants. Indeed, the existence of profit potential should be a principal selling point of any housing program.

3) **Provide tax credits for employers who provide housing for employees.**

One of the emerging issues in housing affordability is the alleged mismatch between the location of an employer, and the high cost of housing within reasonable commuting distance. In a number of expensive markets, such as the Washington, D.C., and New York City metropolitan areas, employees repeatedly have cited difficulty in renting or buying housing near their workplace. Thus, they either turn down a job offer or, more likely, accept the offer and pay too much for their housing, or commute to work excessively long distances to keep their housing costs down.[15] According to a survey by the New Jersey Business and Industry Association, 43 percent of the state's businesses reported difficulty in recruiting or retaining employees due to the high cost of housing.[16]

The potential for participation in employer-sponsored construction, rehabilitation, purchase, and lease programs does exist. According to a three-year study by the American Affordable Housing Institute at Rutgers University, a majority of employers view the idea favorably, with 20 to 35 percent of top-level corporate executives expressing interest in offering such benefits to non-management, non-relocating workers. Currently, only 3 percent of all major U.S. companies have an employee housing plan.[17]

States which are offering or considering such programs include New Jersey, Connecticut, Virginia, North Carolina, Rhode Island, Kentucky, and Oregon. New Jersey perhaps has gone furthest, enacting a demonstration program, HOPE (Homeownership for Performing Employees), which offers $28 million in low-interest mortgage loans to employers, backed by 20 percent employer mortgage guarantees.

A better route than this would be modest state corporate income tax credits for employees. Below-market rate loans merely represent a transfer of wealth from one large set of employees to a smaller set, with companies partly liable for default. The idea of employers rewarding good employees by offsetting their housing costs is a good one, but tax credits up to a moderate cap would be less disruptive of the housing market.

4) **Create housing opportunities for the homeless only to the extent that they support social services intended to foster independence among the homeless.**

During the 1980s and now the 90s, homelessness has been oversold as an unmanageable domestic crisis attributable primarily to a shortage of affordable housing. Such rhetoric is designed to steer the public and Congress to the view that only massive federal housing subsidies can alleviate the problem. In reality, the number of homeless is at maximum in the 500,000-600,000 range, and quite likely about half that. Moreover, the portion of the homeless who suffer from alcoholism, drug abuse, mental illness, or crime is staggering; even Martha Burt of the liberal Washington, D.C.-based Urban Institute estimates that possibly as many as 50 to 60 percent of the homeless may never be able to take care of themselves.[18] The mental health factor alone negates any claim that homelessness is solely a housing issue. A 26-city survey conducted by the U.S. Conference of Mayors in 1987 indicated that roughly one-third of the homeless were mentally ill. The percentage was 45 percent for San Francisco and 40 percent for Louisville, Minneapolis and Seattle.[19]

The American housing stock is capable of housing the homeless, as there are at least 15 year-round vacant dwellings for each homeless person.[20] Moreover, the space in emergency homeless shelters is more than sufficient. According to two separate HUD surveys in the 1980s, shelters were filled only to about two-thirds of their capacity.[21] Interestingly, the number of homeless persons counted in the later (1988) survey— 180,000—is the same as the number counted in shelters by the Census Bureau in its special survey of the homeless in March 1990.

Currently, the states spend about $800 million on various homeless shelter and social service programs. If they must spend any money at all, they should spend it on programs that provide the competent homeless with life skills, including substance abuse counseling and job training.[22] They should use the vast excess capacity of space in state hospitals to house those homeless who cannot be helped. Sound professional decisions made by those knowledgeable about schizophrenia and other mental illnesses, should prevail over maudlin sentiment about the homeless being the "salt of the earth." States should not subsidize nonprofit groups to build or rehab housing for the homeless, as this would merely permanently reserve housing for persons declaring themselves to be "homeless." Washington, D.C.'s disastrous right-to-shelter law (Initiative 17), inasmuch as it encouraged people to do just that, only contributed to homelessness.[23]

An example of state anti-homelessness housing assistance creating self-sufficiency, rather than serving a free lunch, is Massachusetts' Chapter 707 Transitional Housing for Department of Social Services Clients. This program provides rental assistance to service providers who help battered women, pregnant teenagers, and chronically homeless families who are clients of the Department to develop independent living skills. Staffing costs are minimal, and the results are promising.

Not to be discounted as a factor here are the expanded opportunities to place group homes in residential neighborhoods. In 1970, only one state authorized their location in such areas; by 1987, 34 states had such legislation.[24] Under no circumstances, however, should states preempt local authority if an application for a group home is rejected locally. There are many good reasons why residents are apprehensive, indeed fearful, of living near such a facility. To coerce localities into accepting them would be the worst sort of misplaced compassion.

5) Create incentives for tenant management and ownership of public housing.

Most people think of public housing as a federal program, with locally-designated public housing authorities (PHAs) managing individual projects. Less known is that PHAs are state-chartered agencies. States have the power to both grant and revoke an authority's charter. Given the present sorry condition of many housing projects in larger cities, they should exert pressure upon local authorities to do a better job—or else.

When Congress created the public housing program in 1937, it encumbered the federal government only to covering the cost of tax-exempt bonds issued by PHAs to build the projects. By the late-60s, however, many city projects had physically deteriorated, and worse, contained large nonworking welfare populations, a situation that since has gotten even more pronounced.[25] This population, given their inability (and often unwillingness) to contribute to monthly rent, and given the high operating costs they incur through vandalism and crime, caused many of the PHAs to be strapped for cash. Thanks to a number of successful (and misguided) lawsuits by the American Civil Liberties Union (ACLU) and local legal groups funded by the Legal Services Corporation (LSC), housing authorities now have far less leeway than in earlier days to evict destructive, nonpaying tenants.

In response to this, during the late-60s the federal government initiated a physical modernization program, and greatly expanded its then-small operating cost reimbursement program. Together, these activities were appropriated for FY '92 at $5.25 billion, or $3,750 per unit in the 1.4 million-unit system.

What is the current state of public housing? Approximately 100,000 apartments are vacant, with a great many of them uninhabitable; indeed, many occupied apartments are close to being uninhabitable. Apartments, hallways, lobbies, and exteriors have been heavily vandalized and are often under the unofficial domain of gangs and drug dealers. Yet there remain waiting lists for entry. For example, a HUD audit of Detroit's public housing system in the fall of 1990 revealed that 41 percent of all available units were vacant, despite 1,300 eligible households on the Detroit PHA waiting list. Many of the buildings had broken elevators, malfunctioning heating systems, and rodent and insect infestation.[26] A General Accounting Office study of Buffalo's housing projects indicated that as of June 1990, 26 percent of the local PHA's 5,000 units were vacant, many in deep disrepair, yet 2,800 families were on the waiting list.[27] The GAO revealed the housing authority had been spending $240,000 monthly on the vacant units. A 1989 HUD audit of 19 troubled housing authorities, constituting about 184,000 units, revealed close to 35,000, or roughly 20 percent, to be vacant.[28] Many of these authorities for years had padded their payrolls, thus leaving less cash available for maintenance and repairs. While, admittedly, housing projects in smaller cities generally do not have these kinds of problems, and in fact, many of them pay all of their own operating costs, the troubled projects in large cities slowly are draining HUD coffers—and taxpayer patience as well.

The best news about public housing lies with recent privatization efforts, restricted as they may be by federal law.[29] Some of the most successful projects are those in which tenants have taken over from a PHA management responsibility and even ownership. Kenilworth-Parkside (Washington, D.C.), Cochran Gardens (St. Louis), Bromley-Heath (Boston), and one building in Cabrini-Green (Chicago), once granted tenant management, witnessed dramatic improvements in rent collections, safety, cleanliness, and apartment conditions. Accompanying these positive changes were an upsurge in resident pride, and the start-up of several successful small resident-owned businesses. In supporting more of this activity through the new federal HOPE program (Homeownership and Opportunity for People Everywhere) promoted by HUD Secretary Jack Kemp, a public housing tenant can be, as housing expert Irving Welfeld put it, "a consumer to be offered choices, rather than a supplicant who is assigned space."[30]

States can do several things to improve the public housing system. First, they should require PHAs to inform tenants of their management and ownership options under the 1987 Housing and Community Development Act. Section 123 of the Act requires HUD to sell multifamily buildings or groups of buildings to qualified resident management councils that have demonstrated "their ability to manage public housing effectively and efficiently for a period of not less than three years."[31] Second, they should suspend regulatory burdens that inhibit the growth of public housing enterprise. Many states, for example, have their own mini-versions of the federal Davis-Bacon Act requiring payment of the "prevailing" wage on all construction projects receiving $2,000 or more in federal funding. One St. Louis tenant leader complained that complying with Davis-Bacon adds 25 percent to the cost of converting public housing to tenant ownership.[32] Finally, states, as the chartering entity of a housing authority, should pull the plug on authorities that consistently place political patronage above tenant well-being. This would require the courage and patience to combat HUD and local bureaucracies, but it is an option to be considered.

Section B. Strategies to reduce and streamline excessive state and local housing regulation, and high residential property taxation, the effects of which are to constrict the housing supply.

1) Provide incentives to counties and municipalities to ease exclusionary zoning restrictions.

Zoning is a practice that restricts the use of land by density, use, and bulk. While it has had the positive effect of keeping away nuisance land uses that otherwise might lower property values, particularly single-family residential values (and came about more for this than any other reason), there is little question that a price has been paid for this success. Especially in suburban areas, where for decades so much new housing construction has taken place, zoning can leave builders at the mercy of local sentiments. If zoning boards reflect vehement anti-development sentiments of nearby residents, builders frequently are forced either to shelve proposals, scale them down, or revise them to contain housing affordable only to affluent buyers and renters.[33]

Few people realize the delay costs of hearings, negotiations, and appeals in dealing with zoning, or for that matter, all other land use controls. When housing developers hold onto vacant land for development, but must face delays in building on it, they pass their losses onto consumers in the form of higher prices and rents. According to a nationwide survey of builders in the late-70s, for example, each month of delay in the anticipated completion date of a single-family housing project adds about 1 to 2 percent to the final selling price of a dwelling.[34] With the median price of a new home currently about $120,000, this translates into an extra $2,000 per month.

While not all localities engage in exclusionary zoning practices, and while others that do have since eliminated some of them, their barriers are still formidable. The four most important exclusionary techniques are: prohibitions against multifamily and other high-density housing; prohibitions against mobile homes and other manufactured housing; high minimum lot square footage and frontage requirements; and prohibitions against creating accessory units from existing single-family homes.

To overcome these practices, states can: a) mandate that localities include at least a portion of vacant land within their boundaries toward multifamily or higher-density single-family housing; b) provide a bypass system that allows builders an exemption from the zoning ordinance (*e.g.*, Massachusetts' Chapter 774 "anti-snob zoning" law); and c) provide density bonuses to developers where localities already permit multifamily and other high-density housing in its boundaries.[35]

States should avoid at all costs the coercive approach that has emerged from New Jersey's *Mount Laurel* decisions. The prototype of mandated "fair share" strategies, this approach has broken down local barriers, only to have created even worse barriers at the state level. In 1975, after several years in the lower courts, the New Jersey Supreme Court ruled that every local government in the state's developing regions had a responsibility to provide their fair share of housing for low- and moderate-income persons.[36] The Court's striking down of the zoning ordinance of the Township of Mount Laurel as exclusionary was beneficial in and of itself. Yet the Court framed the case as a civil rights issue even more than as an economic issue; by in effect placing "housing rights" above property rights, it set the stage for further frustration and legal action.

In 1983, after the Township had failed to design an "inclusionary" ordinance, the Court clarified its earlier decision. *Mount Laurel II,* as this decision came to be known, required all New Jersey communities to take affirmative action to construct low- and moderate-income housing.[37] This inclusionary mandate was followed two years later by the state's Fair Housing Act, which required all 567 municipalities in the state to submit proposals to the newly created New Jersey Council on Affordable Housing, indicating how they would comply with *Mount Laurel II.* New Jersey has now created a quasi-socialist system of housing production targets. Since building housing for low-income households without resorting to shoddy construction requires some subsidy, *Mount Laurel II,* if strictly enforced, will be a budget-buster. California, Massachusetts, and Maine likewise have enacted inclusionary zoning mandates.

Such measures are not necessary, and states should avoid enacting them. States should be creating opportunities to build and dwell, not inhibiting them in the name of "fairness." An excellent way of liberalizing zoning ordinances to house the less affluent without resorting to these schemes lies with allowing more partitioning of accessory apartments from existing single-family homes. Over a million such apartments easily could be created in this decade if the legal mechanisms were in place,[38] and many older homeowners are enthusiastic about having the opportunity to collect rent from someone else living in their basement or in a spare room.[39]

States should encourage localities to modify their ordinances to allow more of this. They should also emphasize deregulation of zoning and other ordinances when providing shallow housing subsidies. Part of the reason for the success of New York State's Affordable Homeownership Development Program, for example, was that local governments were encouraged to grant zoning variances to builders to relax minimum lot size and detached housing-only requirements.[40]

2) Ease environmental and growth control regulation.

Since the 1970s, states, counties, and municipalities have restricted the supply of land that can be developed for housing or other purposes so as to protect the environment and manage future growth. Just since 1985, some 50 localities in California alone have passed growth control ordinances. Whether taking the form of sewer moratoria, population growth ceilings, building permit ceilings, or prohibition of construction in areas deemed environmentally sensitive, they impose substantial delay costs on developers and increase the price of raw land.

States themselves have enacted strong controls in the past two decades. Many took their cue from the 1973 report of the Rockefeller Brothers Task Force on Land Use and Urban Growth, which argued, "Important developments should be regulated by governments that represent all the people whose lives are likely to be affected by it. Where a regulatory decision significantly affects people in more than one locality, [then] state, regional or even federal action is necessary."[41]

However nobly motivated, such regulation can add significantly to the cost of housing. One study of single-family residential development in Florida a decade ago revealed that the designation of "Development of Regional Impact" to housing proposals under the state's Environmental Land and Water Management Act of 1972 added $4,700 to the price of a new home, with close to 90 percent of this figure attributable to counties, municipalities, special districts, and other state agencies loading their own regulations onto those specified in the Act.[42] With Florida having enacted its Growth Management Act of 1985, a more stringent version of the 1972 legislation, price increases could have only gotten steeper since, even allowing for inflation. This law mandates state-funded local growth control planning and a requirement for localities to provide adequate facilities to accommodate growth. Oregon, Vermont, and California, among other states, have adopted similar stringent legislation.

Nobody disputes the importance of environmental protection as part of the state policy agenda. However, the definition of environmental hazards has grown to the point where a weather-related puddle of water can constitute a "wetland," and applying for and receiving a special development permit can tie up a project for months.[43] Moreover, protecting the environment can be promoted through market incentives; government restrictions are not the only, or even necessarily the most desirable, way of preserving environmental resources. At the least, states should pass legislation to mandate fair compensation to any property owner prevented from developing his land due to such regulation. The *Nollan*[44] and *First English Evangelical Lutheran Church*[45] decisions of the U.S. Supreme Court in 1987 provide ample constitutional justification for such action.

3) Preempt local authority to enact rent control ordinances.

Currently, over 200 localities in the United States, most notably New York City (whose rent control program was taken over by New York State in 1984), New Jersey, and California, place ceilings on residential rents. About 10 percent of the nation's rental housing stock is subject to some form of rent control.

Rent control, good intentions aside, has reduced new housing construction, upgrading and maintenance incentives, property values, vacancy rates, and tenant mobility. Even liberal researchers, such as Brookings Institution Senior Fellow Anthony Downs,[46] have reached such conclusions. Rent control has failed even in its primary goal of protecting the least well-off tenants. Households protected by rent control tend to be middle-class. In 1986, for example, a study by Arthur D. Little, Inc. revealed that 45 percent of the tenants in New York City rent-controlled apartments had incomes of at least $40,000.[47] Author William Tucker, in his recent book, *The Excluded Americans*, concludes from his observations of various rent control laws that their main beneficiaries are "the paperworking class."[48]

Since the early-1980s, Congress intermittently has attempted, without success, to withhold housing assistance from local jurisdictions that enact or retain rent controls. Yet where Washington has been unwilling to act on this score, the states have gone even further. Currently, 18 states (Arizona, Colorado, Florida, Georgia, Idaho, Louisiana, Michigan, Minnesota, Mississippi, Missouri, North Carolina, Oklahoma, Oregon, South Carolina, South Dakota, Texas, Utah, and Washington) have enacted legislation that preempts the ability of counties and municipalities to place ceilings on rents. Another, New Hampshire, has a preemptive judicial mandate.

The main task ahead is for the six states where local rent control is practiced—California, Connecticut, Maryland, Massachusetts, New Jersey, and New York (the District of Columbia also has rent control)—to enact preemptive legislation of their own. While state governments could make exceptions in the case of an aftermath of a natural or man-made disaster, or in the case of voter support of rent control through referendum (preferably with more than a simple majority required), they cannot afford to ignore the principal legacy of rent control: the aggravation, rather than the alleviation, of rental housing shortages.

4) Encourage local easing of building codes and promote the BOCA code.

Frequently cited as barriers to more affordable housing are strict building codes. Enacted principally around the turn of the century to provide safety and design standards to building construction, on occasion they have blocked technological innovation. Trade unions long have had an interest in retaining certain archaic code provisions, and frequently lobby state and local governments to resist updating codes. According to the HUD Task Force on Housing in 1978, "[This] uncoordinated system of differing and increasing regulation is slowing down the building process and making the adoption of current and new cost-saving ideas more difficult and expensive."[49] A study in the 1970s indicated that codes add about 5 to 10 percent to dwelling costs.[50]

These findings may ring even more true today. In Chicago, for example, the local building code raises the cost of installing electrical fixtures by 10 to 30 percent by banning newer, less expensive materials.[51] Bethel New Life, a nonprofit agency that builds and rehabilitates homes for low-income persons, discovered that contractors building $60,000 townhomes in Chicago were building identical dwellings in nearby suburbs for $48,000. The difference lay in the City's mandating of expensive materials and outdated construction methods in its building code.[52]

By contrast, the BOCA (Building Officials and Code Administrators) model code, widely used across the country, allows for frequent updating, provided certain safety and durability standards are met. States should enact legislation mandating the use of the BOCA, or some other modern model code, where evidence is clear that existing local codes significantly add to a contractor's material and labor costs.

5) Create Housing Opportunity Zones in distressed areas in cities.

In 1990, Congress passed the Bush Administration's HOPE proposal, minus several important features, one of which was the Housing Opportunity Zone (HOZ) program. Resembling enterprise zone legislation, the proposal would have HUD declare as HOZs 50 blighted areas. Municipalities would compete for designation by proposing to eliminate regulatory barriers to affordable housing such as excessive zoning requirements, rent control, Davis-Bacon wage requirements, and outdated building codes. The zones would receive low- and moderate-income housing development incentives, including priority for funding under HUD's Urban Homesteading program, in which HUD transfers vacant residential structures to state and local governments at no cost for eventual low-income ownership.

Where Congress failed to act in 1990, the states can act in this year and subsequent years. Just as federal inaction on tax incentives for Enterprise Zones has led to 37 states, plus the District of Columbia, enacting their own largely successful enterprise zone programs, federal inaction here could induce states to enact HOZ legislation. This approach has the advantage of being politically less divisive than proposing subsidized housing in suburban jurisdictions.

6) Allow localities to experiment with site value taxation.

Property taxes remain one of the major components of housing costs, whether for owner-occupied or rental housing. Insofar as taxes on improvements diminish the incentive to make improvements, they are harmful.

Taxing improvements at a lower rate than land is one way to induce property owners to build upon vacant land and make improvements to existing buildings. Such a strategy would stimulate residential construction and rehabilitation precisely in low-income urban areas where the price of land is high, even with a deteriorating housing stock. By discouraging vacant land for speculation, it also would reduce land costs in the suburbs.

The State of Pennsylvania in 1913 mandated that the cities of Pittsburgh and Scranton levy a two-rate real property tax. Under this system, which excludes counties and school districts, buildings would be taxed at half the rate of land. The law was later modified to allow other Pennsylvania cities to do the same, and allow Pittsburgh and Scranton more freedom with the tax. The resulting evidence strongly suggests that cities can expand the supply of affordable housing in this way. During 1979-80, for example, Pittsburgh raised its property tax rate on land from 4.95 percent to 12.55 percent, while keeping its rate on improvements at 2.475 percent. The result was a rapid rise in residential as well as office construction, despite the fact that the nation was in a recession.[53] The two-tiered rate partly explains why Pittsburgh's housing costs have for years ranked among the lowest for any big city in the nation.

During the 80s, Missouri, Wisconsin, California, Massachusetts, Minnesota, and the District of Columbia all considered, though without adopting, similar property tax legislation. The American Legislative Exchange Council (ALEC) proposed several years ago a model "Pro-Enterprise Act" for the states that, through either constitutional amendment or legislation, would give local governments the option to adopt a two-rate real property tax levy, to be phased in on a timetable of their choosing.[54] While advocates of the two-tax system have a tendency to see the idea as a "magic bullet," and are somewhat overheated in their salesmanship, more state governments should consider adopting such a system. The states, of course, should not lose sight of the fact that whether or not land and buildings are taxed at the same rate, the rate on both should be kept low.

Conclusion

State governments need to thoroughly evaluate their housing policies and programs, particularly in this period of fiscal retrenchment. They should avoid, whether through direct expenditures, tax credits/deductions, or bond indebtedness, subsidizing people not requiring help. They should likewise avoid locking themselves into long-term commitments to make households into public charges; today's incendiary politics of housing almost dictates that once granted, long-term housing benefits are next to impossible to remove.

States can indirectly strengthen the housing market through lower taxation, expanded employment and entrepreneurial opportunities, crime control, and welfare reform. A strong economy, and neighborhoods where law-abiding working residents do not fear to tread, may be the best two defenses of all against housing shortages. While the principal leadership in these areas must come from Washington, the states themselves can do much along these lines. That some already have done so provides reason for optimism.

Endnotes

1. Council of State Community Affairs Agencies, *State Housing Initiatives: The 1988 Compendium* (Washington, D.C.: Council of State Community Affairs Agencies, 1988), 7.

2. Margery Austin Turner, "The State Role in National U.S. Policy: Recent Trends and Options for the Future," draft copy (Washington, D.C.: Urban Institute, May 1989), 15-16.

3. The truth is that during fiscal years 1981-89, the HUD budget increased from roughly $15 billion to $20 billion. The "cut" that housing program advocates perennially bemoan took place in authorizations, rather than in expenditures. When Congress authorizes funds, it is setting a spending limit, much as a credit card issuer establishes a credit line for a borrower. It is not "spending" any money.

4. Council of State Community Affairs Agencies, *State Housing Initiatives*, 7.

5. These figures can be found in Irving Welfeld, "Our Nonexistent Housing Crisis," *The Public Interest*, 101 (Fall 1990): 55-61.

6. *Who's Buying Homes in America: Chicago Title and Trust Company's 15th Annual Survey of Recent Home Buyers* (Chicago: Chicago Title and Trust Company, Feb. 1991).

7. U.S. Department of Housing and Urban Development, *Report of the Advisory Commission on Regulatory Barriers to Affordable Housing*, discussion draft (Washington, D.C.: U.S. Department of Housing and Urban Development, 19 Feb. 1991), 7-1, 7-2.

8. Lawrence Litvak and Belden Daniels, *Innovations in Development Finance* (Washington, D.C.: Council of State Planning Agencies, 1979), 136.

9. U.S. Department of Housing and Urban Development, *Report of the Advisory Commission on Regulatory Barriers*, 5-4.

10. U.S. General Accounting Office, *Home Ownership: Mortgage Bonds Are Costly and Provide Little Assistance to Those in Need*, GAO/RCED-88-111 (Washington, D.C.: U.S. General Accounting Office, Mar. 1988).

11. *Ibid.*, 42.

12. Study cited in Richard Bourdon, *Mortgage Revenue Bonds for First-Time Home Buyers: Should the Program Be Continued Beyond 1989?* (Washington, D.C.: Library of Congress, Congressional Research Service, 6 Dec. 1989), 5.

13. Litvak and Daniels, *Innovations in Development Finance*, 138.

14. For information on state housing programs, *see* Council of State Community Affairs Agencies, *State Housing Initiatives*; Frank Keefe and Michael Barker, "Housing and the States," in *Housing and Local Government*, Mary K. Nenno and Paul C. Brophy, et al. (Washington, D.C.: International City Management Association, 1982), 163-79; U.S. Department of Housing and Urban Development, Office of Policy Development and Research, *State Aid to Neighborhoods* (Washington, D.C.: U.S. Department of Housing and Urban Development, 19 Oct. 1984).

15. In some areas of Riverside County in Southern California, people are willing to commute up to 70 miles each way just to be able to afford a single-family home in the $150,000-$200,000 range. *See* Lynn Elber, "Affordable Housing, Unbearable Commute," *Washington Post*, 20 Apr. 1991.

16. Cited in David C. Schwartz and Daniel Hoffman, "Employer-Assisted Housing: A Benefit for the '90s," *Employment Relations Today* (Spring 1990), 21.

17. "Employer-Assisted Housing Gets Boost," *Washington Post*, 6 Apr. 1991.

18. Statement of Martha Burt, in *Rethinking Policy on Homelessness*, A Conference Sponsored by The Heritage Foundation and *The American Spectator*, 14 Dec. 1988, Heritage *Lecture* 194 (Washington, D.C.: Heritage Foundation, 1989), 25.

19. Lilia Reyes and Laura DeKoven Waxman, *The Continuing Growth of Hunger, Homelessness, and Poverty in America's Cities: 1987* (Washington, D.C.: U.S. Conference of Mayors, 1987).

20. According to the 1989 *American Housing Survey*, conducted by the U.S. Census Bureau and HUD (Series H-150-89), there are about 9 million vacant year-round (i.e., excluding seasonal homes) dwellings. The survey is biennial; the results of the 1989 survey were published in July 1991.

21. U.S. Department of Housing and Urban Development, Office of Policy Development and Research, *A Report to the Secretary on the Homeless and Emergency Shelters*, Washington, D.C.: U.S. Department of Housing and Urban Development, May 1984; *A Report on the 1988 National Survey of Shelters for the Homeless* (Washington, D.C.: U.S. Department of Housing and Urban Development, Mar. 1989).

22. For a description of state anti-homelessness programs, *see* Lee Walker, *Homelessness in the States* (Lexington, Ky: Council of State Governments, 1989).

23. *See* Carl F. Horowitz, "Housing Rights Versus Property Rights," Heritage *Lecture* 312 (Washington, D.C.: Heritage Foundation, 1991), 5-7.

24. Lisa L. Leitzell and David T. Somppi, "Perspectives on Group Homes," *Journal of Planning Literature*, vol. 4, no. 3 (Autumn 1989): 365.

25. *For example*, only 12 percent of Chicago's households consist of single-parent families. Yet an astounding 92 percent of Chicago's public housing tenants consist of these households. See John McCormick, "Can Chicago Beat the Odds?" *Newsweek*, 2 Jan. 1989, 25.

26. "Public Housing in Detroit Criticized After HUD Tour," *Washington Post*, 9 Mar. 1991.

27. U.S. General Accounting Office, *Public Housing: Management Issues Pertaining to the Buffalo Municipal Housing Authority*, GAO/RCED-91-70 (Mar. 1991).

28. U.S. Department of Housing and Urban Development, "HUD Troubled PHA Screens," data as of September 30, 1989. For 1990 data, *see* National Center for Neighborhood Enterprise, *The Silent Scandal: Management Abuses in Public Housing* (Washington, DC: National Center for Neighborhood Enterprise, Sept. 1991).

29. To see just how restricted they are, *see* Cassandra Chrones Moore, "Ghetto and Gulag," *National Review* (18 Mar. 1991): 48-49.

30. Irving Welfeld, *Where We Live: The American Home and the Social, Political, and Economic Landscape, from Slums to Suburbs* (New York: Simon & Schuster, 1988), 258.

31. While conservatives can be grateful for this provision, it cannot be ignored that three years is an absurdly long time to demonstrate one's ability to manage housing. There is no real reason, save for protection of bureaucratic turf, why this minimum period could not be six months.

32. Cited in John Scanlon, "People Power in the Projects: How Tenant Management Can Save Public Housing," Heritage *Backgrounder* 758 (8 Mar. 1990), 14.

33. For evidence, *see* Bernard Frieden, *The Environmental Protection Hustle* (Cambridge, MA: MIT Press, 1979); William Tucker, *The Excluded Americans: Homelessness and Housing Policies* (Washington, D.C.: Regnery Gateway, 1990), 140-51.

34. Stephen Seidel, *Housing Costs and Government Regulations: Confronting the Regulatory Maze* (New Brunswick, N.J.: Center for Urban Policy Research, 1978), 32.

35. *See* comments of Anthony Downs, in "Putting Together the Deal," *Builder* (July 1990), 163.

36. *Southern Burlington County NAACP v. Township of Mount Laurel*, 67 N.J. 151, 336 A.2d 713, appeal dismissed and cert. denied, 423 U.S. 808 (1975).

37. *Southern Burlington County NAACP v. Township of Mount Laurel*, 92 N.J. 158, 456 A.2d 390 (1983).

38. *See* Martin Gellen, *Accessory Apartments in Single-Family Housing*, New Brunswick, N.J.: Center for Urban Policy Research, 1985.

39. David Varady, "Factors Affecting Middle-Income Elderly Interest in Accessory Apartment Conversion," *Journal of Architectural and Planning Research*, vol.5, no.1 (1988): 81-87.

40. Howard Husock, "Mocking the Middle Class: The Perverse Effects of Housing Subsidies," *Policy Review* 56 (Spring 1991): 69.

41. William K. Reilly, ed., *The Use of Land: A Citizens' Policy Guide to Urban Growth*, A Task Force Report Sponsored by the Rockefeller Brothers Fund (New York: Thomas Y. Crowell, 1973), 27.

42. James C. Nicholas, et al. *State Regulation/Housing Prices* (New Brunswick, N.J.: Center for Urban Policy Research, 1982), 82-84.

43. Richard Miniter, "Muddy Waters: The Quagmire of Wetlands Regulation," *Policy Review* 56 (Spring 1991): 70-77.

44. *Nollan v. California Coastal Commission*, 483 U.S. 825 (1987).

45. *First English Evangelical Lutheran Church of Glendale v. County of Los Angeles*, 482 U.S. 304 (1987).

46. Anthony Downs, *Residential Rent Control: An Evaluation* (Washington, D.C.: Urban Land Institute, 1988).

47. Arthur D. Little, Inc., *A Tale of Two Cities: Rent Regulation in New York City* (Cambridge, Mass.: Arthur D. Little, Inc., May 1986).

48. Tucker, *The Excluded Americans*, 214-24.

49. U.S. Department of Housing and Urban Development, *Final Report of the Task Force on Housing Costs* (Washington, D.C.: U.S. Department of Housing and Urban Development, May 1978), 35.

50. George Sternlieb and David Listokin, "Building Codes: State of the Art, Strategies for the Future," report submitted to the National Housing Policy Review (Washington, D.C.: U.S. Department of Housing and Urban Development, June 1973).

51. Thom Clark and Hank DeZutter, "The Red Tape Jungle," *Chicago Business*, Jan. 1988, 20.

52. Cited in American Legislative Exchange Council, *Children, Family, Neighborhood, Community: An Empowerment Agenda, The Source Book of American State Legislation*, vol. VII (Washington, D.C.: American Legislative Exchange Council, 1991), 93.

53. For evidence, *see* testimony of Dan Sullivan, Pennsylvania Field Researcher, Center for the Study of Economics, Columbia, Maryland, before the Advisory Commission on Regulatory Barriers to Affordable Housing, U.S. Department of Housing and Urban Development, September 25, 1990.

54. American Legislative Exchange Council, *The Source Book of American State Legislation*, vol. V (Washington, D.C.: American Legislative Exchange Council, 1987), 137-39.

MORAL RELATIVISM AND THE DECLINE OF FAMILY: INITIATIVES FOR THE STATES

Gary L. Bauer
President, Family Research Council, Inc.

Introduction

The states should be little Swedens, to paraphrase Mr. Justice Brandeis earlier in this century.[1] He meant by that, of course, that the states should be the laboratories of representative government. Little was then known of the disastrous effects Swedish socialist policies would have on the family. Those policies have led to a precipitous decline in the birthrate. Illegitimacy has grown. Demands for social services by a rapidly aging population seem insatiable. Socialism, even the ostensibly *democratic* style practiced in Sweden, never leads to the withering away of the state. Instead, it leads to the withering away of peoples. And the withering starts with an assault on the family.

In America, the family had been under assault in a variety of ways before the 1960s. But the rise of the "counterculture" in that decade was endlessly explored and publicized by the media. It provided a quickening drumbeat for anti-family forces. Drugs, alcohol, crime, and illicit sex had certainly been problems throughout American history, but never before the 1960s were there "respectable" authorities who endorsed these vices as "lifestyles."

State legislatures and other state agencies were among the first to feel the pressures of the sexual revolution that began in the sixties. Along with positive reforms that saw millions of minorities and women walking through newly opened doors, the 1960s brought unprecedented pressures to state governments to repeal many of the laws that had provided the basis for stable family life.

The road to the U.S. Supreme Court's infamous *Roe v. Wade*[2] decision was paved in the states. In that 1973 decision, the carefully constructed defenses for human life were swept away in all fifty states. At a time when some State legislatures and courts considered capital punishment for those convicted of murder cruel if not unconstitutional, powerful groups moved vigorously to impose a death penalty on millions of innocent unborn children.

It is no mere coincidence that this same decade saw the beginning of a long period of decline in the well-being of American families. The young Daniel Patrick Moynihan warned of the threat to the black family, in particular, and was roundly criticized. Today, we recognize only too well that we are reaping the whirlwind of the seeds that were sown in that troubled decade.

We see the rise in violent crime, the prevalence of suicide among youth, burgeoning out-of-wedlock pregnancies, abortion-on-demand, unchecked sexually transmitted diseases, and a declining academic performance by Americans. These are the fruits of the sixties.

Then, too, began a coarsening of our public life made inevitable by a flood of dehumanizing pornography. Recently, this debasement has been made infinitely worse by federally-funded obscenity masquerading as art. It is small wonder that best-selling novels depict women as mere objects, or that pundits tut-tut about scenes of unspeakable depravity, but only a few have the courage to call for action against the tide of sleaze. All these trends have combined to threaten the State of the Union.

Focus on the Family and its Washington research and lobbying arm, Family Research Council, are organizations dedicated to defending the home front. The home front has been too long neglected. The ground war in the Persian Gulf, as everyone knows, lasted a mere one hundred hours. Yet more young men were killed in our central cities[3] during those hundred hours than were killed on the battlefield.[4] More Americans have died of AIDS[5] than died in Vietnam combat.[6] More American lives are lost each year in abortion[7] than have died in battle in all our wars.[8] These truths show us that we need a reordering of our national priorities.

Today, we hear a chorus in the prestige press calling for a rejection of the eighties as a decade of greed. These same voices summon up the idealism of the sixties and call for a resumption of the unfinished "march of history." America barely survived the death march of the sixties. In the 1990s, we must reject those siren songs. Rather, we must press on with a basic reform of our institutions and programs that will once again put family first. We now know what the greying flower children of the sixties only dimly perceive: that the family is the department of health, education, and welfare *that works.*

States can and should lead in this needed restoration because states have always been closer to the people than Washington. And, in our federal system, states have always provided the legal protections that the threatened institution of the family relies upon.

In this chapter, I will detail some of the specific threats which will confront state governments in the nineties. I will also outline a series of practical and needed reforms that can be undertaken at the state level. Each of these suggested efforts is based on careful research and reflection. In the 1990s, we may look to the states to provide models for the whole nation and, indeed, for the world. By the turn of the millennium, we may even see Sweden looking to us for a way out of the socialist swamp.

Euthanasia

As anti-family forces work for abortion to eliminate "unwanted" human beings before birth, their allies press on with an attack on the elderly, the ill, and the marginal. Whether labeled "aid-in-dying," "assisted suicide," or "physician-assisted death," proposals to hasten the demise of the sick and suffering—or even of healthy individuals who have tired of life's demands—have taken long, menacing strides in state legislatures and public opinion. Washington State was the first political community on earth to legalize the killing of the unborn by popular referendum. So, there was a dread consistency in the next step. Washington became the first state, in the fall of 1991, to vote on a referendum that could have legalized the administration by physicians of lethal injections for certain patients in their care. This referendum was defeated, but similar proposals have also been discussed in California, Oregon, and Florida.

The case of Dr. Jack Kevorkian and his jerry-built "suicide machine" is well-known. The *New England Journal of Medicine* on March 7, 1991 gave prominence to an account by Dr. Timothy Quill of how he intentionally prescribed sufficient barbiturates for one of his patients to end her own life. The *New York Times* editorialized that, "yes," doctors should be free to "assist in the suicides of terminally ill patients."[9]

The aging of the American population, brought on by the birth dearth and by advances in medical care that have raised life expectancy generally, is a certainty over the next two decades. By the year 2030, there will be more than twice as many Americans over the age of 65 as there are today.[10] The ratio of younger working Americans to older people dependent on Social Security, which stood at 16:1 in 1950, dropped to just over 3:1 in 1970 and 3:1 in 1989. It is expected to decline further to 3:1 by 2010 and to 2:1 by the year 2030.[11] Temptations to expedite the death of thousands upon thousands of elderly Americans, exacerbated by rising health care costs, could be powerful.

Thus, it is vital that State legislators be asked now to take steps to clarify the law and to bar assisted suicide. The legislatures of North Dakota and Michigan have considered such measures. The Michigan Senate adopted a bill in March 1991 by a vote of 26-8 to make it a felony, punishable by up to four years imprisonment and a fine of $2,000, to help anyone commit suicide. In North Dakota, Senate Bill 2332 would also have made assisted suicide a felony, applying the law's strictures to "any person who intentionally or knowingly aids, abets, facilitates, solicits, or incites another person to commit suicide, or prescribes for another person any drug or instrument with knowledge" that the person intends to employ the drug or instrument to commit suicide.

Pornography Victims Compensation

In 1989 the Illinois legislature approved a bill proposed by Rep. Ed Petka amending the State criminal code to permit victims of sexual crimes to bring an action against manufacturers, producers or wholesale distributors of "any obscene material" which proximately caused the criminal act. The statute requires proof by a preponderance of the evidence that the material caused the perpetrator to commit a crime, and it permits recovery of actual damages, court costs, reasonable attorneys' fees, emotional damage, pain and suffering, and loss of consortium.

The legislation is based upon developments in tort law which have extended liability for foreseeable consequences to certain limited classes of defendants. At present, in most states, women have no legal recourse in their own right against producers, manufacturers or distributors of pornography that have direct links to the actions perpetrated against them. All too often, the real culprits are not really liable to the ultimate victims: the battered wives, the rape victims, the abused children.

The evidence of harm associated with exposure to pornography, particularly in its violent and obscene forms, is overwhelming. While pornography may indeed "bore" many of its consumers, there were and are different reactions to this boredom. While some consumers eventually turn away from pornography, many others turn toward progressively harder, more violent, and more perverse forms of it. This part of the pornography market grew throughout the seventies, and is predominant today. These were among the findings of the U.S. Attorney General's Commission on Pornography in 1986.[12]

The phenomenon whereby the addict is driven to ever-harder forms of pornography is called desensitization. To produce the titillation that used to be produced by relatively soft-core material, the addict needs materials that explicitly depict rape, torture, scatological acts, and even dismemberment. A three-year study by Dr. Edward Donnerstein of the University of Wisconsin, done under the auspices of the National Science Foundation, measured the attitudinal effects of exposure to various types of films that linked sex and violence. He found that those who viewed such materials were more prone, as compared with control groups, to underestimate the quantity and seriousness of violence in a particular film, and to give a low estimate to the degree of suffering undergone by a hypothetical rape victim.[13]

Daniel Linz, a colleague of Dr. Donnerstein's, did similar studies using subjects whose psychological testing scores showed them to be of above average aggressiveness. These subjects showed the same level of desensitization after viewing *two* violent pornographic films that the more average subjects had shown after viewing *five*.[14] The Linz subjects exhibited the following attitudes after viewing pornography:

- greater sexual arousal to subsequent depictions of sexual violence against women;

- a greater tendency to endorse deprecatory beliefs about women (e.g., women enjoy sexual violence, women are often responsible for their own rapes, etc.);

- a greater tendency (in a laboratory situation) to punish females.

The tort approach to pornography is new, but the theory behind it is no novelty. A person who has been assaulted by someone who was incited to that crime by pornography is, herself, a victim of pornography. The primary responsibility rests with the assailant, but the producers and purveyors of the material that incited the assailant are also culpable. The harm that resulted was a reasonably foreseeable consequence of their actions. They should be liable to the victim.

Traditionally, tort law demands proof of causation between the act or omission complained of and the harm that the plaintiff suffered. Before the age of mass production and mass communications, this was a fairly straightforward matter. But today, we see more and more plaintiffs who prove that they were harmed by a certain product, and that the defendant manufactured some part of that product, but who have difficulty proving that the defendant's particular product caused the plaintiff's particular injury.

This is the difficulty generally raised concerning tort liability for pornographers. One of the ways the courts have solved it in product liability cases is to reason that if the defendants placed the plaintiff at risk, then they should bear the burden of proving that their particular product did **not** cause the plaintiff's harm. What the plaintiff has to prove is that he or she was injured by a product, and that the defendants manufactured at least some part of that product.

The pornography victims' compensation act under debate in the Congress[15] would require a plaintiff to link a defendant's pornography to an assailant's act by means of expert testimony, the assailant's testimony, or unusual similarity between the pornographic acts depicted and what the assailant did. This is at least as high a causation standard as any seen in the recent products liability cases.

It is time to provide some legal deterrence against producing material that has been shown to turn men into monsters.

Pornography Victims' Compensation II

A second response to the wave of sexual crimes against women, and the need for expanded compensation of victims, would be the imposition of a "sleaze tax" on pornographic and obscene materials, akin to existing "sin taxes" on cigarettes and alcohol.

According to the report of the Attorney General's Commission on Pornography, the U.S. smut industry is a multibillion-dollar enterprise.[16] This profitable industry imposes a variety of other costs on society, however. These costs range from the burden of law enforcement and prosecution of those who violate the obscenity laws to the individual costs borne by women victimized either in the production of pornography or by its effects on criminality among its users. As noted above, systematic research is showing with ever-increasing clarity that pornography, particularly violent and degrading pornography, causes harm to individuals and to society at large.

Tax policy has traditionally taken note of the harm caused by certain substances that, though regulated, enjoy constitutional protection or are otherwise legally available in society. As recently as October 1990 in the Omnibus Reconciliation Bill, the Congress voted to increase excise taxes on alcohol and tobacco in recognition of the physical damage these substances do to both the user and to others, as well as the economic losses associated with health care costs and law enforcement.

A "sleaze tax" on pornography represents sound public policy. The Attorney General's Commission on Pornography reached several conclusions about harm associated with sexually explicit material. With respect to sexually violent portrayals, the Task Force was in agreement that there exists "a causal relationship between sexually explicit materials featuring violence" and actual violence against individuals, and that "the class of such materials" is "on the whole harmful to society."[17] With respect to sexually explicit material depicting "degradation, domination, subordination, or humiliation," the Commission reached a "substantially similar" conclusion: that "substantial exposure to material of this variety is likely to increase the extent to which those exposed will view rape or other forms of sexual violence as less serious than they otherwise would have, will view the victims of rape and other forms of sexual violence as significantly more responsible, and will view the offenders as significantly less responsible."[18]

The Commission divided on the question whether quantifiable harms are caused by non-violent and non-degrading forms of pornography, especially whether non-violent, non-degrading pornography caused sexual violence. It did, however, recognize the social costs associated with the prevalence of sexuality outside of marriage and the attendant costs of sexually transmitted disease, out-of-wedlock pregnancy and childbearing, and other fruits of the promiscuous lifestyle.[19]

A recent systematic review of the research literature on pornography by Larson, Lyons, et al. reached a surprising conclusion: albeit many studies used flawed research designs that would militate against demonstration of harm, "90 percent [of rape studies] show evidence of harm. And 80 percent of the aggression studies show harm."

Given this level of harm, it is difficult to explain why alcohol and tobacco products are heavily taxed, but legally available forms of pornography are not. A system of tax assessment on pornography could exempt material where the sexually oriented matter forms a "small and insignificant part of the whole," an exemption supplied in anti-pornography legislation[20] introduced by U.S. Rep. Tom Ridge and cosponsored by 168 members of the 100th Congress. Excise taxes on alcohol and tobacco products do not rest on the presupposition that all use of such materials is harmful in all cases; neither should a pornography tax.

Funds raised from the "Sleaze Tax" could be devoted to a variety of activities undertaken to counter the impact of sexual harms: support of obscenity enforcement activities, rape crisis and violence against women programs, and the creation of a new Pornography Victims Compensation Fund. The current $125 million Victims of Crime fund in the U.S. Department of Justice draws upon fines paid by convicted defendants in U.S. criminal cases and provides grants to various programs of victim compensation and assistance, including rape crisis centers. Similar funds have been established in a number of states. Expansion of these funds or creation of a segregated sexual crimes fund are possible alternatives for ear marking of pornography excise tax receipts.

Criminalization of Child Pornography Possession

On April 28, 1990, the Supreme Court held in *Osborne v. Ohio*[21] that States are free to criminalize the mere possession of child pornography in one's home. The ruling upheld an Ohio statute that had been defended by the State on the grounds that society's interest in preventing the exploitation of minor children via pornography was so strong as to justify attacking the problem not merely on the supply side (producers and distributors of child pornography), but the demand side (the consumer) as well. The Supreme Court, which had previously held mere possession of pornography in one's home is protected from state intrusion[22] accepted the state's argument.

As a consequence, Congress quickly responded and adopted language at the end of the 2nd Session of the 101st Congress in October 1990 that criminalized possession of child pornography on federal lands.[23] A number of States have taken the same action since *Osborne*. The pernicious child pornography industry enjoys few protectors at any level of the distribution chain today, except the American Civil Liberties Union, which continues to argue that society should protect possession of child pornography once it is produced and transferred to private citizens. *Osborne*, however, deals more realistically with the marketplace for child porn that feeds an inherently criminal industry. With potential constitutional obstacles out of the way, States should now proceed to outlaw the possession of child porn.

Definition of the Family

Definitions of the family have not proven historically troublesome. The family, as the fundamental (and essentially pregovernmental) unit of social organization, is nearly universal. The dictionary and governmental definitions of family in the modern democracies have been so proximate that rarely has it been felt necessary in positive legislation to define the term with precision. Where government has done so, it has generally taken an intuitively traditional course. For example, the U.S. Census Bureau defines family as "two or more persons related by blood, marriage, or adoption and residing together in a household."[24] The heart of the definition is the marital relationship between man and woman with all its generational implications.

Nonetheless, in the past few decades with increasing intensity and effectiveness, organized efforts have been undertaken in city councils, in courts, in State legislatures, in the Executive branches at all levels of government, and in the private sector to consciously redefine the family. Such redefinitions have not been confined, or even truly inspired by, efforts to account for such growing phenomena as single-parent households, although the problems typically encountered by such families are frequently invoked in the cause of family redefinition.

Instead, family redefinition has been pursued as an agenda item for cohabiting couples and homosexual partners. The agenda involves a combination of aims: the first is directed toward breaking down what the advocates of family redefinition see as a "prejudice" in favor of monogamous, heterosexual marital commitment. The other is more practical: family redefinition aims at securing an array of economic benefits and rights that Western society has heretofore reserved for the marital unit.

It is no accident that the first targeted "privileged benefit" of marriage was sexual union. Repeal or constitutional attack on these laws, whether embodied in anti-sodomy statutes (about half of the states retain these once prevalent statutes) or bars to the distribution of contraceptives to unmarried couples (overturned in the U.S. Supreme Court's March 1972 decision in *Eisenstadt v. Baird*)[25], was premised on notions of privacy. For the more far-sighted activists against these laws, however, the prize to be won was the ultimate repeal or deconstitutionalization of the family or marital unit as a protected social entity.

That is where the family redefinition campaign is headed, and its roster of advocates and successes, particularly in recent years, is impressive. To name a few:

- On July 6, 1989, New York State's highest court ruled 4-2 in *Braschi v. Stahl Associates*[26] that a homosexual couple living together must be considered a "family" under New York's rent control regulations.

- In November 1990, the City of San Francisco adopted a "domestic partner" ordinance by referendum permitting cohabiting couples or homosexual pairs to register their relationship with the city for a small fee. In March 1989 the Los Angeles City Council granted a package of employee benefits to domestic partners of city workers. Its actions reflected recommendations by the California State Task Force on the Changing Family, established by law in 1987. Other cities that have granted "domestic partnership" benefits in recent years include Madison, Wisconsin, Seattle and the California cities of Berkeley, Laguna Beach, West Hollywood, and Santa Cruz.[27]

- In 1990, Stanford University moved to the cutting edge of domestic partner promotion and adopted rules granting unmarried couples, including homosexuals, access to dormitories and other campus facilities and benefits previously reserved for married students.

- In December 1990, a major article in *American Demographics* magazine, published by Dow-Jones, predicted that in the 21st century the family would be redefined and domestic partnerships would be recognized in all jurisdictions of the United States. *American Demographics* is a watchword publication for U.S. businesses seeking to detect trends in the American economy.

State and local governments can take the initiative to reverse, or prevent, these trends by adopting general legislation or constitutional amendments to provide a traditional definition of the family as it is to be construed in all government legislation, regulations, or administrative interpretations. Sen. John Marchi of New York introduced one such measure on January 3, 1990,[28] to amend the General Construction Law of New York to overturn the result in *Braschi*. Other states should follow suit, even if only as preemptive legislation.

A second approach would involve the adoption of a state constitutional amendment, as was proposed by the California Family Congress on February 23, 1991. Whether the statutory or constitutional amendment approach is followed, the legislation should begin with a straightforward definition of "family" that would include the variety of relationships established by "blood, marriage, or adoption" and—regrettably necessary—specify that marriage is accessible only to individuals of the opposite sex. These steps alone, whether or not accompanied by delineation of the particular privileges and prerogatives of families, can accomplish a great deal to stem the small but steadily rising tide of "domestic partnership" legislation.

Oftentimes, good people *feel* that the redefinition of the family is inherently wrong, but they do not know how to defend the traditional definition. They want to avoid being judgmental of others. But a recent article in the *New York Times* should show us what is at stake. Polygamists have begun a drive to gain respect and legal recognition for their lifestyle. One polygamist was quoted as saying, "In this liberal age, with all the alternative lifestyles that are condoned it is the height of folly to censure a man for having more than one family." He is, of course, correct that a liberal age cannot distinguish between the family as traditionally understood and as it might be changed. For those who have difficulty defending the traditional family on moral grounds, consider the *costs* of state-paid pensions, medical insurance, and survivor benefits for polygamists. Can anyone demonstrate why "domestic partnerships" should be limited to two individuals? Can anyone doubt that such arrangements will lead inevitably to polygamous relationships?

Opt Out of Title X; Pursue Abstinence

It is ironic that "family planning" has expanded as a public responsibility at the very time the family has been demonstrably declining. In the implicit encouragement many so-called family planning programs give to unmarried sexual conduct, we may see a standing rebuke to the idea of marital fidelity. To encourage family life, we need to discourage nonmarital sexual activity.

In 1970 Congress adopted Title X of the Public Health Service Act, legislation designed to provide grants to agencies conducting family planning programs to prevent unintended pregnancies. In 1978 Congress renewed the program and added specific language authorizing the States to provide birth control devices and prescriptions to adolescents. The legislation stipulated that such services be confidential (i.e., avoid parental involvement).

Over the years, Title X has grown only slowly, but adolescents have become a major part of the program, with estimates of teenage enrollment running as high as 1.5 million in funded clinics. Title X has, however, failed to meet its stated objective of reducing teenage pregnancy. Between two major milestones in the program's existence, teenage pregnancy grew 10 percent. Declines in the teenage *birth* rate have only occurred because of a dramatic explosion in abortions among teenagers.

In recent years, more attention has been focused on the real epidemic: the explosion in teenage sexual activity, whether measured by age of first intercourse (declining), frequency of intercourse (rising among contraceptive users), or number of partners (rising dramatically) per teenager. As a consequence of these developments, sexually transmitted diseases—new in variety and more prevalent—are on the march again among the young.

The historical demise of syphilis in the 20th century is even being reversed:[29]

- Since 1983 congenital syphilis has increased 15 times. Primary, secondary, and early latent syphilis have increased 121 percent since 1985;

- Chlamydia has exploded—4 million cases reported in 1990 (chlamydia poses a considerable threat to future fertility, rising with each recurrence);

- An antibiotic-resistant strain of gonorrhea has developed which has increased 50 percent yearly for the last five years.

Reform of the Title X program has been proposed at the Federal level, as has expansion of an alternative approach (Title XX of the Public Health Service Act) first enacted in 1981. The alternative approach focuses on encouraging teenagers to abstain from sexual intercourse until they enter a mutually faithful, monogamous marriage. States can pursue these issues by enacting their own version of the Title XX program, adding to it mandates (as California has done) that abstinence be taught in any public school program of sex education. Such policies parallel the themes of school anti-drug campaigns, which have successfully emphasized reverse peer pressure to "Say No" to illegal drugs and alcohol.

An additional step some States may be willing to take is to "opt out" of the federal Title X program entirely, as the State of Utah has done from the beginning in order to preserve its option to operate programs without barring parental involvement. Utah has had—and continues to have—an unusually low rate of adolescent pregnancy. The failure of federal initiatives in this area should strengthen the willingness of the states to forego the modest federal subsidy available under Title X and to address more effectively via abstinence programs the underlying causes of teenage pregnancy. The savings to the states in reducing teenage pregnancy by these means are likely to far exceed the modest income received under Title X. An "opt out" effort would take considerable political courage, but it is in line with trends at the Federal level to expand the ability of the states to operate as laboratories for new ideas rather than as mere repositories for federal funds and their accompanying stipulations.

Tax Relief for the Family

State leaders can strengthen the economic health of America's families by easing the crushing burden of taxation on the traditional families with children. The punitive aspect of much of our tax code is in itself a disincentive to family formation.

That the average tax burden on America's families is growing is well recognized. The federal tax burden on a typical family of four grew from 2 percent of family income in 1948 to 24 percent in 1990.[30] At the same time that the Federal tax burden on families has been rising, so has the burden of State and local taxes. In fact, when the Reagan Administration moved to lighten the load on all Americans, many states and localities moved in to impose new taxation. To a considerable degree, families with children have been singled out for this tax punishment. During the same period described above, federal income taxes on single wage earners and childless couples have remained virtually unchanged.

The main reason for this rising income tax burden has been the failure of the personal exemption, the tax code's primary means of adjusting the tax burden for family size, to keep pace with inflation. Had the exemption done so, it would today be pegged at roughly $7,800, rather than $2,150 (where it stands in 1991).

As remiss as the Congress has been in permitting the value of the dependent exemption to erode, many states have been even less sensitive to the anti-family implications of their tax exemption policies. The vast majority of the states have adopted income taxes as a way of meeting current revenue needs. Yet many states have exemptions for dependents worth only a fraction of the federal dependent exemption. Virginia, for example, allows taxpayers to exempt only $800 per dependent. If tax reform is to be complete, efforts at the federal level to raise the dependent exemption must be complemented by parallel efforts in the States. Moreover, state dependent exemptions should be indexed for inflation, so that the family slides no further backward in the treatment afforded it in the tax code.

Another option would be to use monies awarded the states under the federal Title XX Social Services block grants to fund tax relief via an "Earned Income Tax Credit." The State of Wisconsin adopted this approach in 1989, utilizing federal funds to expand a tax benefit designed to provide relief for working parents. The advantage of the EITC approach (Congress dramatically expanded the federal EITC in the 1990 child care package) is that it attracts bipartisan support for an initiative that combines work incentives with low administrative costs. The biggest challenge posed by the EITC is alerting low-income taxpayers to its existence and ensuring that they take advantage of its benefits.[31] Using federal funds to subsidize state tax relief is nonetheless consistent with an empowerment approach that strengthens families rather than making them more dependent on government services.

Increased taxes are taking a toll on families. Due in part to group economic pressure, parents today spend 40 percent less time with their children than did parents in 1965. Not surprisingly, Americans believe "parents having less time to spend with their families" is the single most important reason for the family's decline in our society, according to a recent poll.

Although state legislatures cannot reduce this family time deficit by themselves, or even with the help of Congress, they can help swing the work and family pendulum back in the direction of home by adopting increases in across-the-board tax benefits for children, and by promoting home-based employment. State reforms can lead the way on *home-based employment*. Giving parents an opportunity to do more work for pay from home would help families better manage their income-producing and child-rearing responsibilities. Moreover, encouraging more home-based work is not just good family policy. It is also good energy policy since it would reduce gasoline consumption associated with commuting, good environmental policy since it would reduce automotive air pollution, good foreign policy since it would reduce our dependence on foreign oil, and good anti-crime policy since it would reduce daytime home burglaries.

Accordingly, States should seek to eliminate any burdensome state regulations which inappropriately hinder home-based employment. In addition, consideration should be given to changing state employment policies to facilitate home-based work, flex-time, part-time employment, and flexible benefits plans. In addition states should also consider adopting state "parental preference" policies, which give re-employment privileges to employed women who quit their jobs to care for young children.

This "parental preference" proposal, patterned loosely after existing "veteran's preference" law, is designed to encourage employed mothers to devote more time to raising children when children are young. It would remove obstacles to re-employment, thereby making it less threatening for employed mothers to quit their jobs to stay home with their young children. In addition, a "parental preference" policy would benefit displaced homemakers who unexpectedly find themselves in need of employment after the death or divorce of a spouse.

Adoption

More than a million and a half children are aborted each year[32] even as an estimated two million eligible couples seek a child to nurture and love through adoption. We know that those young mothers who have made adoption plans for their babies are far less likely to continue in a pattern of pre-marital sexual activity. And we know the many benefits that accrue to individuals and society through the blessing of adoptive parenthood. States could act to help:

- Taxes: States could create a state income tax credit in the year of a child's adoption.

- Insurance: States could provide business incentives for companies that give full coverage of adopted children from time of placement to include pre-existing conditions. (Some companies already have this provision). [(Minnesota, 1983; Florida)] States could also mandate coverage of birthmothers' medical expenses by adoptive parents' insurance policies.
- Employee benefits: States could enact laws so that adoption benefits will not be counted as part of an employee's gross income (this would allow for pre-tax adoption benefits). All employee benefits offered to biological parents could also be extended to adoptive parents.

- Education: States should require all school curriculums which address the concept of "family" to include adoption as a positive family-building option.

- Crisis Pregnancy: States could create a voucher system for maternity homes modeled after California's Pregnancy Freedom of Choice Act.

- Adolescent-Family Life: States could create a pool of grant monies for model projects doing adoption counseling/prenatal care, modeled after the federal Title XX Adolescent Family Life Act program.

- Privatization: States could contract out adoption and foster care programs to the private system (Michigan).

- Incentive funding: States could provide incentive monies to agencies which place special needs children quickly (Illinois). They could expand the definition of "special needs" to include minority children, older children and sibling groups (Michigan 1990). States should provide adoption subsidies to special needs children adopted through the private system as well as the public. They could increase adoption subsidies for serious special needs (New York).

- Regulation: States could regulate independent adoptions so that their standards meet those required of agencies. They could allow the agency to include birthmothers' expenses in the fee charged to the adoptive parents.

Divorce

In addition to the national tragedy of families that never form, there is the growing tragedy of families that are broken by "no-fault" divorce. For millions of Americans, the promises of liberation of the sixties have proven hollow indeed. Women and children have been the ones who have suffered most. For them, divorce has too often led to what one writer tellingly called, "a lesser life."

No-fault divorce was introduced for the supposed purpose of eliminating "mess" in those cases where both parties desire divorce. The trend, however, has been towards a *unilateral* right of either party to end the marriage. Thus, only a bit of paperwork distinguishes marriage from cohabitation. Those who make sacrifices in reliance on the marriage contract are deprived of their reliance interest in that contract.

The availability of casual divorce plays havoc with the incentive structures under which marital relationships develop. Anyone can make a commitment and "mean it" at the time. Nevertheless, if one knows that the law will not hold one to that commitment, one's attitude towards it will be vastly diminished.

Monogamous marriage is seen by some sociologists as a triumph of female-imposed discipline against male promiscuity, greatly to the benefit of human society. George Gilder, in *Men and Marriage*, has written that marriage is a *civilizing* institution. But modern divorce law reverses this process, making the exploitation of women by men possible on a heretofore undreamed-of scale.

The time is ripe for state legislatures to re-visit the issue of no-fault divorce. Where no legislation has a reasonable prospect of passage, State lawmakers could still help by holding hearings on the problems and inequities of no-fault divorce. These findings could bring into the public sphere the growing body of scholarly research on the whole question of divorce. The testimony at these hearings would then be available for introduction as evidence in Federal and State court actions.

There is no need to abolish no-fault divorce in those cases where both parties unambiguously wish to end the marriage. But do we really seek a "no-fault" society? Do we really want to tell ourselves that our system of justice is too burdened to be bothered by minor questions of right and wrong? We were promised a Great Society. What we were given is an increasingly No-Fault Society in which individuals are never accountable for their actions and Society itself is placed in the dock. Many people openly advocate "social" spending for all of society's ills, but we can be certain that those advocates will be passing the bill on to those families and individuals who still work to earn their keep.

Parental Choice in Education

No example of individual responsibility is more compelling than the parents' role in the rearing of their own children. And to fulfill that role, parents must make choices about the education of their children. Lamar Alexander, shortly before he was named U.S. Secretary of Education, recognized this: "I don't know how we drifted into telling parents what school their child should attend." "This is America," he told Tennessee editors, "they ought to be able to decide for themselves." This is one of the clearest statements yet of the basic American right of parents to choose the education most appropriate for their children. The challenge to Secretary Alexander, and to education policy makers throughout the country, will be to fashion policies which *empower* parents to make those choices which are consistent with their most deeply held beliefs. The U.S. Supreme Court has repeatedly recognized the *right* of parents to choose non-government schools for the education of their children.[33] And the Court has declared constitutional State income tax deductions for private schools independent of government control.[34]

Millions of Americans are familiar with a basic form of parental choice in education: neighborhood selection. By choosing which neighborhood to live in, parents have traditionally been able to choose good schools. Oftentimes, this meant that those who could afford the best neighborhoods also got the best schools.

Independent schools, including religious schools, "prep" schools, and for-profit training schools, have long afforded a measure of parental choice to those who found the government schools inadequate either for academic or religious reasons, or both. Independent schools include small, inner-city academies that offer structure and motivation to children from low- and moderate-income families. Also included in this group are the prestigious boarding, or college preparatory, schools. "Prep" schools have always appealed to America's elite families. The largest group of independent schools—nearly one out of four in America—consists of religious elementary and secondary schools.

The largest group of these schools—Roman Catholic—educated and assimilated generations of immigrants. Catholic schools provided excellence in a faith-centered curriculum. Catholic schools in the past twenty-five years have been leaders in providing education in the inner cities, including thousands of non-Catholics.

Evangelical schools have been one of the fastest growing groups of new independent schools. Parental concerns for academic quality and their spirited dissent from secular humanism in the public systems have fueled the rise of these new Christian schools. They have joined older associations of Lutheran and Jewish schools in a broadening coalition for choice in education.

All Americans are educated at home. As former U.S. Education Secretary William Bennett said: "Parents are the *first* teachers of their children." Numerous studies have shown parental involvement to be a key factor in children's educational achievement. While most children enroll in some public or private school, it is not surprising that *home schooling* has grown steadily in popularity with parents and in acceptance by the broader educational community. Home-schooled children consistently score high on achievement tests. Their parents show a dedication to their task which causes many others to marvel. Graduates of home schools have gone on to distinguish themselves in some of the most competitive U.S. universities.

Once, almost all Americans who were educated at all were home-schooled—including such distinguished founders of our country as Thomas Jefferson and James Madison. Their families typically hired tutors for their children. Today, home schooling parents have a rich variety of curricula available to them. With sophisticated computer-assisted instruction programs coming "on-line," parents are more able than ever before to meet their responsibilities to their children and to their communities. There has even been a lessening of the legal harassment some home schoolers initially faced. The future prospects for this distinctively American enterprise look bright.

If home schooling is the *ultimate* expression of parental choice in education, it is because it is consistent with the Bible's admonition to parents to "Train a child in the way he should go, and when he is old he will not turn from it."[35] When more and more public schools are forced to install metal detectors to protect students and teachers from violence and disorder, the desperate need for parental involvement, concern, and discipline is made manifest.

A well-developed education policy sees all professionals—teachers, administrators, counselors, and coaches—as *auxiliaries*. Their role is to assist *parents* in exercising their God-given authority over children, not to supplant them.

Happily, parental rights in education have almost always been recognized by our nation's highest courts. The Supreme Court led the way in 1925 with a historic decision striking down an Oregon law that would have forced *every* child to attend public schools. In *Pierce v. Society of Sisters,*[36] the Court rejected any notion that the state had a general power to "standardize its children." The Justices said: "The child is not the mere creature of the state; those who nurture him and direct his destiny have the right, coupled with the high duty, to recognize and prepare him for additional obligations." Subsequent decisions of the Supreme Court have strengthened parental authority (with the glaring exception of teenage sexuality, including abortion). The Court even recognized the right of Amish parents in *Wisconsin v. Yoder*[37] to exempt their children from compulsory high school attendance laws.

Throughout the decade of the 1980s, many innovations were attempted in education. Official government reports termed this "A Nation at Risk." We were concerned about falling student test scores. We were uneasy because of superior performance by youngsters in competitor nations.

We faced an increasingly radicalized and politicized teacher union leadership. For the first time in our history there was a deepening sense that the rising generation would be the first in U.S. history to slip backward in educational achievement. Values were not being "clarified" so much as the well of wisdom was being muddied. All of these conditions called out for reform. The experience of that decade taught us that education reform cannot be achieved without parental leadership. And the key to involving parents is *choice*. As President Ronald Reagan, the first White House champion of parents' rights, said:

> *Choice in education is the wave of the future because it represents a return to some of our most basic American values. Like its economic cousin, free enterprise, and its political cousin, democracy, [parental choice] offers hope and opportunity.*

It is not important to affirm decisions like that of parents to home school their children because a majority of children will be educated in that way in the near future, or even in the distant future. Rather, the action of the states in affirming parents in this way would involve a recognition by government that it is the *servant* of the people. Most Americans believe that. It is a proposition which has distinguished this home of freedom from so many other nations throughout history and throughout the world today.

Germany led the world in many industrial and scientific innovations in the nineteenth century. Germany also led the world in many educational changes. *Kindergarten*—or children's garden—is an example of that earlier drive for educational excellence. But Germany did not teach that *parents* were the ones most responsible for the moral and intellectual development of their own children. The sad legacy of seventy-five years of war, totalitarianism, and untold human suffering, of forty years of national disunity, is only now being healed. In Germany, children were seen as resources of the state. High intellectual and scientific development, universal literacy, and a great cultural heritage proved no barrier to the horrors of the Third Reich when the essential formative role of parents was supplanted by the state.

Communism, too, laid great stress on the education of the young. Literacy campaigns progressed in every Marxist state with vigor at the very time that books (especially religious books) were being suppressed. Great emphasis was always given to math and science instruction in order to assure a productive working class. We see today in the fouled environments of Eastern Europe and Russia, in the corrosive ethnic hatreds that boil below the surface of socialist fraternity, and in the rotting, outmoded industrial plants of the Eastern Bloc the fruits of a policy that ignored the rights of parents.

We are for parental choice in education, therefore, because we are for liberty. And we need to defend parents when they are vulnerable. State bureaucrats who falsely prosecute home schooling parents for child abuse threaten the liberties of every one of us, whether we choose the home school option or not.

Parental choice can exist in a wide variety of contexts, such as:

- Magnet Schools: Originally conceived to aid in public school desegregation plans, magnet schools became popular with parents and students by offering a variety of specialized programs in addition to solid core curricula. Performing arts, languages, science and math, computers, and athletic specialties are among the choices offered to parents of these public school students.

- Intradistrict Choice: A limited form of parental choice, students can be assigned to a selected school *within* a single public school district. Such plans usefully demonstrate the appeal and possibilities of parental choice.

- Interdistrict Choice: Parents and students may select public schools beyond the district in which they live. Minnesota's is the most far-reaching program, allowing broad parental discretion in selecting schools. Other states are following Minnesota's lead.

- Postsecondary Options: Students may select college or vocational programs to attend while completing high school. Such options spur public secondary schools to improve their offerings to retain students.

- Second-Chance Programs: Targeting at-risk students and school dropouts, second chance programs offer students the chance to complete high school despite educational disadvantages. Truants, teenage mothers, recovering alcoholic and drug-dependent students get another opportunity to earn a high school diploma.

- Tuition Tax Credits and Vouchers: Tax credits could be applied to reduce the tax bill of parents who send their children to qualifying private schools. Vouchers operate on the same principle as the G.I. Bill: students may apply government vouchers to the cost of private education up to the covered amount.

- Home Schooling: Parents teach their own children, devoting more time to each child than is possible in even the most elite private schools. No system of parental choice can be deemed to be complete which does not recognize the home-schooling option.

There are benefits for the entire community, not just for parents and their children, in educational choice. Brookings Institution Researcher John Chubb[38] has determined that students in schools that are extensively controlled by politicians and bureaucrats are about *one year behind academically compared to students in schools of choice.* Teachers in schools that parents choose have more freedom to teach. Management in such programs will be school-based. As Governor Tommy Thompson of Wisconsin has said: "The concept of parental choice recognizes that children are not all the same. Schools [of choice] could design curricula to meet specialized needs." Parental choice recognizes, as Hudson Institute scholar Dennis Doyle says, that the *consumer* is sovereign. Improvement comes because it has to come. Competition demands it. Schools of choice would increase *parents'* options and could lure back dropouts and at-risk students. A hazard of some parental choice plans may be the limiting of their scope to public schools only. This would not serve the cause of public school improvement. As Professor John Coons of the University of California, Berkeley Law School says: "Choice confined to public schools may prove largely cosmetic."

The obvious benefits of parental choice in education doubtless account for the growing support the concept receives. Even the National Education Association leadership is unwilling to oppose parental choice openly and absolutely. Their Washington-based spokespersons recently said they only oppose choice that would allow parents to cross district lines or use any tax money for private education. In short, they oppose only the most meaningful expressions of educational choice.

Still, support for the concept grows. Political leaders as diverse as President Bush and Rep. Polly Williams, Jesse Jackson's Wisconsin State Chairman, have supported parental choice in education. Numerous governors are moving to implement choice plans. The Gallup Poll shows 71 percent support nationally for parental choice among local schools; the figure is even higher among minority parents. Business leaders like Xerox Corporation President David Kearns, recently named to be Deputy Secretary of Education, are calling for "the total restructuring of our schools, to be driven by competition and market discipline."

Many religious leaders support parental choice not only because of the educational opportunities it affords and the improvement it brings for the disadvantaged, but also because of the need to sustain the religious values of the community of faith. Parental choice will enable schools public **and** private to resist amoral "value-free" curricula in drug education, family life programs, and sex education.

Conclusion

For many reasons, the United States is unique among nations. Certainly religious liberty and the political freedom it fosters are foremost among them. But our federal system has been an added source of strength which has enabled us to overcome challenges that have defeated other nations. The crisis of the American family has "made in Washington" written all over it. While no federal officeholder ever set out intentionally to undermine the family, it is nonetheless increasingly clear that the effect of federal policy towards the family has been to remove many of the institutional and legal protections that the family needs. Within their constitutional sphere, the States can help to restore the family. Minnesota's Parental Notice Law on abortion provides a model for influencing national policy in a pro-family direction. And state initiatives in the areas I have outlined above can offer new hope to every American family. There is a compelling *political* reason for states to act. Many of the most damaging policies that have been enacted in the past twenty-five years have come over the strenuous objection of state governments, those governments closest to the people. The Union of States will be strengthened when the family union is secured. Let the states lead.

Endnotes

1. *See New State Ice Co. v. Liebman*, 285 U.S. 262, 311 (1932).

2. Roe v. Wade, 410 U.S. 113 (1973).

3. U.S. Department of Justice, *Bureau of Justice Statistics, Sourcebook of Criminal Justice Statistics—1987* (Washington, D.C.: GPO, 1988), 392 (approximately one murder every two hours in cities with more than 1 million population in 1986).

4. *See* John W. Wright, ed., *The Universal Almanac 1992* (Kansas City: Andrews and McNeel, 1991), 34 (38 deaths).

5. *See Ibid.*, 268 (105,277 deaths through 1990).

6. *See Ibid.*, 124 (47,355 battle deaths).

7. *See Ibid.*, 266 (approximately 1.6 million).

8. *See 1992 Universal Almanac*, 124 (approximately 575,000 deaths).

9. Editorial, *New York Times*, 17 Mar. 1991.

10. *1992 Universal Almanac*, 207.

11. Dorcas R. Hardy and C. Colburn Hardy, *Social Insecurity* (New York: Villard Books, 1991), 12, 23, 39.

12. *See* U.S. Attorney General's Commission on Pornography, *Final Report* (Washington, D.C.: GPO, 1986), vol. I, 299-352.

13. *See* E. Donnerstein and L. Berkowitz, "Victim reactions in aggressive-erotic films as a factor in violence against women," *Journal of Personality and Social Psychology*, ch. 41 (1981), 710-24.

14. D. Linz, Sexual Violence in the Mass Media: Effects on Male viewers and Implications for Society (unpublished doctoral dissertation, Madison, Wis.: University of Wis., 1985).

15. S.B. 1521, 101st Cong.

16. *See Final Report*, vol. II, 1353.

17. *Ibid.*, 323-29.

18. *Ibid.*, 329-35.

19. *Ibid.*, 335-47.

20. H.R. 1210, Pornographic Mail Prohibition Act.

21. 110 S.Ct. 1691 (1990).

22. *Stanley v. Georgia*, 394 U.S. 557 (1969).

23. Child Protection Restoration and Penalties Enhancement Act of 1990, 104 Statutes-At-Large, sec. 4818.

24. U.S. Department of Commerce, Bureau of the Census, *Statistical Abstract of the United States 1991* (Washington, D.C.: GPO, 1991), 5.

25. 405 U.S. 438 (1972).

26. 74 N.Y.2d 5201 (N.Y. Ct. App. 1989).

27. Arthur S. Leonard, "Report From the Legal Front," *The Nation*, 2 July 1990, 15.

28. S.6565

29. U.S. Department of Health and Human Services, Centers for Disease Control, Form 732638.

30. *See* Robert Rector and Stuart Butler, "*Reducing the Tax Burden on the Embattled American Family*," *Heritage Backgrounder* (12 Aug. 1991), 845.

31. *See* Rector and McLaughlin, "A Conservative's Guide to State-Level Welfare Reform."

32. 1991 *Statistical Abstract*, 720.

33. *See, e.g., Pierce v. Society of Sisters*, 268 U.S. 510 (1925).

34. *See Mueller v. Allen*, 463 U.S. 388 (1983).

35. Proverbs 22:6.

36. 268 U.S. 5101 (1925).

37. 406 U.S. 205.

38. For a more detailed discussion of educational choice, *see* Chubb and Moe *supra*.

ENERGY AND ENVIRONMENTAL POLICY: A "BIONOMIC" MARKET APPROACH TO REFORM

Dr. John A. Baden
Chairman, Foundation for Research on Economics and the Environment

Introduction: Conservative Environmentalism

Many conservatives, libertarians and classical liberals are strong believers in conservation and stewardship. Nearly all are skeptical of the efficacy, efficiency or equity of centralized command-and-control approaches to the environment. Hence, they often feel frustrated in their attempts to find solutions to environmental problems. But there is hope, for there are ways to achieve environmental goals without sacrificing liberty. Only rarely (for example, in the case of migratory waterfowl that cross state and national boundaries) do solutions to environmental problems require federal action. Most of the time, private property rights, market incentives and voluntary arrangements can be used to reconcile constructively liberty with ecology.

Environmental Politics, Membership, and the Media

To understand current environmental politics it is helpful to examine recent events. For example, the grounding of the *Exxon Valdez* had immense public policy implications. Important questions about the compatibility of petroleum production and environmental quality were thrust into the public spotlight. The spill led critics to question the safety of tanker transport, the importance the oil industry places on environmental protection, and the credibility of the industry as a whole.

Exxon's experience with the spill and events associated with the economic development which preceded it are especially enlightening examples of the degree to which a company that is resource dependent can be exploited politically. This is especially true when a company's environmental problems capture national attention. But the Valdez incident was hardly the first oil spill to become a high moral course.

On January 28, 1969, Union Oil's Platform "A" off Santa Barbara, California, blew out. Three million gallons of oil were released into the

Santa Barbara Channel. The blowout and subsequent environmental damage pitted an apparently careless industry against advocates of environmental quality and protection. Furthermore, Union Oil's poor public relations provided prime fodder for radical environmentalists who equated capitalism with environmental mayhem, boorish insensitivity, and a myopic focus on profits at the expense of the environment.

The message—"oil and ecology don't mix"—became an article of faith for these environmentalists. The Santa Barbara spill conditioned an entire generation's response to the prospect of offshore oil and gas development, and, as a result, the giant field off Santa Barbara's Coal Oil Point is held hostage to emotional seeds planted a generation ago. Despite recent safety advances, the oil and gas industry, and hence consumers, are still paying the price of Union's spill.

The Valdez spill, the worst in U.S. history, could have even greater impacts on the future of America's oil industry and public policy than did the spill off Santa Barbara. When an event such as the Valdez spill occurs, opportunistic politicians exploit it to win points with environmentalists by exaggerating legitimate concerns regarding offshore oil and gas development. Like the 20-year-old errors of Union Oil in Santa Barbara, Exxon's errors will have a lengthy half-life.

So far, the results in the Valdez case have been proposed changes in existing regulations dealing with oil transportation, exploration and development, as well as demand for new and stronger public policy to protect the environment. **Not only the oil industry, but non-oil companies as well, are being pressured to accept a code of conduct demonstrating their environmental responsibility.**

The lack of understanding between the oil industry and the public has a variety of causes rooted in America's political culture. Since the Progressive Era, the public has been highly skeptical of big business in general, and the oil industry in particular. This skepticism has affected the oil industry's relations with the media, and vice versa.

When there is an oil spill, a blowout, or a rupture, there is often a conflict between what industry representatives experience and what the media reports. This was evident in the Santa Barbara blowout of 1969, and several other major spills.[1] This was also true in the Valdez situation when the media quoted New York Judge Kenneth Rohl's comparison of the spill in Prince William Sound to the destruction at Hiroshima. However overstated Judge Rohl's claim, it captures one's attention.

The *Wall Street Journal* captured America's attention after the blowout of Union Oil's platform "A." According to the *Journal*, Fred Hartley, Union Oil's Chairman, walked out to the beach, held up a few sodden birds and said "I'm amazed at the publicity for the loss of a few dead ducks." When asked about the Santa Barbara spill, many people interested in environmental policy recall that comment. They may not remember the specific company, or the name of its crusty CEO, but they remember some insensitive S.O.B. representing big oil saying, in effect, "What the hell, it's no big deal. Who cares except a few wacko ecologists?"

However, that's not what Mr. Hartley really said. A *New York Times* reporter, not actually at the scene, said it, and the *Wall Street Journal* reported it as a direct quote. This was not the *National Enquirer*, the *Star*, or even *Time Magazine*. It was the *Wall Street Journal*, the paper of record for the business world. By treating the story as it did, the paper established a version of the truth nearly universally accepted by the policy elite. A probable consequence of this chain of events is that nearly all Congressmen and Senators were conditioned by this erroneous perception of Fred Hartley's alleged insensitivity.

With the right type of media attention, oil spills can provide the perfect opportunities for environmental groups to increase their membership. By evoking anger and outrage, the media provides reason for people to involve themselves in environmental causes. Examples of this include referring to the Santa Barbara blowout as "an ecological Bay of Pigs," the grounding of the *Exxon Valdez* as "America's Chernobyl," or the Arctic National Wildlife Refuge as "the Yellowstone Park of the 21st Century."

After the accident in 1969, residents of Santa Barbara organized into groups. The first was GOO! (Get Oil Out). GOO! took a militant stance against oil exploration and development, calling for a halt to all drilling in the Santa Barbara Channel. At the national level, the Center for Law and Social Policy was created. The Center was established to specifically fight proposed oil leasing development. In general, environmental organizations benefitted from Union Oil's disaster. One member of such an organization was quoted in *Newsweek* as saying, "That mess did us more good than a million words in Congressional testimony."[2]

President Reagan's appointments of James Watt as Secretary of the Interior and Anne Gorsuch-Burford as head of the EPA also helped environmental groups' funding and membership campaigns. Watt's appointment came when most people were becoming more aware of the environment and the consequences of man's careless activities on environmental quality. As the archfiend who would "sell-it-all-before-the-millennium," Watt was the strongest argument for environmental activism.[3]

Watt's apparent lack of concern for the environment was a boon to environmental organizations, in some instances more than doubling membership. As Lucy Blake, the executive director of the California League of Conservation Voters, said, "you need to create anger and outrage to get people involved."[4] Apparently, she was right.

At the national level, environmental groups have become large, professional organizations/corporations. For example, the Wilderness Society has grown from 37,000 members in 1981 to 295,000 members in

1989. The Sierra Club and the Natural Resources Defense Council have also grown considerably, from 181,773 and 29,600 members in 1980 to 500,000 and 90,000 members, respectively, in 1989. For these three organizations alone, the increase in memberships has been well over 120 percent. This is evidenced by the multimillion dollar budgets of the largest organizations (the "Group of Ten") and their cadres of executives composed of lobbyists, litigators and experts.

Annually, however, most organizations lose members, some with a drop-off rate of as much as 30 percent. (Watt's resignation in 1983 prompted such a loss.) Such high drop-off rates require groups to recruit new members just to stay in the same place. Since most are funded through membership dues and contributions, recruiting is very important.[5] Therefore, to sustain their budgets, they must be sensitive to marketing opportunities.

When we look at the Valdez disaster in perspective, we will see that Exxon, inadvertently, conducted a textbook case of recruitment for environmental groups and for federal action. Environmentalists have used the accident in Prince William Sound to polarize feelings about oil exploration and development in Alaska, and elsewhere in the United States. "Some environmental groups see publicity about the accident and sluggish clean-up efforts as a chance to spur an environmental renaissance."[6]

To strengthen opposition to further leasing, exploration and development in Alaska and elsewhere, environmental groups, after the Valdez accident, held a news conference to chastise not only industry's response to the spill, but the government's as well. In fact, *these groups* are calling for a ban on any further oil exploration and development in Alaska, particularly in the Arctic National Wildlife Refuge, Bristol Bay and offshore in the Chukchi Sea. This increases the value of existing reserves in the Southwest, much as the Wilderness Act of 1964 increased the value of privately owned timberlands because alternative supplies were locked up.

The Sierra Club Legal Defense Fund and the Trustees for Alaska sued Exxon and the Alyeska Pipeline Company on behalf of a coalition of environmental groups. Their stated purpose was to require industry to clean up Prince William Sound and to improve their ability to respond to, and handle, spills.[7] Robert Young, an official in Exxon's Exploration, Land and Regulatory Affairs Department, voiced a concern that can be traced back to the Santa Barbara blowout, when he said, "The spill is being used by environmental groups in an increasingly aggressive phase of wilderness politics."[8] The sentiment of this statement and the pending litigation evidence trends within environmental politics that have been developing over the last twenty years.

Gone are the days when the environmental movement was largely a movement of "nature lovers who joined in the National Audubon Society's Christmas bird count, hiked with the Sierra Club, or fished with the Izaak Walton League."[9] Increasingly, environmental groups are playing a political game: lobbying, publishing and attracting public attention. And the environmental lobby, according to William Proxmire, the former Democratic senator from Wisconsin, is "the most effective one in Washington."[10]

Oil in the Arctic

The conflict between environmental groups and the energy industry has fueled one of the most intense debates in the last few years. In the past, the efforts of environmental groups have focused primarily on lobbying Congress to expand the powers and funding of EPA. In the fight against oil and gas, environmental groups have retained their faith in federal regulation.

The Sierra Club has actively lobbied to influence decisions about oil and gas leasing, not only in Santa Barbara, but Alaska as well. The Club is adamantly opposed to any development in ANWR and is currently filing suit with the Trustees for Alaska against Exxon for the Valdez spill. Michael McCloskey, president of the Club, said the spill "has damaged the credibility of the oil industry in its claim that the prudent development of oil resources in sensitive and delicate environments is possible."[11] Like most other national environmental organizations, the Sierra Club has relied upon and strongly advocates increased government regulation to solve environmental problems.

The Wilderness Society has also actively opposed opening ANWR to oil and gas development. They cite a U.S. Fish and Wildlife Service report that documents the release of large amounts of drilling fluids and reserve pit wastes into the arctic wetlands, endangering wildlife and the ecosystem.[12] As one group put it, "the report confirms that oil development has resulted in serious damage to wildlife and habitat on Alaska's North Slope."[13] George Frampton, Jr., president of the Wilderness Society, believes that oil conservation, not development of wildlife preserves, should be the focus of energy policy.[14]

A report by the Trustees for Alaska, the Natural Resources Defense Council and the National Wildlife Federation, entitled *Oil in the Arctic: The Environmental Record of Oil Development on Alaska's North Slope*,[15] accuses the oil industry of failure to comply with environmental laws and regulations. The report and the oil spill in Prince William Sound support the environmentalists' goal of damaging the public's perception of the oil industry's environmental record in Alaska and elsewhere. As a result, it has become increasingly difficult for even carefully managed oil exploration and development to take place in areas viewed as important for their environmental values.

For the foreseeable future, the United States will depend largely on oil and gas resources, whether imported or domestically produced. Oil and gas do have a potential for environmental damage. However, despite "warnings" by environmental groups that environmental damage is inherent to oil exploration and development, many experts agree that oil development and environmental quality can and do coexist.

Nearly six billion barrels of oil have been produced on the North Slope without significant harm to the environment. While there have been violations of environmental standards, the majority have been quite minor.[16] Government statistics indicate that about 45 percent of the oil spilled into the oceans comes from transportation and less than two percent comes from offshore production.[17] However, the public's perception of environmental damage and pollution results from oil transportation accidents over the last twenty years.

At the national level, the National Audubon Society and the National Wildlife Federation, the nation's largest conservation group, strongly oppose oil and gas development in Alaska, particularly in ANWR. Together with the Natural Resources Defense Council and the Trustees for Alaska, the National Wildlife Federation published a study on the effects of oil development on Alaska's North Slope on wildlife and the environment. The study accuses the industry of creating an alarming number of environmental problems and of violating environmental laws and regulations. The message to the public is that money is far more important to the oil companies than is environmental quality. The conclusion of this group of environmental organizations is that development in sensitive areas of the Arctic is inappropriate.

However, the oil industry has been operating in the Arctic for more than twenty years. Before the Exxon disaster, they could point to their North Slope operations as exemplifying oil development without significant harm to wildlife and ecology. While the accident involved oil transportation and not production, the distinction is blurred in the public's mind. Nevertheless, twenty years of exploration and production, in which over six billion barrels of oil were delivered without major environmental mishaps, is a reasonable record. More importantly, it represents twenty years of moving up the learning curve of how to develop energy resources in fragile environments. It is this record that the oil industry points to when they seek admission to ANWR and other environmentally sensitive areas.

The alternative to "wreck and ruin" development is careful, environmentally sensitive exploration and development. If done deliberately, oil and gas can be extracted with little environmental impact. As the Audubon Society has shown with energy production on its wildlife refuges, oil and ecology do mix—careful exploration, production and transportation can occur while maintaining and even enhancing environmental quality.[18]

Learning from Other States: An Advantage of Federalism

In a September 1989 *Wall Street Journal* article, Dwight Lee argued that Alaska's tax revenues are best considered "common property."[19] Because those revenues are largely paid by consumers and investors outside the state, there is little incentive for taxpayers in Alaska to resist expansion of government programs. And, because no well defined property rights exist to government revenues, the situation encourages a "wasteful special interest race for more government spending now, with little thought given to its long-run consequences." In brief, Alaskans have become addicted to large and often wasteful government programs.

The result of this "race" is profligate spending. A number of wasteful programs and projects have been started and shelved, costing the state hundreds of millions of dollars. Lee provides several good examples of these "budgetary black holes." For example, in 1978 the state began a program to promote barley growing. The state spent over $50 million dollars in loans to farmers, building roads and elevators, and purchasing railroad cars for transport. However, most of the projected barley was never grown. At the same time farmers were taking money from the state to grow barley, they were taking money from the federal government not to.

Faced with a budget deficit, falling oil revenues and declining oil field production, will Alaska's legislators and special interests reduce their demands to maintain current rates of spending? It is not likely. Because of the nature of common property resources (the state budget in this case), users do not face the full costs of their individual actions. It is like two small children sharing a soda. The incentive is to drink as much as possible, as soon as possible, for whatever is conserved may be taken by the other. But, of course, Alaskans are not alone.

Because the governmental money appears to come from elsewhere, politicians and special interests have little incentive to spend responsibly when the funds are raised outside their district. In the case of Alaska, there is no effective mechanism, such as the threat of being voted out of office by out-of-state taxpayers, to constrain their behavior. Here we can so clearly see the key political economy questions: Will politicians continue to promise their constituents endless benefits? Unless citizens increase their recognition of the problem and follow with institutional reforms, the answer is probably yes.

Misguided Environmentalism Inhibits Economic Progress

A recent development may have even more serious consequences for Exxon's and other non-oil corporations' earnings. Responding to pressure from institutional investors holding over one billion dollars in the company's stock, Exxon placed an environmental scientist, Dr. John H. Steele, Senior Scientist at the Woodshole Oceanographic Institution, on its board of trustees.[20] If this addition to the Board anticipates environmental costs and takes appropriate action, it is a useful reform. If, however, it is only a political ploy on the part of Exxon and other companies that follow the trend, it could mean billions of "conscience" dollars with little additional environmental safety.

Environmentalists and investor groups, encouraged by Exxon's acquiescence, have drafted a proposal, termed the "Valdez Principles," designed to "exert economic pressure, possibly including consumer boycotts, on companies that fail to address their concerns," McDonalds recent abandonment of their foam "clamshell" is one such example of response to such threats.[21] The ten principles are analogous to the Sullivan Principles aimed at discouraging corporate investments in South Africa.

The Valdez Principles require an annual, independent environmental audit of each corporation's worldwide operations and public disclosure of the findings. In addition, companies would be required to disclose any environmental or human risks from their production methods or products and any accidents or hazards. Such disclosures may lead to increased litigation against some companies and increased costs of doing business. As outlined, the Valdez Principles are broad and sweeping in their objectives. However, they are also extremely vague. One of the consequences of these new policy proposals is that the future of oil and non-oil firms operating in the U.S. is even more uncertain.

Exploration and Production in Environmentally Sensitive Areas

The National Audubon Society's (NAS) Rainey Preserve in Louisiana shows how well oil and the environment can coexist. Since the mid-1950s, oil companies have run profitable gas wells on the preserve, while maintaining and even enhancing the environment. The fees and royalties they pay are used by the Society to purchase additional land and to fund habitat improvement and environmental education.

The NAS's Corkscrew Swamp Sanctuary in Florida is another example. The Sanctuary, home to many endangered plants and animals, is also home to carefully managed oil development. Clearly, the Audubon Society saw exploration and production as being not only compatible with a sound environment if managed correctly, but also in their best financial interest. The Michigan Chapter of the Audubon Society has had similar success with production in a highly sensitive marsh.

Exploration and production activities have also been permitted in other Florida wetlands and wildlife refuges in Alaska. The oil industry has been allowed to operate in the Big Cypress National Preserve in Southern Florida for over 30 years. Through responsible exploration and production, this development has taken place without harming the ecology or the wildlife of the area. As another example, oil and gas have been produced for more than 25 years in the Swanson River Field which lies within the Kenai National Wildlife Refuge. This development has also taken place without significant adverse environmental impacts.

The Persian Gulf: An Environmental Catch-22

Industry's attempt to attain permission to explore ANWR seemed to be making progress until the *Exxon Valdez* ran aground in Prince William Sound. The result has been a strong political backlash. The image of the industry as insensitive and uncaring has given environmentalists and others reason to believe that oil exploration and production cannot take place in an environmentally sensitive manner.

The persistence of this image will not only increase America's vulnerability to outside events, **it will also increase the environmental risk of impetuous action to open up federal lands if foreign oil is cut off.** The events of 1990 leading up to Operation Desert Storm strongly encouraged advocates of exploring ANWR. But rapid, as opposed to careful development would surely lead to greater environmental destruction. Under these circumstances, if foreign oil is cut off as it was during the embargo of 1973, we are likely to hastily enter ANWR and other environmentally sensitive areas. Development under these conditions is likely to take place with far less regard for environmental impacts or ecological consequences—the very situation that environmentalists and others seek to avoid by blocking new and existing exploration and development.

Energy resources can be developed in an environmentally sensitive manner. This has been shown in Florida, Michigan, Louisiana and elsewhere where oil companies have been given the incentives to do so.

America need not sacrifice its environment or energy security in the face of oil shortages. Rather than prohibiting any and all development, we should provide the incentives to the oil industry to explore carefully and inventory our energy resources. Once we determine the amount of energy reserves available, we can devise a plan to prudently develop these resources should, in the event of an emergency, their value override legitimate environmental concern.

Below, I turn to the task of improving understanding of the political economy of environmental politics. I then use the issue of endangered species to suggest an approach to environmental policy reform that incorporates conservative means to achieve environmental ends.

Market Means to Environmental Ends

While policy analysts recognize that the market provides the means to the environmentalists' ends, few environmentalists understand how an emphasis on market incentives and voluntary action can support their goals. These environmentalists, potential friends of a property rights and market oriented approach to environmentalism, are oftentimes alienated by the antiseptic, business-like nature of this approach. They reject it on the grounds that:

1) economic models neglect what is so important to many, the ethics and the intentions underlying actions;

2) economic models focus upon process—even when the outcome of the process is neither intuitively obvious nor certain; and

3) economic models are based explicitly upon self-interest rather than communitarian or environmental interests.

Unfortunately this gulf between economists and environmentalists is a loss to both economic progress and environmental reform. Economists have the training and inclination to point out environmental problems caused by special interests and perverse institutions. People working in the political economy tradition can help to reconcile liberty with ecology.

As it is, economists have taken three general approaches to dealing with enviros. The first two maintain the traditional rift between economists and potential allies while the third bridges it. The third approach advocates harmonizing economics with ecology in a new "bionomic" perspective where the economy is viewed as an evolving ecosystem, and humans as responsible stewards. The three approaches are:

1) Watermelon, or name-calling approach—Many economists believe that the enviros really have a Marxist/collectivist agenda. In this view, enviros use green paint to camouflage and legitimize an authoritarian, often "red" agenda. These "watermelons" use environmental concerns to legitimize the imposition of their preferences upon others via political coercion. (Authority and expanded government are easily justified if citizens see huge impending ecological losses.) Barry Commoner, Lester Brown, and many other prominent environmentalists assert that today's environmental crisis demands extreme actions backed by governmental force. In their view, freedom must be sacrificed to ecological goods.

These environmentalists are easy targets for economists for they often are sloppy with both data and theory. However, by viewing all enviros as "watermelons," economists alienate themselves from potentially constructive cooperation with people who support environmental groups. Most economists don't resort to *ad hominem* arguments but rather base their criticisms on the scientific merits of proposals for policy.

2) Scientific critique—Many economists note that some enviros grossly exaggerate ecological problems. These economists see the enviros as opportunists who kindle and then exploit people's fears. And some enviros do. For example, the NRDC exploited Alar and Meryl Streep's widespread public recognition to expand their membership and budget. Their PR firm wrote proudly of the success of this enviro flim-flam.

Economists observe that advocates of immediate and often radical environmental reform discount the benefit of additional research. These environmentalists neglect substantial disagreement among scientists on issues such as global warming and declare the issue settled, demanding action now.

"Good Science" is cautious and modest in its claims. It often doesn't support claims that disaster, or even significant damage, is imminent. While this view is intellectually respectable, it alienates the environmental community. It also drives a wedge between ecology and economics, branches of the same Greek root, *oikos*, and hinders the development of "bionomics."

3) Appropriate Economics: A Bionomic Approach to Environmentalism—Many conservatives are conservationists who empathize with enviros and accept their goals if not their means. They advocate noncoercive, market means to achieve them and are highly skeptical of politics, large scale institutions, and force. Again, pointing to the *Exxon Valdez* case they find the command-and-control approach to environmental management ineffective, inflexible and insensitive as well as wasteful. Ultimately, command-and-control bureaucracies respond to special interests more than to a broader public interest.

The fear of concentrated power in private and government sectors leads the free market environmentalist to question large institutions, be it the

Department of Energy, the Forest Service, Exxon, or The Nature Conservancy. Appropriate economics or "bionomics" stresses concepts and processes that share an intellectual heritage with ecology, *e.g.*, spontaneous order, adaptation, and evolution. Below I apply a "bionomic" approach to the problem of dealing with endangered species.

Endangered Values: Species and Property Rights

Ecology and economics share more than the Greek root *oikos*. Both fields of study are concerned with interdependencies. These inter-dependencies are the basis for what might be called the law of unintended consequences. The implementation of a statute like the Endangered Species Act will have unintended consequences, both ecological and economic. We cannot avoid unintended consequences, but we can learn to evaluate policy proposals by always asking, "and then what?" Among these hidden consequences is the impact on the management incentives of private property owners.

In light of the express constitutional requirement of compensation (the 5th Amendment), a foreign observer would probably be surprised that property rights impacts are not seriously considered in public policy debates in this country. Such an observer would surely assume that constitutional provisions reflect central concerns of our society—that social as well as private benefits are expected to flow from the protection of property rights. Like the spotted owl, property rights are threatened, if not endangered. Americans have come to understand the takings clause as a remnant of the past; as a protection for the propertied classes against the efforts of government to provide for the general welfare. It is a view firmly rooted in a half century of judicial attenuation of property rights.

There is no doubt that the Endangered Species Act applies to private lands. Under Fish and Wildlife Service regulations private landowners are prohibited from "taking" or "harming" listed species. According to those regulations, habitat modification can constitute such harm and can therefore be prohibited. There is nothing in the ESA which speaks to the taking or harming of private property rights, but there is such a provision in the 5th Amendment to the Constitution. That provision was designed to avoid the unintended consequences of well-intended government action, for the wise and productive management of privately owned resources.

The pileated woodpecker controversy in Texas and the Southeast and the spotted owl controversy in the Northwest are tips of the icebergs of conflict between endangered species protection and private property rights. The Fish and Wildlife Service is on the verge of listing the

Columbia River Sockeye Salmon as endangered. The Sockeye is only the first of many anadromous fish runs being studied by the FWS. The potential impact for private rights in land and water will make the soon to be announced spotted owl regulations seem mild by comparison.

To date there have been no 5th Amendment challenges to the Endangered Species Act, but pleadings surely have been drafted in anticipation of the FWS critical habitat plan for the spotted owl. Existing takings jurisprudence suggests that the government will prevail in any constitutional challenge to the ESA.

The law of unintended consequences tells us that the public interest might not fare as well. Regulation-induced uncertainties have clear, if unintended, impacts on private resource management. Congress can and should avoid these unintended consequences through the simple remedy of compensation to affected property owners. Congress should do so whether or not the Supreme Court says that the Constitution requires compensation.

Of course the standard objection to compensation is that it is too expensive. The truth of the matter is that we cannot afford not to compensate. Orthodox environmentalists have long advised that there is no such thing as a free lunch. They and our Congress need to understand that the admonition is as true of species preservation as it is of widget production. Here is how they might proceed.

The Endangered Species Act specifically states that economic factors are not to play a role in the decision to list a species as threatened or endangered. But once a species is listed, there are many possible ways to recover it. Economics can play a role in helping to determine the least costly method of recovery.

Under the current system, however, the Fish and Wildlife Service has no incentive to consider economic efficiency. Many biologists even questioned the appropriateness of placing two economists on the recovery task force for the spotted owl. Once a recovery plan is written, the only incentive for public and private land managers to follow the plan is the threat of a lawsuit if they do not.

All of these incentives can be changed by creating a Biodiversity Trust. This fund would be derived from a fixed percentage of the revenues from public land activities, such as logging, mining, and recreation, that impinge on wildlife habitat. If these resources were sold at fair market value, and 10 percent were paid to the biodiversity fund, between $500 million and $1 billion per year would be available.

A biodiversity board of trustees would decide how to use this money. They could buy conservation easements in the areas where disturbances can harm listed species. They could also pay "bounties" to land managers if an endangered species happens to breed successfully on their land.

The trust fund would completely change the incentives surrounding rare and endangered species. Private landowners would support rather than oppose the listing of new species because of the possibility that they could get paid for harboring such species. Trust fund managers would ensure that the most efficient means possible would be used to protect a maximum number of species. In the end, protection would be possible for a wider number of species without all the political turmoil that now surrounds the Endangered Species Act.

Back to Traditional Economic Values

The above example illustrates how a Classical Liberal approach can reconcile America's philosophical traditions with increasing concern for environmental quality. Incentives and voluntary cooperation can emerge as means to ecological integrity, as means to promote a more environmentally sensitive culture. We realize that today, in our society, some of the things with the greatest value have no price at all, do not move through the market, and would in some sense be debased if they carried an explicit price. This understanding does not preclude our using incentives to foster environmental objectives.

We understand that "watermelons" exist as a minority within the environmental community and we understand the importance of science as a check upon unconstrained visions of ecotopians. However, when working with environmentalists, the free market environmentalists do not belabor these points.

I think it is important to stress to these people how to harmonize environmental quality with liberty. An important step is to help environmentalists understand the economy as an evolving ecosystem, where actions have unintended consequences, where prices convey information and incentives and where property rights constrain the uncaring and greedy.

Above all, when working with environmentalists, economists must be modest in their claims of authority and sensitive to the wisdom and insight of others. I hope they find our approach congenial and powerful. The free market environmentalists must establish allies among Sierra Club type environmentalists, for they have far more influence in setting policy than do those of us whose primary commitment is to markets, property rights and voluntary cooperation within a legal framework that protects those resources and values that by their nature do not pass through markets.

Endnotes

1. *See e.g.*, Torrey Canyon, Platform Charlie, Amoco Cadiz, Ixtoc 1.

2. *Newsweek*, 1969.

3. Paul Rauber, "A Nasty Split Rocks the Environmental Movement: With Friends Like These . . .," *Mother Jones* (Nov. 1986): 35-49.

4. Peter Borrelli, "Environmentalism at a Crossroads," *Amicus Journal* (Summer 1987), 24-37.

5. Paul Rauber, 35-49.

6. Caleb Solomon and Allanna Sullivan, "For the Petroleum Industry, Pouring Oil is in Fact the Cause for Troubled Waters," *Wall Street Journal*, 31 Mar. 1989.

7. Philip Shabecoff, "As Senate Begins Oil-Spill Inquiry, The Industry Is Roundly Rebuked," *New York Times*, 20 Apr. 1989.

8. *Seattle Times/Seattle*, 23 Apr. 1989, *P-I*.

9. Borrelli, 24-37.

10. Borrelli, 26.

11. Eliot Marshall, "Valdez: The Predicted Oil Spill," *Science*, 7 Apr. 1989, p. 20.

12. *Wilderness*, Spring 1988.

13. Philip Shabecoff, "Alaska Oilfield Report Cites Unexpected Harm to Wildlife," *New York Times*, 11 May 1988, p. 1.

14. Source: Foundation for Research on Economics and the Environment.

15. *Oil in the Arctic: The Environmental Record of Oil Development on Alaska's North Slope* (NRDC, Inc., 1988).

16. *Oil and Gas Journal*, 1 Feb. 1988.

17. *Wall Street Journal*, 31 Mar. 1989.

18. *See* John Baden and Richard Stroup, "Saving the Wilderness: A Radical Proposal," *Reason*, July 1981.

19. Dwight Lee, "A Bigger Oil Spill That No Alaskan Seems to Notice," *Wall Street Journal*, 20 Sept. 1989.

20. "Exxon Head Seeks Environmentalist to Serve on Board," *New York Times*, 12 May 1989.

21. *See* "Who Will Subscribe to the Valdez Principles?" *New York Times*, 10 Sept. 1989.

A PRO-GROWTH TAX AGENDA FOR
THE STATES IN THE 1990's

Stephen Moore
Director of Fiscal Policy Studies, Cato Institute

Across the nation, in the state capitals from Albany, New York to Sacramento, California, governors and state legislators are sending out budget distress signals. The *New York Times* recently called the current plight of state governments "a fiscal calamity."[1] Some economic analysts believe that the budget outlook for the states is worse than at anytime since the Depression.

While this might be an exaggeration, there is no question that not since the recession of the early 1980s have the states had to combat the levels of red ink that confront them in 1992.[2] Two-thirds of the states spent more money in 1990 than they collected in tax receipts. According to the National Association of State Budget Officers, the states have chopped their aggregate budget reserves in half since 1989 (see Table 1). The fiscal deterioration is most urgent in those states east of the Mississippi, but also has begun to invade some of the midwestern and western states as well. California, Texas, Connecticut, Florida, Maryland, Washington, New Jersey, New York, Rhode Island, and Virginia must tackle estimated deficits of at least $1 billion this year. New York Governor Mario Cuomo faces a staggering $4 billion budget shortfall.

In response to this fiscal breakdown, many governors and legislatures are naturally investigating new revenue raising options. In 1990, for instance, half the states raised a combined $10 billion in new taxes. Last year states raised $18 billion in new taxes, making 1991 the largest tax increase year ever.[3] This year that mark could easily be eclipsed: an estimated two-thirds of the states are contemplating a long menu of new taxes. The most popular options include: raising income tax rates (or, in states such as Texas, Tennessee and Florida that do not currently have one, introducing an income tax), imposing new taxes on professional services, hiking the sales tax rate, boosting "sin" taxes on alcohol and cigarettes, closing loopholes and eliminating exemptions, charging user fees for government services, experimenting with fees on new development, and imposing commuter taxes on people who work inside the state but live outside its boundaries.

Table 1
TOTAL BALANCES AS A PERCENT OF EXPENDITURES, FISCAL 1989 TO FISCAL 1991

Region/State	Total Balances ($ in millions)			As a Percent of Expenditures		
	Fiscal 1989	Fiscal 1990	Fiscal 1991	Fiscal 1989	Fiscal 1990	Fiscal 1991
NEW ENGLAND						
Connecticut	$102	$157	-$379	1.8 %	-2.5 %	-5.8%
Maine	188	65	7	12.7	4.3	0.4
Massachusetts	-442	-1,226	41	-3.5	-9.1	0.3
New Hampshire	35	-30	-5	6.1	-4.9	-0.8
Rhode Island	51	3	6	3.6	0.2	0.4
Vermont	24	11	8	4.0	1.9	1.3
MIDEAST						
Delaware	185	172	124	17.0	14.7	9.8
Maryland	482	178	136	8.8	3.0	2.1
New Jersey	411	1	181	3.6	0.0	1.5
New York	0	0	0	0.0	0.0	0.0
Pennsylvania	497	263	139	4.5	2.2	1.1
GREAT LAKES						
Illinois	541	395	275	4.6	3.0	2.0
Indiana	690	690	492	13.8	12.5	8.2
Michigan	480	391	441	6.8	5.4	5.8
Ohio	815	810	439	9.2	8.6	4.3
Wisconsin	375	243	99	6.9	4.2	1.6
PLAINS						
Iowa	95	71	1	3.6	2.5	0.0
Kansas	371	270	127	17.2	11.3	5.1
Minnesota	946	828	532	15.9	12.5	7.4
Missouri	110	57	47	2.9	1.4	1.1
Nebraska	340	299	148	34.5	25.0	10.0
North Dakota	65	75	61	11.9	14.2	12.2
South Dakota	39	38	11	9.4	8.6	2.3

SOUTHEAST						
Alabama	74	97	-47	2.3	3.0	-1.3
Arkansas	0	0	0	0.0	0.0	0.0
Florida	199	240	228	2.1	2.4	2.0
Georgia	433	37	37	6.8	0.5	0.5
Kentucky	48	87	202	1.4	2.5	4.7
Louisiana	655	546	199	16.3	12.4	4.4
Mississippi	108	26	-32	6.0	1.4	-1.6
North Carolina	157	222	141	2.4	3.2	1.8
South Carolina	146	109	115	4.7	3.3	3.2
Tennessee	228	165	100	6.7	4.4	2.6
Virginia	0	0	-556	0.0	0.0	-8.4
West Virginia	66	100	0	4.5	5.8	0.0
SOUTHWEST						
Arizona	1	6	14	0.0	0.2	0.4
New Mexico	113	108	107	6.4	5.9	5.5
Oklahoma	309	298	346	12.1	11.0	11.6
Texas	297	550	75	2.3	3.7	0.5
ROCKY MOUNTAIN						
Colorado	135	111	44	5.7	4.4	1.6
Idaho	89	84	52	12.5	9.5	5.7
Montana	67	85	67	17.3	19.7	14.8
Utah	119	104	108	7.9	6.4	6.4
Wyoming	112	51	65	29.0	11.8	17.7
FAR WEST						
Alaska	163	268	283	7.2	10.9	10.9
California	1,109	694	1,578	3.1	1.7	3.8
Hawaii	629	456	313	28.2	17.0	11.1
Nevada	67	110	95	8.9	14.4	10.8
Oregon	296	311	306	15.2	14.1	12.8
Washington	516	771	645	9.0	12.1	9.5
TOTAL	$12,538	$9,082	$7,412	4.8%	3.3%	2.5%
District of Columbia	-217	-217	-217	-7.6	-7.0	-6.7

The tax agenda of state lawmakers and special interest groups appears to be on a direct collision course with citizen groups whose resistance to new taxes may be more pronounced today than at anytime since the 1978 tax revolt launched in California with Proposition 13. For instance, in New Jersey, angry taxpayers voted out the Democratic majority in the state legislature to protest Governor Florio's taxes. In Connecticut some 50,000 taxpayers attended a rally in front of the state capitol in Hartford to protest the imposition of a new state income tax. In the past two gubernatorial elections, eight tax raising governors were unceremoniously dumped by angry voters and four others chose to step down rather than face a hostile electorate. This year, in several states—including Michigan, Mississippi, New Jersey and Connecticut—serious tax relief initiatives are gaining political momentum.

This combination of dire state fiscal conditions with overwhelming voter disapproval of significant new taxes has left lawmakers in an understandable quandary about what tax reform agenda they should be pursuing in the short term and for the remainder of the 1990s. On the one extreme is the path chosen by Governors James Florio of New Jersey, Lowell Weicker of Connecticut and Pete Wilson of California, who each tried to close a budget deficit by ramming a major tax hike through the legislature. This strategy has ignited unprecedented state taxpayer fury. On the other extreme, is the more conservative fiscal blueprint involving no new taxes now being pursued by Governors Douglas Wilder of Virginia, John Engler of Michigan and William Weld of Massachusetts.[4] They vow to tackle their states' deficits through spending restraint alone.

This chapter broadly outlines the principles that should guide state legislators in constructing a pro-growth tax policy for the 1990s. These principles are drawn mainly from the major state fiscal policy lessons of the 1970s and 1980s. They can be summarized as follows:

- The most critical tax reform agenda for the states today is to *aggressively reduce tax burdens down to normal historical levels* while restraining the growth rate of state expenditures to the rate of inflation or per capita income growth. On balance state taxpayers today are not under-taxed. Overall state tax burdens are higher than they have ever been in history.

- The second principle of tax reform is that *revenue increases are no assurance of long-term fiscal health* and may impede fiscal balance. The states in the most desperate fiscal condition today are those that experienced unusually rapid, not slow, revenue growth during the 1980s. The fiscal chaos in those states—particularly in the troubled Northeast—has been due to double-digit inflation of state budgets during the past decade.

- The third principle of state tax reform is that *tax increases may severely damage the state's economic performance.* In the 1970s and again in the 1980s the states with the most impressive performance in generating economic growth, rising incomes, and new employment were those which reduced tax burdens, while the tax-raising states generally experienced sluggish economic expansion.

- The fourth principle of tax reform is that *states must resist increases in corporate and individual income tax rates that may seem appealing on fairness grounds, but have particularly destructive economic effects.* Although the overall tax burden has a negative impact on a state's economic performance, some taxes are more economically destructive than others. The most destructive taxes are highly progressive marginal income tax rates. Excise taxes and direct government user fees appear to have a less damaging impact.

- The final principle of state tax reform is that *policymakers must consider the effects that interstate tax competition have on new tax raising options.* They should be particularly careful about keeping their tax system competitive with neighboring states or they will discover that excessive tax rates may even lose revenues for the state.

Achieving fiscal balance without harming the economic climate of the state is the central challenge facing state policymakers today. The task will be especially difficult, given recent actions by the courts and the federal government. Increasingly, the courts are judicially mandating state/local tax increases for education and other purposes. Meanwhile, last year's bipartisan federal budget agreement raised state expenditure requirements—by approving non-reimbursed mandated spending for programs such as Medicaid—and raided the states' traditional tax base—by increasing the federal gasoline tax and introducing new federal excise taxes. Nonetheless, the budget squeeze in the states is anything but a justification for raising taxes. Rather, state policymakers can balance the budget most expeditiously by adopting a strategy of selective tax *cuts* aimed at expanding the state treasury's tax base through economic growth.

Are the States Undertaxed?

A recent analysis by the National Conference of State Legislatures suggests that twenty to thirty-five states will be raising taxes in 1991 to close budget shortfalls.[5] State lawmakers complain that the national economic slowdown and the residual effects of the citizens' tax revolt of the late 1970s has depleted state treasuries of revenues needed to pay for vital state services. Yet few states can make a convincing case for new taxes this year. Figure 1 shows that per capita state tax burdens have been climbing steadily since 1960. Even as a percentage of GNP, Figure 2 shows that state taxes climbed to a new peak in 1989 (the most recent year for which official Census Bureau data is available).

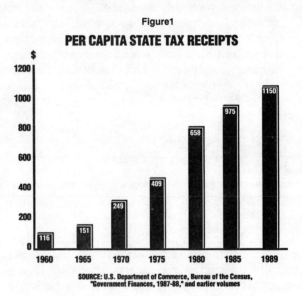

Figure1

PER CAPITA STATE TAX RECEIPTS

SOURCE: U.S. Department of Commerce, Bureau of the Census, "Government Finances, 1987-88," and earlier volumes

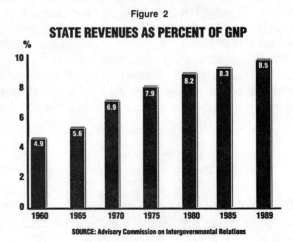

Figure 2

STATE REVENUES AS PERCENT OF GNP

SOURCE: Advisory Commission on Intergovernmental Relations

Many state officials also insist that new state taxes are necessary to replace steep declines in federal aid to state and local governments. But in fact, federal aid in recent years has been climbing not falling.[6] In constant 1982 dollars federal payments to state and local governments slipped from a high water mark of $110 billion in 1978 to $91 billion in 1987. By 1991 these payments were back up to a new peak of $111 billion. The current fiscal plight of the states cannot be reasonably blamed on declining federal aid when these payments have *risen* by over 20 percent in real dollars in the past four years.

The recent budget deterioration of the eight northeastern states—Connecticut, Maine, Massachusetts, New Hampshire, New Jersey, New York, Rhode Island, and Vermont—is a case study in how new taxes can be a double-edged sword for state governments.[7] Thanks to rapid economic growth in the 1980s, tax revenues grew by an enormous 80 percent between 1981 and 1988 in those eight states. That was a 20 percent faster rate of revenue expansion than experienced in all other states. In fact, even over the more recent 1987-1990 period, tax receipts in the eight northeastern states grew more rapidly than in the rest of the nation—22 percent versus 20 percent in all other states. (see Table 2) Yet the bottom panel of the table shows that despite this faster revenue growth, these eight states had negative budget reserves of 2 percent in 1990 while the 42 other states had 4 percent positive balances.

What, then, is the explanation for the northeastern states being awash today in red ink? Their plight can be summarized concisely: rapid revenue growth invited unbridled spending expansion on programs that now cannot be cut back. As the *Washington Post* recently summarized the situation: "The main reason for budget shortfalls from Concord to Trenton has been...mushrooming spending that doubled and tripled many outlays in these prosperous states."[8] Indeed, between 1981 and 1989 outlays escalated by 173 percent in Connecticut, 137 percent in Massachusetts, 145 percent in New Jersey, 116 percent in New York, and 115 percent in Maine and New Hampshire. This data would suggest that higher taxes are not a formula for budget balance but expenditure growth.

Careful empirical research confirms this tax and spend relationship. Examining state budget data from 1952 through 1982, former U.S. Treasury Department economists Michael Marlow and Neela Manage conclude: "The results of our tests indicate that tax receipts cause expenditures at the state level of government."[9] In other words, historically, raising taxes has been a false prescription for attaining fiscal balance in the states: a lesson the eight states of the Northeast are now painfully learning.

Table 2

Taxes and Budget Reserves in the Northeastern States

General Tax Revenues

State	1987	1990	% Change 1987-90
Connecticut	4,742	6,112	29%
Maine	1,118	1,419	27%
Massachusetts	6,964	8,272	19%
New Hampshire	538	568	6%
New Jersey	9,339	11,407	22%
New York	24,688	29,229	18%
Rhode Island	1,187	1,461	23%
Vermont	482	588	22%
Total Northeast			22%
All Other States			20%

Budget Reserves

State	1987	1990
Connecticut	4.9	-2.5
Maine	8.1	4.3
Massachusetts	1.1	-9.1
New Hampshire	9.8	-4.9
New Jersey	7.9	0.0
New York	0.7	0.0
Rhode Island	12.5	0.2
Vermont	14.0	1.9
Total Northeast	3.0	-2.0
All Other States	3.0	4.0

Source: National Association of State Budget Officers, *Fiscal Survey of the States*, 1988, 1989, 1990 editions.

The Effect of New Taxes on State Economic Performance

For many decades the conventional wisdom among economists and experts in public finance was that state tax burdens had very little impact on the economic performance of the individual states. The standard argument was that factors, such as the quality of the infrastructure, proximity to markets, quality of the work force, cost of living, quality of education, availability of natural resources, and energy costs, were substantially more important in determining the standard of living in a state than were taxes. For instance, one prominently cited study concluded that "empirical evidence that taxes affect interregional business location decisions is almost nonexistent."[10]

Yet over the past ten years this verdict has been overturned. Virtually all of the recent research on state economic development finds that taxes play a vital role in determining growth rates. Today, the overwhelming consensus opinion is that low tax states economically outperform high tax states.

Taxes and Economic Growth Rates

In a landmark 1982 study, economist Robert Genetski of the Harris Bank in Chicago compared each state's taxes as a percentage of income with each state's income growth between 1963 and 1980. Although he did not find a systematic relationship between average tax burden and income growth, he did uncover "an inverse relationship between *changes* in state relative tax burdens and state relative economic growth."[11] According to Genetski, "Those states with decreasing relative tax burdens tend to experience subsequent above average income growth. Those states with increasing relative tax burdens tend to experience subsequent below average growth."

A 1988 study by A.B. Laffer Associates confirms this relationship. The Laffer study reveals that "during the 1980-1986 period, a negative and significant relation [emerged] between changes in states' relative tax burdens and their rates of economic growth."[12] Laffer Associates has found that fully one-third of "a state's economic performance is associated with changes in the average tax rates relative to the national average."

Table 3 underscores this negative relationship in an easy to understand non-statistical fashion. The table compares the real per capita income growth and the job growth in the five states that raised taxes most rapidly between 1978 and 1987 to the five states that made the deepest tax reductions. The "tax reduction" states saw per capita income rise by an average of 8.5 percent over the period, while in the five "tax increase" states growth fell by 1.1 percent. Similarly, the average unemployment rate in the "tax cut" states fell by half a percentage point, while joblessness rose by 2.6 percent in the "tax increase" states.

Case Study 1: Massachusetts

Massachusetts in particular is a microcosm of how changes in tax burdens can dramatically affect the economic fortunes of a state. Between 1970 and 1978 the state's tax burden as a percentage of personal income

Table 3

Taxes and State Economic Development in the 1980s:
Five Highest Tax-Increase States and the Five Highest Tax-Cut States

	Percentage Change Between 1978-1987 in:		
	State/Local Tax Revenue Per $1,000 Income	Real Per Capita Income	Unemployment Rate* (percentage points)
Ohio	+14.1	+3.6	+1.6
Wyoming	+13.4	-19.6	+5.3
Utah	+4.9	-3.5	+2.6
North Carolina	+4.2	+15.4	+0.2
Iowa	+3.8	-1.3	+1.5
Average 5 Highest Tax-Increase States**		-1.1	+2.6
California	-20.1	+8.8	-1.3
Massachusetts	-17.5	+30.1	-2.9
North Dakota	-12.5	-2.9	+0.4
Montana	-11.7	-5.1	+1.2
Arizona	-11.6	+11.7	+0.1
Average 5 Highest Tax-Cut States		+8.5	-0.5

*State Unemployment rate in 1987 minus state unemployment rate in 1978.
**Excluding Alaska
Source: National Conference of State Legislatures, " Interstate Tax Comparisons and How They Have Changed Over Time," Legislative Finance Paper No. 66, 1989; U.S. Department of Commerce, Bureau of Economic Analysis, unpublished data on state income growth; and U.S. Department of Labor, Bureau of Labor Statistics, unpublished data, 1989.

rose by twenty percent—third fastest in the nation—and per capita income plummeted. The state earned the derisive nickname "Taxachusetts" and was quickly "on its way to becoming a banana republic," recalls University of Massachusetts Professor Ralph Whitehead, Jr.[13]

In 1980 the state passed Proposition 2 1/2, modeled after California's Proposition 13, and shortly thereafter it substantially cut capital gains taxes. Within five years of the passage of these two tax cuts, the state's relative tax burden had been slashed by almost 25 percent, and by 1986 its per capita income had risen by almost 30 percent—five times faster than the national average. This economic success was quickly touted as the "Massachusetts miracle." Then, beginning in 1986, because of surging state government spending, Massachusetts began to raise taxes again; as theory would predict, its economic revitalization has subsequently stalled. Its bond rating has been lowered twice in the past two years, as its budget deficit has skyrocketed. Thanks to new taxes, the "Massachusetts miracle" is now the "Massachusetts mirage."[14]

Case Study 2: New Hampshire and Vermont

Vermont and New Hampshire are two neighboring northeastern states which have much in common.[15] But their tax codes are widely dissimilar. In 1987 New Hampshire had a lower per capita tax burden as a percentage of personal income than any of the fifty states (12 percent), while Vermont ranked 36th (17 percent of personal income). Further, the per capita dollar tax burden was $1,965 in New Hampshire but $2,251 in Vermont.

Yet, despite the lower tax burden, from 1975 through 1987 New Hampshire's tax revenues grew more quickly than Vermont's. The reason: New Hampshire's economy prospered over the period. According to a study on the fiscal systems of New Hampshire and Vermont by Professor Colin Campbell of Dartmouth University and by Rosemary Campbell: "More rapid economic growth in New Hampshire than in Vermont accounts for most of the larger increase in tax revenue in New Hampshire. From 1975 to 1987, New Hampshire's population grew by 27.3 percent compared to 14.3 percent in Vermont, and personal income rose by 299 percent in New Hampshire compared to 216 percent in Vermont." But even New Hampshire has ignored the fiscal policy lesson in recent years and has thus suffered a reversal of fortune. By enacting a series of tax increases from 1988 through 1990, New Hampshire has surrendered some of its comparative advantage on taxes and is now suffering a severe recession.

Taxes and Employment Growth

Statistical studies reveal that the number of new jobs created within a state is also adversely affected by rising tax burdens. Economists Michael Wasylenko and Therese McGuire in a 1985 study found that between 1973 and 1980 the overall tax effort (taxes as a percentage of income) in a state had "a negative and statistically significant effect on overall employment growth and on employment growth in manufacturing, retail trade and services."[16]

This negative relationship between taxes and employment applies to cities as well as states. Princeton economist Ronald Grieson investigated employment growth during the 1960s and early 1970s in two major U.S. cities: New York and Philadelphia.[17] He found that every 30 percent increase in city income taxes during this period caused an 11 percent decline in manufacturing employment in Philadelphia and a 10 percent decline in New York City. Grieson estimated that New York's taxes were "perhaps above the revenue maximizing point." In other words, the city might have increased revenues if it had imposed a lower tax rate. Wasylenko and McGuire also found that sales taxes, which are traditionally thought not to impair employment opportunities, "had a negative and statistically significant effect on wholesale trade employment." The single stipulation to this general finding was that when the increased taxes were used to fund education, the effect on employment of taxes was positive.

Taxes and Business Investment

Perhaps the most destructive effects of high taxes is in discouraging new business investment. A 1982 survey of corporate executives of high technology firms by Robert Premus for the Joint Economic Committee also found that businesses are attracted to areas that impose low taxes.[18] Table 4 shows that most corporations when choosing plant locations, regard as "very important" both the general level of taxes in a region and the tax burdens of states within a region. The study found that whether taxes fall directly on workers or businesses is not as important as the overall level of taxes in the state. The report explains why:

> State and local taxes influence the willingness of high technology companies to invest in a region for two interrelated reasons. First, the portion of the tax bill that falls directly on business will result in a reduction in the rate of return on investment in new technologies. Second, the portion of the tax that falls on workers will result in a reduction in real after-tax income and make it more difficult for high technology companies to attract and hold skilled labor. As a result, in a tight labor market, state and local taxes are likely to be forced onto the businesses in the form of tax-compensated wage increases, reducing further the rate of return on investment in the region.

This is only one of a series of studies that have come to the same conclusion. James A. Papke, a professor of business at Purdue University, reviewed over two dozen studies on the influence of tax burdens on business investment.[19] He concludes from this comprehensive review of the literature: "There is now widespread recognition among a variety of public finance scholars that taxes are an important factor in the plant location decision process. Recent evidence suggests [the effect] is discernible and not inconsequential."

Case Study 3: New York

The classic case of high average tax burdens chasing away investment is New York State.[20] In the 1970s state and local governments in

Table 4

Taxes and State/Regional Business Investment
Survey of 691 Executives of High Technology Firms

Rank	Factor	Percent Responding "Important" or "Very Important"
Top Five Factors that Influence Regional Plant Locations		
1	Labor Skills/Availability	89
2	Labor Costs	72
3	Tax Climate Within Region	67
4	Academic Institutions	59
5	Cost of Living	58
Top Five Factors that Influence Plant Locations within Region		
1	Availability of Workers	96
2	State and/or Local Taxes	85
3	Local Attitudes Toward Business	82
4	Property and Construction Costs	79
5	Transportation for Workers	76

Source: Robert Premus, "Location of High Technology Firms and Regional Economic Development," Joint Economic Committee, 1982.

New York had so appreciably shrunk their corporate tax base due to high tax burdens, that higher taxes were producing lower, not higher, revenues. Over half a million people left New York in the 1970s, causing a loss of state and local tax revenues of $640 million. According to a 1976 New York State Special Task Force on Taxation formed to investigate the flight of people and capital:

> There is evidence that the present tax structure is, in many respects, counterproductive, fostering as it has an exodus of business, industry, and individuals, eroding the tax base, and shifting the burden of taxation relentlessly down the income scale. Either New York reduces tax levels now, or New York, by inaction, will suffer an even greater revenue loss through further erosion of its tax base.

Undeterred, in the 1980s New York further raised its massive tax burden. From 1983 to 1988 its state taxes as a percentage of personal income rose by just less than 10 percent. As should have been expected, the 1990 Census reveals that New York was one of the biggest losers of population and business in the 1980s.

What Are the Most Economically Damaging State Taxes?

The above brief sample of case studies and empirical research on state taxes and economic performance demonstrates that today there is nearly unanimous agreement in the economics and public finance fields that higher overall tax burdens will harm a state's economy. Similarly, by pursuing a course of tax reduction, policymakers can stimulate job creation, business investment, and income growth. This means that policymakers concerned about how tax actions will affect the economy of the state should concentrate less on **what types of taxes to raise or cut, and more on the overall tax burden in the state.**

Nonetheless, lawmakers who feel compelled to raise taxes may at least wish to pursue the least destructive tax increase option. Alternatively, states with an opportunity to cut taxes may wish to identify and eliminate those current taxes that have particularly pernicious effects. For this reason, state policymakers often are interested in the issue: What taxes are the most damaging to the state economy?

Unfortunately, there is far from universal agreement on this point. Unlike Alaska, which taxes oil that is exported into other states, few states have the luxury of exporting their tax burdens, so every tax does some degree of harm. (Even commuter taxes often deter new business investment in a state.) One of the reasons that general conclusions are elusive on the question—What is the ideal state tax code?—is that the answer may depend on the unique circumstances of the individual states. For example, small states, such as New Jersey, with large population segments living near the border of other states may suffer more loss of retail sales from a high sales tax than large states, such as Texas, where it may be highly inconvenient for residents to travel outside the state to shop and escape the tax. Similarly, a state may suffer less loss of business and population by raising its income tax if it is surrounded by states with still higher income tax rates, than if it is surrounded by low income tax states.

With this caveat plainly stated, there are some tentative conclusions that can be drawn about the economic effects of specific types of taxes. These conclusions may be thought of as holding true under most, but not all, circumstances. They are as follows:

1) **The Most Depressive Tax Increase Is a Rise in Personal Income Tax Rates.**

Governors and state legislators are naturally drawn to the income tax as the "fairest" tax, because it is progressive and based on the ability to pay.[21] New Hampshire and Texas are two states which have never had an income tax but are now considering one. Most of the evidence, however, reveals income taxes are the single most anti-growth tax. In 1982 the Joint Economic Committee (JEC) of the U.S. Congress substantiated this.[22] The JEC compared the tax policies in the 16 fastest income growing states and the slowest income growing states from 1970 to 1979. The results, shown in Table 5, demonstrate that income growth in a state is inversely related to:

- The level of state and local tax burdens,
- The changes in state and local tax burdens,
- The amount of *income taxes* levied in the state, and
- The *progressivity* of the income tax rates in the state.

Table 5

Differing Tax Policies of High and Low Growth States

Tax Measure	High Growth States 1970-1979	Low Growth States 1970-1979
Change in State/Local Taxes Per $1,000 Income, 1970-1979	+$0.80	+$7.51
State/Local Personal Income Taxes Per $1,000 Income, 1970	$7.10	$14.90
Change in State/Local Personal Income Taxes Per $1,000 Income, 1970-1979	$4.89	$8.08
State/Local Corporate Income Taxes Per $1,000 Income, 1970	$2.90	$6.26
State Income Tax Progressivity, 1970*	3.30 percent	5.40 percent

*Highest marginal tax rate minus lowest marginal tax rate. The higher the percentage, the more progressive a state's tax code.
Source: Ricard K. Vedder, "State and Local Economic Development Strategy: A Supply Side Perspective," Joint Economic Committee, October 1991.

These relationships were found to be statistically significant. The conclusion of the study was as follows:

> The evidence is strong that tax and expenditure policies of state and local governments are important in explaining variations in economic growth between states—far more important than other factors frequently cited such as climate, energy costs, the impact of federal fiscal policies, etc. It is clear that high rates of taxation lower the rate of economic growth, and that states that lower their tax burdens are rewarded with an enhancement in their economic growth. Income taxes levied on individuals and

corporations are particularly detrimental to growth, more so than consumption-based taxes or user charges that do not reduce incentives to work or form capital. Progressive taxation not only lowers the rate of economic growth compared with proportional or regressive taxation, but in the process hurts the very persons that progressive taxes are designed to help: the poor.

Case Study 4: Iowa

A 1987 study by the Iowa Tax Education Foundation entitled "The Iowa Exodus: Why Are People Leaving the State?" interviewed 251 former Iowans who moved out of the state in 1980s.[23] The report found that the state's very high income tax rates were a major factor in explaining the out-migration. It tells this sobering tale:

During the 1980s Iowa has experienced a significant population loss. Between 1980 and 1987 80,000 Iowans left the state. Sayings such as—"Will the last Iowan who leaves please shut off the lights"—were common.

Our survey results reveal that Iowans leave for a variety of reasons. Job opportunities, Iowa's overall tax situation, and the Iowa personal income tax appear to play the largest role in people's decision to leave.

Older people, high income individuals, and high net worth Iowans are very sensitive to Iowa taxes. In fact, Iowa's personal income tax plays a very significant role in the decision making process of these individuals.

Perhaps most disturbing is the fact Iowa is losing the very people it needs to spark economic development and growth. As evidenced in this sample, Iowa is losing both its new generation of young professionals and its crop of wealthy individuals who are needed to fund future economic growth.

Case Study 5: Illinois

Illinois is now facing the same problems thanks to its rising personal income tax rate. In 1989 the state passed a temporary 20 percent income tax surcharge which now the new governor Bob Edgar wishes to make permanent. According to an economic analysis of the tax surcharge by the Chicago-based Heartland Institute, the tax would have a devastating effect on the state in the 1990s if made permanent.[24]

Based on our study of the experiences of other states, we would predict an annual loss of $400 million in personal income that would have been created during the coming decade in the absence of the tax increase. This lost personal income corresponds to an annual loss of approximately 10,000 jobs that otherwise would have been created.

During the course of the 1990s, then, a permanent 20 percent increase in the personal income tax rate could cost the residents of Illinois approximately $5 billion in lost income and 100,000 jobs.

Case Study 6: New Jersey

In 1990, faced with a $1 billion plus budget deficit and a court mandated education reform program, Governor James Florio approved a $2.8 billion tax increase. Although the new taxes include substantial increases in excise taxes including an increase in the sales tax from 6 to 7 percent, the major tax change was in the income tax rates. Florio doubled the top marginal rate to 7 percent for individuals earning over $75,000, one of the highest top rates in the nation. The ambitious program is being viewed as a national experiment on the effects of new taxes on a state's economic pulse. An initial economic analysis by the New Jersey-based economics consulting firm Polyconomics predicts "a severe economic recession" in New Jersey with growth as much as 3 percent lower than it would otherwise be by 1992.[25] The report continues:

> State tax revenues could decline by approximately 5 to 10 percent by 1992 with property tax revenues of local governments possibly declining by as much as 20 to 30 percent. Net relocation of corporate offices to the state will turn negative, eliminating about half the demand for mid-range ($250,000 to $500,000) homes, and about two-thirds of the demand for new office space....

A vicious cycle of declining property values and declining tax revenues, combined with higher property tax revenue requirements, will throw many New Jersey communities into fiscal crisis.

Already some of these dire predictions appear to be proving highly accurate. Real estate values in New Jersey have dropped substantially over the past twelve months and unemployment has climbed from below to above the national average.

In sum, the empirical and state by state evidence suggests that governors and state legislators first and foremost should resist increases in personal income tax rates in redesigning their tax codes. Indeed, a pro-growth strategy would involve substantial reductions in this tax.

2) Corporate Income Taxes Deter Growth.

Corporate income taxes are only slightly less anti-growth than personal income taxes. Corporate taxes have a particularly negative effect on state employment opportunities. Economist Robert Newman in 1983 examined state employment growth between 1957 and 1973 and uncovered evidence that high corporate taxes reduce state employment in "capital-intensive industries."[26] Newman concludes that each 10 percent rise in the corporate income tax leads to a 1.4 percent decline in employment.

Later, in a 1985 study Timothy Bartik of Vanderbilt University reported an even stronger employment effect. Bartik found that the plant location decisions between 1972 and 1978 of Fortune 500 companies were significantly influenced by state corporate tax policies.[27] According to Bartik:

> A 10% increase in a state's corporate income tax rate (for example, from 4.0% to 4.4%) is estimated to cause a 2-3% decline in the number of new plants. A 10% increase in a state's average business property tax rate (for example, from 2.0% to 2.2%) is estimated to cause a 1-2% decline in the number of new plants....These changes in business location patterns put some limitations on the ability of states to redistribute income away from corporate stockholders, both in state and out of state, and toward other state residents.

An amendment to this general conclusion is that business taxes which are aimed at taxing out of state corporate subsidiaries—so-called "unitary taxes" are enticing but should be avoided. The evidence suggests that out-of-state firms are discouraged from locating subsidiaries in states with unitary taxes. This is because the unitary tax charges out-of-state corporate branches for government services they do not directly benefit from.[28]

3) State Sales Taxes May Be Less Harmful than Income Taxes But Often Have Unintended Consequences.

State sales taxes are generally believed to have a less damaging economic and employment impact than state corporate and personal income taxes. For instance, Ohio University economist Richard Vedder, who is one of the nation's leading experts on interstate tax competition and the author of several prominent studies on the subject, contends that "the optimal state and local fiscal policy would be one in which the overall tax burden is comparatively low, coupling high sales taxes with low income and property taxes."[29]

Although this seems to be the prevailing viewpoint among economists who have studied the issue, sales taxes can have very negative effects under certain circumstances. Sales taxes may deter retail sales and may raise the cost of living in a state, which may mean higher labor costs and more inflation. The earlier cited study by Wasylenko of Pennsylvania State University and McGuire of City College of New York which investigated the effects of state taxes on employment in six industries did uncover negative effects from the sales tax. In particular, they found that between 1973 and 1980, "the sales tax had a negative and statistically significant effect on wholesale trade employment."[30]

Case Study 7: Washington and Oregon

The two neighboring western states of Washington and Oregon have pursued divergent sales tax policies, thus providing a testing ground for the hypothesis that sales taxes may harm retail sales activity. The *Wall Street Journal* reports that in 1986 the sales tax in Washington's major city, Seattle, was 8.1 percent, while in Oregon's major city, Portland, there was no sales tax.[31] General merchandise sales in 1986 were 69 percent higher in Portland than in Seattle even though income was 18 percent higher per person in Seattle. Forty percent of all new jobs in Portland are in the retail trade sector. As one Portland store owner noted: "It's not that Portland people are living high. It's that others are coming here to shop."

Case Study 8: New Jersey

In some cases, very high excise taxes on particular big-ticket items may even cost the states revenues. That is, higher sales tax rates may lead to *lower* revenues from the tax. Consider the market response to Governor James Florio's new 7 percent sales tax imposed on heavy trucks in 1990. According to an investigative story by the *Times of New Jersey*, after the imposition of the tax, truck sales dropped by 90 percent.[32] In the last two months of 1990 only 49 trucks were sold with the new tax, compared to 623 sales during a comparable period in 1989. The paper reported of the tax later repealed:

> The new levy on heavy trucks was a complete failure. Expected to raise $44 million each fiscal year, the tax effectively killed off the truck sales industry in the state.

Worse yet, the tax drove business into other states, where the vehicles were registered—costing the state hundreds of thousands of dollars in lost motor vehicle registration fees.

Case Study 9: Massachusetts and New Hampshire

In 1990 the accounting firm Price Waterhouse studied the impact of selected excise taxes on retail sales and tax receipts in various states.[33] It too found that heavy excise taxes can have unintended consequences because of cross-border competition between states. Because excise taxes artificially inflate the price of goods and services relative to the price in neighboring states, the researchers discovered:

- Massachusetts has a five percent sales tax while New Hampshire has none. Moreover, Massachusetts charges a higher excise tax on alcohol and cigarettes than does New Hampshire. As a result, between 1975 and 1988 42 percent of New Hampshire cigarette sales and 29 percent of its distilled spirits sales were to Massachusetts residents.

- For New Hampshire this meant $23 million in extra tax revenues, $104 million in higher retail sales, and 800 added jobs. For Massachusetts the tax differential meant $27 million of lost tax revenue, $133 million of foregone sales, and 1,500 lost jobs.

Case Study 10: Illinois and Indiana

Price Waterhouse also compared the excise taxes of Illinois and Indiana.[34] The researchers found a similar effect of high excise taxes. In 1988 the gasoline tax was 5 cents per gallon lower in Indiana than in Illinois. An estimated 15 percent of all gasoline sales in Indiana were to Illinois residents. This tax advantage induced $425 million average annual higher sales and $63 million higher annual tax revenues in Indiana than in Illinois over the 1975 to 1988 period.

The conclusions of the Price Waterhouse cross-border study bear repeating:

1) A state with high sales and excise taxes relative to surrounding states can lose significant tax revenues and retail activity when residents purchase goods out of state.

2) A small state can dramatically increase its effective tax base by having competitive sales and excise taxes. In fact, any state where a relatively large number of another state's residents live close-by has the potential to gain substantially from cross-border activity.

3) Competition for cross-border sales exists on a commodity by commodity basis. A state which enjoys a favorable cross-border trade in one commodity should realize that it may be losing sales in other commodities because of unfavorable tax differentials.

In sum, sales taxes may at first brush appear to be an appealing method of raising revenues with minimal effects on the state economy, but policymakers must be cognizant of the effects of interstate tax competition and the effects of higher excise taxes on particular industries.

4) Tax Abatement Schemes and Government Subsidies to Corporations Are Not Preferable to Lower Overall Taxes.

In the 1970s and 1980s many states became involved in smokestack chasing. This describes a situation when a state offers tax abatements, subsidies, and other special considerations to corporations that locate factories within their boundaries. The most prominent examples of state bidding wars include Diamond Star, General Motor's Saturn plant, and the Superconducting Super Collider. On the one hand, offering selective tax relief to specific large companies or employers may provide high profile successes of economic development. And even at the reduced tax rates, the new businesses probably provide substantial economic benefits to the state.

Yet there is very little evidence that states with aggressive tax relief programs designed to lure identified companies are particularly successful at picking winners and improving the overall economic condition of the state. In fact, most of the evidence suggests otherwise. According to economist Joseph Bast of the Heartland Institute in Chicago: "Yes, selective tax abatements and subsidies can attract new business and retain existing businesses. But every dollar of subsidy awarded to a favored firm is one dollar taken away from another firm....The subsidy or abatement may not produce as much value as it would have had it been retained by the state's taxpaying firms."[35]

To be sure, tax abatements may in some cases provide useful and visible benefits to the particular state. Indeed, the very fact that states pursue this activity is proof that taxes are a significant factor in businesses location decisions. States with very high tax rates may benefit disproportionately from offering selective tax abatement incentives. But the bulk of the evidence suggests that in terms of bang for the tax dollar, this economic development strategy is inferior to one of general tax reduction for all the businesses and workers in a state.

Conclusion

State policymakers will be closely scrutinizing a wide range of tax options in the coming years to conquer record budget shortfalls and to meet emerging social needs. If they follow the orthodox view of the 1950s, 1960s, and 1970s, they will ignore the economic ramifications of these tax options. Many legislators insist on ignoring recent history and continue to cling to the outmoded belief that taxes are inconsequential to growth.

Today the almost universal evidence indicates that the states' relative economic performance is intricately linked to their tax burdens. The research of the 1980s shows that taxes not only matter, they matter a lot. In the 1970s and 1980s, low tax states and states with declining tax burdens have created more jobs, have experienced faster income growth, and have attracted more new businesses than high tax states. The overall tax burden, as opposed to the composition of taxes, appears to be the most important fiscal policy variable in explaining differences in economic growth. In short, there is no such thing as a pro-growth tax.

The states which prosper in the 1990s will be those that heed the lessons of the last two decades. They will restrain the growth of expenditures, hold the tax burden to minimal levels, monitor the tax developments of neighboring states to maintain a competitive tax code, and resist calls for increases in personal and corporate income taxes. This is a proven pro-growth tax reform strategy for the 1990s.

Endnotes

1. "80's Leave States and Cities in Need," *New York Times*, 30 Dec. 1990, pp. 1, 16.

2. Ellen Perlman, "After a Bad '90, States Brace for '91," *City and State*, 13 Aug. 1990.

3. National Association of State Budget Officers, *Fiscal Survey of the States* (Sept. 1990).

4. Warren Brookes, "Second Front Against Spenders?" *Washington Times*, 11 Mar. 1991, pp. D1-2.

5. National Conference of State Legislatures, "State Budget and Tax Actions 1990," (Aug. 1990).

6. The data on federal aid to states is from Office of Management and Budget, "Budget of the United States Government, Fiscal Year 1992."

7. A more complete history of the fiscal plight of the northeastern states can be found in Stephen Moore, "Taxes, Economic Growth, and Budget Deficits: What Washington Can Learn from the States," Heritage Foundation *Backgrounder*, 25 July 1989.

8. "Northeast Scrambling to Pay the Bills," *Washington Post*, 16 Apr. 1989, p. A-30.

9. Michael Marlow and Neela Manage, "Expenditures and Receipts: Testing for Causality in State and Local Government Balances," *Public Choice* (1987), 243-55.

10. Michael Wasylenko, "The Location of Firms: The Role of Taxes and Fiscal Incentives," *Urban Government Finance: Emerging Trends*, ed. R. Bahl (Beverly Hills, Cal.: Sage, 1981).

11. Robert J. Genetski, "The Impact of State and Local Taxes on Economic Growth: 1963-80," (Harris Bank, Chicago, Ill., 17 Dec. 1982).

12. Victor A. Canto, "The State Competitive Environment, 1987-88 Update," (A.B. Laffer Associates, Feb. 1988).

13. *Quoted* in Warren Brookes, "Top Growth States Have Tax Sense," *Insight*, 27 Oct. 1986, p. 51.

14. Foundation for Economic Research, "New Massachusetts Reserves: A History and Analysis, 1983-88," (Needham, Mass.: Oct. 1988).

15. The analysis in this section is based on Colin D. Campbell and Rosemary G. Campbell, "The Fiscal Systems of New Hampshire and Vermont, an Update, 1975-87" (The Henley League, Ltd., 1988).

16. Michael Wasylenko and Therese McGuire, "Jobs and Taxes: The Effect of Business Climate on States' Employment Growth Rates," *National Tax Journal* (vol. 38, 1985), 497-511.

17. Robert Grieson, "The Effects of Business Taxation on the Location of Industry," *Journal of Urban Economics* (Apr. 1977), 170-85; and Robert Grieson, "Theoretical Analysis and Empirical Measurement of the Effects of the Philadelphia Income Tax," *Journal of Urban Economics* (July 1980), 123-37.

18. Robert Premus, "Location of High Technology Firms and Regional Economic Development," Joint Economic Committee, 1982.

19. James A. Papke, "Research on Taxation and Industry Location: A Survey of the Empirical Evidence" (Purdue University, Center for Tax Policy Studies, Paper No. 7, July 1986).

20. *See* Bruce Bartlett, *Reaganomics,* Chapter 5, "Taxation and Regional Growth and Decline," 1981.

21. This was the argument James Florio, Governor of New Jersey, used to push through his 1990 record tax hike. Also, Connecticut Governor Lowell Weicker is trying to impose a first-ever state income tax on the grounds of fairness.

22. Richard K. Vedder, "State and Local Economic Development Strategy: A Supply Side Perspective," Joint Economic Committee, Oct. 1981.

23. Iowa Tax Education Foundation, "The Iowa Exodus: Why Are People Leaving This State," 1987.

24. Joseph Bast, *Coming Out of the Ice* (Chicago, Ill: The Heartland Institute, 1988), 55.

25. David Goldman, "New Jersey's Fiscal Counter-Revolution and Its Consequences," *Polyconomics* (Morristown, N.J.: July 1990).

26. Robert Newman, "Industry Migration and Growth in the South," *Review of Economics and Statistics,* vol. 65, pp.76-86.

27. Timothy Bartik, "Business Location Decisions in the United States: Estimates of the Effects of Unionization, Taxes, and Other Characteristics of States," *Journal of Business and Economic Statistics* (Jan. 1985): 14-22.

28. Bast, *Coming Out of the Ice.*

29. Richard K. Vedder, "Rich States, Poor States: How High Taxes Inhibit Growth," *Journal of Contemporary Studies* (Fall 1982): 19-32.

30. Wasylenko and McGuire, 509.

31. Gary Eisler, "Portland, Oregon: Washington's Bargain Basement," *Wall Street Journal,* 25 Jan. 1989.

32. "Heavy-Truck Tax Abolished Amid Partisan Sniping," *Times of New Jersey,* 20 Nov. 1990, pp. A1, A10.

33. "The Tax Incentives and Economic Consequences of Cross-Border Activity," American Legislative Exchange Council, *The State Factor* (July 1990).

34. *Ibid.*

35. Bast, *Coming Out of the Ice.*

FISCAL DISCIPLINE MECHANISMS: CONTROLLING THE GROWTH OF GOVERNMENT

Duane A. Parde
Legislative Director, ALEC

State lawmakers are constantly confronted with powerful economic and fiscal pressures. Changing demographics, constituent demands for services, federal mandates, and "boom or bust" economic cycles all require careful attention to the full range of state budget policies. State tax and fiscal policies which are moderate and well-managed ensure the efficient use of taxpayer dollars and engender support and confidence for state government. State economic policies can also encourage business expansion, entrepreneurship, and job creation. On the other hand, state economic policies which are not well-managed lead to wasteful spending, high rates of taxation, and constant deficits. Fiscal discipline mechanisms help to protect taxpayers from the "give-and-take" of the political process that can lead to irresponsible fiscal policies.

The debate in America concerning fiscal discipline mechanisms has been hard fought ever since Thomas Jefferson voiced concern over the lack of a balanced budget requirement in the U. S. Constitution. The fact that a balanced budget amendment to the U. S. Constitution is still debated in the Congress attests to this point. Fortunately, the budget process in most states differs significantly from the federal process in terms of diversity and the degree of fiscal discipline.

Fiscal discipline mechanisms can be defined as institutional controls that establish limits on political decisions pertaining to budgetary matters.[1] Examples of fiscal discipline mechanisms include balanced budget provisions, line-item veto authority, super-majority requirements, and tax and expenditure limits (TELs). In all, 49 states require balanced budgets, 43 governors have line-item veto authority, 21 states limit taxation and expenditures, and seven states require a super-majority vote of the legislature to raise taxes.

Numerous studies have been conducted over the years on the effects of fiscal discipline mechanisms. Perhaps the most comprehensive study on this subject was published by the Advisory Commission on Intergovernmental Relations (ACIR) in a 1987 report entitled "Fiscal Discipline In the Federal System: National Reform and the Experience of the States." The report specifically evaluated: the effect of state balanced budget requirements on state deficits, surpluses, and spending; the effect of constitutional debt limits on long-term debt; the effect of gubernatorial vetoes on spending and the effect of fiscal discipline on tax revenues.

The ACIR report found substantial evidence that the major fiscal discipline mechanisms are effective in controlling the state budgetary process.

The study found that in 1984, states with the most disciplined fiscal process:

- Had per capita surpluses of 0.8 to 1.0 percent higher than all other states.

- Had per capita spending that ranged between $156 and $192 lower than other states.

- Experienced lower per capita taxes about $170 than other states.

The ACIR report concludes that:

> The major state mechanisms of fiscal discipline are associated with the effects their proponents claim for them, and such findings are, for the most part, statistically significant. . . . The results do suggest that, contrary to the assertions of some critics of fiscal restraints, such devices may play a significant role both in reducing the size of state budget deficits and in holding down the rate of growth of state spending.[2]

Moreover, the report points to evidence that fiscal discipline mechanisms may be associated with less government regulation of the economy. This is an added advantage because government regulations, like taxes, raise the cost of doing business. This is most likely the result of two factors: 1) states with stringent fiscal discipline mechanisms have a more controlled budgetary process, thereby providing a more stable environment for business, and 2) the political philosophy in these states is such that lawmakers may be less likely to over-regulate the economy.

Opponents of fiscal discipline mechanisms argue, among other things, that lawmakers should not be limited in their ability to raise and spend tax revenues in order to provide government services. They also cite several studies conducted by organizations (i.e., National Association of State Budget Officers) that conclude that such constraints are not effective, complicate the budget process, and force lawmakers to rely on certain expenditures and revenues that are not covered by the limits.[3]

While even the most stringent fiscal discipline mechanisms contain certain exceptions, such as in case of natural disasters, the critics do present several legitimate points. Lawmakers are rather ingenious, and if they are determined to circumvent some constraints they can usually find a way. For instance, the state of Oregon circumvented its statutory cap on appropriations in fiscal 1987-89 when the legislature "temporarily" exempted capital spending from limitation. However, to more effectively counter this problem, experts on the issue recommend that fiscal discipline mechanisms should be constitutional and not statutory. Constitutional limits have been proven more effective, if for no other reason than they are more difficult to circumvent.[4] The debate concerning fiscal discipline mechanisms will continue. Nevertheless, substantial research does indicate that, when properly constructed and implemented, fiscal discipline mechanisms provide effective controls on the growth of government.

Tax and Expenditure Limits

Forty-nine states currently have constitutional or statutory balanced budget requirements. In addition, twenty states have enacted stringent institutional mechanisms to limit the growth of government by defined economic factors, commonly referred to as tax and expenditure limits, or "TELs."

Tax and expenditure limits are constitutional or statutory provisions which constrain increases in the maximum rate of taxation or spending by such factors as the yearly increase in the consumer price index, the increase in state personal income, or to changes in state population. TELs incur popular taxpayer support because they establish "across-the-board" limits on state spending and taxation, and they force government to set priorities and manage its activities in a more accountable manner.

In the absence of a clearly defined bottom line, governments pursue a perpetual quest for new and increased taxes in order to fund additional spending. TELs constrain the perpetual growth of government by requiring public officials to set spending priorities within revenue limits. When a state is required to balance its budget each fiscal year and, at the same time, maintain a lid on spending, both deficits and spending growth (beyond a certain defined percentage) can be eliminated.[5]

History of TELs

The history of tax and expenditure limits can be traced to the 19th century. However, the first modern TEL was enacted by New Jersey in 1976 as part of a school finance reform package which included the state's first income tax. The New Jersey TEL placed a statutory cap on government spending, not to exceed the annual increase in per capita income. New Jersey's lead was followed by Colorado and Rhode Island, which both enacted statutory limitations on the yearly growth of general fund appropriations in 1977.

Nevertheless, the popularity of TELs did not become evident until 1978. In California that year, voters approved Proposition 13, a constitutional amendment promoted by Howard E. Jarvis, to limit property tax levies to 1 percent of assessed valuation and freeze assessments at 1975 levels. The following year, California taxpayers struck again when they approved a similar measure, Proposition 4 (Gann limits), which limited the growth of state taxes and expenditures to a formula based on growth in state population and on either growth in state personal income or the U. S. Consumer Price Index (inflation). Both Proposition 4 and 13 were unique at the time in that they were voter-approved initiatives that placed constitutional limits on the government's ability to increase taxes and spending beyond growth in the economy.

The popularity and success of the California initiatives prompted similar actions in other states. Lawmakers, faced with this new-found taxpayer power, were forced to begin reducing the share of state and local tax burdens—which had been rising in real terms from 11.32 percent per $100 of personal income in 1970 to 12.15 percent in 1977. During the first tax revolt, 1978-82, 14 states adopted TELs, eight states enacted legislation indexing their income taxes for inflation, and numerous states enacted sales tax exemptions for food, prescription drugs, and consumer utility bills.[6]

Effectiveness of Tax and Expenditure Limits

Starting in the mid-1980s, economists began to assemble evidence on the impact of TELs and other fiscal discipline mechanisms on the state fiscal process. Several such studies conducted by Dr. Barry W. Poulson at the University of Colorado indicate that TELs are effective in controlling the growth of government in relation to the economy. Dr. Poulson has examined the states that have adopted TELs and found that the restraints have had a significant impact in reducing the rate of growth of state government. Dr. Poulson's work indicates that the rate of growth in government measured against growth in state income increased steadily up to the point when TELs were imposed, and has since declined. The evidence demonstrates that states with stringent TELs have been more effective in controlling the rate of government taxing, spending, and borrowing than were states that had not enacted such limits.[7]

Until 1987 few states actually encountered the limits imposed on taxes and spending by TELs. This delay is primarily attributable to the recession during the early 1980s that adversely affected state budgets. However, the economic recovery of the mid-1980s increased state revenues dramatically and, for the first time, several of the state TELs were triggered. For instance, during the 1986-87 fiscal year California

Spending/Taxes in States TELs
vs.
All Others

	Spending as % of Personal Income			Tax as % of Personal Income		
	1979	1987	% Change	1980	1987	% Change
TEL States	5.5	5.7	+4	6.1	6.0	-2
Non-TEL States	5.4	5.9	+9	6.5	6.6	+2

Source: Stephen Moore, "What the States Can Teach Congress About Balancing the Budget," *Heritage Foundation Backgrounder* 751 (Washington, D.C.: THe Heritage Foundation, 6 Feb. 1990).

surpassed its spending limit by $1.1 billion. Because of the limits imposed by the state's TEL, legislation was enacted in the following fiscal year that provided for the rebate of the funds to personal income taxpayers based on their 1986 state tax liability.[8]

Nevertheless, one common defect does seem to impair the effectiveness of most TELs. On average, approximately 44 percent of state-appropriated funds are outside of the general fund and are, therefore, excluded from many TELs.[9] The solution to this problem is not dismissing the value and purpose of TELs, but in expanding the scope of TELs and strengthening the limits (constitutional versus statutory limits).

Summary

In the past few years, state and local tax burdens have risen to their pre-1979 level of approximately $12 per $100 of personal income. Similarly, state spending is at an all-time high in relation to the economy. Therefore, it is no wonder that taxpayers are again actively engaged in efforts to limit the growth of government and safeguard their incomes. This "rebirth" of the tax revolt was made evident in 1990, when ballot initiatives to limit taxes and spending appeared in 10 states—a record number.

Tax and expenditure limits are an effective method to control the growth of state government and promote fiscal responsibility. Tax and expenditure limits do so by changing the starting point in the budgetary debate. Once enacted into law, TELs serve as a constant reminder to lawmakers of the costs of extravagant fiscal policies.

SURVEY OF STATE TAX & EXPENDITURE LIMITS

State	Enacted	Statutory (S) Constitutional (C)	Provisions
Alaska	1982	C	Expenditures. Limited to inflation & population growth.
Arizona	1978	C	Expenditures. Spending limited to 7% of personal income.
California	1979	C	Expenditures. Annual appropriations limited to changes in cost of living and population growth.
Colorado	1977	S	Expenditures. General fund appropriations limited to 7% annual increase.
Delaware	1982	C	Expenditures. Limited to 98% of estimated general fund revenue and prior year's unencumbered funds.
Hawaii	1978	C	Expenditures. Spending increase limited to the annual percentage change in personal income for 3 prior calendar years.
Idaho	1980	S	Expenditures. Limited to 5 1/3% of total increase in state personal income.
Louisiana	1979	S	Revenues. Increase limited to percent of state personal income.
Massachusetts	1986	S	Revenues. Limited to average growth of wages and salaries of previous 3 years.
Michigan	1978	C	Revenues. Limited to a ratio and the greater of state personal income in prior calendar year or average state personal income over previous 3 calendar years.
Missouri	1980	C	Revenues. Limited to a ratio and the greater of state personal income over previous 3 calendar years.
Montana	1981	S	Expenditures. Biennial spending cannot exceed prior biennium spending plus growth in percentage of average state personal income of 3 prior calendar years.
Nevada	1979	S	Expenditures. Limits increases in executive budget requests to the rate of inflation & population growth.
New Jersey	1976*	S	Expenditures. Limits spending for state operations & capital outlays to increase in FY state per capita income.
Oklahoma	1985	C	Expenditures. Limited to 12% annual increase, or 95% of certified revenue.[10]
Oregon	1979	S	Expenditures. Increase in state appropriations limited to growth of personal income of prior 2 years.

Rhode Island	1977	S	Expenditures. Governor's budget limited to 6% annual increase.
South Carolina	1980	S	Expenditures. Limits spending to annual growth in personal income over 3 preceding years, or 9.5% of total state personal income, whichever is greater.
Tennessee	1978	C	Expenditures. Limits spending to growth in state personal income.
Texas	1978	C	Expenditures. Limited to estimated future growth in state personal income.[11]
Utah	1979	S	Expenditures. Limits spending increase to 85% of growth in personal income.
Washington	1979	S	Revenues. Limits tax revenues to average rate of growth of state personal income over 3 years.

Source: ACIR, *Significant Features of Fiscal Federalism* (Jan. 1990). (New Jersey's TEL expired in 1983)

Endnotes

1. Advisory Commission on Intergovernmental Relations (ACIR), "Fiscal Discipline in the Federal System: National Reform and the Experience of the States."

2. *Ibid.*, 45.

3. Marcia Howard, "State Tax and Expenditure Limitations: There Is No Story" (National Association of State Budget Officers, 1988).

4. *For example, see* Barry W. Poulson, "Constitutional Tax and Spending Limits," available from ALEC (Washington, D.C., 1987).

5. *For example, see* Barry W. Poulson, "Tax Revolt is Alive and Well," available from ALEC (Washington, D.C., 1987).

6. ACIR, *Significant Features of Fiscal Federalism* (Washington, D.C.: ACIR, 1990).

7. Poulson, *supra*, note 12.

8. Howard, *supra*, notes 11, 16.

9. *Ibid.*

10. In March 1992, Oklahoma voters approved SQ640 which "requires a statewide vote on any future state tax increase legislation that fails to get approval of three-fourths of both houses of the Legislature." *Daily Oklahoman*, 11 Mar. 1992.

11. *See* Michael D. Weiss, "The Texas Tax Relief Act After 12 Years: Adoption, Implementation and Enforcement. (San Antonio, Tex: Texas Public Policy Foundation, 1991).

THE ROLE OF THE STATES IN AMERICA'S FISCAL FUTURE

Lewis K. Uhler

President, National Tax Limitation Committee

More than 200 years of the history of the United States has blurred the relationship that originally existed between the states and our government in Washington. The only way to appreciate the role of the states today is to recall their origin as separate sovereign states following the Revolutionary War, linked loosely through the Articles of Confederation. The states created the federal government; and in so doing, they retained both the power and responsibility to discipline it. Unfortunately, over the years Washington has become a spoiled child on an unlimited allowance. As a result, it has become haughty, arrogant, self-centered, unruly, intermeddling and spendthrift. Worst of all, it has become disdainful of its parents (the states), causing them no end of grief.

In the role for which the federal government was initially created—national defense and foreign affairs—it has done reasonably well of late. But in its domestic role it has been a failure on almost every front. Domestic spending is on virtual automatic pilot. There is no meaningful oversight of most programs. Washington stirs up controversy in nearly everything it does with regard to the arts, family matters, education, poverty, homeless programs, etc. In short, Washington has "flunked" domestic programs and policy. Shouldn't we demand that it devote itself to those functions which only the central government can perform—national defense and foreign affairs—and give people problems back to those closest to the people? Such suggestions make many legislators cringe. They become downright uneasy about challenging the federal government lest it retaliate by interrupting the flow of funds and canceling a program or project.

Hence, the first and foremost consideration in disciplining Washington and enhancing the role of the states is that of *attitude*—the attitude of state legislators about themselves and their role (and that of their states) in the federal system. State legislators must not only understand that they have the constitutional and practical political power to control Washington, but they must finally make a decision and believe it essential that they do so.

What follows is a history of state powers, the role of states in America's fiscal future and some ideas on making changes in Washington and the states a reality.

The States as Masters of Washington

When the states came together in Philadelphia in 1787, each of them was a sovereign entity. They were each willing to give up some sovereignty in exchange for enhanced mutual security. Being extraordinarily jealous of their respective powers, they gave the central government only those powers specifically enumerated in a contract we call the Constitution. Our present federal government is the creature of the states; and although it has abrogated many of the contractual restraints on its authority, the Constitution still reserves to the states the ultimate power to control, shape and discipline the federal government.

Only the states may change the Constitution, because the ratification process is the exclusive province of the people of the states. Furthermore, the states have co-equal authority with Congress to propose or initiate amendments to the Constitution. When Edmund Randolph presented the Virginia Plan to the delegates at Philadelphia, he proposed that only the states have the power to initiate amendments (James Madison was the principal architect of the Virginia Plan). Only later in the debate over the amendment process did the Federalists succeed in achieving a co-equal power on the part of the Congress to initiate or propose amendments.

Although the carefully circumscribed and limited powers of the federal government established at Philadelphia have been expanded enormously by an activist Supreme Court and over-reaching presidents and congresses, the explicit amendment process remains in place. The states, therefore, are the principals in the amendment process, and each state legislator is an agent who, acting under the authority provided in the federal Constitution, can change the rules by which Washington plays the game. Most state legislators have no idea of the enormous power which they possess to discipline an errant Washington—*if* they are only willing to exercise that power. Whatever the states don't like about Washington and want to change, they can. Their legislators must merely muster the political will and courage to assert themselves.

The state resolution process of Article V is a powerful tool just waiting to be used. Through it, the states may pass resolutions forcing Congress to convene a citizen convention to propose an amendment on any subject desired by the states. While the process has never come to fruition, it has been used effectively early in this century in the direct election of United States Senators. The U.S. Senate consistently refused to propose an amendment for the direct election of U.S. Senators. The states began passing Article V resolutions to that effect, and when the number of state resolutions had reached just one shy of the requisite two-thirds, the U.S. Senate capitulated and approved an amendment, grandfathering in the terms of the sitting members of the U.S. Senate.

It is now time that this process be used once again. In the debates regarding the Constitution following the convention at Philadelphia, people were deeply concerned at the prospect that a strong central government might usurp powers and become oppressive to the people. In response, advocates of the Constitution consistently indicated that the states represented the bulwark and final protection against an over-reaching federal power. In *Federalist* No. 28, Hamilton addressed the issue in the following way:

> It may safely be received as an axiom in our political system that the state governments will, in all possible contingencies, afford complete security against invasions of the public liberty by the national government. Projects of usurpation cannot be masked under pretenses so likely to escape the penetration of select bodies of men, as of the people at large. The legislatures will have better means of information. They can discover the danger at a distance; and possessing the organs of civil power and the confidence of the people, they can at once adopt a regular plan of opposition, in which they can combine all the resources of the community. *They can readily communicate with each other in the different states and unite their common forces for the protection of their common liberty.* (Emphasis added.)

Hamilton's appreciation of the continuing role of the states as ultimate masters, not servants, of the federal government, permeated the thinking of the Founders. Over the years Washington, D.C. has come to dominate, with the states and state legislators feeling subservient to Washington, primarily, I believe, because of the "fiscal handout" role exercised by Congress. Until the legislators and the states quit viewing themselves as lap dogs of Washington, they will not be able to counter its power and force. It would be a very useful exercise if state legislators were to commence the process of *instructions* to their congressional delegations, telling them that the states no longer intend to respond to Washington's commands to jump by simply asking "how high."

Whatever the states find objectionable in the federal government, they can change. They just need to muster the political will and courage to do so. The state resolution process of Article V is just waiting to be used.

Article V State Resolutions for the
Balanced Budget Amendment:
A "Demonstration" Project of State Power

The fiscal excesses of the government of the United States continue unabated—in fact, they are growing worse. Our annual deficits—exacerbated by the savings-and-loan debacle—are unconstrained and *unpredictable*. Our national debt limit is being increased to $3.4 trillion to accommodate the new debt. The national debt as a percentage of GNP is the highest since World War II. Tax revenues in (fiscal year) 1991 are expected to increase *automatically*—without one change in the tax law—by nearly $80 billion. But federal spending will increase even more as Congress adds new, expensive programs. Inflation has returned to a rate which will cut the value of the dollar in half in 15 years. Real interest rates remain at unprecedented levels.

When we try to fix blame or focus responsibility for these problems, everyone ducks. There is no way to impose responsibility, because authority under our form of government has been fractured *intentionally* by the Founders and spread around among the various branches in what we have come to know as "checks and balances." This may sustain *balance* between the branches, but it is not sufficient to provide a *check* on the federal government *as a whole*. As a total institution, Washington is in a *runaway* mode.

What we are experiencing is a constitutional *breakdown* which can be addressed only by repairing the Constitution itself. We can limit the fiscal excesses of the government created by our Constitution *only* by placing fiscal limits within the Constitution itself.

The people of America agree with this premise overwhelmingly. Whether they understand it intellectually or merely know it and "feel" it instinctively, Americans want constitutional fiscal discipline—known generically as a "balanced budget amendment"—by a majority of four-to-one in most polls.

Congress has been given the power and authority to revise and correct "errors" in the Constitution by proposing amendments to it. What has been Congress's response to our fiscal crisis and to Americans' demand for a balanced budget amendment? Congress has refused to act.

As recently as July 18, 1990, the House of Representatives voted down HJR 268, a balanced budget amendment—having earlier rejected overwhelmingly a strong tax-limitation provision for the Amendment. Other than a favorable Senate vote in 1982, Congress has failed to approve such an amendment on several occasions.

Congress's refusal to impose constitutional fiscal discipline upon itself has been predictable. The unlimited power to spend, tax and borrow provides Congress as an institution, and members individually, with enormous political power. They are unwilling to relinquish that power.

The Founders understood that at times reforms, which might run counter to the self-interest of Congress, would nevertheless be essential to the sound operation of the federal system. Hence, the Founders provided an alternative method for *proposing* amendments to the United States Constitution. The medium fashioned by the Founders was a citizen convention under Article V of the Constitution to be convened for purposes specified in resolutions passed by two-thirds of the states. In providing us with this alternative method of initiating corrections to the Constitution, the Founders placed *their* faith in the common sense and good judgment of "we the people" to shape the destiny of the Republic. It is time that we the people assert our constitutionally-authorized power and demand an Article V convention for the purpose of imposing fiscal discipline on Washington.

The recent rejection by the House of an amendment without a strong tax limitation element demonstrates that we cannot expect Congress to craft voluntarily an amendment of the kind which the current fiscal crisis demands. Not only must we limit taxes and spending and reduce the size of the federal government, but we must protect the states and local units of government from federally-mandated program costs. Furthermore, the current savings-and-loan scandal, and the uncertainties surrounding other loan and guarantee programs of the federal government, make it essential that we restrain the power of Congress to extend to special interests credit and loan guarantees for which the taxpayer must ultimately pick up the tab. It will take taxpaying citizens to achieve these reforms.

We have been pursuing the state-resolution option in order to achieve federal fiscal reform. We are very close to success, having obtained the support of 29 state legislatures. We must obtain five more resolutions as quickly as possible. Then citizens brought together for such a purpose would write the amendment—or Congress would be forced to do it. The latter is by far and away the more likely outcome.

Why would Congress be more likely to approve a sound amendment after the 34th state has acted? Simply because Congress's current choice is between an amendment and no amendment. Congress prefers no amendment. When Congress's choice is between convening a convention of citizens under Article V to draft such an amendment—or drafting the amendment itself—Congress will propose the amendment. Congress is not about to allow "mere" citizens to design a limitation on its fiscal powers. Members realize that public attitudes toward Congress might lead a convention to adopt punitive enforcement mechanisms such as monetary penalties or banishment from office of members who failed to honor the amendment's requirements.

One would think that the desirability of the state resolution/Article V citizens convention process would be obvious. The fact that the Founders themselves were the authors of Article V should sanctify it and place it beyond criticism. But that is not the case. Big-spending special interests and a few well-meaning but misguided conservatives have fashioned the specter of a citizen convention that would destroy America as we know it. Whether driven by the notion of a conspiratorial group waiting to take over a convention or by conjuring up an image of a torch-bearing street mob, they are terrified by the thought of citizens coming together, certain that it would lead to a "runaway convention."

Let's dissect the "runaway" convention bogeyman and find out what makes it tick. Opponents of an Article V convention contend that it surely will run amok, because there is no way to limit it; that the only kind of a convention which may be convened under Article V is an *open* convention that may consider all parts of the Constitution.

Such a claim is without foundation in terms of authority, historical precedent, common sense or political reality. The Founding Fathers intended to provide two *co-equal* methods by which amendments to the U.S. Constitution might be *proposed*. One was through Congress, and the other through the states. In *Federalist* No. 43, Madison states: "It [the power to amend the Constitution], moreover, equally enables the general and the state governments to originate the amendment of errors, as they may be pointed out by the experience on one side, or on the other."

We know that Congress can and has proposed single, discrete amendments without opening up the entire Constitution to consideration of revisions. (Remember, whenever it is in session, Congress is a general constitutional convention, since at any time that two-thirds of its members agree, they can propose any amendment or amendments they wish.) To be on an equal footing with Congress, the states have the same discrete amendment authority. Furthermore, Article V refers specifically to the application of the various states as being the triggering device leading to the convening of a convention: ". . . on the application of the legislatures of two-thirds of the several states, [Congress] shall call a convention. . . ." The resolutions themselves are the very "foundation" upon which a convention would be constructed. If those resolutions say, as they do in this instance, that the states want a convention for the *"sole, limited and exclusive purpose of proposing a balanced budget amendment,"* the states are triggering a limited, not a general, convention. This is not to say that the states could not call for a general convention, but they would have to do so pursuant to a convention call which explicitly states that objective. (Again, ours does not.)

Those who profess fear that a convention might "run away" are caught in a very uncomfortable contradiction. They acknowledge that Congress is under no duty to convene a convention until 34 resolutions on the same subject have been received. However, they contend that once 34 resolutions have been delivered to Washington, Congress can no longer be guided by those applications and is obligated to convene a convention that is entirely absent any guidelines as to subject matter or, for that matter, any rules as to its conduct, etc. While the Constitution is silent as to the details of an Article V convention, it is very clear that Congress has the responsibility to shape and convene such a convention. Congress, which has absolutely no institutional interest in convening a convention, let alone an open convention, will look to the resolutions and seek to make the scope of such a convention as narrow as possible.

Those preoccupied with a "runaway convention" conveniently ignore the fact that the work product of a convention must be ratified by the legislatures of 38 states before it becomes law. So the "runaway convention" argument is very misleading. The dire results predicted by the purveyors of doom could not come from a runaway convention but from runaway ratification, a total failure of the entire amendatory system or process.

Over the past several years, vigorous efforts have been made by a front group of the AFL-CIO and other liberal big-spending organizations, misleadingly entitled the "Committee to Protect the Constitution," to rescind the Article V balanced budget amendment resolutions that have been passed in some 32 states. More recently, the big spenders have been joined by the John Birch Society and others on the right who predicate their opposition on the existence of a sinister conspiracy to destroy our Constitution and nation. Where we have had full, fair hearings and votes, allowing us time to refute the doomsday claims of the runaway conventioneers, the resolutions have been upheld. Rescission has succeeded in three states, primarily through sneak attacks where resolutions have been rushed through without hearing or debate.

Our escalating resistance to further rescissions is testimony to the strength of our position, which is supported by every serious legal study of the issue, including the landmark studies by the American Bar Association (1974) and the United States Department of Justice (1989), as well as by many scholars and experts, such as the late Senator Sam Ervin, former Attorney General Griffin Bell, constitutional law professor John Noonan (now a federal Appeals Court Judge), William Van Alstyne (Duke University Law School), and Prof. Aaron Wildavsky (former president of the American Association of Political Scientists).

It is clear that as state legislators become increasingly familiar with the arguments and the people and organizations involved, they support the propriety and efficacy of the Article V state resolution process as a means of obtaining fiscal discipline at the federal level.

The time is increasingly ripe for obtaining the final five state resolutions that will push the balanced budget amendment effort over the top. Ensuing events will demonstrate the efficacy and safety of the process at the same time we are enjoying the substantive benefits of constitutional fiscal reform.

Once Congress comes to realize that the states are both able and willing to use the state resolution process to initiate amendments and therefore impose discipline upon the federal government, the states will be back in the game as real players that Congress simply cannot ignore. Other needed reforms, such as preventing unfunded federal mandates, realignment of functions between Washington and the states, allocation of revenue sources, congressional term limitation, etc., will be available as discrete Article V resolution objectives.

The States Should Provide Leadership by Example for Washington and Local Governments

The old notion of do as I do, not as I say, should be the watchword for the states. Leadership by example in an era of empty rhetoric and broken promises is the only meaningful language left. The states have it within their power to set the example on several important fronts:

1. Those states that have not already done so should adopt firm constitutional tax and spending limits for themselves and their local governments. If they have adopted legislative control devices in the past, they should move to constitutional limitations. If they have adopted constitutional limitations, they should review them to see if they are working properly rather than try to circumvent or undermine them, as many states have done.

The combination of state fiscal restraints, such as balanced budget requirements, line-item vetoes, augmented by tax and expenditure limitations (TELs), have had a positive effect on holding down state taxes and spending. In its 1987 report entitled "Fiscal Discipline in the Federal System: National Reform and the Experience of the States," the Advisory Commission on Intergovernmental Relations (ACIR) concluded:

> The major state mechanisms of fiscal discipline are associated with the effects their proponents claim for them, and such findings are for the most part statistically significant . . . the results do suggest that contrary to the assertions of some critics of fiscal restraints, such devices may play a significant role both in reducing the size of state budget deficits and in holding down the rate of growth of state spending.[1]

Dr. Barry Poulson, Professor of Economics at the University of Colorado, investigated the effectiveness of TELs in controlling the growth of government. The evidence indicates that the states with stringent TELs have been more effective in controlling the rate of government taxing, spending and borrowing than were states that had not enacted such limits.[2]

In his Heritage Foundation study, economist Stephen Moore demonstrated that states with TELs have been more effective in holding the line on spending and taxes than those without.[3]

	Spending as % of Personal Income			Tax as % of Personal Income		
	1979	1987	% Change	1980	1987	% Change
TEL States	5.5	5.7	+4	6.1	6.0	-2
Non-TEL States	5.4	5.9	+9	6.5	6.6	+2

Spending/Taxes in States TELs vs. All Others

Source: Stephen Moore, "What the States Can Teach Congress About Balancing the Budget," *Heritage Foundation Backgrounder* 751 (Washington, D.C.: The Heritage Foundation, 6 Feb. 1990).

But what of such taxing and spending limitations? Do they help or hinder the economic growth of a state? Is there a payoff in terms of economic expansion, jobs, capital formation as a result of belt tightening and the hard effort of fiscal discipline? The evidence is clear that there is.

Thomas L. Wyrick, Associate Professor of Economics, Southwest Missouri State University, studied the Missouri State TEL, commonly referred to as the Hancock Amendment, which was approved by Missouri voters November 4, 1980. Wyrick concluded, ". . . Missouri incomes have increased by about 1.76 percent relative to the U.S. average due to the adoption of Hancock . . . to place the gain in perspective, it rivals the impact of a five million unit increase in U.S. car output. In dollar terms, it represents a contribution of about $1.3 billion annually to the state personal income. Total accumulated state personal income since January 1981 has exceeded $500 billion, so Hancock appears to have stimulated more than $8.5 billion worth of additional income during the eight years since it took effect." Wyrick concluded, "The findings of this study lend support to the view that tax policy exerts an important influence on the economy. The following chart shows Missouri's per capita personal income since 1980, and what it would have been without the 1.758 percent annual gain earlier attributed to the Hancock effect."[4]

**Missouri Per Capita Income,
With and Without Hancock Amendment**

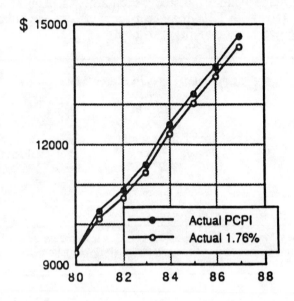

Without tax and expenditure limitations as part of their constitutions, states are at liberty to and inclined toward increasing taxes and spending whenever time and circumstances—especially a budget crunch—justify it. Such policy is a high risk approach for a state's economic health, as numerous studies have revealed. One of the leaders in the field, Dr. Richard K. Vedder, Distinguished Professor of Economics, Ohio University, has concluded from his studies that ". . . other things equal, the higher the level of state and local taxes, the lower the rate of economic growth; the growth enhancing aspects of state expenditures are more than offset by the growth retarding effects of higher taxes needed to finance the expenditures; state and local taxes adversely impact on the percentage of the work age population that actually work; . . . a growth maximizing strategy would call for low taxes, with heavy emphasis on sales taxation, and with a low proportion of expenditures going for public assistance and other growth inhibiting transfer payments." Dr. Vedder concludes, "Evidence is overwhelming . . . that state and local taxes can and do have an inverse impact on the rate of economic growth. Any state or local jurisdiction levying new taxes should not delude itself into thinking that human economic behavior in that state will not be impacted

Dr. Vedder has also noted that the lag time between tax and spending decisions and their impact on the state's economy has declined to approximately 18 months. Even a high-tax state can set its economy on a new course simply by initiating a reduction of taxes and tax rates. The trend line of taxes has significant influence on economic growth activities.

The evidence is clear that legislators can help their state improve its economic future by the fiscal discipline which a strong constitutional tax and expenditure limitation provision can assure. In so doing, they set the proper example both for Washington and for local governments within the state.

2. State governments have a propensity to shift program costs to other levels of government within the state without paying the bill. So-called "mandated programs" satisfy a politician's urge to "do good" without suffering the political consequences of having to pay for it. States should either send along the money for functions they require to be performed or impose sufficient discipline upon themselves to resist the temptation to pass the programs in the first place. At most, they make those functions for which they are unwilling or unable to pick up the tab discretionary at the local level. This would be the example Washington desperately needs.

3. Those states whose leadership has a tradition of citizen service should restore a public service, non-careerist mentality to its legislature and statewide offices by one or more of the following limitations and reforms: (1) limit the terms of legislators and statewide officers (preferably to no more than eight years in each office); (2) eliminate pensions for legislators; (3) control the legislature's budget if it has grown much faster than the growth in the state's budget; (4) encourage gainfully employed individuals to participate as legislators by limiting the regular session of the legislature to not more than one week per month throughout the year. Legislative sessions of several consecutive months are historic anachronisms linked to the difficulty of travel in the early days of our nation and the reality that most early legislators (and members of Congress) were farmers who could be absent only during the winter months. Legislators wanted to make only one round-trip to the capital, remaining there long enough to get the business done and get home for planting.

These reforms are in keeping with the times, would mitigate against political careerism and would accommodate significantly broader participation in the legislative process. The states can provide a healthy example for the nation's capitol, where careerist self interest dominates the political landscape.

The States Should Demand a Restoration
of Their Powers: Return to Federalism

For most of our nation's history, states have jealously guarded their rights and prerogatives from an over-reaching central government. With the advent of a federal government that has put its nose in every corner of domestic policy (since the Roosevelt era, with the explosive expansion during the Kennedy-Johnson era), all of that has changed. Now people go hat in hand to Washington for federal largesse, fearing fiscal and regulatory retaliation if they don't hew the line. It is high time for an "attitude adjustment hour" in which the states demand a review of the allocation of functions, making the states the dominant players in the development of domestic policy and in its administration.

Of course, this recommendation runs entirely counter to conventional wisdom. The pragmatist will insist that we must have our fair share of federal funds or we will be bankrupt. But to the extent that the states are fed up with Washington's intermeddling, mal-administration, wastefulness, etc., the pragmatist, as well as those legislators driven by a desire for sound public policy (in keeping with the Founders' intentions), should band together and initiate a national meeting of state legislators, governors and others to debate these great issues as we enter the third century of our nation's existence.

The threshold issue should be to challenge the entire array of functions performed by government, recognizing that government at whatever level is an inefficient deliverer of goods and services. We know this to be true intuitively but need not rely on intuition. Recently, both the Rand Corporation and the World Bank completed studies of the effect taxes and government spending have on economic growth. Independently, each concluded that big government means slower economic growth, less wealth and lower paying jobs.[6] These studies found that for every 10 percent of a nation's total income that is taxed and spent by its government, the average growth rate of that nation's economy is reduced by 1 percent annually.[7] One percent per year might not sound like much, but its impact can be enormous. The compounding effect over a generation can transform an economy. The very high level of total taxes in the U.S. at all levels of government (over 40 percent of national income) seriously retards growth of the economic base of the nation. Reducing that percentage makes everyone in our nation richer. Doing nothing constitutes a policy decision to impoverish our nation over the long term in favor of immediate gratification of some special-interest demand.

Once over that hurdle, the burden of proof should be borne by those who insist that the federal government ought to be involved in any domestic program such as health, welfare, education, housing or transportation. The corollary burden of proof should answer why the federal government should not be restricted to those activities envisaged for it by the Founders, to wit: national defense, foreign policy, international security, relations between the states, maintenance of federal properties and installations and general administrative affairs of the federal structure.

Function allocation decisions must be followed closely by the challenge of privatization, competition and choice. The opportunities for privatization and the introduction of choice and competition in education, corrections, and transportation have exploded on the political scene, offering the opportunity for vast improvements in the services which it has fallen to government's lot to provide. The potential here is limited only by our own creativity.

Conclusion

The role of the states in America's fiscal future has never been greater. The states can force change in Washington through their federal constitutional power. They can lead by example, putting their own houses in order in the process; they can assert themselves in terms of the allocation of functions between levels of government and in alternatives to government provision of services at whatever level of government. The potential is here; now it is only a matter of will.

Endnotes

1. ACIR, "Fiscal Discipline in the Federal System: National Reform and the Experience of the States" (1987), 45.

2. *See*, *supra*, Duane Parde, "Fiscal Discipline Mechanisms" 7.

3. Steven Moore, "What the States Can Teach Congress about Balancing the Budget," *Heritage Backgrounder* 751 (6 Feb. 1990).

4. The Hancock Amendment and the Missouri Economy, *Southwest Missouri Economic Review*, 1989, 5.

5. Vedder, "Do Tax Increases Harm Economic Growth and Development," Arizona Issues Analysis Report No. 106, 20 Sept. 1989, issued by the Barry Goldwater Institute for Public Policy Research.

6. Charles Wolf, Jr., *Markets or Governments: Choosing Between Imperfect Alternatives* (Cambridge, Mass.: MIT Press, 1988); Keith Marsden, "Links Between Taxes and Economic Growth: Some Empirical Evidence," *World Bank Staff Working Paper #605* (Washington, D.C. 1983).

7. Wolf, *op. cit.*, 146.

STATE INCOME TAXATION FUELING GOVERNMENT, STALLING THE ECONOMY

Prof. Thomas R. Dye
Florida State University

What are the consequences of adopting a state income tax? Does an income tax accelerate the growth of government activity? Does an income tax retard the growth of private income, earnings, and investment?

Fueling Government Growth

Income taxation has fueled the growth of government throughout the twentieth century. All advanced Western nations levy direct taxes on individual incomes, but nowhere is this tax as important as in the United States. The national government grew exponentially following the adoption of the Sixteenth Amendment in 1913, and today income and payroll taxes constitute more than three-quarters of federal revenue. Following the federal example, American state governments have increasingly financed their own growth from income taxation. Wisconsin enacted the first modern, enforceable state income tax in 1911, and more than half the states had adopted income taxation by 1940. Today forty-one states tax all forms of individual income and three additional states tax non-wage income. Only six states assess no personal income tax (see Table 1). Connecticut was the most recent state to enact an income tax in 1991.

Stalling the Economy?

Economists have long debated the economic consequences of income taxation. The central issue has been the impact of income taxation—particularly high marginal tax rates—on the incentives of individuals to engage in productive activity.

Traditional economic theory argued that income taxation had little adverse effect on work, savings, or investment. It was believed that, when income was taxed, individuals would work harder and save more in order to maximize their after-tax income, thus overcoming the disincentives of the income taxation. According to a leading liberal economist, Joseph A. Pechman of the Brookings Institution:

Taxation is only one of many factors affecting work incentives. This makes it extremely difficult to interpret the available statistical evidence or the results of direct interviews with taxpayers. The evidence suggests that income taxation does not greatly reduce the amount of labor supplied by workers and managers who are the primary family earners. Work habits are not easily changed, and for most people in a modern industrial society there is little opportunity to vary their hours of work or the intensity of their efforts in response to changes in tax rates. Nearly all people who are asked about income taxation grumble about it, but relatively few say that they work fewer hours or exert less than their best efforts to avoid tax.[1]

In contrast, supply side economists in recent years have identified significant disincentive effects of high rates of income taxes—disincentives to enter or remain in the workforce, to bear additional economic risks, to make more productive investments, to accept more demanding jobs, or to expend additional time and energy in generating additional income. According to economist James D. Gwartney:

> In the past, most economists believed that tax rates on income exerted little adverse influence on the incentive of individuals to engage in productive activity.
>
> During the late 1970s and early 1980s, the traditional view underwent a serious reevaluation. Challengers to the traditional view argued that high marginal tax rates induced taxpayers to reduce their work time and engage in more tax avoidance, and even illegal tax evasion. The proponents of this view argued that when high marginal tax rates take a major share of the income from additional work, some individuals will respond by increasing their vacation time and absenteeism, while reducing their overtime hours. Others will allocate more time to untaxed household activities, such as fixing their cars, painting their houses, and producing additional home-prepared meals, rather than allocating more time to working, purchasing new cars, buying new houses, and eating meals at restaurants. Still others will take jobs with lower pay but higher nonmonetary benefits and allocate more time to real-estate investments with attractive tax benefits. Business ventures designed to show an accounting loss to shelter taxable income will also flourish. These alternatives are perfectly legal. However, some individuals will also use illegal means to evade the payment of taxes.[2]

In brief, income taxes lower the rate of return for individuals, families, and firms on their work, savings and risks. Lowered rates of return reduce the incentive to engage in these economic activities.

TABLE 1
INCOME TAXATION IN THE STATES, 1990

States Without Income Taxes	States Taxing Interest, Dividends, and Capital Gains Only
Alaska	New Hampshire
Florida	Tennessee
Nevada	
South Dakota	
Texas	
Washington	
Wyoming	

States Taxing Adjusted Gross Income (Rate ranges in parentheses)

Alabama (2.0-5.0)	Kansas (4.5-6.0)	New York (4.0-7.5)
Arizona (2.0-8.0)	Kentucky (2.0-6.0)	North Carolina (6.0-7.0)
Arkansas (1.0-7.0)	Louisiana (2.0-6.0)	North Dakota (2.6-12.0)
California (1.0-9.3)	Maine (2.0-8.5)	Ohio (0.7-6.9)
Colorado (5% fed)[1]	Maryland (2.0-5.0)	Oklahoma (0.5-6.0)
Connecticut (4.5)	Massachusetts (5.0-10.0)	Oregon (5.0-9.0)
Delaware (3.2-7.7)	Michigan (4.6)	Pennsylvania (2.1)
Georgia (1.0-6.0)	Minnesota (6.0-8.0)	Rhode Island (23% fed)[1]
Hawaii (2.0-10.0)	Mississippi (3.0-5.0)	South Carolina (3.0-7.0)
Idaho (2.0-8.2)	Missouri (1.5-6.0)	Utah (2.6-7.2)
Illinois (3.0)	Montana (2.0-11.0)	Vermont (25% fed)[1]
Indiana (3.4)	Nebraska (2.0-5.9)	Virginia (2.0-5.8)
Iowa (0.4-10.0)	New Jersey (2.0-3.5)	West Virginia (3.0-6.5)
	New Mexico (1.8-8.5)	Wisconsin (4.9-6.9)

[1]State income taxes determined as a percentage of federal income tax liability.

STATES WITH INDIVIDUAL INCOME TAX

- STATES WITH NO INDIVIDUAL INCOME TAX
- STATES WITH NO TAX ON WAGE INCOME

How Federalism Accentuates the Negative

Federalism, by providing the option of moving from one jurisdiction to another, accentuates the disincentive effects of higher taxes in any one jurisdiction. People confronting high *federal* taxes have the options of working less and enjoying more leisure, saving less and consuming more goods and services, or avoiding new entrepreneurial endeavors that risk their time and money as a way of accommodating themselves to high taxes. *People confronting high state and local taxes have an additional option: migrating to jurisdictions with lower taxes.* It is certainly easier to move within the United States than between the United States and other countries. Thus, mobility should accentuate the growth-retardant effects of high taxes in any single jurisdiction.

It is not only the total tax burden that affects economic growth but the types of taxes governments choose. Consumption-based taxes, notably state sales taxes, may not have the same debilitating impact on productivity as corporate or individual income taxes. It is true that sales taxes must be paid out of personal income, but it is consumption that is being taxed directly, not work, savings, or investment. Indeed, by raising the costs of consumption relative to the costs of savings, sales taxes may have a modest beneficial effect on savings.

In contrast, individual income taxation directly taxes the return on earnings, dividends, interests, and rents. Progressive income taxation has the most harmful effect because it substantially lowers the rate of return on work and savings of the most productive people. Relatively modest aggregate tax burdens can have a very adverse effect on economic growth if these burdens are carried disproportionately by the most productive individuals and firms. Federalism accentuates the harmful effects of progressive state and local income taxation. The most productive people are usually the most mobile, and a highly progressive state income tax is a strong incentive to move.

A Design for Research

The eight most recent states to enact personal income taxes (excluding Connecticut's 1991 adoption)—Illinois, Maine, Michigan, Nebraska, New Jersey, Ohio, Pennsylvania and Rhode Island—provide an "experimental" group. These states enacted income taxes between 1964 and 1977 (see Table 2). "Time series" observations of government growth and economic performance *before* and *after* their adoption of income taxation can indicate the consequences of their decision. (Connecticut is excluded, of course, because post-adoption data has yet to be generated.) The hypotheses can be simply stated: the adoption of an income tax accelerates the growth of state government while at the same time slows the growth of the state economy.

A time series research design applied to each of the eight states that adopted income taxation over the past three decades will allow us to observe economic performance before and after adoption in these states. A hypothetical visual portrayal of the effect of adopting an income tax on growth in total personal income is shown in Figure 1. Annual observations of a state's total personal income *before* the adoption of an income tax, when converted to a trend line, allows us to project income growth into the post-adoption years. If the actual growth in personal income *after* the adoption of an income tax falls below the projected trend line, we can infer that the difference between actual and projected post-adoption performance is a *cost* of income taxation. This cost represents the economic losses incurred by a state as a result of adopting an income tax.

TABLE 2
STATES ADOPTING AN INCOME TAX, 1969-1976

State	Year of Adoption	Initial Tax Rates	Rates in 1988
Illinois	1969	2.5% flat	3.0% flat
Maine	1969	1.0-6.0%	2.0-8.5%
Michigan	1967	2.9% flat	4.6% flat
Nebraska	1967	10% of federal tax liability	2.0-5.9%
New Jersey	1976	2.0-2.5%	2.0-3.5%
Ohio	1971	0.5-3.5%	0.7-6.9%
Pennsylvania	1971	2.3% flat	2.1% flat
Rhode Island	1971	15% of federal tax liability	23% of federal tax liability

Results from Eight State "Laboratories"

The results of time series observations *before* and *after* the adoption of state personal income taxes for the eight most recent states to enact these taxes (excluding Connecticut) are presented in Figures 2 and 3. *State government spending* is observed for each of the eight states in Figure 2, and *total personal income* is observed in Figure 3. While each state possesses a separate record of government spending and economic growth, their similarities in response to income taxation are striking.

Figure 1

**Research Design: Assesing the effect of adopting
a state income tax on growth of personal income.**

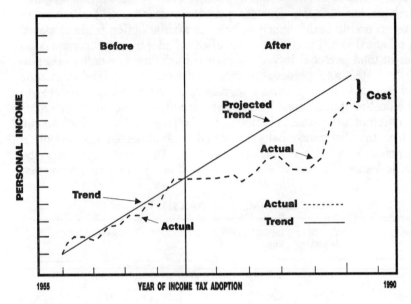

These similarities strengthen our inferences about the impact of state personal income taxes.

Accelerating Government Growth. Adopting an income tax is a general prescription for accelerating government growth. In six of the eight states that adopted an income tax in recent years, state government spending accelerated rapidly following enactment. Dramatic rises in state government spending were recorded in Illinois, Maine, Michigan, Nebraska, New Jersey, and Ohio. Of course, state government spending rose both before and after adoption of an income tax. But Figure 2 shows that the *rate of increase* following the adoption of an income tax was significantly higher than the rate of increase prior to doing so. Each of these six state governments began spending significantly more than pre-adoption-based forecasts. Note that all of these observations are in *constant dollars*, insuring that the effects observed are not a product of inflation.

It is true that government spending did not accelerate in Rhode Island following income tax adoption; and in Pennsylvania, growth in state government spending actually slowed. The experience in these states indicates that income tax adoption does not always produce accelerated government spending.

Retarding Economic Growth. Adopting an income tax is a general prescription for slowing economic growth. In six of the eight states that adopted an income tax in recent years, personal income growth slowed significantly following enactment. Personal income continued to grow in these states, but as shown in Figure 3 the *rate of increase* was significantly lower following adoption of income taxation. Personal income growth fell below pre-adoption based forecasts in Illinois, Michigan, New Jersey, Ohio, Pennsylvania, and Rhode Island. In New Jersey and Rhode Island personal income growth appeared to recover in the late 1980's, but the adverse effects of their adopting an income tax lasted for almost a decade.

There were no apparent adverse effects of income tax adoption in Maine and Nebraska. Thus, state income taxation does not invariably produce an economic slowdown.

Estimating Losses. The estimated losses in personal income experienced by the citizens of each state adopting an income tax are presented in Table 3. These estimates were calculated by subtracting the forecasted personal income based on the pre-adoption trend line from the actual post adoption experience each year. (This cost is represented for each in Figure 3 by the area between the post adoption trend line and the line representing actual personal income levels.) For example, we estimate that the citizens of Illinois lost personal income totaling $237 billion in *constant dollars* between 1969 and 1988.

Regression Tests for Intervention Effects

Income tax adoptions were modeled as interventions in time series regressions for each state for both total state expenditures and total personal income growth. Income tax adoption is included in each regression problem as a dummy variable:

$$Y = a + b_1 T + b_2 D + b_3 (DT) + e$$
Where:
    Y = total state expenditures, or total personal income
    T = year
    D = income tax adoption

The equation assumes that both the slope and the intercept values may be changed by adoption of an income tax.

Figure 2

The Effect of Income Tax Adoption
On Government

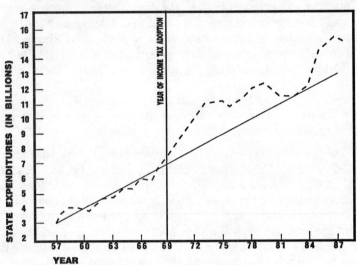

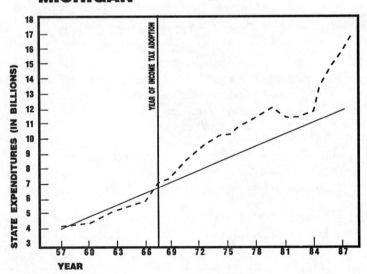

MAINE

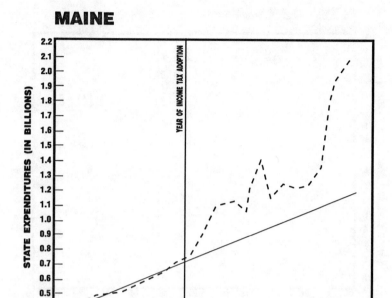

NEBRASKA

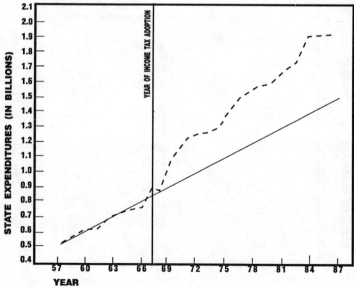

NEW JERSEY

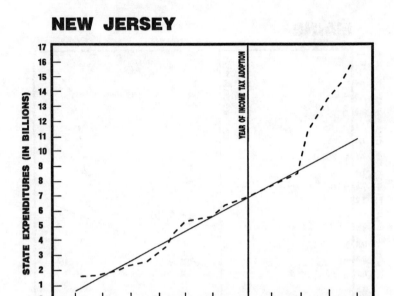

OHIO

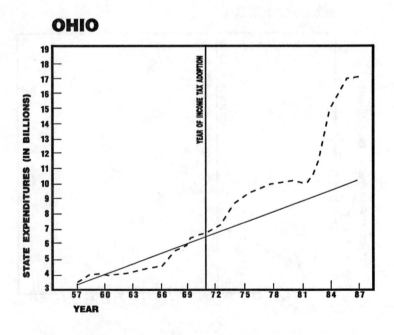

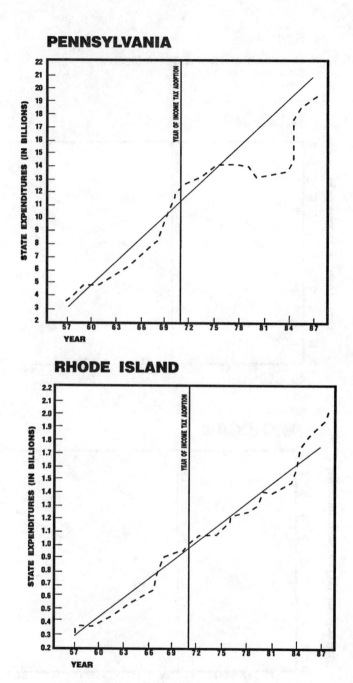

PENNSYLVANIA

RHODE ISLAND

Note: State expenditures are in constant dollars.

Figure 3

The Effect of Income Tax Adoption
On Economic Growth

ILLINOIS

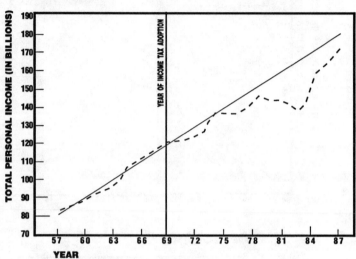

MICHIGAN

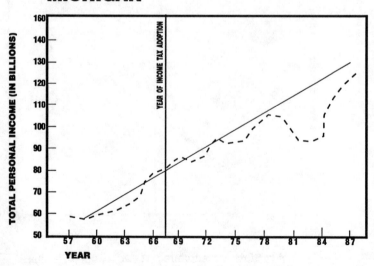

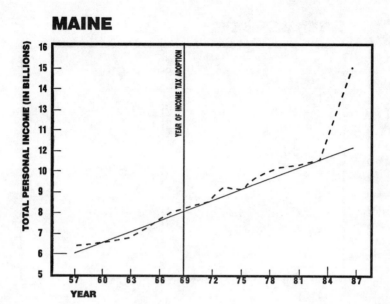

MAINE

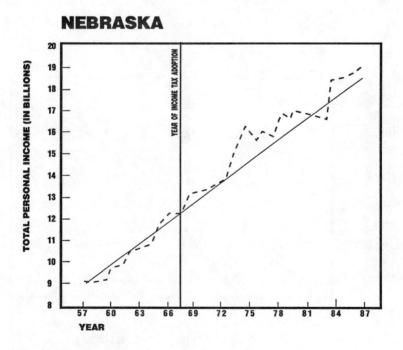

NEBRASKA

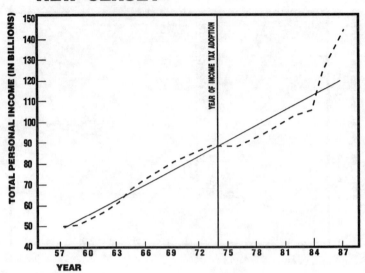

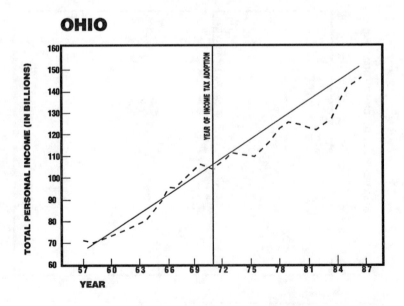

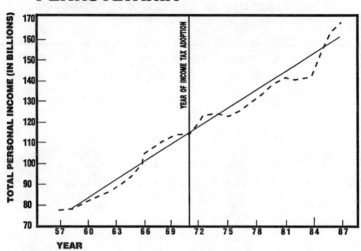

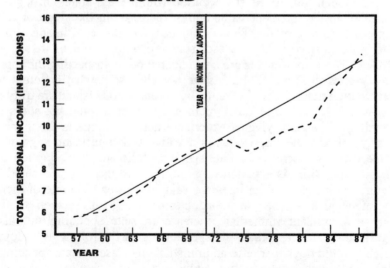

Note: Total personal income is in constant dollars.

TABLE 3
ESTIMATED LOSSES IN TOTAL PERSONAL INCOME
ATTRIBUTED TO THE ADOPTION OF AN INCOME TAX
(millions of constant dollars)

YEAR	IL	ME	MI	NE	NJ	OH	PA	RI
1968				--				
1969			2475	--				
1970	-1625	--	-2219	--				
1971	-3789	--	-2640	--				-164
1972	-3689	--	-308	--		-1672		-21
1973	-690	--	1599	--		543		-149
1974	-3924	--	-3265	--		-2200		-644
1975	-9276	--	-9684	--		-8368		-1106
1976	-10180	--	-7228	--		-7312		-1088
1977	-9401	--	-4212	--	-6220	-5586	-2533	-1082
1978	-8796	--	-2203	--	-5772	-4225	-2877	-1034
1979	-9265	--	-3292	--	-6420	-4442	-1640	-1082
1980	-15494	--	-8836	--	-6082	-8283	-2963	-1241
1981	-17155	--	-14080	--	-6290	-11821	-3965	-1365
1982	-23450	--	-21152	--	-7761	-17244	-8161	-1635
1983	-28406	--	-23703	--	-6162	-18924	-10048	-1385
1984	-22285	--	-20122	--	-2310	-14745	-7350	-947
1985	-18934	--	-14468	--	8320	-12389	-486	-694
1986	-18833	--	-12570	--	11315	-12349	830	-434
1987	-17591	--	-13070	--	15671	-11864	3478	-68
1988	-14621	--	-11829	--	20711	-9897	6851	309

State spending increases occurred within these states through both
increases in the intercept value and/or increases in the slope or rate of
state spending growth. The T-statistics for the coefficients for the
intercept and slope values for each state regression problem are shown in
Table 4. These coefficients are best understood by inspecting the separate
state graphs in Figure 2. Each state reveals a somewhat different post-
intervention trend. But only Pennsylvania and Rhode Island are truly non-
conforming in terms of our hypotheses that an income tax spurs state
spending. (The Pennsylvania experience actually suggests the inverse of
our hypothesis: the slope value is negative and significant, suggesting a
reduced rate of increase in state spending following the adoption of an
income tax.) **Illinois** experienced an immediate increase, indicated by a
significant increase in the intercept value, followed by a rate of increase
not much greater than the pre-adoption slope. **Maine** experienced not
only a significant immediate increase in state spending but also a
significantly greater rate of spending growth following adoption.
Michigan did not experience an immediate increase in state spending but
embarked upon post-adoption annual rate of spending growth that
eventually led to much higher levels of spending than forecast on the
basis of pre-adoption trends. **Nebraska** exhibited roughly the same

pattern; a significant increase in slope leading to a higher level of state spending. State spending in **New Jersey** was not significantly affected by the adoption of an income tax for several years; but then in the late eighties state spending leaped dramatically, giving the state a significant slope increase. **Ohio** also experienced a very significant change in the rate of increase in state spending. In both New Jersey and Ohio the increase in slope was sufficient to cause declines in the intercept value.

Personal income in the states was also affected by both decreases in the intercept value and/or declines in the slope or rate of increase in personal income. The T-statistics for the coefficients for the intercept and slope values for each state for total personal income are shown in the last two columns of Table 4. Again, it is easier to interpret these values by inspecting the separate state graphs in Figure 3. Maine and Nebraska failed to conform to our hypotheses that an income tax adversely affects economic growth. (Maine experienced a significant increase in the rate of personal income growth after adopting the tax, as indicated by a significant positive slope coefficient.)

TABLE 4
INTERVENTION EFFECTS OF INCOME TAX ADOPTION,
TIME SERIES REGRESSIONS ON PERSONAL INCOME AND
STATE SPENDING, EIGHT STATES

| | T Statistics for Income Tax Adoption | | | |
| | State Spending | | Personal Income | |
	Intercept	Slope	Intercept	Slope
Illinois	3.56*	0.53	3.23*	-3.55*
Maine	1.99*	2.83*	(-4.54*)	(3.66*)
Michigan	-0.50	1.98*	2.95*	-2.01*
Nebraska	-1.05	2.84*	1.38	-0.04
New Jersey	-4.58*	4.85*	-7.13*	6.74*
Ohio	-1.27*	4.42*	2.48*	-3.22*
Pennsylvania	(2.93*)	(-2.44*)	0.29	-1.23
Rhode Island	-1.95	1.53	2.89*	0.45

Note: An asterisk indicates statistical significance at .05 level
Figures in parenthesis contradict hypotheses.

Illinois, Michigan, and Ohio experienced significant declines in their rate of income growth following income tax adoption, as indicated by a significant negative slope coefficients. Pennsylvania also experienced a decline in the rate of income growth, but the slope coefficient did not meet the standard .05 level of significance. Rhode Island experienced a significant drop off in personal income, following a brief, two year lag; however, its rate of growth was relatively unaffected and the state eventually regained its losses. New Jersey also experienced a significant loss in personal income for a decade following adoption of an income tax; however its dramatic economic growth after 1984 more than made up for its losses. This recovery produced a significant positive slope for all post-adoption years, even though the New Jersey economy performed poorly for a decade following adoption.

Summary of Findings and Forecasts

Economic forecasting is admittedly risky business. We can look backward and observe what happened in other states following the adoption of an income tax. We can observe that in six of the eight states to adopt an income tax over the past twenty-five years (excluding Connecticut's 1991 adoption) *state government spending grew rapidly*. The *rate of increase* in state spending was significantly higher in these states following enactment of the tax. Moreover, in six of the eight states that adopted an income tax, *personal income growth* slowed significantly following enactment.

It is always possible to suggest alternative explanations for these increases in state spending and declines in economic growth in any of the states under study. But the frequency of these observed effects, and the similarities in state experiences, add to the credibility of our inference that these effects were a result of the adoption of state income taxation.

Economic growth and growth in government spending can be projected forward to the year 2000 for any state based upon trend lines. These projections can be based on long-term or more recent observations. We chose a best-estimate forecast based on the years 1977-1988, which envisioned healthy economic growth rate.

Endnotes

1. Joseph A. Pechman, *Federal Tax Policy*, 5th ed. (Washington, D.C.: Brookings Institution, 1987), 76-77.

2. James D. Gwartney, *Economics: Private and Public Choice* (New York: Harcourt Brace Jovanovich, 1990), 113-114.

Appendix

Data Source

U.S. Department of Commerce, Bureau of the Census, Governments Division *State Government Finances* Series GF published annual.

Government Expenditure Concepts

> The expenditure reporting categories comprise all amounts of money paid out by a government and its agencies, with the exception of amounts for debt retirement, and for loan, investment, agency, and private trust transactions. Note that expenditures include payments from all sources and funds, including amounts spent from borrowing and from previous period balances, as well as from current revenues. Included in this category are expenditures of business-type government corporations and agencies. Transactions not considered as expenditures include payments for debt retirement, extension of loans, purchase of securities, and payments to the Federal Government of monies withheld for income tax or Social Security (OASDH) purposes.
>
> [*State Government Finances*, p. vi]

For information regarding data contained in this report, contact **Henry Wulf**, Governments Division, Bureau of the Census, Washington, D.C. 20233 (telephone 301-763-7664).

Financial data published by individual state agencies does not always coincide with federal data owing to differences in definitions and categories of revenues and expenditures.

LOTTERIES ARE A BAD BET

Prof. Patrick R. Anderson
Florida Southern College

Egged on by the $200 million a year in fantasy-inducing government-paid advertisements, Americans now spend more than $16 billion a year —up from $2 billion a decade ago—on ever-smaller chances of winning ever-larger sums of money (The biggest jackpot so far is the $115 million that Pennsylvania paid out in April 1991). On average, each citizen of Massachusetts spends almost $1 a day on lottery tickets.[1]

From 1982 to 1988, lottery revenues increased a staggering 288 percent. Per capita spending on lotteries in states that sponsor the games increased from $39 in 1982 to $189 in 1988.[2]

Yet even with the increased popularity of state-sponsored and owned lotteries, questions remain about the wisdom of government promotion of gambling. Should the state entice those with low incomes and minimal job skills to wager their bread and butter money on the lotteries?

What is the long-term effect of state-sponsored gambling on the moral and civic values of the citizenry? If revenues from lotteries come in under their projections, will the state turn to other forms of vice to legalize for revenue purposes, prostitution? drugs? cock fights? Before a lottery is adopted in a state, perhaps the main question to be asked is, will it work? Is this the most efficient way of raising revenue and the most equitable?

A Lottery Is a Regressive Form of Taxation

The entire debate about state-operated lotteries is a result of the pressure for more revenues for the states. Within this present context, lotteries are purely and simply viewed as a means of raising revenues from the citizens of the state who are either inclined, or can be enticed, into playing the lotteries. Since the result is to clearly function as a tax, the lotteries must be judged by the manner in which they function, which includes a consideration of those from whom the state raises revenue.

State-operated lotteries follow a pattern in developing the games which are played by the gamblers. Usually they turn to the daily "numbers" game to hike revenues which level off and decline after the start-up period for the lottery.[3]

The "numbers" or player selection lottery games generate the major portion of the revenue derived from state-operated lotteries. From 1976 through 1979, Maryland's lottery netted $145 million for the state, and $138 million of it was from the daily numbers game. Since Pennsylvania introduced its daily numbers game in 1977, 70 percent of its income has come from the daily numbers game.[4] In fiscal 1982, 88.8 percent of New Jersey's lottery income was from daily numbers games.[5]

There can be no reasonable doubt that the daily numbers game, the one upon which most of the state-operated lotteries depend for their main source of revenue, appeals primarily to the poor and less educated members of our society. Its appeal is based on the illusory promise and the desperate hope of a big win.[6]

Most forms of gambling are highly regressive when viewed as forms of taxation. This is not a new conclusion. It was clearly demonstrated by the research done in connection with the Presidential Commission on the Review of the National Policy Toward Gambling. Of the 11 different types of gambling reviewed, all but two, casinos and illegal sports booking bets, were regressive. When Nevada residents were surveyed, even casino gambling was found to be regressive. The only reason that casino gambling was not regressive for the population of the United States as a whole is that poor people outside of Nevada lacked the funds to travel to Nevada, which was the only state with legal casino gambling when that study was made.[7]

Daniel B. Suits, an economics professor at Michigan State University, has pointed out on several occasions that low-income lottery players wager a disproportionately high percentage of their income on the lottery, with the numbers game having the primary appeal.[8]

Perhaps the most conclusive evidence of the manner in which lotteries appeal to poor people is the fact that their outlets are concentrated in poorer neighborhoods.[9] One highly informative study was done in New Castle County, Delaware, in 1979. The study found no lottery outlets in the upper-income neighborhoods where 17,630 persons lived. There was one lottery outlet for every 17,774 persons in upper-middle income neighborhoods. There was one lottery outlet for every 5,032 persons in the lower-middle to middle-income neighborhoods. There was one lottery outlet for every 1,981 persons in the poorest neighborhoods.[10]

State-operated lotteries are a regressive and inefficient way to raise taxes. A form of taxation is regressive if it draws a larger percentage of its revenue from the poorer citizens than from middle- and upper-class citizens. It is regressive if a poorer person spends a higher percentage of his or her income on the activity than does the person of modest or affluent means. Such is clearly the case with the lottery.

State-operated lotteries are among the most regressive forms of legalized gambling. They are almost twice as regressive as pari-mutuel wagering on horses. The conclusions of the study of the Presidential Commission have been supported by a number of other studies which have reported remarkably similar results. In all of the studies, persons with incomes below $5,000 spent a much larger percentage of their personal income on the lottery. The most revealing comparison is the amount spent on the lottery out of every thousand dollars of income. In Connecticut, the figure was 14 times greater for those with incomes below $5,000 than for those with incomes of $25,000 or more; in Massachusetts, 15.5 times greater; in Maryland, regarded as perhaps the state with the most successful state lottery, the figure was 21.5 times greater.[11] One of the few forms of gambling which was more regressive than state-operated lotteries was the illegal numbers game.[12] But that same game is now being run by state-operated lotteries in a number of "player choice" games, which was not the case when most of these studies were conducted. The state-operated lotteries of today are even more regressive than four of the five studies demonstrated.

The player selection games, which represent the main source of revenue for state lotteries, have been identified as having a disproportionate drawing from lower socioeconomic groups. One of the earliest studies to detect this heavy appeal was conducted by Dr. Mark Abrahamson, Professor of Sociology, University of Connecticut. That study concluded: "Connecticut Daily Numbers primarily attracts poor, long-term unemployed and less educated participation. It generates State revenue in a regressive manner and should be discontinued."[13]

It might also be instructive to note some relevant information which can be derived about lottery regressivity from persons and organizations associated with the lottery industry. Scientific Games, Inc., a subsidiary of Bally, Inc., is a leading supplier of products for the operation of state-operated lotteries. Scientific Games, Inc., is such a strong advocate of state-operated lotteries that it serves as a catalyst in states considering the adoption of state-operated lotteries. Published reports have indicated that Scientific Games has spent in excess of $2.1 million in California in getting the lottery issue on the ballot,[14] approximately $200,000 in Arizona,[15] $150,000 in Oregon,[16] perhaps another $150,000 in Colorado and the District of Columbia,[17] hired a lobbyist in Missouri, and spent unidentified amounts in states such as West Virginia, Louisiana, Mississippi, and New Mexico.

These funds were expended in a variety of ways: for petition circulators, for lawyers fees, for promotion campaigns, and other activities connected with the development of a campaign for legalization of a state lottery. Clearly, Scientific Games is fully involved with the marketing and development of state-operated lotteries.

In 1982 Daniel Bower, president and co-founder of Scientific Games, Inc., addressed the Fourth Annual Gaming Conference and International Gaming Congress at the Dunes Hotel in Las Vegas, Nevada.[18] On that occasion he identified the principal players of the three different forms of lottery games being played: the weekly draw game, the instant game, and the player selection game. These different games were introduced chronologically in that general sequence and each form of the lottery represented an approximate tripling of the activity being realized by the preceeding game.

The weekly draw game attracts players "most likely to be white male, and on the middle to lower side of the occupational scale. A majority of the players are age 55 or older." The dollar instant game is most likely to be played by those who are white and male, but somewhat younger than those playing the weekly draw game. The big attraction, however, is the player selection game, which in some states represents almost 90 percent of the net sales of the lottery. According to Bower, the player "is most likely to be a nonwhite male employed as a laborer or service worker. Most players have less than an eighth grade education and few have more than a high school education."

In expounding on the merits of the development of the "video lottery," considered to be the "state of the art for the future," Bower noted that it will attract a new group of consumers not yet attracted by existing forms of the lottery. This group is "younger, better educated, more affluent and higher in occupational status." Surveys he quoted in this address indicate an awareness that white-collar, upper-income individuals do not presently play the lottery. Thus it seems clear that the proponents of the lottery are aware that their product attracts individuals on the lower income strata of society, on the low end of the educational and professional ladder.

Public Gaming Magazine carried a series of articles describing a study conducted by Dr. John Koza, chairman and chief executive officer of Scientific Games. Dr. Koza received a Ph.D. in computer science from The University of Michigan. The study conducted was of participation in the lottery in New Jersey. The most instructive part of the study was reported in Part IV of the series.[19] In that article, Koza identified the leading neighborhoods in terms of their participation in the four kinds of games sponsored by the New Jersey lottery. The New Jersey lottery at the time of the study had the instant game and three forms of the player selection game: Pick 3, Pick 4, and Pick 6 (New Jersey abandoned the weekly draw game because it was less profitable than the other games).

Since Koza identified the leading four neighborhoods for each form of the lottery, a total of 16 possibilities existed in determining the leading lottery players. Of the 16 possibilities, only 2 neighborhoods were either middle-class or upper-class level in income, both with the instant game. The other two neighborhoods which showed up among the leaders in playing the instant game were identified as follows:

- Older Population, Lower-Middle Income, Eastern Europeans, North-eastern U.S., and

- Older Population, Lower-Middle Income, Low Value, Very Old Housing.

The kind of neighborhood which was the leader in both Pick 3 and Pick 4 was identified as Black Neighborhood, Older Population, Old Rental Housing. This neighborhood was the fourth leading neighborhood in playing Pick 6. The frequency with which this kind of neighborhood played Pick 3 was 2.46 times greater than average, 2.29 greater than average for Pick 4, and 1.23 times greater than average for the Pick 6 game.

A second leading neighborhood in playing the player selection games sponsored by the lottery is identified as Older Population, Lower-Middle Income, Small Towns. This neighborhood was third in Pick 3, fourth in Pick 4, and second in playing Pick 6. The neighborhood which was identified as Older Population, Lower-Middle Income, Eastern Europeans, northeastern U.S., which was the leader in the instant game, was second in both Pick 3 and Pick 4 and third in Pick 6. The other neighborhood to note is identified as Hispanic Neighborhood, Poor Families, Very Old Housing. This neighborhood was identified as being fourth in Pick 3, third in Pick 4, and second in Pick 6. Thus, of the 16 possibilities, only two of the neighborhoods represented income levels classified as middle-class or above.[20] The public policy conclusion is that a state should not sponsor a lottery which is calculated to have a disproportionate appeal to individuals from the lower socioeconomic classes of our society, thereby extracting a disproportionate share of state revenue from them.

A Lottery Will Knowingly Appeal Disproportionately to Ethnic Minorities

Objective studies which have focused on the regressivity of the lotteries have dealt with ethnic identification less precisely than would have been desired. However, it now is apparent that state lotteries have a dramatic appeal to ethnic minorities which transcends even lottery regressivity.[21] Abrahamson's study of gambling in Connecticut reported the following conclusion about the state's daily numbers game: "The Connecticut daily lottery attracts predominantly black, low income, daily bettors who continue to play the illegal numbers game at the same time . . . . "[22] This was true despite original restrictions about the sale of these tickets in lower socioeconomic neighborhoods, restrictions which subsequently were eliminated.

This contention is further demonstrated by the quote from Bower mentioned earlier: "The player selection games in the U.S. primarily attract the low-income, minority market. The player is most likely to be a nonwhite male employed as a laborer or service worker."[23] Koza's study further demonstrates the dramatic appeal that state-operated lotteries have to ethnic minorities. In Part I of his study, he indicated that blacks and Hispanics played the Pick 4 game with 1.99 the frequency of the average population (almost double). The Pick 3 game attracted blacks and Hispanics with 1.97 times the frequency of the average population.[24]

One Michigan legislator, Representative Joe Young, Jr. (D-Detroit) began raising these concerns in 1983. Lottery officials had apparently very little data on who played the lottery. However, according to officials of Market Opinion Research of Detroit, the proportion of blacks who play is higher than whites, and among those who play, blacks play with greater frequency. "This sort of data is not lost on Young, who is black, and who has concerns that Michigan's lottery, subtly or otherwise, preys on inner-city residents and is, in effect, a tax on poor people and black people." This conclusion seemed to be reinforced by statistics indicating that 47 percent of the Michigan on-line lottery outlets were in the Detroit city limits.[25]

Further inquiry is needed into this apparently conscious direction and marketing of the player selection games to ethnic minorities. The indication is that state lotteries knowingly derive a significant percent of their income from games directly targeted to blacks and Hispanics.

A Lottery Is an Unstable Source of Revenue for States

States that have implemented a state-owned and operated lottery have found them to be an undependable source of income. During 1990, California dropped 11.3 percent in its lottery sales. Sales in Oregon dropped 11 percent; Pennsylvania, 7.5 percent; Washington, 2.4 percent; New Jersey, 0.8 percent. In fact, of the 33 states with lotteries, sales in six of them declined and several others barely recorded gains because of the recession, the Persian Gulf crisis and the maturation of older lotteries that no longer excite players.[26]

States where the profits from a lottery are earmarked suffer even more. In California where education gets one-third of lottery revenues, the school districts have had to hustle to make up the difference in decreased contributions. Since lottery revenues have never represented more than three percent of statewide school funding in California, lawmakers have routinely used it to supplant, rather than supplement, education dollars from other sources.[27] Relying on revenues from a lottery may be a poor public policy tool for states, especially when a state is already spending more than it is taking in.

A Lottery Will not Reduce
Illegal Gambling but Will Stimulate It

One of the main arguments advanced for the legalization of state lotteries is that legalization will cut into illegal gambling and thereby cut off a major source of funds for organized crime. This contention is not supported by evidence. It is understandable that a society would be concerned about organized crime. In 1980, *Forbes* magazine ran a series of articles on organized crime that estimated the income of organized crime at $150 billion per year.[28] Of that amount, approximately $22 billion was projected to result from illegal gambling activity. Income from organized crime derived from illegal gambling serves as seed money for drug traffic.

In January 1984, an interview was conducted with Mr. Sean Mc-Weeney, chief of the organized crime section of the criminal investigative division of the FBI. Mr. McWeeney declined to speculate on the amount of income organized crime derives from illegal gambling, but he did express disagreement with the idea that legalization of a form of gambling will reduce the amount of illegal gambling and thereby reduce organized crime's association with gambling.

"The major problem is credit," McWeeney said. "Legal gambling creates new gamblers who switch over to illegal gambling when their money is exhausted. They switch to the illegal games because they can get credit." Although acknowledging that he did not possess statistics, he did estimate that organized crime derives more income from its involvement with illegal lotteries than from its more publicized involvement with casinos. "Small individual bets by themselves don't seem significant. But millions of these small bets provide an enormous source of income which can then be used in other organized crime activities like the narcotics trade." "Those who go overboard in their betting are likely to wind up getting involved with loan sharks. Only then, when they are unable to pay the exorbitant fees, do they run into the violent aspect of organized crime," said McWeeney.

Compared with other forms of legal (and illegal) gambling, lotteries represent the worst bet for gamblers. Lotteries have the lowest odds of winning of any form of gambling. The primary reason is that, on average, only about half the money bet on lottery tickets is ever returned to winners. States are in the business of running lotteries to make money, and they regularly take half the revenues right off the top.

On the average, 16 percent of gross lottery sales goes to pay for the administration and promotion of the games. About 35 percent of the money raised by lottery sales goes into the state's budget. This means that, on average, less than half of the money bet on lotteries is paid out to bettors—the lowest payout of any form of gambling. In some cases it's even worse. According to the Indiana Fiscal Policy Institute, New York paid only 39 percent of lottery receipts back in winnings, and Kansas only 44 percent in 1988.[29]

In comparison, consider the average payout rates of other forms of legal gambling:

Craps 98%

Roulette 95%

Slots 75-95%

Jai Alai 85-87%

Horses 83-87%

Lotteries 49%[30]

The conclusion from law enforcement sources and studies seems to have disputed for a number of years the idea that legalization of a form of gambling will have the effect of reducing illegal gambling. In 1974, the Fund for the City of New York and the Twentieth Century Fund sponsored a Task Force on Legalized Gambling. Two relevant conclusions were stated by that Task Force:

> Legalized gambling probably cannot simultaneously serve the objectives of both maximum gains in revenues and improved law enforcement. A policy designed solely to maximize public revenue from gambling may conflict with other policies in the public interest.

> The law enforcement benefits of legalization are more important than the revenue potential. But even though legalization of certain specific games may make a noticeable dent in the volume of illegal gambling, legalization of most forms of gambling—unless accompanied by greatly increased law enforcement efforts—will not eliminate illegal gambling operations.[31]

One of the forms of legalized gambling which the Task Force thought promising was the legal numbers game. This optimism seems unjustified, however. Captain Dennis Deneen, vice control commander for the Chicago police is quoted as saying: "Our biggest problem right now is the illegal booking of the state lottery."[32]

This is a situation which has also been noted in Washington, D.C. "Washington's illegal numbers racket is booming, with profits as large as they've ever been, despite the introduction of the District's first legal gambling last August," according to D.C. police officials. " . . . . Matching the illegal game against the legal lottery 'is like two guys in a boxing ring, one with an arm tied behind his back,'" said Howard Klein, associate publisher of *Gaming Business* magazine in New York and an expert on legal and illegal lotteries. "We expect the illegal numbers game to continue to flourish in spite of any legal games," Inspector Kris Coligan, chief of the D.C. police morals division, said. "Obviously, a legalized lottery is not going to stop the illegal numbers game that we have now," said former Police Chief Maurice Turner, citing a similar pattern in other cities where legalized gambling has been introduced.[33]

The matter was made worse in Washington, D.C., by the use of preprinted slips to be used in connection with the legal numbers game. But these slips can be used by the operators of the illegal games, making arrest and prosecution for illegal gambling almost impossible. "With the use of official government-sanctioned bet slips, numbers operators would be able to tell police that their slips were meant for use in the legal game even if they were instead planned for use in the illegal game."[34]

In 1978, hearings in Florida by the Senate Permanent Subcommittee on Investigations stated the following conclusion: "Thus, while the level of illegal lottery activity cannot be labeled 'wide open' it is definitely widespread." The report indicated that one operation alone grossed in excess of $10 million. Lottery operators were discovered to have clear links with organized crime families both in Florida and in the New York/New Jersey areas.[35]

A study financed by the National Institute of Law Enforcement and Criminal Justice, the research arm of the LEAA, contained the following statements:

> Police efforts against gambling could not be reduced, even with legalization, because there is no evidence that legalized wagering decreases illegal gambling . . . .[36]

> Major system wide gambling-related corruption scandals in the recent past have been more likely to occur in cities where organized crime was thought to be directly involved in illegal gambling.

Senator Strom Thurmond's Judiciary Committee took testimony from Lt. Colonel Justin J. Dintino, commander of the Intelligence Division of the New Jersey State Police. Mr. Dintino is a member of the Presidential Commission on Organized Crime. The following excerpt is instructive:

> Sen. Thurmond: "In other words, you're saying that when you legalize gambling it has increased other gambling, is that right?"

> Dintino: "Yes, in other words, when you introduce gambling to an area where they never had gambling before, you now develop a whole new group of individuals who start to gamble. Now, as a result of that, they may initially start out with legal gambling, but some of those people will

turn to the illegal gambling because maybe it offers them higher payments and there are no tax payments that have to be made."[37]

Mr. Austin McGuigan, former Chief State's Attorney of the State of Connecticut, successfully prosecuted the operators of the lottery on two separate occasions. He suggested that, upon legalization of gambling, including the lottery, the states, rather than pretending to regulate the activity, should post a sign which says something like the following: "The state does not guarantee the honesty or integrity of this game." Mr. McGuigan's comments seem appropriate. A sufficient number of instances of corruption have occurred to indicate that state-operated lotteries are not free of corruption. Ample evidence exists to indicate the proliferation of illegal gambling under the umbrella created by a state-operated lottery. Establishment of lotteries does not carry with it sufficient funding for the law enforcement necessary to guarantee the honesty of the game and to control the growth of illegal gambling which takes place within the state.

A Lottery Will Contribute to
Growth in the Number of Problem Gamblers

In 1981, the American Psychiatric Association classified compulsive gambling as a mental disorder. Thus, compulsive gambling is recognized as a disease, an illness, in the same vein as drug addiction or alcoholism. Estimates vary as to the number of compulsive gamblers in the nation, just as estimates vary about the number of drug addicts in the nation. Most estimates suggest the number of compulsive gamblers total eight million. This means that there are about eight million persons in our nation who are unable to control their urge to gamble.

The introduction of a state lottery places the state in a paradoxical role in relation to these individuals. If we are to take seriously the mandate to "promote the general welfare," our nation and our states must provide medical attention for these individuals just as we seek to do for the drug addict. Yet the introduction of a state-operated lottery would put the state in the position of being the huckster that promotes the very activity which is detrimental to the health of the individual. The constant promotions on television, the daily announcement of the winners, the conduct of an activity which is glorified by newspapers and television reporting—all of this carries with it the imprimatur of the state, legitimatizing the activity which for some will grow beyond their ability to control.

A few samples of information may dramatize slightly the seriousness of the problem. Many of us noted with sadness the plight of the 19 year old boy who wagered $6,000 on a lottery drawing and attempted suicide after losing rather than have a confrontation with his father over the squandering of his savings.[38] Although this example is extreme, other kinds of personal tragedy are almost as severe, although not as widely publicized. Perhaps the most dramatic growth in compulsive gambling has been among women. Earlier studies had identified the problem as essentially a man's problem. But Arnie Wexler, vice president of the National Council on Compulsive Gambling, has stated that about 25 percent of the compulsive gamblers are now women.[39] In 1977, New York City police chaplain Msgr. Joseph Dunne estimated that perhaps 1,500 of the 25,000 New York City policemen might have a gambling problem that would require professional counseling to help overcome.[40] Gerald T. Fulcher of the Delaware Council on Gambling Problems states that 86 percent of compulsive gamblers have committed felony crimes while pursuing their addiction. A study seriously needed is one which would seek to identify the amount of money lost through the commission of these crimes by compulsive gamblers. The amount would stagger the imagination and would serve as an antidote for myopic projections about the good that legalized gambling does for a state's economy. Fulcher cites estimates from the American insurance industry which indicate that about 40 percent of "white collar crime" is committed by compulsive gamblers. In addition, he cites studies that almost 20 percent of wife abuse cases involve domestic tension resulting from compulsive gambling.[41]

Mr. Thomas J. O'Brien, director of the New Jersey Division of Gaming Enforcement asserts, "We're creating a whole generation of gamblers in this country. The person with access to funds will be increasingly susceptible to committing crimes such as embezzlement."[42] Perhaps the biggest time bomb is the problem of compulsive gambling among teenagers. An address at a thoroughbred racing meeting contained the following warning:

> Someone on the lottery commission also wants to put lottery tickets in slot machines, where you can go right into any place, press a button, put your money in, and get your ticket. It is also going to be available to high school students. Their lunch money is going to go in there like it has gone into all of those video games.[43]

A 1979 study on compulsive gambling in New Jersey was conducted by Mr. Rickey Greene of the New Jersey Department of Health, Alcohol, Narcotic and Drug Abuse Unit. I simply note some of the highlights of his study:

- Individuals who are probable compulsive gamblers are five times as likely to have been married three or more times than the population in general.

- The average compulsive gambler affects four to ten other individuals.

- One study indicates that there are as many women compulsive gamblers as there are men.

- Studies indicate that in excess of 90 percent of compulsive gamblers began gambling prior to age 21.

- Lottery tickets are highly accessible to children since they are sold in locations which are readily available, such as candy stores, supermarkets, and news stands.[44]

In 1981, committee hearings were held on the subject of compulsive gambling by the Assembly Institutions, Health and Welfare Committee of the New Jersey Legislature. One of those testifying was Mr. Robert Klein, a specialist counselor at the Atlantic City High School, working with problems of addiction such as compulsive gambling. He had conducted a survey among Atlantic City High School students regarding their gambling behavior. He noted the following results:

- 72% of the students gambled in the casinos in New Jersey.
- 69% started gambling at the age of 16.
- 6% started gambling at the ages of 10-12.
- 9% started gambling before the age of 10.
- 6% shoplift to get money to gamble.
- 3% sold drugs to get money to gamble.[45]

If 72 percent of the students have gambled at one time or another, or with some frequency, in casinos, with all of the attempts at regulation and control, how can we seriously contend that lottery sales can be conducted so as to assure that children do not take advantage of the greater availability of lottery tickets? We can't.

One last statement from New Jersey seems appropriate. Mr. Walter Read, Chairman of the New Jersey Casino Control Commission made the following statements in 1984:

> Fifteen years ago there were no women and no teenagers in Gamblers Anonymous. Today there are 20% teenagers and 20% women. A common profile of a compulsive gambler today would be someone under 30 years of age and $85,000 in debt.[46]

The lottery industry insists that its product is not a major contributor to the problem of compulsive gambling. It should be noted, however, that neither the casino industry nor the pari-mutuel industry regards its product as the primary cause of growth in compulsive gambling. Attempting to separate the lottery industry from the problem of compulsive gambling is inconsistent with the way in which the lottery industry views itself and, in turn, is viewed by other parts of the gambling industry. In an editorial explaining why the pari-mutuel industry should not look at the lottery as an opponent, Irving Babson made the following statement: "Over the past five years we have taken the position repeatedly that, rather than take away players, *lotteries create risk takers* in the most cost-effective, efficient manner possible."[47] (Emphasis added.) Such an outlook is perfectly consistent with the attitude expressed by one representative of the casino industry at a recent Conference on Gambling and Risk Taking held in Atlantic City. In a discussion of the lottery industry, Mr. Vern Kite, Director of Planning and Economic Research, Harrah's East, made the following statement: "Lotteries are a way to educate people about a way of entertainment. They can learn about it at home. Then they will look to Atlantic City as a destination for our type of entertainment."

These viewpoints recognize that a state-operated lottery more widely distributes points of contact between the gambling industry and potential clients. By going into the business and residential communities, gambling is made more respectable, especially since it carries with it the imprimatur of the state. The study of gambling in New Jersey conducted by Koza is also informative at this point. By using his figures on the percentage of New Jersey adults who are regular players, it was possible to make some estimates on the amount of money wagered by the "regular" players of the different lottery games:

- Instant game. The per capita expenditure was $12, and the figure for the 16% who played twice monthly or more often was $63.15.

- Weekly game (Pick 4). The per capita expenditure was $18-19, and the figure for the 14% who played twice monthly or more often was $126.

- Lotto game (Pick 6). The per capita expenditure was $26-27, and the figure for the 22% who played twice monthly or more often was $110.

- Daily game (Pick 3). The per capita expenditure was $73-74, and the figure for the 13.1% who played weekly was $505. The figure for the 4.7% of the adults who played daily was $991.

These figures clearly demonstrate that the lottery has the kind of attraction that can become addictive. This is especially true for the daily game, which provides both the immediate gratification and a sufficiently large prize to provide the "action" desired.

There is no doubt that the problem of compulsive and problem gambling is increasing dramatically. The Presidential Commission Report is worth remembering in this regard: "The Commission's research has shown that the availability of legal gambling creates new gamblers. A government that wishes merely to legitimatize existing illegal wagering must recognize the clear danger that legalization may lead to unexpected and ungovernable increases in the size of the gambling clientele."[48] The Report also stated:

> By directly engaging in the promotion of a gambling business, a State takes on the responsibility of insuring that the enterprise is conducted in the best interests of the people. Indeed, the State as lottery entrepreneur has a special fiduciary responsibility to its citizens; since the presumption exists that the State is acting on behalf of the people, it has an obligation to inform them of its intentions to profit from the participation. Accordingly, the State must take care to inform the public fully as to the odds and character of the games being offered, and to avoid any misleading practices in its advertisements and promotional activities . . . . The states should conscientiously disseminate information about the probabilities involved in winning a prize, and should scrupulously limit their lottery advertisements to those informing the public of the existence and nature of the games offered, rather than actively encouraging them to participate.[49]

The Report continues: "In this context, the States have the responsibility to police themselves. Should they fail in this responsibility, Congress should consider giving the Federal Trade Commission the explicit authority to set and enforce compulsory guidelines."[50]

At the press conference connected with the jackpot in Illinois, which produced a $40 million jackpot, one of those attending was Governor Jim Thompson who had publicly purchased tickets for the jackpot. Governor Thompson is quoted as saying: "I think it's terrific. There are no losers in the Illinois Lottery . . . ."[51] How far is this quote from being exactly the kind of state action about which the Presidential Commission Report was warning?

It is clear that no other form of legalized gambling will bring the activity more visibly into the community. Those who choose to utilize the services of a casino or a racetrack have to travel to that facility to engage in gambling. This is not so with the lottery. Because of its greater availability, it has much greater potential for doing exactly what the Presidential Commission warned against: encouraging people to gamble rather than simply allowing those to gamble who might choose to do so. The lottery goes into the community with its outlets. It goes on television and advertises under the banner of the state's name. One has to look long and hard for information about how poor the chances of winning are.

Conclusion

Lotteries are a bad bet for the state as a revenue source. Although lotteries produce a very small percent of a state's revenue needs, an inordinate amount of legislative and bureaucratic time is spent on lottery management, expansion, advertising, and, less frequently, control. Lotteries place the state government in business, which is bad enough, for states do not properly engage in business to raise revenues. States do not traditionally operate cattle ranches, oil fields, or shoe factories for profit. But, with the lottery, the state engages in the business of promoting and selling lottery tickets.

Lotteries are harmful to some people. This fact is demonstrated by the fact that children are not allowed to purchase lottery tickets. How can something that is harmful to children be good for the state? In other forms of vice, the state, if it profits at all, does so by taxation. With lotteries, the state becomes the pusher. The state uses its considerable power and resources to entice, to encourage people to engage in what is essentially a harmful behavior . . . gambling. The proper role of government is to protect the weakest members of the society, to encourage citizens to pursue the American dream of success and security. In our society this dream can truly be realized through thrift, hard work, and savings. Rather than enticing its citizens with that achievable goal and the legitimate means to achievement, lottery states entice their citizens to waste their limited resources on a futile, get-rich-quick dream. The state becomes a huckster, pushing lottery tickets as the avenue to success and security. That is not the proper role of government.

Endnotes

1. Viewpoint, "Private State Lotteries," *Economist*, 1989.
2. Amy Bayer, "Are Lotteries A Ripoff?," *Consumers Research*, Jan. 1990, p. 11.
3. *Chicago Tribune*, 2 Mar. 1990, sec. 1, p. 6.
4. *Ibid.*
5. "Lucky for New Jersey: New Jersey State Lottery 1982 Annual Report," 2.
6. *New York Times*, 23 Sept. 1980, p. 23; *Rochester Democrat and Chronicle*, 27 Mar. 1983, p. 3B; *Wall Street Journal*, 23 Feb. 1983, sec. 2, pp. 31-32.
7. "Gambling in America: Final Report of the Commission on the Review of the National Policy Toward Gambling" (Washington: 1976), 91.
8. Daniel B. Suites, "Gambling Taxes: Regressivity and Revenue Potential," *National Tax Journal*, vol. 30, no. 1 (Mar. 1977): 22-29; Daniel B. Suites, "Economic Background for Gambling Policy," *The Journal of Social Issues*, vol. 35, no. 3 (1979): 52-57; *Christian Science Monitor*, 12 May 1982, p. 10; "Gambling as a Source of Income," in *Michigan's Fiscal and Economic Structure*, ed. Harvey E. Brazer (Ann Arbor: The University of Michigan Press, 1982), 828-853.
9. G. Robert Blakey, "State Conducted Lotteries: History, Problems and Promises," *The Journal of Social Issues*, vol. 35, no. 3 (1979): 63-64; *Christian Science Monitor*, 12 May 1982, p. 10; Dudley E. Sarfaty, "A Need to Guard Against a Gambling Dependent State," *Engage/Social Action*, vol. 11, no. 8 (Sept. 1983): 14; "The Impact of State Sponsored Gambling on the Community: A six-month study conducted in New Castle County, Delaware, by the Delaware Council on Compulsive Gambling."
10. "The Impact of State Sponsored Gambling on the Community: A six-month study conducted in New Castle County, Delaware, by the Delaware Council on Compulsive Gambling."
11. M. Spiro, "On the Tax Incidence of the Pennsylvania Lottery," *National Tax Journal* 27 (1974): 57-61; R.E. Brinner and C.T. Clotfelter, "An Economic Appraisal of State Lotteries," *National Tax Journal* 28 (1975): 395-404; Suits, "Gambling Taxes: Regressivity and Revenue Potential," 19-35.
12. Suits, "Gambling Taxes: Regressivity and Revenue Potential," 24-29.
13. Mark Abrahamson, Director, and John N. Wright, Assistant Director, "Gambling in Connecticut, A Research Report Funded by the Connecticut State Commission on Special Revenues" (Storrs, Conn.: Nov. 1977), ii.
14. *Washington Post*, 19 Mar. 1985, p. A14.
15. Bill Curry, "State Lotteries: Roses and Thorns," *State Legislatures* (Mar. 1984), 16.
16. *Oregon Statesman Journal*, 24 July 1984.
17. *Arkansas Democrat*, 12 Dec. 1983.
18. Daniel W. Bower, "Video Lottery Devices: A New Generation of Players," Fourth Annual Gaming Conference and International Gaming Congress, 1982 (Philadelphia: Laventhol & Horwath, 1982), 23-24.
19. Dr. John R. Koza, "Who is Paying What: Part IV of a Series," *Public Gaming*, June 1984, pp. 50ff.
20. *Ibid.*
21. S. C. Drake and H. Cayton, "Policy: Poor Man's Roulette," in *Gambling*, ed. R.D. Herman (New York: Harper and Row, 1967).

22. Mark Abrahamson, Director, and John N. Wright, Assistant Director, "Gambling in Connecticut, A Research Report Funded by the Connecticut State Commission on Special Revenues" (Storrs, Conn.: Nov. 1977), 33.

23. Bower, 23-24.

24. Dr. John R. Koza, "Who is Playing What: Part I of a Series," *Public Gaming*, June 1984, pp. 50ff.

25. *Detroit Free Press*, 23 June 1983.

26. *Dallas Times Herald*, 22 July 1991, p. A-6.

27. *Ibid.*

28. James Cook, "The Invisible Enterprise," *Forbes*, 29 Sept. 1980, pp. 60-71.

29. Bayer, *Op. cit.*, 11.

30. The South Carolina Policy Council Education Foundation.

31. "Easy Money." Report of the Task Force on Legalized Gambling sponsored by the Fund for the City of New York and the Twentieth Century Fund (Millwood, New York: Kraus Reprint Co., 1975), 2.

32. "Gambling Rage Out of Control?," *U.S. News and World Report*, 30 May 1983, p. 28.

33. *Washington Post*, 26 Apr. 1983, pp. A1, A8.

34. *Washington Post*, 29 May 1983, pp. B1, B9.

35. U.S. Congress, Senate Permanent Subcommittee on Investigation, *Organized Criminal Activities—South Florida and U.S. Penitentiary: Hearings before the Senate Permanent Subcommittee on Investigations, Part 3*, 95th Cong., 2nd sess., 24-25 Oct. 1978, pp. 750, 818.

36. *Crime Control Digest*, 10 Apr. 1978, pp. 3-5.

37. *Organized Crime Digest*, Feb. 1983, 3.

38. *Progress*, Nov. 1983.

39. *Arkansas Democrat*, 26 Dec. 1983.

40. *Crime Control Digest*, 7 July 1977, 5-6.

41. Gerald T. Filcher, "In Response: Legalized Gambling, Who Are Its Victims?," *State Legislatures*, Oct. 1981, pp. 20-21.

42. *Wall Street Journal*, 23 Nov. 1983.

43. *The Blood-Horse*, 12 May 1984, p. 3443.

44. Ricky Green, "A Preliminary Study on Compulsive Gambling in New Jersey," July 1979. Green is an employee of the New Jersey Department of Health, the Alcohol, Narcotics and Drug Abuse Unit.

45. Public Hearings on Compulsive Gambling, before the Assembly Institutions, Health and Welfare Committee, 8 Apr. 1981, p. 3A.

46. "Regulation 1984," *Public Gaming*, Feb. 1984, p. 18.

47. *Gaming and Wagering Business*, Nov. 1984, p. 2.

48. *Gambling in America*, 2.

49. *Ibid.*, 159.

50. *Ibid.*, 158.

51. *Tennessean*, 4 Sept. 1984, p. 1.

THE CONSERVATIVE ACTIVIST'S PRIMER
ON DIRECT DEMOCRACY

Patrick B. McGuigan
Chief Editorial Writer, Daily Oklahoman

For a long time, conservatives neglected long range planning in the politics of direct democracy, even though this brand of politics in which "citizen legislators" can directly write laws, circulate petitions calling for a popular vote on the issue in question and, if the requisite valid names are garnered, gain a statewide verdict from their fellow citizens has recently dominated the political agenda in some states.

The exceptions to this neglect prove how useful direct initiative action can be for conservatives: much of the recent, scattered progress in reduction of state and local taxation, and the occasional surprises for social issues conservatives, have come in instances where their compatriots had either planned ahead for years, or when they had the wisdom to exploit shifts in popular attitudes toward given issues.

Business interests have certainly discovered, in the last three election cycles, how ill-advised was their former neglect of direct democracy. In California alone, corporate interests have had to spend hundreds of millions of dollars over the last decade, mostly to oppose activist liberal initiatives. For the most part this money was spent in a manner best described as reactive.

No effort is made here to speculate why the politics of direct democracy has not had on the right the focus and sustained concentration of energy/resources it clearly merits. Nor is much attention devoted to a question which divides many conservatives: "should" conservatives participate in the initiative and referendum process, with its populist anti-establishment flavor?

Direct Democracy: Knowing the Terms

This much is clear: if business interests do not play pro-actively on the legislative field of direct democracy, their foes—the Ralph Naders, the Public Interest Research Groups, the anti-utility activists and all the rest—will continue to dominate.

For multi-issue, anti-tax or social issues conservatives, the dilemma is similar: if they do not play on this field, their foes, whether sycophants for big government or supporters of abortion on demand or advocates of the radical homosexual agenda, will control what issues get voted on in state and local referenda.

In short, there is no reason in the world for leftists to dominate in the various states the process of circulating initiatives, qualifying them for popular votes, and seeking the concurrence of fellow citizens. Just as conservatives would be foolish to leave the halls of Congress and state houses to their foes, they will be foolish if their long range goals, strategic and tactical planning and specific objectives are not pursued, whether in a defensive or an offensive mode, in the arena of direct legislation.

Alexis de Toqueville once asserted that eventually every important question of public policy in America becomes the subject of a lawsuit. McGuigan's corollary to that observation might be this: if an issue is being considered in a legislative body anywhere in the country, expect it to become (if it's not already) the subject of a state or local ballot proposition somewhere, at some point. Virtually every significant issue of regulation, taxation or private-public partnership now facing corporate America has been or will soon be a subject of direct popular concern somewhere in the United States.

In part this is true because of the sheer extent of direct democracy in the country. In his book, *Direct Legislation: Voting on Ballot Propositions in the United States,*[1] Professor David Magleby of Brigham Young University provided the best short sketch of direct democracy's "spread" in the contemporary United States: "Twenty-six states currently provide for some form of initiative or popular referendum; of that number, twenty-one provide both, three provide [popular] referendum only, and two provide only the initiative. Of states having initiative, twenty-one permit the statutory initiative and seventeen permit the constitutional initiative. Five states have both the direct initiative and the indirect initiative, while fifteen have only the direct initiative and three only the indirect initiative. Popular referendums are permitted in twenty-five states and are generally limited to statutes, but every state except Delaware submits all legislatively derived constitutional amendments to a vote of the people."

To expand on this a bit[2], the way words are used in descriptions of ballot activity is often confusing. For example, the word referendum has a precise dictionary meaning, but in application its meaning is nebulous. In essence, any yes/no vote of the people is a referendum (or, as it is sometimes called, a plebiscite). The term referendum means, simply, a vote of the people. Referendum, thus, is often used to refer to all ballot measures but for purposes of clarity most analysts now use the terms "ballot measures" or "ballot questions" or even "ballot propositions" when speaking of referenda in general, and one of the more specific terms (defined below) when discussing the types of ballot measures.

Referred measures are those ballot questions which come to the ballot as a result of legislative action, constitutional edict, or some mandate of state government. Such proposals can be constitutional amendments, statutes, bonds, advisory questions or other sorts of issues. Referred measures are by far the most common type of ballot propositions.

Initiatives are those ballot questions which come to the ballot as a result of citizen petitioning. Such proposals can be either constitutional or statutory, depending on the provisions of the particular state or locality in which the proposal originates.

Perhaps the rarest of all forms of direct democracy is the popular referendum (often, and confusingly, called simply a referendum). Those states and localities which have the popular referendum allow citizens to circulate petitions calling for a vote of the people on legislation already passed by the legislature.[3]

A variety of democratic mechanisms confront voters with yes/no choices which, while not considered referenda, form a vital part of American governance.

As an example, the recall mechanism is even less understood than the initiative. Under recall provisions, a sufficient number of valid signatures can force a yes/no popular vote on the retention of a public official. Although seldom utilized, this is one of the most powerful political devices available. Its potential was demonstrated in the Michigan legislative recall drives of 1983-84 (which actually switched control of one legislative chamber) and, with absolute clarity, in the recall against Arizona Governor Evan Mecham in 1987-88. A threatened recall drive against Arizona U.S. Senator Dennis DeConcini sparked by both his pro-gun control votes and involvement in the Keating 5 scandal never came to fruition in 1990, but dominated political discussion in the state for a time.

Closely related to the recall mechanism which is triggered as a result of citizen activism is the provision for reconfirmation or popular retention votes. Simply put, this device gives the electorate a chance, after a designated term, to decide whether or not an elected or appointed official should continue for another term of office.[4]

The town meeting, the American version of a community decision making process which still prevails in Switzerland, continues as the preferred method of governing in some New England jurisdictions. At these meetings, any adult citizen comes to annual meetings at which the community decides upon pending local issues in a relatively free forum.[5]

Direct Democracy: A Decade of Drama

Americans regularly face a variety of ballot propositions at the state and local levels which impact on business, regulation of the marketplace, social justice/morality and other conservative concerns. The most consistent propositions impacting conservative interests this past decade dealt with taxation and utilities/environmental concerns. However, Equal Rights Amendments were frequent ballot questions in the 1960s and 1970s and in the last half of the 1980s both "gay" rights and abortion propositions faced popular scrutiny. Here is a sketch of direct democracy this past decade.[6]

1980: Reagan Cometh

In November 1980, voters in a particularly environment-sensitive state rejected the Maine Nuclear Referendum (which would have shut down the Maine Yankee Power Plant at Wiscasset) by a 3-2 count. At the time the initiative drive attracted national and international attention because it was the first such popular vote since the 1979 Three Mile Island accident in Pennsylvania.

On the same day Americans elected tax cut champion Ronald Reagan to the presidency in 1980, tax slashing initiatives patterned after California's Proposition 13 failed in Arizona, South Dakota, Nevada, Michigan, Utah and Oregon. But voters in Massachusetts gave solid approval to Question 2 (best known as Proposition 2 1/2), a statutory initiative which slashed government revenue sources in the state some conservatives had called "Taxachusetts." Referred tax "shift" efforts (increasing tax burdens on upper income voters while providing some relief to other citizens) lost in Michigan and Ohio.

While other tax-related referenda in a variety of states had mixed results, the energy industry was the object of a successful North Dakota initiative increasing the oil extraction tax, while Oregonians passed a severance tax and defeated an increase in the motor fuels levy.

Recovering somewhat from their disappointment a few weeks earlier in Maine, anti-nukers won new regulatory schemes in Montana, Oregon and Washington state but supporters of nuclear power turned back the most aggressive efforts in Missouri and South Dakota.

Proposition 10, a stringent anti-smoking proposal in California, was solidly rejected, while a tough bottle deposit initiative lost in Montana.

The election which brought Republicans control of the U.S. Senate also saw Arizonans approve deregulation of the trucking industry. Texans took a step away from the old populist anti-banking regulations, assenting to installation of automatic tellers around the state, but Colorado voters defeated Issue 4, the populist oriented effort to regulate mortgage rates.

North Dakota voters demonstrated some anti-business sentiments in approving Initiative 7, making the State Industrial Commission a housing agency to manage home mortgage financing for low and moderate income persons and retaining the ban on PAC contributions to candidates for public office in the state.

1981: All This, and Tax Shifts, Too

On May 19, 1981, Michigan voters defeated Governor William Milliken's tax shifting Proposal A, which pleased neither tax cutters nor supporters of increased state spending.

In the November 1981 statewide elections, voters in 12 states and the District of Columbia faced a total of 48 ballot questions. Only six of the measures were initiatives. The remaining 42 propositions were referred.

On the environmental front, Maine voters solidly rejected the Energy Commission Initiative, while Washington state voters approved a proposal to require future voter consent before the issuance of utility construction bonds. In a local election in Austin, Texas, voters passed a proposal to withdraw the city from partial ownership of a nuclear power plant.

On fiscal matters, voters in 1981 offered a similarly diverse perspective. While District of Columbia voters solidly rejected the Educational Tax Credit Initiative, Washington state voters approved elimination of the state inheritance tax. Meanwhile, in Houston, Texas, citizens rejected a massive property tax cut by a narrow margin. On a range of other issues, 1981 brought some surprises. Perhaps the biggest upset of the year was the unforeseen defeat of the Ohio FAIR Initiative, a proposal to make reapportionment of legislative and congressional districts less partisan. Ohio voters also defeated a proposal to introduce "free enterprise" into the Buckeye State's worker's compensation laws.

1982: Not Everything Froze

California voters in June 1982 breathed temporary new life into the tax revolt through approval of three focused initiatives, two eliminating state gift and inheritance taxes, and one (a Howard Jarvis initiative) indexing the state income tax to inflation. On that same ballot, a hefty 62 percent of the electorate rejected the controversial Peripheral Canal (a rare example of a popular referendum), which would have authorized a huge project to transfer water from Northern to Southern California.

On November 2, 1982, voters in 42 states and the District of Columbia considered a total of 237 ballot questions. A total of 52 of the 237 measures were on the ballot as a result of citizen petitioning (51 initiatives, one popular referendum). The remainder were all submitted to the electorate through the legislature or state constitutional mandates.

The public that year faced what might have been the most controversial selection of ballot propositions to appear in one year in modern political history. Citizens registered clear sentiments against high taxes, and overwhelmingly approved proposals to provide special tax breaks for the elderly at a time of general economic difficulties. Voters gave solid approval to the historic nuclear weapons freeze propositions, a harbinger of a trend to place national and international questions on state and local ballots. However, voters also gave solid approval to measures toughening state criminal justice procedures.

Liberal and environmental initiative activists had some things to cheer in 1982, but suffered overwhelming defeats on Bottle Bill Initiatives (Arizona, California, Colorado and Washington) and some other issues. (In fact, pro-nuclear forces won in Maine and Idaho, while the anti-nuke side prevailed in Massachusetts and Montana.) The environmental defeats came despite a political season in which environmentalists exhibited intense levels of professionalism, dedication and commitment of impressive resources.

Tax increase and business regulatory ballot measures were generally frowned upon by the voters, indicating to some observers a popular unwillingness to advance the liberal agenda through the initiative process.

But as the rest of the decade showed such analysis should not be overstated. The nuclear freeze measures were a huge success and provided a model for subsequent actions (such as the nuclear free zone propositions).[7]

The November 1982 results saw another tax indexing victory in Maine, while moderate tax reduction/limitation proposals of various types passed in West Virginia, Colorado and Alaska. An aggressive tax cut effort lost narrowly, by only 13,000 votes out of roughly 1 million cast, in Oregon.

Business interests faced a mixed reception in 1982, while faring well on two particularly significant ballot questions that year. In Arkansas, voters gave strong approval to Constitutional Amendment 60, which raised the maximum allowable interest rate on retail purchases from 10 percent to 17 percent. Meanwhile, in Washington state the electorate crushed a proposal to limit retail interest rates to 12 percent.

"Enterprise zones" called for in referred measures lost in Arizona and South Carolina, Coloradans rejected legalization of wine sales in grocery stores, and Montanans decided to stick with their liquor license quota system. Idahoans approved Initiative Petition 2, establishing a denturitry board, Mainers narrowly rejected an attempt to end milk price controls, Michiganders rejected the initiative which would have banned due on sale clauses in real estate transactions. But Nebraskans gave 56.5 percent approval to Initiative 300, the statutory proposal banning corporate farm ownership.

1983: This Was an "Odd" Year?

The November 3, 1983, "odd year" ballots saw a total of 50 statewide ballot measures in 10 states and the District of Columbia. Five of the propositions were initiatives, while 45 were referred measures.

The results in various states provided several surprises for political analysts. Two tax reduction/limitation initiatives lost big in Ohio, delivering a serious blow to tax cut activists, though not signaling an end to the tax revolt as some observers maintained at the time. Major bonds passed around the country, while Maine voters declined the opportunity to reimpose a ban on the state's moose hunt. A proposal calling for preservation of an historic landmark secured popular consent in the nation's capital city, but Ohio voters in the biggest surprise of the election declined to increase the state drinking age from 19 to 21.

1984: You Tell Me What it Means.

The concept of state-level industrial planning suffered crushing rejection in Rhode Island in a special June 12, 1984 referendum. The state's "Greenhouse Compact" an economic game plan designed to foster $500 million in private investment as a result of $250 million in public financing lost 4-1 despite (or perhaps because of populist reaction to) support from a range of state, business and organized labor leaders.

Life, the quality of life, death and taxes: these were among the themes facing voters who considered 237 propositions in 44 states and the District of Columbia on November 6, 1984. Voters that year faced 40 initiatives and 197 referred measures. Although the total number of initiatives was a sharp drop from the 52 citizen-sparked measures of 1982, several duly-qualified initiatives were bumped from statewide ballots as a result of judicial actions in the closing weeks of the 1984 campaigns. Of the 40 statewide initiatives that remained on the ballot, 20 secured popular consent, a much higher approval rate than the historic norm (over time, only one-third of statewide initiatives have passed).

With few exceptions, Orwell's year of reckoning provided heartbreaking defeats for tax reduction activists and corporate interests generally opposed the major tax slashing efforts. The Michigan "voter's choice" initiative designed to slash taxes to 1981 levels and require popular approval of future tax hikes suffered 60-40 percent rejection, Howard Jarvis' "Save Prop 13" initiative lost with a 54.7 percent negative verdict in California, a Nevada tax cut/limitation initiative lost handily, and the Oregon Taxpayers Union lost its second close battle in a row, falling 20,000 votes short (out of 1.1 million cast) with its Prop 13 "clone" initiative.

Liberals enjoyed three notable successes with environmental/utility propositions (two in Oregon, one in South Dakota), but suffered a significant defeat in Missouri.

Alaskans gave solid approval to a Libertarian Party-sparked initiative abolishing the state Transportation Commission and opening the state to increased competition. In Arizona, a dizzying array of five propositions dealing with the state health care industry yielded widespread popular confusion on election day. The two measures most objectionable to the industry were initiatives designed significantly to increase state regulation of hospitals. The remaining three propositions were referred to the electorate by the legislature. In apparent anger over the confusing choices they faced, voters rejected all five.

Two additional Arizona propositions had implications for business interests. The electorate rejected a measure to forbid public employee strikes, but narrowly consented to a repeal of the state's "little Davis-Bacon" requirement that the state pay "union scale" wages on tax-funded construction projects.

Generally, voters in 1984 remained difficult to categorize and the results were, to put it mildly, all over the map. Neither liberals nor conservatives could point to consistent results supporting their agenda, although conservatives appeared to enjoy a slight advantage because of several significant victories on social justice and moral questions.

1985: Holding Pattern

On September 17, 1985, Oregon voters crushed a proposal to create a state sales tax, the seventh time since 1933 the state electorate had said no to the idea.

On November 1985 ballots, voters in nine states and the District of Columbia pondered 53 statewide questions. Only one of the measures was an initiative (in Maine, where environmentalists won a temporary victory in their ongoing fight with the nuclear power industry), but another was a popular referendum (in D.C., where voters overturned the city council's modest revisions in rent controls).

A third vote of interest came on November 12 in South Dakota, where citizens delivered a crushing 83 percent negative verdict to the Dakota Compact, a measure which would have allowed the state to form a waste disposal agreement with North Dakota. That statewide vote was necessitated by a 1984 initiative.

1986: Something for Everyone

The June 3, 1986, California primary ballot brought a 63 percent victory for Proposition 51, the "tort reform" initiative. The outcome was a defeat for the state's trial lawyers, and a victory for the insurance industry in what was characterized as the "clash of the titans" in the state. The measure was nicknamed the "deep pockets" initiative because while it retained "joint and several liability" for all "economic damages" medical costs, property damage, lost wages and so forth it returned to the state's pre-1978 theory of "strict liability" to govern all awards for "pain and suffering" and other intangibles.[8]

The noted American humorist and political sage, Will Rogers, used to say about the weather in his native Oklahoma, "If you don't like it, just wait a minute." [9] Similarly, the 1986 elections produced results so mixed that, in isolation, they could please or displease just about anyone. All told, voters in 43 states faced a total of 226 statewide ballot propositions on November 4, 1986. Of the total, 184 measures were referred to the people, while the remaining 42 measures came to the ballot as a result of citizen petitioning: 38 were initiatives flowing directly from citizen draftsmanship, while four were popular referenda voter consideration of items already enacted by the Legislature. Significantly, voters in 1986 returned to historic patterns, nationally rejecting roughly two of every three initiatives, while approving the vast majority of the questions submitted by legislators.

In sum, voters registered a mixed picture on highly contentious social justice issues, and most efforts of candidates to manipulate the processes of direct democracy were unsuccessful. The tax revolt made a modest comeback, while environmentalists continued to find sympathy from most of the electorate. "Don't tread on me" was the message in most ballot campaigns impinging on individual liberties, but Americans really don't like drugs and drug traffickers.

On economic regulation, Americans were not predictable, preferring to look at such questions on a case by case (industry by industry) basis. Lotteries were OK with voters, parimutuel betting was tolerable, but casinos were still no good. The electorate would not automatically curb the litigious society, but they wanted their guns. Californians chose not to limit the pay of top end public servants, but residents of other states thought their legislators were being paid quite enough. Popular concern about AIDS was a cutting edge issue in at least one ballot campaign (the state ERA in Vermont), but Californians did not want to quarantine AIDS carriers. Americans of all ethnic backgrounds like English, and sent the message in several votes that they want their children taught it and commerce conducted with it.

Of the three biggest surprises in 1986, two dealt with contentious moral questions. The major shocker in the country was the defeat of the Equal Rights Amendment in Vermont, a state national feminist leaders handpicked to start a comeback. The second surprise came in Arkansas, where voters narrowly rejected (318,357 to 317,753) an initiative to forbid taxpayer financing of most abortions. (Less surprising were similar results on referenda in Massachusetts, Rhode Island and Oregon.) The third big surprise, of particular concern to business interests, was the fairly substantial victory Idaho voters gave to that state's right to work proposal. Despite intense opposition from the forces of organized labor, a hefty spending disadvantage and polls showing that the measure would lose, voters gave a comfortable 54 percent consent to the right to work idea. Further, most analysts believed that popular interest in the confrontation benefitted the successful effort of conservative Republican Senator Steve Symms (who backed the right to work side) to turn back a challenge from popular moderate Democrat Governor John Evans (who sided with the unions).[10]

Taxes were again a key issue in 1986. After a shutout of tax eduction/limitation propositions in 1984, the tax revolt made a modest comeback. Aggressive tax limitation proposals received popular consent in Massachusetts, Montana and in California (Howard Jarvis's "last hurrah"). Alaskans reaffirmed the tax limit first enacted in 1982, while Oregonians overwhelmingly rejected a sales tax proposal and Washingtonians turned thumbs down on a modest sales tax to finance environmental programs.

Offsetting these results, Colorado voters strongly rejected an initiative which would have required popular consent for future tax hikes, Montanans rejected abolition of the state's modest property tax levy, and Oregonians rejected the fifth initiative since 1978 designed substantially to reduce property taxes and limit future increases. The defeat of the Oregon measure was undoubtedly the biggest disappointment to tax cutters.

Environmentalists enjoyed most of the election returns, with the notable exception of those from Oregon. Efforts to move aggressively against toxic waste problems secured popular approval in California, Massachusetts, New Jersey and New York (a hefty $1.45 billion bond). The California measure, opposed by Governor George Deukmejian, easily passed with 62 percent of the vote. In Washington state, a legislatively-referred measure taking a slap at the possible Hanaford nuclear waste site won 82 percent support.

However, a trio of Oregon initiatives were, somewhat surprisingly, rejected. One would have prohibited nuclear power plant operations until a waste disposal site is licensed, while another would have toughened the legal definition of radioactive waste. The biggest disappointment for environmentalists was the rejection of the initiative designed to make Oregon the first "nuclear free zone" state, a rejection coming in the wake of popular approval of local NFZs all over the country during the previous several years.[11]

One regulatory issue which many thought would be a "comer" in initiative politics after the 1986 election involved the provision of measured phone service. Deregulation and the break-up of AT&T brought lower long distance rates, but a subsequent move toward higher local rates, especially in the form of limits on the number of local calls users can make before a measured (per call and length of call) rate comes into play. In Oregon and Maine, initiatives were approved in 1986 requiring phone companies to continue the provision of low cost rates for local phone usage. In the November 1986 "tort reform" confrontations, it was an even split: trial lawyers prevailed narrowly in Arizona, while the opposition coalition won in Montana (only to see the victory eviscerated in subsequent judicial construction).

1987: Prelude to an Initiative Explosion

The 78 statewide propositions on the ballots in 11 states and the District of Columbia in November 1987 made it the most crowded odd-year ballot of the 1980s. But only five of the questions were initiatives. In D.C., voters defeated a bottle bill initiative 55 percent to 45 percent, after an expensive campaign which nonetheless was one of the most effective instances of corporate coalition building in an initiative campaign that decade. The same day, voters in Virginia and Ohio continued a trend of the last six years, approving state lotteries to boost government revenues without direct tax increases. Lone Star State voters said "yes" to county option pari-mutuel horse racing and betting.

In Maine, the nuclear power industry continued its string of impressive victories, turning back another shutdown effort, this time with 58 percent support for keeping the Maine Yankee plant at Wiscasset open.[12]

1988: An Electorate Liberal on Economics, Conservative on Culture

On the same day Americans chose divided government at the federal level, opting for both a Republican president and a still-solidly Democratic Congress, they reflected additional political contradictions in the choices they made in direct "yes/no" votes on 230 statewide ballot questions.[13] The 1988 elections saw the greatest number of initiatives and popular referenda on a November ballot since the 1930s. The November picture found a total of 50 initiatives, four popular referenda and 176 proposals submitted to the electorate through legislative action or constitutional requirements.

Americans frequently stuck to traditional preferences when they pondered issues as varied as "gay" rights and insurance regulation. But at the same time, the environmental movement had its strongest showing in several election cycles, voters in some states opted for new taxes, several states enacted heightened regulation of business including Ralph

Nader's hugely controversial Proposition 103 in California and every tax reduction or limitation initiative (save for a non-contentious measure in Nevada) suffered popular rejection.

The big surprises in 1988 included a shocking defeat of the National Rifle Association (NRA) in the popular referendum confrontation surrounding the "gun ban" commission in Maryland.[14] Additionally, after years in which they lost most such confrontations, pro-lifers in 1988 celebrated a clean sweep in three (Colorado, Michigan and Arkansas) battles over abortion funding restrictions.

The biggest defeat for corporate interests in 1988 came in California, where voters approved the Nader-inspired initiative mandating a 20 percent reduction in rates and an elected (rather than appointed) insurance commissioner. Although the state Supreme Court subsequently gave modest relief to the industry, in truth the narrow popular approval of the measure was a shocking outcome in a campaign which saw at least $70 million in insurance industry money spent on five conflicting initiatives, to only $1-2 million for Nader and his allies. The insurance industry's own "no fault" initiative garnered a more than 4-1 popular rejection. Despite their antipathy to insurance companies, the state's trial lawyers were not too happy with the electorate, which only narrowly rejected a tort reform proposal to cap lawyers' contingency fees at 10 percent of judgments. The trial lawyers' own preferred initiative was crushed. Nader and his allies around the country understandably predicted they would push additional "Ratepayers Revolt" initiatives in 1989 and 1990, on the model of Proposition 13, the taxpayers revolt initiative of 1978. But whereas Prop 13 gathered nearly 2-1 backing, Proposition 103 gained only 51 percent support, a much weaker position from which to build a national movement. Nonetheless, it is likely there will be Prop 103 "clone" efforts in the years just ahead.[15]

California Proposition 99, a 25 cent hike in the cigarette tax, garnered very high support despite a multi-million dollar opposition campaign. In Missouri, a constitutional amendment leaving in place a modest tax to finance soil and water conservation, and state parks, passed easily. A new tax financing ambitious hazardous waste cleanup passed comfortably in Washington state.

Environmentalists had their best day at the ballot in many years, but did not get everything they wanted. The California chemical industry took another hit as the electorate approved a complex initiative further heightening "toxic" disclosure requirements.

But voters rejected several of the most aggressive environmental efforts. With even losing presidential candidate Michael Dukakis in the opposition camp, Massachusetts voters rejected another nuclear power plant shutdown initiative 2-1. A litter control/recycling initiative lost in Montana, and a major extension of the Oregon Indoor Clean Air Act was also rejected. Perhaps the most disappointing result for environmentalists came on the South Dakota strip mining initiatives and in solid citizen rejection of a Nebraska proposal which once looked as if it could trigger the state's withdrawal form a multi-state radioactive waste disposal compact.

Perhaps the most intriguing observation about the 1987-88 election cycle which might still have implications for the 1990s was the fact that the mix of propositions which secured ballot status did not have a dominant philosophical strain, in contrast to some past elections.

In the mid-1970s, as the initiative device surged after decades of dormancy, environmental activists led the charge. In the era 1978-80, tax revolt activists led another surge in utilization of the initiative, while the nuclear weapons freeze campaign of 1982 dominated the first off-year elections of the Reagan era. In 1984, 1986 and again in 1988, however, a full range of political perspectives were represented in the mix of initiatives and referenda securing ballot status.

In terms of the actual results on ballot propositions, there were reasons to believe after the 1988 elections that some traditional patterns of direct democracy were changing. In 1987-88, the electorate showed increasing willingness to approve aggressive initiatives of the Left and Right, favoring regulatory and tax increase efforts of the Left, and many of the moral preferences of the conservatives.

It was an election full of surprises and nuances, with voters delivering stunning defeats to such well-organized and well-financed interests as the insurance industry, Planned Parenthood and the National Rifle Association. With important exceptions, the American electorate of November 8, 1988, was generally liberal on economic issues of regulation but not, apparently, ready to embrace broad new categories of taxation. On the other hand, voters were conservative when considering questions impacting upon the nature of the shared American culture, and in matters of personal and societal morality.[16]

1989-90: The Path Not Taken

In a variety of statewide votes scattered through the first half of 1989, voters rejected the interpretation some had placed on the previous fall's results: that they were ready to accept hefty tax hikes. As former Delaware Governor Pete du Pont put it:

> Voters in two frequently liberal states, Oregon and Wisconsin, have the same message as those in a swing state (Pennsylvania) and a conservative southern state (Louisiana). In all four instances, supporters of tax 'reform'—the word the political establishment still hopes will serve to mask tax increases on the citizenry—significantly outspent their

opponents. But the message in every case was the same: 'No New Taxes.'[17]

Voters in nine states faced a range of 55 statewide ballot questions on November 7, 1989, with contentious initiative battles sparking special interest in Maine and Washington state. Around the country the electorate in candidate races delivered victories to supporters of abortion on demand, but in direct local ballot questions on another moral question, increased legal rights for homosexuals, conservative forces prevailed in five separate confrontations. Additionally, the national electorate appeared distinctly conservative as it considered taxing and spending questions. That conservatism was somewhat ameliorated, however, by a frequent willingness to approval significant bonding propositions.

In Washington state, voters buried the Children's Initiative, Initiative 102. It would have increased government spending $360 million or children and family services. The sweeping measure was easy to organize against, even though it enjoyed initial 70 percent support. The state corporate community late in the campaign broke solidly against the initiative's hefty spending (and implied tax) hikes. Supporters of the initiative included the National Education Association, which poured more than $100,000 into the race. The measure lost 2-1.

In Michigan, elements of the business community were once again pitted against government educators. Proposals A and B, while separate tax increase proposals, were cast as essential supports for schooling in the state. Traditional anti-tax activists such as Brooks Patterson and Richard Headlee were joined by James Barrett of the state Chamber of Commerce. Governor James Blanchard might have gone too far with his aggressive fundraising in support of the initiatives, as even the cautious *Detroit News* stood against what it called his "goon squad tactics." Both sides spent heavily in this battle, but the conservative foes enjoyed the traditional advantages of those seeking "no" votes.

In Maine, supporters of a controversial advisory initiative to ban testing of the cruise missile garnered a narrow 52 percent victory. Another Maine initiative, to impose new campaign finance restrictions on candidates for public office, lost rather handily.

In the Lone Star State, Texans rejected both a legislative pay hike and an increase in per diem payments. A variety of bond propositions passed around the country. Utahns approved a bid for the 1998 Winter Olympics.

The most controversial local issues in the country were those dealing with increased legal rights for homosexuals and lesbians. The defeat for "gay" activists in all five confrontations is one of the year's most significant developments, with the results in San Francisco a particular surprise.[18]

On December 5, 1989, North Dakota captured some national attention briefly for a dramatic statewide election which saw citizens reject eight ballot measures. The results were an incredible slap at Democrat Governor George Sinner, as citizens defeated three separate tax increases. His high water mark was only 46.51 percent in support of his 1 percent general sales tax hike. Other rejected issues concerned games of chance, mandatory seat belts and sex education.[19]

In the lowest turnout (39%) for a primary election since 1928, California voters on June 5, 1990, approved three out of five initiatives slated, and gave assent to all 12 referred measures. Perhaps the most significant question was Proposition 111, an increase in the state gas tax to finance road construction. Republican-backed reapportionment initiatives, designed to prevent a repeat of a notorious Democrat gerrymander after the 1980 census, suffered solid rejection. The outcome was not terribly surprising, in that only Democrats faced meaningful primary battles.

On the same day, Alabama voters gave 89 percent approval to an English Language Amendment, making theirs the eighteenth state to designate English as the preferred language. And, in North Dakota, voters still said "no" to taxes, rejecting on June 12 a statutory initiative providing for various sales tax increases for education.

As 1990 wore on, activists in the nuclear free zone (NFZ) movement suffered a series of unexpected defeats. Thus, voters began to reverse a pattern of victories NFZs had enjoyed all over the country earlier in the 1980s.[20]

In the fall of 1990, direct democracy in America reached its greatest peak in modern history.[21] Whether the issue was taxes, environment, morality, gambling or public holidays, citizens all over the country turned more than ever to the processes of direct democracy.

A modern record of 68 of the ballot measures reached the ballot as a result of citizen petitioning.[22] Sixty-two of the 68 were initiatives, and the remaining 6 were popular referenda. In all, 169 state questions on fall ballots were referred through legislative action or other requirements.[23]

The upward trend over the past decade is compelling evidence of declining citizen confidence in the traditional processes of representative government. In fall 1982, the year of the nuclear weapons free campaign, 52 statewide measures on fall ballots were citizen petitions. The total dropped off to 40 in 1984, nudged up to 42 in 1986, and jumped to 54 in 1988.

California led the hit parade in fall 1990, with an astonishing 28 statewide questions but "only" 13 of those were initiatives.

At the risk of some oversimplification, for a time it looked as if the 1990 election might be remembered as the first volley in a voter revolt designed to change the way government operates. The term limitation initiatives (which all passed) were the clearest manifestation of this, but the various tax cut and related efforts were notable for their focus on process: heightened popular control over state finances, and reduced legislative options to increase government spending. Even liberal initiative efforts included campaign rhetoric which mirrored conservative critiques of legislative bodies as grid-locked and dominated by special interests.

In the 1980s, the number of status quo shattering initiatives prevailing in California had crept upward, to roughly half. If that percentage had manifested itself in the nationwide results in 1990, it would have been the clearest sign yet that voters had lost their faith in the institutions of representative government.

Instead, only 20 of the 62 citizen-sparked measures considered on November 6 prevailed. The percentage which succeeded in November (32.26%)[24] was precisely in line with the historical success ratio for initiatives. Thus, traditional victory patterns were sustained for direct democracy but within the context of much higher utilization of the process than in the past.

Here is a sketch of how the election went for particular "issues clusters."

Although tax reduction activism was notable throughout the nation including in New Jersey, where incumbent Democrat U.S. Senator Bill Bradley nearly suffered the upset of the decade, in direct votes on issues the tax cut movement was disappointed in most cases. Tax cut/limitation initiatives lost narrowly in California and Colorado. Negative votes also came for reduction efforts in South Dakota (54.7%) and Utah (55.8%).

Perhaps the most draconian initiative of the year, Massachusetts Question 3 (another aggressive proposal from Citizens for Limited Taxation) garnered a 59.9 percent negative vote. However, tax reduction activists played a significant role in the Bay State's political turmoil that year, which saw a Republican elected for the first time in decades, and a number of Democrat legislative incumbents surprised. Crushing losses for tax reduction initiatives came in Montana and Nebraska.

Victory for tax revolt came in Oregon, where citizens gave 52.4 percent to property tax limitations which, however, were partially offset for purposes of public education. The tax cut victory came even though its foes enjoyed a 12-1 spending advantage.[25] A successful initiative in Nevada (72.4%) got its second popular endorsement (as required by the state constitution), thus creating a constitutional prohibition on the imposition of any state personal income tax.

Tax increase efforts lost statewide in California, Nevada and Montana, and in dozens of local jurisdictions.

Legalized gambling, in a variety of referred measures, continued to offer an attractive means of government revenue enhancement in an era of recession. In an early October referendum, Louisiana voters gave 69.3

percent approval to establishment of a state lottery. On November 6, voters in Minnesota consented to assignment of proceeds from future lotteries to environmental and natural resource purposes. New Jersey voters agreed to allow parimutuel horse racing on Sundays, and Nevadans consented to charitable private lotteries. In a bit of a surprise for outside observers, Rhode Island Referendum 3 to allow off-track betting in Pawtuckett, accompanied by property tax relief, suffered 63.4 percent rejection.

In perhaps the most notable pro-gambling initiative victory of the year, Coloradans approved Question 4, a constitutional initiative allowing legalized gambling in Black Hawk, Central and Cripple Creek. In Arizona, Proposition 200 (a statutory initiative) was approved, assigning state lottery dollars to the Parks Board and Game & Fish Commission.

However, gambling-related initiatives lost overwhelmingly in North Dakota and Ohio. In the Buckeye State, the issue was a pilot program of casinos in Lorain. Defeat of this constitutional initiative continued the virtually uniform pattern of intense popular suspicion toward casinos, and more ready acceptance of other forms of wagering.

It was surprising that educational policy making was not more of an issue in direct popular votes. The one major confrontation came in Oregon, where the constitutional initiative Ballot Measure 11 faced an intense, overwhelming negative media blitz financed by the National Education Association (NEA-union).

Backers of the Oregon initiative designed what could have been the first American system of full parental choice in education, mandating complete open transfer in government schools as well as use of parental vouchers to send children to private schools. After a vigorous NEA-financed legal challenge forced supporters of the initiative to drain their resources in courtroom battles, the measure remained on the November ballot, where it faced one of the most astounding media assaults of the year.

Opponents of the initiative broadcast television advertisements claiming passage of the initiative would result in schools serving the Ku Klux Klan. (This charge had a certain historic irony to it, coming as it did in a state where public officials early in this century, influenced by the Klan and other nativist elements, tried to shut down Catholic schools. Eventually the religious schools won a landmark decision in the U.S. Supreme Court.)

After running well in some early polls, undecided opinion broke strongly against the initiative late in the campaign, and the proposal lost overwhelmingly (67.8% no). The campaign demonstrated clearly that any popular votes on parental choice in education will face well-funded opposition.[26]

Other education-related ballot propositions were much less contentious, although an Arizona initiative mandating a classroom improvement program garnered a 66 percent negative verdict. A $45.7 million New Mexico bond issue for capital improvements for education earned a 51.5 percent negative verdict, perhaps the victim of an even stronger tide against other initiatives on the ballot. Georgians approved a constitutional measure creating an educational trust fund, whereas Kansans declined to grant public officials greater flexibility in educational operations.

The environment is a perennial theme in American direct democracy, and in 1988 environmentalists had enjoyed one of their best days in year.

In terms of issues considered, 1990 was another big year for consideration of environmental questions. However, environmentalists had their worst election results in many years, as citizens turned thumbs down on one sweeping environmental measure after another.

The big ticket item came in the big ticket state, California. Proposition 128 was what the Associated Press called "an ecologists dream." It included comprehensive restrictions on offshore drilling, use of pesticides, limits on oil and gas production, reduced emissions of many pollutants, and a $300 million bond program for acquisition of redwood lands.

Supporters called their 39-page, 31,000 word initiative the Environmental Protection Act of 1990, and it soon had the nickname "Big Green" for short. Foes, however, called it an economic disaster. Businesses organized earlier than normal in such campaigns, and challenged the initiative on every front. One of the nation's best political consulting firms in direct democracy campaigns, Woodward & McDowell, signed on with the corporate interests. Even though environmentalist supporters had, as one analyst put it in the summer of 1990, "pushed all the right buttons," foes were able to demonstrate that the initiative went too far.[27] As a result, Big Green's support steadily declined, until an election eve California Poll showed it losing 43 percent to 41 percent.[28]

The overwhelming spending advantage foes enjoyed dominated the final days of the campaign, and the initiative suffered 63.6 percent rejection. Californians also rejected initiatives to mandate acquisition of redwood lands and limits on logging, an expanded pesticide management program and other questions.

The picture was largely the same in the rest of the country. Arizonans rejected Proposition 202, an initiative to create a waste reduction, recycling and management plan. Missouri voters crushed (75.1% no) an initiative creating a Natural Streams Commission. In what must have been particularly bitter losses for environmentalists, Oregonians solidly rejected another attempt to shutdown the Trojan nuclear power plant, and an initiative mandating packaging goals in state. In Washington state, an initiative to require that local land use plans conform to a state plan was crushed under a 75.1 percent negative mandate. And, in New York state, a $1.975 billion environmental quality bond act was narrowly rejected.

Californians approved just one environmental question, Proposition 132, an initiative creating a Marine Protection Zone off the coast, and prohibiting certain fishing nets after 1993. Another modest bright spot for the environmental movement was a modest bond issue given 66 percent consent in Nevada, giving the green light to $47.2 million for park facilities, parks, and wetlands.

The environment was not the sole issue of concern to business interests in 1990. Mainers, who are politically liberal, but in some respects culturally conservative, gave only 52.5 percent consent to a statutory initiative allowing many stores to remain open on Sundays. A Massachusetts advisory question on whether or not the state should require radio and television to provide free and equal time to all political candidates secured 54 percent support. In New Jersey, Public Question 2, a referred statute, gained 56.3 percent backing to allow Sunday horse racing and parimutuel betting.

The much-vaunted passage in 1988 of California Proposition 103, the Ralph Nader insurance rate-slashing initiative, did not carry over into the next election cycle. Three Arizona initiatives on various aspects of insurance coverage each experienced crushing negative verdicts. In North Dakota, a statutory initiative to allow rebates to insurance consumers was rejected 88.6 percent - 11.4 percent.

In a broad category of questions relating to legal rights and/or criminal justice, the results were mixed. Oregonians did approve an initiative for mandatory seat belt usage, while Floridians (where earlier in the 1980s a law allowing concealed weapons had been passed) overwhelmingly created a three-day waiting period for gun purchases. Concerned about drug abuse and stronger strains of cannabis than in past decades, Alaskans reversed themselves and, 54.3 percent - 46.7 percent, re-criminalized possession of small quantities of marijuana, approving an initiative initially pushed only by a grass roots conservative housewife. Arizonans gave 57.1 percent approval to a victims bill of rights initiative. California Proposition 139 gained 63.5 percent support, permitting the use of prison inmate labor for work, except in strike or lockout situations. Californians defeated complicated initiatives raising some taxes, rewriting corporate tax provisions, creating drug treatment programs and other provisions. A $20.25 million bond for corrections was defeated in Maine, while in North Carolina a $200 million bond for prison and youth facilities garnered extremely narrow popular consent.

Some of the most contentious popular votes of the year again focused on abortion, and the pendulum this time swung back toward supporters of abortion on demand. In Nevada, pro-lifers had challenged via a popular referendum petition a controversial statute on access to abortion, but citizens gave the law 63.5 percent approval. In Oregon, a constitutional initiative banning abortion except in the "hard cases" of rape and incest suffered 67.7 percent rejection. In a bit of a surprise, Oregon Ballot Measure 10 (a statutory initiative requiring parental consent before abortions could be performed on minor women) also lost, albeit narrowly, 52 percent - 48 percent. That result was widely attributed to a "spillover negative" from the other abortion-related measure.

In other social justice/moral propositions, voters in the District of Columbia went along with changes their city council had made in the Homeless Shelter Act. In New Jersey, voters narrowly defeated a $135 million bond issue for low income housing grants and the homeless.

In Arizona, voters acting through a popular referendum overwhelming rejected replacement of the traditional Columbus Day holiday with one honoring the late Dr. Martin Luther King, Jr. Citizens more narrowly rejected (50.8%) the law creating a paid state holiday in honor of King and civil rights.

The most significant political development of 1990 might have been the emergence of the term limitation movement, a new wrinkle in the politics of direct democracy. After years of discussion among conservative activists and some idealistic liberals, suddenly in this election cycle the term limit concept caught fire.

In Oklahoma, conservative businessman Lloyd Noble II of Tulsa bankrolled an initiative campaign to place 12 year caps on the service of members of the state legislature. Noble prevailed upon retiring Governor Henry Bellmon, a fellow Republican, to place the initiative on the September 18 runoff election ballot. In a campaign with lots of popular discussion through radio, television and newspapers, but relatively little paid advertising, the initiative was never seriously challenged.

As a result, the Sooner State became the first in American history to cap legislative service, when 67.3 percent of the citizens agreed with Noble's bright idea. [29]

The success in Oklahoma attracted international attention, and served as a prelude to approval of initiatives in Colorado and California. State Senator Terry Considine, a successful businessman, promoted the Colorado initiative, which included a legally severable provision applying the limitation to members of Congress, as well as legislators. Considine's measure gained 71 percent consent. [30] In California, Attorney General John van de Kamp had pushed a term limitation combined with public financing of elections. Voters rejected that solidly, but gave 51.8 percent approval to a conservative initiative putting a six year limit on legislative service, and reducing the size of legislative staff.

The term limitation initiatives sparked a national movement which showed every sign of continuing in 1991. But there were other 1990 ballot propositions dealing with the political process itself.

In Arizona, Arkansas and New Mexico, propositions to increase legislative salaries or per diem gained only 32.6 percent, 46.2 percent, and 25.1 percent support, respectively. Oklahomans had, in September, approved an ethics commission initiative on the same day they backed the term limitation. Arkansans joined in the act in November when they gave 65.7 percent approval to Initiative 1, a statutory initiative dealing with political conduct and disclosure.

Direct democracy itself was the focus of a California initiative, Proposition 137, to require popular approval of any statute dealing with the initiative process. Voters rejected the measure, 55.3 percent - 44.7 percent. In Montana, however, voters remembered how qualified initiatives had been stripped from recent ballots, so they gave 56.2 percent agreement to CA 21, a referred measure mandating that qualified ballot questions would get future ballot status if results were ever invalidated for other questions.

Maryland and Montana voters, by 60 percent and 82 percent verdicts, respectively, chose not to hold state constitutional conventions. Coloradans approved a referred measure creating a presidential primary structure.

Conservative Initiative Activism: Thinking About the Future

Those who have read this essay will tend to be women and men already involved in, or at least interested in, politics. Therefore, they can draw many of their own lessons about what worked, or did not, in particular election years, and what those results might mean for the future.

In terms of an issues agenda, conservative prescriptions for what ails America have not changed dramatically in the decade since the rise of Ronald Reagan to the presidency thrust conservative policy proposals into the limelight.

Conservatives believe government at all levels is too big, that it taxes too much and that it is too intrusive into the economy. Further, conservatives believe government has, particularly through judicial activism and social change agency in the schools, fed the collapse of those traditional moral values which undergird American success.

Quite frequently, citizens will agree with these conservative assumptions in direct popular votes. However, most of the tax reduction and limitation propositions to succeed in the past decade (a point I will reiterate below) were those crafted to the needs and realities of the state in which the successful question was listed. And, as the historical narration above demonstrated, broad-based coalitions (such as those which coalesced in the 1989 anti-tax campaigns in several states, including Michigan) are the surest route to the adequate funding and citizen activism needed to sustain successful statewide initiative campaigns, whether pro-active or reactive.

There is no short route to success, no laundry list of conservative ballot initiatives which will guarantee success in any state. Rather, the broad list of conservative public policy objectives, perhaps many of the questions covered elsewhere in this book, or fresh versions of the successful initiatives described above must be adapted to the situation prevailing in each state.

That adaptation to your state's or your community's particular needs can take place after careful study of essays such as this one, and the books cited here (particularly Tom Cronin's masterpiece). To succeed, I'd recommend that you think about direct democracy along the lines sketched in the concluding pages of this essay, where I offer a few modest thoughts on how conservative initiative activists can begin to plan their activism for the 1990s.[31]

First, remember that your direct democracy activism is part of a bigger picture. Meaningful activism through the processes of the initiative, referendum and recall is but a subset of practical political activism at all levels federal, state and local. Too many conservatives fail to recognize that the political struggle is but a subset of the larger battle for the soul of America, its economic ethos, its politics, its culture. Conservatives need to carry their message into all aspects of American society. Political activism in the arena of direct democracy is but a part of what is needed to take back the American culture.

Second, as former House Speaker Tip O'Neill, the Massachusetts Democrat, often put it, "All politics is local." This maxim might seem to contradict the first point, but it does not. The political culture of a state, its traditions, as well as its current political realities, can have as much to do with the success of a particular initiative as anything else. In the late 1970s, after California voters passed the landmark Proposition 13 tax cut, tax reduction activists all over America crafted "copy cat" initiatives and pushed them in their states. Nearly all of them failed. The tax reduction initiatives which have succeeded in the past decade have for the most part been those tailored to the political and fiscal realities of a particular state.

Third, you must study direct democracy, which has political dynamics in some ways similar to those in other aspects of American politics, but which in some respects are unique. One factor contributing to the unpredictable nature of this branch of politics is the wide range of regulation or lack thereof found in the various states. Twenty-six states have one aspect or another of direct democracy state-wide, and most of the remainder have it at the local level. Signature requirements vary from as little as two percent of voters in North Dakota to as much as fifteen percent of the votes cast in the last election in Wyoming. Only careful research of your state or local provisions (at the county courthouse, state capital or political party headquarters) can answer questions about the provisions in your jurisdiction.

The time frames for initiative campaigns vary widely. Procedural hurdles in states such as Maine and Alaska necessitate that initiative petitions be turned in as early as January of an election year, in order to get on the November ballot. In Florida and Nevada, initiatives turned in as late as August can theoretically make the November ballot. Most states fall somewhere in between but increasing legal challenges (see below) make it more and more common for initiative activists to submit their petition names to state officials early.

Signature verification methods vary widely in the states. Typically, names are turned into the secretary of state's office. In some states, the initiative text must be approved in advance. In fact, if your state's initiative system operates honestly, this is actually a good idea because it will save your group the grief of having collected signatures, only to have them invalidated due to a technical violation in the initiative text.

Methods for signature gathering (or petition circulation) vary from state to state. In Oklahoma and Colorado, initiatives can still gain ballot status with mostly volunteer petition gatherers. In California, however, campaigns typically rely on professional signature collection firms, supplemented by grass roots activists.

For most of the country, a typical initiative petition campaign (especially at the local level) is still a grass roots oriented, low dollar affair, featuring neighborhood door-to-door signature gathering, petition tables at county and state fairs, or big city shopping malls. But that folksy methodology might not be the best route for your campaign. Don't be sentimental about this; put your volunteer activists to work, yes, but take the serious, substantive steps which will result in your policy proposal actually getting to the ballot.

The processes of direct democracy are ideologically neutral. Further, the electorate is generally more sympathetic to legislatively referred measures than to initiatives. Over time, two out of three referred measures pass. For initiatives, only one out of three initiatives pass. For any status quo changing initiative, you will face the burden of proof in most voters' minds: they will be inclined to vote no, unless you give them compelling reasons to vote yes.

States increasingly have "single subject" rules, meaning that an initiative question may only raise one substantive policy issue. This should mean that initiative measures, whether liberal or conservative, must be fairly narrow in their impact. However, the courts from state to state are inconsistent in enforcement of the "single subject" rule. You'll have to study carefully what "single subject" has meant in past initiative battles in your state or community.

Voter turnout, and therefore the timing of an election, may have a significant impact on your proposal's success or failure. Voter "drop off" or fatigue may hurt you, or help you. "Drop off" is the term used to describe the reality that fewer voters generally cast their ballots on propositions than on such "top of the line" races as the presidency, U.S. Senate, gubernatorial or other statewide races.

Some studies have found this "drop off" is about 12 percent, but often it is much greater than that. Occasionally it is less: more citizens voted in the June 1978 California Proposition 13 vote than in the gubernatorial primary that same day. Similarly, Oklahoma voters have on several occasions participated in higher numbers in propositions than in candidates races. Generally, however, there is a drop off for propositions. Research your state's recent political history in order to speculate wisely on what might happen in a popular vote on the issue you are pushing.

Campaign spending and disclosure requirements vary dramatically from state to state, and sometimes the disclosure rules for propositions are different than for candidate races. Know the rules for your state.

Initiative campaign spending is accelerating. Either have lots of money already in hand, or recognize you will need to raise it through direct mail or by other means. Spending will not guarantee your victory though, historically, money can be a contributing factor in opposing initiatives, with the evidence murkier when it comes to support spending. Still, only a meaningful budget will enable you to react quickly to your foes as an initiative campaign unfolds.[32]

Fourth, careful planning is a must for conservative initiative activism. You might, rarely, be able to take advantage of a political dynamic that suddenly emerges in the electorate and ride it to victory. But usually, political success results from working very hard for a long time and then getting lucky.

Morton Blackwell, the former Reagan Administration public liaison officer with a life-time commitment to conservative politics, often says conservatives act as if they will win in politics because "our heart is pure, and our cause is right." Those are reasons why you can get up every morning, and look yourself in the mirror. They can be predicates to effective action, but cannot substitute for a serious, professional approach to the realities of politics.

Don McIntire of Oregon, whose successful property tax reduction initiative was one of the conservative bright spots of 1990, offers an observation which incorporates both of the preceding points: his group "did not try to duplicate the language and structure of tax initiatives from other states; we crafted a tax limitation initiative that was unique to Oregon and reasonable in its goals. The process included many re-writes and reviews by constitutional attorneys to ensure that the initiative would withstand the toughest possible challenge in court." [33]

Fifth, McIntire's last remark prefaces this: any serious initiative activism in this day and age must take into account the pervasive role the courts are playing in direct democracy. In 1984, a half dozen duly-qualified conservative-leaning initiatives were stripped from statewide ballots, even though they had gained ballot status under the rules existing at the time.[34]

In the 1991 election cycle, anti-initiative judicial activism had a dramatic effect on the course of initiative politics. In Missouri, an initiative to slash the size of the legislature from 160 to 103 members, restrict salary increases and create an ethics commission was stripped from the ballot in October. Governor John Ashcroft, a rare example of a multi-issue conservative Republican governor, was dismayed, saying, "Never before has the will of hundreds of thousands of Missourians been so plainly disregarded by politicians and the courts."

Just weeks earlier, in Illinois, the state Supreme Court stripped from the ballot an innovative initiative to create a special tax committee in the legislature. The National Taxpayers United of Illinois had played by the rules, garnering more than 450,000 signatures, in order to get their policy idea considered by fellow citizens. The court, in a hugely controversial ruling which nonetheless has stood through this writing, ripped the initiative from the ballot.[35]

The point of these examples is that serious initiative players need careful legal strategies as well as political strategies. Even when you plan well and carefully, you may still get stripped from the ballot. In Oklahoma, Lloyd Noble II anticipated from day one that his aggressive and historic term limitation initiative would face serious legal challenge. Fortunately, he was able to garner the pro bono help of two bright conservative "good government" lawyers (one of whom was a legislator) to draft and re-draft his initiative before it ever entered the field seeking signatures. The result of this process was perhaps the most carefully crafted (and surprisingly short) initiative in Oklahoma history, so well-written, in fact, that its foes despaired of a successful legal challenge, and let the proposition go to a popular vote.

Sixth, remember that patience is a virtue. "Rome was not built in a day" the old expression goes. Conservatives might offer their own thought: the liberal welfare state was not built in a day. Similarly, conservatives will not bring their policy alternatives into law without the kind of life-long commitment of energy and resources liberals deployed in construction of their agenda at the national level from 1932-1969.

To underscore this point, consider yet again the case of the Oregon tax reduction activists, who lost at least five statewide votes during the lifetime of the late Ray Phillips. Phillips, the Howard Jarvis of Oregon, refused to give up after his initiative lost in 1978. He kept experimenting with slightly different versions of the same, simple property tax reduction initiative. After his death, his philosophical descendants came back once more and, in 1990, secured the one meaningful tax reduction initiative victory of the year. They just kept at it, moderating their proposal slightly each time, until they found the formula for tax relief their fellow citizens could endorse.

Seventh, do not underestimate how far your opponents will go to defeat you. The Oregon parental choice/educational tax voucher initiative campaign in 1990 certainly demonstrated that some liberal foes of conservative policy ideas will do whatever is necessary including crafting powerful, outrageously unfair television advertisements to defeat proposals (or people) with which/whom they disagree.

Many liberals are honorable, and will meet you fairly on the field of political battle. Some are not, and they will lie because they correctly perceive the threat conservative victories hold for the substantial "territory" liberals still control in our politics and culture. Further, they will lie with multi-million megaphones called paid advertising and free media (the evening news).

To counter them, you must either purchase your own "megaphones" or figure out ways to get your message on the television evening news, on the radio news breaks and on the front pages of local newspapers.[36]

Conclusion

Whether or not to participate directly in the writing of citizen initiatives, petition circulation, legal jousts surrounding ballot status, the subsequent campaigns for enactment, and the post-election legal fights which are increasingly common these are decisions each conservative (for that matter, liberal) group must make for itself. There can be no doubt, however, that American politics is in an era in which few organized interests can afford merely to react to the latest assault on their values via the processes of direct democracy. Therefore, it seems apparent to this writer that conservatives must play on the direct democracy field.

One of the few political consultants to write extensively about business community interests in direct democracy, and to devote some thought to ways in which to build pro-active agenda, is Dr. Richard Ryan of Tarrance & Associates, the Houston, Texas, firm with extensive experience in California initiative campaigns. Ryan's observations bear repeating at some length. Conservatives will agree that, with a word changed here or there, he offers a wise approach for any serious political player. Dr. Ryan observes:

- "The initiative process can be a direct threat to business interests, differing as it does from familiar legislative lobbying efforts."

- "Business industrial groups and trade associations must become knowledgeable about campaign methodology including polling, communication theory, political advertising, direct mailing, etc."

- "Corporate decision-making must involve electoral as well as consumer predilections."

- "Trade associations should create campaign-experienced groups to identify problems and to manage initiative campaigns competently, both defensively and offensively, across the states."

- "In states where direct initiatives are not yet practiced, business and industry should oppose their introduction to save money in the long run."

In the view of this writer, who has regularly monitored direct democracy since 1980, that last recommendation is wrong. By and large, and on the whole, the impact of direct democracy has been no more, perhaps less, deleterious to business interests (and to conservative social, cultural and other interests) than for instance, high-powered and "creative" litigation from the nation's trial lawyers, regulatory schemes promoted by professional bureaucrats in state and local governments, sustained activity in legislative bodies on the part of anti-business/ anti-conservative politicians such as Ohio Democrat Senator Howard Metzenbaum, and outrageous anti-democratic edicts from all levels of the American judiciary. The point is, I'll stack up the results in direct democracy against the results in legislative bodies, in the litigious society and in the regulatory state. Any day. Any year.

But these recommendations come from one of the nation's smartest political analysts with a personal perspective sympathetic to most conservative values. Therefore, I recommend they receive serious consideration from each reader. Dr. Ryan notes "caveats for business" which serve equally well to guide the thinking of multi-issue conservatives:

- "Existing demographic constituencies (i.e. Republicans and Democrats) seldom obtain in issue campaigns. Extensive early research among potential voters on the issue is therefore the *sine qua non* of success."

- "Concept formulation is uniquely important. For example, is the no-growth constituency actually pro-environment or is it anti-jobs? The answer depends not on fact, but on who and where you are."

- "Many political issues require expansion in order to be fully developed and understood. In issue campaigns, reduction rather than expansion are required in order to arrive at the desired emotional "yes" or "no" vote. Sometimes that necessitates over-simplification to the point of becoming intellectually unbuttoned."

- "Scheduling is particularly important. In an important utility referendum in Indiana some years ago, only the votes of a narrow constituency were sought. So the election was set for Christmas Eve!"

Regardless of whether or not one accepts each of Ryan's assertions and recommendations, there is little doubt of the accuracy of his fundamental conclusions for business interests and, again by extension, for all serious players in politics. His thoughts, expanding the phrase "business community" to include all conservatives, offer a useful close for my own essay:

> Issue campaigning is increasing in frequency because of the heightened dominance of single-issue groups, because of the legislative gridlock created by powerful opposing lobbies in many legislatures, because of the increasing legislative timidity among all lawmaking bodies from Congress to city Council and because of increasing voter disenchantment with traditional political process. All of which means that the business community must better prepare itself for political battle directly in the marketplace of ideas and issues.[37]

Endnotes

1. David Magleby, *Direct Legislation: Voting on Ballot Propositions in the United States* (Baltimore and London: The Johns Hopkins University Press, 1984), 36.

2. Much of this discussion of direct democracy definitions is adapted from Patrick B. McGuigan, *The Politics of Direct Democracy: Case Studies in Popular Decision Making* (Washington, D.C.: Free Congress Foundation, 1985), 25-26. Some copies remain available for purchase for $6.95 from: Publications Department, Free Congress Foundation, 717 Second Street, N.E., Washington, D.C. 20002, telephone: 202-546-3000.

3. An excellent "short form" summary of initiative and popular referendum petition requirements was provided by the now-defunct Initiative Resource Center of Berkeley, California. Its founder was David Schmidt, who for many years edited *Initiative News Report*, a one-time competitor to my own newsletter in the nation's capital. Schmidt now lives in the San Francisco area and remains one of the nation's most knowledgeable observers of direct democracy.

4. For an understanding of the recall device, *see especially* Thomas E. Cronin, *Direct Democracy: The Politics of the Initiative, Referendum and Recall* (Harvard University Press, 1989), 125-156. This book, still available through bookstores, is in my opinion the best book ever written on the politics of direct democracy.

5. Town meetings continue to play an interesting role in our politics. Russian author Aleksandr Solzhenitsyn, when he first came to the United States, had an interesting experience at a Vermont town meeting. *See* Michael Scammel, *Solzhenitsyn: A Biography* (New York and London: W.W. Norton and Co. 1984), 955-957.

6. Although many specific citations are offered throughout the following text, the sketch for the years 1980-83 is adapted from my book, *The Politics of Direct Democracy*. The 1984-88 era is drawn from two now-defunct Free Congress Foundation sources: my newsletter, "The Initiative and Referendum Report," and Stu Rothenberg's quarterly journal, *Election Politics*, for which I wrote an overview of the election results every two years. The material for the last two years is original writing for this essay, with citations provided.

7. The nuclear freeze movement is the focus of the 35-page Chapter IV in my 1985 book, *The Politics of Direct Democracy*.

8. For background on this campaign and the other 1986 tort reform initiatives, *see* Kristin R. Blair, "Of Torts and Men," *Free Congress Judicial Notice* (Apr. 1987).

9. This discussion is adapted from *Election Politics* (Winter 1986-87): 16-19.

10. I covered this particular campaign in more detail than usual. My post-mortem on the Idaho right to work campaign is "Idaho's a Gem for Right to Work, Free Congress Initiative and Referendum Report" (Feb./Mar. 1987), 4-15.

11. For background, *see Free Congress Family, Law & Democracy Report*, Jan. 1989. In the fall of 1989, the U.S. Justice Department challenged the constitutionality of one of the most famous NFZs, that of Oakland, California.

12. The five initiatives on "state" ballots in 1987 were the start of a modest surge in initiative usage. David Schmidt discusses this in his book *Citizen Lawmakers: The Ballot Initiative Revolution* (Philadelphia: Temple University Press, 1989), 214.

13. For more detail, *see Election Politics* (Winter 1988-89): 18-21.

14. For an overview of the 1988 results with particular detail on the Maryland results, *see Free Congress Initiative and Referendum Report* (Dec. 1988): 15-24.

15. Detailed analysis of the pro-life referenda, particularly the Michigan vote, is found in Catherine Deeds, "Pro-Lifers Celebrate Historic Initiative Victories in Three States," *Free Congress Initiative and Referendum Report* (Dec. 1988): 1-6.

16. A look at the Proposition 103 results is provided from two post-election analyses: Kristin R. Blair, "Nader, Lawyers and Insurance," *Free Congress Family, Law & Democracy Report* (Feb. 1989): 6-10; Harvey Rosenfield's "True Confessions," "How Voter Revolt Won," *FLD Report* (Apr. 1989): 12, 17-18.

17. Pete du Pont, "Voters to Polls: No New Taxes," *Family, Law & Democracy Report* (June 1989), 7, *see also*, 1-6.

18. McGuigan, "1989 Verdict In Except North Dakota," *Family, Law & Democracy Report* (Dec. 1989), 1-3; *see also*, 4-9.

19. McGuigan, "'People Power' Buries Dakota Tax Hikes," *Family, Law & Democracy Report* (Jan. 1990), 9-10.

20. *Family, Law & Democracy Report* (July 1990), 16-17.

21. Some of the following discussion is adapted from Patrick B. McGuigan and John P. Keast, "Direct Democracy '90: Firestorm," *Daily Oklahoman*, 25 Oct. 1990.

22. 62 of those were on November 6 ballots, six others were scattered on earlier fall 1990 ballots.

23. Of the total, Matt Miller of the Free Congress Foundation listed 145 referred measures as falling on Nov. 6 ballots; the remainder were on earlier ballots, most of them in Louisiana, which had (as usual) a crowded early October ballot. *See* "1990 Ballot Measures: A Move Toward Citizen Control," Free Congress Foundation special report, 1991. This useful report provides the final results of every statewide proposition in the country that November.

24. *See* Matthew M. Miller, Free Congress special report, note 23 above.

25. John P. Keast, "Seizing the Initiative," *Free Congress Foundation Empowerment* (Jan. 1991), 1. *See also* Don McIntire, "Oregon Property Tax Cut," *Free Congress Foundation Empowerment* (Jan. 1991), 3.

26. A first-rate, honest post-election assessment of the Oregon education choice initiative campaign is found in *Free Congress Empowerment* (Feb. 1991), 1-3.

27. Ann Bellamy Stoneburner, with Patrick B. McGuigan, "California: Big Green or Big Mistake?," *Family, Law & Democracy Report* (July 1990), 1-5.

28. Associated Press, *Tulsa World*, 6 Nov. 1990.

29. The story of this initiative intrigued me, and eventually I wrote the first short history of the campaign. The paper is entitled, "Better Sooner than Later: How the Oklahoma Term Limitation Initiative Came to Pass," prepared for delivery at the 1991 annual meeting of the Western Political Science Association in Seattle, Washington, Mar. 21-23, 1991. Single copies are available upon request.

30. Terry Considine, "Coloradans Back in Charge," *Free Congress Empowerment* (Jan. 1991), 2.

31. Although my Initiative and Referendum Report and its successor, the *Family, Law & Democracy Report*, is no longer published there, the Free Congress Foundation still offers the best available regular source of information on what is and is not working for conservatives in the politics of direct democracy. The newsletter "Empowerment" only six months old but cited several times in this essay is available for $30 a year from the Foundation's Publications Department: 717 Second Street, N.E., Washington, D.C. 20002, telephone: 202-546-3000.

32. The preceding paragraphs are adapted and updated from McGuigan, *The Politics of Direct Democracy*, 33-43.

33. McIntire, "Oregon Tax Initiative," *Free Congress Empowerment* (Jan. 1991), 3.

34. See the appendix, Pat McGuigan, *The Politics of Direct Democracy: Case Studies in Popular Decision Making* (Washington, D.C.: Free Congress Foundation, 1985).

35. Thomas Jipping, "Judges Take the Initiative," *Free Congress Empowerment* (Jan. 1991), 7.

36. In the foregoing, I have adapted to this discussion some of the lessons learned in a different kind of politics, and offered at length in Patrick B. McGuigan and Dawn M. Weyrich, *Ninth Justice: The Fight for Bork* (Washington, D.C.: Free Congress Foundation, 1990). The book is available in B. Dalton and Waldenbooks stores, and also available from the Free Congress Foundation's Publications Department for $21.95, or for the same price, plus $1.50 for handling, from University Press of America, National Book Network, 4720 Boston Way, Lanham, MD 20706.

37. *See* the Aug.-Sept. 1989 issue of the Tarrance & Associates newsletter, 1-2.

TERM LIMITATION

Terry Considine
Colorado State Senator

Thomas Jefferson was disappointed with the Constitution. Jefferson was Ambassador to France during the summer of 1787, and did not take part in the drafting of the foundation document of our government. But one of its principal architects, his friend, James Madison, kept him well informed. In December of 1787, Jefferson wrote to Madison with a detailed critique of the proposed Constitution. Jefferson was most concerned about the absence of a Bill of Rights. Madison, Hamilton, and the other drafters of the Constitution didn't disagree about what those rights should be. But Madison and the others felt that since the new federal government being created by the Constitution, it would be restricted to the powers specifically enumerated in the document, a Bill of Rights was unnecessary.

Jefferson thought otherwise. "To say, as Mr. (James) Wilson (of Pennsylvania) does, that a Bill of Rights was not necessary, because all is reserved in the case of the general government which is not given, while in particular ones, all is given which is not reserved, might do for the audience to which it is addressed; but it is surely a *gratis dictum*, the reverse of which might just as well be said, and it is opposed by strong inferences from the body of the instrument, as well as from the omission of the cause of our present confederation, which had made the reservation in express terms."[1] In the end, Jefferson prevailed. The states were reluctant to ratify the document unless a Bill of Rights was added, but accepted the new instrument of government expecting subsequent amendments.

We have seen often in the last 200 years how right Jefferson was to insist upon inclusion of a Bill of Rights. Far more of our constitutional law has been litigated on the basis of the first Ten Amendments than upon grounds from the core document. What bothered Jefferson almost as much as the omission of a Bill of Rights in the new Constitution was the failure to impose limits on the length of service by federal office-holders" . . . The second feature I dislike, and strongly dislike, is the abandonment in every instance of the principal of rotation in office," Jefferson had written to Madison.[2]

Rotation in office—limits on the number of consecutive terms of the president, senators and representatives—wasn't omitted from the

Constitution because a majority of the Founding Fathers opposed the concept. In addition to a Bill of Rights, the Articles of Confederation had contained a limit on the terms of the members of the Continental Congress. As with a Bill of Rights, the drafters of the Constitution hadn't included term limits simply because they didn't' think they were necessary. We'd just fought a revolution to free ourselves from the dictates of the "Kings, priests and nobles" who governed Europe. Surely the American people had the good sense not to perpetuate a ruling class over here. The requirements for frequent elections ought to be enough.

Even so, the absence of term limits—especially for the president and members of the senate—was a rallying point for anti-federalists at the state conventions called to ratify the Constitution. "If the office is to be perpetually confined to a few, other men of equal talents and virtue, but not possessed of so extensive an influence, may be discouraged from aspiring to it," warned Melanchton Smith during New York's convention.[3] In the end, the warnings of Jefferson, Smith and others went unheeded, and the Constitution was ratified without a provision limiting the tenure of officeholders.

We have learned to our sorrow that Jefferson was as much on the mark about term limits as he had been about a Bill of Rights. Just 59 percent of registered voters, and only 36 percent of potential voters, bothered to cast ballots on election day, 1990. Many pundits and political leaders say the low turnout indicates there is something wrong with the voters. We've become lazy and complacent, they say. Only in government is customer resistance to a product thought to indicate there is something wrong with the customer. In the business world, when people avoid a product in the numbers and proportions Americans stay away from the polls, people think there might be something wrong with the product.

Election day 1990 was a victory for the status quo in Washington. In the House of Representatives, 96 percent of incumbents who sought re-election won. The average victory was almost 2:1. In the U.S. Senate, only one incumbent lost. This ratification of the powers-that-be didn't happen because people were satisfied with the job their elected representatives were doing. According to the most recent pre-election Gallup Poll, fewer than half of the American people (48%) approved of the job President Bush was doing. Less than a third (32%) approved of the job Congress was doing. More than two thirds of those polled (69%) thought our country was headed in the wrong direction. The 1990 election was typical. In 1988 and in 1986, 98 percent of incumbents in the House of Representatives won. In 1984, 95 percent won.

The problem isn't only in Washington. I live in Colorado, one of the most open, honest states in the union, with a near even balance between registered Republicans and registered Democrats. Yet in Colorado in 1990, 86 percent of incumbents who sought re-election to the State House of Representatives won. The re-election rate for the Colorado senate was 94 percent. Only one incumbent state senator has been defeated in Colorado since 1982. No incumbent elected governor has lost since 1962. Incumbents are in even better shape in the legislatures of other states. In California in the last three elections, only three incumbent state legislators have been defeated at the polls.

At a time when politicians, federal and state, rank below used car salesmen in surveys of public esteem, incumbent officeholders seem all but immune to effective challenge. Why? Because before the people spoke on November 6th, the special interests had had their say. Money talks. And in American politics today, special interest money often matters more than popular votes.

As of October 17, 1990, incumbent members of the U.S. House had raised $156.5 million to their challengers' $27 million, an advantage of nearly 6 to 1. Incumbent senators had raised $105.9 million by that date, compared to their challengers' $27.5 million, an advantage of more than 3 to 1. And this doesn't take into account the advantages incumbents gain from their free mailing privileges and their huge, taxpayer-financed staffs. Most of the incumbents' money came from people and entities who could not vote for them. The typical House incumbent received 47.7 percent of his or her campaign funds from the Political Action Committees (PACs) of special interest groups. The typical Senate incumbent received 40.4 percent of his or her campaign funds from PACs. When we add to the river of PAC money large contributions from "heavy hitters" who live outside the district or the state in which the Congressman or Senator is running, the typical incumbent received roughly two-thirds of his or her campaign funds from people who weren't eligible to vote for him or her.

If he who pays the piper calls the tune, it's no wonder Congress is as unresponsive as it is to the will of the people. However, Congress is not the only unresponsive elected body. At my request, the Legislative Counsel here in Colorado did a study on the source of campaign funds for incumbents in the state legislature. In the three elections studied (1984, 1986, 1988) incumbent state representatives and senators raised roughly three times as much money as did their challengers. Two-thirds of the incumbents' money came from PACs, corporations and labor unions (it is legal in Colorado for corporations and unions to contribute directly to candidates for state offices). Only a third of the challengers' money came from PACs and special interest groups.

As government has grown more remote, government has grown more corrupt. Pirates were permitted to loot savings & loan associations because they shared their booty with powerful Members of Congress— including the Speaker of the House and Committee Chairmen—who kept the regulators at bay. You and I will have to pay at least $300 billion— $1,200 for every man, woman and child in the country—to clean up the mess. And the economic health of our country has been put in jeopardy. These are only the Members who have been caught overstepping the lax boundaries set by the House and Senate. There are many others who engage in shady practices that are not against the law . . . because Congress makes the rules.

Rep. Gene Taylor (R-Mo.) retires from Congress . . . and pockets $325,000 in campaign contributions. It isn't against the law. But it's wrong. Rep. Dan Rostenkowski (D-Ill.), chairman of the House Ways & Means Committee, decides to hold a big party to celebrate the 200th anniversary of the committee. He leans on business and labor unions for $750,000 in contributions to throw the party. Diamond Jim Brady was never so greedy. Boss Tweed was never so arrogant.

Our elected officials pay more attention to their pay and perquisites than to the needs of the people. Americans were asked to make sacrifices last year. Spending for social programs was cut. Taxes were raised. But the huge Congressional pay raise was untouched.

In Washington and in many of our state capitols, "iron triangles" are solidifying. Coalitions of legislators, bureaucrats and special interest groups keep programs going without regard for cost, need, or effectiveness. Government is run less and less for the benefit of those who need its services, or for the taxpayers who pay for those services. Increasingly, government is being run for the benefit of the people who are being paid to provide the services. The longer lawmakers remain in office, the less they see themselves as representatives of the people who elected them in the first place, and the more they become revenue collectors for the bureaucracy.

The government of the People, by the People, and for the People that Abraham Lincoln hoped would never perish from this earth is being replaced by a government of the special interests, by the special interests, and for the special interests. We have, as Thomas Jefferson warned, created for ourselves a ruling class. Turnover in the U.S. House of Representatives in the 1980s was comparable to that in Britain's House of Lords. The only way you leave the House of Lords is feet first. And our ruling class isn't ruling us very well. The principal job of Congress is to produce a budget each year. But Congress hasn't balanced a budget in 30 years, and has completed work on the budget on time only once in the last ten years.

Most of the economic problems afflicting America today reflect failures of government. The S&L scandal and the burgeoning crisis in bank deposit insurance are egregious examples. So are the scandals in public housing. A more serious problem—more the responsibility of state and local governments than the federal—is the skyrocketing cost and declining quality of public education. Crime-infested streets and a crumbling infrastructure—streets, roads and bridges in disrepair—are other examples. We are governed much. But we are not governed well. Fortunately, the old Jeffersonian notion of rotation in office is enjoying a renaissance. More freedom, and more open, honest and effective government may follow in its wake.

On September 18, 1990, Oklahoma became the first state in the Union to limit the terms its state legislators can serve when voters in Oklahoma's primary voted, 67 percent to 33 percent, to limit Oklahoma lawmakers to a total of 12 years service in the state House and Senate combined. California and Colorado followed on November 6. Californians voted, 52 percent to 48 percent, for Proposition 140, which restricts state legislators to eight consecutive years of service in the Senate, six consecutive years in the House, and which slashes legislators' staff and pension benefits. Coloradans voted, 71 percent to 29 percent, for Amendment 5, which restricts the Governor, state executive officers, and state legislators to eight consecutive years in the same office. The Colorado initiative was the most noteworthy, because it also restricts Colorado's U.S. Senators and Congressmen to 12 consecutive years in the same office. The trend to term limitation is so strong that the *Washington Post's* trendy style section has declared term limits "in" for 1991, and incumbency "out".

The term limit measures drew predictable fire from lawmakers, special interest groups, and some quarters of academia. California Assembly Speaker Willie Brown called them "racist" and "unconstitutional" . . . although it is difficult to imagine how a measure which affects all lawmakers equally is "racist," or how an amendment to a state constitution can be "unconstitutional." The more restrained arguments against term limits were as follows:

1. Term limits aren't needed.

2. There are better ways than term limits to make elections fair.

3. Term limits will deprive government of valuable experience.

4. Term limits would transfer power from the legislative to the executive branch.

5. Term limits would transfer power from elected officials to appointed ones.

6. Term limits would deprive voters of choice.

7. It's unconstitutional (in the case of the Colorado initiative) for a state to limit the terms of its federal representatives.

Let's examine each of these.

Term limits aren't needed.

Those who make this argument acknowledge incumbents usually win elections, but insist there is sufficient turnover from other causes to keep fresh blood circulating in Congress and in the state legislatures. "Two thirds of the current House Members weren't there in 1980," the *New York Times* noted in an editorial.[4] Charlie Roos, a columnist for Denver's *Rocky Mountain News*, noted: "Colorado has 35 state senators. How many who were there ten years ago will still be in office in 1991? At most, seven." Colorado has 65 representatives. How many who were there ten years ago will still be there in 1991. At most, seven."[5]

Term limit supporters note that the typical Member of Congress serves more than twice as long as Congressmen did a century ago. Moreover, in a healthy democracy, such turnover as does occur in elective office ought not primarily to be the result of death, retirement, indictment, or ambition (running for a higher office). Most of it ought to occur at the polls.

There are better ways than term limits to reform elections.

Those who make this argument acknowledge that incumbents enjoy huge advantages, and that competition is leaching out of our democracy. But the way to make elections more competitive, they argue, is through restricting the advantages of incumbents, by such means as campaign finance reform, competitive districting, restricting the free mail privileges of incumbents, and so forth. These will do the trick. We don't need to "throw the baby out with the bathwater" by the draconian step of term limitation.

Supporters of term limits tend also to favor other election law reforms. But they contend those who favor campaign reform without term limits have things backward. In an ideal world, it might be possible to have campaign reform without term limits. But in the real world, incumbents have legislated extra advantages for themselves—PACs, gerrymandering, free mailing privileges, huge staffs, etc.—in order to perpetuate themselves in office. They will not enact meaningful campaign reforms **unless** they can no longer remain in office indefinitely. Only when terms are limited, and there is no longer so strong an incentive to cheat, will Congress and the legislatures be willing to put challengers on a more equal footing.

Term limits will deprive the government of valuable experience.

Roll Call, the "newspaper of Capitol Hill," put it this way: "Will the following Members start packing their bags: Sens. Bob Dole (R-Kan.), Sam Nunn (D-Ga.), Richard Lugar (R-Ind.), J. Bennett Johnston (D-La.), and Reps. Tom Foley (D-Wash.), Bob Michel (R-Ill.), Dick Gephardt (D-

Mo.), Henry Hyde (R-Ill.). . . ."[6]   University of Colorado political science Professor Walter Stone agreed: "A limitation on terms would greatly reduce the amount of expertise in the legislature. Contemporary questions of public policy are complex, and those who would influence national policy must have the relevant expertise."[7]

Supporters of term limits, however, make a number of responses. First, the assumption behind this argument attacks the core of democracy. It assumes the complexities of government are beyond the ken of the ordinary citizen, and must be vested in a mandariante which acquires its expertise over long years of service. But ours was to be a citizen government, representative of the people. The Founding Fathers believed holding public office was a public service to be performed for a limited time, not a lifetime job.

Second, there is the question of what kind of experience is most valuable in Congress and the state legislatures. Experience in living away from home and spending other people's money? Or broad experience in life? Third, term limits, which apply only to tenure in a particular job, could result in greater overall experience in government. Sam Rayburn's complaint about the "whiz kids" in the Kennedy Administration (I wish some of them had run for sheriff once) would be greatly ameliorated. Members of Congress now loathe to give up safe seats would be less reluctant to accept appointments in the executive branch. (Dick Lugar would make a great Secretary of State; Sam Nunn a fine Secretary of Defense.) There would be greater interchange between state and federal office, and between the executive and legislative branches. More Cabinet and sub-Cabinet officers would have the broader political understanding that can come only from facing the voters. More lawmakers would acquire an appreciation for the difficulties in administering some of the laws Congress and the state legislatures pass.

Fourth, term limits would still permit public careers of considerable length. Sen. William Armstrong (R-Colo.) held elective office continuously from 1963 until 1991, followed by his retirement after two terms in the U.S. Senate. At no time in his career as a state representative, state senator, Congressman and United States Senator would he have run afoul of the term limits Coloradans enacted last November. Finally, there is the common sense observation that we've got the most experienced Congress, and some of the most experienced state legislatures, in history, and they're not doing such a hot job. Citizen legislatures of earlier eras did a better job of making national policy.

Term limits would transfer power from the legislative to the executive branch.

Professor Stone says: "If we arbitrarily limit their time in office, we make the legislature—whether Congress or the state legislature—a less than equal partner in the setting of public policy."[8] Since the President is restricted by the Twenty-second Amendment to two consecutive terms, and the terms of the governors of 30 states are limited by law, some would argue term limits on the legislative branch only even things up. But if Congress were to lose some ground to the executive, would that be so bad?

Most analyses of the U.S. government today give Congress the upper hand over the president. The president's lack of a line item veto (possessed by 47 governors) has tied his hands not only in matters of domestic policy but also in foreign policy, historically nearly the exclusive purview of the president. Congress has used its power more for narrow pork barrel spending than for making broad public policy. If term limits were to shift some power from 535 congressmen and senators who tend to represent their districts alone to the one American elected by all the people, it is difficult to imagine this as a tragedy.

The situation with legislatures varies from state to state. Colorado has what is known as a "weak governor" system. The legislature has more control over the budget and other important items than is the case in many other states. This has tended to make the governor more a cheerleader than a leader. In Colorado, term limits will tend to equalize power among the branches. In other states, that may not be the case.

A major assumption of those who argue term limits would leach power from the legislature to the executive is that inexperienced lawmakers would tend to defer more to executive branch bureaucrats. But my observation of Congress, and my experience in the Colorado legislature, tends to indicate otherwise. It is the more junior, not the more senior, members who are more likely to challenge the executive on policy matters, and who are more likely to do their own work than to rely upon staff or outside expertise.

Term limits would transfer power from elected officials to appointed ones.

This is a corollary of the executive/legislative branch argument, expanded to include transfer of power from lawmakers to their staffs as well as to executive branch appointees. Those who make this argument with regard to Congress are unfamiliar with how Congress really works. Congressional staffers are wholly creatures of their employers. Congress is in many ways the last plantation. Senators and representatives have exempted themselves from the hiring and firing rules they have applied to everyone else. The most powerful staffers are those who serve the longest serving members. There are, for instance, few staffers more powerful than those who work for Rep. Jamie Whitten (D-Miss.). Their power is derived in part from his prominence, and in part from the attenuation of his faculties (the nonagenerarian Whitten's mental and physical capacities are not what they used to be), which causes Whitten to be more reliant on staff advice than younger, more vigorous members are. The only really effective way to break their power is to remove the member. It is true that very able staffers likely would find employment with a new senator or congressman if their present employer were barred from seeking re-election. But their influence—at least initially—is not likely to be as great as it was with their former boss(es). Furthermore, if this were thought to be a serious problem, there is a simple remedy: Don't permit congressional staffers to serve in the same job for more than 12 years.

In state legislatures, circumstances vary. Legislators in big states like California have large staffs. But when voters in California limited the terms of their legislators, they solved the staff problem by reducing the size of legislative staffs as well. In small states like Colorado with citizen legislatures, there is no large staff on which to rely. We share a secretarial pool and are helped by an intern or two, and that's it.

Term limits would deprive voters of choice.

The argument here is that voters shouldn't be deprived of the opportunity to vote for a favored lawmaker simply because he or she had been in office for a long time. I call this the "let them eat cake" argument. The evidence is clear that the overwhelming effect of long term incumbency is to deny voters meaningful choice. And if it were his or her popularity—and not the enormous advantages of incumbency—that gets a legislator, or congressman, or senator re-elected time after time—he or she could run for another office or, (under Colorado's rules) seek again the office formerly held after sitting out a term.

It's unconstitutional for a state to limit the terms of its U.S. Senators and Representatives.

Maybe. Maybe not. It's an unsettled area of law. No state has ever tried to limit the terms of its federal representatives before. And in our system of jurisprudence, the courts don't issue advisory opinions. Nothing in the Constitution forbids a state from limiting the terms of its own U.S. senators and representatives, and the Ninth and Tenth Amendments say that anything the Constitution is silent on is reserved to the states, or to the people. But the Constitution is, as Justice Holmes once observed, what the judges say it is. Our Founding Fathers would be astonished to learn that flag burning is constitutional, and prayer in public schools is not. We won't know for sure whether federal term limits are constitutional unless and until the Supreme Court rules on the question. But if recent federal case law is any guide, it is very likely that term limits like Colorado's will be upheld.

Constitutional attacks on state laws limiting ballot access typically are premised on the "Qualifications Clauses" or the equal protection clause of the Fourteenth Amendment. Article 1, Sections 2 and 3 of the Constitution set forth the qualifications to be a representative or a senator. A representative must be 25, a citizen of the United States for seven years, and a resident of the state from which he or she was elected. A senator must be 30, a U.S. citizen for nine years, and also a resident of the state at the time of his or her election.

Although neither the Constitution or any of its drafters said so, some constitutional commentators have expressed the view that these qualifications of age, citizenship and residency are exclusive, and any attempt to add to them would be unconstitutional. And a state supreme court (Maryland) has struck down a statute that required a candidate be a resident of the district he was seeking to represent.[9]

But Article 1, Section 4 of the Constitution gives states the right to set the "Times, Places and Manner" of holding elections for U.S. senators and representatives. Federal courts have ruled that Article 1, Section 4 gives states the right to prevent Independent candidates from running for Congress if they have changed their status and party affiliation within 11 months of the election;[10] to prevent a candidate defeated in a primary from running as an Independent,[11] and to require a state court judge to resign his judgeship before he could run for Congress.[12] The constitutional question hinges on whether term limits are an "additional qualification" which some feel is prohibited by Sections 2 and 3 of Article 1, or an exercise of the state's authority to regulate "the Times, Places, and Manner" of conducting elections. The weight of federal case law supports the latter interpretation.

It is worth noting that no federal court has ever ruled that the qualifications clauses are in fact exclusive. There is a federal case in which the Supreme Court ruled that Congress may impose no additional qualifications for sitting in the House or Senate.[13] But this is a different question from whether or not the states may impose restrictions. The federal government is supposed to have only those powers specifically delegated to it by the Constitution, and the implied powers required to carry out the functions specifically delegated. The Ninth and Tenth Amendments make it plain that all powers not given to the federal government are reserved to the states, or the people thereof. In other words, the states can do things the federal government is forbidden to do.

The Fourteenth Amendment provides no help to term limit opponents either. On those occasions when the courts have intervened in state election laws—as they did in the reapportionment cases, the poll tax cases, and the civil rights cases—it was to protect the rights of voters, not the convenience of candidates. Since term limits apply equally to all who are similarly situated, and their effect is to make elections more competitive, if the courts used the same logic applied in the reapportionment cases, they would be more likely to mandate term limits than to invalidate them.

In any event, it is unlikely that the question ever will be litigated. Before a lawsuit can be brought, a plaintiff must have standing to sue—he or she must be able to claim some injury. The term limits enacted in Colorado are prospective—they don't go into effect until 2002—so no incumbent can claim injury until then. The political fate of the term limit movement likely will have been settled before then. Either the "Colorado Idea" of state imposed federal term limits will have spread sufficiently to bring about a federal Constitutional amendment, or the drive will have fizzled out. Rebutting the arguments against term limits is not the same as making a case for them. Here are some of the arguments term limit supporters use:

Limitation of power.

If the philosophy underlying the American system of government could be expressed in a single sentence, it would be Lord Acton's: Power corrupts. From the Founding Fathers, to the Progressives, to the present day, Democrats in America have striven to restrict the power of the privileged; to preserve choice, opportunity and control for ordinary people. This is why we have a federal, rather than a national, system of government. It is why the powers of government—executive, legislative and judicial—are divided among three separate, but equal, branches. It is why we have a bicameral legislature.

As times have changed, Americans have discovered that some additional protections besides those provided by the Founding Fathers were needed to prevent abuses of power. During the Progressive era we added the secret ballot, direct primaries, and the initiative and referendum, not to replace representative government, but to curb abuses of it. The Twenty-second Amendment limiting the terms of the president is another example. Limits on the terms of members of Congress or state legislatures is in the same vein.

Term limitation is as American as apple pie.

As noted above, Thomas Jefferson was a firm believer in term limits. He was by no means alone. Terms limits were applied to the Continental

Congress during the Revolutionary War and in the Articles of Confederation government which preceded adoption of the Constitution. Abraham Lincoln supported rotation of office. Term limits for the president and for legislators were incorporated into the Confederate constitution. Presidents Truman, Eisenhower and Kennedy—and now President Bush—have endorsed term limits for members of Congress.

Elections will be more competitive.

Term limits will revitalize representative government. In Congress— and in all too many state legislatures—virtually the only competitive races are those in which no incumbent is running. By substantially increasing the number of races for open seats, term limits will go a long way toward making elections meaningful again.

More will have the opportunity to serve.

For citizen government to function, a broad range of citizens should have the opportunity to hold office. With term limits, doors that are now closed will be opened.

Government will be more representative.

Limited terms should change the way lawmakers view themselves and their jobs. A legislator who views holding public office as a hiatus in private life to which he or she will soon return sees the job differently from the career politician. He or she is more likely to take firm stands on controversial issues, and less likely to cater to special interest for votes or campaign contributions. The views of constituents are likely to mean more than the views of the bureaucracy.

Leadership positions will go to the most able.

Limited terms would permit able newcomers to rise to positions of power and responsibility more quickly. Committee chairmanships and other plum assignments would be less likely to be doled out on the basis of seniority, and more likely to be awarded on the basis of ability. "A Congress invigorated by frequent infusions of new blood would be a more responsive, more democratic, more varied place," predicts *New Republic* editor, Hendrik Hertzberg. "The term limit would leave Congress little choice but to elect its chiefs democratically, on the basis of the policies and the leadership qualities of the candidates."[14]

The people want them.

Perhaps the best argument for term limits is that the people want them. Opinion surveys consistently show nearly two-thirds of all Americans— black, white, male, female, young, old, liberal, conservative, Republican, Democrat—favor term limitation. In Colorado, our term limit initiative carried every single county with at least 60 percent of the vote. As Sen. Robert LaFollette (R-Wis.) said in his maiden speech to the U.S. Senate: "In a representative democracy the common judgment of the majority must find expression in the law of the land. To deny this is to repudiate the principles upon which representative democracy is founded."[15]

The Future for Term Limits

Lawmakers are the only demographic group in America that does not favor term limitation. In Colorado, the state senate rejected by a 2-1 margin the term limit measure Colorado's people later approved with 71 percent of the vote. A Gallup Poll in January, 1990, indicated that although two-thirds of the American people favored limits on the terms of members of Congress, nearly three-quarters of Congressmen were opposed. Lawmakers are as unlikely to vote to limit their own terms as they are to put an end to PACs or to cut their own pay. And since it is the lawmakers who make the laws, how then can term limits be enacted?

Colorado has shown the way. Twenty-two states besides Colorado have the initiative and referendum. These include states such as California, Ohio, Michigan, Massachusetts, Florida, Illinois. . . states which elect almost one-half of the members of the U.S. House of Representatives. If each of these states were to pass term limit initiatives like Colorado's— limiting the terms of both state legislators and the state's federal representatives—it wouldn't be long before a large number of those who sit in the U.S. House would have had their terms limited. This is likely to alter their views on whether or not to support a U.S. Constitutional Amendment to limit tenure in Congress.

This is, in fact, very much how direct election of U.S. senators came about. The Constitution originally specified that senators were to be elected by state legislatures, not by the people, and the Senate saw no reason to change that. Four times, the House sent to the Senate a proposed Constitutional Amendment to provide for direct election of senators. But none of the measures received even so much as a hearing in the upper house. But, beginning in Oregon, states with the initiative and referendum passed laws which, in effect, required the legislature to select the winner of a popular election. Before long, a majority of new senators were in fact being directly elected. In 1912, the Senate saw the handwriting on the wall, and ratified de jure—by passing the 16th

Amendment—what was already the practice de facto in nearly half the nation.

As more and more initiative states adopt term limits, the issue will become more popular for candidates in state legislative and U.S. House races in states which don't possess the initiative and referendum. It is hard to resist an idea whose time has come. Thomas Jefferson's idea couldn't be coming to the fore at a more appropriate time. We are on the verge of a new century, a new millennium, a rapidly changing new world in which geo-economic competition is replacing geopolitical competition.

For America to survive and prosper in this Brave New World, we must make all of our institutions more efficient. We must, in effect, reinvent government. We cannot expect to go forward with governmental structures bound to the wasteful, inefficient, corrupt "iron triangles" of the past. Circumstances change, but principles and values do not. Our guides for the future must be those faithful principles which led us to such greatness in the past—liberty and representative government, government "Of the People, By the People, and For the People," restrictions on the power of the privileged, and promotion of the general good over the special interests.

Term limits are not a new idea. But they are a new way of advancing the old values that have served us so well. Term limits will make government more representative, more responsive, more responsible. Term limits will give us lawmakers with more vigor, more vision, more openness to new ideas. Term limits will give elections more meaning, give the people more control over the direction of their government.

Endnotes

1. Adrienne Koch and William Peden, eds., *The Life and Selected Writings of Thomas Jefferson* (New York: Random House, 1944).

2. *Ibid.*

3. Smith, a prominent merchant and former member of the Continental Congress, was opposed to ratification of the Constituion. His speech is reprinted in *The American Constitution: For and Against*, ed. J.R. Poole (New York: Hill and Wang, 1987).

4. Editorial, *Rocky Mountain News*, 23 Feb. 1990.

5. Charles Roos, "Promises, Promises: Who Believes Them, Anyway," *Rocky Mountain News*, 1 June 1990.

6. Editorial, *Roll Call*, 16 Feb. 1990.

7. Walter Stone, "Limiting Terms of Officeholders Would Not Serve Democracy," *Boulder Camera*, 13 May 1990.

8. *Ibid.*

9. *Hellman v. Collier*, 217 Md 93, 141 A. 2d 908, 910 (1958).

10. *Storer v. Brown*, 915 U.S. 724 (1974).

11. *Williams v. Tucker*, 382 F. Supp. 381 (1974).

12. *Clements v. Fashing*, 475 U.S. 957 (1982).

13. *Powell v. McCormick*, 395 U.S. 486 (1969).

14. Hendrik Hertzberg, "Twelve is Enough," *New Republic*, 14 May 1990, 26.

15. *Congressional Record*, 23 Apr. 1906.

CUTTING STATE DEFICITS:
THE ROLE OF PRIVATIZATION

Dr. Lynn Scarlett
Vice President of Research

and

Robert W. Poole, Jr.
President, Reason Foundation

Introduction

The U.S. Department of Commerce reported in mid-1990 that state and local operating budgets, including capital outlays, are sinking deeply into the red, continuing a trend that started in 1986. The estimated annual shortfall for state and local governments at the end of the first quarter of 1990, for example, had reached $44.9 billion, compared with $35 billion in 1989. Moreover, the economic slowdown in 1990-91, which has resulted in a seven percent decline in corporate tax revenues, will further constrain public finances.

In this context, calls for tax increases have emerged, set forth on the grounds that sizable budget cuts are not possible without sacrificing essential state services. However, as an alternative, privatization offers a key mechanism for reducing budget expenditures without cutting services, since considerable empirical evidence exists of cost savings resulting from privatization. As such, it offers a means of avoiding tax increases. A Reason Foundation study of just three state services in California— corrections facilities, highway maintenance, and developmental centers— found savings potential of $339 million dollars.[1]

Recent surveys show fiscal pressures playing a key role in privatization decisions at the local government level. A 1988 survey by the International City Management Association of 4,870 local governments found that the most significant impetus to contracting out of local services was internal fiscal pressure to reduce service costs.[2] Over 80 percent of respondents cited internal fiscal problems as a decisive factor in their decisions to privatize, with external fiscal pressures resulting from legal and constitutional restrictions on raising taxes also playing a significant role (see Figure 1).

Figure 1: Factors Prompting Consideration
of Private Alternative Service Delivery

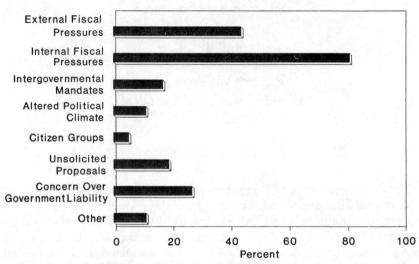

Source: ICMA, Baseline Data Report, 1988, Vol.21, No.6, p.5.

In its sixth annual public finance survey, *American City & County* confirmed in 1990 that some local jurisdictions were, in fact, turning to privatization in response to budget problems.[3] Some 23.2 percent of respondents said they had privatized some services to cut budgets, while 52.2 percent imposed or raised user fees. Among cities and counties, areas most frequently targeted for reduced budget outlays were social services, infrastructure repairs, garbage collection, and housing rehabilitation—each representing opportunities for increased privatization.

State Government Privatization Trends

While privatization has taken hold firmly among local governments, state governments have been somewhat slower to move toward more contracting out and privatization. However, growing budget constraints in the 90s along with continued demand for a wide array of public-sector services have prompted state governments increasingly to look to privatization as a key policy option (see Figure 2).

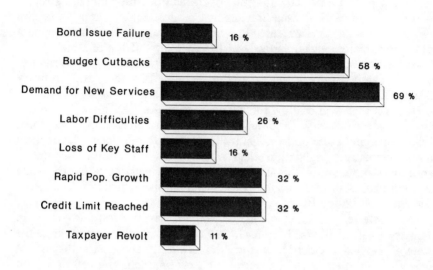

Figure 2: Factors That Could Push States Toward Privatization

- Bond Issue Failure — 16 %
- Budget Cutbacks — 58 %
- Demand for New Services — 69 %
- Labor Difficulties — 26 %
- Loss of Key Staff — 16 %
- Rapid Pop. Growth — 32 %
- Credit Limit Reached — 32 %
- Taxpayer Revolt — 11 %

Source: 1989 Survey by Deloitte & Touche, New York.

Many states already contract out to the private sector for provision of a variety of services, including, for example, highway maintenance and prison construction and operation. But opportunities for additional privatization activity exist among the states. And some states are already moving toward greater use of privatization.

For example, in 1989 Utah created a Privatization Policy Board to explore ways of using the private sector for service provision at both the state and local levels. The Board noted that garbage collection privatization could offer not only significant savings but also more revenues from taxes paid on the purchase and operation of capital equipment. Taxes on a $100,000 privately owned garbage truck, for example, would yield $10,223.

Other states are also under pressure to explore privatization options. Arizona is considering legislation akin to California's AB680, allowing for private-sector highway construction and operation under long-term leases. The legislation would amend the state code Title 28 to allow for private development of new roads or leasing of existing state-owned roads to the private sector. Behind this legislative drive is the state's desire to find funding for its largely unfunded 230-mile urban freeway system.

Florida, too, is considering legislation to allow for construction and operation of private tollways. A 1990 version of the bill (SB 60) had received support from both Democrats and Republicans and failed to pass only because of problems with other portions of the highway bill.

And Ohio's Senate Committee on Competition is looking at privatization, including possible privatization of prison facilities. In Montana a report was submitted to Gov. Stan Stevens that proposed possible privatization of some 30 state services, including prison operations, case management of some social services, and sale of the state's retail liquor stores.

Similar recommendations for privatization were made by the Washington Research Council and the Connecticut Business and Industry Association. Already, legislators in Connecticut have introduced legislation that would allow the governor to make cuts in staff positions as deemed necessary in order to achieve privatization, work force reductions, and structural reorganizations. And Rhode Island lawmakers have introduced legislation that would create a special legislative commission to study the increased use of privatization by the state government. South Carolina is considering similar legislation to create a privatization policy board.

Other states are also considering broad privatization measures. In January 1991, a bill was introduced in North Dakota that would direct the state's Legislative Counsel to study the feasibility and desirability of the privatization of some state government services, including determination of whether state government agencies are competing unnecessarily and unfairly with the private sector and the advisability of restricting that governmental competition. The states of Washington and Wyoming are both considering a law that would prohibit government agencies from competing with the private sector. And a bill was introduced in the New York legislature that would require the governor to include with the annual executive budget recommendations regarding which government services should be privatized. In a move that could restrict privatization, legislators in Oregon have introduced legislation that would require public hearings before any public employer could contract with the private sector to perform duties or services currently performed by public employees.

Much recent state-level action regarding privatization has focused on correctional facilities. Pennsylvania, for example, is already moving forward with plans for some privatization of prison construction using lease-purchase arrangements. The state is seeking bids from private developers for three 1,000-cell prisons, including one maximum- and two medium-security facilities. The Department of Corrections will own and operate the facilities, but savings are expected by using the private sector to build the facilities, since private developers are not subject to state public works process constraints. Under current plans, the state will lease the prison facilities from the developers for twenty years, with an option to buy the facilities at the end of that time.

Indiana, too, has introduced legislation that would authorize the Department of Corrections to enter into contract with private vendors to operate, manage, and maintain correctional facilities. Massachusetts and Nebraska are also considering legislation relating to prison privatization. Oklahoma is considering a bill that would authorize that inmates in the custody of the Department of Corrections could be incarcerated in private facilities. South Dakota is considering legislation that would allow cities and counties to contract with the private sector to operate and maintain correctional facilities, detention centers, and work camps. Texas, too, is considering a bill that would allow for the conversion of certain correctional facilities operated by the Board of Criminal Justice to facilities operated by private vendors or counties; Texas has already obtained a number of new prisons via privatization. Proposed legislation in Wyoming would allow counties to contract with private facilities to house prisoners convicted of misdemeanors. Legislators there are also considering a bill that would allow the Board of Charities and Reform to contract with private entities to construct, lease, acquire, improve, operate, or manage correctional facilities.

Mississippi is considering legislation that would allow municipalities to contract out for fine collection and probation oversight. New Hampshire, by contrast, has introduced legislation that would put a moratorium on privatization of correctional facilities. The same bill would create a private prison task force to further look at the concept. New Mexico has introduced legislation that would give its Corrections Department broad regulatory, inspection, and enforcement authority over all privately operated correctional facilities in the state. New Mexico is also considering legislation that would restrict the construction of private jails or prisons to house out-of-state prisoners.

The state of Washington is looking at another area that might be suitable for privatization—public transit. A proposed bill there would require public transit operators to seek competitive proposal on at least ten percent of its fixed-route bus service on an annual basis. The legislation is similar to a bill passed in Colorado requiring the contracting out of 20 percent of Denver's transit system.

This current state activity underscores that numerous states are considering privatization. However, these efforts typically remain sporadic. As budget constraints push legislators to look for ways to cut public-sector expenditures, privatization of a broad array of services could offer significant savings potential without jeopardizing key programs. At the state level, four key areas of privatization offer the most immediate opportunities:

- Infrastructure privatization, especially highways;
- Prison privatization, including facilities for all levels of security;

- Fleet and highway maintenance; and

- Incentives and requirements for local-government contracting, particular of such services as transit, solid waste, and welfare caseload operations.

Privatization Policy Recommendations

A. Highway Infrastructure

Private Construction and Operation. A 1988 national report, "Fragile Foundations," notes that infrastructure has received a declining share of GNP since 1961.[4] As a result, federal, state, and local governments face pressing needs to maintain, rebuild, and construct new infrastructure. Some estimates put dollar requirements at over $1 trillion for the decade of the 1990s.

Failure to invest adequately in infrastructure has left states and cities with congested freeways, deteriorating highways and bridges, inadequate wastewater treatment facilities, and overcrowded airports. Privatization can offer a mechanism for better meeting these needs. For states, a key area will be highway privatization coupled with introduction of road pricing in congested areas.

The 1987 federal highway bill, which for the first time permitted some states to use federal aid on toll highways, received support in a 1990 review by the General Accounting Office.[5] That report noted that three of the nine eligible states had started construction on their toll roads, five others were in the design/review stage, and one (Colorado) had dropped out. The GAO report found that being able to charge tolls helped states to increase their total new-highway investment, and also that tolls provide a dedicated source of funds for maintenance. The report also stressed the importance of automatic vehicle identification (electronic) technology in reducing costs of toll collection and ensuring speedier traffic flows by eliminating the need for vehicles to stop in order to pay tolls.

In July 1990, the American Road and Transportation Builders Association announced the creation of a Private-Public Ventures Advisory Council. The group's first project is a nationwide study on the use of private enterprise for highway projects. And in its 1991 proposal for a new highway bill the Bush Administration stressed the increased use of tolls and a major expansion of the role of the private sector in providing "toll roads, bridges, tunnels, bus lanes, transit facilities, and perhaps even maglev and high-speed rail facilities," according to a speech by DOT Secretary Samuel Skinner.

Tolls and Congestion Pricing. However, for privatization to be feasible, three changes in institutional structures and user incentives are required. Infrastructure privatization requires that:

1. Some form of user-based funding be implemented to generate not only revenue streams to provide a return on investment but also to provide a market test to pinpoint which projects are likely to have the highest demand;
2. Revenues be dedicated to operation, capital investment needs, and maintenance of the facility generating the user fees;
3. Market pricing be implemented that gives incentives for economizing on facility usage. For example, congestion pricing on roads helps allocate road use according to time-of-day usage, while gasoline taxes have no impact on demand driving patterns.

These concepts have gained increasing academic and political support. For example, the idea of charging directly for highway use, especially in urban areas, gained support from a major 1989 Brookings Institution book, *Road Work*, which argued for replacing today's indirect user tax and trust fund approach with direct user charges: demand-based congestion prices in urban areas and axle-weight fees for intercity highways.[6] In addition, the 1990 Clean Air Act's supporting report from the House Public Works & Transportation Committee notes that "tolls have long been recognized control measures which discourage automobile travel demand...Experience with toll facilities indicates that financial incentives on a tolled facility greatly increase the average vehicle ridership on that facility."

Demonstration of the effectiveness of congestion pricing also exists. In 1974, Singapore began requiring display of a purchased sticker to enter its downtown and reduced auto traffic by 40 percent. In 1990, Singapore announced plans to convert the existing system to electronic toll collection (ETC) by 1993. In Europe, three Norwegian cities—Bergen, Oslo, and Trondheim—have created toll rings around their downtowns. All three are converting them to ETC, and Trondheim will be the first to charge time-varying tolls, higher during rush hours. The Netherlands has announced plans for electronic congestion pricing in Amsterdam, Rotterdam, Utrecht, and The Hague as part of its National Environmental Policy Plan for reducing urban air pollution. Cambridge, England's local authority is planning for that city to become the first in the United Kingdom to implement congestion pricing on local city streets. In the United States, urban tollways exist in Miami, Orlando, Tampa, Chicago, Houston, and Dallas, among others. All charge flat-rate tolls, and only one—the Dallas North Tollway—has thus far converted to ETC (which makes flexible pricing easy to implement).

However, concern about automobile emissions has stimulated interest in congestion pricing in California's major population centers. In early 1990, the Bay Area Economic Forum produced a transportation plan aimed at enabling the Bay Area to reach compliance with state and federal emission-reduction mandates. Key to the plan, which was eventually rejected by the Metropolitan Transportation Commission, was congestion pricing on major bridges and freeways.

The Southern California Association of Governments, composed of all Los Angeles-area local governments, endorsed a congestion-pricing concept to address traffic and air pollution problems. Several states are either actively considering toll roads and congestion pricing or have already begun the privatization process. California, for example, after passing legislation (AB680) to permit the building of four private toll roads, completed its selection process in late 1990 for the first four projects. A number of other states are pursuing private tollway laws and/or projects:

- **Arizona**: In December, 1990 the Arizona Department of Transportation announced it would be requesting consideration of an AB680-type bill in the 1991 session. The chairmen of both House and Senate transportation committees have supported the idea.

- **Florida**: A private tollway bill was reintroduced at the end of 1990, and is modeled after Virginia's 1988 private tollway law.

- **Minnesota**: A private tollway bill was expected to be introduced in the legislature early in 1991 and is expected to pass. It would permit the blending of public and private funding, allow incorporation of existing roads into private projects, and rules out public utility-type regulation. For monopoly routes, a limit on rate of return would be set.

- **Mississippi**: At the local level, the town of Flowood hired a firm to conduct a feasibility study of a $60 million private tollway linking Jackson to the Jackson International Airport.

- **Virginia**: After the passage of legislation in 1988 to permit private tollways, plans for construction of a 14-mile extension of the existing Dulles Toll Road were introduced. The project won final state approval in 1990 and the private group preparing the $227 million project is now assembling the funding and pursuing a permit from the Corps of Engineers.

To address highway infrastructure needs, states should move to encourage public-private partnerships and privatization. It is not likely that federal monies will be available for the full infrastructure needs of the states, including new construction and renovation of existing facilities.

In addition to offering states a new source of infrastructure funding, some evidence suggests that private-sector projects can be built at lower cost than publicly built projects.

B. Corrections Facilities

The steep rise in the prison population over the last decade has left many states hard-pressed to meet their total prison needs. Consider that in 1977 there were 300,024 prisoners in federal and state prisons. A decade later that population had increased to 581,601—a growth of 94 percent. Over 90 percent of these prisoners were held in state correctional facilities. Budget constraints have left states without adequate resources to build new correctional facilities.

Privatization, both of existing prisons through operating contracts, and of new prisons through private construction (and also possibly operation), can help states meet their prison needs at lower cost and without the upfront capital expenditures required through public construction and operation. Through lease-financing techniques, governments can overcome existing budget constraints on large facility expenditures. Lease-financing—including straight leases, lease/purchase, and lease-back arrangements through which the government rents the prison facility from the private owner/builder—can spread construction costs over the long term. The lease approach, according to a Reason Foundation study, can avoid time delays and associated costs that are often incurred in the bond-floating process.

Three factors are fueling the continued privatization of prison operations: 1) At least 43 states are under court order to improve prison conditions and reduce crowding, yet face budget constraints that inhibit their ability to construct new prisons; 2) state and federal prison populations have increased some 90 percent over the past decade, prompting an acute need for additional space; and 3) current efforts suggest that operating-cost savings of 5 to 13 percent can be achieved through privatization.

At the federal level, two legislative proposals were introduced that would have encouraged prison privatization, but neither bill was acted upon. The first, the Prison Privatization Financing Act (HR 4814) would have made prisons eligible to compete for tax-exempt private activity bond financing under existing state volume caps. The second, the Omnibus Crime Bill (HR 4079) would declare a five-year national emergency giving the Attorney General the authority to contract with private firms to the greatest extent possible to finance, build, operate, and perhaps own federal prisons. To date, neither bill has moved forward in Congress.

However, prison privatization nonetheless continues apace. A number of states already permit the private sector to play a major role in developing and operating prisons and jails. These states include Florida, Kentucky, Louisiana, New Mexico, Texas, and Tennessee (see Table 1).

Table 1

STATE & LOCAL CORRECTIONS PRIVATIZATION

State	Facilities Contracted or Privately Developed	Security Level
Alabama	Tuscaloosa Detention Facility	min.,med.
	Holman Correctional Facility	max.
	Station Correctional Facility	min.,med.
	Bhan Work Release	
California	34 work–furlough facilities	
	Six Return–To–Custody facilities	
	1 substance abuse treatment facility	
Florida	Orange Correctional Inst.	close
	Charlotte Correctional Inst.	close
	Gulf Work Camp	min.,med.
	Quincy Vocational Center	close
	West Palm Beach CCC	min.
	Okaloosa Correctional Inst.	close
	Franklin Work Camp	min.,med.
	Hardee Correctional Inst.	close
	Jackson Correctional Inst.	
	Monroe County Jail	
	Escambia Correctional Inst.	close
Iowa	Bids are not final so names cannot be provided	
Louisiana	Winn Parish Prison	
Minnesota	Ramsey County Womens Correctional Facility	
Mississippi	Jesco/James Martin	max.
Missouri	Potosoi Correctional Center	max. level 5
New Mexico	Grant Women's Prison	min., med., & max.
	Santa Fe County Jail	
Tennessee	Department of Youth Dvp. Authority	
	Hamilton County Penal Farm	
	Shelby County Correctional Facility	
Texas	Venus Pre–Release Center	min.
	Cleveland Pre–Release Center	min.
	Kyle Pre–Release Center	min.
	Bridgeport Pre–Release Center	min.

SOURCE: *Privatization Report, Aptil 7, 1990 (Alexander Research & Communications) and Reason Foundation Files.*

A 1987 National Institute of Justice report noted that some 1200 adults were held in secure, privately operated prison facilities. And numerous jurisdictions contracted to the private sector to operate non-secure facilities.[7] By 1989, the number of adults held in privately operated corrections facilities had climbed to over 3,000. Plans were underway to contract out another 2,500 beds pending completion of new prisons, suggesting that the trend toward contracting out continued through 1990. A 1990 Reason Foundation report, "A California Budget Assessment Project," notes that 11 states have privately developed or operated prison facilities.[8]

At least three of these facilities—one in Alabama, one in Mississippi, and one in Missouri—are maximum-security facilities. The U.S. National Institute of Justice in 1989 reviewed the corrections privatization experience in Hamilton County, Tennessee.[9] The study compared the private-sector cost of running the Hamilton County Penal Farm to what the county auditor estimated it would cost the county to operate the same facility. That study found savings of **at least** four to eight percent using the most conservative estimates, and if the county's downward biases were eliminated, the real savings over the first three years of operation would have been from five to fifteen percent.

In another comparison of costs, when a private firm agreed in 1986 to operate a minimum-security facility in Kentucky, the estimated state operating costs were $28.62 per inmate per day. Including capital costs the tally came to $32 per day. Based on this estimate, state savings from the privatization came to 21 percent. Privatization has the potential of promoting both greater efficiency in construction and management of prison facilities and to improve quality (or effectiveness). In particular, improvements can come from:

1. **Greater efficiency in construction.** This results in part from savings from faster construction or renovation through use of such techniques as modular construction and "design-build" construction management. Public-sector costs for prison construction range from $50,000 to nearly $100,000 per prison bed. The average figure is around $58,000 for maximum-security cells, and $46,000 and $26,000 for medium- and minimum-security facilities, respectively. Building time is typically around 2½ years. Private-sector construction has already shown potential for significant savings. For example, a review of costs for building one private-sector minimum-security facility showed costs of about $14,000 per bed, and construction time of 5½ months.

2. **Increased management efficiency.** This results in part from more flexibility in purchase of prison goods and services, lower cost of

equipment purchases as a result of private-sector incentives to keep costs as low as possible, and optimum utilization of staff.

3. **Construction quality improvements.** This can result from greater flexibility in site selection, personnel, and material; flexibility in design and use of building technology. Design innovations can in turn lower operating costs. For example, a Reason Foundation study on prison privatization notes that "each guard position eliminated by virtue of improved prisoner oversight and control capabilities—be it through construction of cell tiers and connecting hallways permitting more efficient personal surveillance or via deployment of centralized video technology and computerized locking systems—in effect (over a 24-hour day, seven-day week) means a reduction of five guards and five salaries in actual manpower expenditures."[10]

4. **Improvements in management quality.** This can result from greater use of merit pay, for example. One key state action to promote prison privatization would be the development of contract guidelines. These guidelines should include provisions requiring: 1) guarantees of at least modest cost savings; 2) assurances of prisoner rights and legal recourse if rights are violated; 3) flexibility for the private provider regarding introduction of efficiency measures; 4) protection of existing employee rights by addressing the issues of job retention and collateral benefits; and 5) contract monitoring provisions to reinforce the idea that the intermediate and ultimate responsibility for prison quality rests with the state.

A Reason Foundation report on the potential for prison privatization in California noted that cost savings could range from 10 to 40 percent.[11] Even using the lowest estimate, that would translate into savings for the state of some $212 million, a figure almost equal to the proposed 1990-91 budget increase for prisons.

To facilitate privatization, states should form task forces to develop specifications and draft contract language for the operation of each adult correctional institution. This approach has already been taken in California for "return-to-custody" facilities (a community correctional program) and has been done for other types of correctional facilities in other states and local governments. In addition, states should move to contract out the management and operation of existing facilities to qualified private firms. It may be advisable to permit no firm to operate more than five institutions within the state at one time in order to insure competition. Contracts and/or specifications should not limit bidders to certain salary levels, benefits, or operational approaches, though some provisions for preserving existing public-sector employee benefits may be required.

C. Fleet and Highway Maintenance

Fleet Maintenance. A 1990 survey by the Mercer Group reported that counties frequently cited fleet maintenance as a key target for privatization.[12] In part, this growing interest in privatization is a consequence of well-documented successes of contracted fleet maintenance. At the state level, fleet maintenance represents a promising target for savings, given the record of such privatization at the local level.

The County of Los Angeles program, in which it contracted out to Holmes & Narver Services, Inc. (HNSI) the maintenance of its entire fleet, offers a notable example of potential savings from privatization. The HNSI contract, awarded in 1988, was one of the largest local government maintenance contracts with the private sector in history, totaling $10 million for one year with an estimated overall value of $60 million. The contract was five times larger than any similar local government fleet maintenance contract. Under the contract, Holmes & Narver maintained 6,500 county vehicles, including 1,800 heavy vehicles and the entire fleet of the sheriff's department.

Though the contract has been terminated because of a contract dispute (and contracts with three new private firms have been signed), the HNSI experience in Los Angeles County offers important information regarding both potential problems with such contracts and implications for public-sector savings and service-quality.

Early problems under the contract surfaced. First, as a consequence of the inaccurate records the county had kept of its fleet maintenance prior to privatization, actual work had been underestimated. Moreover, upon taking over maintenance of the fleet, HNSI faced a backlog of some 850 vehicles, double what had been anticipated. And the county had inaccurate information on the actual condition of the fleet in terms of age and mileage. This resulted in early problems for HNSI, with the contractor initially not keeping the backlog to expected levels.

However, after initial adjustments HNSI brought the backlog down to an average of 200 vehicles. The backlog rate—the number of vehicles awaiting repair as a percentage of the total fleet—is now below 4 percent by the end of 1990, which is the lowest rate since the county began keeping records. This essentially means that at least 200 more vehicles per day are available to county department users than were on line prior to privatization. A survey of county departments showed that 88 percent of users rated HNSI service as excellent or good.[13]

Cost savings after the first year were at least $1.5 million. HNSI representatives argue that actual savings are much higher but their claim is difficult to document, since the county kept inaccurate records. For example, it did not keep any records of dozens of small repairs. Given the first-year savings, HNSI estimates of savings over seven years (the five-year contract, plus an expected two-year extension) will mount to $14.7 million.

The Los Angeles County privatization program offers other key experience for governments considering contracting out. With public employee opposition representing the most significant barrier to contracting out, the county implemented its programs with what amounts to a "no lay-off" policy. Staff reductions are handled through attrition, and employees are offered positions either with the contractor or in other county departments. As an incentive to department managers, their departments receive a percentage of any savings resulting from privatization.

Highway maintenance. Highway maintenance costs in some states have exceeded the rate of inflation over the past decade. For example, in California, expenditures for highway maintenance have risen at an annual rate of 6.9 percent over the past decade. A number of studies have found that contracting for road or street maintenance activities yields savings of up to 30 percent or more. One California study by University of California professor Robert Deacon found that cities contracting for street maintenance services were paying only 70 percent as much as cities using in-house forces for these services.[14]

Another study found that cities using in-house forces for asphalt repaving had 96 percent higher costs than cities relying on contractors.[15] And in a Reason Foundation study comparing the city of Los Angeles, which uses in-house forces for asphalt resurfacing and street cleaning, and the county of Los Angeles, which uses contractors, city costs were 106 percent more per mile paved and 56 percent more for street cleaning per curb mile.[16] A joint study by the Council of State Governments and the Urban Institute noted that "the practice of contracting for a portion of road and bridge maintenance and repairs is well-established in many states."[17] Hawaii, for example, contracts for 90 percent of its maintenance work. Florida's Department of Transportation, along with the state's large counties, contracts out all construction, reconstruction, and maintenance work except signing. And Texas bids out most of its reconstruction and maintenance work in accordance with a competitive bidding statute. Other large urban states increasingly contract out road maintenance (see Table 2).

Thus, in several of the nation's largest states, most or nearly all reconstruction and maintenance work is contracted out. In addition, the Canadian province of British Columbia recently contracted out 100 percent of its highway maintenance program to dozens of private companies, including newly formed firms composed of the former public employees who previously provided the same basic service. In fact, the province made special efforts to encourage contractors to hire the public

Table 2

**EXTENT OF CONTRACTING FOR STATE ROAD MAINTENANCE:
LARGE URBAN STATES**

State	Maintenance Services Contracted
California	Some
Florida	All except signs
Illinois	None except some signs
Michigan	Very little
New Jersey	Some -- increasing
New York	Some
Pennsylvania	Most
Texas	Most

SOURCE: *Adapted from The Private Sector in State Service Delivery: Examples of Innovative Practices, Allen, et al., The Council of State Governments and The Urban Institute, Washington, D.C., 1989, p. 141.*

employees currently performing the work. It actually helped employees form their own companies to take over highway maintenance and gave them a five-percent preference on the bids.

In the United States, Pennsylvania is the leader in contracting for highway maintenance. According to the Council of State Governments and the Urban Institute, the state contracts for 50 to 80 percent of paving, 95 percent of roadside insecticide spraying, 95 percent of bridge maintenance, and 50 percent of tar and chip roadway surface treatment. The state commissioned a consulting firm to compare the work of a private contractor and state employees between 1980 and 1981. Using that comparative data, the consulting firm found that a 12-percent reduction in state personnel would result in costs savings of 5.6 percent, and contracting all road maintenance and repair would cut costs 10.6 percent.

The cost savings from contracting for highway maintenance range from 10 to 106 percent, depending on the particular maintenance service. A useful mid-range of between 25 to 50 percent cost savings is provided by the Privatization Cost Savings Database developed jointly by the Reason Foundation and the Law and Economics Center at the University of Miami in a study, *The Role of Privatization in Florida's Growth.*[18] These figures are derived from numerous studies and publications, as well as from being used in the extensive literature addressing the relative efficiency of alternative delivery systems.

States should consider privatization of highway maintenance by developing specifications and contract language/conditions to encourage bidders to employ current maintenance workers, including steps to facilitate the formation of firms composed of and owned by the employees currently providing the service (as British Columbia has done). Contracts and/or specifications should not limit bidders to certain salary levels, benefits, or operational approaches. To enhance competition, states might consider dividing their road networks into regions which would serve as contract areas. Firms would bid to maintain these specified areas.

D. Promotion of Local Government Contracting

While states can achieve significant cost savings from contracting out some state operations, additional opportunities for state-level savings could come from legislation to require local governments to open some services to competitive bidding. This process could not only reduce local government costs but also result in potential savings for states.

One possible model for U.S. state governments that would encourage local government privatization is the British Local Government Act, passed in 1988. The law requires all local governments to contract competitively for six basic local services: refuse collection, food services, street cleaning, janitorial, grounds/building maintenance, and vehicle maintenance. Municipal contracting accelerated dramatically in 1989 and 1990 as a result of the law. Cost savings from contracting out the services to private contractors or bid-winning in-house departments have ranged from 10 to 40 percent. The law allows council-run service organizations (in-house agencies) to compete in the process; however the contracts must go to the lowest bidder. The bill has resulted in a streamlining of their operations by local governments in order to compete with the private sector. The effects of such a program among the states could be significant. A Reason Foundation study of the state of California found that such a program could save the state over $870 million annually.[19]

In California, the state controller estimated in fiscal year 1988-89 that total budget requirements for all California counties were close to $20 billion. The state provided some $7.1 billion, or 35 percent, of these funds. For cities, total expenditures in 1987-88 were over $15 billion, with the state (and its counties) providing approximately $1.4 billion or about 9 percent of these funds.

The Reason study notes that, according to the state's Legislative Analyst, "the largest [general government program] over much of the last ten years has been aid to local governments. This aid, which is funded primarily by motor vehicle license fees (VLF) and is apportioned to cities and counties for general purposes according to population, has been growing at an annual average rate of 9.1 percent since 1984-85. In the 1981-82 through 1983-84 period, the state reduced VLF subventions as part of its overall budget-balancing strategy."[20]

Since all states allocate some portion of their budgets to local governments, the British Local Government Act of 1988 could serve as a useful model with cost-savings potential for the states. The Reason Foundation study found that passing a California Local Government Act to require that local governments open up certain service provision to competition from private firms would better ensure the state government that its money is being spent efficiently. By requiring that city governments solicit bids for such activities as emergency medical services, street lighting, street repairs and maintenance, public transit, solid waste disposal, and parks and recreation administration, the state could save a minimum of $416 million. By requiring that the counties competitively contract out services for some public facilities, health and sanitation, and recreation and cultural services, the state could save at least $458.9 million.

States, to benefit from local government privatization potential, should develop "local government contracting acts" similar to Britain's Local Government Act and a recent Phoenix, Arizona program that permits competition between in-house service agencies and private contractors. Such state laws should include provisions to ensure that in the comparison of in-house and contractor bids: 1) all additional local government costs involved in contract operation including contract development, bidding/recruitment expenditures, and monitoring costs are added to contractor bids; and 2) a private, independent auditor verify the in-house bid based on generally accepted accounting principles, including all indirect costs (e.g., legal and administrative overhead), retirement benefits, and opportunity costs (e.g., rental space income forgone by letting the in-house agency use public property).

A key problem faced by states in implementing such programs is how to capture some of the savings from local privatization. Existing legal relationships between states and counties and cities may make it difficult to ensure that municipal government competitive-contracting savings can be easily captured by the state via reduced state aid. One method proposed for California was to amend the laws regulating the disbursement of motor vehicle fees in lieu of tax revenue to require cities to shift that revenue to their respective counties in an amount equal to at least some portion of competitive-contracting savings. Counties, in turn, would have their categorical grants reduced by at least a portion of the total amount of both their own and their cities' competitive contracting savings. This mechanism would allow the state to benefit from the local government savings but would also allow local governments to capture some of the benefits from those savings.

Transit Service. By passing local government privatization acts, states could, for example, encourage local governments to privatize transit service. Contracting for transit service is a well-established, though not widespread, practice among local governments. A 1985 survey showed that 300 public agencies contracted for transit services at the local level.[21] And some states—for example, Texas, Washington, Illinois, Virginia, and California—use private-sector contracting for bus service. The state of Pennsylvania is also exploring the concept of competitive contracting for urban mass transportation services. Legislation has been introduced that would require that 10 percent of public transportation services be opened to competitive bidding.

The state of Colorado has already passed legislation requiring that Denver contract out at least 20 percent of its transit services. That legislation may be expanded to require contracting of 50 percent of transit services provided by the Denver Regional Transportation District under provisions of a recently introduced bill (SB 113).

In California, the California Bus Association has actively sought over the past four years to open local bus routes to private bus firms. In the wake of these efforts, key major competitive contracts have been awarded with an annual value over $65 million. These include contracts in San Diego County, Orange County, Los Angeles County, and the San Francisco Bay Area. Particularly notable is the contracting of service in the Foothill Transit District, an area carved out of the Southern California Rapid Transit District, the nation's second-largest bus system. With costs cut by 40 percent as a result of this privatization and ridership up 80 percent, this experiment in privatization may be expanded.

Despite these successes, several barriers continue to constrain privatization efforts. Public employee opposition remains a key barrier. However, disputes about service quality and cost also limit privatization efforts. Critics argue that both hidden costs and large transition costs actually mean few cost savings are actually achieved. And they argue that service quality declines. Transit expert Roger Teal examined these criticisms and concluded that they are either ill-founded or overstated.[22] For example, Teal found that administration and monitoring costs actually represent a small portion—about 6 percent—of overall transit budgets. These costs are insufficient to overcome typical cost savings from privatization.

Teal also found that transition costs, while sometimes significant, do not erode cost savings but can delay such savings. Federal law prohibits the laying off of public workers through privatization of bus service. As a result, jurisdictions that introduce privatization must use attrition and early retirement methods to reduce any transit staff not hired by the private firm. This slows the realization of cost-savings from trimming and reorganizing workforces. However, Teal nonetheless found significant cost savings over the longer term, specifically by year three of contract operations.

Though Teal acknowledges problems of comparability between public- and private-sector transit service delivery, he finds data that strongly indicate cost savings in the range of 22 to 39 percent for private, fixed-route service and over 50 percent for demand-responsive service. These conclusions can be drawn by comparing data in cases where a jurisdiction first contracted its transit service to a public agency and subsequently switched to private contractors. Since the service packages were virtually identical, this facilitates the public- versus private-sector cost comparison.

Nor are cost savings the result of initial "low-balling" by private contractors in order to obtain contracts. In a survey of 14 private-service providers with over 5 years contracting experience, Teal finds that cost savings are maintained.[23] Private contractor prices declined in real terms while public-sector prices climbed 30 percent above the rate of inflation between 1974 and 1984. Though public transit costs have recently slowed somewhat, costs still rose at an average annual rate of 4 percent in real terms between 1980 and 1986. On the other hand, competitively contracted systems declined in real terms during that same period by 1.7 percent. Over five years this would amount to a cost differential of 32 percent.

Teal notes that cost savings appear to be more robust under competitive bidding circumstances.[24] Contracts that require the private provider to purchase large numbers of vehicles may reduce competition, since only large, national companies can afford the high capital investment associated with such contracts. This, in turn, can reduce cost-savings from privatization.

On the issue of service quality, Teal's findings are more equivocal. He notes that quality of service comparisons are varied, with some studies showing marked improvements under private contracting and others showing problems with service quality. Teal also concludes on the issue of safety that "little empirical evidence is currently available to illuminate this issue. While the data (are) too mixed to support strong conclusions, (the data) does suggest that private contractors may have difficulty matching the accident record of public agency operations."[25] Again, however, the data are equivocal, with some areas showing little difference in the accident records of public and private operators.

Social Services. State and local officials are increasingly turning to the private sector—both for-profit and nonprofit—to handle a variety of social services, even including welfare case loads. The 1988 ICMA survey reported that private firms operate some 45 percent of all homeless shelters and 30 percent of homeless food programs under contracts with local governments.[26] About 25 percent of local public health programs and programs for the elderly are operated by private contractors. And nearly 35 percent of drug and alcohol treatment programs, mental health programs, and programs for the retarded are operated by private contractors.

The Mercer Group prepared a report on state rehabilitation agencies in 1990 to explore privatization trends and practices.[27] Of 22 state agencies surveyed, 91 percent used some form of privatization. Both private, nonprofit organizations and private, for-profit organizations provided service under contract to public agencies. Privatized services included employment training programs, vocational evaluation, placement services, and physical therapy programs.

Of particular note is the Brown County, Wisconsin contracting of general relief welfare programs. In 1986, the Wisconsin state legislature modified statutes to require county governments to handle general relief. Brown County opted to privatize this service. A 1990 study by the Wisconsin Policy Research Institute (WPRI) compared the contracted-out general relief program with that of other counties and also with the publicly operated program that the contracted program replaced.[28]

While program differences made precise comparisons impossible, the Institute adjusted for such differences in order to compare costs and service. Over the final five years during which the city of Green Bay had operated a general relief program, its administrative costs had gone from $189,700 in 1982 to $411,800 in 1986. By contrast, WPRI found that "total administrative costs for the two years following privatization were $226,000 in 1987 and $219,000 in 1988."[29]

The WPRI report concluded that the privatized service is more efficient than the city's program, in part because the city program required more extensive data collection and other costly procedures. As a result, the city employed twice as many people as the private contractor to operate the program. Nor did privatization savings come at the expense of employee recompense and benefits. The WPRI study found that the private contractor paid rates comparable to public providers.

And service quality also compared favorably with public-sector operations. The contractor must operate the program according to published guidelines established by the county that regulate procedures and eligibility, and ensure that benefits are distributed equitably. Benefit levels have not declined under the program's private-sector administration. To the extent that states directly operate a variety of social services, they should consider contracting out for their provision. In addition, however, passage of local government privatization legislation could foster privatization at the local level, with potential savings accruing to states to the degree that they support such local social service activities.

Privatization—General Trends and Results

General Trends. Most survey information on privatization in the United States has focused on the local level, with little attention to state-level activity. However, the local government information does offer relevant information regarding potential savings from privatization and barriers to privatization that are relevant to state legislators considering privatization. Some 99 percent of respondents to the 1988 survey on privatization by Touche Ross, ICMA, and the Privatization Council reported that they contracted out at least one service. Moreover, of these, 80 percent said they achieved savings of 10 to 40 percent through privatization. While that survey was not updated again for 1990, other surveys show trends in contracting out to be stable or increasing.

In its 1990 update of its 1988 survey, The Mercer Group found increased use of privatization for areas such as wastewater treatment facilities.[30] The survey looked at 120 cities, counties, and special districts (see Figure 3).

Figure 3: Cities' Contracting Practices

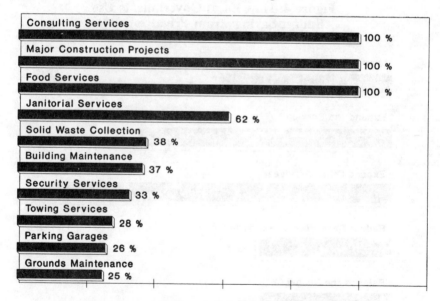

Service	Percentage
Consulting Services	100 %
Major Construction Projects	100 %
Food Services	100 %
Janitorial Services	62 %
Solid Waste Collection	38 %
Building Maintenance	37 %
Security Services	33 %
Towing Services	28 %
Parking Garages	26 %
Grounds Maintenance	25 %

Source: Privatization Survey, The Mercer Group, Inc., October, 1990, p.8.

At least 26 percent of respondents of the Mercer survey contracted out janitorial services, solid waste collection, building maintenance, security services, towing services, management and maintenance of parking facilities, and grounds maintenance. Some 25 percent or more contracted out some human resources services, landscaping and parks maintenance, food and medical services, data processing, landfilling, and wastewater services. They found a slight falling back of 1988 trends toward privatization across jurisdictions. However, a number of individual jurisdictions, particularly smaller ones, actually increased use of contracting out. They also found a move toward sale of some public services—for example, of excess data processing capacity or crime lab use—to neighboring jurisdictions.

The Mercer Group noted that "the results of privatization have been overwhelmingly positive. That's the word from 97 percent of the cities, 99 percent of the counties, and 81 percent of the special districts that have tried it." The survey reports that fully 100 percent of respondents claim to have achieved financial savings through contracting out, and 45 percent claim that improved quality of work also was a significant benefit.

Figure 4: How Local Governments Use
Budget Savings from Privatization*

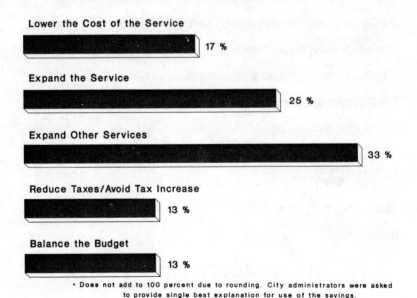

Lower the Cost of the Service
17 %

Expand the Service
25 %

Expand Other Services
33 %

Reduce Taxes/Avoid Tax Increase
13 %

Balance the Budget
13 %

* Does not add to 100 percent due to rounding. City administrators were asked to provide single best explanation for use of the savings.

In a third of the cases examined in a report of the National Commission on Employment Policy, privatization savings were used to expand other services. In one-quarter of the cases, savings were used to expand the privatized service, and in 17 percent of the cases they were used to lower the cost of the service to recipients (see Figure 4).

Privatization Obstacles. The 1988 ICMA survey found that public employee opposition posed the most important obstacle to contracting out, with 39.3 percent of respondents citing it as a barrier.[31] However, of the nine other potential barriers listed in the ICMA survey, all but one were cited within five percentage points of 30 percent, indicating that no single barrier other than public employee opposition predominated (see Figure 5).

The Mercer Group survey confirmed this picture, with employee opposition cited as the most important barrier to privatization—41 percent of respondents from cities and 50 percent from counties indicated employee opposition as a problem. Opposition by elected officials was also cited as an obstacle, but by considerably fewer respondents—22 percent of counties and 20 percent of cities. Likewise, citizen opposition was cited by 24 percent of citizens and 17 percent of counties.

Figure 5: Obstacles Encountered in Privatization

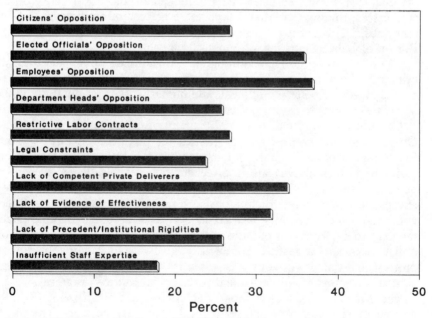

Source: ICMA, Baseline Data Report, 1988, Vol.21, No.6, p.9.

Given the continued opposition to privatization by the public employees, the findings of a 1989 study by the National Committee on Employment Policy (NCEP) are noteworthy.[32] In that study, "Long-term Employment Implications of Privatization,'" NCEP reviewed the employment effects for 34 city and county services privatized over the last 10 years.

The 34 services examined had 2,213 public employees. After privatization, 7 percent of these were laid off, 58 percent were hired by the private contractor, 24 percent were placed in other government positions, and 7 percent retired. This conforms to a U.S. Government and Accounting Office study that showed only 5 percent of public employees displaced through privatization. In addition, the NCEP report found that while government employment decreased as a result of privatization, private sector jobs increased, though there was a net job reduction of 12.5 percent. Services with the greatest job losses were street cleaning and garbage collection, while employment gains after privatization were more frequent for human services like hospital care and public safety.

Notably, the NCEP study found that, contrary to frequent claims by opponents of privatization, worker wages under privatization were not significantly reduced in most cases, though employee benefits were typically less for private-contractor employees. Labor turnover, a key indicator of job satisfaction, was also not unusually high for private-sector providers of public services. NCEP looked at the "quit rate" of 25 contractors, finding that after 3-5 years 35 percent of employees had left their jobs.[33] This compares to the mean for all jobs, as noted by the U.S. Bureau of Labor Statistics, of about 40 percent.

Key cost-cutting measures through privatization do not appear to come primarily from reductions in employee wages. Rather, reductions in overhead, use of better equipment, and higher worker productivity make key contributions to savings, according to the NCEP study (see Figure 6).

Contract Information. In its 1990 survey of privatization, The Mercer Group examined contract characteristics for privatization efforts. They found that over half of all city, county, and special district contracts reviewed in their survey are in effect for one year. Between 27 and 40 percent of the remaining contracts last from one to three years. The key exception was for infrastructure projects, including wastewater treatment contracts, which typically last 20 to 30 years. Average contract sizes ranged widely, from tens of thousands of dollars annually to multi-million dollar contracts. Largest city contracts typically are for major construction projects and transit system management. At the county level, the largest contracts are for public works and some social service programs.

The Mercer Group also looked at contract forms, finding that 90 percent of city contracts and 79 percent of county contracts are fixed-

Figure 6: How 32 Contractors Cut Local Service Costs*

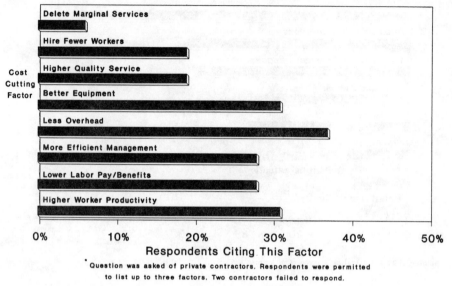

Source: Partnership Focus, June 1990, p.22.

price contracts. The remainder are either cost-plus contracts, incentive contracts, or contracts involving a percentage of profits. The survey also found that the majority of contracts let by cities, counties, and special districts are competitively bid.

Contrary to one popular argument against privatization, The Mercer Group results revealed that most jurisdictions have found sufficient contractors to bid for privatization contracts. Only 9 percent of cities and 8 percent of counties said they had trouble getting enough contractors to conduct competitive bidding. However, special districts had more difficulty, with some 30 percent saying there had not been sufficient numbers of contractors bidding on projects.

A number of factors influenced public-sector decisions regarding choice of a contractor, with potential service quality cited by 59 percent as a key factor and 40 percent citing financial considerations. Among important financial considerations were low price (cost effectiveness), financial stability, and willingness to put up bonds (see Figure 7).

Figure 7: Critical Success Factors for Contracting

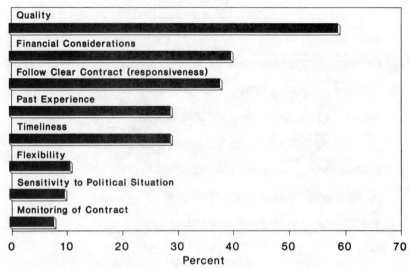

Source: 1990 Privatization Survey, The Mercer Group, Inc., October, 1990, p.24.

Summary

One constraint in looking at financial implications of privatization continues to be the inadequate accounting practices of public agencies. The Mercer survey found that 45 percent of cities and 58 percent of counties believed that local governments do not keep their costs in such manner as to be easily comparable with outside bids. Indeed, the inadequacy of local government accounting practices explains in large part the often widely divergent assessments regarding cost savings from privatization which they produce.

Privatization has proven a useful tool for local governments to achieve cost savings while maintaining quality public services. That same experience has been repeated in the limited privatization that has thus far occurred among state governments, particularly through prison privatization, as well as privatization of some maintenance and social service activities. With state legislators facing tight fiscal constraints, more systematic attention should be given to the potential of privatization. In a study of the California budget, the Reason Foundation found that privatization could yield substantial savings that could cut the budget deficit by at least one-third. All states could form task forces to explore savings potential from privatization across all state expenditure categories.

In addition, states should pay particular attention to prison privatization, since corrections facility expenditures make up significant items in state budgets. Likewise, highway maintenance and infrastructure privatization should be key targets for privatization. In addition, consideration of legislation along the lines of laws passed in Britain to encourage local government contracting out could yield benefits to both state and local governments.

Portions of this chapter were adapted from the Reason Foundation's *Privatization 1991* report and from other Foundation publications on privatization.

Endnotes

1. Philip Fixler and William Eggers, "California Budget Assessment Project: Addressing the 1990-91 California Budget Shortfall" (Santa Monica: Reason Foundation, June 1990).

2. "Trends and Issues in the Use of Intergovernmental Agreements and Privatization in Local Government," *Baseline Date Report 21* (Washington, D.C.: ICMA, Nov./Dec. 1989), 5.

3. Joe Morris, "No More Magic," *American City & County* (Apr. 1990), 66-67.

4. "Fragile Foundations," National Council on Public Works Improvement (Feb. 1988).

5. "Highway Financing: Participating States Benefit Under Toll Facilities Pilot Program" (Washington, D.C.: General Accounting Office, Dec. 1990).

6. Kenneth A. Small, Clifford Winston, and Carol A. Evans, *Road Work* (Washington, D.C.: Brookings, 1989).

7. "Research in Brief" (Washington, D.C.: National Institute of Justice, June 1987).

8. "California Budget Assessment," 6-10.

9. Charles Logan and Bill McGriff, "Comparing Costs of Public and Private Prisons: A Case Study," *Research in Action* (Washington, D.C.: National Institute of Justice, Sept./Oct. 1989).

10. Samuel Jan Brakel, "Privatization and Corrections" (Santa Monica, Calif.: Reason Foundation, Jan. 1989), 6.

11. "California Budget Assessment," 6-10.

12. The Mercer Group, "1990 Privatization Survey" (Atlanta, Ga.: The Mercer Group, Oct. 1990).

13. Jerome Premo, "A Partnership That Works: L.A. Fleet," presentation to the Privatization Council Fourth National Conference, Washington, D.C., June 12, 1990 (Orange, Calif.: Holmes & Narver Services 1990).

14. Reported in "California Budget Assessment," 11.

15. *Ibid.*

16. "Savings A.S.A.P.: Alternative Service Delivery Assessment Project," by Reason Foundation and University of Miami, Law and Economics Center (Santa Monica: Reason Foundation, Nov. 1988).

17. Reported in "California Budget Assessment," 11.

18. *The Role of Privatization in Florida's Growth*, by Reason Foundation and University of Miami, Law and Economics Center (Santa Monica: Reason Foundation, 1986).

19. "California Budget Assessment," 17.

20. Reported in "California Budget Assessment," 16.

21. Roger Teal, "Issues Raised by Competitive Contracting of Bus Transit in the U.S.A.: Part I," *Journal* (Mar./Apr. 1990): 8.

22. Roger Teal, "Cost Savings from Competitive Contracting: Part II," *Journal* (May/June 1990): 5.

23. Teal, "Issues Raised by Competitive Contracting: Part I," 13.

24. *Ibid.*

25. Roger Teal, "Cost Savings from Competitive Contracting: Part III," *Journal* (Nov./Dec. 1990): 10.

26. "Culture, Recreation, and Health—Ensuring the Quality of Life," *Special Data Issue* 12 (Washington, D.C.: ICMA, 1989).

27. "Study of Privatization Practices in Selected State Rehabilitation Agencies," report prepared by The Mercer Group for the Georgia Division of Rehabilitation Services (Atlanta: The Mercer Group, Dec. 1990).

28. Daniel J. Alesch, "Privatizing Welfare in Brown County, Wisconsin," *Wisconsin Policy Research Institute Report* (May 1990).

29. *Ibid.*, 22.

30. "1990 Privatization Survey," The Mercer Group.

31. "Trends and Issues in the Use of Intergovernmental Agreements and Privatization," ICMA, 9.

32. "Long-term Employment Implications of Privatization," report prepared by Dudek & Company for the National Committee on Employment Policy, Washington, D.C., *Research Report No. 89-04* (Mar. 1989).

33. *Ibid.*, 35-36.

REJUVENATING THE ROLE OF STATE POLITICAL AND GOVERNMENTAL INSTITUTIONS IN THE AMERICAN FEDERAL SYSTEM

Gregory S. Davidson

Clerk, Texas House Committee on Public Safety

At best, the general perception of state government is divided. Some see state capitols as the very temples of democracy: oracles created by "legislators who saw in the dramatic possibilities of architecture a means of expressing the spirit of liberty."[1] Others, see state government as the "ready tool of every monopolistic and reactionary interest seeking to block and hamstring national liberal measures."[2]

Those of us working in state government or serving as elected or appointed state officials fall somewhere between these two extremes of opinion. For many of us, an interest in state government and state politics is almost intuitive. In many instances, it represents a personal desire to fulfill civic duty and responsibility. We actually enjoy serving the public interest in places such as Sacramento, Springfield, Denver, Nashville, Albany, Austin, Madison, Lincoln, Jefferson City, Raleigh, and Tallahassee. Although at times we find it difficult to understand why others fail to share our enthusiasm for state government and politics, we understand and often share the sense of frustration that any government generates.[3]

The prevailing perception of American government holds that an interest in state government is at best, rather quaint, and at worst, a boorish waste of time, or terribly misguided. To this understanding, Washington, D.C., is the true center of American politics, the vortex of national and international political decision-making. The wellspring of American culture and political life lies somewhere inside the Beltway, not beyond it. Congress, the Supreme Court, the presidency, and the Washington social and political scene are the key elements of American politics, institutions are the appropriate focal point for the proper study of the modern American state. Adherents to this persuasion see state governments as corrupt backwaters teeming with notorious political characters such as George C. Wallace, Lester Maddox, Orvil Faubus, and Huey P. Long.

Fortunately, those who have been paying attention to domestic political development over the last thirty years have noticed something quite revolutionary occurring throughout the nation. Time and time again, the ability of the national government to govern the lives of individual citizens from Washington has proven to be inadequate. The growing federal debt, an irresponsible federal congress, and legislative decisions handed down by an elite cadre of federal judges only serve to accentuate the runaway nature of the national government. Meanwhile, perceptive political observers have noticed the dawning of a new era for American government. New attitudes toward governing our country and revitalized institutions have emerged over the last quarter century in American state governments. Names like Long, Wallace, Faubus, and Maddox have been replaced with names like Babbitt, Carter, Clinton, Dukakis, Deukmejian, Kunin, Martinez, Perpich, Reagan, Roemer, Thompson, Waihee, Wilder, and Wilson—a diverse group representing a truly pluralistic approach to governing the nation.[4]

The first part of this paper examines the decline of the state governments during this middle part of this century and the development of a Washingtonian orientation to American government and politics. The second part of the paper surveys the revitalization of state governmental institutions and politics that placed state governments on an equal footing with each other and the federal government. The final part of the paper adds a brief proviso concerning the movement of modernization that goes beyond restoring states to their rightful role in a federal system by a program that specifically seeks to reconstruct state governments in the image of the federal government.

The old paradigm of American government that focused exclusively on the federal government is giving way to a new theory in which state governments are seen as active participants in a revitalized federal system of government. The time seems ripe for a new theory of organization for the entire American state, one in which diversity and innovation are encouraged and the American entrepreneurial spirit is unleashed on the pressing political and social issues of the day. The time seems right for a new theory of government that balances state and national interests in a reinvigorated system that is closer and more responsive to the people it seeks to govern. This paper seeks to cast American state governments and political institutions as the appropriate and just mechanisms for governing the vast and diverse American state.

Restoring the State's Role in a Federal System

Ask the average person on the street for a definition of a federal government and you will more than likely receive a feeble answer that refers to the president, the Congress, the U.S. Supreme Court, or the vast bureaucracy in Washington, D.C. Unfortunately, if you were to ask the average political scientist the same question, you would likely get some version of the same response. As an organizational concept, federalism can be extremely rich in its possibilities and genuinely alive in its ability to order the American state. However, in the United States, federalism has lost most of its potency as a concept that vigorously protects the rights and liberties of Americans. Its eventual emasculation could signal the end of freedom and diversity in American governmental and political regime.

A Federal System of Government

A federal system of government is an arrangement of political power which involves the joining of several sovereign entities by means of an agreement for some mutual benefit or trust. A federal system involves the combination of at least two unique governments and results in the creation of a new government to carry out the agreed to principles which bind the constituent governments together. "Each," according to John C. Calhoun, "within its appropriate sphere, possessed all the attributes and performs all the functions of government. Neither is perfect without the other. The two combined form one entire and perfect government."[5] By its nature, then, federalism seeks to achieve a proper balance between a central government representing unity and its various constituent states representing diversity.

Political scientist William H. Riker has described federal systems of government in terms of two extremes.[6] In a minimal federal system, the rulers of the federation can make decisions in only narrowly restricted categories of action without obtaining the approval of the rulers of the constituent units. In a maximal federal system, the rulers of the federation can make decisions without consulting the rulers of the constituent governments in all but one narrowly restricted category of action. Riker refers to the minimal system as "peripheral," and the maximal system as "centralized."[7]

Federalism can then be understood as an attempt to balance competing powers in a spatially diverse system of government. A robust federal system of government almost by definition requires that there be a certain level of tension between the central government and the peripheral governments. It is this tension between unity and diversity that creates a dynamic and healthy system of government. However, domination by either the central government or any one of the constituent states discombobulates the whole system and the structural efficiency of the entire federal system of government is thwarted. This loss of balance between the federal and state governments is precisely what has happened to the modern conception of federalism in America.

American Federalism at Mid-Century[8]

Throughout the history of the United States, the federal government has continually encroached upon the sovereignty of the individual states that make-up the American nation. National institutions and politicians have grown in number, size, and stature to dominate state governments and state political institutions. Using Riker's description of various federal systems, the federal system drafted by the founders was clearly a peripheral system. They kept the important political decision-making institutions closest to the people in the states. However, during the last one-hundred and fifty years, certain powers have been at work to transform the modern theory of American federalism into a centralized federal state and have clearly thwarted the Federalists' great experiment. "An identifying feature of centralized federalism," Riker notes, "is the tendency, as time passes, for the rulers of the federation to overawe the rulers of the constituent governments."[9] Centralized federal governments, Riker says, tend to become more like unitary or imperial governments. Like most post-war American political theorists, Riker favors this movement toward centralization. Peripheral federal systems gradually fall apart until they are easy prey for their enemies. In a fashion typical of political writing during the Cold War era, Riker thinks centralized federal governments are better able to function in a hostile world. "It is this deference between gradual disintegration and gradual solidification that explains the contrast between the failure and relative rarity of ancient and medieval peripheralized federalisms and the success and the popularity of modern centralized ones."[10]

As an organizational concept, federalism in the Post-War era was placed on the verge of extinction by the proponents of the modern welfare state. New Deal programs designed by Roosevelt's "Brain Trust" to supplement the ability of the states soon became so entrenched that it was virtually impossible to return the programs to the states for fear of great, irreversible damage to the *status quo*. Roosevelt's New Deal welfarism may have sidetracked socialism in America, but it left its own legacy to be endured by future generations of Americans.

To build up their case for an all-powerful national government, proponents of the national welfare state had to dispense with their rivals in state and local governments. Typical of the intellectual attitude toward federalism was Harold Laski's pronouncement that "the epoch of federalism is over." Federalism "inhibits the mergence of necessary standards of uniformity" and "it leaves the backward areas a restraint, at once parasitic and poisonous, on those which seek to move forward."[11] The nation was, according to this analysis, in need of a new theory of organization which would usher in a new era of human relations and political development in the United States.

The transformation of the American state toward a unitary state was seen by many political and economic theorists as the next step in the progression of American political development.[12] The short-term success of nationalization undertaken by New Deal welfarism placed increased attention on the federal government as a provider of basic goods and services from cradle to grave.[13] Social and political planners saw the development of the national welfare state as just another step toward international welfarism. Gunnar Myrdal claimed that:

> The plain fact is this: When once the national Welfare State has come into existence and build its moorings firmly in the hearts of the peoples who in the democracies of the Western world have the political power, there is no alternative to international disintegration except to begin, by international cooperation and mutual accommodation, to build the Welfare World.[14]

State governments, under this theory, would be neatly folded into national governments, which would in turn be folded into international governments, which would eventually be folded into a one-world government. States in general were seen by these intellectuals as impediments to the development of a single, unified American state. The new American state, according to their incantation of American democracy, was to be unitary and classless, one which would promote egalitarianism and discourage diversity, and one which could silently wither into the pages of history. Federalism, as a system of government which seeks to preserve a balance between unity and diversity, was seen by these international intellectual adventures as a roadblock to the integration of the international welfare state.

It was vital to the success of this paradigm of American government and politics that the states be discredited so that the role of the federal government could gradually increase. Thus, those intellectuals who embarked upon this political agenda had a vested interest in undermining any amount of sovereignty remaining from the colonial period. State constitutions and charters, the basic documents which laid the blueprint for the new American state after the Revolutionary War, were vilified while the federal Constitution was exalted. The power of the states and their unique place in American government was neatly clipped and trimmed to fit the research program of certain New Deal, Post-War, intellectual movements.

Their arguments against the states, of course, were legion. State governments were corrupt and incapable of securing the freedoms and liberties of their citizens. State governments were antiquated. Constitutions were holdovers from the Reconstruction era and statues were written to protect one socioeconomic class from another. State legislatures were bastions of special interests and full of crooks seeking to steal the public weal. State courts were parochial backwaters which rarely affirmed their own presence.

At the same time that government and politics in the states and localities was being portrayed in the literature as provincial and arcane, the federal government was being portrayed as international and modern. State politicians were corrupt and inept in the affairs of state. Politicians in Washington, D.C., were virtuous and effective, and were in fact creating the state of tomorrow while solving the problems of the day. State courts were backwaters and state constitutions were arcane and outdated. The United States Supreme Court was the new liberator and the United States Constitution was portrayed as the modern canon of political and social salvation. The new paradigm of American government was powerful, not only in its conceptual underpinnings, but also in the intellectual power which was placed behind the theory. The members of the Rooseveltian Brain Trust devoted their entire political and intellectual lives to promoting and enacting the new paradigm.[15] If the federal government was destined to increase, they were determined that state governments had to decrease. If, according to this theory, the American state was to wither away, the states were destined to be the first leaves to fall.

Atrophy of the States

Given the low level of expectation placed on state governments and the power of the intellectual movement that sought their demise, it is no surprise that the states did indeed fall into disrepair and disrepute. By 1949, Robert S. Allen declared that "state government is the tawdriest, most incompetent, and most stultifying unit of the nation's political structure."[16] Allen charged that

> In state government are to be found in their most extreme and vicious forms all the worst evils of misrule in the country. Venality, open domination and manipulation by vested interests, unspeakable callousness in the care of the sick, aged, and unfortunate, criminal negligence in law enforcement, crass deprivation of primary constitutional rights, obfuscation, obsolescence, obstructionism, incompetence, and even outright dictatorship are widespread characteristics.[17]

Allen surmised that state legislatures are the

> 'bawdy house of state government' and are 'without exception . . . as a whole, a shamble of mediocrity, incompetence, hooliganism and venality . . . State legislatures are the most sordid, obstructionist, and anti-democratic law-making agencies in the country. Their annals are filled with the blackest pages of corruption, frustration of popular will and public

good, obscene irresponsibility, and the squandering and pilfering of fabulous natural resources and rights.'[18]

Other commentators have been less strident but just as concerned about the demise of the states. James Reichley noted that:

> [T]he problems, the tribulations, the opportunities for future development of state governments are of utmost importance to every American because the American political system has, to a great extent, been based and constructed on the fact of the existence of the states. If the states should fail to meet the challenges that are being put to them during the seventh decade of the twentieth century, the only alternatives, short of chaos, would be an enormous expansion of the resources and authority of local government or acceleration of the present trend toward complete assumption of governmental responsibility by the national government ... [which] would, carried to its logical extreme, almost surely undermine if not destroy the political freedom, regional diversity, and social and economic flexibility which have thus far characterized the American system.[19]

Such was the prominent viewpoint of American federal theory during the middle third of the Twentieth Century. The system had become one-sided. And like any one-sided relationship, it was doomed for tough times. The intellectuals claimed that their observations were vindicated and that the extinction of state government was more than justified. The era of the sovereign state in an American federal system had long since passed. The states, they argued, could just as easily be replaced by regional administrative units that would be subordinate to the ever-expanding national government.

So, without an active role to play in the affairs of state, many states accepted the new role assigned them by the mid-century version of federalism and soon became a series of small, disjunct fiefdoms run by parochial despots interested only in their own personal gain. Atrophy set in. The mid-century version of federalism was poised to proceed with the states as mere administrative units for the national government. Federalism as a creative balance between diversity and unity was about to be replaced by a single, unitary state.

Muddied by the influence of several regional despots, the role of state governments in a federal system seemed inextricably tied to racism. William Riker concluded his analysis of federalism with the comment that if one "approves of the Southern white racists, then one should approve of American federalism" and if one "disapproves of racism, one should disapprove of federalism."[20] Rexford G. Tugwell, one of the three charter members of Roosevelt's Brain Trust, even went so far as to propose a new constitution to replace the U.S. Constitution of 1789. Tugwell's new constitution, of course, abolished the existing state governments and replaced them with regional republics which resembled geographic administrative units rather than sovereign states.[21] Thus, it is easy to see how state governments had been emaciated by almost a half-century of inattention and neglect.[22] The proverbial baby was about to be thrown out with the bath water. The future of the states in the American system of government was very much in question.

Revitalizing State Governmental Institutions

Twenty-five years ago, political scientist Roscoe Martin explored the question of why states were not functioning effectively in the American federal system. Martin claimed that the answer could be found in certain "palpable deficiencies of the state and their governments."[23] Martin neatly cataloged these deficiencies in an analysis which will serve as a good general summary of the charges made against the states at mid-century. Surprisingly, many of these same charges are still held against the states even to this day.[24]

First, Martin claimed that *state constitutions were not equipped* to organized a modern state. State constitutions were drafted to serve the needs and purposes of an agrarian society and almost uniformly reflect a narrow, restrictive point of view. These constitutions were lengthy and contained excessive attention to detail which sacrificed flexibility and severely restricted the actions of state government to foresee and react to every contingency it faced.

Second, according to Martin, state governments and state political institutions were *not representative of the electorate* because of mal-apportioned legislatures which were typically rural in nature. This in turn called into question the legitimacy of the state legislature as the main organ of representation in a society that was becoming more urban in nature.

Third, states were *not organized for proper administration*. The function of the executive branch in many states was fractured through plural executives who dispersed political authority to the point of inefficiency. Governors were weak and unable to cope with immediate demands because of limited staff resources and constitutional barriers to action. The leadership ability of state chief executives was also hampered because of their short terms of office that constantly kept them running for office.

Fourth, Martin charged that state governments were *reluctant to fully utilize their available tax resources*. State governments existed mostly on property taxes and state programs expanded or contracted as property owners were able or willing to support them.

Fifth, state governments were *not willing to expand programs* to meet the vast problems of modern metropolitan America. Martin chides state governments as the protectors of the *status quo* and bastions of Nineteenth-Century agrarianism.

Finally, Martin concludes his analysis with the claim that state governmental leaders *do not seek new horizons.* The state man, Martin says, is oriented toward the land and his values are oriented toward the agrarian way of life. The state mind is provincial in thinking which occurs within the limits of a rigid moral code which all must profess.

> [T]hree overriding deficiencies flow from the state of mind and mythology which grip the states. The first is in orientation—most states are governed in accordance with the rural traditions of an earlier day. The second is timeliness—the governments of most states are anachronistic; they lack relevance to the urgencies of the modern world. The third is in leadership—state leaders are by confession cautious and tradition bound, which ill-equips them for the tasks of modern government.[25]

Martin summarized his analysis by stating that state constitutions were outmoded and inflexible; that the legislatures, once identified as the keystone of the democratic arch, were beholden to rural interests and were not representative of modern America; that the resources of state government were inadequate; that the atmosphere was not congenial to the introduction of new programs; and that state horizons were severely limited by prevailing mythology.

Given the diminished role of state governments and their eventual atrophy under widespread neglect, Martin's assessment of state government seems reasonably accurate for the period. The fallacy, however, has been the continued application of this assessment twenty-five years later. Significant events have taken place in the states over the last quarter-century which call into question the continued application of this analysis to American state government.

The Turning Point: Change in the States

In response to these and other similar charges made by American intellectuals at mid-century, state leaders and concerned citizen action groups began a process to improve state political institutions that resulted in the revitalization and rejuvenation of state governments as active participants in the federal system.

State Constitutions

In response to the charge that state constitutions were not equipped to handle the organization of the modern state, state leaders embarked upon a campaign to renew and revitalize state constitutions. Between 1940 and

1990, fifteen states adopted completely new state constitutions. The 600,000 word Georgia Constitution which was notorious for its length[26] was replaced with a new document only 25,000 words in length.[27] Even in states which chose not to adopt entirely new documents, constitutions have been amended in piecemeal fashion to remove arcane words and provisions and remove some of the statutory material which had worked its way into state constitutions. Constitutional initiative and referendum continue to distinguish the heritage of state constitutions from the staid legacy of the national constitution.

Even more important than the changes that have taken place in the text of these documents is the rediscovery of the state constitutions by state courts. In many respects, state constitutions flesh out the basic provisions of government framed by the United States Constitution.[28] State constitutions were the original guarantors of personal rights and liberties under law[29] before being brushed aside by the doctrine of incorporation created by the federal courts.

Representative Government

The sporadic redistricting of state legislative districts that created a wide disparity between rural and urban control of state legislatures has been replaced by the periodic redrawing of legislative districts after each new census.[30] Numerous reform movements and efforts to improve state legislatures have swept through the states over the past twenty-five years, some with resounding success and others with questionable consequences.[31] The Council of State Governments, the National Conference of State Legislatures, the American Legislative Exchange Council and other organizations have played a key role in improving the effectiveness of state legislatures. Citizen's groups such as the Citizens Conference on State Legislatures and the League of Women Voters have provided the impetus for dramatic change in many state legislatures throughout the nation by issuing research reports detailing specific deficiencies in the organization and operation of state legislatures. For the most part, state legislatures have responded well to the charge to improve their general operations and have accepted reforms that have increased their representativeness and made them independent institutions capable of governing a diverse population.

Organized for Administration

Like state legislatures, the executive branches of most states have undergone a tremendous transformation over the past half-century. Chief executives have been granted greater formal powers which allow them to balance the powers of the legislative branch. Governors have been given greater political security in the form of longer terms of office in an attempt to broaden executive institutional control over the bureaucratic agencies of the state. In 1940, almost half of the governors were elected for brief, two-year terms of office which gave them little time to devote to establishing long-term policies and programs. By the mid-1980s, only four states elected their chief executive to a two-year term.[32] This greater political security has allowed governors to venture into efforts to control the bureaucracy of state government through appointments and periodic reorganization. Almost half of the governors can authorize administrative reorganization through executive order, and all but eight governors retain full responsibility for budget-making which initiates the process by which state agencies are funded.[33]

Not only have the formal powers of the executive office increased, but so has the prestige of the office. In an exhaustive analysis of governors since 1950, Larry Sabato chronicled the passing of governors who were perceived as "flowery old courthouse politicians', 'machine dupes', 'political pipsqueaks' [sic], and 'good-time Charlies'," and concluded that, for the most part, "the nation's governors are capable, creative, forward looking, and experienced."[34] Sabato clearly details how the quality and experience of American state governors has improved over the last quarter-century to provide a healthy and robust collection of chief executives.

Resources and Programs

Against the charge that state governments do not fully utilize their tax resources to support public programs stands the experience of the past twenty-five years of diversification of the state tax base and development of new state programs and services. Where state tax-structures had been traditionally dependent on the wealth of property owners through an ad valorem tax, current tax structures now draw upon sales and gross receipts taxes, income taxes, severance taxes, and many different types of taxes to fund state and local government. All states generate revenue through licensing fees and some form of a sales or gross receipts tax.[35] Forty-five states have personal income taxes and 46 states have corporate income taxes.[36] The total revenue in 1988 from state government tax sources for all fifty states was over $264 billion.[37]

Protected from massive public deficits by constitutional balanced-budget requirements, most states have operated on a pay-as-you-go basis. This restriction has forced state leaders to grapple with the true desire of citizens to tax themselves in turn for services derived from state governmental services. Unlike the national government which can pander to every constituency seeking public dollars, state leaders have been institutionally cajoled into responsible taxing politics by citizens groups seeking to limit government to the business of basic services and ending massive redistribution programs.

Horizons

Finally, against the charge that state governmental leaders do not seek new horizons and innovations stands a body of innovative public policy which rivals anything to come out of Washington, D.C., over the past fifty years. Sunset laws that periodically review the effectiveness of state agencies and programs; the executive line-item veto which allows state governors the power to eliminate pork-barrel programs from the state budget; initiative, referendum and recall which seek to increase political participation: the list could go on and on with truly innovative and effective policy proposals that have been implemented in state governments throughout the nation. Most of these innovations cannot even receive formal consideration inside the Beltway because of the radical change associated with such proposals. If anything, it is the officials elected to serve in the federal government who seem imperiled by threats to the status quo and unable to respond to the changing needs and demands of the citizenry.

Experimenting with Structural and Political Alternatives

So far we have seen that the role of the state governments in American federalism had been severely reduced by the New Deal and its intellectual legacy. Given the low level of expectations, and the subsequent atrophy of the states under such a strong, centralized form of federalism, it is not surprising that state governments and political institutions did indeed conform to the mold and fell into a state of disrepair and disrepute. Faced with a turning point, states could resign themselves to their new role in the centralized form of federalism popular at mid-century, or they could set about to revitalize and rejuvenate state governmental institutions and reassert their place in a balanced system of federal government. We have seen that most states have answered the challenge and have undertaken massive campaigns to reinvigorate their political institutions and political systems. However, as with any movement, there have been diverse strains of thought concerning the changes which have transpired in state government over the past twenty-five years. Some efforts have been aimed at truly rejuvenating the existing political institutions and political traditions and heritage of state governments, while others have simply been an effort to clone the Washington, D.C., paradigm and transpose it into the states under the cloak of reform or modernization.

Modernization or Rejuvenation?

There is a distinction to be drawn between the rejuvenation and modernization of state political institutions and politics. Modernization of state government has been for the most part, an effort to conform state politics and political institutions to the Washingtonian model of government. This movement has taken several forms. For example, the professionalization movement in state legislatures seeks to conform state legislators to the Washingtonian model of a full-time, professional politician who is elected by a constituency to spend most of his time in some far away capitol pondering the effects of public policy. Or, for example, the recent increase in judicial activism by state courts clearly reflects the judicial fiat wielded by the federal courts. Or consider the rapid growth of the state bureaucracy. State capitol buildings which at one time housed the entire apparatus of state government, have been dwarfed in many states by massive state office buildings built to house the ever-increasing state bureaucracy, which is directly analogous to the burgeoning federal bureaucracy in Washington. For the most part, change at the state level over the past thirty years has been oriented toward implementing a Washingtonian mode of government in the states.

The modernization movement concerning state legislatures provides a good example of how reformers at the state level have attempted to recast state legislatures in the form of the United States Congress. The most comprehensive study of American state legislatures was conducted by a self-styled organization called the Citizens Conference on State Legislatures.[38] The group commissioned a study of the fifty American state legislatures that culminated in a rank-order listing of each legislature according to criteria developed by the study and a whole host of suggestions concerning the improvements that should be made by each state. The report was widely read and well received by state governmental leaders and had a tremendous impact on the modernization movement in state legislatures. However, many reformers failed to consider the normative nature of the study.

The study began with a certain set of assumptions about what a modern legislature should look like and proceeded to measure state legislatures according to those judgments. The study developed five "bare necessities" of what a modern legislature should be. It should be (1) functional, (2) accountable, (3) informed, (4) independent, and (5) representative. The criteria, which came to be known as the F.A.I.I.R. criteria, categorized legislative performance in various areas of legislative organization and structure. According to the model, the professional state legislature would be one in which legislators were full-time, staffs were large, compensation was high, committees were manageable, facilities were large, the number of legislators was small, the leadership was responsive, and the rules and procedures were open and fair. For example, the criteria developed by the study evaluated state legislatures according to the length of time the legislature was in session. The report suggested unlimited legislative sessions where legislatures could devote the time necessary to developing public policy. The report, however, failed to examine how increasing the legislator's time in session also decreases the legislator's time in the district. One of the great hallmarks of American government was the citizen-legislator, an individual that devoted a certain period of time to public service in the legislature and then returned home to live in the community under the very laws that he had passed while in session. The normative nature of the F.A.I.I.R. criteria, however, failed to measure the adverse impact that removing legislators from the community would have on the quality of the accountability provided by the political system.

The theory held that once legislators were professionalized, they would be independent from all the external impediments to good lawmaking such as the special interest lobbyists, overbearing governors, or judicially active courts. This, however, has failed to be the case. Political scientist Alan Rosenthal has warned legislative theorists that modernized state legislatures are following the same path into excessive fragmentation that has been blazed by the United States Congress. Rosenthal has noted the fragmentation of the committee system at the state level with independent committee chairmen wielding power within their own policy fiefdom. Legislative staffs have become highly specialized and divorced from the interests of the legislators. Constituencies and interest groups have been fragmented with each striving to protect its own self-interest. According to Rosenthal, the "one quality that distinguished the new breed of full-time, professional politicians from the old breed of part-time, citizen legislators is ambition."[39]

Rosenthal points out that amateur legislators were willing to devote a few years to public service and then return to the private sector to continue their private career.[40] The political risk involved with legislative service is relatively low for citizen-legislators since they can always return to their previous occupations. Conversely, since professional legislators have somewhat severed their connections in going off to the state capitol to ponder the great issues of the day, their risk involved with legislative service is extremely high. They have no other career to return to after leaving the legislature. Thus, "survival has become the primary consideration for members" of professional legislatures.[41] This observation is certainly substantiated by looking at a longitudinal analysis of the legislative turnover since the professionalization movement has existed. In 1935, legislative turnover was estimated to be about 40 percent in state houses and about 20 percent in state senates.[42] In 1963, the turnover in state legislatures was reduced to approximately 34 percent in both houses.[43] By 1988, this figure had dropped to 19.1 percent for state houses and 17.5 percent for state senates.[44]

In 1949, political scientist V.O. Key, Jr. concluded that one-party control of political institutions inhibits effective leadership and governance.[45] At that time, 18 legislatures were controlled by Democrats, 17 were controlled by Republicans, and 13 were divided.[46] Of the 7,636 legislators serving in state legislatures in 1950, 4,072 (53%) were Democrats and 3,235 (42%) were Republicans. Over forty years later, of the 7,461 legislators serving in state legislatures in 1990, 4,469 (59%) were Democrats and 2,927 (39%) were Republicans.[47] The Democrats controlled both chambers in 29 state houses, the Republicans controlled eight, and twelve were split between the two parties.[48] So while the proponents of the modernized state legislature claim that they have made state legislatures more representative, the partisan control of state legislative bodies has become an even more distinctive feature of the political landscape since Key issued his general warning against one-party control.

Thus, while the modernization movement has claimed to have competent, professional state legislators as its goal, it has produced questionable results. While it has erased the rural-urban distinction in most legislatures, it has skewed the partisan balance of state legislatures by insisting on retaining politicians with no ambition or capability other than politics. And while it claimed to have as a goal of producing state legislators that were technically competent to analyze the confusing intricacies of public policy, it has instead produced a group of professional politicians imbedded in a political system that they have created to assure their own return to office.

The California legislature has developed the Washingtonian model further than any other legislature in the country. Under the tutelage of Jesse Unruh, the California legislature was modernized to provide legislators with more time, more pay, more staff, more resources and more anything else deemed necessary to professionalize the legislature. However, even in the land of endless opportunity, the desirability of a full-time, professional legislature based on the Washingtonian model is beginning to be questioned.[49]

Against this theory of the professional legislator stands the theory of the legislator as a citizen first, elected official second. The citizen-legislator is a rich concept in American state politics that thrives on the responsibility of the legislator to live under the very laws that he adopted while sitting as a public official in some distant capitol. The citizen-legislator is accessible to the constituency and is responsive to the needs of the community from which he is elected. The citizen-legislator spends most of the time surrounded by "non-governmental" type people and is capable of being more in tune with the needs and desires of his constituency. On the other hand, many states have succumbed to the professional model of legislative behavior and have sequestered state legislators in state capitol buildings by means of continuous legislative sessions[50] and full-time salaries which only serve to further distance the professional legislator from the constituency. So, in an attempt to reform existing state political institutions, leaders jettisoned a distinctive trait of state government and replaced it with a system that perpetuates imbedded incumbents concerned only with their own political perpetuation. The professionalization movement has made some positive contributions to the efficiency and operations of state legislatures, but for the most part it has carried with it excess baggage that in several instances was worse than the practice it sought to replace.

So, it is easy to see how respectable reform movements can desecrate the very institutions that make state governments distinct from the federal government. Modernization was presented to state leaders as a means of making state governments more effective, and in many cases, it achieved just that. However, in several respects, modernization has taken the step over the line and promoted a particular political agenda that goes beyond a concern about more effective institutions.

Against this concept of modernization of state governments and politics is a theory of rejuvenation. This concept takes existing political institutions and returns them to their intended purposes in an attempt to revitalize their mission and purpose. Instead of conforming state political processes and institutions to a Washingtonian model, rejuvenation preserves their uniqueness and guarantees the diversity necessary for a robust system of government. Thus, the fact that the governor in North Carolina does not have veto powers over legislative enactments does not necessarily mean that the executive article of the North Carolina Constitution should be rewritten to give the governor the same power enjoyed by other state executive officers. Rather, the interaction between the North Carolina legislature and the governor should be studied to help understand how the veto empowers governors. Perhaps the North Carolina model is preferable to modern governing. Serious theorists should at least explore the institutional arrangement before dismissing it out of hand and erasing it through some self-styled modernization movement. Perhaps the people of North Carolina have it right and the other forty-nine states are in error. Or, for instance, what should theorists make of the Texas Legislature that is still only part-time and meets regularly only once every two years. Should this legislature be dismissed as being arcane and outdated (read: non-modern) or should it be studied to determine its strengths and weaknesses.

Diversity in institutional arrangements will produce a richer dialogue on the functions and purpose of American government than what has been imposed on the American people over the last half-century. The restoration movement should not be based on theories that will only replicate the major deficiencies of the national government. The true error of the modernization movement is that instead of merely restoring state governments to their appropriate place in American government, the modernization movement was a homogenization movement that sought to recreate state institutions according to the Washingtonian paradigm. In one respect, the modernization movement was another attempt at reconstruction. A movement to rejuvenate state political institutions would continue until the restoration had been made complete and state institutions were functioning according to some level of internal competence. Then, once the institutions had been invigorated and energized by some serious rethinking of the purpose and mission of state government, state leaders could then set out on an agenda of political development based on their own blueprints according to the desires of the people the government is established to govern.

Conclusion

For the better part of this century, state governments have suffered under a theory of government proposed by "Washington-centric" political theorists whose main concern was the creation of a single, unified national state directed by social planners and economists located deep in the bowels of the Washington bureaucracy. Their main concern was the collapse of capitalistic democracy and the inevitable rise of a socialistic state in its place. Subnational, state governments were seen by these theorists as impediments to the burgeoning realization of a single, unified national state which would eventually wither into the pages of American history.

The collapse of centralized governments in Eastern Europe and the reform efforts undertaken by the former Soviet republics have severely damaged this theory of a centralized, all-powerful national government which directs the affairs of state from a single vantage point. We are entering a Post-Washington era in American government and politics. Optimistically, if the failures of the national government do not collapse the whole system, this new era will be one of expansion and diversity and innovation. The old paradigm focused on the federal government. The new paradigm will focus on the partnership between all levels of government to create a thriving American state. The era of social engineering and planning from Washington, D.C. is ending. It remains to be seen if it will be replaced by a system of social engineering and planning from fifty state capitols, or if it will be replaced by fifty, distinct and unique polities striving to govern a diverse culture and population.

Endnotes

1. Henry-Russell Hitchcock and William Seale, *Temples of Democracy, The State Capitols of the USA* (New York: Harcourt Brace and Jovanovich, 1976), 3.

2. Robert Sharon Allen, "The Shame of the States," in *Our Sovereign States*, ed. Robert Sharon Allen (New York: Vanguard Press, Inc., 1949), viii.

3. Throughout this paper, I will use the terms "state government" and "state politics" to refer to the fifty state governments and political systems that comprise the United States of America. However, the use of this collective term emphasizes one of the themes of this paper which is the fallacy of treating all state governmental and political systems as if they were the indistinguishable. The use of these terms and this approach in general echoes a failure of analysts to recognize the unique development and nature of each state as an active and vigorous polity within the United States. Until this point is widely conceded, I suppose it will be necessary to follow suit and continue to refer to state polities in the collective.

4. For a current perspective, *see* Allen H. Neuharth, *Profiles of Power: How the Governors Run Our 50 States* (Washington, D.C.: Gannett New Media Services, Inc., 1988).

5. John C. Calhoun, *Discourse*, 85.

6. William H. Riker, *Federalism: Origin, Operation, Significance* (Boston: Little, Brown and Company, 1964), 5-8.

7. For an interesting application of this analysis *see also* William H. Riker, *Soldiers of the States, The Role of the National Guard in American Democracy* (Washington, D.C.: Public Affairs Press, 1957). Riker analyzes the role of the militia with respect to the distinctions between the peripheral and centralized forms of federalism.

8. David M. Ricci has postulated the existence of a mid-century liberal matrix which he has used to analyze the intellectual development of the social sciences in the post-war period. This matrix represented the universe of discussion and debate which constituted the catch-all frame of reference within which most American scholars investigated and spelled out the meaning of American society. Ricci describes this matrix as an "intellectual mold within which certain ideas were patently valid and commendable, while others appeared harmful and deserved condemnation." Ricci, *The Tragedy of Political Science, Politics, Scholarship, and Democracy* (New Haven: Yale University Press, 1984), 100-101. In the context of this article, I conceive of American federalism at mid-century as a subset of Ricci's broader description. The term "mid-century" roughly refers to the middle third of the twentieth century or it can be strictly understood to be those years between 1933 and 1966. However, since periodization tends to be as much of an art as it is a science, I reserve the right to extend the mid-century period in either direction to account for the antecedents and consequences of the period.

9. Riker, *Federalism*, 7.

10. Riker, *Federalism*, 8.

11. Harold Laski as quoted in Terry Sanford, *Storm Over the States* (New York: McGraw-Hill Book Company, 1967), 22.

12. Joseph A. Schumpeter, *Capitalism, Socialism, and Democracy* (London: Allen and Unwin, Ltd., 1942).

13. Milton and Rose Friedman, *Free to Choose: A Personal Statement* (New York: Avon, 1980), 82.

14. Gunnar Myrdal, *Beyond the Welfare State, Economic Planning and Its International Implications* (New Haven: Yale University Press, 1960), 176 (emphasis in original).

15. *See for example*, Rexford Tugwell, "The Experimental Roosevelt," *The Political Quarterly* 21 (1950): 239-62.

16. Allen, "The Shame of the States," in *Our Sovereign State*, vii.

17. Allen, vii.

18. Allen, xxxi.

19. James Reichley, ed. *States in Crisis: Politics in Ten American States, 1950-1962* (Chapel Hill, North Carolina: The University of North Carolina Press, 1964), 256-57.

20. Riker, *Federalism*, 155.

21. *See for example* Rexford G. Tugwell, *A Model Constitution for a United Republics of America* (Santa Barbara, California: The Center for Democratic Institutions, 1970).

22. Malcolm Jewell, "The Neglected World of State Politics," *Journal of Politics* 44 (August 1982): 638-657.

23. Roscoe Martin, *The Cities and the Federal System* (New York: Atherton Press, 1965), 47.

24. The following sections flesh out Martin's categories to create a framework of analysis for many of the charges that were leveled against state governments during the mid-century period. The authors of *Modernizing State Government, A Statement on National Policy by the Research and Policy Committee of the Committee for Economic Development* (New York: Committee for Economic Development, 1967), identified the inactivity of state governments under four major categories: (1) geographic handicaps, (2) outmoded structures (such as archaic constitutions, unresponsive and ineffective legislatures, weak executives, and uncoordinated courts systems), (3) inadequate use of resources, and (4) political weaknesses. The authors of *The Question of State Government Capability* (Washington, D.C.: Advisory Commission on Intergovernmental Relations, 1985), assessed the criticisms against the states according to functional categories such as state constitutions, state legislatures, governors and their offices, executive branch reorganization and central management, the judiciaries, openness and access, finances, and financial administration. Considering the variety of complaints against state governments, Martin's can at least be seen as representative of the various claims.

25. Martin, 79.

26. *Book of the States, 1980-81*, "Table 1 - General Information on State Constitutions" (Lexington, Ky.: Council of State Governments, 1980), 16.

27. *Book of the States, 1990-91*, "Table 1.1 - General Information on State Constitutions" (Lexington, Ky.: Council of State Governments, 1990), 40.

28. Donald S. Lutz, "The United States Constitution as an Incomplete Texas," 496 The *Annals of the American Academy of Political and Social Science* (Mar. 1988), 26-27.

29. Gordon S. Wood, *The Creation of the American Republic* (New York: Norton, 1969), 271-272.

30. *See* William C. Havard and Loren P. Beth, *The Politics of Mis-Representation, Rural-Urban Conflict in the Florida Legislature* (Baton Rouge: Louisiana State University Press, 1962). *See also Baker v. Carr*, 369 U.S. 186 (1962), *Reynolds v. Sims*, 377 U.S. 533 (1964), and *Maryland Committee for Fair Representation v. Tawes*, 377 U.S. 656 (1964).

31. For a good summary of several attempts at modern reform, *see* Ann O'M Bowman and Richard C. Kearney, *The Resurgence of the States* (Englewood Cliffs, N.J.: Prentice-Hall, Inc., 1986), 76-97.

32. Bowman and Kearney, *Resurgence of the States*, 62.

33. *Book of the States, 1990-1991*, "Table 2.4 - The Governors: Powers" (Lexington, Ky.: Council of State Governments, 1990), 67-68.

34. Larry Sabato, *Goodbye to Good-time Charlie: The American Governorship Transformed*, 2nd ed. (Washington, D.C.: Congressional Quarterly, Inc., 1983), 1-2.

35. *Book of the States, 1990-91*, "Table 6.25 - State Government Tax Revenue, By Type of Tax, 1988" (Lexington, Ky.: Council of State Governments, 1990), 331-332.

36. *Book of the States, 1990-91*, "Table 6.25 - State Government Tax Revenue, By Type of Tax, 1988" (Lexington, Ky.: Council of State Governments, 1990), 331-332.

37. *Book of the States, 1990-91*, "Table 6.25 - State Government Tax Revenue, By Type of Tax, 1988" (Lexington, Ky.: Council of State Governments, 1990), 331-332.

38. John Burns, *The Sometimes Governments: A Critical Study of the 50 American Legislatures* (New York: Bantam Books, 1971). *Also see* A.E. Buck, *Modernizing Our State Legislatures* (Philadelphia: American Academy of Political and Social Science, 1936).

39. Alan Rosenthal, *Governors and Legislatures, Contending Powers* (Washington, D.C.: CQ Press, 1990), 63.

40. Alan Rosenthal, *Legislative Life: People, Process, and Performance in the States* (New York: Harper and Row, 1981), 63.

41. Alan Rosenthal, "The Legislative Institution: Transformed and at Risk," in *The State of the States*, Carl E. Van Horn, ed. (Washington, D.C.: CQ Press, 1989), 93.

42. Charles S. Hyneman, "Tenure and Turnover in Legislative Personnel," *Annals of the American Academy of Political and Social Science*, vol. 135 (1935), 21-31.

43. Duane Lockard, "The State Legislator" in *State Legislatures in American Politics*, ed. Alexander Heard (Englewood Cliffs, N.J.: Prentice-Hall, 1966), 103-104.

44. *Book of the States, 1990-91* "Table 3.4 - Membership Turnover in the Legislatures: 1988" (Lexington, Ky.: Council of State Governments, 1990), 124.

45. V.O. Key, Jr., *Southern Politics in State and Nation* (Knoxville, Tenn.: University of Tennessee Press, 1949 [1984]), 298-310.

46. *Book of the States, 1950-51* (Lexington, Ky.: Council of State Governments, 1950), 112. In this analysis, Republican or Democrat controlled legislatures are defined as legislatures in which both chambers are composed of a majority of members from the same political party. Divided legislatures are ones in which a majority of the members in each chamber are from opposite parties, or one in which one chamber has an equal number of members from each political party.

47. *Book of the States, 1990-91*, "Table 3.3: The Legislators - Numbers, Terms, and Party Affiliation" (Lexington, Ky.: Council of State Governments, 1990), 123.

48. *Book of the States, 1990-91*, "Table 3.3: The Legislators - Numbers, Terms, and Party Affiliation" (Lexington, Ky.: Council of State Governments, 1990), 114.

49. For a perspective on the failures of the professional legislature in California, *see* Rob Gurwitt, "California Here We Come: The Professional Legislature and Its Discontents," *Governing* (Aug. 1991), 65-69; Richard Zeiger, "The Luster is off the California Model," *California Journal* XXI, No. 6 (June 1990), 299-302; and Dan Walters, et al "Legislature - Professional and Paralyzed," in the *California Political Almanac, 1989-1990* (Santa Barbara, Cal.: Pacific Data Resources, 1990), 131-138.

50. In 1950, only seven states (California, Maryland, Massachusetts, New Jersey, New York, Rhode Island, and South Carolina) held annual legislative sessions; *Book of the States 1950-51* (Lexington, Ky.: 1950), 106, 109. By 1990, all but seven states (Arkansas, Kentucky, Montana, Nevada, North Dakota, Oregon, Texas) meet annually; *Book of the States, 1990-91*, "Table 3.2 - Legislative Sessions: Legal Provisions" (Lexington, Ky.: 1990), 119-122.

MODERN TORT AND THE DECLINE
OF INNOVATION

Peter Huber
Senior Fellow, The Manhattan Institute

It is one of the most ubiquitous taxes we pay, now levied on virtually everything we buy, sell, and use. The tax accounts for 30 percent of the price of a stepladder and over 95 percent of the price of childhood vaccines. It is responsible for one-quarter of the price of a ride on a Long Island tour bus[1] and one-third of the price of a small airplane.[2] It will soon cost large municipalities as much as they spend on fire or sanitation services.

Some call it a safety tax, but its exact relationship to safety is mysterious. It is paid on many items that are risky to use, like ski lifts and hedge trimmers, but it weighs even more heavily on other items whose whole purpose is to make life safer. It adds only a few cents to a pack of cigarettes, but it adds more to the price of a football helmet than the cost of making it. The tax falls especially hard on prescription drugs, doctors, surgeons, and all things medical. Because of the tax, you cannot deliver a baby with medical assistance in Monroe County, Alabama. You cannot buy several contraceptives certified to be safe and effective by the Food and Drug Administration (FDA), even though available substitutes are more dangerous or less effective. If you have the stomach upset known as hyperemesis, you cannot buy the pill that is certified as safe and effective against it.[3] The tax has orphaned various drugs that are invaluable for treating rare but serious diseases. It is assessed against every family that has a baby, in the amount of about $300 per birth,[4] with an obstetrician in New York City paying $85,000 a year.[5]

Because of the tax, you cannot use a sled in Denver city parks or a diving board in New York City schools.[6] You cannot buy an American Motors "CJ" Jeep[7] or a set of construction plans for novel airplanes from Burt Rutan, the pioneering designer of the *Voyager*.[8] You can no longer buy many American-made brands of sporting goods, especially equipment for amateur contact sports such as hockey and lacrosse. For a while, you could not use public transportation in the city of St. Joseph, Missouri,[9] nor could you go to jail in Lafayette County in the same state.[10] Miami canceled plans for an experimental railbus because of the tax.[11] The tax has curtailed Little League and fireworks displays, evening concerts, sailboard races, and the use of public beaches and ice-skating rinks.[12] It temporarily shut down the famed Cyclone at the Astroland amusement park on Coney Island.

The tax directly costs American individuals, businesses, municipalities, and other government bodies at least $80 billion a year, a figure that equals the total profits of the country's top 200 corporations.[13] But many of the tax's costs are indirect and unmeasurable, reflected only in the tremendous effort, inconvenience, and sacrifice Americans now go through to avoid its collection. The extent of these indirect costs can only be guessed at. One study concluded that doctors spend $3.50 in efforts to avoid additional charges for each $1 of direct tax they pay.[14] If similar multipliers operate in other areas, the tax's hidden impact on the way we live and do business may amount to a $300 billion dollar annual levy on the American economy.

The tax goes by the name of *tort liability*. It is collected and disbursed through litigation. The courts alone decide just who will pay, how much, and on what timetable. Unlike better known taxes, this one was never put to a legislature or a public referendum, debated at any length in the usual public arenas, or approved by the president or by any state governor. And although the tax ostensibly is collected for the public benefit, lawyers and other middlemen pocket more than half the take.

The Innovator Departs

As the tort system has expanded steadily in the past two decades, innovation has been suppressed on many fronts. Safety has been set back, not advanced. And the consumer has ended up worse off, even in his personal security, than he would have been had the legal system been slower to rush to his rescue.

Who flees most quickly for shelter from the baying new tort pack? Those quickest on their feet, of course—the person of action, the company of initiative, the mover, the shaker, and the doer. When it comes to liability problems, the bold innovators are the most fleet-footed of potential defendants. More often than not, they have adjusted to the threat of liability by doing less. *Not* innovating is a remarkably easy thing to do.

In the very markets where the legal pursuit has been the most intense in recent years—on the trail of exotic drugs, contraceptives, pesticides, small planes and cars, hazardous waste disposal, and medical procedures— the mood among suppliers has become most sullen, hostile, defensive, and then coldly stagnant. Soon tired of running, the fox has retreated to its burrow and refused to come out.

Research expenditures by U.S. companies working on contraceptives peaked in 1973 and plummeted 90 percent in the next decade. Steroidal oral contraceptives in this country underwent no significant changes after 1976, and no truly new contraceptive chemical entities have been introduced since 1968. Clinical tests of a contraceptive implant system called Capronor, developed by the National Institutes of Health, were stalled for more than a year for lack of liability insurance.[15] The implanted contraceptive Norplant, which releases a hormone for five years, was developed by the New York Population Council and as of 1986 was on the market in five other countries. But no American firm dared to market it at home. A new and effective IUD, the Copper-T 380A, won FDA approval, but no major firm was willing to market it for several years.[16] In late 1987, one tiny company finally announced that it would sell the product, at a price vastly above the cost of manufacture, and without any liability insurance (which was, in any event, unavailable), presumably on the assumption that if a wave of lawsuits struck, bankruptcy would provide a quick and clean exit from the market.[17] So the United States, a leader in contraceptive research and marketing well into the early 1960s, has today lost its edge and its hunger for progress. Research on other aspects of reproduction has suffered as well. "Who in his right mind," the president of a major pharmaceutical company asked in 1986, "would work on a product today that would be used by pregnant women?"[18]

The story has been much the same in other high-tech markets favored with attention from the liability system in recent years. Between 1965 and 1985, the number of U.S. vaccine manufacturers shrank by more than half; by 1986 the nation depended on a single supplier for vaccines against polio, rubella, measles, mumps, and rabies. In the 1960s there were eight U.S. manufacturers of whooping cough vaccine; by 1986 there were only two. And only two major companies, Merck and Lederle Labs, were still investing heavily in vaccine research.[19] America, once the world leader in this technology so vital to the public health, was quickly losing ground here too.

Consulting engineers report that they systematically favor old products over new ones in their design specifications, fearing (quite correctly) that newer design options carry a greater risk of liability, whatever real decrease in risk they might actually represent.[20] Liability-conscious universities decline to license patents to small companies, despite the fertile environment they offer for innovation, fearing that anyone suing over a patent-related product would be sure to go for the university's deep pocket as well.[21] Liability concerns forced a Virginia engineer to abandon his business of designing better hand controls for cars used by the handicapped,[22] a business he had set up after his own son had been crippled in a motorcycle accident.

America, land of the Wright brothers, has lost even its appetite for innovation in small planes. Burt Rutan, the pioneering designer of the *Voyager*, didn't have the resources to compete with larger manufacturers, but he had a cheaper way of getting his products out into the marketplace. He sold construction plans for novel airplanes to do-it-yourselfers, who built the planes in their garages. But in 1985, fearful of the lawsuits that would follow if a home-built plane based on his designs crashed, he stopped selling the plans.

As the new tort system has advanced, in whatever field, technologists have fallen back; it is that simple. The phenomenon runs so contrary to the accepted articles of faith in conventional legal circles that many doggedly refuse to acknowledge the facts at all. The conventional theories declare, quite emphatically, that sharper liability should spur more innovation. How can the facts dare to be otherwise? The answer is that the accepted theories are wrong.

The theories depend, first of all, on a fine-tuned and highly predictable legal process which consistently disfavors more dangerous products and favors safer ones. The success of the new liability engine thus depends on great precision in the courts. But the legal assembly line relies on unskilled workers, heavily pressed for time and with many extraneous factors—sympathy for the victim most especially—on their minds. This introduces a great uncertainty into the system. And there are limits to the total uncertainty—scientific plus regulatory—that any endeavor can tolerate. With innovative science and technology that limit is reached much sooner than with the old and familiar.

Worse still, the new tort theoreticians penned a book of new legal rules that discouraged innovation at every turn. From the innovator's perspective, much of the damage was done at the very beginning, when the courts replaced negligence with strict liability. The negligence standard had inquired whether the technologist—the human actor on the scene—was careful, prudently trained and properly supervised. Who is most likely to pass a negligence test? The best and the brightest—the technologists working at the leading edge of their professions. It is at the frontiers of science, after all, that the best engineers, pharmacologists, doctors, and chemists typically congregate. Under the new legal standards, however, the people themselves, and their good care, good training, and good faith, were quite irrelevant. The new legal inquest concerns the product itself and its alleged defects. Where once human conduct had been its focus, the tort system now places technology itself in the dock.

This seemingly modest change sharply tilted the system against innovation. The reason lies in quite understandable human psychology. Jurors can make reasonably sensible intuitive judgments about people—even about professionals—because we are all in the people-judging business every day of our lives. But jurors are not experts about technology itself, and intuition here is a terrible guide. When a juror is asked to categorize technologies—as distinct from their inventors or managers—as good, bad, or ugly, the answers follow a quite predictable pattern. Age, familiarity, and ubiquity are the most powerful legitimizing forces known to the layperson. The inexpert juror is predisposed at every turn to identify technologies that are novel, exotic, unfamiliar, or adventuresome as unwelcome and fraught with danger—in short, defective.

It is a matter of human nature, an instinct as ancient as the species itself. Mothers who stay at home underestimate the familiar risks of their own environment—electric sockets, bottles of cleaning fluid, pediatric services, and cars, while overestimating the less familiar hazards of chemical pollution and nuclear power. Blue-collar workers see too little threat in their familiar cigarettes, alcohol, and construction-site environments, and too much threat in the less familiar hazards of air travel or high-tech medicine. People everywhere underestimate the risks they know well and face every day and overestimate those that are new and foreign. The familiar is safe, or at least bearable enough, no matter how appallingly dangerous it may be in reality. The unfamiliar is suspect, intrusive, and probably dangerous, no matter how reassuring the statistics may be.

The predisposition of juries is not by any means the end of the anti-innovation problem, however. When the search for product defects grew too convoluted, the courts shifted their attention to warnings. Gilt-edged safety warnings, that is, where how you pronounce it counts for everything. Exhaustive detail is the modern rule. It will not suffice to warn of a risk of death; the seller must warn specifically of the risk of stroke or serum sickness or acute encephalopathy. It will not suffice to warn the prescribing doctor of a drug's hazards; the drug company must somehow also get the information to the patient too. Grossly obvious risks must be flagged, but so must risks that arise only from the most bizarre and unexpected forms of consumer abuse.

How can any defendant learn to satisfy such requirements? Only through long perseverance in the market and in the courts. The warnings on oral contraceptives have been honed for thirty years, to the point where they run on for several pages of densely detailed text. No equivalent detail can be provided for a truly new IUD, because the risks are much less familiar—even if their general nature is known and even if the IUD is demonstrably safer, overall, than the pill it could replace. So the new law of warning further sharpens the anti-innovation bias of the new tort system.

Another blow to the innovator's peace and progress comes from the insurance side of the business. The general idea in modern tort law is that all goods must come gift-wrapped in a special-purpose insurance contract. When can such wrapping be found at any reasonable price? The availability of insurance depends largely on an accumulation of accident experience. That is something that established technologies always have and truly innovative ones never do. Insurance is easiest to find when a good has been used by many people for many years, so that the frolics and caprices of tort liability have been as far as possible washed out and the statistics of experience speak for themselves. Innovation necessarily starts without an established market, and so is often condemned to start without insurance as well. For the prudent businessperson, a start without insurance is often worse than no start at all.

Orphan drugs reveal some of these problems in particularly tragic circumstances. Only a few hundred American children suffer from cystinosis, a fatal kidney disease. About 2,000 adults suffer from Charcot-Marie-Tooth disease, a rare nerve disorder (unrelated to teeth) that severely impairs motor function. About 1,000 suffer from leprosy and experience an extremely painful allergic reaction on their skin. A tiny number suffer from a rare but incapacitating disease characterized by uncontrollable twitching of the eye muscles.[23] There are some 5,000 other orphan diseases that shorten lives or bring agonizing disability to tiny groups. Therapies are available or under development for some 500 of them.[24] But insurance is often all but impossible to obtain. Chemie Grunenthal, for example, a West German company that once supplied thalidomide to American leprosy victims, announced in 1986 that it planned to abandon the U.S. market to avoid the risk of liability that might arise if, for example, the drug was used in excess or fell into the wrong hands.[25] Until recently, another West German chemical company supplied Americans with botulinum, a paralytic poison that is just right for controlling the eye-twitching disease, but the company cut off supplies in 1986 for similar reasons.[26] Orphan drugs are condemned, in a sense, to be perennial newcomers to the commercial world and are therefore forever uninsurable under the modern rules. Business realities take care of the rest.

The law's attitude to safety improvements made after an accident has also changed for the worse. The old law strictly barred a plaintiff from offering any evidence of such conduct—the redesign or recall of a product, a postsale or postaccident change in a process, or the addition of a new safety system.[27] The logic for the rule was simple: safety improvements must be encouraged, and so should never be used to condemn past shortcomings. But in the 1960s, this rule too came under direct attack.[28] The courts proceeded in the usual way, fashioning one exception and then another, then yet another. Evidence of subsequent remedial measures was first admitted to impeach witnesses, then to prove that the defendant controlled the premises in question, then to show that conditions had changed since the time of the accident or that changes in design were feasible. The exceptions nibbled away at the rule until some courts were emboldened to sweep the tattered remains aside entirely. An Illinois appellate court simply declared that the rule shouldn't apply in strict liability cases because the focus was on the product itself, not on the defendant's conduct.[29] The California Supreme Court then picked up the idea in a landmark ruling in 1974.[30] New York and other states followed quickly.

Incredibly, the logic offered in these rulings was exactly what had been used earlier to *exclude* evidence of the plaintiff's contributory negligence before the accident. The product was on trial, the courts argued, not the people. So the plaintiff's personal conduct *before* the accident was irrelevant. But somehow the defendant's conduct *afterward* was perfectly relevant and admissible, because it would shed light on the product itself. None of this made any real sense except as a way of imposing more liability more often.

Many courts have also reset the clock on litigation, so that a suit can be filed years or even decades after the car gear box, herbicide, or strip-mining machine, was designed or used. Defects in technology, like negligence in human conduct, depend critically on the context of time and place. The best-designed cars of 1950 were clearly deficient by 1980 standards, as were the best medical procedures, industrial chemicals, pesticides, or home appliances. The problem is especially acute in mature industries with long-lived products. When the sun never sets on the possibility of litigation, each improvement in method, material, or design can establish a new standard against which all of your earlier undertakings, of no matter what vintage, will then be judged. Finding a way to do better today immediately invites an indictment of what you did less well yesterday or twenty years ago.

No wonder the strong temptation today is to leave well enough alone in the hope that somehow the courts then will too.[31] The pattern is consistent: a shift in the jury's focus from negligence to design defects; a legal obsession with perfectly phrased and endlessly detailed warnings; a rigid demand for universal, special-purpose accident insurance; the use of remedial efforts in the aftermath of an accident to indict whatever came before; and no effective time limit on litigation, so that even the normal pace of technological evolution becomes legally dangerous to the technologists. No one could have brought together five elements better calculated to entrench the status quo and scare off innovators of every description.

But mightn't this slowdown be a blessing in disguise? Technological adventure is known to be dangerous. Perhaps innovation deserves that extra measure of deterrence that the new tort system provides so generously. Everything supports this conclusion, especially our most common instincts and intuitions about the safety of the familiar and the hidden danger of the novel and innovative.

But the facts are otherwise. Whatever intuition may tell us, newer is generally safer than older in the modern technological world. Slowing down the pace of innovation did not advance safety in the least; it set it back sharply. We know for sure that since the turn of the century, life has been growing steadily safer in America, and at a rapid pace.[32] Most major diseases, including even most forms of cancer, have been on the decline, at least when one adjusts for the overall aging of the U.S. population. What accounts for these favorable trends? Innovation, technological change, and the economic growth they made possible. There is hardly a product in use today — a car, plane, boiler, municipal water system, drug, vaccine, or hypodermic syringe — that is not many times safer than its counterpart of a generation or even a decade ago.[33]

The liability system behaves as if the opposite were true. In 1977, for example, small-plane manufacturers paid a total of $24 million in liability claims. By 1985, their payout was $210 million. Companies like Beech, Cessna, and Piper curtailed or suspended production; they quickly discovered that the new-model planes, carrying a 50 percent surcharge for liability insurance, could no longer compete with used planes already on the market. Aircraft technology, however, had been advancing steadily, so the new models kept off the market were notably safer than the old ones people went on using instead. Worse still, small-plane development has traditionally been the richest source of aerodynamic research and innovation for the aircraft industry in general, so what private pilots and hobbyists lose today, the public will likely lose a decade or two later in commercial aviation.[34]

Small cars like Ford's Pinto, Honda's Civic, and Toyota's Corona, became magnets for liability claims as well. If the new tort theories were correct, the escalating awards against manufacturers of these cars deterred sales. And what then? It is possible, of course, that those who would otherwise have bought a new Pinto took the bus instead or bought a Mercedes. But it seems likely that many of them nursed along the old family car for a few more years instead or bought a clunker from Honest Eddie's used-car lot. Did liability deter? Certainly. Did it make life safer? In all likelihood, it did just the opposite.

Counting the bodies that have fallen because of things that might have been done better but weren't will always remain an exercise in speculation—just as it is impossible to count, with any precision, the accidents that were successfully deterred by the expansion of tort law. But the difficulty of taking any exact census should not lead anyone to suppose that no one has died. One surely cannot say that every single time the tort system slows down or cuts off innovation it thereby impedes safety. But by all indications that is the result more often than not.

Just What Is Deterred?

"We are here on earth to help others," W.H. Auden once remarked, "but what the others are here for I cannot say." The designers of the modern tort system were of much the same mind. They were not going to spend a great deal of time worrying about just what drug manufacturers might or might not contribute to the larger scheme of public health and welfare; the lawyers' business was to see to it that people who caused accidents paid, and people who suffered accidents got paid, and that was that.

So does the new tort jurisprudence deter? Yes, certainly, it deters all sorts of things. But just what are those things? When you think about this quite different question the answer doesn't seem by any means as attractive as when you don't think about it. This much is clear: What is risky in legal terms often has little to do with what is risky in the physical world. When put to the test, the new tort system has failed to discriminate effectively among good risks and bad ones. It has been indifferent to, when not deliberately disdainful of, individual needs and individual responsibilities.

When it encourages improvement at all, the new tort system promotes the trivial and marginal change. Today's oral contraceptive manufacturer does work hard to fine-tune the warning, or microscopically adjust the hormonal balance in the pill. The drill press designer adds an extra hair guard or hand shield. The doctor administers more tests, shoots more X-rays, and piles on a paper trail of his own. Large companies hire risk managers, industrial hygienists, consumer psychologists, and quality control experts in droves. The individuals and institutions all vigorously insist that they are working relentlessly to improve safety and cut their exposure to avoid liability. How could they claim otherwise? Due diligence on safety matters is still at the heart of a successful liability defense, most especially when punitive damages are at issue. No car maker, pesticide designer, or pediatrician should be eager to admit publicly to anything but the most tireless effort on safety matters.

The effort is there, but it is incremental, aimed at perfuming the violet and painting the lily. Liability-driven safety management has become a mirror image of the legal process itself—fussy, cumulative, bureaucratic, and preoccupied with paper. The risk-reduction initiatives that are encouraged by liability undoubtedly do some good some of the time. But the threat of liability also postpones or prevents the sharp break from tradition, the profound change in method or material, design or manufacture. And the sharp break, the occasional bold leap forward, is all-important in the quest for safety.

The picture is no brighter when the makers and doers are retreating rather than advancing. Yes, one can always point to some bad products driven off the market by litigation, to the overall benefit of the public health and safety. But the list of safety-enhancing products also banished is at least equally long, with safety consequences that have been even more grave. Yes, some incompetent doctors and irresponsible waste haulers have been forced out of business, as they richly deserved to be. So too have been many competent and much-needed ones. Some worthless or even dangerous innovations have been forestalled, but only because innovation across the board has been slowed, and innovation remains the most vital, long-term promoter of safety that we know.

Conclusion

The designers of the modern tort system started their crusade, in the early 1960s, under a banner of safety, prudence, and progress, but despite their best intentions they ended up fighting for the opposite side. They tackled products and services one at a time, all but ignoring the subtle trade-offs between the risks in front of them and the risks that were not in court. They engaged the risks of human creation, overlooking the still graver risks of the natural world. They ignored the ample evidence that new is generally safer than old, and set in place rules that entrench the status quo and repel all who endeavor to change it. They took the ancient parable of a man who stopped by the roadside for a stranger in need of help and rewrote it as a Kafkaesque nightmare of lawsuits, stigma and shame. The courts' proudest and most earnestly touted objective was to make life safer. It has been their most ignominious failure.

This article is adapted from Peter Huber, *Liability: The Legal Revolution and Its Consequences* (Basic Books, Inc., 1988).

Endnotes

1. R. Hanley, "Insurance Costs Imperil Recreation Industry," *New York Times*, 12 May 1980, p. A1.

2. "General Aviation Tort Reform Considered," *The Executive Letter*, Insurance Information Institute (18 Aug. 1986); *see also* "Business Struggling to Adapt as Insurance Crisis Spreads," *Wall Street Journal*, 21 Jan. 1986.

3. T. R. Reid, "Insurance Famine Plagues Nation," *Washington Post*, 23 Feb. 1986, pp. A1, A6.

4. Lester Thurow, "In Suit-Happy Society, the Economy Ends Up Suffering the Damages," *Los Angeles Times*, 15 Dec. 1985, Part IV, p. 3.

5. "Business Struggling to Adapt as Insurance Crisis Spreads," *Wall Street Journal*, 21 Jan. 1986, p. 31.

6. "Sorry, Your Policy is Canceled," *Time*, 24 Mar. 1986, p. 16; Advisory Commission on Liability Insurance, *Insuring Our Future, Scope of the Problem* (Report of the Governor's Advisory Commission on Liability Insurance to Governor Cuomo, State of New York, 7 Apr. 1986).

7. "Insurance Famine Plagues the Nation," *Washington Post*, 23 Feb. 1986, p. A6.

8. P. Huber, "Who Will Protect Us from Our Protectors?," *Forbes*, 13 July 1987, p. 56.

9. R. Lindsey, "Soaring Liability Premiums Threaten Some Bus Lines," *New York Times*, 29 Dec. 1985, p. A16.

10. "Business Struggling to Adapt as Insurance Crisis Spreads;" *see also* Editorial, "Liability Insurance in Crisis," *New York Times*, 4 Mar. 1986, p. A26.

11. "Business Struggling to Adapt as Insurance Crisis Spreads."

12. "Insurance Famine Plagues Nation," *Washington Post*, 23 Feb. 1986, p. A1; *New York Times*, 12 May 1980, p. A1.

13. *Chief Executive*, Summer 1986, p. 32.

14. "Defensive Medicine: It Costs, But Does It Work?" 257 *J.A.M.A.* 2801 (May 1987).

15. Cf. "Birth Control: Vanishing Options," *Time*, 1 Sept. 1986, p. 78.

16. E. Connell, "The Crisis in Contraception," *Technology Review* (May-June 1987): 47. As one observer has noted, "a pharmaceutical company would have to be altruistic to the point of suicidal to market an IUD today." Quoted in "Birth Control: Vanishing Options."

17. T. Lewin, "Birth Control Device Returning for Sale in U.S.," *New York Times*, 18 Oct. 1987, p. 30.

18. John Carson-Parker, "The Liability Crisis; Who's At Risk," *Chief Executive* (Summer 1986): 19.

19. "Business Struggling to Adapt as Insurance Crisis Spreads," *Wall Street Journal*, 21 Jan. 1986, p. 31.

20. D. Dimond, "Know-How or No Way?" *Insurance Rev.* (Oct. 1987): 34.

21. *Ibid.*

22. Michael Brody, "When Products Turn Into Liabilities," *Fortune*, 3 Mar. 1986, p. 20.

23. P. Boffey, "Loss of Drug Relegates Many to Blindness Again," *New York Times*, 14 Oct. 1986, p. C1.

24. N. R. Kleinfield, "'Orphan' Drugs: Caught in Limbo," *New York Times*, 20 July 1986, Sec. F, pp. 1, 27.

25. *Ibid.*

26. *Ibid.*

27. *E.g., Columbia & P.S. Railroad Company v. Hawthorne*, 144 U.S. 202 (1892).

28. *See* J. Hoffman and G. Zuckerman, "Tort Reform and the Rules of Evidence: Saving the Rule Excluding Evidence of Subsequent Remedial Actions," 22 *Tort & Ins. L. J.* 497 (Summer 1987).

29. *Sutkowski v. Universal Marion Corporation*, 5 Ill. App. 2d 313, 281 N.E.2d 749 (1972).

30. *Ault v. International Harverster Company*, 13 Cal. 3d 113, 117 Cal. Rptr. 812, 528 P.2d 1148 (1974).

31. T. Lewin, "Insurance a Liability for Some: Costs Rise Prohibitively," *New York Times*, 8 Mar. 1986, p. 35; S. Johnson, "Malpractice Costs vs. Health Care for Women," *New York Times*, 14 July 1985, p. A14; V. Schwartz, "The Post-Sale Duty to Warn: Two Unfortunate Forks in the Road to a Reasonable Doctrine," 58 *N.Y.U.L.Rev.* 892 (1983).

32. *See* E. Crouch and R. Wilson, *Risk/Benefit Analysis* (New York: Ballinger, 1982), 3; *New York Times*, 9 July 1984, p. A15.

33. Bruce N. Ames, "Six Common Errors Relating to Environmental Pollution," testimony for California Assembly on Water, Parks and Wildlife (1 Oct. 1986).

34. D. Dimond, "Know-How or No Way?"

SUE CITY: THE CASE AGAINST
THE CONTINGENCY FEE

Walter K. Olson

Senior Fellow, The Manhattan Institute

For years the New York City firm of Morris Eisen P.C. ran one of the nation's biggest personal-injury law practices, employing 45 lawyers and handling hundreds of cases at a time. Like all law firms that specialize in injury lawsuits, it worked on contingency—keeping a share of its clients' winnings, if any ("no fee unless successful").

It all came undone in 1990 when a federal grand jury indicted Eisen and seven persons associated with his firm on charges that included bribing witnesses and court personnel, suborning false expert testimony, doctoring photographs, and manufacturing other physical evidence. Among those charged along with Eisen were two lawyers, a former office manager, and four private investigators who worked regularly with his firm.[1]

Federal prosecutor Andrew Maloney detailed the charges. "They produced an eyewitness to two automobile accidents," he said. "The witness was never at either accident and, at the time of one accident, he was serving time on a forgery charge."[2] In another case, where one of Eisen's employees claimed to have tripped at a racetrack parking lot, Maloney said one of the suspects used a pickax to widen a pothole so it could be blamed for the supposed incident. Two of the group were charged with causing a witness to give false testimony in another lawsuit where an injured woman claimed that a bus driver had signaled for her to cross the street into traffic; New York City settled the case for $1 million. Altogether the 19 lawsuits where wrongdoing was alleged had brought in $9 million in awards and settlements, of which the lawyers had pocketed an estimated $3 million in contingency fees, along with some additional sum to cover their reported expenses.[3]

Around the rest of the country a wave of similar scandals was breaking. A front-page series in the *Miami Herald* told how a North Miami legal practice had conspired to manufacture and exaggerate injury claims. Florida prosecutors followed with a 32-count indictment of three lawyers, two doctors, and three associates.[4] A federal indictment charged two New Jersey lawyers and a doctor with 58 counts in an alleged scheme of massive fraud in auto-accident claims.[5]

America's legal profession, it seems, is being cleaned up. Or is it? What may be needed is not just more crackdowns like those underway, but a rethinking of the modern American wisdom on legal ethics.

Temptations for Dishonesty

Lawyers as a profession face unusual temptations to engage in unethical conduct. No one knows better how to skirt or evade the law than someone trained in it, and huge amounts of money can hang on the choices made when no one is looking over a lawyer's shoulder. This can be tempting enough for the ordinary lawyer who guides inexperienced clients through large financial transactions. It can be even more tempting for the trial lawyer who specializes in lawsuits or threats of lawsuits. Litigation is mostly about the violent and chancy redistribution of wealth. It abounds in opportunities for perjury-coaching and witness-tampering, the faking of evidence, and the bribing of court personnel, all for what can be dizzyingly high stakes. It offers many chances for dishonest persons to become rich.

A job that offers enormous rewards for unscrupulousness will attract many unscrupulous people, and corrupt many people of ordinary character. Yet most of the ways to sort out the bad apples are not very promising. Criminal prosecution, disbarment, and other heavy-duty disciplinary measures can help in the few cases where abuses can be brought to light and proved conclusively. In practice, only a few relatively flagrant cases of lawyer misconduct are caught and corrected in this way, mostly embezzlement of client funds and the like. Advance screening of bar applicants for "good character" is a subjective affair that can imperil the merely unpopular applicant along with the shady one; it has fallen largely into disuse. Civil lawsuits against lawyers provide occasional recourse for victimized clients but next to none for victimized opponents. What is really needed is a reduction in the temptations for dishonesty within the practice of law itself.

Ethics in Sports

The ethical rules of many professions share a common underlying principle: if temptations are allowed to get out of hand, many will yield. To put it in raw dollar terms, if under system A people can grab $1,000 by telling a lie, and under system B they can grab $1 million by telling the same lie, more people—not all, but more—will tell the lie under system B. No system could block all chances to profit from lying, cheating, and corner-cutting; that would be hopelessly utopian. Rather, a practical system of ethics tries to fence off the steepest and most slippery slopes. It lowers the rewards for dishonesty not to zero but to a point where most people will resist.

One of the standard ethical rules of professional sports forbids athletes to bet on their games. There are obvious reasons for not letting them bet against their own teams. The reasons for not letting them bet in favor are in the end no less compelling. Some athlete-gamblers would throw their strengths into certain contests at the expense of the season as a whole. More generally, kneeing and below-the-belt gouging of opponents would run wild: badminton would soon get as mean as hockey, and who can think what hockey itself would be like?

Likewise doctors have never been allowed to charge contingency fees—to place, in effect, bets with their patients on the success of their therapies. Under such a system, doctors would dispense with their fees if a patient remained sick. If, on the other hand, he rallied, they would charge higher than normal fees. And if the patient got well enough to go back to work, doctors might even arrange to take a share of his future earnings.

Why would this be unethical? In part because it would tempt doctors to depart from honesty. Under such a fee arrangement some doctors would portray transient maladies, best treated by doing nothing, as life-threatening to scare patients into promising a whopping contingency. Some would cure an illness with harsh remedies that left the body vulnerable to worse assaults later on. Some would allow patients who were still sick to believe they were cured, perhaps administering feel-good potions toward that end. Falsification of test results, bedside charts, and autopsy findings would go on constantly. Even doctors of ordinary integrity would feel their objectivity subtly disoriented, and the truly unscrupulous would find chances to become very rich indeed.

And so the custom arose of paying doctors by the hour, whether their patients recovered miraculously, feebly, or not at all. By achieving a surprise cure a doctor might hope to get valuable word-of-mouth and repeat business. But that is the difference between more and some, not between feast and famine. Many of the subsidiary rules of medical ethics, such as the separation of medicine from pharmacy, follow similar lines. By shielding doctors from a financial interest in drug-dispensing, we avoid clouding their decision whether to prescribe or withhold drugs in borderline cases.

America's Legal Exceptionalism

In virtually every other country, society has deemed that lawyers, like doctors, should be shielded from the temptations of the contingency fee. The English common law, French and German civil law, and Roman law all agree that it is unethical for lawyers to accept such fees. In 1975 British judges strenuously opposed even a closely regulated version of the fee, in which a contingency suit could go forward so long as leading lawyers verified its reasonableness. They explained that lawyers would no longer make their cases "with scrupulous fairness and integrity."[6]

The American exception on contingency fees developed naturally and inevitably from a wider and more profound American exception on legal fees in general, an exception that is central to understanding the problems of our legal system. America is the only major country that denies to the winner of a lawsuit the right to collect legal fees from the loser. In other countries, the promise of a fee recoupment from the opponent gives lawyers good reason to take on a solidly meritorious case for even a poor client. Oxford's Patrick Atiyah notes that "the reality is that the accident victim with a reasonable case should be able to find a lawyer with equal ease in England and America."[7]

At first much of America tried a not very promising substitute for the contingency fee: volunteer legal service. Lawyers were supposed to make a reasonable effort to handle a poor person's claim for free when it appeared meritorious. When a suit of this sort was a money claim, and it succeeded, the now not-so-penniless client might offer the lawyer a grateful recompense, but was not obliged to do so. The system was based on two-way altruism, first from the lawyer, then from the beneficiary.

Systems that depend too heavily on pure altruism do not tend to chug along forever. Without a legal right to recover fees in case of victory, lawyers did not donate enough time to these pro bono publico cases, and some meritorious claims slipped through the cracks. The straightforward solution of shifting fees to the losers of lawsuits was obstinately resisted. So, amid misgivings and reluctance, the contingency fee was admitted state by state; Maine was the last state to legalize it, in 1965.

Restrictions confined the use of the fee to the necessary cases. The arrangement was to be discouraged unless a client was too poor to pay the normal freight. Most important, lawyers could represent only plaintiffs on this basis, and never defendants, either civil or criminal. And although contingencies were permitted in most money claims, they were disallowed in many other kinds of lawsuits, divorces in particular.

The older American legal ethicists emphasized the need for vigilance against the special corrupting dangers of the contingency fee. Lawyers were to recognize that taking a share in the spoils subjected them to a sort of moral vertigo that should be shunned when not necessary and handled with tightrope care when it was. They would have to cultivate a special humility and detachment when they worked on this basis, trying harder than other lawyers to remember that winning wasn't everything, struggling to forget that victory in the case at hand might bring personal riches or that loss might bring a financial blow. In short, the system was asked to run on a new kind of altruism, the self-restraint of lawyers with fortunes at stake.

"My Ads Can Make You Millions"

Just as salesmen paid on commission step forward and make eye contact when the customer walks in the store, so contingency-fee lawyers have a strong incentive to get clients interested in the merchandise. For such reasons the standard American text on legal ethics, by Judge George Sharswood of Pennsylvania, said the fee gave "an undue encouragement to litigation."[8] Street-level views could be much more scathing. By the 1920s one federal prosecutor was calling the fee the "arch tempter to the ambulance chaser" (as well as the fount of "false claims, witness fixing, and perjury").[9]

With their incentive to go for volume, contingency-fee lawyers have long done far more than their share of advertising and solicitation, both lawful and unlawful. "My custom TV ads can make you millions," promises a full-page pitch on page three of the December 1985 *Trial*, the magazine for injury lawyers. "Twenty-seven lawyers have become millionaires while running my custom TV commercials, 9 are multi-millionaires, and 22 are close (net worth between $450,000 and $975,000)," claims independent producer Paul Landauer. "Some started with less than nothing! One borrowed $6,000 to go on the air and took in an off-shore injury case the second week that settled for $3.8 million." Smart lawyers, he explains, know that attracting clients "in bunches and droves" increases the odds of getting a "big one." "I give you an elegant, 100-percent custom, 'dream lawyer' image the TV audience can't wait to call."

Cultivators of Discontent

The initial step of getting potential clients to dial the operators standing by to receive their call is but the first in the encouragement of litigation. That encouragement naturally extends to every stage of the dispute. The true cultivator of discontent does not sow the seeds of grievance and then retire while the seedlings grow or wither as Nature ordains. He waters and fertilizes the tender shoots to a state of garish bloom.

The popular television show *L.A. Law* has made famous the character of divorce lawyer Arnie Becker. In one episode, a woman comes in who is thinking of splitting up with her husband: they haven't been fighting, but they seem to have drifted apart; maybe it's time to work out a parting of the ways. As Arnie drops a word here and a hint there, her mood subtly changes. She begins to feel annoyed at her hubby, then downright aggrieved; by the next commercial she is howling for his scalp on toast.

This style of consciousness-raising or client education can be applied to virtually any legal problem. Someone walks into the office in a far from combative frame of mind, feeling there is something to be said for both sides, not at all in the right mood for litigation services. The entrepreneur can artfully lay out the full gravity of the other side's conduct. The client who wants help in rescheduling overdue bills can begin to appreciate how irresponsible the banks were to send him so many credit cards. The frightened tenant behind on the rent can realize, the thought coming as if unbidden, that the landlord's delay in repairing the sink is really little short of depravity.

None of this would have surprised old-time lawyers in the least, and it was one reason for the insistence on detachment and passivity that runs through their writings on the lawyer/client relationship. Yes, lawyers were to apprise clients fully of their rights and options, but it was best done clinically, so as not to inflame any latent feelings of fear, rage, envy, or avarice. If the case did proceed to litigation, the client as "master of his suit" was to provide the impetus not only for the initial filing but for any major escalation of the battle. Given a client of lawful intent, the ideal lawyer did not try to shape even his attitudes, let alone his story.

Client Loses Control

If you hire a contingency-fee lawyer you surely know already about the great advantage of giving him a piece of the action: he gets a powerful incentive to bring in the absolutely biggest cash amount. But the absolutely biggest cash amount may not be what you want.

You may not, for example, be feeling angry enough to fire off every arrow in your quiver of legal rights. Maybe it strikes you as a little rough to sue the nurse as well as the doctor and hospital just to get a few dollars more, or to brand your ex-business partner as a racketeer as part of your action seeking a fairer division of the enterprise property. You may not want to pry into the other side's private life or invite prying into your own. Then, too, litigation can end in many ways. The bitterest marital fallings-out have been known to end in a miraculous reconciliation. (Most states still forbid contingency fees for obtaining divorce decrees because they so clearly give the lawyer a reason to sabotage any such development.) A new management might take over at the work place where you were fired and offer you a job instead of back-pay settlement. The magazine you sued for libel might print your side of the story. In a University of Iowa study of libel complainants interviewed after their suits were over, by far the majority said they would have been satisfied at least initially with a correction or retraction instead of cash damages.[10]

But, if someone else fronted the money to get you into court, the action is no longer yours alone. You have a new partner in your lawsuit, maybe a senior partner, to whom words of forgiveness butter no parsnips and gestures of mercy pay for no beach front condos. You will be pushed toward high-ticket strategies, although they may end in hatred or self-reproach.

Timing is a common source of conflict between lawyer and client interests. Most litigants tire of their fights, if not at first, then after a while, and at some point would rather get on with their lives than hold out for a little more. The lawyer with a big war chest has an incentive to make you wait in order to go for the extra money. Every so often the roles are reversed: some clients have complained, and at least one legal-malpractice suit has charged, that lawyers settled too early for a low figure because they needed help with the office cash flow.

Hiring a lawyer on an hourly fee puts you in control of the direction of your affairs, much as a taxi fare gives you wide discretion to name your own destination and hop off where you want. The contingency fee takes you along for someone else's ride, aboard a high-powered machine typically geared to breaking altitude records. With luck, it might be a ride to riches. But it is best not to complain about the steering. And although you may think you have the right to change lawyers in mid-lawsuit if things get too ugly, just try it.

Costs to Third Parties

There is no denying that contingency fees have certain productivity advantages. Paying people only if their efforts culminate in success definitely coaxes more effort out of them. The question is whether the effort is aimed in the right direction. Much of the economy is run on a fee-for-results basis. Farmers get paid for cabbages based on how many edible cabbages they come up with, not how many hours they spend in the cabbage patch. Realtors and travel agents work on straight commission. So, for that matter, do authors who hope to make royalties past the advance on their books: if the product doesn't sell, they may get no recompense for an extra hundred hours of work.

Not all occupations are like cabbage, house, or book selling. Contingency fees tend to be disfavored in professions to whom the interests of others are helplessly entrusted, where misconduct is hard to monitor. Accountants have long been barred from accepting contingency fees ("I'll pay you twice your normal rate if my taxes go down, the bank stays happy, and I survive the next annual meeting without being voted out"); we hope they will stay independent enough to tell their clients unwelcome truths. Salesmen are not always paid on commission in part because the hustle factor in salesmanship can be turned in a destructive direction: commissioned salesmen, although they outperform the hourly variety, are also more tempted to use high-pressure sales techniques and manipulative tactics that "make their numbers look good" to the boss.

Contingency fees are particularly frowned on where the costs of abuse fall on third parties who are not taking part voluntarily. Giving traffic cops contingency fees by hinging their bonuses on how many tickets they write arouses widespread anger because it so obviously tempts the officer to be unfair to the motorist. The same is true of giving tax collectors contingency fees by hinging their bonuses on how many deductions they disallow or how many assets they seize. Giving soldiers contingency fees for successful attacks, by letting them loot the towns they capture, was long favored as a way of encouraging warlike zeal, but came under gradual ethical control as civilization progressed; we now give out medals and ribbons instead of the contents of civilian homes.

Dangers for Society

Giving lawyers contingency fees encourages similar abuses of both the client and the public. In the classic underworld injury racket, the operator, after pocketing the defendant's tender of settlement, gives the accident victim whatever pocket change it is thought should satisfy him, or just dumps him back on the street with no money at all. (Any back talk from the victim and his original accident will seem minor in relation to the troubles that await him.) Most clients of today's litigation industry fortunately do not get treated that badly. But many are quite surprised to discover at the end of a suit that the lawyer's claimed "expenses"— copying, filing costs, expert witness fees, and so forth—have somehow ballooned to represent a huge share of the settlement on top of the contingency fee itself. Some naive souls never find out how much the defendant paid to settle, but take the lawyer's word for it.

But the dangers of the contingency fee go beyond the exploitation of clients. After all, alert clients can be on guard against being exploited by their own lawyers; as the abuses are more widely publicized, more may learn to avoid the lawyers who get too greedy in bill reckonings. The real problem with the contingency fee derives not so much from the conflicts it creates between the interests of lawyer and client, as from the even more dangerous conflicts it creates between their interests and everyone else's.

In truth, many clients are delighted to find a lawyer who is much more ruthlessly committed to winning than the hourly-fee lawyer who represents their opponent. They seek the operator who knows how to turn a worthless or low-value claim into a cash bonanza even if he keeps most of the extra money for himself. If they are made to cooperate in truth-shading or worse, they are not bothered. Some are only too glad to think up new embellishments of their own.

The case against the contingency fee has always rested on the danger it poses not to the one who pays it, but to the opponent and more widely to justice itself. As other nations recognize, it can yoke lawyer and client in a perfectly harmonious and efficient assault on the general public. The designated opponents are far from the only ones victimized by wrongful or overzealous litigation. Every lawsuit sweeps in third parties who are forced to expend time, energy, and money without compensation, and surrender their privacy by answering under oath the probing questions of a hostile lawyer. The cost to taxpayers of running the system are far from trivial; more broadly, lawsuits tend to paralyze productive initiative by keeping rights in a state of suspense. We all pay for needless litigation.

Enthusiastic First Resort

The most common justification for the contingency fee is that it provides the "key to the courthouse" for people of modest means. But injury lawyers tend to oppose the method all other countries use to provide that key: an hourly fee paid by the losing opponent. And it turns out that they happily charge contingency fees to middle- and upper-income clients who could easily afford to pay on an hourly basis.

In fact, mysteriously, the contingency fee has become the only way most clients can get a lawyer for injury cases, even if they would rather pay an hourly fee. Some clients suspect that a phone call or two from a lawyer, or a letter on his stationery, may be all they need to get a satisfactory resolution of their problem. They might feel that giving their lawyer a third of the amount won in such a case would be an undeserved windfall. But they are out of luck. A report from the Federal Trade Commission showed that 97 percent of lawyers took injury cases only on contingency, refusing to consider hourly rates, however generous.[11] Lawyers seem to have come to the conclusion that a good injury case is a plum and, damn it, they have a right to a share, as befits a player. They are also loath to undercut the "going rate" fee percentage, even when success in a case seems virtually assured. In some of the rougher towns like Detroit and Kansas City the going rates over the years have been reported to run at 40 and even 50 percent.

As lawyers have discovered how very profitable this kind of practice can be, more of them have gotten over their scruples. The contingency fee is coming to be seen as the basis of an industry boldly and openly run for profit, as an enthusiastic first resort for the general case rather than a troubled last resort for the special. And in a trend that is full of implications for the future, the fee is spreading to litigation over employment matters, child support, will contests, copyrights, taxes, and, perhaps most ominously, divorces.

In Texas, where the contingency-fee industry is unusually well developed, it is having a profound effect on commercial litigation. Texas lawyer John O'Quinn may represent a one-man wave of the future. His full-page Yellow Pages ad, as quoted in a *Wall Street Journal* report, says he is dedicated to "helping injured people obtain cash damages" and promises an "attorney on call 24 hours a day." State bar officials have accused him of using runners to acquire injury cases.[12] What makes O'Quinn an interesting and apparently a very, very rich man is that he also applies his personal injury case methods—appealing to populist resentment—to otherwise routine disputes between businesses, with astonishing success. His most startling victory came in 1988 when a jury awarded $600 million to one of his clients, an Ohio natural-gas producer, in a contract dispute with the giant Tenneco Corporation.[13]

A Professional's Obligations

For centuries the practices of law, medicine, accounting, pharmacy, and other professions have been seen as fundamentally different from those of, say, agriculture, metalworking, and clothes-making, not because the former pursuits are more important or difficult, but because they pose special dangers of abuse and unethical conduct. Professionals face distinctive ethical responsibilities that would be unnecessary and indeed wrongheaded to impose on other persons. These responsibilities have gradually crystallized in the form of long-evolved codes of professional ethics.

A typical tenet of these codes is that a professional practice should not be run purely "as a business." Ethical codes commonly require members to charge per-hour fees rather than contingency fees based on a client's satisfaction or success. Even more common are rules restricting the gung-ho "chasing" of business through advertising and more direct promotional methods.

Such rules plainly curb competition, and many free-market supporters have denounced them as advancing a profession's collective interest at the expense of society's. Critics have cheered over the last 15 years as professions have been forced to relax or abandon their former ethical rules, under pressure from antitrust suits and adverse court decisions.

The case against untrammeled professional competition is seldom heard at length these days, but should not be dismissed lightly. It proceeds from the observation that competition tends to stimulate output of a service and tailor it more closely to what customers want. These normally fine results can be problematic in a professional context.

Consider first the stimulation of output. Overselling—the hustling of customers to buy things they would probably do better without—is perhaps a venial offense in the selling of home freezers and encyclopedias, but somewhat more ominous when applied to amphetamine pills and divorces. Auto salesmen are free to encourage impulse buying of sports cars, but surgeons may have a duty to discourage unnecessary surgery.

Perhaps, lest we fall into paternalism, it is best to recognize the client's right to be self-destructive. Trouble is, many dubious professional services harm someone other than the one who pays for them. A great deal of medicine is practiced on infants or on feeble or unconscious persons at the (perhaps misguided) behest of family members and others. There is likewise a steady market for faked medical reports, forged prescriptions, and undeserved audit options, all of which facilitate fraud aimed at third parties. The unethical doctor or accountant, far from being shunned by clients, may be in hot demand—which may be one reason to shield both professions from too strong a financial incentive to give clients what pleases them.

Of course the deliberate insulation of producers from consumer sovereignty is a dangerous thing. It seems likely that many of the old bans—on price advertising by druggists and opticians, for example—were of little importance in curbing abuse and did badly undercut market efficiency. We may also wish on libertarian grounds to uphold an individual's right to offer services to consenting clients even if the consequence is to expose third parties to hard-to-detect abuse. But however strong the case may be for deregulating the practice of medicine and accounting—while, one hopes, allowing outraged colleagues to shun the maverick, which our antitrust laws currently forbid them to do—there is no case at all for extending the principle to the practice of law.

Lawyers are delegated certain quasi-governmental powers to invoke compulsory process. In particular, they can initiate lawsuits that impose huge unrecompensed costs on what frequently turn out to be innocent opponents. As we know from the case of pollution, the opportunity to impose costs on other people is likely to be overused unless it is regulated or priced in some way. In no way does it violate individual rights to demand of those who seek to wield this coercive power that they submit in exchange to certain rules to prevent its overuse.

Reprinted with permission from *Policy Review*, Winter 1991. Excerpted from his recent book *The Litigation Explosion: What Happened When America Unleashed the Lawsuit* (Dutton/Truman Talley Books). Copyright 1991 by Walter K. Olson.

Endnotes

1. Dennis Hevesi, "Three Lawyers Accused of Using Bribes and Faked Evidence," *New York Times*, 12 Jan. 1990; Wade Lambert and Wayne Green, "Personal-Injury Lawyers Charged With Fraud," *Wall Street Journal*, 12 Jan. 1990.

2. *Ibid.*

3. *Ibid.*

4. Joe Starita, "Insurance Mill Enriches Lawyers, Doctors," *Miami Herald*, 9 Oct. 1988.

5. "U.S. Court Rules Law Firm's Client Files Can Be Searched in Criminal Inquiry," *Wall Street Journal*, 4 Aug. 1989.

6. Gordon Crovitz, "Contingency Fees and the Common Good," *Wall Street Journal*, 21 July 1989.

7. Patrick Atiyah, "Tort Law and the Alternatives: Some Anglo-American Comparisons," *Duke Law Journal* 1002, 1017 (1987).

8. George Sharswood, *An Essay on Professional Ethics* (T. & J. Johnson & Co., 1907).

9. Quoted in Murray Teigh Bloom, *The Trouble With Lawyers* (New York: Simon and Schuster, 1968), 138.

10. Gilbert Cranberg, "In Libel, Money Isn't Everything," *Wall Street Journal*, 13 July 1989.

11. Cited in Gordon Crovitz, "Contingency Fees and the Common Good."

12. Wayne Green, "Bar Groups Take on Ambulance Chasers," *Wall Street Journal*, 28 Sept. 1988.

13. Dianna Solis, "O'Quinn Defeats Tenneco With Emotion," *Wall Street Journal*, 16 Dec. 1988.

AN OVERVIEW OF THE HISTORIC ROLE OF THE STATES IN AMERICAN GOVERNMENT AND THEIR POSITION IN THE FUTURE

Professor M. E. Bradford

University of Dallas

The problem of federalism and of the proper division of the responsibilities of government between the nation and the states has been with our country from its beginnings. For the Revolution itself had been made *by the states which speak in the Declaration*—made for local self-government and against remote and potentially arbitrary power. And therefore no one could be properly surprised when, in 1787-1788, as the original Constitution of the United States was sent out by the Continental Congress to be evaluated by the people of the several states represented in the Great Convention, the document provoked various reactions among them. Because of a widespread concern for the future integrity of state and local power, in many states there was a popular majority opposed to ratification—indeed, perhaps in most. North Carolina and Rhode Island actually refused to affirm what had been proposed in Philadelphia—at least for a time. Moreover, New Hampshire adjourned its first convention without deciding anything. And until the business had been carefully maneuvered, Massachusetts, New York and Virginia remained unwilling to accept what the Framers had made. Eventually the Constitution was ratified. But in every ratifying convention which recommended amendments, part of the suggestion for refinement in the proposed instrument of fundamental law was that it should include an overt guarantee reserving to the commonwealths joined in the Union (and to their citizens) all the powers not specifically granted to the general government. Indeed, the call for such an amendment was *the primary proposal* wherever amendments were recommended. What North Carolina requested was also the request of Virginia, New Hampshire, Rhode Island, Massachusetts and New York. And the most important part of what all of the Antifederalists meant by "a bill of rights"—a restriction on the outreach of the national government toward authorities and responsibilities not rightfully within its scope. Federalism, a division of sovereignty between its sources in historic communities organized by state and township and a national power with real but limited authority over legitimately national concerns, is what was new about American government—the *novus ordo seclorum* of the nation's motto. Our new political arrangement not covered in ancient or modern political theory, insisted on unity of sovereignty: a division leaving both levels of government with some security against the potential excesses of the other acting on its own. Generally, though the federal balance took some injury from Chief Justice Marshall in *Marbury v. Madison* (1803),[1] this arrangement remained intact until 1869, when it was finally, after the fact, revised by the High Court in the case of *Texas v. White*.[2]

Yet even after Appomattox and the military defeat of the doctrine of reserved state powers, federalism survived in the constitutional rectitude of those Democrats and moderate Republicans who defended the Union in order to restore what it had been before the War Between the States. As Phillip S. Paludan has taught us in his *A Covenant With Death*, the Midwesterners who dominated the Chase, Waite and Fuller Courts were not like their radical Republican counterparts on the proper construction of the Constitution.[3] They wanted preservation, not innovation—a Constitution not instrumental but primarily procedural in its functions, operating to promote no doctrine not announced in the letter of its text, leaving to the states all of the roles they had played when they first combined to be both one and, in some sense, many—when they made a Union: that is, unless the states had themselves amended the Constitution, shifting the federal balance in some particular. Paludan, Charles Fairman and Michael Benedict give us the story of this unlikely and unexpected federalism.[4] But the point is that, until the 1890's, the states of the United States retained most of their original capacities and protections against federal intrusion upon their rightful functions. Indeed, until late in the 1930's, little changed even though certain kinds of attenuation were visible before the beginnings of the judicial revolution of Franklin Roosevelt's second term.

Before the great collapse of 1937, the failure of the will in the High Court once it was faced with the general popularity of the New Deal, the drift of the prevailing constitutional theory implemented by the Court and Congress brought about only an incremental erosion of the balance of federalism—the cases leading up to *Lochner v. New York* (1905)[5] and the triumph of substantive due process, or the memorable *Schenck v. United States* (1919),[6] which discouraged routine restrictions on speech endangering neither the operations of government nor the public peace. These and other limitations on the authority of the states made inroads in the plan of the Framers, as did Republican supports for railroads and other internal improvements and Supreme Court opinions concerning trial procedures in state courts. For there was, for judge or legislator, no fame to be earned and no glory in merely upholding the Constitution—always a psychological disadvantage faced by American Conservatives.

By slow and steady stages, American federalism was undermined. And then was soon abandoned when Franklin Roosevelt got the Court he had wanted. At this time, most constitutional restraints on action by government in areas where some thought "good works" were more important than regard for proper limits on the scope of federal law were replaced by a doubtful reading of the Fourteenth Amendment and an ahistorical, reckless jurisprudence of incorporation and implied powers. I will not rehearse the familiar story of what happened to the federal principle during and since the Warren Court. For my point is that federalism in our political system was initially undone, *issue* by *issue*, case by case, and that, when it was overturned altogether, the backbone had already been cut away from it by a series of particular deviations justified circumstantially by legislators, judges and Presidents who had ceased to value the federal division of powers or other restraints upon Leviathan before some ostensibly sacrosanct cause moved them to give up on such mere legal formalities altogether.

Now the way to change the centralized and statist condition we are in is by an inversion of the gradual process which originally brought us to this pass. I assume that the sentiment for such a reversal already exists. Nothing makes the case for federalism so well as its absence, with alternative arrangements demonstrating clearly that calling upon Washington for assistance in every difficult situation ends up being more the source than the solution to the problems of the Republic. Yet though we can agree that Washington cannot adequately solve all of the problems of policy, police, finance and self-regulation which confront our communities, there is no single inclusive action (apart from the election of a President with the proper views) that we might take to restore agency to the states. Nothing will, at this stage in our history, serve that purpose except a series of particular projects better undertaken at the state level than by the general government: projects like those recommended by the essays gathered in this volume.

The initiatives proposed (or warned against) in *Making Government Work: A Conservative Agenda for the States* have in common their disposition to put important functions of contemporary government back into the hands of the states, arguing that they belong there because they can be more readily and effectively performed at that level than under federal supervision or by a federal substitute. This is of course the case with educational priorities, since the responsibility for public education still belongs primarily to state and local governments. The more that responsibility stays at that level, the healthier federalism will be. The difficulty is that most studies of American education call for more and more federal funding (and regulation) of this basic function. The same is true of law enforcement and the regulation of crime. Failure of state educational and law enforcement programs to measure up to ideologically imposed standards generated in the federal courts or by legislative fiat has often resulted in usurpations by Washington performed with the authority of "good causes." The states are dispossessed of their responsibilities because they have not been careful of the recently discovered rights of some classification or group of citizens. In these two areas what remains of federalism is definitely under fire. But a great many Americans are concerned about the success of the states in dealing with education and crime.

In the present, the inclination of many state governments to turn to lotteries to avoid adopting unpopular taxes is obvious. Patrick Anderson is clearly correct in suggesting that such legislation gives the division of powers a bad name. And (apart from what might be done by constitutional amendment) term limitation is exclusively a state question, touching officers of state government. Initiative and referendum also belong to state politics, to be arranged by provisions of state constitutions, but are growing to be more and more popular as a method for protecting the people against their elected representatives. Such policies and procedures are I believe by their nature hostile to the ambitions of the general government to do for the people whatever they ostensibly cannot do "so well" for themselves.

Dinesh D'Souza's discussion of political correctness and Tex Lezar's remarks on fighting crime address timely issues in a forceful and persuasive fashion. They confront the ideology of domestic radicalism in its most virulent form. And the same might be said about the essays by Huber and Olson on tort reform, or by Greg Davidson on particular initiatives at the state level which could contribute to the visible stature of state institutions, and to the force of arguments that more business should be left in their hands.

Yet it is in the essays which deal with great practical concerns in the area of public policy—concerns not utterly distorted by the influence of ideology yet nonetheless intractable in their difficulty and impossible to resolve with either spending or frugality by government—that this book is most exceptional: in the treatments of health insurance regulation by John Goodman and Edmund F. Haislmaier and in the commentary on the impact of privatization on state budgets by Robert W. Poole, Jr. and Lynn Scarlett. For the authors of these essays recognize that in an era of limited resources it is sometimes better to improve a situation than it is to make an heroic attempt to resolve it altogether—and in the process aggravate the demand to give up on fiscal restraint and to tax and spend, wherever "need" can be discovered and emotionally portrayed.

Indeed, *Making Government Work: A Conservative Agenda for the States* says a lot about taxes—and about the environment, health care, the danger of moral relativism, housing policy, the politics of educational theory, the decline of family and the need for welfare reform. Within its scope are most of the pressing concerns that now dominate the arena of public policy as we may observe it in the various state legislatures.

Altogether it is an absolutely timely book—one which reminds us that conservatives need to take the initiative in debating such questions, to recognize how their values apply in coming to political and prudential conclusions and to avoid mere negative posturing about overgovernment after the adversary has written the laws and we are left, because of our silence and unwillingness to participate in the crafting of imperfect or incomplete solutions, with nothing to do but complain.

Federalism, wrote the English scholar K. C. Wheare, is a "method of dividing powers so that the general and regional governments are each, within a sphere, coordinate and independent." He said further "that each government should be limited to its own sphere and, within that sphere, should be independent of the other."[7] *A movement in the direction of such decentralization is going on all over the world—except in the United States.* But even here, riding the wave of intelligent suggestions for public policy that might prove how well (and inexpensively, unobtrusively) the states can tend to their own affairs, that movement has good prospects. For our country is still various and multiple in its essential character, glorying in the enrichment and strength which come out of the Pennsylvania Dutch, the North Dakota Scandinavians and the Scotch Irish of the South producing and organizing, each in their own way, very different cultures—with different industries, different agricultural products, different religious configurations and (within a few general constraints) different laws. Federalism *does* require a written Constitution, but not a Constitution to make us all the same. Or to prevent experiments at the state level which, in the end, might reshape national policy and will at the least protect us all in ensuring that we will be governed by those most directly responsive to us, who will themselves have to live with the social, legal and economic arrangements they have made. Thus something of the ancient liberties which our fathers intended for themselves and their posterity might be once again made secure, liberties inseparable from the preservation of the federalist model of government. For the desire for that security is everywhere to be observed, in every corner of the land.

Endnotes

1. 1 Cr. (5 U.S.) 137 (1803).

2. 7 Wall (74 U.S.) 700 (1869).

3. *A Covenant With Death: The Constitution, Law and Equality in the Civil War Era* (Urbana, Ill.: University of Illinois, 1975).

4. Michael Benedict. *A Compromise of Principle: Congressional Republicans and Reconstruction, 1863-1869* (New York: Norton, 1974); *see also* Charles Fairman, *Reconstruction and Reunion, 1864-1888*, Part I, Vol. VI of the Oliver Wendell Holmes' Devise *History of the Supreme Court of the United States* (New York: MacMillan, 1971).

5. 198 U.S. 45 (1905).

6. 249 U.S. 47 (1919).

7. James McClellan. *Liberty, Order and Justice: An Introduction to the Constitutional Principles of American Government* (Washington, D.C.: Center for Judicial Studies, 1989), 180.